Handbook of Research on Innovations in Information Retrieval, Analysis, and Management

Jorge Tiago Martins
The University of Sheffield, UK

Andreea Molnar
University of Portsmouth, UK

A volume in the Advances in Knowledge
Acquisition, Transfer, and Management (AKATM)
Book Series

An Imprint of IGI Global

Managing Director:	Lindsay Johnston
Managing Editor:	Keith Greenberg
Director of Intellectual Property & Contracts:	Jan Travers
Acquisitions Editor:	Kayla Wolfe
Production Editor:	Christina Henning
Development Editor:	Courtney Tychinski
Cover Design:	Jason Mull

Published in the United States of America by
Information Science Reference (an imprint of IGI Global)
701 E. Chocolate Avenue
Hershey PA, USA 17033
Tel: 717-533-8845
Fax: 717-533-8661
E-mail: cust@igi-global.com
Web site: http://www.igi-global.com

Library of Congress Cataloging-in-Publication Data

Handbook of research on innovations in information retrieval, analysis, and management / Jorge Tiago Martins and Andreea Molnar, editors.
    pages cm
  Includes bibliographical references and index.
  ISBN 978-1-4666-8833-9 (hardcover) -- ISBN 978-1-4666-8834-6 (ebook) 1. Information technology--Research--Handbooks, manuals, etc. 2. Information services--Handbooks, manuals, etc. 3. Information science--Sociological aspects--Handbooks, manuals, etc. 4. Information storage and retrieval systems--Handbooks, manuals, etc. 5. Management information systems--Handbooks, manuals, etc. I. Martins, Jorge Tiago, 1984- editor. II. Molnar, Andreea, 1984- editor.
  T58.5.H3528 2016
  003'.54--dc23
                                            2015024010

This book is published in the IGI Global book series Advances in Knowledge Acquisition, Transfer, and Management (AKATM) (ISSN: 2326-7607; eISSN: 2326-7615)

British Cataloguing in Publication Data
A Cataloguing in Publication record for this book is available from the British Library.

All work contributed to this book is new, previously-unpublished material. The views expressed in this book are those of the authors, but not necessarily of the publisher.

For electronic access to this publication, please contact: eresources@igi-global.com.

Advances in Knowledge Acquisition, Transfer, and Management (AKATM) Book Series

Murray E. Jennex
San Diego State University, USA

ISSN: 2326-7607
EISSN: 2326-7615

Mission

Organizations and businesses continue to utilize knowledge management practices in order to streamline processes and procedures. The emergence of web technologies has provided new methods of information usage and knowledge sharing.

The **Advances in Knowledge Acquisition, Transfer, and Management (AKATM) Book Series** brings together research on emerging technologies and their effect on information systems as well as the knowledge society. **AKATM** will provide researchers, students, practitioners, and industry leaders with research highlights surrounding the knowledge management discipline, including technology support issues and knowledge representation.

Coverage

- Cognitive Theories
- Cultural Impacts
- Information and Communication Systems
- Knowledge acquisition and transfer processes
- Knowledge management strategy
- Knowledge Sharing
- Organizational learning
- Organizational Memory
- Small and Medium Enterprises
- Virtual Communities

IGI Global is currently accepting manuscripts for publication within this series. To submit a proposal for a volume in this series, please contact our Acquisition Editors at Acquisitions@igi-global.com or visit: http://www.igi-global.com/publish/.

Titles in this Series

For a list of additional titles in this series, please visit: www.igi-global.com

Societal Benefits of Freely Accessible Technologies and Knowledge Resources
Oswaldo Terán (Universidad de los Andes, Venezuela) and Jose Aguilar (Universidad de los Andes, Venezuela)
Information Science Reference • copyright 2015 • 362pp • H/C (ISBN: 9781466683365) • US $175.00 (our price)

Contemporary Issues Surrounding Ethical Research Methods and Practice
Chi B. Anyansi-Archibong (North Carolina A&T State University, USA)
Information Science Reference • copyright 2015 • 376pp • H/C (ISBN: 9781466685628) • US $205.00 (our price)

Organizational Knowledge Dynamics Managing Knowledge Creation, Acquisition, Sharing, and Transformation
Constantin Bratianu (Bucharest University of Economic Studies, Romania)
Information Science Reference • copyright 2015 • 349pp • H/C (ISBN: 9781466683181) • US $210.00 (our price)

Strategic Data-Based Wisdom in the Big Data Era
John Girard (Middle Georgia State College, USA) Deanna Klein (Minot State University, USA) and Kristi Berg (Minot State University, USA)
Information Science Reference • copyright 2015 • 312pp • H/C (ISBN: 9781466681224) • US $205.00 (our price)

Handbook of Research on Maximizing Cognitive Learning through Knowledge Visualization
Anna Ursyn (University of Northern Colorado, USA)
Information Science Reference • copyright 2015 • 572pp • H/C (ISBN: 9781466681422) • US $325.00 (our price)

Information Seeking Behavior and Technology Adoption Theories and Trends
Mohammed Nasser Al-Suqri (Sultan Qaboos University, Oman) and Ali Saif Al-Aufi (Sultan Qaboos University, Oman)
Information Science Reference • copyright 2015 • 321pp • H/C (ISBN: 9781466681569) • US $200.00 (our price)

Handbook of Research on Scholarly Publishing and Research Methods
Victor C.X. Wang (Florida Atlantic University, USA)
Information Science Reference • copyright 2015 • 589pp • H/C (ISBN: 9781466674097) • US $335.00 (our price)

Collaborative Knowledge in Scientific Research Networks
Paolo Diviacco (Istituto Nazionale di Oceanografia e di Geofisica Sperimentale (OGS), Italy) Peter Fox (Rensselaer Polytechnic Institute, USA) Cyril Pshenichny (Geognosis Project, ITMO University, Russia) and Adam Leadbetter (British Oceanographic Data Centre, NERC, UK)
Information Science Reference • copyright 2015 • 461pp • H/C (ISBN: 9781466665675) • US $200.00 (our price)

www.igi-global.com

701 E. Chocolate Ave., Hershey, PA 17033
Order online at www.igi-global.com or call 717-533-8845 x100
To place a standing order for titles released in this series, contact: cust@igi-global.com
Mon-Fri 8:00 am - 5:00 pm (est) or fax 24 hours a day 717-533-8661

List of Contributors

Table of Contents

Detailed Table of Contents

Chapter 1

    Ramona Trestian, Middlesex University, UK
    Faisal Zaman, University College Dublin, Ireland
    Gabriel-Miro Muntean, Dublin City University, Ireland

Being able to react fast to exceptional events such as riots protests or disaster preventions is of paramount importance, especially when trying to ensure peoples' safety and security, or even save lives. This chapter presents a study on the use of fully anonymized and highly aggregated cellular network data, like Call Detail Records (CDRs) in order to connect people, locations and events. The goal of the study is to see if the CDR data can be used to detect exceptional spatio-temporal patterns of the collective human mobile data usage and correlate these 'anomalies' with real-world events (e.g., parades, public concerts, soccer match, traffic congestion, riots protests etc.). These observations could be further used to develop an intelligent system that detects exceptional events in real-time from CDRs data monitoring. Such system could be used in intelligent transportation management, urban planning, emergency situations, network resource allocation and performance optimization, etc.

Chapter 2

    Alireza Amrollahi, Griffith University, Australia
    Mohammad Tahaei, University of Tehran, Iran
    Mohammad Khansari, University of Tehran, Iran

Since 2001 Wikipedia has grown up to one of the most important sources of knowledge worldwide. The voluntarily and independent nature of the project has made it a very unique case of Information Systems with various elements which could affect the way each article is developed. In this paper by referring to the DeLone& McLean model of Information Systems success and considering the body of research in the field, the measures for evaluating the effectiveness of wiki articles have been identified. Then using a sample of 804 articles in Wikipedia and Structural Equation Model (SEM) method the model has been validated. The findings indicate that in the context of Wikipedia open content, system quality and information quality could be merged together and after this simplification, they can affect use and user satisfaction in open content platforms such as Wikipedia.

Chapter 3

Muhammad Ibrahim, Monash University, Australia
Manzur Murshed, Federation University Australia

Ranking a set of documents based on their relevances with respect to a given query is a central problem of information retrieval (IR). Traditionally people have been using unsupervised scoring methods like tf-idf, BM25, Language Model etc., but recently supervised machine learning framework is being used successfully to learn a ranking function, which is called learning-to-rank (LtR) problem. There are a few surveys on LtR in the literature; but these reviews provide very little assistance to someone who, before delving into technical details of different algorithms, wants to have a broad understanding of LtR systems and its evolution from and relation to the traditional IR methods. This chapter tries to address this gap in the literature. Mainly the following aspects are discussed: the fundamental concepts of IR, the motivation behind LtR, the evolution of LtR from and its relation to the traditional methods, the relationship between LtR and other supervised machine learning tasks, the general issues pertaining to an LtR algorithm, and the theory of LtR.

Chapter 4

Salim Lahmiri, ESCA School of Management, Morocco

This paper compares the accuracy of three hybrid intelligent systems in forecasting ten international stock market indices; namely the CAC40, DAX, FTSE, Hang Seng, KOSPI, NASDAQ, NIKKEI, S&P500, Taiwan stock market price index, and the Canadian TSE. In particular, genetic algorithms (GA) are used to optimize the topology and parameters of the adaptive time delay neural networks (ATNN) and the time delay neural networks (TDNN). The third intelligent system is the adaptive neuro-fuzzy inference system (ANFIS) that basically integrates fuzzy logic into the artificial neural network (ANN) to better model information and explain decision making process. Based on out-of-sample simulation results, it was found that contrary to the literature GA-TDNN significantly outperforms GA-ATDNN. In addition, ANFIS was found to be more effective in forecasting CAC40, FTSE, Hang Seng, NIKKEI, Taiwan, and TSE price level. In contrary, GA-TDNN and GA-ATDNN were found to be superior to ANFIS in predicting DAX, KOSPI, and NASDAQ future prices.

Chapter 5

Jenny Grant Rankin, Northcentral University, USA

In the field of Education, computerized data systems are used to manage, retrieve, and analyze information. Educators view this information in the form of data reports, which educators use to inform decisions that impact students. These decisions are frequently undermined by misunderstandings concerning the data and its implications. Yet data systems and their reports typically display data without any guidance concerning the data's proper analysis. In a quantitative study, medicine labeling conventions were applied to data systems to embed guidance in the proper use of contents. Among 211 educators of varied backgrounds and roles, data analyses were found to be 307% more accurate when a report label/footer was present, 205% more accurate when a 1-page reference sheet was present, and 273% more accurate when a reference guide was present. Findings hold implications for those who provide or use tools for high-stakes information retrieval, analysis, and/or management, particularly in Education.

Analytics (discover and communication of patterns, with significance, in data) of Big Data (basically characterized by large structured and unstructured data volumes, from a variety of sources, at high velocity - i.e., real-time data capture, storage, and analysis), through the use of Cloud Computing (a model of network computing) is becoming the new "ABC" of information and communication technologies (ICTs), with important effects for the generation of new firms and for the restructuring of those ones already established. However, as this chapter argues, successful application of these new ABC technologies and tools depends on two interrelated policy aspects: 1) the use of a proper model which could help one to approach the structure and dynamics of the firm, and, 2) how the complex trade-off between information technology (IT) and communication technology (CT) costs is handled within, between and beyond firms, organizations and institutions.

In this chapter the authors explore the relationship between Information Systems and Organization Development, highlighting the value that Holistic Change Interventions can introduce when applied to IS/IT areas, mobilizing Individuals, Groups and the whole Organization to promote Organizational Effectiveness. A "soft" approach to Organizational Change is proposed, focusing on main internal aspects which are determinant for Organizational Performance, including Organizational Culture and Values, Leadership, Work Teams, and Employee Engagement. The approach is illustrated by a successful "real-world" Transformational Change Program which has been developed, within an IT Unit of a major financial organization, following an Action Research paradigm. The intervention has integrated two main cycles – a first one covering the strategy determination and behavioral preparation for further action, and a second one devoted to a coordinated implementation of strategic actions which have emerged from the first cycle – where communication, engagement, action and improvement have been the most relevant attributes of the whole process. From a Research perspective this successful Change intervention has served to develop and test, within context, a Framework of Critical Success Factors for Holistic Change, which is described on its management implications, and covering distinct areas and dimensions. Also, the high potential of Action Research, to promote Holistic Change within real organizational settings, and, simultaneously, to address complex research issues, questions, objectives, and test hypothesis, is deeply illustrated within this chapter.

In face of growing global competition, the ability of organizations to effectively use information technologies to deliver innovation and creativity is widely recognized as an important competitive advantage. In this context, knowledge of how to apply creativity techniques to information systems planning becomes particularly relevant. This chapter presents a framework for the introduction of creativity in Information Systems Planning. The framework aims at promoting the development of innovative Information Systems, which traditional methods of requirements elicitation fail to address. Finally, we discuss how the framework was implemented at a public organization to identify information systems opportunities.

Chapter 9

This chapter seeks a deeper understanding of stakeholder dynamics as a critical social component influencing IT strategy alignment. Perez-Batres et al. (2012) recognized the paucity of research on alignment dynamics, mainly stakeholder dynamics. Stakeholder theory, primarily Mitchell et al. (1997) identification model, is used to determine stakeholders' saliency throughout an ICT strategic project in a Saudi public hospital. However, stakeholder theory is static and does not help in tracing how saliency is gained and lost through time, and hence interpreting the influence on the alignment process. Therefore, this research utilizes the appreciative systems concepts of Geoffrey Vickers as dynamizing instrument to understand saliency dynamics and their influence. Results show that stakeholder dynamics resides in the nature of the relationship they pursue with each other.

Chapter 10

This chapter applies the principle of reflective practice - as the capacity to reflect on action - so as to engage in a process of continuous learning about the implementation of an e-learning platform at the Polytechnic Institute of Santarem, Portugal. The chapter begins with an introduction to the role of reflective practice, a discussion of fundamental e-learning principles and an overview of the e-learning platform's information architecture. In addition, two methodological tools support the reflective thinking process and the extraction of recommendations: social network analysis and visualization of structured discussion forum activity, and an inductive thematic analysis of the postings to the platform's unstructured fora.

Chapter 11

The investigation of information systems (IS) development usually relies on two different research approaches, namely, quantitative approach and qualitative approach. Both approaches are equally important and useful to the development of IS theories. No research approach should be considered to be superior or inferior to the other. However, the mainstream of Chinese IS research mainly follows the quantitative approach, whereas the qualitative approach is generally viewed as "too soft" or not scientific enough. As a qualitative approach, desk case-study research approach has been widely accepted and applied in a number of IS research in the West. However, in China, this approach is merely considered as an effective approach for teaching, but not valid for scientific research investigations. Thus, Chinese

IS research have neglected a number of important experiences, viewpoints and lessons, which can be elicited from IS case-studies occurred in the past. This chapter generally aims at introducing and discussing the desk case-study approach in IS research. Specifically, this chapter discusses this approach through four incremental research stages, namely, defining the research question, establishing theoretical framework from literature review, case-study selection, and theory formulation through case-study analysis. Furthermore, two exemplary research projects are presented in this chapter to further clarify and substantiate the research methods, tools and processes. It is expected that by formulating a rigorous research framework and specifying incremental processes of theory development, this research approach could be accepted and used by Chinese IS scholars in the future.

Chapter 12

Guo Chao Peng, The University of Sheffield, UK
Miguel Baptista Nunes, The University of Sheffield, UK

The research reported in this paper aimed to identify and explore potential cultural, operational, managerial, organisational and technical barriers and risks that can affect successful long-term exploitation of Enterprise Resource Planning (ERP) systems in Chinese SOEs. The study adopted a mixed-methods research design, which consisted of a questionnaire survey and a follow-up multiple case study. Business-oriented and human-related challenges associated with management deficiencies in Chinese SOEs were found to be the main triggers of the complicated network of ERP exploitation barriers and risks. The importance of these crucial business and organisational barriers however are often underestimated by SOE managers. This study thus concluded by suggesting that Chinese SOEs need to become more aware of the critical importance and the networked nature of the organisational barriers identified. Properly managing this type of ERP obstacles can help Chinese SOEs to mitigate and remove other ERP challenges and risks and thus ensuring long-term success in ERP post-implementation.

Chapter 13

John N Walsh, University of Limerick, Ireland
Fergal McGrath, University of Limerick, Ireland

The objective of this chapter is to present a case study of the development of a strategy to increase eParticipation among a number of disadvantaged communities in the city of Limerick in Ireland. The chapter's authors' acted as facilitators for the strategy development process. The strategy group consisted of multiple educational, developmental and community and local government representatives. Given the participants' differing perspectives and interpretations the strategy development attempted to be as inclusive and transparent as possible and information technology was used that provided shared spaces using a wiki and allowing the sharing of the information (strategy document) as it emerged through various iterations.

Chapter 14

This chapter presents the development of a new human-machine interface - a wheelchair controlled by the recognition of human hands' static gestures. The application will allow the occupant of an intelligent wheelchair to communicate with certain objects in order to facilitate their daily life. The suggested methodology draws on the use of computational processes and low-cost hardware. The development of the application involved dealing with computer vision issues in a comprehensive way. It was based on the steps of video image capture, image segmentation, feature extraction, pattern recognition and classification. In terms of its relevance and impact, the application described in the chapter promotes a more natural and intuitive mode of interaction for disabled individuals, which is expected to improve their quality of life.

This chapter reveals the roles of business process modeling (BPM) and business process reengineering (BPR) in eGovernment, thus describing the concepts of eGovernment and BPM; BPM methodologies; business process modeling notation (BPMN); the importance of BPR in government-to-citizen (G2C) e-commerce; the relationship between BPM and eGovernment-based citizen satisfaction; the application of BPR in eGovernment; and the implementation of eGovernment through BPM. eGovernment is a modern trend that is driven by the advances in BPM and BPR as well as the aspirations of citizens who place increasing demands on governments' service. By modeling business processes in eGovernment, public sector organizations can achieve improvements in transparency and reduction in costs and resource requirements, resulting in improved business performance and compliance. The chapter argues that applying BPM and BPR in eGovernment has the potential to enhance public sector performance and achieve organizational goals in public sector organizations.

The study reported in this chapter evaluates how the Customer Experience Management System (CEMS) used by a University's Student Support Services (StuSS) responds to the objectives of capturing, storing, extracting, interpreting, distributing, using and reporting customer experience information for creating organisational value. Theoretically, the study draws on the concept of organizational ambidexterity. Concerning the research design, the study was undertaken using qualitative methods of data collection and interpretivist methods of data analysis. It has been inductively discovered that the availability of customer experience information obtained through the CEMS allows StuSS to respond effectively to different student needs. Organizationally, there is clarity concerning the ownership and management of customer relationships. Individual student data is collected, coordinated and distributed across lines of business. Because of this, StuSS is able to consistently identify customers across touch points and channels. Further suggestions are advanced to improve StuSS's analytical investigation capability to derive descriptive and predictive customer information, through applying data mining models to the information that is currently collected.

Research conducted around the topic of open innovation has been mainly empirical in nature and primarily focused on firms. For a better understanding of open innovation, it is important to conduct further research beyond the "firm environment", particularly in areas related to public policy. This chapter addresses the topic of open innovation, relating it to public policy, analyzing the framework conditions that can stimulate the development of open innovation in organizations. More specifically, the chapter uses the Portuguese public policies as a case study. A methodology is proposed and discussed for analyzing the degree of openness in public policy, concerning policy orientation to support the development of open innovation.

Research Knowledge production is the result from knowledge processes that happen at diverse networks spaces. Those spaces are supported by a cascade of systems (Data Management Systems, Information Management Systems, Knowledge Management Systems, Evaluation Systems and Monitoring Systems) that must be aligned to avoid formation of silos and barriers to the flows of information and knowledge. The energy that powers consists of the people and their connections; so there is crucial to understand and govern formal and informal networks. By take a holistic approach, we propose to join benefits of an efficient knowledge management with the implementation of knowledge governance mechanisms in order to improve Research Knowledge production and its impacts.

Preface

Our aim in editing this book was to present original research that advances knowledge on the production, discovery, recording, storage, representation, retrieval, presentation, interaction, dissemination, use and evaluation of information and on the tools, techniques and processes associated with such practices.

Traditional accounts of information science as a discipline relate it to the practice of information sense making and to the concrete ways in which information can be organised, searched, accessed and mediated through different technologies and techniques. Therefore, this field of research emphasises the micro and macro conditions and methods available for individuals and organisations to get hold of relevant information for their different activities (e.g. business, public administration, education and training, personal development, etc.).

The variety of understandings, platforms and problems introduced by different social actors, business models, behavioural patterns and technologies contributes greatly to the density of information science as a discipline and to the complexity of its implications: from the implementation and evaluation of retrieval systems to the strategies that operationalize the management of information resources; from the principles of knowledge and information organisation to the socio-technical fit and strategic alignment of systems designed to store, manage and share information effectively.

Departing from a definition of information science as the discipline that examines information systems in their social, cultural, economic, historical, legal and political contexts, this book seeks to take stock of innovative directions the discipline has developed into. The result, we hope, is an enhanced understanding of novel ways in which both users and the social systems they are embedded into change through the use of information and information technology.

The primary audiences are researchers, developers, managers, strategic planners, doctoral students and all others interested in state-of-the art knowledge in the field of information. A common concern with the future of information science and with the skills required to successfully navigate the contemporary digital contexts will be the element uniting these diverse audiences. Moreover, the multifaceted nature of the big questions of information science is of interest to a wide range of backgrounds such as management science, computer science, cognitive and behavioural science, education, etc.

In terms of structure and contents, there are six sections to the book. In Section One, we present developments in, and approaches to information retrieval. Using fully anonymized and highly aggregated cellular network data (e.g. call detail records - CDRs) as a starting point, Trestian, Raman and Muntean explore the possibility of connecting people, locations and certain types of events. More specifically the chapter explores the use of CDR data to detect exceptional spatio-temporal patterns of collective human mobile data usage and correlates these 'anomalies' with real-world events such as parades, public concerts, traffic congestions or riots. This is particularly relevant as the observations reported in the chapter can inform the further development of an intelligent system that detects exceptional events in real-time based on CDRs data monitoring. The potential areas of application are manifold and include smart cities and network resource allocation.

Amrollahi, Tahaei and Khansari focus on the analysis of Wikipedia as an information system. The chapter applies the DeLone& McLean model of information systems success to measure the effectiveness of Wikipedia articles. Given the popularity of Wikipedia and its large volume of users, the study is of great relevance, particularly as the findings confirm the impact of content quality and content presentation on Wikipedia user satisfaction.

Finally, Ibrahim and Murshed offer an insight into how learning to rank (LtR) for information retrieval has gained a lot of interest in the recent years. In a comprehensive and detailed chapter the authors introduce LtR and discuss how it relates to other information retrieval methods, situate LtR in relation to supervised machine learning tasks (e.g. classification, regression, ordinal classification), and discuss LtR algorithms.

In Section Two we take a closer look to theory, principles, and procedures in information analysis. Lahmiri presents the use of intelligent systems for stock market predictions. More specifically, the chapter compares three artificial neural network architectures used for the prediction of next day individual stock price using past values. The three soft computing models compared are the adaptive neuro-fuzzy inference system (ANFIS), the time delay neural network (TDNN), and the adaptive time delay neural network (ATDNN).

Rankin raises the timely question of educators facing the widespread use of computerized data systems to manage, retrieve, and analyze student and teaching-related information without embedded usage guidance to ensure each data content is properly understood and appropriately used. As remedial action the chapter identifies formats through which data systems can embed data usage guidance in order to improve educators' data analysis accuracy.

A final conceptual paper is presented by Cavalcanti, where the interrelations between analytics (discovery and communication of data patterns, with significance, in data) of big data (large volumes of structured and unstructured data), through the use of cloud computing is discussed. The argument coalesces around the proposed Architecture-Governance-Growth Model, which holds the key to the complex trade-offs between information technology and communication technology costs, which are common to contemporary organizations.

In Section Three we unpack the reciprocal relationship between information systems and organizations and the impacts that these relationships create. Henriques and O'Neill demonstrate that the interaction between human behavior and information systems continues to be an exciting area of research. Their chapter discusses how human behavior plays an essential role at every stage of the lifecycle of information systems, from development to adoption, deployment, and use. The emphasis however is on change management within the information technology department of a financial institution. Therefore, the chapter focuses on the associated opportunities and challenges, at individual, team, and organizational levels of analysis.

The engagement with challenging disciplinary and interdisciplinary perspectives in information systems research is further accomplished by Santos, Amaral, S. Mamede and Gonçalves, and their proposed framework for the embedding of creativity in Information Systems Planning. This topic is particularly relevant for information systems planning research, as achieving the right balance between creativity and control has always been problematic. The chapter describes the process of introducing creativity in information systems planning in detail and presents an action research case study where the framework was successfully applied to identify opportunities for the development of information systems at a large public sector organization.

In seeking a deeper understanding of stakeholder dynamics as a critical social component influencing information systems strategy alignment, Alghaith conducts an analysis of stakeholder saliency dynamics in a strategic information systems project within a Saudi public hospital. This analysis is attained through the innovative combination of stakeholder theory and appreciative systems concepts. The results indicate that information systems strategy and project management are not static. Indeed, in face of changing events in the context of the project stakeholders choose to maintain, elude, or modify relationships. This in turn causes them to lose or gain saliency and influence during the project's trajectory.

In Section Four we consider the development and management of information systems with a particular focus on identifying effective project management practices. Taking the perspective of the reflective practitioner, Potes Barbas offers an engaging narrative where the implementation of an e-learning system at a Portuguese Higher Education Institution is critically appraised. The description of the implementation process is punctuated with a literature-informed discussion of the use of information and communications technologies in universities, as well as of the impacts of using e-learning systems in educational practice on learners and on educators. Situating the chapter within the research agenda of educational informatics, the author seeks to present practical knowledge that is of relevance to the design and facilitation of learning environments that are supported by e-learning systems.

In a refreshing position paper, Zhou and Baptista Nunes advocate the use of desk research methodology in information systems research, arguing that when conducted rigorously it can contribute to the identification of useful experiences, viewpoints and lessons, directly extracted from information systems management case studies. The chapter focuses particularly in the context of China, where the interest in information systems research is flourishing, yet where the use of qualitative research approaches is still in its infancy. The authors illustrate their proposed approach to conducting desk research with a structured presentation of two case studies: establishing information systems project risk checklist, and identifying knowledge sharing barriers in Chinese healthcare referral services.

Reinforcing the argument that research on information technologies in China is gaining increasing attention in the information systems community, Peng and Baptista Nunes examine the barriers and risks affecting long term enterprise resource planning (ERP) systems success, in the specific context of Chinese state-owned enterprises. The authors conducted an exhaustive exploration of potential cultural, operational, managerial, organizational and technical barriers and risks, which culminated in the identification of business-oriented and human-related challenges. These, associated with management deficiencies in Chinese state-owned enterprises, are the main triggers of a network of ERP systems exploitation barriers and risks.

In Section Five we reflect on the ways in which society is being reshaped in the ubiquitous presence of information systems. Walsh and McGrath explore the mechanisms of e-participation, i.e. the use of information technology-supported participation in government and governance processes. The specific context of the research reported in this chapter is the city of Limerick, Ireland, where the authors attempted to foster the engagement of disadvantaged communities with the formal politics sphere through the use of shared wiki spaces. The wiki spaces operated as a platform of engagement where participants contributed to the production of a strategy document, and in this sense the chapter enhances our understanding of management practices in relation to community digital strategy.

Moving into the substantive field of human computer interaction, Guerra Lopes presents a novel system that exploits human-machine interfaces based on the recognitions of hands static gestures to enhance the mobility of wheelchair occupants. The chapter details how the development of the system - based on video image capture, image segmentation, feature extraction, pattern recognition and classification – contributes to a model of interaction that is natural and intuitive, thus facilitating the experience of differently abled citizens.

Subsequently, Kasemsap discusses how information systems are not only changing the way organizations store and process information, but also the ways in which citizens interact with their governments. The chapter offers a conceptual discussion into how citizen-centered eGovernment services can be attained. A discussion of the relationship between business process modeling and government-based citizen satisfaction is the theoretical foundation for the proposition of business process reengineering in eGovernment services.

Finally, in Section Six we explore the concept of knowledge management as a set of practices related to the use of knowledge as a crucial factor to add and generate value. Kouassi, Martins and Molnar propose the use of organizational ambidexterity theory to frame the evaluation of a customer experience management system in a Higher Education Institution. Ambidexterity is presented as the organizational ability to remain aligned and efficient in current business demands while simultaneously being flexibly adaptive to environmental changes. Typically this requires achieving a balance between knowledge exploration and knowledge exploitation activities. The use of a student oriented customer experience management system is evaluated against this theoretical framework, in a context where the experience of students as customers is increasingly valued, and where the adoption of strategic information systems to guide decision making is growing.

Continuing with research on innovation and knowledge processes Bob Santos proposes to extend the open innovation paradigm to the analysis of public policy incentives. Mainstream research on open innovation tends to focus on the use of non-linear thinking and disruptive creative solutions in the context of firms. However, the availability of external knowledge for firms to assimilate is critical to open innovation. Using Portugal as a case study, this chapter proposes to analyse how public policy endeavours to promote organizations' open innovation practices and proposes a conceptual framework for analyzing the degree of openness in public policy mechanisms.

A final conceptual chapter is presented by Pinho and Pinho, who put forward a reflection on the need to govern academic research knowledge. In times of increasing pressure to deliver high quality inputs and impactful research, and when multiparty interdisciplinary research consortia become commonplace, the article discusses academic research activity monitoring and evaluation and the need to strategically align the variety of knowledge and information management systems used by academics within Higher Education Institutions.

We owe particular thanks to the authors of this volume for the high level of the contributions, but also for their cooperation and patience, and for responding so generously to reviewers' comments and editorial suggestions. Our heartfelt thanks are also extended to the reviewers who undertook anonymous assessment of the chapters.

In preparing this book we wanted to be forward looking and to develop the current theoretical and practical understanding of information science as a fascinating field that continually evolves into productive directions as individuals' and organisations' information needs and behaviours expand and grow in complexity. We trust that this volume will contribute in that regard.

Jorge Tiago Martins
The University of Sheffield, UK

Andreea Molnar
University of Portsmouth, UK

Chapter 1
Spotted:
Connecting People, Locations, and Real–World Events in a Cellular Network

Ramona Trestian
Middlesex University, UK

Faisal Zaman
University College Dublin, Ireland

Gabriel-Miro Muntean
Dublin City University, Ireland

ABSTRACT

Being able to react fast to exceptional events such as riots protests or disaster preventions is of paramount importance, especially when trying to ensure peoples' safety and security, or even save lives. This chapter presents a study on the use of fully anonymized and highly aggregated cellular network data, like Call Detail Records (CDRs) in order to connect people, locations and events. The goal of the study is to see if the CDR data can be used to detect exceptional spatio-temporal patterns of the collective human mobile data usage and correlate these 'anomalies' with real-world events (e.g., parades, public concerts, soccer match, traffic congestion, riots protests etc.). These observations could be further used to develop an intelligent system that detects exceptional events in real-time from CDRs data monitoring. Such system could be used in intelligent transportation management, urban planning, emergency situations, network resource allocation and performance optimization, etc.

INTRODUCTION

In the ever-evolving telecommunication industry, smart mobile computing devices have become increasingly affordable and powerful, leading to a significant growth in the number of advanced mobile users and their bandwidth demands.

This, together with the improved next generation telecommunications infrastructure, motivates the continuing uptake of the mobility around the world. People can now connect to the Internet from anywhere at any time, while on the move (e.g. on foot, in the car, on the bus, stuck in traffic etc.) or stationary (e.g., at home/office/airport/coffee

DOI: 10.4018/978-1-4666-8833-9.ch001

bars, etc.). The number of mobile users increases continuously as the penetration of both fixed and mobile broadband solutions becomes more affordable for the masses and more accessible around the globe. The connection to the Internet is possible and can be done via wireline or wireless solutions. Depending on the user location, wireless connectivity is enabled by different Radio Access Technologies (RATs) such as: Global System for Mobile Communications (GSM), Enhanced Data Rates for GSM Evolution (EDGE), Universal Mobile Telecommunications System (UMTS), High Speed Packet Access (HSPA), Long Term Evolution (LTE), Worldwide Interoperability for Microwave Access (WiMAX), Wireless Local Area Networks (WLAN), Wireless Personal Area Network (WPAN), etc. The use of all these RATs is rapidly spreading, covering various geographical locations in an overlapping manner.

Additionally, this increasing expansion of the telecommunication infrastructure could bring economic, social and technological benefits especially to the far reaching regions. For example, it can bring education to the remote regions; it can contribute to enabling innovations in healthcare (e.g., remote monitoring and diagnostics), smart grid solutions, social networking sites, economy, etc.

One of the key characteristics of these mobile networks and the mobile computing devices is that every time they are used a digital signature is recorded. Voluntarily or not, whenever people interact with the telecommunications networks or any type of social media platform, they leave behind digital traces. All these traces have become a powerful tool to analyze human behavior patterns. For example, the data collected by the cellular telecommunications systems referred to as Call Details Records (CDRs) is done in regular basis for billing and troubleshooting purposes. Moreover these CDRs contain the information details about every call carried within the cellular network, including information about the location, call duration, call time, and both parties involved in the conversation. Thus, there is an increase in-

terest on making use of the information provided by the CDRs in order to analyze human mobility cheaply, frequently and especially at a very large scale. To this end, three main reasons could be identified in using the CDR data, such as: their usage incur insignificant additional costs as they are already being collected by the network operators to help manage their networks; they can be used for large-scale analysis as they are collected for all the active cellular phones within a network reaching billions of users worldwide; and they can be used for timely analysis as they are collected continuously for each incoming or outgoing calls and text message. Even though the importance of the CDRs is obvious, they have two important limitations that need to be mentioned as well: (1) they are sparse in time, as they are collected only when the mobile device is initiating or receiving calls or exchanges text messages; and (2) they are coarse in space as they record only the location of the communication tower the mobile device is connected to.

In general, understanding the human mobility patterns could have broad applicability on a wide range of areas, such as: network resource optimization, mobile computing, transportation systems, urban environment planning, events management, epidemiology, etc.

This chapter will explore the use of anonymized CDRs containing both voice-calls and SMS activities, from a cellular network in Ivory Coast in order to connect people, locations and events. The goal of this study is to identify the exceptional spatio-temporal patterns of the collective human activity from fully anonymized and highly aggregate cellular network data, like CDRs, and correlate these 'anomalies' with real-world events (e.g., parades, public concerts, soccer match, traffic congestion, etc.). These observations could be further used to develop an intelligent system that detects exceptional events in real-time from CDRs monitoring. The benefits of such systems could be threefold:

- The network operators could benefit by detecting congested cells and optimize their network resources in advance of an exceptional event (Zang et al., 2007), e.g., make use of the Wi-Fi offloading solutions, enabling adaptive bandwidth allocation to their radio cells, etc.;
- The society could benefit from intelligent transportation and urban planning and management (Isaacman et al., 2010);
- The individual could benefit from traffic information and prediction, emergency management (Bagrow et al., 2011). For example, a real-time event detection system could be used in case of emergency situations, such as riots protests which could be more efficiently handled if detected and handled on time.

In this context, the research questions of this study are:

- Can the CDR data be used to detect exceptional spatio-temporal patterns of the collective human mobile data usage?
- Can we correlate these exceptional usage patterns to real-world events?

The rest of the book chapter is organized as follows: the related work section provides a comprehensive classification, comparison and analysis of the state-of-the-art approaches in using user-generated mobile data in modeling human population movement for specific areas; the third section describes the datasets used in this study and provides information about the data collection methodology and characteristics; the fourth section provides an in-depth analysis on the datasets in order to identify hotspots and correlate people, locations and events during the period of the recorded data; the fifth section looks into connecting people and locations from the dataset; whereas the sixth section connects people, locations and real-world events from the spatio-temporal patterns identified in the dataset; the seventh section provides an analysis on the user mobility and activity, and finally the conclusions of this study are presented in the last section.

RELATED WORKS

In the current environment, the mobile network operators are laying at the intersection of the emerging technologies such as big data analytics, location-based services, or machine-to-machine communications. By taking advantage of these technologies, especially big data, will offer the mobile operators real opportunities to gain a complete view and understanding of their operations as well as their customers. The aim of big data analytics is to correlate every source of information in order to generate a transparent end-to-end view of all the customers' interactions with the mobile operator. In this way the mobile operators could benefit in terms of: routing optimization and Quality of Service by real time network traffic analysis, identifying fraudulent behavior from call data records, individualized marketing campaigns using location-based or social networking technologies, analyze the customer behavior to develop new products, etc. Apart from the benefits brought to the network operators, this big data analysis could help the community as well, such as: city planners could use the data to identify places to extend the public transport, the data could help study the human behavior in case of emergency situation, the data cloud also help studying the epidemic spread, etc.

Recently, there has been extensive academic research related to the use of user-generated traffic in mobile communications networks as a powerful tool to analyze human behavior. As billions of people around the world own at least one mobile device, the data from the mobile communications networks could help study different aspects of human mobility and their interactions on a large scale.

As there is a wide amount of research on the use of user-generated traffic within the mobile communications networks aiming to understand different aspects of human people movement and interaction, this section provides a comprehensive survey of the current research and classifies the wide range of solutions into six broad categories, based on their applications: (1) definition of the universal law for human mobility – this category includes solutions that are using the CDR data to characterize the human mobility; (2) urban planning and real-time traffic forecast – this category includes solutions that are using the CDR data in order to estimate real-traffic volumes on the commuting routes and provide real-time traffic forecast; (3) human localization and mobility patterns – this category includes solutions that make use of CDR data in order to identify important locations in humans' live; (4) context-aware applications – this category includes solutions that make use of the CDR data to correlate anomalies behavior from the data to real-world events; (5) subscribers churn and privacy – this category includes solutions that make use of the CDR data in order to predict the churning rate and avoid privacy risks; and (6) health management – this category includes solutions that make use of the CDR data in order to understand the spreading of the infectious diseases and their correlation with the human mobility. All these categories and their solutions are introduced in the following sections.

Definition of the Universal Law for Human Mobility

When looking into understanding the human mobility patterns, several works tried to define some basic laws governing the human motion. Gonzalez te al. (2008) showed that individuals follow simple reproducible patterns despite the diversity in their travel history. The study was conducted by tracking the position of a number of 100,000 anonymized mobile phone users over a six month period. The authors state that the 100,000 individuals were randomly selected from a sample of more than 6 million anonymized mobile phone users. The location of the communication tower the users were connected to when they initiated or received a call or a text messages was used by the authors in constructing the user's time-resolved trajectory. The authors observed that individuals present significant regularity in their trajectories as they often return to several of their highly frequented locations (e.g., home, work). A second data set with the location of 206 mobile phone users over one week period was used to validate the results.

Song et al. (2010a) used empirical data on human mobility to show that the predictions provided by the continuous time random walk (CTRW) models conflict with the empirical results. The authors made use of two data sets: (1) the first dataset contains the CDRs of 3 million anonymized mobile phone users over a one year period; (2) the second dataset contains the hourly location record of 1,000 anonymized users who signed up for a location-based service, over a two week period. The authors explore the limitations of the traditional random walk models and propose a new individual mobility model that takes into consideration the exploration and the preferential return of the individual. The exploration refers to the probability of the individual moving to a new location. As the authors state, observing the trajectory of an individual long enough it becomes harder to find unexplored locations within the vicinity of their home or workplace. The preferential return refers to the probability of the individual returning to one of the previously visited locations. It has been shown that human tend to return to the highly visited locations, like home or workplace, which is not considered by the random walking models. The authors state that the proposed model adds an improvement over the traditional random walk models by capturing the specifics of human mobility.

A study on the limitations of predictability in human mobility is provided by Song et al. (2010b). The study is conducted using the CDRs of 50,000 anonymized mobile phone users over a three months period. The 50,000 individuals were selected from a sample of 10 million anonymized mobile phone users, following the criteria: more than two locations visited and an average call frequency higher than 0.5 hour[1] The authors observe that most of the individuals can be well localized within a specific neighborhood with only few users traveling widely. The study shows that there is a probability of 93% that the human location could be predicted regardless of how far the person travels within the preferred locations.

Noulas et al. (2012) try to identify a universal law for human mobility using data from a large set of Foursquare users. More specifically, the authors collected the data from public check-ins that users made on the location-based social network, Foursquare. The authors study the movement of 925,030 users around the globe covering 5 million places in 34 metropolitan cities, over a six months period. The authors model the urban mobility and show that the distance is not enough to define a universal law for human mobility. The authors also show that the place density is the key component of urban movement and propose the use of rank-based mobility preferences in order to reproduce the movement distribution as observed in the real data.

Kung et al. (2014) explored the universal patterns in human home-work commuting using a broad range of datasets. The authors used the CDRs from different parts of the world and study the mobility pattern at the country level and city level. Five datasets were used: (1) the first dataset provided by Orange telecom, contains the CDRs of 50,000 randomized subscribers of Ivory Coast over 150 days; (2) the second dataset provided by Orange telecom, contains the CDRs of 2 million users from Portugal over a 2 years period; (3) the third dataset provided by Saudi Telecom Company, encompasses the data from 14 million devices in Saudi Arabia; (4) the fourth dataset provided by AirSage, contains the signaling data of 2 million mobile devices over 4 months period in the Greater Boston area; and (5) the fifth dataset provided

by Octo Telematics, contains the GPS traces of 99,000 cars over a period of one week in Milan metropolitan area. The study showed that it is possible to identify common commute features even though the datasets are highly different in nature. The authors used the vehicle GPS data from Milan to compare it against the other datasets that are more agnostic to different commute methods and showed that the constant travel time hypothesis applies at the aggregate level only. Another study that looked into the use of CDRs in sampling the human mobility is provided by Ranjan et al. (2012). The dataset used consists of CDRs from over 500,000 anonymized mobile phone users over one month period (July 2011) in San Francisco bay area. The authors differentiated between the voice calls and SMS and compared the voice call and SMS sampling processes against an artificially imposed sampling process, such as Poisson point process. The authors demonstrated that the imposed Poisson sampling process yields better results of the user's spatio-temporal behavior particularly as the activity rates vary.

Palchykov et al (2014) showed that human mobility can be predicted by using a simple model based on the frequency of the mobile phone calls between two locations and their geographical distance. The authors use the data provided by Orange for Ivory Coast, consisting of CDRs from 50,000 anonymized mobile phone users collected over a 150 days period. Using only the aggregated call data and the geospatial information as inputs, three different models were tested: the gravity model, the communication model based on the number of calls between two locations, and a modified version of the radiation model. The results showed that out of the three models the communication model is the most accurate in this setting.

Table 1 presents a summary of the solutions presented under this subsection, highlighting the main differences between them, such as: the number of users identified in the dataset, the period of collection of data, the location and the type of data collected.

Table 1. Definition of the Universal Law for Human Mobility- Solutions Summary

Ref.	Application	Number of Users	Period Covered	Location	Data Type	Main Findings
(Gonzalez et al., 2008)	defining individual human mobility	-100,000 anonymized mobile phone users -206 anonymized mobile phone users	- 6 moths for the 100,000 users and one week for the 206 users	- not mentioned	- CDRs – identity of the closest communication tower when the user initiates or receives a call or a text message	Humans follow simple reproducible patterns, despite the diversity of their travel history.
(Song et al., 2010a)	defining individual human mobility	-3 million anonymized mobile phone users -1,000 users who signed up for a location based service	- one year for the 3 million users - two week for the 1,000 users	- not mentioned	- CDRs – identity of the closest communication tower when the user initiates or receives a call or a text message	Human tend to return to the highly visited locations, like home or workplace, which is not considered by the random walking models.
(Song et al., 2010b)	limitations of predictability in human mobility	-50,000 anonymized mobile phone users	- 3months	- not mentioned	- CDRs – identity of the closest communication tower when the user initiates or receives a call or a text message	There is a 93% probability that the human location could be predicted regardless of how far the person travels within the preferred locations.
(Noulas et al., 2012)	universal law for human mobility	-925,030 Foursquare users	- 6 month	- 5 million places in 34 metropolitan cities/four continents/11 countries	- check-in data of Foursquare users	The transiting probability from one place to another is inversely proportional to a power of their rank, that is, the number of intervening opportunities between them.
(Kung et al., 2014)	universal patterns in human home-work commuting	-50,000 anonymized mobile phone users for Ivory Coast - 2 million users for Portugal - 14 million devices for Saudi Arabia - 2 million mobile devices for Boston -99,000 cars for Milan	- 150 days from December 1, 2011 to April 28, 2012 for Ivory Coast - 2 years from January 1, 2006 to December 31, 2007 for Portugal - 4 months from July to October 2009, for Boston - one week period for Milan	- Ivory Coast, Portugal, Saudi Arabia, Boston, Milan	- CDRs – identity of the closest communication tower when the user initiates or receives a call or a text message - GPS data	The home-work time distributions and average values within a single region are largely independent of commute distance or country, despite the substantial spatial and infrastructural differences.
(Ranjan et al., 2012)	human mobility	-500,000 anonymized mobile phone users	- one month, July 2011	-San Francisco bay area	- CDRs – identity of the closest communication tower when the user initiates or receives a call or a text message	Although the CDR can be used to sample significant locations, such as home and work, in some cases it may incur biases in capturing the overall spatio-temporal characteristics of individual human mobility.
(Palchykov et al., 2014)	human mobility	-50,000 anonymized mobile phone users	-150 days from December 1, 2011 to April 28, 2012	- Ivory Coast	- CDRs – identity of the closest communication tower when the user initiates or receives a call or a text message	The human mobility can be predicted by using a simple model based on the frequency of the mobile phone calls, between two locations and their geographical distances.

Urban Planning and Real-Time Traffic Forecast

Several works explored the use of cellular network data for urban planning and real-time traffic forecast.

Isaacman et al. (2010) look into the mobility patterns of two cities, such as Los Angeles and New York. This study could further help at investigating the environmental impact of daily commutes. The datasets used consist of CDRs from hundreds of thousands of users containing information about three events types in the cellular network: incoming voice calls, outgoing voice calls, and data traffic exchanges. The CDRs were collected over 62 consecutive days from March 15, 2009 to May 15, 2009 in Los Angeles and New York areas. The study shows that the people living in Los Angeles tend to travel on a regular basis, 2 times farther than people in New York. Moreover, New Yorkers tend to take 2 to 6 times longer trips than Angelenos. Additionally, the authors observe that in terms of commuter distance within the city, the Los Angeles area is more homogeneous than the New York area.

Yuan et al. (2012) propose a framework referred to as DRoF, Discovers Regions of different Functions (e.g., educational areas, entertainment areas, historic oriented areas, etc.) in a city using a combination of both human mobility data among different regions and points of interests (POI). The proposed framework is evaluated using large-scale and real-world datasets consisting of two POI dataset of Beijing collected in 2010 and 2011, and two 3 month GPS data used to represent human mobility, generated by 12,000 taxi cabs in Beijing in 2010 and 2011. The authors state that their proposed solution outperforms other two baseline methods that base their findings of functional regions solely on POIs or mobility data.

Calabrese et al. (2011) present a real-time urban monitoring platform that makes use of a broad range of datasets in order to provide a visualization map of the vehicular traffic status and the pedestrians' movement. The platform was tested for the city of Rome in Italy. The authors aim to provide a visualization tool that gives a qualitative understanding of how the mobile phone data and vehicle real-time location data could be used to provide valuable services in the context of urban planning and tourist management.

Di Lorenzo et al. (2011) combine the use of people trajectories and geographical preferences in order to propose a method for evaluating human spatio-temporal activity patterns. The authors used two datasets covering the state of Massachusetts consisting of the individual human trajectories extracted from anonymous mobile phone traces and the geographical features of places in the area, such as land use. The data was collected over a 4 months period from one million unique devices. The authors define a measure of land use distribution used to characterize the human activity on a specific day, and they have identified 4 distinct patterns that can be mapped to a specific number of kilometers traveled in the day. The authors state that these patterns can be further integrated into activity-based transportation models.

Ratti et al, (2006) introduced Mobile Landscapes project, an application in the metropolitan area of Milan that enables the graphic representation of the intensity of urban activities using location data from cell phones. A similar study is presented by Pulselli et al. (2008), where the authors develop a real-time monitoring technique of population density in Milan based on the data from cell phones. The study shows that there is a correlation between the intensity corresponding to the social activity and the density of people.

Another work that looked into urban planning is presented by Becker et al. (2011). The authors present an experimental study using 13 driving routes and two train routes leading to the suburban city of Anytown. Two mobile phones were used for active voice calls during the commuting over the 15 routes, and obtained the CDRs corresponding to their calls. The authors propose two algorithms, one based on Earth Mover's Distance and a second one based on the signal strength data, for matching handoff patterns to the routes. The results show that their proposed algorithms in combination with CDRs could be used to determine the relative traffic volumes on the roads.

A summary of the solutions is presented in Table 2, highlighting the main differences between them, such as: the number of users identified in the dataset, the period of collection of data, the location and the type of data collected.

Human Localization and Mobility Patterns

One of the first studies that provided evidence of geographic correlation between users' interests within a cellular network was conducted by Trestian et al. (2009). The authors categorized the user interests into six groups based on the type of the application they are accessing, such as: mail, social networking, trading, music, news, and dating. The main focus of the study was to correlate these users' interests with their location, e.g., home or work. Their results showed that in general the users tend to spend a significant fraction of their time in their top three locations only. Additionally, the authors showed that the location affects the applications the users are accessing. For example, at certain locations users might be interested in accessing one particular type of application regardless the time of day.

Another study that focuses on identifying important locations in humans' live from mobile data traces was conducted by Isaacmanc et al. (2011). The study was conducted using a dataset containing CDRs from hundreds of thousands of phones, over a 78 days period in Los Angeles and New York. The authors propose several algorithms based on logistic regression that are used to identify important places from CDRs and then apply semantic meaning to these important locations, namely Home and Work. The authors state that their algorithms identify the key locations with media errors under one mile.

Zang et al. (2007) propose a dynamic profile-based paging/location management technique in order to increase the efficiency of the location management process within a cellular network. In order to propose their solutions, the authors examine the data from a network operator providing CDMA2000 with support for voice, data and SMS services to their customers. The per call measurement data traces contain: the call starting time, the call duration, the mobile identification number, the initial cell, the final cell, the service type, the call direction and the number of pages. The data was collected from hundreds of thousands of users over a one month period in three locations: Manhattan, Philadelphia, and Brisbane. The authors state that the proposed solution increases the average paging success rate across voice/data/SMS calls above 90% in Brisbane and 85% in Manhattan. Additionally such a mechanism could reduce the signaling overhead by up to 90% at a cost of a small increase in paging delay.

Hasan et al. (2013) conducted a study to analyze the human mobility dynamics and their activity patterns. The study was conducted on datasets with Tweets from Twitter that contain the check-ins linked from Foursquare. The data was collected over almost one year, from February 25, 2010 to January 20, 2011 from New York, Chicago, and Los Angeles. However, the study is mainly based on a sample of 3256 users from New York. The authors propose the following activity categories: home, work, eating, entertainment, recreation and shopping with 94.5% of the check-ins from the study appertaining to any category. From this study the authors observe that in general people do not select their destination in a random manner, rather the selection is done base on the popularity of the specific place. The authors show that the relationship between the popularity of a place and the probability of the place being selected as a destination can be described by a scaling law.

Motahari et al. (2012) investigated the impact of temporal factors on the randomness and the size of mobility and the spatial distribution. The study

Table 2. Urban Planning and Real-Time Traffic Forecast – Solutions Summary

Ref.	Application	Number of Users	Period Covered	Location	Data Type	Main Findings
(Isaacman et al., 2010)	-environmental impact of daily commutes	-hundreds of thousands of anonymized identifiers	-62 days from March 15, 2009 to May 15, 2009	Los Angeles and New York	-CDRs - incoming voice calls, outgoing voice calls, and data traffic exchange	The study highlights significant differences in mobility patterns between different human populations from two different cities.
(Yuan et al., 2012)	- urban planning	- 12,000 taxi cabs for GPS data	-year 2010 and 2011 for the POI data sets -two 3 month GPS data in 2010 and 2011	Beijing, China	-POI - coordinates and category like restaurants and shopping malls -GPS trajectory datasets representing human mobility	By using both human mobility among regions and points of interests (POIs) located in a region when identifying the functions of a region, is more efficient than using the baseline methods that are solely based on POIs or human mobility.
(Calabrese et al., 2011)	-real-time urban monitoring	- 30,000 calls -7268 buses for GPS data -43 taxies for GPS data	-weekday	Rome, Italy	-mobile phone position information, call in progress, SMS sending, handover, etc. -GPS data -real time traffic noise from sensor networks	The use of mobile equipment (ME) location-based monitoring, from ME data together with other type of real-time-information, e.g., taxis and buses positions could help developing a real-time control system for cities.
(Di Lorenzo et al., 2011)	-human spatio-temporal activity patterns	-one million unique devices	- 4 months	Massachusetts	-individual human trajectories extracted from anonymous mobile phone traces -geographical features of places	The authors define a new measure of land use distribution referred to as *lud* used to characterize human activity on a specific day. The *luds* can be mapped back to a specific number of kilometers traveled during the day as well as home locations.
(Ratti et al., 2006)	-urban planning	- not mentioned	-16 days from April 19 to May 4, 2009	Milan, Italy	-CDRs – identity of the closest communication tower when the user initiates or receives a call or a text message	Graphic representation of the intensity of urban activities using location data from CDRs.
(Becker et al. 2011)	-urban planning	13 commuter routes and 2 train routes, using two phones for maintaining active voice calls and collecting the data	- Fall of 2010, March 2011	Anytown, USA	-CDRs– identity of the closest communication tower when the user initiates or receives a call	Cellular handoff patterns can be used to identify which routes people take through a city. CDR data can be using to determine the relative traffic volumes on roads.

was conducted on CDRs collected from several thousands of users in San Francisco area. Two temporal factors were considered in the analysis: the day of the week and the time of the day. The authors studied how these temporal factors impact four characteristics of human mobility, such as: location entropy, radius of gyration, step size, and spatial probability distribution of user locations. The results show that the spatial distribution is most concentrated during work hours and most scattered on the weekends. However, a different pattern is observed during the non-working hours of weekdays where the spatial distribution is concentrated around home, work and the commute path. The authors state that by considering the temporal factors, the place predictions mechanisms can improve their accuracy by 15% compared to the case without the temporal factors.

A summary of these solutions is presented in Table 3, highlighting the main differences between them, such as: the number of users identified in the dataset, the period of collection of data, the location and the type of data collected.

Context-Aware Applications

As previously seen, there are many studies analyzing the mobility patterns and the dynamics of human mobility within specific areas and under various temporal factors. It has been shown that human mobility especially in urban areas can be predictable to some extent, by taking into consideration the daily routines of the mobile users. However, in case of unusual activities that arise from a specific context such as various social events: concert, football game, religious pilgrimage, etc. more studies are needed.

Xavier et al. (2013) analyzed the human mobility and the workload dynamics of a cellular network during large scale events such as New Year's Eve. The study was conducted on dataset containing the CDRs from a number of up to 100,000 users from three large Brazilian cities, such as: Belo Horizonte, Recife, and Salvador. In order to compare their findings, the authors analyzed other datasets without events, and another large-scale event such as a soccer match. The authors observed that the number of calls during the New Year's Eve celebration increased by a factor between 6.7 and 12.6 as compared with a regular day without events. While in the case of the soccer match, when compared with a no event day, the growth factor is lower, indicating the importance of the event.

Calabrese et al. (2010) used the CDRs from one million devices over one month period to analyze the crowd mobility during special events happening in Massachusetts and Greater Boston areas. The study shows that there is a strong correlation between the locations the people are living in and the locations of the special events will be taking place. For example, the probability of people attending an event is higher if people live close to that specific location of the event. Moreover, the events of the same type show have similar spatial distributions of origins. Thus, the authors state that for future events it can be partly predicted where people will come from.

Bagrow et al. (2011) present a study on understanding the human communication and mobility patterns under large scale special events. The authors identified four important emergency events that happened between January 2007 and January 2009, namely: (1) a bombing without fatalities; (2) a plane crash with a significant number of fatalities; (3) an earthquake with mild damage and no casualties; and (4) a power outage. For comparison purposes, the authors explored other non-emergency social events, such as: sports games and several rock concerts. The results show that the emergency events cause a sharp increase in the number of outgoing calls and text messages, in the immediate location of the event. However in the case of non-emergency events, there is a gradual increase in the call activity. The authors observe that the call activity is stronger in the immediate proximity of the emergency event, dropping rapidly as the distance from the event increases.

Table 3. Human Localization and Mobility Patterns – Solutions Summary

Ref.	Application	Number of Users	Period Covered	Location	Data Type	Main Findings
(Trestian et al. 2009)	-correlation between people's application interests and mobility properties	-281,394 users	-seven days	large metropolitan area of 1,900 square miles (approx. 5,000 square kilometers)	-packet data session details containing: local timestamp, anonymized user identifier, anonymized IP-Address, correlation identifier, base station identifier, the URL accessed	The users tend to spend a significant fraction of their time in their top three locations only and the location affects the application type the users are accessing.
(Isaacman et al., 2011)	-identifying important places in people's lives	-hundreds of thousands of phones	-78 consecutive days from November 15, 2009 to January 31, 2010	Los Angeles New York	-CDR containing information about voice calls and text messages	By using temporally sparse and spatially coarse location information from CDRs, key locations can be identified with media errors under one mile.
(Zang et al., 2007)	-location management	-1,061,000 users in Manhattan -543,000 users in Philadelphia -404,000 users in Brisbane	- one month, from February 2 to February 28, 2006	Manhattan, Philadelphia, Brisbane	-per call measurement data, containing: call starting time, call duration, initial cell, final cell, service type, call direction, number of pages, etc.	By making use of call and mobility data the paging efficiency in a cellular network can be improved, by reducing the signaling load (up to 80%) at the minimal cost of increase in paging delay (less than 10%)
(Hasan et al., 2013)	-urban human mobility and activity patterns	- a sample of 3256 users from a dataset of 20,606 users for New York	- one year, from February 25, 2010 to January 20, 2011	New York, Chicago, Los Angeles	Tweets with check-in services from Foursquare	There is a strong influence of urban context on people's destination choices. People do not select their destination in a random manner but on the popularity of the specific place.
(Motahari et al., 2012)	-mobility characteristics and location prediction	- several thousands of users	- 4 days, 16 days, and 3 months	San Francisco	-CDRs including voice, SMS, and data sessions	By considering the impact of temporal factors on mobility patterns, the prediction mechanism can improve their accuracy by 15%.

Another interesting study is presented by Batty et al. (2003), where the authors analyzed the discrete dynamics of small-scale spatial events.

The authors make use of swarm intelligence to construct a model to help simulating small-scale spatial events involving local movement with

Table 4. Context-aware Applications – Solutions Summary

Ref.	Application	Number of Users	Period Covered	Location	Data Type	Main Findings
(Xavier et al., 2013)	-understanding human mobility during large-scale events, such as New Year's Eve	10,000 to 100,000 users	New Year's Eve, 9:45PM to 2:30AM, 2012	Three large Brazilian cities: Belo Horizonte, Recife, and Salvador	-unique user identifier, geographical locations of the antennas, time instant of the call's start and end	The number of calls during New Year's Eve increased by a factor between 6.7 and 12.6. The number of calls during the soccer match is lower (factor of 3.4).
(Calabrese et al., 2010)	-analyzing crowd mobility during special events	One million devices	July 30 to September 12, 2009	Massachusetts Greater Boston	-CDRs - identity of the closest communication tower when the user initiates or receives a call or a text message	The probability of people attending an event is higher if people live close to that specific location of the event.
(Bagrow et al., 2011)	-understanding the communication and mobility patterns under large scale emergency events	10 million subscribers	Three years of activity, from January 2007 to January 2009	Western European country	-CDRs - identity of the closest communication tower when the user initiates or receives a call	In case of emergency events the communication spikes in the cellular network are both spatially and temporally localized.
(Batty et al. 2003)	-agent-based models of mobility in carnivals and street parades	Not mentioned	Two days over the Notting Hill Carnival in 2001	London, United Kingdom	-cordon count at 38 entry points, video footage, 1022 images -data on entry and exit volumes at the subway station -bus volumes at setting down locations	Congestion and safety problems could be resolved by introducing controls that make use of agents using swarm intelligence, and rerunning the model until a 'safe solution' is reached.

congestion, crowding, and panic and safety issues. The model runs in an iterative fashion using intelligent agents until a safe solution is reached. The authors developed the model to simulate the route changing in the 2 days Notting Hill Carnival in London.

Table 4 presents a summary of these solutions, highlighting the main differences between them, such as: the number of users identified in the dataset, the period of collection of data, the location and the type of data collected.

Subscribers Churn and Privacy

One of the top challenges for network operators is the understanding of the subscriber churn and the developing of methods and strategies for customer retention in order to reduce the subscriber loss.

Han et al. (2013) conducted an empirical analysis on a large scale dataset containing the CDRs and tariff plans information for 4 million prepaid subscribers between August 2008 and June 2009. A sample of 10,000 subscribers along with their identified 690,000 friends was used for the analysis. The authors observed that over the eleven month the average churn rate was 2.07%. The authors analyze the influence of peer on churn and notice that the churning probability increases by 3% if there is a friend who churns. However, in the case where two or more friends churn the churning probability increases by 1% only.

Andrews et al. (2013) studied the user behavior in relationship to the quota balance and/or time to the end of the quota period. The study was conducted on the CDRs containing both voice calls and SMS, for 1.6 million subscribers over a 6 week span period. The results show that the call duration varies with the user balance, with the first call after top-up lasting longer than the other calls.

In terms of subscriber privacy, De Montjoye et al. (2013) present a study on the privacy bounds of human mobility. The study was conducted on a large scale dataset containing 1.5 million individu-als collected over a 15 month period in a western country. The authors observe that the human mobility traces are highly unique and having the hourly information of the individual's current com-munication tower location, four spatial-temporal points are enough to uniquely identify 95% of the individuals. The authors conclude that even coarse datasets provide little anonymity.

Zang et al. (2011) presented a study in which they show that publishing anonymized location data could lead to privacy risks. The study is

Table 5. Subscribers Churn and Privacy – Solutions Summary

Ref.	Application	Number of Users	Period Covered	Location	Data Type	Main Findings
(Han et al., 2013)	-peer influence on subscribers churn	-4 million prepaid subscribers	August 2008 to June 2009	European Country	CDRs and tariff plans	The churning probability increases by 3% if there is a friend who churns.
(Andrews et al., 2013)	-understanding the quota dynamics	-1.6 million prepaid mobile subscribers	6 weeks	Not mentioned	CDRs for calls and SMS	The first call after the top-up lasts longer than the other calls.
(De Montjoye et al., 2013)	-privacy bounds of human mobility	-1.5 million people	15 months, from April 2006 to June 2007	European country	CDRs - identity of the closest communication tower when the user initiates or receives a call or a text message	Four spatial-temporal points are enough to uniquely identify 95% of the individuals.
(Zang et al., 2011)	-subscriber privacy	-25 million cell phone users	3 months from February to April 2010	All 50 states of the US	CDRs - identity of the closest communication tower when the user initiates or receives a call	To avoid the privacy risks, the data needs to be coarse in either time domain, with short periods of time of the order of a day, or space domain, strictly higher than the cell level.
(De Mulder et al., 2008)	-subscriber privacy	-100 human subjects	One academic year, 2004-2005	MIT, Cambridge, US	call logs, Bluetooth devices in proximity, cell tower IDs, application usage and phone status	It is possible to identify users within a cellular network, based on their previous movement with an accuracy of 80%.

conducted on a large dataset covering all the 50 states of the US and including 25 million cell phone users over a 3 months period. The authors state that the data needs to be coarse in either time domain, with short periods of time of the order of a day, or space domain, strictly higher than the cell level. In a previous study, De Mulder et al. (2008) observed that it is possible to identify users within a cellular network, based on their previous movement with an accuracy of 80%. The study was conducted on 100 human subjects with data collected over one academic year period.

A summary of these solutions is presented in Table 5, highlighting the main differences between them, such as: the number of users, the period of collection of data, the location and the type of data collected.

Health Management

One important area that gained significant interest over the past years is the use of user-generated mobile data in the area of health management. Several works studied the spreading of the infectious diseases and their correlation with the human mobility identified from mobile phone data. Wesolowski et al. (2012) analyzed the travel pattern of 15 million individuals over one year period in Kenya and combined the data with a simple transmission model of malaria. The analysis identifies specific routes from mobile phone data that contribute to the malaria epidemiology on regional spatial scales. The authors state that such studies could add significant improvements to the malaria control programs.

Another work that focused on the strategic elimination planning of malaria spreading is presented by Tatem et al. (2014). The dataset used contains the CDRs from 1.19 million unique SIM cards over a period of 12 months in Namibia. The authors analyzed the human mobility patterns from the mobile phone call dataset and mapped it to the malaria case-based risk maps built on satellite imagery. By combining both information datasets,

the authors show how the human population movements connect malaria transmission risk areas.

Frias-Martinez et al. (2011) proposed an agent-based model system designed to simulate virus spreading using agents characterized by their individual mobility patterns. The authors use real CDRs data to identify the human population movements, which is then used to build the agents' mobility behavior and social network models. In this way the agents' behavior mimics the real population's mobility and social patterns. The dataset used for the study contains CDRs from 2.4 million unique cell phones, collected over a 5 month period during the H1N1 flu outbreak, in one of the most affected Mexican cities.

Bengtsson et al. (2011) investigated the use of mobile phone data records in order to improve the response to disasters and outbreaks, such as earthquakes. The datasets used in the study cover two periods and contain records from 2.8 million SIMs in Haiti area. The first dataset covers the period starting six weeks before an earthquake until 5 month after the earthquake. Whereas the second dataset covers the two weeks period of the early phase of the cholera outbreak. The study shows that the information about the human population movement from the CDRs can be used to estimate the magnitude, distribution and the trends in population displacement during a disaster. Moreover the authors state that the method is feasible to use for near real-time monitoring of population movement during infectious disease outbreaks.

Table 6 presents a summary of these solutions, highlighting the main differences between them, such as: the number of users identified in the dataset, the period of collection of data, the location and the type of data collected.

DISCUSSIONS

The ubiquity of mobile phones and the increasing amount of data they are generating produced a major shift towards the use of massive phone

Table 6. Health Management – Solutions Summary

Ref.	Application	Number of Users	Period Covered	Location	Data Type	Main Findings
(Wesolowski et al., 2012)	-impact of human mobility on malaria	-15 million individuals	One year, between June 2008 and June 2009	Kenya	CDRs- identity of the closest communication tower when the user initiates or receives a call or a text message	Specific routes that contribute to the malaria epidemiology can be identified from mobile phone data.
(Tatem et al., 2014)	- strategic malaria elimination planning	1.19 million unique SIM cards	12 month period from October 2010 to September 2011	Namibia	CDRs- identity of the closest communication tower when the user initiates or receives a call or a text message	The human population movements identified from mobile phone call datasets connect to malaria transmission risk areas.
(Frias-Martinez et al., 2011)	-modeling the epidemic spread	2.4 million unique cell phone numbers	5 month period from January 1 to May 31, 2009	Mexican city	CDRs- identity of the closest communication tower when the user initiates or receives a call or a text message	By using an agent-based system to model the virus spreading, the peak number of individuals infected by the virus could be reduced by 10%, if government mandates would impose restricted mobility. The peak of the pandemic could be postponed by two days.
(Bengtsson et al., 2011)	-response to disasters and outbreaks	2.8 million SIMs	6 month period from December 1, 2009 to June 18, 2010 and 2 week period from October 15 to October 23, 2010	Haiti	CDRs- identity of the closest communication tower when the user initiates the first call each day (for the first dataset) and each call (for the second dataset)	The information about human population movement from the CDRs, can estimate the magnitude, distribution and the trends in population displacement during a disaster.

data sets collected by the network operators giving rise to new research domain across computing and social science by examining issues in behavioral and social science from Big Data perspective.

This section provides a comprehensive survey of the current research on this topic in the form of a categorization and comparison of the exist-ing solutions. Six broad categories are identified based on the application of the use of CDR data: (1) definition of the universal law for human mobility; (2) urban planning and real-time traffic forecast; (3) human localization and mobility; (4) context-aware applications; (5) subscribers churn and privacy; and (6) health management.

As we have seen in this section, the use of large-scale mobile data has great potential in several areas, from the statistical modeling of human mobility and the definition of universal laws (Gonzalez te al., 2008) to real-time traffic monitoring conditions that would help in transportation planning and management (Isaacman et al., 2010). Song et al. (2010b) showed that there is a 93% probability that the human location could be predicted and that humans tend to return to the highly visited locations, like home or workplace, in contrast to the random walking models (Song et al., 2010a). However, a study presented by Ranjan et al. (2012) showed that although these CDRs can be used to sample these significant locations, like home and work, there are cases in which it may incur biases in capturing the overall spatio-temporal characteristics of individual human mobility. This is because these human mobility prediction models highly depend on the frequency of the mobile phone calls generated by the mobile user.

The use of CDRs could also help in terms of urban planning and real-time traffic forecast. By examining the CDR data from a city in US, Becker et al. (2011) showed that the cellular handoff patterns could be used to identify which routes people are taking through the city, which could in turn help to determine the relative traffic volume of the roads. Moreover, Hasan et al. (2013) showed that people do not select their destination in a random manner, but there is a strong influence of the urban context, basing their decision on the popularity of the specific place.

Several studies looked at analyzing the data under unusual activities what could arise form a specific context, such as social events: concerts, football games, religious pilgrimage, or even emergency situations, like floods or earthquakes. Calabrese et al. (2010) showed that the probability of people attending an event is higher if people live close to that specific location of the event. This information could be useful for event organizers in strategic marketing and events locations selection.

In case of emergency events, Bagrow et al. (2011) analyzed the communication and mobility patterns under several important emergency scenarios, like bombing, place crash, earthquake and power outage. The authors observed that the communication spikes in the cellular network are both spatially and temporally localized.

The big data analysis could also help the network operators in understanding their subscribers churn. In this context, Han et al. (2013) showed that the churning probability increases by 3% if a friend of the subscriber churns. Another interesting study was presented by Zang et al. (2011), who looked at the subscriber privacy. The authors showed that to avoid the privacy risks, the anonymous CDR data needs to be coarse in either time domain, with short periods of time of the order of a day, or space domain, strictly higher than the cell level.

However, out of all these areas where analyzing the CDR could bring benefits, the most interesting use of CDRs is in the field of health management. Before starting using the CDR data, the field of spread disease modelling relied on extrapolating trends from census data and surveys. Integrating the use of CDRs which are empirical, immediate and updated in real-time could improve the way to model the spread of diseases. As we have previously seen, Wesolowski et al. (2012) and Tatem et al. (2014) made use of CDR data to map the malaria outbreaks in Kenya and Namibia, respectively. Frias-Martinez et al. (2011) used the CDR data to monitor the public response to government health warnings during Mexico's swine-flu epidemic in 2009. Bengtsson et al. (2011) used the CDRs to model the population movements and to provide estimates of where aid was most wanted during a cholera outbreak in Haiti in 2010.

All these studies have shown that understanding the humans' mobility patterns by using user-generated mobile data could be a crucial component in various areas, such as: network optimization opportunities for cellular network operators in handling the explosive growth in traffic observed from CDRs; transportation planning and management, modeling commuting flows, content delivery services, context-aware applications, health management, etc. However these findings are limited by several factors, such as: the size of the dataset used, the location of the data collection, or the interaction frequency of a particular individual with the network. For example the size of the datasets in these studies varies from one day or two days period up to 3 years period, which might impact the results of the various studies. Another factor that might impact the results is the location, various studies were considered in different parts of the world, from European cities to US cities, and other various development countries. The frequency of the interaction of an user with the mobile network, will impact the amount of CDRs and thus the predictability of the mobility patterns, and other findings.

The aim of this chapter is to explore the use of the anonymized CDRs containing both voice-calls and SMS activities to identify the exceptional spatio-temporal patterns of the collective human activity and correlate these 'anomalies' with real-world events (e.g., parades, public concerts, soccer match, New Year's Eve, etc.). The study is carried out with CDR data collected from 50,000 randomly selected customers from a cellular network in Ivory Coast over a 150 days period. Similar studies, like Xavier et al. (2013) looked into understanding human mobility during large-scale events such as New Year's Eve. However, the dataset size is limited to one day data collection over New Year's Eve from three large Brazilian cities, such as: Belo Horizonte, Recife, and Salvadore. Calabrese et al. (2010) analyzed the crowed mobility during special events. However, the CDR data is limited to one and a half month data collection from July 30 to September 12, 2009 in Massachusetts and Greater Boston areas.

DATA COLLECTION METHODOLOGY AND CHARACTERISTICS

Data Collection and Preprocessing

The study presented in this chapter makes use of the anonymized CDR provided by the Orange Group within the Orange Data for Development (D4D) challenge. The CDRs are anonymized phone calls and SMS exchanges between five million Orange customers in Ivory Coast. The anonymized CDRs were collected from a random set of cellular phones over 150 days, between December 1, 2011 and April 28, 2012. The territorial expanse of the dataset on Ivory Coast is illustrated in Figure 1. The Ivory Coast is located in West Africa having an area of 322,462 square kilometers and an estimated population of 20 million inhabitants. The political capital of Ivory Coast is Yamoussoukro whereas the biggest city is the port city Abidjan. The country telecommunications sector is dominated by mobile telephony with Orange being one of the leaders in the market, recording around five million customers (a quarter of the entire population). For the purpose of this study, there are four sets of data provided by Orange Group and described in the following sections.

Dataset 1: Antenna-to-Antenna Communication

The first dataset contains the aggregated number of calls as well as the calls durations within one hour, between any antennas pair. The dataset was stored in 10 files each corresponding to a 14 days interval. All the datasets are provided in Tabulation Separated Values (TSV) file format. For the Antenna-to-Antenna dataset each line stores information about the date, time, originating antenna, terminating antenna, number of voice calls, and the duration of the voice calls in minutes for a given hour.

Figure 1. Territorial expanse of the dataset – Ivory Coast

Dataset 2: Individual Trajectories-High Spatial Resolutions Data

The second dataset provides high resolution individual movement trajectories of 50,000 randomly sampled customers split into consecutive two-week periods starting with December 5, 2011 and ending with April 22, 2012. The data was stored in 10 TSV files, and in order to protect the customers' privacy new random identifiers for each customer are chosen in every two-week time period. Each line in the file contains the following information: customer identification number, connection date and time and the antenna identification number the customer is connected to.

Dataset 3: Individual Trajectories – Long Term Data

The third dataset contains the long term, low spatial resolution trajectories of the 50,000 randomly selected customers. The low spatial resolution is obtained by replacing the antennas identifiers with the sub-prefectures of the antenna the customer is located in. Ivory Coast has a total number of 255 sub-prefectures, which are local administrative regions. Figure 2 illustrates the sub-prefectures and their identifiers along with the Orange antennas locations, as identified from the datasets. There are a total number of 1238 antennas, and as can be noticed not all the sub-prefectures have cell phone towers.

Figure 2. Ivory Coast sub-prefectures and Orange antennas location

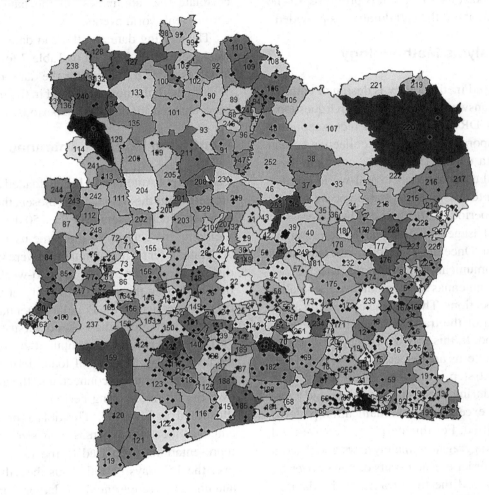

Each file in this dataset contains information on customer identification number, connection date and time and the sub-prefectures identifier that contains the antenna the user is connected to. The dataset covers the period starting with December 1, 2011 until April 14, 2012.

Dataset 4: Communication Subgraphs

The fourth dataset contains information on the communication subgraphs of 5,000 randomly selected individuals (egos). The communication between the randomly selected egos and their second order neighbors was divided into two-weeks periods starting December 5, 2011 over the 150

days of the observation period. Each file indicates if there was communication between every customer's pair by providing the source customer id and the destination customer id.

Limitations of the Datasets

Although the CDRs represent a good source of location information they have several significant limitations: (1) they are generated only when the mobile device is engaged in a voice call or exchanges text messages, thus no information about application usage type (voice/text/data) is available; (2) the location granularity is at cell tower level or sub-prefectures, no information about the exact user location is provided; (3) no information about the call duration is provided.

Data Analysis Methodology

Our proposed methodology is designed with the purpose of answering two main research questions: (i) can the CDR data be used to detect exceptional spatio-temporal patterns of the collective human mobile data usage? (ii) Can we correlate these exceptional usage patterns to real-world events?

In order to answer these questions, we first try to identify periods in the dataset where there is an exceptional usage or anomaly in the communication pattern. Once these periods with anomalies in the communication pattern are detected, we identify the antennas that present these anomalies and their locations. This is done by looking at the distribution of the traffic per antennas for each given period. In this way the exceptional spatio-temporal patterns are detected.

The next step is to identify the events that happened during that particular time and location where exceptional communication patterns were identified. For this purpose, we have used online news aggregators, mainly news.google.com services in order to find events or news covering the country and the time frame of the dataset. Keywords such as 'soccer', 'football', 'parades', 'concerts', etc. were used to find information about potential events for that particular spatio-temporal location. In this way, we were able to identify major events of national importance collocated with the spatio-temporal pattern found in the datasets.

IDENTIFYING HOTSPOTS

This section presents an in-depth analysis on the datasets to correlate people, locations and events during the 150 days of recorded data. The study aims on identifying hotspots with highly loaded antennas, analyze the human activity pattern and

correlate the 'anomalies' in the patterns with certain real-world events.

The starting date and the end date of each 2 week period file is listed in Table 7 for the data in Dataset 2 and Table 8 for the data in Dataset 3, along with the notations used in the rest of the book chapter, for each of the periods.

Identifying HotSpot Antennas

The HotSpot Antennas or highly loaded antennas are defined as the antennas that present the highest number of active users over the 150 days period, including the activity of the same user. Popular Antennas refer to the antennas that were visited by distinct users over each of the two-week period, thus excluding the repeated activity of the same user. Consequently, the Popular Antennas are the antennas with the highest user diversity.

Dataset 2 is used to compute the overall antennas activity (in terms of load, defined as the total number of users connected to the antennas) over the full monitoring period. The results are illustrated in Figure 3. The dots represent the antennas locations whereas their size and color representation is reported to the load intensity over the 150 days period. Thus, heavily loaded antennas are represented by larger points and higher intensity color.

The Cumulative Distribution Function (CDF) of the number of active users recorded at each antenna over the 150 days period is illustrated in Figure 4. The average load over the 150 days equals to 38333 active users and the standard deviation is about 38138 active users. This means that around 70% of the antennas have a load within one standard deviation to the mean, as seen in Figure 4. Considering only the top 5% of the antennas, the number of active users is within 147000-235000 over the full 150 day period. Figure 5 illustrates the location of the top 5% of highly loaded antennas on the Ivory Coast.

Using Dataset 2, the total number of users registered at each antenna (antenna activity) for

Table 7. Dataset 2 Recorded Periods

File	Start Date dd/mm/yyyy	End Date dd/mm/yyyy	Notation
SAMPLE 0	05/12/2011	18/12/2011	Week1-2
SAMPLE 1	19/12/2011	01/01/2012	Week3-4
SAMPLE 2	02/01/2012	15/01/2012	Week5-6
SAMPLE 3	16/01/2012	29/01/2012	Week7-8
SAMPLE 4	30/01/2012	12/02/2012	Week9-10
SAMPLE 5	13/02/2012	26/02/2012	Week11-12
SAMPLE 6	27/02/2012	11/03/2012	Week13-14
SAMPLE 7	12/03/2012	25/03/2012	Week15-16
SAMPLE 8	26/03/2012	08/04/2012	Week17-18
SAMPLE 9	09/04/2012	22/04/2012	Week19-20

Table 8. Dataset 3 Recorded Periods

File	Start Date dd/mm/yyyy	End Date dd/mm/yyyy	Notation
SAMPLE A	01/12/2011	15/12/2011	A
SAMPLE B	16/12/2011	30/12/2011	B
SAMPLE C	31/12/2011	14/01/2012	C
SAMPLE D	15/01/2012	29/01/2012	D
SAMPLE E	30/01/2012	13/02/2012	E
SAMPLE F	14/02/2012	28/02/2012	F
SAMPLE G	29/02/2012	14/03/2012	G
SAMPLE H	15/03/2012	29/03/2012	H
SAMPLE I	30/03/2012	13/04/2012	I
SAMPLE J	14/04/2012	28/04/2012	J

each 2 week period, was computed. Figure 6 illustrates a boxplot intended to show the distribution of the total number of users per antenna for each period. The boxplot can be interpreted in the following way:

- The line in the box represents the median value for the dataset
- The lines above and below the median (the upper and lower bounds of the box) represent the upper quartile and the lower quartile, which are used to give an indication of the distribution of the values within the dataset relative to the median
- The top whisker indicates the greatest value of the dataset excluding the outliers
- The bottom whisker indicates the least value of the dataset excluding the outliers
- The outliers indicate those values that are significantly higher or lower for the rest of the values within the dataset. In this work the outliers are defined using the 3/2 rule, meaning that the values that are more than 3/2 times of the upper quartile and the val-

Figure 3. Orange antennas location and activity over 150 days

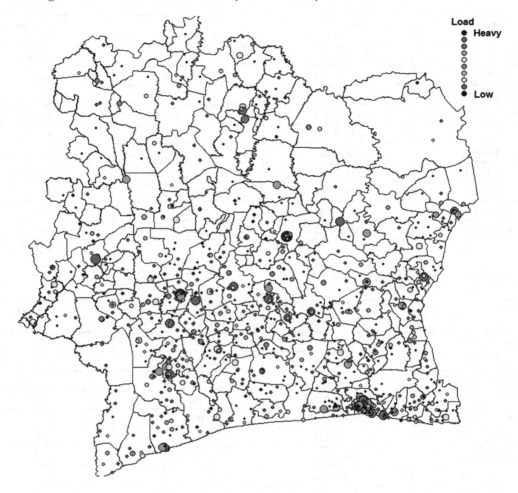

ues that are less than 3/2 times of the lower quartile are defined as outliers. In this case, the upper whisker goes as far as the first data point before the 3/2 cut-off.

Looking at Figure 6, and following the variation of the maximum value of the total number of users, the upper whisker, for each period, we can notice that there is a noticeable increase at the beginning of February (i.e., Week 9-10). For this period, the upper quartile is higher, meaning that there are more antennas with a total number of active users greater than the median value. Another peak in the upper whisker is visible at the end of March, beginning of April. For this period, the median

value is higher and it can be noticed that there is an increased number of antennas that have a total number of active users greater than the median. This is represented by a higher upper quartile.

Looking at the outliers, we can notice that for each period there are a significant number of outliers. These outliers are in fact the antennas located in highly populated areas, as identified in Figure 5, that have an increased number of active users compared to the rest of the antennas spread out around the country. It can be noticed that there are several antennas that have a significant user activity at the end of December and beginning of January (i.e., week 3-4 and week 5-6) with the

Figure 4. CDF of the number of active users at each antenna over 150 days

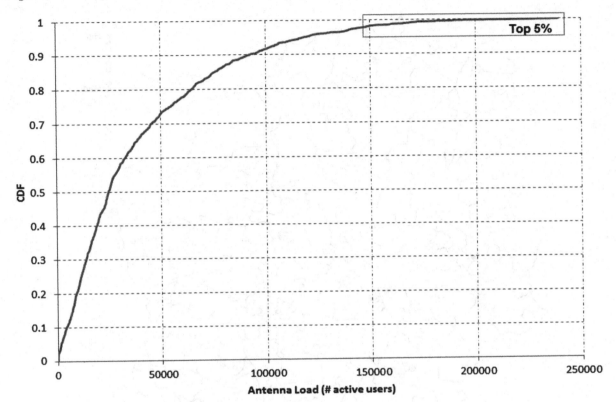

highest value for a outlier recorded at the end of February, beginning of March (i.e., week 13-14)

When analyzing the most Popular Antennas it was not possible to make the computation over the overall 150 days period as the dataset provides different random user identification number for each two-week period and the number of distinct users that were connected to each antenna over the time period is needed. Thus the top 5% of each two-week period was computed and their intersection was selected as the most Popular Antennas over the 150 days period. The top most Popular Antennas and their location are illustrated in Figure 7.

The total number of distinct users registered at each antenna (user diversity) for each 2 week period, was computed. Figure 8 illustrates a boxplot intended to show the distribution of the total number of distinct users per antenna for each period.

Looking at Figure 8, and following the variation of the maximum value of the total number of distinct users, the upper whisker, for each period, we can notice that there is an increase at the end of December and beginning of January (i.e., week 3-4) and beginning of February (i.e., Week 9-10). For these periods, the upper quartile is also higher, meaning that there are more antennas with a total number of distinct active users greater than the median value. Another noticeable peak in the upper whisker is recorded at the end of March, beginning of April (i.e., week17-18). For this period, the median value is higher and it can be noticed that there is an increased number of antennas that have a total number of distinct active users greater than the median. This is also represented by a higher upper quartile for this period. Noticeable peak values for the outliers are recorded at the end of December, beginning of January, beginning of February and end of March,

Figure 5. Top 5% of HotSpot Antennas over 150 days

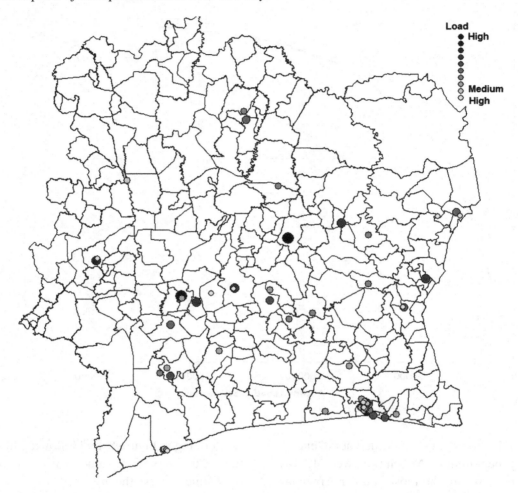

beginning of April. In this study, we will focus on analyzing the data in these periods, as they also correspond to the highest periods for the total number of active users as illustrated in Figure 6.

Identifying HotSpot Sub-Prefectures

From Dataset 3 the overall activity of each sub-prefecture over the full monitoring period of 150 days is computed. Figure 9 illustrates the sub-prefectures of the Ivory Coast and their activity over the 150 days period, with their color representation reported to the load intensity. Thus, heavily loaded sub-prefectures are represented by higher intensity color. Comparing the sub-prefectures activity

map in Figure 9 with the indicative population map of Ivory Coast provided by Map Action[1] as illustrated in Figure 10, it can be noticed that data usage activity is mostly registered in the densely populated areas, as expected.

Using Dataset 3, the total number of active users registered in each Sub-Prefecture over each two-week period, was computed. Figure 11 illustrates the boxplots with the outliers as in Figure 11a and without the outliers as in Figure 11b. The boxplots are intended to show the distribution of the total number of active users per Sub-Prefectures for each period. Looking at Figures 11a and 11b, and following the variation of the maximum value of the total number of active users, the upper

Figure 6. Antennas Activity over 150 days

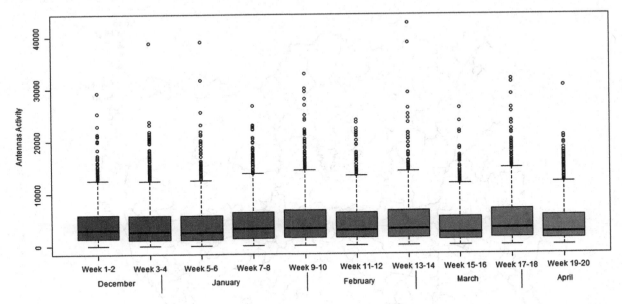

whisker, for each period, as well as the variation of the median values and the maximum values of the outliers, we can see that there are a number of noticeable periods as previously identified when analyzing the data from Dataset2, such as the end of December and beginning of January, with an increase in the maximum values for the outliers, the end of January and beginning of February with the maximum value for the upper whisker and increase in the values for the outliers, and the end of March and beginning of April period which records the maximum values for the outlier, the median value, the upper quartile and the upper whisker.

CONNECTING PEOPLE AND LOCATIONS

Considering the study on Antennas Activity and User Diversity only, by intersecting the top identified HotSpot Antennas with the top identified Popular Antennas, a set of highly loaded and high user density antennas were detected, over the full 150 days period. Taking the location coordinates of these antennas, it was possible to identify their position within a certain sub-prefecture, hence city. The results show that the highly loaded and high user density antennas are spread across three cities, such as: Bouake, Yamoussoukro, and Abidjan, as illustrated in Figure 12. These findings have significant impact and they can be correlated to the important cities of the country. Bouake is the second largest city in the Ivory Coast, Yamoussoukro is the official political and administrative capital, while the economic capital of the country and the city with the highest population density is Abidjan.

These observations could be leading to the correlation between antennas activity and user density within a cellular network and their geographical location. Thus by analyzing the user activity and their mobility patterns within a cellular network only, it is possible to identify the major cities/locations within a country/city.

Understanding the people-location interaction could represent a potential for location-based services. For example time-independent interactions

Figure 7. Top Most Popular Antennas over 150 days

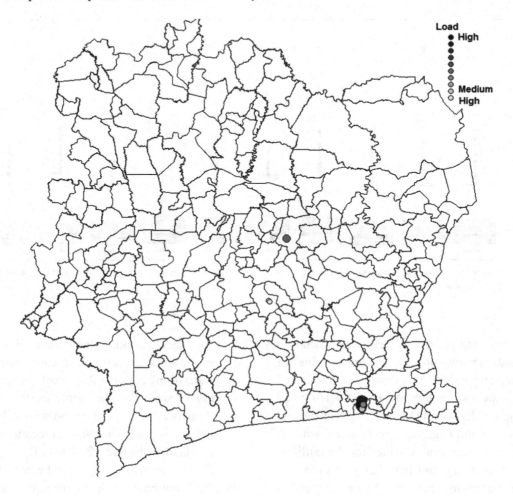

refer to overlapping trajectories between distinct people irrespective of the actual time of overlap. This information is very useful in social recommender systems which are based on location-based tagging services (Biancalana et al., 2011). In these social recommender systems, users make use of the location-based services in order to obtain and share information (tags) about the points of interest in their surroundings.

In order to explore the idea on how many distinct people are likely to meet each other in a time-independent manner, the user diversity at the antennas over each of the two-week period for the full 150 days is analyzed, as previously listed in Figure 8. Considering the overlap in trajectories

between users, irrespective of the actual time of overlap, the results show that over the 150 days period, the maximum number of distinct users per antenna was registered at the end of December (i.e., week 3-4), represented in Figure 8 by the outlier with the maximum value of 2295 distinct users. This could be interpreted as the fact that over the 150 days period, a maximum number representing 4.5% of the total 50,000 customers monitored, share the same location at a certain cell tower irrespective of the time and day. This type of interaction is the basis for location-based tagging services, as mentioned above.

From a lower resolution point of view, when looking at the study on the sub-prefectures ac-

Figure 8. User Diversity over 150 days

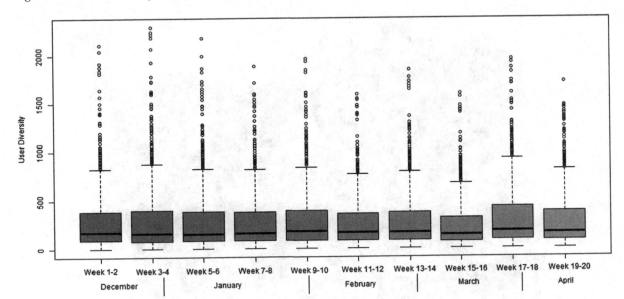

tivity as illustrated in Figure 9, the city with the highest activity is Abidjan (Sub-Prefecture ID 60), followed by Yamoussoukro (Sub-Prefecture ID 58), Bouake (Sub-Prefecture ID 39) and San Pedro (Sub-Prefecture ID 122).

CONNECTING PEOPLE, LOCATIONS, AND REAL-WORLD EVENTS

From the spatio-temporal patterns of the collective customers' activity within the mobile network traffic datasets introduced previously, the correlation between people, locations and events is analyzed. Specifically the interest is on studying the correlation between exceptional patterns detected in the mobile usage within a cellular network and real-world events such as public concerts, parades, soccer matches, riots protests, etc.

Understanding the exceptional data usage patterns could significantly improve the spatial and temporal awareness when taking decisions. An example would be in the case of event management, when organizing parades/carnivals/concerts, etc.

From the previous observations on the sub-prefectures activities several peak periods are detected and highlighted below:

- **New Year's Eve:** As we previously observed from the above studies the first substantial increase in the total number of distinct users and the total number of active users per antenna for each of the two week period (see Figure 6 and Figure 8), is recorded at the beginning of January. This increase in users' diversity and antennas activity could be correlated with the New Year's Eve period. The detailed view of the overall antennas activity distribution during the 10 days with pre- and post-New Year's Eve periods is illustrated in Figure 13. It can be noticed that as the New Year's Eve is approaching, the values of the upper whiskers and the values of the outlier are increasing. For the first day of the New Year, the median value is higher and it can be noticed that there is an increased number of antennas that have a total number of

Figure 9. Sub-Prefectures Activity over 150 days

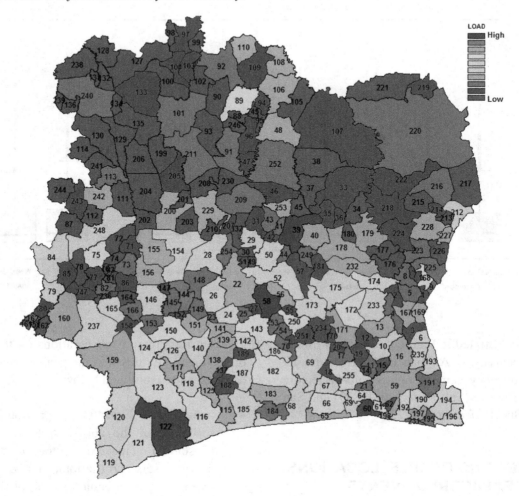

active users greater than the median. For example, looking at the upper whisker, it can be noticed that there is a 40% increase in the users' activity on this first day of the New Year when compared to the previous day. This is also represented by a higher upper quartile for this day, as well as a maximum outlier. After the first of January the antennas activity is decreasing.

- **Soccer Match:** As noticed in Figure 11a, another increase the sub-prefectures activity is at the end of January, beginning of February. This increase in user activity during this period overlaps with the duration of the Africa Cup of Nations 2012, also

known as Orange Africa Cup of Nations, which took place between 21st of January and 12th of February. In order to study if the increase in users' activity is due to the Africa Cup of Nations game, we looked at the total number of active users during the day with the final when Ivory Coast played against Zambia, and was defeated after a dramatic penalty shootout. The game started at 7:30pm on Sunday February 12th, and went through the penalty shootout, with duration of around 2h. Figure 14 lists the total number of active users on hourly basis for 12th of February and the next day, as well as the total users' activity a week later

Figure 10. Ivory Coast Indicative Population Map[1]

during the same days of the week, Sunday and Monday. From Figure 14, it can be noticed that from 7:30pm to 9pm there is a decrease in users' activity, marking the importance of the event. After the game, the users' activity started increasing with a peak around 11pm when the activity was about 96% higher than the activity at the same hour and same day of the week but a week later. The increase in users' activity is noticeable during the next day after the game, on February 13th when compared to a Monday's activity without any events, a week later.

- **Carnivals/Parades:** Another noticeable antennas activity and users' diversity over the 150 days period, is recorded at the beginning of April. Looking only at the antenna with the highest load and highest user diversity over the full monitoring period (Antenna ID 257), we compute the total number of active users and the total number of distinct users registered per day at this Top HotSpot Antenna, for each of the two-week period. Figure 15 and Figure 16 illustrate a boxplot intended to show the distribution of the total number of distinct users and total number of active users, re-

Figure 11. Sub-Prefectures Activity over 150 days: a) without outliers and b) with outliers

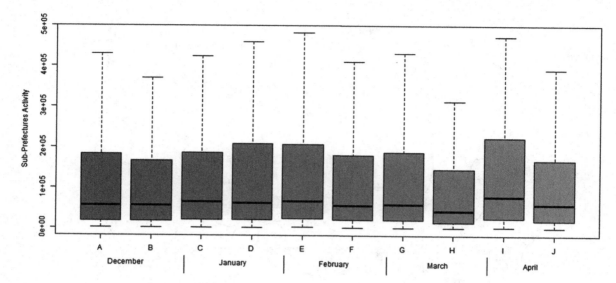

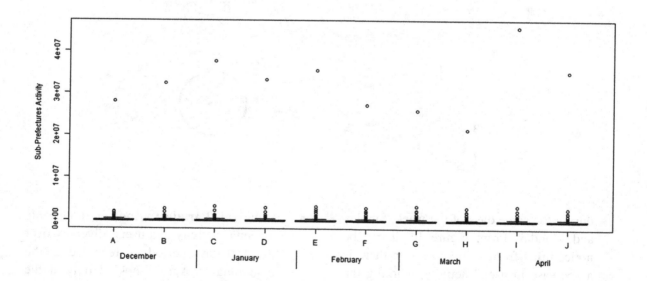

spectively, at the Top HotSpot Antenna, per day for each two-week period. Looking at Figure 15 and Figure 16, and following the variation of the maximum value of the total number of distinct users and the maximum value of the total number of active users, respectively, represented by the upper whisker, for each period, we can notice that in both cases, there is a peak increase at the end of March, beginning of April (i.e., week 17-18). This means that there is a significant increase in the antenna's activity for this period, compared with the rest. Looking at the location of this antenna it can be noticed that it is located within Bouake city.

Figure 12. Connecting people and locations

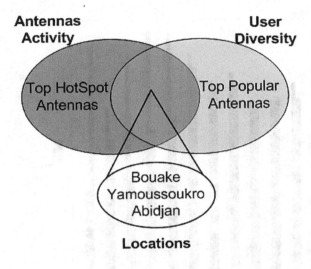

Taking these observations and looking at the real-time events happening in that specific location during exactly the same period with the increase in users' activity and users' diversity, we come to know about the annual Bouake Carnival. Consequently, these pattern exceptions in the antenna usage might be correlated with the real-world event, such

as: Bouake Carnival. The Bouake Carnival is a week-long carnival happening each year around the ending of March through the first week of April and attracts thousands of visitors.

Figure 17 illustrates the total number of distinct users and the total number of active users recorded at the Bouake Antenna, for each day of the week during the Week 17 and Week 18 periods. It can be noticed that both the total number of distinct users and the total number of active users increases in Week 18 when compared with the previous Week 17. This is because of the Bouake Carnival which is happening throughout the first week of April, when people come from all over the world to attend the festival, with a peak activity on Friday and Saturday as spotted in Figure 17.

- **Weekends:** In order to study the users' behavior during the week days and weekends, we computed the total number of active users per antenna over each day of the week during the full monitoring period. Figure 18 illustrates a boxplot intended to show

Figure 13. Antennas Activity over New Year's Eve

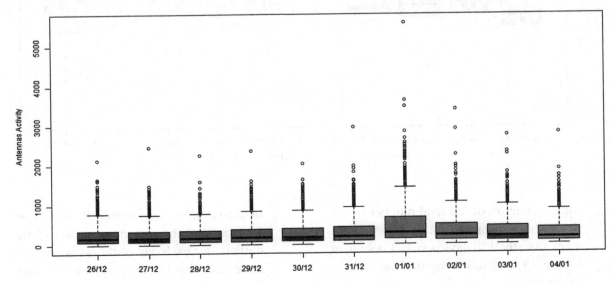

Figure 14. Antennas Activity during Orange Africa Cup of Nations Final

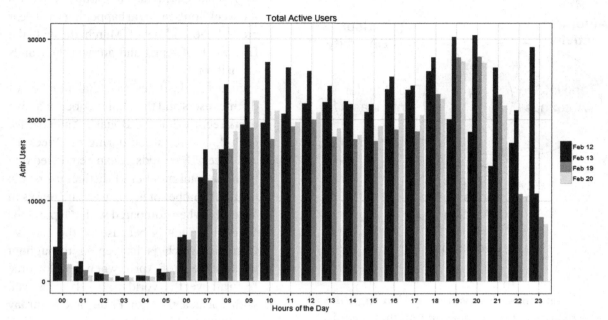

Figure 15. Top HotSpot Antenna Activity over 150 days

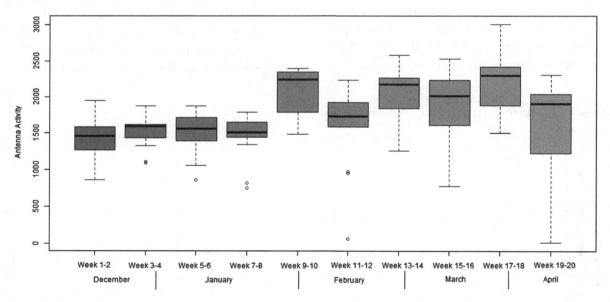

the distribution of the total number of active users per antenna for each day of the week over the 150 days period. Looking at Figure 18, and following the variation of the maximum value of the total number of active users, represented by the upper whisker, and the maximum values of the outliers, for each day of the week, we can notice that there is an increase on Fridays. For this day, the median value is higher and

Figure 16. Top HotSpot Antenna User Diversity over 150 days

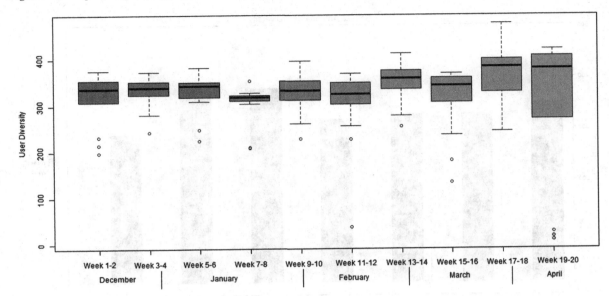

it can be noticed that there is an increased number of antennas that have a total number of active users greater than the median. This is represented by a higher upper quartile for this day. During the weekend the activity is decreasing marking the importance of these days.

USERS MOBILITY AND ACTIVITY

In order to get a more general view of the user mobility, the CDF of the number of distinct locations visited by any of the 50,000 customers over Week17-18 period is computed. The Week17-18 period was selected as is the period with the highest recorded antennas activity and user diversity, thus the highest user mobility period. The CDF is illustrated in Figure 19. The average number of distinct locations is around 8 and the standard deviation is 9.81. This means that 70% of the users

have less than 8 distinct locations, whereas around 9% of the customers have been seen in more than 20 distinct locations.

Looking at the customers' activity during week days as illustrated in Figure 18, it can be noticed that the users tend to be more active as the weekend is approaching and less active as the working days start.

In order to have a higher resolution on customers activity, on hourly basis we computed the total number of active users per antenna over each hour of the day for Wednesdays, Fridays, and Sundays during the full monitoring period. Figure 20 illustrates the boxplots intended to show the distribution of the total number of active users per antenna on an hourly basis for the three days mentioned. Looking at Figure 20, and following the variation of the maximum value of the total number of active users, represented by the upper whisker, it can be noticed that during the night hours there is not much traffic during

Figure 17. Bouake Antenna Total User Diversity and Total User Activity for each day of Week17-18

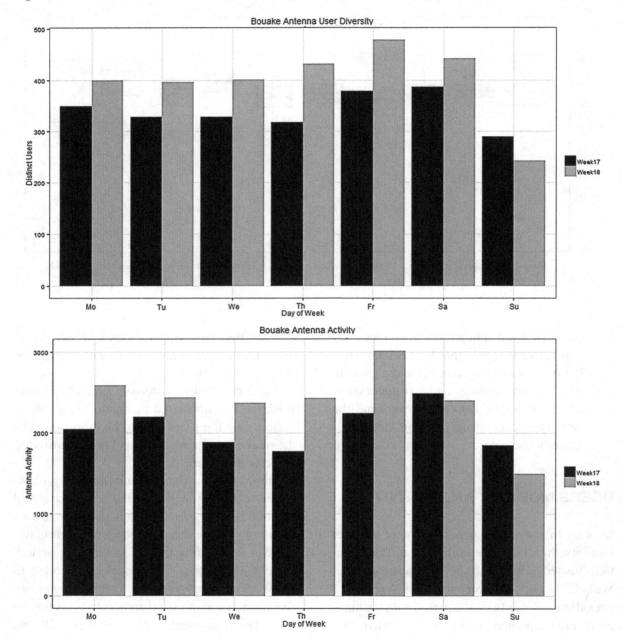

work days however there is an increase in the traffic during weekends. It can be noticed that the users also tend to communicate more before and after working hours with a smaller activity during work. However, during the weekend, there is reduced activity, users communicating more on late hours as well, with reduced activity during morning hours.

Figure 18. Antennas Activity on Week Days over 150 Days Period

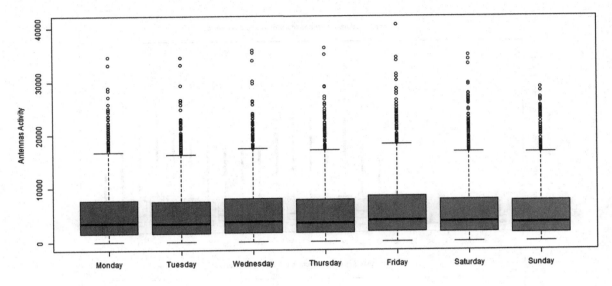

Figure 19. CDF of the number of distinct locations visited by each user over Week17-18

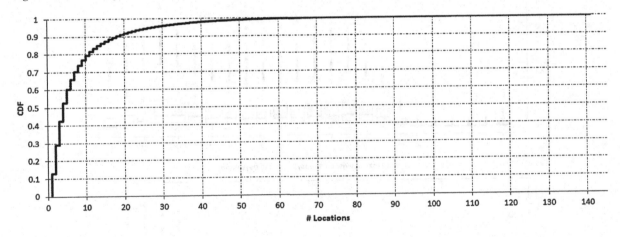

CONCLUSION

This book chapter aims to familiarize the readers with the use of fully anonymized and highly aggregated cellular network data, like Call Detail Records (CDRs) in order to provide various insights in human mobility patterns and other related areas. It presents a comprehensive survey of the current research on this topic. The survey also provides a useful categorization based on

the application of the use of CDR data, where six solution categories are defined: (1) definition of the universal law for human mobility; (2) urban planning and real-time traffic forecast; (3) human localization and mobility; (4) context-aware applications; (5) subscribers churn and privacy; and (6) health management. The major findings from these solutions are addressed and summarized.

The book chapter also presents a study that explores the use of these anonymized CDRs con-

Figure 20. Antennas Activity on Wednesdays, Fridays, and Sundays over 150 day period

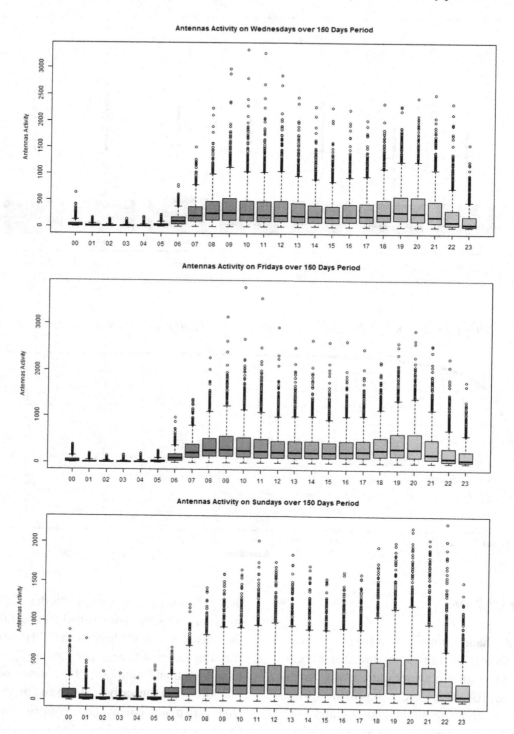

taining both voice-calls and SMS activities, from a cellular network in Ivory Coast over a period of 150 days. The aim of the study is to identify exceptional events in the communication patterns and associate them to real-time events in order to connect people, locations, and events. The study shows that by analyzing the users' activity and users' diversity within the mobile communication network the important cities of the country could be mapped to the hotspot antennas, such as: Bouake, Yamoussoukro, and Abidjan. It has been seen that the CDR data can be used to detect exceptional spatio-temporal patterns of the collective human mobile data usage and that these 'anomalies' in the usage patterns could be associated to real-world events (e.g., soccer match, parade/carnival, etc.). For example, high user network activity was identified at the beginning of February, collocated with the final of Africa Cup of Nations where Ivory Coast played against Zambia. The users' activity on the day with the game was compared against the users' activity on the same day of the week without similar events. It has been noticed that during the game playout, there is a decrease in users' activity, marking the importance of the event. However, there is significant increase in the users' activity during the period following the game and the next day, when compared with other days without events.

When exploring the idea of how many distinct people are likely to meet each other irrespective of the time and day, we came to know that w maximum number of 4.5% of the total 50,000 customers share the same locations at a certain cell tower during the 150 days period. This information is useful for social recommender systems, where users make use of these location-based services to share and obtain information about various points of interests.

Understanding the exceptional data usage patterns could significantly improve the spatial and temporal awareness when taking decisions and this knowledge could be further used to develop an *intelligent system that detects exceptional events in real-time* from CDRs monitoring. For example, a real-time event detection system could be of crucial importance to ensure people's safety in case of emergency situations, such as riots protests which could be more efficiently handled if detected on time.

ACKNOWLEDGMENT

We would like to thank the D4D Challenge committee and the Orange Group for Development and Initiative for the datasets provided in this study.

REFERENCES

Andrews, M., Bruns, G., Dogru, K. M., & Lee, H. (2013). Understanding Quota Dynamics in Wireless Networks. *Proceedings of the third conference on the Analysis of Mobile Phone Datasets. NetMob. Cambridge, USA.* doi:10.1145/2663494

Bagrow, J. P., Wang, D., & Barabási, A.-L. (2011). Collective Response of Human Populations to Large-Scale Emergencies. *PLoS ONE*, 6(3), e17680. doi:10.1371/journal.pone.0017680 PMID:21479206

Batty, M., Desyllas, J., & Duxbury, E. (2003). The discrete dynamics of small-scale spatial events: Agent-based models of mobility in carnivals and street parades. *International Journal of Geographical Information Science*, 17(7), 673–697. doi:10.1080/1365881031000135474

Becker, R. A., Caceres, R., Hanson, K., Loh, J. M., Urbanek, S., Varshavsky, A., & Volinsky, C. (2011). Route Classification Using Cellular Handoff Patterns. *Proceedings of the 13th International Conference on Ubiquitous Computing* (pp. 123–132). New York, NY, USA: ACM. doi:10.1145/2030112.2030130

Bengtsson, L., Lu, X., Thorson, A., Garfield, R., & von Schreeb, J. (2011). Improved Response to Disasters and Outbreaks by Tracking Population Movements with Mobile Phone Network Data: A Post-Earthquake Geospatial Study in Haiti. *PLoS Medicine*, 8(8), e1001083. doi:10.1371/journal.pmed.1001083 PMID:21918643

Biancalana, C., Gasparetti, F., Micarelli, A., & Sansonetti, G. (2011). Social Tagging for Personalized Location-Based Services. *Social Recommender Systems (SRS), a Workshop of the ACM Conference on Computer Supported Cooperative Work*. Retrieved from http://citeseerx.ist.psu.edu/viewdoc/download?doi=10.1.1.475.8892&rep=rep1&type=pdf

Calabrese, F., Colonna, M., Lovisolo, P., Parata, D., & Ratti, C. (2011). Real-Time Urban Monitoring Using Cell Phones: A Case Study in Rome. *IEEE Transactions on Intelligent Transportation Systems*, 12(1), 141–151. doi:10.1109/TITS.2010.2074196

Calabrese, F., Pereira, F. C., Di Lorenzo, G., Liu, L., & Ratti, C. (2010). The Geography of Taste: Analyzing Cell-phone Mobility and Social Events. *Proceedings of the 8th International Conference on Pervasive Computing* (pp. 22–37). Berlin, Heidelberg: Springer-Verlag. doi:10.1007/978-3-642-12654-3_2

De Montjoye, Y.-A., Hidalgo, C. A., Verleysen, M., & Blondel, V. D. (2013). Unique in the Crowd: The privacy bounds of human mobility. *Scientific Reports*, 3. doi:10.1038/srep01376 PMID:23524645

De Mulder, Y., Danezis, G., Batina, L., & Preneel, B. (2008). Identification via Location-profiling in GSM Networks. *Proceedings of the 7th ACM Workshop on Privacy in the Electronic Society* (pp. 23–32). New York, NY, USA: ACM. doi:10.1145/1456403.1456409

Di Lorenzo, G., & Calabrese, F. (2011). Identifying human spatio-temporal activity patterns from mobile-phone traces. *Proceedings of the 2011 14th International IEEE Conference on Intelligent Transportation Systems (ITSC)* (pp. 1069–1074). doi:10.1109/ITSC.2011.6082974

Frias-Martinez, E., Williamson, G., & Frias-Martinez, V. (2011). An Agent-Based Model of Epidemic Spread Using Human Mobility and Social Network Information. *Proceedings of the 2011 IEEE Third International Conference on Privacy, Security, Risk and Trust (PASSAT) and 2011 IEEE Third Inernational Conference on Social Computing (SocialCom)* (pp. 57–64). doi:10.1109/PASSAT/SocialCom.2011.142

González, M. C., Hidalgo, C. A., & Barabási, A.-L. (2008). Understanding individual human mobility patterns. *Nature*, 453(7196), 779–782. doi:10.1038/nature06958 PMID:18528393

Han, Q., & Ferreira, P. (2013). Determinants of Subscriber Churn in Wireless Networks: The Role of Peer Influence. *26th European Conference on Operational Research, Telecommunication, Networks, and Social Networks Stream, Roma, Italy*. doi:10.1145/2639968.2640057

Hasan, S., Zhan, X., & Ukkusuri, S. V. (2013). Understanding Urban Human Activity and Mobility Patterns Using Large-scale Location-based Data from Online Social Media. *Proceedings of the 2Nd ACM SIGKDD International Workshop on Urban Computing* (pp. 6:1–6:8). New York, NY, USA: ACM. doi:10.1145/2505821.2505823

Isaacman, S., Becker, R., Cáceres, R., Kobourov, S., Martonosi, M., Rowland, J., & Varshavsky, A. (2011). Identifying Important Places in People's Lives from Cellular Network Data. Proceedings of the 9th International Conference on Pervasive Computing (pp. 133–151). Berlin, Heidelberg: Springer-Verlag. Retrieved from http://dl.acm.org/citation.cfm?id=2021975.2021988

Isaacman, S., Becker, R., Cáceres, R., Kobourov, S., Rowland, J., & Varshavsky, A. (2010). A Tale of Two Cities. *In Proceedings of the Eleventh Workshop on Mobile Computing Systems & Applications* (pp. 19–24). New York, NY, USA: ACM. doi:10.1145/1734583.1734589

Kung, K. S., Greco, K., Sobolevsky, S., & Ratti, C. (2014). Exploring Universal Patterns in Human Home-Work Commuting from Mobile Phone Data. *PLoS ONE*, *9*(6), e96180. doi:10.1371/journal.pone.0096180 PMID:24933264

Motahari, S., Zang, H., & Reuther, P. (2012). The Impact of Temporal Factors on Mobility Patterns. *Proceedings of the 2012 45th Hawaii International Conference on System Science (HICSS)* (pp. 5659–5668). doi:10.1109/HICSS.2012.572

Noulas, A., Scellato, S., Lambiotte, R., Pontil, M., & Mascolo, C. (2012). A Tale of Many Cities: Universal Patterns in Human Urban Mobility. *PLoS ONE*, *7*(5), e37027. doi:10.1371/journal.pone.0037027 PMID:22666339

Palchykov, V., Mitrović, M., Jo, H.-H., Saramäki, J., & Pan, R. K. (2014). Inferring human mobility using communication patterns. *Scientific Reports*, *4*, 6174. doi:10.1038/srep06174 PMID:25146347

Pulselli, R. M., Romano, P., Ratti, C., & Tiezzi, E. (2008). Computing Urban Mobile Landscapes through Monitoring Population Density Based on Cell-Phone Chatting. *International Journal of Design & Nature and Ecodynamics*, *3*(2), 121–134. Retrieved from http://www.witpress.com/elibrary/dne-volumes/3/2/346 doi:10.2495/D&NE-V3-N2-121-134

Ratti, C., Pulselli, R. M., Williams, S., & Frenchman, D. (2006). Mobile Landscapes: Using location data from cell phones for urban analysis. *Environment and Planning. B, Planning & Design*, *33*(5), 727–748. doi:10.1068/b32047

Song, C., Koren, T., Wang, P., & Barabási, A.-L. (2010a). Modelling the scaling properties of human mobility. *Nature Physics*, *6*(10), 818–823. doi:10.1038/nphys1760

Song, C., Qu, Z., Blumm, N., & Barabási, A.-L. (2010b). Limits of Predictability in Human Mobility. *Science*, *327*(5968), 1018–1021. doi:10.1126/science.1177170 PMID:20167789

Tatem, A. J., Huang, Z., Narib, C., Kumar, U., Kandula, D., & Pindolia, D. K. et al. (2014). Integrating rapid risk mapping and mobile phone call record data for strategic malaria elimination planning. *Malaria Journal*, *13*(1), 52. doi:10.1186/1475-2875-13-52 PMID:24512144

Trestian, I., Ranjan, S., Kuzmanovic, A., & Nucci, A. (2009). Measuring Serendipity: Connecting People, Locations and Interests in a Mobile 3G Network. *Proceedings of the 9th ACM SIGCOMM Conference on Internet Measurement Conference* (pp. 267–279). New York, NY, USA: ACM. doi:10.1145/1644893.1644926

Wesolowski, A., Eagle, N., Tatem, A. J., Smith, D. L., Noor, A. M., Snow, R. W., & Buckee, C. O. (2012). Quantifying the Impact of Human Mobility on Malaria. *Science*, *338*(6104), 267–270. doi:10.1126/science.1223467 PMID:23066082

Xavier, Z. F. H., Silveria, M. L., Almeida, M. J., Malab, S. H. C., Ziviani, A., & Marques-Neto, T. H. (2013). *Understanding Human Mobility Due to Large-Scale Events. Third conference on the Analysis of Mobile Phone Datasets. NetMob. Cambridge, USA*. Retrieved from http://perso.uclouvain.be/vincent.blondel/netmob/2013/NetMob2013-abstracts.pdf

Yuan, J., Zheng, Y., & Xie, X. (2012). Discovering Regions of Different Functions in a City Using Human Mobility and POIs. *Proceedings of the 18th ACM SIGKDD International Conference on Knowledge Discovery and Data Mining* (pp. 186–194). New York, NY, USA: ACM. doi:10.1145/2339530.2339561

Zang, H., & Bolot, J. (2011). Anonymization of Location Data Does Not Work: A Large-scale Measurement Study. *Proceedings of the 17th Annual International Conference on Mobile Computing and Networking* (pp. 145–156). New York, NY, USA: ACM. doi:10.1145/2030613.2030630

Zang, H., & Bolot, J. C. (2007). Mining Call and Mobility Data to Improve Paging Efficiency in Cellular Networks. *Proceedings of the 13th Annual ACM International Conference on Mobile Computing and Networking* (pp. 123–134). New York, NY, USA: ACM. doi:10.1145/1287853.1287868

KEY TERMS AND DEFINITIONS

Big Data: An extremely large and complex data set of structured and unstructured data that cannot be processed using traditional data processing applications.

Call Details Records: A data record containing information about the recent usage of the telecommunication system related to a telephone call or short message service.

Churn Rate: The amount of customers that discontinue their subscription to a specific service during a given time period.

Hotspot Antenna: A telecommunication tower that serves a relatively high number of customers in comparison to others.

Privacy: The protection of sensitive personal information that customers provide during the communications transaction.

Radio Access Technology: The type of underlying physical connection method for a wireless communication environment.

User Diversity: The amount of distinct users that are seen at the telecommunication tower over a given period.

ENDNOTE

[1]   http://www.mapaction.org/component/mapcat/mapdetail/2383.html.

Chapter 2
Measuring the Effectiveness of Wikipedia Articles:
How Does Open Content Succeed?

Alireza Amrollahi
Griffith University, Australia

Mohammad Tahaei
University of Tehran, Iran

Mohammad Khansari
University of Tehran, Iran

ABSTRACT

Since 2001 Wikipedia has grown up to one of the most important sources of knowledge worldwide. The voluntarily and independent nature of the project has made it a very unique case of Information Systems with various elements which could affect the way each article is developed. In this paper by referring to the DeLone& McLean model of Information Systems success and considering the body of research in the field, the measures for evaluating the effectiveness of wiki articles have been identified. Then using a sample of 804 articles in Wikipedia and Structural Equation Model (SEM) method the model has been validated. The findings indicate that in the context of Wikipedia open content, system quality and information quality could be merged together and after this simplification, they can affect use and user satisfaction in open content platforms such as Wikipedia.

INTRODUCTION

Wikipedia has started as a "user-written online encyclopedia" in 2001 and fast expanded to one of the biggest sources of knowledge which is available freely online (Tapscott & Williams, 2008). Although its growth rate has been variable over

time (Manjoo, 2009), it has been one of ten top rated websites according to Alexa ranking (www.alexa.com).

Wikipedia has been started as an independent project and after 2003 it has been part of the non-profit Wikimedia foundation. The aim of the project at first was to develop a free, collaboratively

DOI: 10.4018/978-1-4666-8833-9.ch002

edited and multilingual internet encyclopedia but the idea soon extended to other websites such as: Wiktionary (collaborative dictionary), Wikibooks (free textbooks), Wikiquote (Collection of quotations), etc. Now after 11 years Wikipedia has more than 22 million articles in 285 languages (over 3.9 million in English) and it is estimated to have 365 million readers worldwide.

In Wikipedia there are specific regulations for adding, improving, editing and deleting articles which are free or open content (OC) and everyone could participate in these processes. The process which undergoes for an article from beginning to a mature or reliable article involves many different steps and many stakeholders play different roles in this process.

The collaborative structure of the project makes it possible for everyone to contribute in the project by adding new content and editing available content. Moreover, volunteer members monitor the developed content and by various mechanisms deal with problematic content (including: copyrighted content, unstructured content, and the content which its correctness is suspicious). The structure of the website makes it possible for even anonymous users to edit (most of the) content. As a result of this open editing model, the quality of Wikipedia's content has often been questioned (Javanmardi, Ganjisaffar, Lopes, & Baldi, 2009). Although various research studies have positively reported the quality of Wikipedia posts in comparison by other sources (Adler & De Alfaro, 2007; Chesney, 2006; Giles, 2005; Gorgeon & Swanson, 2009; Kramer, Gregorowicz, & Iyer, 2008; Wilkinson & Huberman, 2007b), a pessimistic viewpoint still exist in academia in regards to validity of Wikipedia posts as "scientific references".

Moreover the success of Wikipedia has inspired many others to use the same idea for sharing their knowledge in thousands of wikis all over the world and shaped new paradigm for collaborative work. Today; wikis have been used for different purposes as part of enterprise information systems (Albors,

Ramos, & Hervas, 2008; Yates & Paquette, 2011). It has also inspired a new form of sourcing by which an organizational task is performed by a large group of people and has been later named crowdsourcing (Howe, 2006a, 2006b, 2008). This model has been used in various contexts in practice (Anderson, 2011; Brabham, 2008a, 2008b, 2009), and attracted much attention from researchers and academia (Amrollahi, Ghapanchi, & Talaei-Khoei, 2014a; Behrend, Sharek, Meade, & Wiebe, 2011; Pedersen et al., 2013).

This attention from both research and practice perspectives shows the importance of Wikipedia as both a source of knowledge and a new paradigm in information systems. Although many aspects of the website has been studied in the information systems literature and related areas, the process which leads to development of an effective success has not been studied in the literature.

In the current research we aim at understanding the process by which a Wikipedia post succeeds initial steps of development and becomes reliable, useable, effective or successful for its audience.

Findings of this research may help foundations like Wikimedia to better advance their products. Businesses that use wiki-type systems as their knowledge management or other information systems can also benefit the result of research for advancement of these systems.

To gain a better understanding of the factors that result in the effectiveness of wiki articles and the measures by which this effectiveness could be measured, we use current body of research in success of Information System. The most cited research in this category is "DeLone and McLean model of IS success" (Delone, 2003).

Information systems evaluation models have been already used to evaluate the effectiveness of IS in various context including e-government, open source software, financial systems, and collaborative systems (Alavi & Leidner, 2001; Ding, Hu, Verma, & Wardell, 2009; Gil-Garcia, 2012; Horsti, Tuunainen, & Tolonen, 2005; Pitt, Watson, & Kavan, 1995; Rai, Lang, & Welker,

2002). These papers usually study a number of systems and evaluate the fitness of the model to that context based on this study. The current study, however, uses different approach and studies different articles in one system (Wikipedia) for success evaluation. The logic behind using the model of IS success for Wikipedia articles (instead of comparing different wiki-type systems) is based on the followings facts:

- Articles in Wikipedia are independent entities
- Each articles in Wikipedia has its own developers, administrators and process of development
- Previous researches have shown various development processes for different articles in Wikipedia
- Wikipedia covers variety of topics and it is a source for people with different interests to contribute and use (Spoerri, 2007)

The above mentioned facts show the need for study of each article as an independent IS and develop a model which reflects the success of these articles in general. The current study seeks the answer for the following research question:

RQ: How a successful content is developed in Wikipedia?

In the remaining of the paper, after a review of the literature on Wikipedia, and the success of information systems and Open Source Software (OSS), we discuss the research model, the measures for each construct and relevant hypotheses. The paper then explains the process of validating the research model in which the data of 804 articles have been used for analyzing research hypotheses with structural equations model. This is followed by the discussion of the results and finally we conclude the paper in the last section with possible implications for practice and future research directions.

BACKGROUND

In order to draw a picture of the current state of research in the field, we review two different areas which together shape the context of current research: Wikipedia and success of information systems (IS).

Wikipedia

The success of Wikipedia as well as its unique features and providing open access to the records and statistics about its articles have caused a great attention from research community. Jullien (2012) in his review paper mentioned "inputs, process, outcomes" framework for categorizing different fields of research about Wikipedia. In the input category of research, internal rules and process of content development and motivation of the users have been subject of attention by researchers. Topics like conflicts between members and how to resolve it (Morgan, Mason, & Nahon, 2011), demographics of contributors (Glott, Schmidt, & Ghosh, 2010), and effect of contextual and longitudinal factors (Antin, 2011; Bryant, Forte, & Bruckman, 2005; Dejean & Jullien, 2012; Forte & Bruckman, 2008) on motivation have been studied in this category.

In the "process" category activities and role of contributors, the structure of projects and articles, and the organization and governance of the project have been studied. Various stakeholders in the project (Huvila, 2010), interrelations between articles (Capocci et al., 2006), structure of the teams (Chen, Ren, & Riedl, 2010; Kittur & Kraut, 2008; Nemoto, Gloor, & Laubacher, 2011), forms of leadership (Choi, Alexander, Kraut, & Levine, 2010; Halfaker, Kittur, Kraut, & Riedl, 2009; Halfaker, Kittur, & Riedl, 2011; Zhu, Kraut, & Kittur, 2012), and evolution of posts and contributors (Otto & Simon, 2008) have been subject of research papers in this category.

The last category is "evaluation" in which process quality, user experience, and product

Table 1. Summary of researches about effectiveness of Wikipedia articles

Reference	Measure of Effectiveness	Affecting Factor(s)
(Brändle, 2005; Lih, 2004; Ortega & Izquierdo-Cortazar, 2009; Wilkinson & Huberman, 2007a; Wöhner & Peters, 2009)	Labeled as featured article	More edits and editors
(Adler et al., 2008)	Labeled as featured article	Author's contributions life-length
(Mcguinness et al., 2006)	Labeled as featured article	Internal reference to the article
(Stein & Hess, 2007)	Labeled as featured article	Having experienced editors
(Ransbotham & Kane, 2011)	Labeled as featured article	Having a fine tune of experimented editors and fresh newcomers
(Wilkinson & Huberman, 2007a)	Labeled as featured article	More discussion on the talk page
(Blumenstock, 2008; Hasan Dalip, André Gonçalves, Cristo, & Calado, 2009; Lipka & Stein, 2010)	Labeled as featured article	The length and basic quality of the writing,
(Poderi, 2009)	Labeled as featured article	Longer articles, but less edit and contributors
(Nemoto et al., 2011)	Labeled as featured article	More centralized network and more members
(Arazy & Nov, 2010)	Quality (measured by external experts)	Having a small team, very committed and having people very invested in Wikipedia and peripheral contributors
(Lam, Karim, & Riedl, 2010)	Quality of decision of article deletion	Larger groups, experienced members, administrator's point of view
(Choi et al., 2010)	Newcomers' edit activity	Welcome messages, assistance and constructive criticism
(Lam et al., 2010)	Users' experience	Accuracy of information
(Stvilia, Al-Faraj, & Yi, 2009)	Labeled as featured article	Language of the article

Summarized from (Jullien, 2012)

quality have been studied (Jullien, 2012). Both internal measures (Carillo & Okoli, 2011; Poderi, 2009) and external measures (Stvilia & Gasser, 2008; Wöhner & Peters, 2009) have been used to evaluate the quality of Wikipedia with different perspectives. Many studies addressed quality and the process of advancement in Wikipedia. Some of these papers study single post (Gorgeon & Swanson, 2009) or the Wikipedia as a whole (Giles, 2005). Other studies have also mentioned different measures of effectiveness and studied effect of this. It entails various internal and external factors and interrelation between them. Table 1 summarizes findings of different researches about effectiveness of Wikipedia. This table reflects various references which studied quality of Wikipedia articles, the

measure by which they studied effectiveness or quality of each post, and the factor they propose to affect this effectiveness.

However as concluded by De Laat (2010),evaluation of the Wikipedia articles' is still a work in progress. To best of our knowledge (neither in the review which conducted by Jullien (2012) nor our independent search) there is no research in which the effectiveness or success of Wikipedia posts has been evaluated in terms of interrelated models.

Success of Information Systems

Measuring the tangible and intangible benefits of IS has been a question for organizations since the late 1970s (Delone, 2003). Among many different models of IS success, work of Delone (2003) has been attracted the most attention and has been deployed to many different areas. Figure 1 illustrates the revised model of IS success.

This model has been widely used for evaluation of various types of information systems. Table 2 shows a number of these studies.

For the purpose of adapting the general model of IS success with context of research, we focus on the research on success of Open Source Software, which is similar to open content in many ways:

- They are both provided freely to people
- Open content providers (especially Wikipedia) use free/open software licenses as the basis of their licensing[1] term.
- In both OSS and OC, audience of the product actively participates in the development activities
- Founders and pioneer people in Wikipedia have been inspired by free software movement (Rosenzweig, 2006)

- Other researchers already have proven the similarities of OSS and OC communities in some aspects (Ortega & Izquierdo-Cortazar, 2009)

In the OSS context many factors have been cited to be influential on the success of the IS. This includes factors such as: number of developers (Subramaniam et al., 2009), norms and values (Stewart & Gosain, 2006a), structure of social network (J. Wu, Goh, & Tang, 2007), sponsorship (Amrollahi, Khansari, & Manian, 2014b), license type (Stewart, Ammeter, & Maruping, 2006), technical specification of the project, project status (Stewart & Gosain, 2006b), and number of downloads (Amrollahi, Khansari, & Manian, 2014a).

The initial research on success of OSS usually expands existing theories to this context (Crowston et al., 2003; Crowston, Annabi, Howison, & Masango, 2005; Crowston et al., 2006; Sagers, 2004). Future studies, however, have developed several

Figure 1. Delone & McLean model of IS success (Delone, 2003)

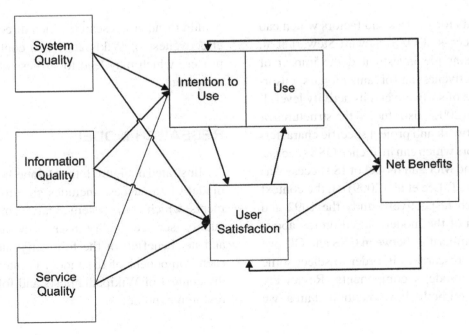

Table 2. Use of Delone & McLean model of IS success in various areas of information systems

Number	Area of Information Systems	Reference
1	Knowledge Management Systems	(Halawi, McCarthy, & Aronson, 2007; M. Jennex & Olfman, 2005; M. E. Jennex & Olfman, 2006; M. E. Jennex, Smolnik, & Croasdell, 2007; Kulkarni, Ravindran, & Freeze, 2007)
2	Electronic Business	(Cao, Zhang, & Seydel, 2005; Delone & Mclean, 2004; Eikebrokk & Olsen, 2007; Horsti et al., 2005; B. Xiao & Benbasat, 2007)
3	Electronic Government	(Gil-Garcia, 2012; Gil-Garcia, Chengalur-Smith, & Duchessi, 2007; Gil-García & Pardo, 2005; Hussein, Karim, & Selamat, 2007; Teo, Srivastava, & Jiang, 2008)
4	Open Source Software	(Crowston, Annabi, & Howison, 2003; Crowston, Howison, & Annabi, 2006; S. Y. T. Lee, Kim, & Gupta, 2009; Sen, 2007; Subramaniam, Sen, & Nelson, 2009)
5	Enterprise Resource Planning	(Chien & Tsaur, 2007; Dezdar & Ainin, 2011; Morton & Hu, 2008; J.-H. Wu & Wang, 2006; Xue, Liang, Boulton, & Snyder, 2005)
6	Marketing and Customer Relationship Management	(Avlonitis & Panagopoulos, 2005; Gounaris, Panigyrakis, & Chatzipanagiotou, 2007; McCalla, Ezingeard, & Money, 2003; McCalla, Ezingeard, & Money, 2004; Tsai, Chou, & Leu, 2011)
7	Health and Medical Information Systems	(Chatterjee, Chakraborty, Sarker, Sarker, & Lau, 2009; Häyrinen, Saranto, & Nykänen, 2008; Lau et al., 2012; Otieno, Hinako, Motohiro, Daisuke, & Keiko, 2008; Petter & Fruhling, 2011; Shahmoradi, Ahmadi, & Haghani, 2007)
8	Project Management Systems	(Kaiser & Ahlemann, 2010; S.-K. Lee & Yu, 2012; Raymond & Bergeron, 2008)
9	Educational Systems	(Holsapple & Lee-Post, 2006; Limayem & Cheung, 2008; Lin, 2007; Ozkan & Koseler, 2009; Wang, Wang, & Shee, 2007; Yi, Liao, Huang, & Hwang, 2009)
10	Decision Support Systems	(Ben-Zvi, 2012; Lynch & Gregor, 2004; Popovič, Hackney, Coelho, & Jaklič, 2012)

measurements for success and factors which can affect the success of OSS. Stewart Stewart et al. (2006) for example investigated the impact of license restrictiveness and organizational sponsorship on usage of software and its activity level. J. Wu and Goh (2009) also studied the structures of the social network and project specific characteristics as factors which can influence OSS success.

Delone and McLean model of IS success was used by (S. Y. T. Lee et al. (2009)) in the context of OSS which respectively study the 1992 and 2002 version of the model. Based on the above mentioned similarities between OSS and OC, we refer to these researches in order to select some measures of model's components. Reviewing the literature on both above mentioned area, we couldn't find any research which directly targets effectiveness of Wikis and open content or the process which may lead to success of this type of content.

RESEARCH MODEL

As illustrated in Figure 1, the Delone and McLean model of IS success includes six different elements which are: system quality, information quality, service quality, user, user satisfaction, and net benefits. In the following subsections, each component of the model is interpreted in the context of Wikipedia posts and followed by research hypotheses.

System Quality

This is the measure of the information processing system itself (DeLone & McLean, 1992). While the information processing is done by the same tool in all Wikipedia articles (MediaWiki software), we could omit these item from our model or merge it with information quality. This could be compared with the modification which performed by S. Y. T. Lee et al. (2009) on Delone and McLean model of IS success to adapt the model with the context of open source software. The factor could be also considered as the developers' power to work with software which is a critical aspect of OC development.

In fact many developers of Wikipedia are knowledgeable people in the field but less familiar with the software and related regulations (e.g. copyright law); so what they develop is a set of words and sentences about the topic. We believe that these kinds of articles are less effective in Wikipedia. For this reason we measure the number of internal links to other articles and number of multimedia material in each article for this component.

H1a: Increase in quality of the Wikipedia posts (in form of using more features) will increase the number of visits for each post.

H2a: Increase in quality of the Wikipedia posts (in form of using more features) will increase user satisfaction about each post.

Information Quality

This construct is dedicated to measure the output of the system (DeLone & McLean, 1992) and it may be the most important element in evaluation of OC contents. As we mentioned before, we refer to items which are directly connected to the quantity and quality of transferred knowledge for this element.

It is important to note that the conventional indicator in literature which is "labeling the article as featured article" is inefficient in our research while it is a binary (Yes/No) indicator and little amount of articles are featured when they are selected randomly.

Anyway we can also merge system and information quality and make another construct called "Content quality". This new construct in the model results in a new alternative model in the context of open content. Both models have been tested in order to understand which one is best fitted to our data.

H3a: Increase in quality of the Wikipedia posts (in form of better content) will increase the number of visits for each post.

H4a: Increase in quality of the Wikipedia posts (in form of better content) will increase user satisfaction about each post.

H1b: Increase in quality of the Wikipedia posts (in form of both better features and better content) will increase the number of visits for each post.

H2b: Increase in quality of the Wikipedia posts (in form of both better features and better content) will increase user satisfaction about each post.

Service Quality

It has been added to the old model of IS success in order to take the service of IS department in to the account (Delone, 2003) and in context of OSS it has been defined as the quality of services provided by the community (S. Y. T. Lee et al., 2009).

In Wikipedia we also mentioned the quality of community service in revising and editing the articles and the length of talk page for each article as measures of service quality.

H5a: Increase in the quality of services which is provided by community in discussion page of each post will increase the number of visits for each post.

H6a: Increase in the quality of services which is provided by community in discussion page of each post will increase user satisfaction about each post.

H3b: Increase in the quality of services which is provided by community in discussion page of each post will increase the number of visits for each post.

H4b: Increase in the quality of services which is provided by community in discussion page of each post will increase user satisfaction about each post.

Use

It is the degree and manner in which users utilize the capabilities of an information system (Petter, DeLone, & McLean, 2008). More than simple indicator of number of visits (or download), the reuse of software code is indicated in the context of OSS as a measure of use construct (Crowston et al., 2003).

Number of links to content on the internet (as citation, definition, etc.) can be an indicator of reuse of that content. Although it was impossible for us to count all the links to an article on the internet, but we know that number of external links to a webpage is an important factor for the ranking of the result in search engines (Page, 2001). Therefore, we measured the reuse of an article via the rank of the article in Wikipedia when we search it on internet.

User Satisfaction

Although this is rather a subjective measure, but recently Wikipedia has initiated the "Rate this page" section for its articles which is a decent indicator of user satisfaction from that page.

Based on the literature on OSS success, we also evaluated developers' satisfaction through the absorption power of each article and the number of developers who have at least one contribution for each article.

H7a: Increase in user satisfaction about each post will increase the number of visits for each post.

H5b: Increase in user satisfaction about each post will increase the number of visits for each post.

Net Benefits

It is the extent to which IS are contributing to the success of individuals, groups, organizations, industries, and nation (Petter et al., 2008). It is an important and critical factor for IS success and it may be more important for Wikimedia articles, when it needs to understand how Wikipedia improves the knowledge of people and how it is useful for business (i.e. donators). But all measures we found in the literature (such as improved decision-making, improved productivity, increased sales, cost reductions, improved profits, market efficiency, consumer welfare, improving knowledge and teaching ability) were subjective or very hard to measure in the context of Wikipedia.

Even Crowston et al. (2003) declares that the measurement of individual and organizational impacts (the equivalent constructs in 1992 revision) are unusable in the context of OSS as a result of the problems with definition and measurement of the element.

So according to our research method and source of data which do not let us to survey subjective matters, we omit this construct from the current version of the research. Figures 2 and 3 illustrate the final proposed research model for Wikipedia and Table 3 shows different measures we used to evaluate them.

RESEARCH METHOD AND DATA COLLECTION

In order to evaluate the research model we used Structural Equation Model (SEM) method has

Figure 2. The proposed research model-a of Wikipedia success

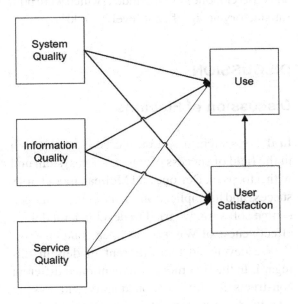

Figure 3. The proposed research model-b of Wikipedia success

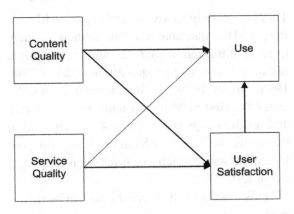

been used and analyzed the model with Amos student software (Arbuckle, 2006).

We gathered the data of 1100 random articles in English Wikipedia. These articles have been selected between January and February 2013 and cover a variety of topics and areas.

In the next step we surprisingly noticed that about 141 (13%) of them have less than 20 words lengths. Because these short articles in Wikipedia are usually stubs which do not convey any in-depth information about the topic and they usually only introduce the topic, we omitted them from the pool in order to prevent any outlier data. The final sample of the research contains 804 articles which is an adequate sample size for our research. These articles also cover a variety of subjects like: history, entertainment, politics, art, technology, science, etc.

Table 3. Measures for each construct of the model

Construct		Measure
System Quality*	Content Quality**	Number of internal links Number of multimedia material
Information Quality*		Number of references Number of external links Length of article (number of words)
Service Quality		Edit intervals (average time between edits) Number of minor edits Number of major edits Length of talk page (number of words)
Use		Number of visits (in last three months) Rank of page in search engine
User satisfaction		Page rates (average of 4 rates) Number of contributors

*Constructs of first model
**Constructs of second model

Data Analysis

The current study uses Structural Equation Modeling (SEM) for data analysis. This method is widely used in information systems and management research for analyzing quantitative data (Chin, 1998; Straub, 1999; Van der Heijden, 2004). We tested the first SEM model with Amos software and result is depicted in Table 4. As depicted in the table, the effect of System quality on both Use and User satisfaction has not been supported in our test.

This confirms that combining information quality and system quality may result to better findings. Therefore, we examine the second model with Amos software. The result is shown in Table 5.

As it could be seen in the model, except the effect of User satisfaction on Use, all other research hypotheses have been approved by the path analysis. We also studied validity of both model in

AMOS software by CFI (Comparative Fit Index) and GFI (Goodness-of-Fit Index) which were both satisfactory at significant level of 0.001.

DISCUSSION

Discussion of Findings

In this research, based on the body of research in the field of success of information system and with a focus on DeLone and McLean model of IS success and its implications in the context of open source software, we tried to develop a model for effectiveness of Wikipedia's open content.

We developed two different models in this regard: In the first model we mentioned different constructs for Information quality and System quality. By system quality, we meant the features of articles which entail ability of working with

Table 4. Result of path analysis using research model-1 (Standardized Regression Weights)

				Estimate	P
H1a	Use	<	System Quality	-4.964	.983
H2a	User Satisfaction	<	System Quality	.000	.983
H3a	Use	<	Information Quality	-1.133	***
H4a	User Satisfaction	<	Information Quality	.000	***
H5a	Use	<	Service Quality	14.225	***
H6a	User Satisfaction	<	Service Quality	.001	***
H7a	Use	<	User Satisfaction	546.363	NS

*** Significance at the 0.001 level

Table 5. Result of path analysis using research model-2 (Standardized Regression Weights)

				Estimate	P
H1b	Use	<	Content Quality	-1.600	***
H2b	User Satisfaction	<	Content Quality	.000	***
H3b	Use	<	Service Quality	14.427	***
H4b	User Satisfaction	<	Service Quality	.001	***
H5b	Use	<	User Satisfaction	540.515	NS

*** Significance at the 0.001 level

Mediawiki software and deep understanding of the Wikipedia rules. In contrast information quality refers to simple textual power of an article and its appropriateness in terms of ascertainably.

In the second model we combined two constructs together and build content quality which refers to both informational and technical aspects of developing an open content on Wikipedia.

The validation of two models showed us that the second model better fits the real of Wikipedia articles. Therefore, it can be concluded that dividing technical and informational properties of Wikipedia posts is not advised in study of effectiveness of Wikipedia articles.

As shown in Tables 3 and 4, although the estimates of regression is supported in our analysis, estimated value is around zero for the effect of content quality and service quality on user satisfaction. The impact of service quality on use is also supported by the test and it does not provide support for the impact of user satisfaction on use.

Probably the most interesting result of the research is the negative impact of content quality on use. In other words the current study indicates that when the quality of an article improves (in terms of length, number of multimedia material, references and links to external resources) less views and reuse of the article will occur.

We believe that the reason for this impact is related to the demand of users for concise and summarized content on Wikipedia. An in-depth study about this impact needs evaluation of user behavior in Wikipedia.

Implications for Practitioners

Businesses and practitioners in various areas can use principles of Wikipedia for various organizational purposes such as: knowledge management (Schaffert, 2006; Wagner, 2004), software development (Louridas, 2006; W. Xiao, Chi, & Yang, 2007), strategic planning (Amrollahi, Ghapanchi, & Talaei-Khoei, 2014b; Dobusch & Kapeller,

2013; Whittington, Cailluet, & Yakis-Douglas, 2011), and any other form of organizational collaboration. However, effective use of these tools and techniques needs considering a number of factors which were studied in the current research.

The quality of Wiki posts in terms of both content quality and presentation of the content is an important factor which this study found to affect the number of reads and user satisfaction in Wikipedia. This could be extended to other types of Wiki websites. It could be implied by practitioners in selecting the Wiki platform: easy platforms and software systems which make it easy for content developers to submit their idea and content can increase the effectiveness of posts. Moreover, training the volunteer developers for better use of the system is another method for increasing the effectiveness according to the current study.

In the current study, number of references, external links, and length of the article have been mentioned as indicator of content quality. It could be compared with previous quantitative studies on Wikipedia (Lam et al., 2010).

The quality of service which is provided by other members in discussion page of each post or by editing the post can also significantly affect use of each post. Practitioners should consider this factor as an important success factor for Wiki posts and more than initiating new articles, encourage the volunteers and contributors in their organization to edit other posts and participate in discussion about the quality of the article which have been already submitted.

The effect of user satisfaction on use which is mentioned in Delone and McLean model of IS success, has not been supported by the current study in the context of Wikipedia posts. It may indicate that used measures of user satisfaction (page rate and number of contributors) are not adequate for evaluating user satisfaction. For this reason future studies and practices should look for better evaluation of users' satisfaction through qualitative and quantitative methods.

Limitations

The source of data for our research was limited to information of articles on Wikipedia and we do not go further in order to understand the subjective matters such as beliefs of different parties about the constructs and variables of model, their relationships.

Finally, our study was limited to articles in Wikipedia. Although this website is the most important case of open content, it is not the only wiki-type system in the world and currently thousands of others exist and work on the Internet. These systems have surely different specifications and dimensions from Wikipedia and for this reason we cannot introduce our model as a "general model for effectiveness of open content".

FUTURE RESEARCH DIRECTIONS

Wikipedia and its role in distribution of knowledge over the internet has been subject of attention by many research to date. However, most of the studies so far have focused on quality of single post (micro level) and in the review of the current body of knowledge; no macro level study could be found which develop a model for effectiveness of these articles.

This study is a first attempt to develop this model base on the previous literature on IS success. Future research could expand this model and add new components that increase the adaptability of the model with this context or develop. This study also calls for future qualitative research that could end in specific models for this context.

CONCLUSION

The study of Delone and McLean for evaluation of IS success has been widely accepted in different areas. In this paper, we attempted to study if the model is compatible with open content articles in Wikipedia. For this purpose, we developed two different models and evaluated the model with data of 959 articles.

Although there are different empirical studies about the effectiveness of OC content, but we do not find any research about evaluation of model with success models or evaluation of interrelation of different constructs of OC effectiveness.

The findings could benefit Wikipedia and other OC websites to better evaluate and improve its effectiveness. It may also help practitioners to manage effectiveness of knowledge management system. The negative effect of quality measurements on use of OC may also be a unique finding in the D&M based research.

REFERENCES

Adler, B. T., Chatterjee, K., De Alfaro, L., Faella, M., Pye, I., & Raman, V. (2008). *Assigning trust to Wikipedia content*. Paper presented at the Proceedings of the 4th International Symposium on Wikis.

Adler, B. T., & De Alfaro, L. (2007). *A content-driven reputation system for the Wikipedia*. Paper presented at the Proceedings of the 16th international conference on World Wide Web. doi:10.1145/1242572.1242608

Alavi, M., & Leidner, D. E. (2001). Review: Knowledge management and knowledge management systems: Conceptual foundations and research issues. *Management Information Systems Quarterly*, 25(1), 107–136. doi:10.2307/3250961

Albors, J., Ramos, J. C., & Hervas, J. L. (2008). New learning network paradigms: Communities of objectives, crowdsourcing, wikis and open source. *International Journal of Information Management*, 28(3), 194–202. doi:10.1016/j.ijinfomgt.2007.09.006

Amrollahi, A., Ghapanchi, A., & Talaei-Khoei, A. (2014a). *A systematic review of the current theory base in the crowdsourcing literature.* Paper presented at the ANZAM 2014 Conference, Sydney, Australia.

Amrollahi, A., Ghapanchi, A., & Talaei-Khoei, A. (2014b). *Using Crowdsourcing Tools for Implementing Open Strategy: A Case Study in Education.* Paper presented at the Twentieth Americas Conference on Information System (AMCIS 2014).

Amrollahi, A., Khansari, M., & Manian, A. (2014a). How Open Source Software Succeeds? A Review of Research on Success of Open Source Software. *International Journal of Information and Communication Technology Research, 6*(2), 67–77.

Amrollahi, A., Khansari, M., & Manian, A. (2014b). Success of Open Source in Developing Countries: The Case of Iran. [IJOSSP]. *International Journal of Open Source Software and Processes, 5*(1), 50–65. doi:10.4018/ijossp.2014010103

Anderson, M. (2011). Crowdsourcing Higher Education: A Design Proposal for Distributed Learning. *MERLOT Journal of Online Learning and Teaching, 7*(4), 576–590.

Antin, J. (2011). *My kind of people?: perceptions about wikipedia contributors and their motivations.* Paper presented at the Proceedings of the SIGCHI Conference on Human Factors in Computing Systems. doi:10.1145/1978942.1979451

Arazy, O., & Nov, O. (2010). *Determinants of wikipedia quality: the roles of global and local contribution inequality.* Paper presented at the Proceedings of the 2010 ACM conference on Computer supported cooperative work. doi:10.1145/1718918.1718963

Arbuckle, J. L. (2006). IBM SPSS Amos Student.

Avlonitis, G. J., & Panagopoulos, N. G. (2005). Antecedents and consequences of CRM technology acceptance in the sales force. *Industrial Marketing Management, 34*(4), 355–368. doi:10.1016/j.indmarman.2004.09.021

Behrend, T. S., Sharek, D. J., Meade, A. W., & Wiebe, E. N. (2011). The viability of crowdsourcing for survey research. *Behavior Research Methods, 43*(3), 800–813. doi:10.3758/s13428-011-0081-0 PMID:21437749

Ben-Zvi, T. (2012). Measuring the perceived effectiveness of decision support systems and their impact on performance. *Decision Support Systems, 54*(1), 248–256. doi:10.1016/j.dss.2012.05.033

Blumenstock, J. E. (2008). *Size matters: word count as a measure of quality on wikipedia.* Paper presented at the Proceedings of the 17th international conference on World Wide Web. doi:10.1145/1367497.1367673

Brabham, D. C. (2008a). Crowdsourcing as a model for problem solving an introduction and cases. *Convergence (London), 14*(1), 75–90. doi:10.1177/1354856507084420

Brabham, D. C. (2008b). Moving the crowd at iStockphoto: The composition of the crowd and motivations for participation in a crowdsourcing application. *First Monday, 13*(6). doi:10.5210/fm.v13i6.2159

Brabham, D. C. (2009). Crowdsourcing the public participation process for planning projects. *Planning Theory, 8*(3), 242–262. doi:10.1177/1473095209104824

Brändle, A. (2005). Too Many Cooks Don't Spoil the Broth.

Bryant, S. L., Forte, A., & Bruckman, A. (2005). *Becoming Wikipedian: transformation of participation in a collaborative online encyclopedia.* Paper presented at the Proceedings of the 2005 international ACM SIG-GROUP conference on Supporting group work. doi:10.1145/1099203.1099205

Cao, M., Zhang, Q., & Seydel, J. (2005). B2C e-commerce web site quality: An empirical examination. *Industrial Management & Data Systems*, *105*(5), 645–661. doi:10.1108/02635570510600000

Capocci, A., Servedio, V. D., Colaiori, F., Buriol, L. S., Donato, D., Leonardi, S., & Caldarelli, G. (2006). Preferential attachment in the growth of social networks: The internet encyclopedia Wikipedia. *Physical Review E: Statistical, Nonlinear, and Soft Matter Physics*, *74*(3), 036116. doi:10.1103/PhysRevE.74.036116 PMID:17025717

Carillo, K., & Okoli, C. (2011). Generating quality open content: A functional group perspective based on the time, interaction, and performance theory. *Information & Management*, *48*(6), 208–219. doi:10.1016/j.im.2011.04.004

Chatterjee, S., Chakraborty, S., Sarker, S., Sarker, S., & Lau, F. Y. (2009). Examining the success factors for mobile work in healthcare: A deductive study. *Decision Support Systems*, *46*(3), 620–633. doi:10.1016/j.dss.2008.11.003

Chen, J., Ren, Y., & Riedl, J. (2010). *The effects of diversity on group productivity and member withdrawal in online volunteer groups.* Paper presented at the Proceedings of the SIGCHI Conference on Human Factors in Computing Systems. doi:10.1145/1753326.1753447

Chesney, T. (2007). An empirical examination of Wikipedia's credibility. *First Monday*, *11*(11). doi:10.5210/fm.v11i11.1413

Chien, S.-W., & Tsaur, S.-M. (2007). Investigating the success of ERP systems: Case studies in three Taiwanese high-tech industries. *Computers in Industry*, *58*(8), 783–793. doi:10.1016/j.compind.2007.02.001

Chin, W. W. (1998). Commentary: Issues and Opinion on Structural Equation Modeling. *Management Information Systems Quarterly*, *22*(1), vii–xvi. doi:10.2307/249674

Choi, B., Alexander, K., Kraut, R. E., & Levine, J. M. (2010). *Socialization tactics in wikipedia and their effects.* Paper presented at the Proceedings of the 2010 ACM conference on Computer supported cooperative work. doi:10.1145/1718918.1718940

Crowston, K., Annabi, H., & Howison, J. (2003). Defining open source software project success.

Crowston, K., Annabi, H., Howison, J., & Masango, C. (2005). *Effective work practices for FLOSS development: A model and propositions.* Paper presented at the System Sciences, 2005. HICSS'05. Proceedings of the 38th Annual Hawaii International Conference on. doi:10.1109/HICSS.2005.222

Crowston, K., Howison, J., & Annabi, H. (2006). Information systems success in free and open source software development: Theory and measures. *Software Process Improvement and Practice*, *11*(2), 123–148. doi:10.1002/spip.259

De Laat, P. B. (2010). How can contributors to open-source communities be trusted? On the assumption, inference, and substitution of trust. *Ethics and Information Technology*, *12*(4), 327–341. doi:10.1007/s10676-010-9230-x

Dejean, S., & Jullien, N. (2012). Enrolled since the beginning. an assessement of the Wikipedia contributors' behavior regarding their first contribution: Marsouin working paper.

Delone, W. H. (2003). The DeLone and McLean model of information systems success: A ten-year update. *Journal of Management Information Systems, 19*(4), 9–30.

DeLone, W. H., & McLean, E. R. (1992). Information systems success: The quest for the dependent variable. *Information Systems Research, 3*(1), 60–95. doi:10.1287/isre.3.1.60

Delone, W. H., & Mclean, E. R. (2004). Measuring e-commerce success: Applying the DeLone & McLean information systems success model. *International Journal of Electronic Commerce, 9*(1), 31–47.

Dezdar, S., & Ainin, S. (2011). Measures of success in projects implementing enterprise resource planning. *International Journal of Business Performance Management, 12*(4), 334–353. doi:10.1504/IJBPM.2011.042012

Ding, D. X., Hu, P. J.-H., Verma, R., & Wardell, D. G. (2009). The impact of service system design and flow experience on customer satisfaction in online financial services. *Journal of Service Research.*

Dobusch, L., & Kapeller, J. (2013). *Open Strategy between Crowd and Community: Lessons from Wikimedia and Creative Commons.* Paper presented at the Academy of Management Proceedings. doi:10.5465/AMBPP.2013.15831abstract

Eikebrokk, T. R., & Olsen, D. H. (2007). An empirical investigation of competency factors affecting e-business success in European SMEs. *Information & Management, 44*(4), 364–383. doi:10.1016/j.im.2007.02.004

Forte, A., & Bruckman, A. (2008). *Why do people write for Wikipedia? Incentives to contribute to open–content publishing.* Paper presented at the Proceedings of 41st Annual Hawaii International Conference on System Sciences (HICSS).

Gil-Garcia, J. R. (2012). *Enacting Electronic Government Success.* Springer. doi:10.1007/978-1-4614-2015-6

Gil-Garcia, J. R., Chengalur-Smith, I., & Duchessi, P. (2007). Collaborative e-Government: Impediments and benefits of information-sharing projects in the public sector. *European Journal of Information Systems, 16*(2), 121–133. doi:10.1057/palgrave.ejis.3000673

Gil-García, J. R., & Pardo, T. A. (2005). E-government success factors: Mapping practical tools to theoretical foundations. *Government Information Quarterly, 22*(2), 187–216. doi:10.1016/j.giq.2005.02.001

Giles, J. (2005). Internet encyclopedias go head to head. *Nature.com.*

Glott, R., Schmidt, P., & Ghosh, R. (2010). Wikipedia survey–overview of results. *United Nations University: Collaborative Creativity Group.*

Gorgeon, A., & Swanson, E. B. (2009). *Organizing the Vision for Web 2.0: A Study of the Evolution of the Concept in Wikipedia.* Paper presented at the Proceedings of the 5th international Symposium on Wikis and Open Collaboration. doi:10.1145/1641309.1641337

Gounaris, S. P., Panigyrakis, G. G., & Chatzipanagiotou, K. C. (2007). Measuring the effectiveness of marketing information systems: An empirically validated instrument. *Marketing Intelligence & Planning, 25*(6), 612–631. doi:10.1108/02634500710819978

Halawi, L. A., McCarthy, R. V., & Aronson, J. E. (2007). An empirical investigation of knowledge management systems' success. *Journal of Computer Information Systems, 48*(2).

Halfaker, A., Kittur, A., Kraut, R., & Riedl, J. (2009). *A jury of your peers: quality, experience and ownership in Wikipedia.* Paper presented at the Proceedings of the 5th International Symposium on Wikis and Open Collaboration. doi:10.1145/1641309.1641332

Halfaker, A., Kittur, A., & Riedl, J. (2011). *Don't bite the newbies: how reverts affect the quantity and quality of Wikipedia work.* Paper presented at the Proceedings of the 7th international symposium on wikis and open collaboration. doi:10.1145/2038558.2038585

Hasan Dalip, D., André Gonçalves, M., Cristo, M., & Calado, P. (2009). *Automatic quality assessment of content created collaboratively by web communities: a case study of wikipedia.* Paper presented at the Proceedings of the 9th ACM/IEEE-CS joint conference on Digital libraries. doi:10.1145/1555400.1555449

Häyrinen, K., Saranto, K., & Nykänen, P. (2008). Definition, structure, content, use and impacts of electronic health records: A review of the research literature. *International Journal of Medical Informatics*, *77*(5), 291–304. doi:10.1016/j.ijmedinf.2007.09.001 PMID:17951106

Holsapple, C. W., & Lee-Post, A. (2006). Defining, Assessing, and Promoting E-Learning Success: An Information Systems Perspective*. *Decision Sciences Journal of Innovative Education*, *4*(1), 67–85. doi:10.1111/j.1540-4609.2006.00102.x

Horsti, A., Tuunainen, V. K., & Tolonen, J. (2005). *Evaluation of electronic business model success: Survey among leading finnish companies.* Paper presented at the System Sciences, 2005. HICSS'05. Proceedings of the 38th Annual Hawaii International Conference on. doi:10.1109/HICSS.2005.253

Howe, J. (2006a). Crowdsourcing: A definition. *URL*. Retrieved from http://www.crowdsourcing.com/cs/2006/06/crowdsourcing_a. html

Howe, J. (2006b). The rise of crowdsourcing. *Wired magazine*, *14*(6), 1-4.

Howe, J. (2008). *Crowdsourcing: How the power of the crowd is driving the future of business.* Random House.

Hussein, R., Karim, N. S. A., & Selamat, M. H. (2007). The impact of technological factors on information systems success in the electronic-government context. *Business Process Management Journal*, *13*(5), 613–627. doi:10.1108/14637150710823110

Huvila, I. (2010). Where does the information come from. *Information Research*, *15*(3), 28–28.

Javanmardi, S., Ganjisaffar, Y., Lopes, C., & Baldi, P. (2009). *User contribution and trust in Wikipedia.* Paper presented at the Collaborative Computing: Networking, Applications and Worksharing, CollaborateCom 2009, 5th International Conference. doi:10.4108/ICST.COLLABORATECOM2009.8376

Jennex, M., & Olfman, L. (2005). Assessing knowledge management success. [IJKM]. *International Journal of Knowledge Management*, *1*(2), 33–49. doi:10.4018/jkm.2005040104

Jennex, M. E., & Olfman, L. (2006). A model of knowledge management success. [IJKM]. *International Journal of Knowledge Management*, *2*(3), 51–68. doi:10.4018/jkm.2006070104

Jennex, M. E., Smolnik, S., & Croasdell, D. (2007). *Towards defining knowledge management success.* Paper presented at the System Sciences, 2007. HICSS 2007. 40th Annual Hawaii International Conference on. doi:10.1109/HICSS.2007.571

Jullien, N. (2012). What We Know About Wikipedia: A Review of the Literature Analyzing the Project (s).

Kaiser, M. G., & Ahlemann, F. (2010). Measuring Project Management Information Systems Success: Towards a Conceptual Model and Survey Instrument.

Kittur, A., & Kraut, R. E. (2008). *Harnessing the wisdom of crowds in wikipedia: quality through coordination.* Paper presented at the Proceedings of the 2008 ACM conference on Computer supported cooperative work. doi:10.1145/1460563.1460572

Kramer, M., Gregorowicz, A., & Iyer, B. (2008). *Wiki trust metrics based on phrasal analysis*. Paper presented at the Proceedings of the 4th International Symposium on Wikis. doi:10.1145/1822258.1822291

Kulkarni, U. R., Ravindran, S., & Freeze, R. (2007). A knowledge management success model: Theoretical development and empirical validation. *Journal of Management Information Systems, 23*(3), 309–347. doi:10.2753/MIS0742-1222230311

Lam, S. K., Karim, J., & Riedl, J. (2010). *The effects of group composition on decision quality in a social production community*. Paper presented at the Proceedings of the 16th ACM international conference on Supporting group work. doi:10.1145/1880071.1880083

Lau, F., Price, M., Boyd, J., Partridge, C., Bell, H., & Raworth, R. (2012). Impact of electronic medical record on physician practice in office settings: A systematic review. *BMC Medical Informatics and Decision Making, 12*(1), 10. doi:10.1186/1472-6947-12-10 PMID:22364529

Lee, S.-K., & Yu, J.-H. (2012). Success model of project management information system in construction. *Automation in Construction, 25,* 82–93. doi:10.1016/j.autcon.2012.04.015

Lee, S. Y. T., Kim, H.-W., & Gupta, S. (2009). Measuring open source software success. *Omega, 37*(2), 426–438. doi:10.1016/j.omega.2007.05.005

Lih, A. (2004). Wikipedia as participatory journalism: Reliable sources? metrics for evaluating collaborative media as a news resource. *Nature*.

Limayem, M., & Cheung, C. M. (2008). Understanding information systems continuance: The case of Internet-based learning technologies. *Information & Management, 45*(4), 227–232. doi:10.1016/j.im.2008.02.005

Lin, H.-F. (2007). Measuring online learning systems success: Applying the updated DeLone and McLean model. *Cyberpsychology & Behavior, 10*(6), 817–820. doi:10.1089/cpb.2007.9948 PMID:18085970

Lipka, N., & Stein, B. (2010). *Identifying featured articles in Wikipedia: writing style matters*. Paper presented at the Proceedings of the 19th international conference on World wide web. doi:10.1145/1772690.1772847

Louridas, P. (2006). Using wikis in software development. *Software, IEEE, 23*(2), 88–91. doi:10.1109/MS.2006.62

Lynch, T., & Gregor, S. (2004). User participation in decision support systems development: Influencing system outcomes. *European Journal of Information Systems, 13*(4), 286–301. doi:10.1057/palgrave.ejis.3000512

Manjoo, F. (2009). Is Wikipedia a victim of its own success? *Time Mag, 174*.

McCalla, R., Ezingeard, J.-N., & Money, K. (2003). A behavioural approach to CRM systems evaluation. *Electronic Journal of Information Systems Evaluation, 6*(2), 145–154.

McCalla, R., Ezingeard, J.-N., & Money, K. (2004). The Evaluation of CRM Systems: A Behavior Based Conceptual Framework.

Mcguinness, D. L., Zeng, H., Silva, P. P. D., Ding, L., Narayanan, D., & Bhaowal, M. (2006). *Investigation into trust for collaborative information repositories: A Wikipedia case study* Paper presented at the Workshop on Models of Trust for the Web.

Morgan, J. T., Mason, R. M., & Nahon, K. (2011). *Lifting the veil: The expression of values in online communities*. Paper presented at the Proceedings of the 2011 iConference. doi:10.1145/1940761.1940763

Morton, N. A., & Hu, Q. (2008). Implications of the fit between organizational structure and ERP: A structural contingency theory perspective. *International Journal of Information Management, 28*(5), 391–402. doi:10.1016/j.ijinfomgt.2008.01.008

Nemoto, K., Gloor, P., & Laubacher, R. (2011). *Social capital increases efficiency of collaboration among Wikipedia editors.* Paper presented at the Proceedings of the 22nd ACM conference on Hypertext and hypermedia. doi:10.1145/1995966.1995997

Ortega, F., & Izquierdo-Cortazar, D. (2009). *Survival analysis in open development projects.* Paper presented at the Emerging Trends in Free/Libre/Open Source Software Research and Development, 2009. FLOSS'09. ICSE Workshop. doi:10.1109/FLOSS.2009.5071353

Otieno, G. O., Hinako, T., Motohiro, A., Daisuke, K., & Keiko, N. (2008). Measuring effectiveness of electronic medical records systems: Towards building a composite index for benchmarking hospitals. *International Journal of Medical Informatics, 77*(10), 657–669. doi:10.1016/j.ijmedinf.2008.01.002 PMID:18313352

Otto, P., & Simon, M. (2008). Dynamic perspectives on social characteristics and sustainability in online community networks. *System Dynamics Review, 24*(3), 321–347. doi:10.1002/sdr.403

Ozkan, S., & Koseler, R. (2009). Multi-dimensional students' evaluation of e-learning systems in the higher education context: An empirical investigation. *Computers & Education, 53*(4), 1285–1296. doi:10.1016/j.compedu.2009.06.011

Page, L. (2001). Method for node ranking in a linked database: Google Patents.

Pedersen, J., Kocsis, D., Tripathi, A., Tarrell, A., Weerakoon, A., Tahmasbi, N., et al. (2013). *Conceptual foundations of crowdsourcing: A review of IS research.* Paper presented at the System Sciences (HICSS), 2013 46th Hawaii International Conference on. doi:10.1109/HICSS.2013.143

Petter, S., DeLone, W., & McLean, E. (2008). Measuring information systems success: Models, dimensions, measures, and interrelationships. *European Journal of Information Systems, 17*(3), 236–263. doi:10.1057/ejis.2008.15

Petter, S., & Fruhling, A. (2011). Evaluating the success of an emergency response medical information system. *International Journal of Medical Informatics, 80*(7), 480–489. doi:10.1016/j.ijmedinf.2011.03.010 PMID:21501969

Pitt, L. F., Watson, R. T., & Kavan, C. B. (1995). Service quality: A measure of information systems effectiveness. *Management Information Systems Quarterly, 19*(2), 173–187. doi:10.2307/249687

Poderi, G. (2009). Comparing featured article groups and revision patterns correlations in Wikipedia. *First Monday, 14*(5). doi:10.5210/fm.v14i5.2365

Popovič, A., Hackney, R., Coelho, P. S., & Jaklič, J. (2012). Towards business intelligence systems success: Effects of maturity and culture on analytical decision making. *Decision Support Systems, 54*(1), 729–739. doi:10.1016/j.dss.2012.08.017

Rai, A., Lang, S. S., & Welker, R. B. (2002). Assessing the validity of IS success models: An empirical test and theoretical analysis. *Information Systems Research, 13*(1), 50–69. doi:10.1287/isre.13.1.50.96

Ransbotham, S., & Kane, G. C. (2011). Membership turnover and collaboration success in online communities: Explaining rises and falls from grace in Wikipedia. *MIS Quarterly-Management Information Systems, 35*(3), 613.

Raymond, L., & Bergeron, F. (2008). Project management information systems: An empirical study of their impact on project managers and project success. *International Journal of Project Management, 26*(2), 213–220. doi:10.1016/j.ijproman.2007.06.002

Rosenzweig, R. (2006). Can history be open source? Wikipedia and the future of the past. *The Journal of American History, 93*(1), 117–146. doi:10.2307/4486062

Sagers, G. (2004). The influence of network governance factors on success in open source software development projects.

Schaffert, S. (2006). *IkeWiki: A semantic wiki for collaborative knowledge management.* Paper presented at the Enabling Technologies: Infrastructure for Collaborative Enterprises, 2006, International Workshop. doi:10.1109/WETICE.2006.46

Sen, R. (2007). A strategic analysis of competition between open source and proprietary software. *Journal of Management Information Systems, 24*(1), 233–257. doi:10.2753/MIS0742-1222240107

Shahmoradi, L., Ahmadi, M., & Haghani, H. (2007). Determining the most important evaluation indicators of healthcare information systems (HCIS) in Iran. *Health Information Management Journal, 36*(1), 13. PMID:18195393

Spoerri, A. (2007). *Visualizing the overlap between the 100 most visited pages on Wikipedia for September 2006 to January 2007.*

Stein, K., & Hess, C. (2007). *Does it matter who contributes: a study on featured articles in the german wikipedia.* Paper presented at the Proceedings of the eighteenth conference on Hypertext and hypermedia. doi:10.1145/1286240.1286290

Stewart, K. J., Ammeter, A. P., & Maruping, L. M. (2006). Impacts of license choice and organizational sponsorship on user interest and development activity in open source software projects. *Information Systems Research, 17*(2), 126–144. doi:10.1287/isre.1060.0082

Stewart, K. J., & Gosain, S. (2006a). The impact of ideology on effectiveness in open source software development teams. *Management Information Systems Quarterly*, 291–314.

Stewart, K. J., & Gosain, S. (2006b). The moderating role of development stage in free/open source software project performance. *Software Process Improvement and Practice, 11*(2), 177–191. doi:10.1002/spip.258

Straub, K. (1999). 1999 and beyond: IT's impact on the business of healthcare in the new millennium. *Health Management Technology, 20*(2), 40, 42–43. PMID:10346476

Stvilia, B., Al-Faraj, A., & Yi, Y. J. (2009). Issues of cross-contextual information quality evaluation—The case of Arabic, English, and Korean Wikipedias. *Library & Information Science Research, 31*(4), 232–239. doi:10.1016/j.lisr.2009.07.005

Stvilia, B., & Gasser, L. (2008). An activity theoretic model for information quality change. *First Monday, 13*(4). doi:10.5210/fm.v13i4.2126

Subramaniam, C., Sen, R., & Nelson, M. L. (2009). Determinants of open source software project success: A longitudinal study. *Decision Support Systems, 46*(2), 576–585. doi:10.1016/j.dss.2008.10.005

Tapscott, D., & Williams, A. D. (2008). *Wikinomics: How mass collaboration changes everything.* Penguin.

Teo, T. S., Srivastava, S. C., & Jiang, L. (2008). Trust and electronic government success: An empirical study. *Journal of Management Information Systems, 25*(3), 99–132. doi:10.2753/MIS0742-1222250303

Tsai, W.-H., Chou, W.-C., & Leu, J.-D. (2011). An effectiveness evaluation model for the web-based marketing of the airline industry. *Expert Systems with Applications, 38*(12), 15499–15516.

Van der Heijden, H. (2004). User acceptance of hedonic information systems. *Management Information Systems Quarterly*, 695–704.

Wagner, C. (2004). Wiki: A technology for conversational knowledge management and group collaboration. *Communications of the Association for Information Systems, 13*(1), 58.

Wang, Y.-S., Wang, H.-Y., & Shee, D. Y. (2007). Measuring e-learning systems success in an organizational context: Scale development and validation. *Computers in Human Behavior, 23*(4), 1792–1808. doi:10.1016/j.chb.2005.10.006

Whittington, R., Cailluet, L., & Yakis-Douglas, B. (2011). Opening strategy: Evolution of a precarious profession. *British Journal of Management, 22*(3), 531–544.

Wilkinson, D. M., & Huberman, B. A. (2007a). Assessing the value of cooperation in Wikipedia. *arXiv preprint cs/0702140.*

Wilkinson, D. M., & Huberman, B. A. (2007b). *Cooperation and quality in wikipedia.* Paper presented at the Proceedings of the 2007 international symposium on Wikis. doi:10.1145/1296951.1296968

Wöhner, T., & Peters, R. (2009). *Assessing the quality of Wikipedia articles with lifecycle based metrics.* Paper presented at the Proceedings of the 5th International Symposium on Wikis and Open Collaboration. doi:10.1145/1641309.1641333

Wu, J., & Goh, K. Y. (2009). *Evaluating longitudinal success of open source software projects: A social network perspective.* Paper presented at the System Sciences, 2009. HICSS'09. 42nd Hawaii International Conference on.

Wu, J., Goh, K.-Y., & Tang, Q. (2007). Investigating success of open source software projects: A social network perspective.

Wu, J.-H., & Wang, Y.-M. (2006). Measuring ERP success: The ultimate users' view. *International Journal of Operations & Production Management, 26*(8), 882–903. doi:10.1108/01443570610678657

Xiao, B., & Benbasat, I. (2007). E-commerce product recommendation agents: Use, characteristics, and impact. *Management Information Systems Quarterly, 31*(1), 137–209.

Xiao, W., Chi, C., & Yang, M. (2007). *Online collaborative software development via wiki.* Paper presented at the Proceedings of the 2007 international symposium on Wikis. doi:10.1145/1296951.1296970

Xue, Y., Liang, H., Boulton, W. R., & Snyder, C. A. (2005). ERP implementation failures in China: Case studies with implications for ERP vendors. *International Journal of Production Economics, 97*(3), 279–295. doi:10.1016/j.ijpe.2004.07.008

Yates, D., & Paquette, S. (2011). Emergency knowledge management and social media technologies: A case study of the 2010 Haitian earthquake. *International Journal of Information Management, 31*(1), 6–13. doi:10.1016/j.ijinfomgt.2010.10.001

Yi, C.-C., Liao, P.-W., Huang, C.-F., & Hwang, I.-H. (2009). Acceptance of mobile learning: a respecification and validation of information system success.

Zhu, H., Kraut, R., & Kittur, A. (2012). *Effectiveness of shared leadership in online communities.* Paper presented at the Proceedings of the ACM 2012 conference on Computer Supported Cooperative Work. doi:10.1145/2145204.2145269

KEY TERMS AND DEFINITIONS

External Links (in Wikipedia Posts): A reference or hyperlink to an online material outside of Wikipedia.

Information System Success: A series of models in information systems research which provide a holistic view about the effectiveness of an information system.

Internal Links (in Wikipedia Posts): A hyperlink to another page in Wikipedia which explains a term in more details.

Multimedia Material (in Wikipedia Posts): Any image, video, or audio material which can be found inside a Wikipedia article.

Open Content: A piece of content which is provided to viewers with an open-type license.

Wiki: A form of content development in which several authors contribute in development of a piece of content.

Wikipedia: Is the first and the most well-known wiki-type website that provide information about various topics in form of an encyclopedia.

ENDNOTE

[1]	The initial license for Wikipedia was GFDL which is created for software manuals that come with free software programs licensed under GPL.

Chapter 3
From Tf-Idf to
Learning-to-Rank:
An Overview

Muhammad Ibrahim
Monash University, Australia

Manzur Murshed
Federation University Australia

ABSTRACT

Ranking a set of documents based on their relevances with respect to a given query is a central problem of information retrieval (IR). Traditionally people have been using unsupervised scoring methods like tf-idf, BM25, Language Model etc., but recently supervised machine learning framework is being used successfully to learn a ranking function, which is called learning-to-rank (LtR) problem. There are a few surveys on LtR in the literature; but these reviews provide very little assistance to someone who, before delving into technical details of different algorithms, wants to have a broad understanding of LtR systems and its evolution from and relation to the traditional IR methods. This chapter tries to address this gap in the literature. Mainly the following aspects are discussed: the fundamental concepts of IR, the motivation behind LtR, the evolution of LtR from and its relation to the traditional methods, the relationship between LtR and other supervised machine learning tasks, the general issues pertaining to an LtR algorithm, and the theory of LtR.

1. INTRODUCTION

In the last few decades, there has been an overwhelming increase in the volume of digital data due to the proliferation of information and communications technology. Getting the required information from this vast ocean of data has eventually become so formidable that people started using machines from late 1980's[1] to get assistance, thereby giving rise to information retrieval (IR) systems (i.e., search engines). In general, the task of an IR system is to return a ranked list of 'items' to the users in response to specific information need. This task appears in many domains such as document ranking, recommender system, automatic question answering, automatic text summarization, online

DOI: 10.4018/978-1-4666-8833-9.ch003

advertising, sentiment analysis, web personalization, and so on. In fact, any task which presents the user on-demand a list of items ordered by a utility function is a ranking task. In this chapter, we survey only the document ranking research works without any loss of generality, as most of the discussed techniques are applicable to other ranking domains as well. We use the terms IR ranking and document ranking interchangeably throughout the chapter.

1.1 Scope of the Chapter

Several standard books on IR (e.g., Manning, Raghavan & Schütze, 2008) are available in the literature. These books, however, do not cover the learning-to-rank (LtR) systems with appropriate emphasis, mainly because these systems have emerged as a promising IR direction only a few years ago. There are a few survey papers on LtR; some of these are more focused on detailed discussion of the technical aspects of the LtR algorithms (Li, 2011; Liu, 2011), while some others are too short (Phophalia, 2011; He, Wang, Zhong & Li, 2008). Therefore, these reviews provide very little assistance to someone who, before delving into technical details of different algorithms, wants to have a broad understanding of the LtR systems, and their evolution from and relation to the traditional IR methods.

This chapter is complementary to the existing few surveys in the sense that we focus on the evolution of the LtR systems from the conventional methods. It also elaborately discusses some aspects of LtR that have so far been less-emphasized. Specifically, our main goals are the following:

1. Familiarise the readers with the fundamental concepts of IR from scratch by emphasising on intuitive explanations.
2. Discuss the motivation behind LtR; how it has evolved from and relates to the traditional IR methods.

3. Show the relationship between LtR and other supervised machine learning tasks, namely, classification, regression, and ordinal regression.
4. Discuss the general issues pertaining to the LtR algorithms. That is, to give a big picture of the existing LtR algorithms before delving into technical details of individual algorithms. Some of these issues are: relationship between LtR and other machine learning tasks and developing taxonomy of LtR algorithms.
5. Relate the theory of LtR to various loss functions of existing LtR algorithms.

This chapter is not a comprehensive survey of all LtR algorithms—in fact, it is not feasible to discuss all of them in a single chapter as the number of research papers on LtR is more than a hundred, nor does it discuss the technical details of different algorithms.

1.2 Organization of the Chapter

The rest of the the chapter is organized as follows.

*   Section 2 defines the ranking problem in IR.
*   Section 3 explains why existing search engines are not sufficient.
*   Section 4 describes the term *relevancy* with a simple but concrete example.
*   Section 5 briefly discusses three popular IR models, namely, cosine similarity, BM25, and Language Model, with an emphasis on intuitive explanations.
*   Section 6 argues why the traditional IR models need further improvement, and hence a remedy can be found by using the supervised machine learning framework. Here some very basic concepts of machine learning are presented. Then the strategies for preparing a training set of LtR is de-

scribed which is important to understand the problem definition of LtR. This is followed by the mathematical formulation of the LtR problem.

- Section 7 emphasizes on the importance of evaluation metrics in IR, and discusses three widely-used IR metrics, namely, NDCG, precision, and MAP—all of these are explained in both intuitive and mathematical ways, and most of the times with examples.
- Section 8 mentions some challenges of designing an LtR system as to why it is not as straightforward as some might be tempted to contemplate.
- After presenting the foundation of knowledge necessary to comprehend an LtR system in the previous sections, Section 9 explains three major tasks of supervised mahcine learning: classification, regression, and ordinal regression. The understanding of these techniques is crucial because LtR is inherently related to these tasks. This section also compares the above-mentioned supervised machine learning tasks, which is followed by a comparison between LtR and its closest counterpart among these three tasks, namely, the ordinal regression.
- Section 10 explains the core issues of any LtR algorithm without referring to any specific algorithm. Thus the reader, before delving into the technical details of an LtR algorithm, will get a big picture of what and how should an LtR algorithm do. Here two important things, among others, are discussed: (1) the loss function, and (2) the optimization algorithm.
- Section 11 briefly discusses some representative LtR algorithms. Although the goal of the chapter is to avoid technical details of the algorithms as much as possible, some LtR algorithms are explained at a

higher level so that the readers are able to relate their knowledge gained in the previous sections with the existing algorithms.

- Section 12 briefly describes the theoretical foundation of LtR, which is followed by the linkage between the theory and the loss functions.
- Sections 13 highlights the current trends in LtR research.
- Sections 14 and 15 summarizes and concludes the chapter, respectively.

2. THE RANKING PROBLEM IN INFORMATION RETRIEVAL

Suppose a user is in need of some information. She concocts a query in a natural language which reflects her information need. She then submits the query to an IR system expecting the system to return a list of relevant documents with respect to her information need. Note that the returned list is not necessarily expected with respect to just the submitted query because a query concocted by the user is just one out of many possible ways of representing the information need. For example, suppose the information need is: *does the Java programming language have any feature for splitting a string*? One query for this information need may be *string separation in java*; whereas another query may be *java string split*.

Now the system has a large pool of documents. From the given query, the system first elicits what the actual information need is – so the system takes the query as a surrogate to the original information need (the original information need is unseen to the system). Then it uses its estimated information need to rank all the documents of the collection based on their degree of relevance to the information need. It then presents only the top few documents (which are sorted in decreasing order of the degree of relevance) to the user because usually the corpus of the documents is

Figure 1. An Information Retrieval System Interacting With User

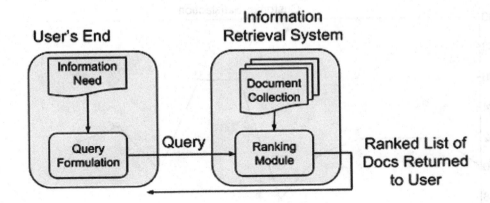

very large while the number of relevant documents for a particular query is very small. Figure 1 depicts the scenario. As the user is interested in only highly-relevant documents, retrieving all documents that are highly-relevant to the query and placing them in the top part of the presented list is crucial from the retrieval system's perspective.

3. AREN'T EXISTING SEARCH ENGINES ENOUGH?

Today we are quite familiar with the search engines so much so that when any new research on information retrieval is presented, perhaps the first obvious question comes into the mind of a layman: *is the research going to reinvent the wheel*?

The following are some reasons as to why people still do and will be doing active research in IR:

- As mentioned in Section 1, ranking a set of items has a large number of applications besides the conventional search engines. Different tasks may need different ranking functions. The ranking function of a typical search engine may not solve the problem of ranking of, for example, automatic question answering systems.
- Commercial search engines may perform badly in some special scenarios such as, the case when a query is very long and/or ambiguous. Specific research should continue for these types of difficult scenarios.
- Commercial search engines have huge computational resources (computing power, storage etc.). But small organizations who are in need of specific search facilities on their own collection of documents may not have so much recources. Hence research should be there as to how we can give better searching facility with limited resources.
- Data is increasing day by day. Even the state-of-the-art IR systems struggle to cope with such large volume of data in an efficient and effective way. Moreover, the format of data, the requirement of the users etc. are ever-changing. Therefore, research has to be carried out in these directions.
- The core algorithms of many of the existing commercial IR systems were results of academic research. An example is the PageRank algorithm (Page, Brin, Motwani & Winograd, 1999) – Google's[2]

Figure 2. U.S. customer satisfaction with Google from 2002 to 2014 (index score)[5]

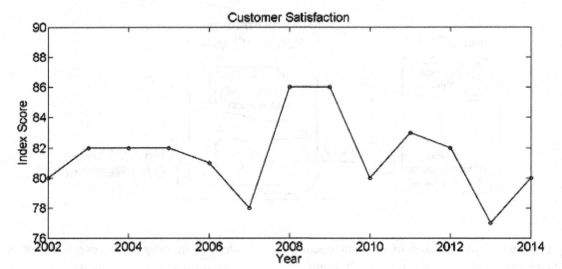

one of keys to success. Also, Yahoo![3] and Microsoft[4] are believed to be using LtR techniques for their commercial search engines which have been invented recently in the academia. Therefore, it is natural to expect that new breakthrough in performance of IR systems will come from academic research.

- The ultimate judge of an IR system is the users. Figure 2 shows that user satisfaction fluctuates heavily in course of time. Therefrore, even though exisitng search engines are deemed reasonably smart today, in order to continue to quench the ever-thirsty user satisfaction, research on how to further improve them should continue.

- Commercial IR systems are proprietary, i.e., they do not disclose details of their algorithms. But many organizations need custom search engines due to their security and privacy concerns. Moreover, their own engines can be tuned in a better and specific way for their particular applications. Hence, research should be devoted in this direction.

4. WHAT DOES RELEVANCY OF A DOCUMENT MEAN?

Since the number of documents of a typical collection is very large, there is a high monetary cost for consulting human experts to search for any required information. Thus in the early era of IR research, how machines can replace human experts with as much accuracy and as fast as possible gained significant research interest.

In order to do this, in the first place we need to know how a human expert gives verdict to a document (relevant or not) with respect to a query[6]. After that, the same reasonings should be captured by a machine as much as possible. Now the solution to this problem, i.e., finding the exact reasons that prompt a human expert to label a document as relevant (or irrelevant) with respect to a query, requires investigating topics from different fields such as cognitive psychology, information science etc. Some of the early IR researchers such as Schamber, Eisenberg & Nilan, (1990) discussed these in details.

Let us give a simplified but concrete example. Suppose a user wants to know about the situation of wastage of food in the developed countries at present time. So she may ask a human expert who has access to a corpus of documents: *I want to know about the current situation of the food wastage in the developed countries*[7]. Now given this information need, the human expert, before commencing searching the document corpus, tries to elicit the main information need from this query by applying a number of tasks to the query. For example, he (1) selects the key words (e.g. *current, situation, food, wastage, developed, countries*) from the query and excludes some words from his consideration such as *I, want, to, about, the* etc.; (2) elicits the roots of the selected words instead of as they are presented in the query (e.g. *wastage -> waste, developed -> develop, countries -> country*) and treats these roots similar to the original query-words; (3) identifies the phrases from the query (e.g. *developed countries, food wastage, current situation*); (4) applies some grammatical rules (e.g. *the food wastage in the developed countries* is related to the phrase *current situation*, *in the developed countries* is related to the phrase *food wastage*); (5) treats some synonyms of the query-words as similar to the original words (e.g. *status: situation* etc., *develop: modern* etc., *country: territory* etc.); and so on. These are just a glimpse of a large number of processing a human expert usually applies to a submitted query for eliciting the information need as much concisely and precisely as possible. He then starts to scan the documents one by one and ranks each document according to how much information related to the information need it contains. How exactly human performs this judgment is, again, quite complicated, and leads to the problem of natural language understanding (Li & Xu, 2012). As such, if anyone wants to solve the ranking problem exactly as a human expert does, he/she eventually has to land in the fuzzy area of Artificial Intelligence research where there is a core and still unanswered question: *can machines replace human*? In order to tackle the problem in

a feasible way, IR researchers adopt approaches that use several simplifying assumptions. Some of these approaches are explained in the next section.

Note that there are many levels of approximations in the whole process of ranking performed by IR systems. The query submitted by a user is an approximation to her original information need. The query is converted into a particular query representation by the IR system (e.g. bag-of-words model as described in the next section). The documents are also converted according to a particular document representation scheme. The query representation and the document representation are then taken by a ranking function as input which itself can be effective or not. Figure 3 depicts some of these approximations. But the relevance of the ranked list of documents produced by a ranking function is judged based on the original documents (not the document representations), the original information need (not even by the query, let alone one out of many possible query representations), and by the user herself. Therefore, the ranking problem in IR is deemed inherently a difficult task due to many levels of approximations involved in the whole process.

5. TRADITIONAL APPROACHES

While designing a ranking algorithm, incorporating all criteria a human expert employs to judge a document is not a trivial task. When IR research for building ranked retrieval systems[8] started back in the 1970s, researchers started with the simplest assumptions. One important distinction researchers still maintain is that the IR researchers deal with comparatively more general retrieval models (e.g., bag-of-words model to be described in a short while), whereas Natural Language Processing (NLP) research community is primarily concerned with more specialized techniques built for narrower and specific domains (e.g. parts of speech tagging, named entity recognition, pars-

Figure 3. Many Levels of Approximations Involved in the Ranking Process

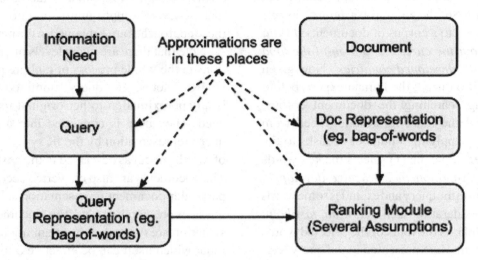

ing etc.). For instance, in our example given in the previous section, we have listed five tasks a human expert usually performs on a query. Out of those, tasks 1 (known as *stopword removal*), 2 (known as *stemming*), and 5 can be considered as IR tasks, whereas the tasks 3 and 4 can be considered as NLP tasks. Nevertheless, there exists a large overlap between these two fields of research.

Bag of Words Model. One of the earliest, simplest but effective and still-used assumptions in IR research is the bag-of-words model (Salton, Wong & Yang, 1975). It assumes that (1) the words of a document have no relationship with each other, implying that the order of the words does not matter; and (2) the position of a word in the document is of no importance. Figure 4 shows a sample document and its bag-of-words representation (stemming and stop-word removal are performed). The bag-of-words model can be used to represent both the documents and the queries. The main criticism of this model is that these assumptions do not hold in many instances. For example, (1) if *Hong* comes in a document, the probability of coming *Kong* after that is very high, so there is a high correlation between these two words, i.e., they are not independent;

(2) if two consecutive query words appear in a document consecutively, and appear in another document sparsely, then the former document is likely to be more relevant than the later because it captures the information need represented in the query more accurately (for example, if the query contains "developed countries" in it, then intuitively a document contains it as it is more likely to be relevant than a document which contains "developed" at some paragraph and "countries" in another paragraph); and (3) as for an example relating to the position of the words, if a query word appears in the first paragraph of a document while in the last paragraph of another document, then the former document is likely to be more relevant to the query than the latter one. In spite of its limitations, this model simplifies many otherwise complicated issues and it also gives reasonable performance (when used in conjuction with a scoring function as described next). In this chapter, we shall be assuming the bag-of-words model unless otherwise stated.

In the next few subsections we briefly describe some conventional ranking functions. More detailed discussion of these and other traditional models can be found in Manning *et al.*, (2008).

Figure 4. A Document and Its Bag-of-words Representation

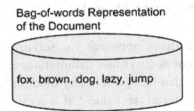

5.1 Vector Space Model

One of the earliest methods for solving the ranking problem is the Vector Space Model (VSM) (Salton *et al.*, 1975; Salton & Buckley, 1988). It is based on two simple ideas: (1) the more the occurrences of the words[9] of a query a document contains, the more likely is that the document be relevant with respect to the query; and (2) the weight of a rare term (across the whole collection of documents) present in the query is higher than that of a comparatively more frequent term. Elaborately, suppose a query is consisted of two terms, t_1 and t_2. If is rarer than t_2 across the collection, then if document *A* has t_1 but not t_2, and document *B* has t_2 but not t_1, then the VSM treats *A* to be more relevant than *B*. The intuition behind this assumption is that a document containing a more frequent term may be relevant to many queries because frequent term means it is also likely to be frequent in the queries; but the rare term in a document also implies that it is rare in the query as well. Thus when a user types a rare term in the query, possibly she is looking for the few documents that contain the rare term in question.

This model treats the query as a separate document (using the bag-of-words assumptions), and then computes the cosine similarity among the documents and the query. Elaborately, it represents every document (and the query) as a vector in the space of all of the distinct words present in all the documents as follows: initially all distinct terms across the entire collection are collected, and the number of occurrences of each term in each docu-

ment of the entire collection is computed (only once). In doing so, every document (and the query when it is submitted by the user) becomes a point in a very high dimensional space of terms. Suppose *q* and *d* are the bag-of-words representation (i.e., two vectors in the term space) of a query and a document over a collection *C*. Then the VSM score, i.e., the estimated degree of relevance for *d* with respect to *q* is given by:

$$score(d, q) = \sum_{t \in q} tf(t, d) idf(t, C) \qquad (1)$$

where *tf(t, d)* is the term frequency — the number of occurrences of *t* in *d*, and *idf(t, C)* is the inverse document frequency — a measure which computes the rarity[10] of term *t* in the collection *C*. This score is widely known as tf-idf score. After computing scores of all the documents, they are ranked in decreasing order of the scores and presented to the user.

The similarity score measured by Equation 1 is also called *cosine similarity* which can be efficiently computed using a vector dot product. This involves using unit vectors instead of original ones. Hence the query and document vectors are *Euclidean length-normalized*. This conversion to unit vectors also offsets the unwanted bias of long but verbose documents[11]. But it has some drawbacks with regard to long documents containing many topics (hence not verbose). Advanced methods like pivoted length normalization (Singhal, Salton, Mitra, & Buckley, 1996) have been proposed to deal with these problems.

5.2 Probabilistic Model I: Binary Independence Model

The use of probabilistic approach for solving the ranking problem is also quite mature (since 1970s). It assumes that there is a binary random variable $R_{d,q}$ which takes the value 1 if a document d is relevant with respect to a query q; and 0 otherwise[12]. Manning *et al.*, (2008, Ch. 11) states the *Probability Ranking Principle* as follows: "*If the retrieved documents are ranked decreasingly on their probability of relevance (w.r.t. a query), then the effectiveness of the system will be the best that is obtainable*". The basic assumption is that the relevance of each document is independent of the relevance of other documents. The Binary Independence Model (BIM) represents the documents and queries by binary vectors and assumes that the terms are independent of each other. Then using Bayes rule, it computes

$$P(R = 1 \mid q, d) = \frac{P(d \mid R = 1, q)P(R = 1 \mid q)}{P(d \mid q)}$$

(2)

The probabilities in the right hand side of the above equation are approximated from the collection and the use of bag-of-words model (independence of the terms) simplifies the probability calculation. Then the documents are ranked in decreasing order of these probabilities.

Taking this model as a general framework, many scoring functions have been proposed. Among these, Okapi BM25 (*Best Match 25*) model (Jones, Walker & Robertson, 2000), which incorporates terms frequency (and hence, unlike BIM, not binary) and length normalization, has been mainly used till date by the IR community due to its empirical superiority. BM25 score can be derived from BIM using term frequency and inverse document frequency.

5.3 Probabilistic Model II: Language Model

The Language Model (LM) for IR (Ponte & Croft, 1998) is also a probabilistic model; but it takes a different approach than the BIM model. It assumes that when a user wants to concoct a query, she already has some relevant document(s) in her mind that she wants the IR system to retrieve. She then creates a query consisting of some distinctive (i.e., discriminative) terms present in those documents by which it is easy to single out them from the other documents of the collection. As the user is assumed devising the query using some relevant documents in her mind, the query can be thought of "being generated" exclusively from those relevant documents, and not by other (irrelevant) documents of the corpus. As such, if we model the probability $p(q \mid d)$, then for the relevant documents in the user's mind, the probabilities will be higher. So this probability can be used as a relevance score in order to rank a document. Alternatively, we could model $p(d \mid q)$ using Bayes rule, in doing so, we can also incorporate prior probability of the document (for example, popularity of the document). Concretely:

$$p(d \mid q) = \frac{p(q \mid d)p(d)}{p(q)}.$$

(3)

The probabilities are computed from the collection, and the independence of the terms is assumed for simplicity in probability calculation. After computing $p(d \mid q)$ for each document, they are ranked in decreasing order of the probabilities.

5.4 Discussion of Traditional Models

VSM is simple, both at conceptual and implementation levels, and yet effective to some extent. Its downsides include: there can be many variations of the term frequency and inverse document frequency, and it is not obvious which combination is the best; thus it has less theoretical foundation as Nallapati (2004) points out. BIM and its descendants have strong theoretical foundation because of using probabilistic framework. But its performance is hindered mainly due to some impractical assumptions such as independence of the terms, independence of the scores of the documents etc. Nonetheless, its performance is in general better than VSM, and in fact, its popular descendants (such as BM25 and its extensions) are considered as one of the baseline methods till today (Chapelle & Chang, 2011). The LM approach is also a good generative model and its performance is comparable to that of the BM25 model (Nallapati, 2004). Note that the terms frequency and inverse document frequency are at the heart of these probabilistic models; but these models use these count-based metrics in different ways than VSM.

All the above models can be treated as unsupervised models because the true relevance labels of the documents are not explicitly utilized. The next section discusses the use of supervised methods.

6. LEARNING-TO-RANK APPROACH

In this section we begin the discussion on LtR methods.

6.1 Motivation

All the traditional approaches have an inherent bottleneck: they have several tunable parameters. For example, in the VSM, one can use either tf-idf or some other variations of it such as log(tf-idf) etc. (Taylor, Guiver, Robertson & Minka, 2008). The BM25 model also has some tunable parameters. Traditionally people have been selecting the best settings of these parameters on trial-and-error basis. That is, one can try over a set of rule-of-thumb values: for each combination of these values, the performance of the model is evaluated either by

explicit human judges or by standard IR evaluation metrics (will be described in Section 7). Thus the best combination of the parameters is then chosen for a particular model.

Generally this strategy has been shown empirically to work with acceptable performance (Metzler & Croft, 2007; Dang, Bendersky & Croft, 2013). But the following reasons have paved the way to consider more complex techniques.

1. Although some researchers such as Taylor *et al.* (2008) applauded traditional models by saying: "*They are robust and generalize well,*" which means that these models often work well on new corpora with the default parameter settings, none claims that one model always wins over the others in all types of collections and queries[13]. We can think of each model as giving a score indicating the degree of relevance of a document with resect to a query. (As such, we can also call the score of a model as the relevance measurements.) Hence a natural tendency could be to combine more than one model at the same time in order to get better accuracy.

2. As time passed on, incorporating more than one relevance measure has become not only a choice, but also a necessity; as more and more relevance measurements have started to emerge in the research community. For example, one can compute separate tf-idf scores for different parts of a documents such as the title, abstract and the body (Robertson, Zaragoza, & Taylor, 2004). Also, term proximity based features have turned out to be important (Metzler, Strohman & Croft, 2006). For web search, the link information (e.g. the popularity of a web page) has turned out to be important as well along with standard relevance measurements like count based ones[14].

3. The availability of vast user log data from commercial web search engines started to lure the designers of search engines to

use complex methods because most of the traditional models cannot incorporate these additional information collected from the users.

Given the importance of using more than one models, if we want to use a linear combination of different models (i.e., relevance measurements), we need to optimally select the weights (i.e., coefficients) of each measurement in a (linear) combination. Or, even further, we can think of using a nonlinear combination. A combination of different models can be used to generate a final score for a document d with respect to a query q in the following way:

$$score(d,q) = \alpha_1 g_1(r_1(d,q)) + \alpha_2 g_2(r_2(d,q)) + ... + \alpha_N g_N(r_N(d,q))$$

(4)

where $r_i(d, q)$ is the relevance score predicted by ith model, α_i is the weight of ith model, and $g_i(.)$ is a function which decides how the score of ith model will be used, for example, if $g_i(r_i(d,q)) = r_i(d,q)$, then the combination of the models is a linear one, otherwise it is nonlinear. N is the number of models to combine.

Now the job is to find a solution to Equation 4, i.e., to find the α_i's and g_i's. To this end, supervised machine learning framework can be used. Instead of tuning the parameters manually by trial-and-error, a supervised learning algorithm is given some data (in our case, relevance measurement scores for the query-document pairs) along with appropriate ground truth labels (in our case, the relevance judgements made by human experts). Together these data are called the training data. An algorithm then learns a model/function (in our case, an appropriate linear/nonlinear combination of different scores), which can not only predict labels for these training data, but also for any future data with some performance guarantee. The process of building a model from the

training set is called learning or training. By using supervised learning framework an overall ranking model, which uses different (base) ranking models in an effective way, can be designed. More on it is discussed in the next section.

6.2 Supervised Learning Framework

For the readers who are not familiar with supervised mahcine learning, in this section we briefly discuss some key concepts. Among many available in the literature, some useful resources for understanding these methods are Hastie, Tibshirani, & Friedman (2009), and Alpaydin (2004).

Suppose we have a data set consisting of M data points (also called instances, training examples etc.), each has N dimensions (also called features, or attributes). Each point has a ground truth label which can be discrete (also called categorical) or continuous. We call the data set along with the labels as training data. As an example, suppose each data point is a house, and each of the N dimensions describes a feature of the house, for example, size of the house, number of floors of the house, whether or not the house has garage etc. The label is the price of the house, which in this case is a continuous variable. The task of the supervised learning method is to learn a function (also called model, hypothesis etc.) from the data which takes a data point (house in our example) as input (this is called training or learning phase), and predicts a label (price in our example) as output (this is called testing or evaluation phase). Note that the test data point may not be in the training set, i.e., the function should be able to predict for the unseen data point (if the test data point were in the training data, then there would have been no need to learn the function, rather a simple table-lookup would have been enough). Figure 5 depicts the general framework.

The major dimensions of a supervised learning framework are: the task (e.g. classification or regression which will be discussed in Section 9), the family of possible functions to be considered

Figure 5. Supervised Learning Framework

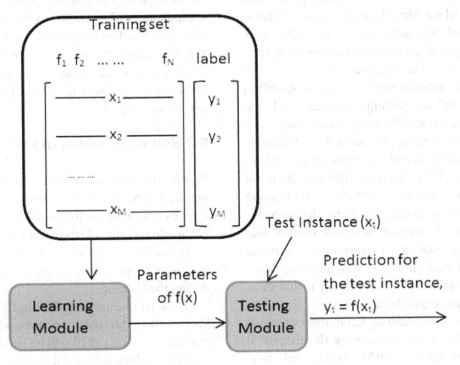

as potential solution, and the loss function which is optimized over the training data.

Since the hypothesis space is very large thereby making the search for the global best hypothesis computationally infeasible, the learning algorithms are approximation algorithms because they use some simplifying assumptions. As such, the learnt model's prediction is prone to error, but there is high probability that the prediction will be below some threshold value. This is called *PAC (Probably Approximately Correct)* model: *approximately* because of the threshold error, and *probably* because of the probability involved.

There are primarily two approaches for solving a supervised learning problem: generative and discriminative. A generative model finds out the actual process which *generates* the training data (and test data). That is, it finds out the probability distribution of the generated the training data. As the test data are assumed to be generated from the same distribution, it uses the learnt distribution in

order to assign a label to a test instance. On the contrary, a discriminative model finds a function which can *discriminate* between different labels. It is a minimalist approach in the sense that it does only what is absolutely necessary. Generative models use more assumptions than discriminative models. A good comparison between these two approaches is made by Ng & Jordan, (2001).

Since discriminative algorithms (such as support vector machine (SVM), logistic regression, artificial neural network etc.) are mainly used in LtR (as will be discussed in Section 11), now we briefly describe how it works. The algorithm first selects a function from a fixed set of candidate functions. Using this function, it then tries to predict the labels of the instances of the training data. Then it calculates the performance based on some predefined loss function which measures the deviation of the predicted labels from the ground-truth labels. Then it optimizes (i.e., minimizes) that loss function over the training set by modifying the selected function. It stops when a predefined accuracy level is achieved. Finally the performance of the model over some unseen test data set is reported as its generalization performance (i.e., how well it performs on unseen data).

Note that we do not want the learning algorithm to "memorize" the training data because (1) the training data is normally noisy, so learning every details of the patterns present in the training set is likely to result in bad performance in test (unseen) data; and (2) even if the training data is not noisy, memorizing every details of the training set will result in taking very 'hard' decisions for test instances. This problem is called *overfitting*. The other extreme case is learning a too simple model from the training set which actually does not capture actual patterns present in the data. This problem is called *bias*.

As for the theoretical underpinnings of supervised learning algorithms, using the Empirical Risk Minimization (ERM) framework borrowed from Statistical Learning Theory, it can be shown that learning the exact target function from the training data is NP-hard. Even learning the optimal function from a particular family of functions (for example only linear functions) is also NP-hard. Hence people use heuristics which involves making different assumptions in the problem formulation, confining to only a small subset of candidate functions for learning, using surrogate loss function instead of using the true loss function etc.

In order to learn a good prediction function, there must exist some pattern in the training set of a supervised learning task which is captured by a learning algorithm. For example, if the values of the features are completely random, then there is no characteristic or pattern of the data for the learning algorithm to learn. That is, there must be some features which have an effect in deciding the labels, or, in other words, which have correlation with the labels—be it loose or strong. As such, LtR training data should also have some learnable pattern, and it does have. The reason is, we use

the base rankers as features. These base rankers are indicators of relevance to some extent as we have discussed in Section 5, so we can expect that the higher the relevance label of a query-document pair, the higher the scores of the base rankers for that query-document pair across this particular query[15].

6.3 Relevant Issues of LtR

Now that the motivation for using supervised learning algorithms to solve the ranking problem has been established, the following issues should be taken into account: (1) the nature of training data; (2) the family of supervised models to consider; and (3) the type of loss function to be optimized during the training.

We defer discussing the 2nd and 3rd issues until Section 10; by then some crucial background of the evaluation metrics of IR will be laid out. The first issue, as explained next, will aid in understanding the mathematical formulation of the LtR problem.

6.3.1 Preparation of Training Data

The preparation of training data is a critical aspect of supervised learning. The accuracy of the model heavily depends on the quality of the training set. As discussed in the previous section, the training data of supervised learning framework contains instances, each having a set of feature values and a ground truth label. In LtR, the instances are the query-document pairs and the ground truth labels are their degree of relevances with respect to different queries. The steps for preparing a training data can be summerarized as follows.

Step 1: *Query selection.* A number of sample queries are collected. This sampling may be performed with replacement from the query logs of existing IR systems so that popular queries appear more frequently than unpopular queries, thereby gaining more weight in the training data (Chapelle & Chang, 2011).

This way the true distribution of different types of queries of real world scenario can be maintained in the training data.

Step 2: *Document selection and labelling.* IR systems has a large number of documents that, in order to be included in a training set, should be labelled according to their degree of relevance with respect to various queries selected in Step 1. The relevance labels may be in different ranges, for example, from 0 up to 4 (0 means completely irrelevant and 4 means the highest relevance). For each query, however, collecting human judgement of relevancy for all the documents is not practical as (1) the number of documents of the collection is usually very large—millions, or even billions; so labeling all these documents for even a single query is impractical; (2) the number of relevant documents is very small as compared to their irrelevant counterparts[16]. As a result some alternative feasible techniques such as the *depth-k pooling* are practised (which will be discussed shortly).

Step 3: *Feature extraction.* After selecting the queries and labelling the documents, features need to be extracted. Since a single document may be relevant to some queries but irrelevant to some others, a document in a training set should be associated with a particular query[17] (note that there is no such concept in the training sets of most other supervised learning tasks such as classification and regression as will be discussed in Section 9). Thus an instance in the training set is a query-document pair, and the features should include any information useful for predicting the label. Any "raw" scoring function such as cosine-similarity, BM25, language model etc. may be used as features as well as any other information that may have some affect in deciding the labels such as the possibility of being spam, popularity of a document etc.[18]

We now describe a method called *pooling* or *depth-k pooling* (Harman, 1995; Chapelle & Chang, 2011), which is typically used to label the selected documents (cf. Step 2 mentioned in this section).

Depth-k Pooling

The basic idea here is to use multiple base rankers in order to retrieve as many relevant documents as possible for a query using the following steps.

Step 1: For a particular query, a number of simple ranking functions (e.g. tf-idf scoring function) are applied to the documents. We call these as base rankers.

Step 2: The top k documents of each of the base ranker's returned lists are collected and merged.

Step 3: These selected documents are labeled explicitly by human judges. Sometimes multiple judges are employed for labelling a single query-document pair and the resultant judgements are combined.

Some typical values for k reported in the literature are: 1000 (Qin *et al.*, 2010) for a collection size of 1 million, 100000 (Cossock & Zhang, 2006), 5000 for a collection size of 500 million (Craswell, Fetterly, Najork, Robertson & Yilmaz, 2009), *"tens of thousands of documents"* (Chapelle & Chang, 2011). Note that the commercial search engines have millions, or, even billions of documents in their collection.

Now let us discuss how human judgements are collected for the selected documents. For a query, a judgement can be given for each document or for each pair of documents. In the former case, each document is assigned a relevance label out of some possible values such as highly relevant, partially relevant, and irrelevant. In the latter case, each pair of documents is considered, and instead of assigning any explicit label, the preference of one document over the other is judged. In the former case, the judgement process is comparatively more difficult, but requires less number of judgement. The later case requires too many judgements (in quadratic order of the documents) (Niu, Guo, Lan & Cheng, 2012).

Instead of using a number of base rankers, following Qin *et al.* (2010), a single simple-to-compute base ranker like BM25 may be used. This strategy requires less computational time. However, some relevant documents may not be included in the training set thereby making it less informative.

The rest of the documents that are left out by the base ranker(s) are generally treated in two ways: (1) they can be treated as irrelevant (Qin *et al.,* 2010), which has an issue that many of them might be highly relevant; or (2) they can be discarded altogether, which has also an issue that the information from otherwise a bigger training set will be ignored.

Problems of Pooling Strategy. These include: (1) Many highly relevant documents may miss out in the initial list if the base rankers are not effective, thereby losing important information from the training set[19]. (2) If a single base ranker e.g., BM25 is used, the documents in the training set will have an unwanted bias from this score. Quite often the BM25 scores of the top k documents are higher, but some of these documents are labeled as irrelevant by the human judges. However, the converse is not observed, i.e., document of the training set labelled relevant by a human judge has significantly low BM25 score. In other words, all the relevant documents in the training set have higher BM25 scores. Thus the base ranker's scores, unlike other scores present in the training set, have a biased effect in the learning process; but this score is not fully accurate (otherwise there would have been no need for using multiple scorers at all), and the main goal of the learning is to learn the weights of the scores (including BM25) automatically from the training data. To mitigate this problem, Qin *et al.* (2010) advocate to include

some manually selected relevant documents that have low BM25 scores.

Despite its problems, the pooling approach is widely used by the IR community (Pavlu, 2008; Chapelle & Chang, 2011). For example, people affiliated with Microsoft (Qin *et al.*, 2010) and Yahoo! (Cossock & Zhang, 2006) reported this strategy in the literature. Research in sampling better training data for LtR problem is still in its infancy (Macdonald, Santos & Ounis, 2013; Niu *et al.*, 2012; Dang *et al.*, 2013).

Before concluding this discussion, we note some points below.

1. From the theoretical point of view, the query and its associated documents form a group structure in the training set (which is one of the key differences between LtR and other machine learning tasks). These groups are usually considered i.i.d. (independent and identically distributed) as the grouping depends on the selection of the queries from the query pool (cf. Step 1 of the training data creation process). But the documents associated to a query are not i.i.d. because a base ranker is biased to select the relevant documents (Xia, Liu, Wang, Zhang & Li, 2008). This aspect makes theoretical analysis of some LtR algorithms difficult (elaborated later in Section 10).

2. The higher the number of relevant documents in a training set, the better the learning of a ranking function. Usually the number of relevant documents is very small; so an LtR algorithm should be given as much information about those relevant documents as possible (Dang *et al.*, 2013). As alluded earlier, research on how to make the training set more effective is yet to be matured.

3. At a conceptual level, the LtR perspective of the ranking problem can be thought of reasonably different to the bag-of-words model (Li & Xu, 2012). In LtR, unlike the bag-of-words model, a document is no longer

represented by a vector of, for example, tf-idf scores of its terms; rather it is represented with respect to a query and by a set of features. However, the bag-of-words model is used to generate many of the features, though it can also make use of features derived from term-dependency relationship as opposed to bag-of-words.

4. The LtR methods have been empirically shown to outperform the best conventional approaches like BM25 and language models (Metzler & Croft, 2007; Dang *et al.*, 2013; Zhang, Kuang, Hua, Liu & Ma, 2009; Nallapati, 2004). More on this will be discussed in Sections 11.

5. The features (raw scores) are themselves prone to error, hence LtR data is noisy. For example, for a particular document, if one score shows some behavior, another score may show a loosely correlated behavior. Also, the ground truth labels judged by humans may vary from one judge to another (Niu, Lan, Guo, Cheng & Geng, 2014). More research should be done on how to effectively deal with the noisy nature of LtR training data.

6.4 Problem Formulation of Learning-to-Rank

With some background on LtR training data acquisition laid out, we are now at a stage to formalize the LtR problem. Suppose we have a set of m queries $Q = \{q_1, q_2, ..., q_m\}$, where each query q is associated with a set of n_q documents $D_q = \{d_1^q, d_2^q, ..., d_{n_q}^q\}$. Each query-document pair $\langle q, d_j^q \rangle$ corresponds to a feature vector $x_j^q = \psi(q, d_j^q) \in \mathbb{R}^N$ and a relevance label y_j^q, such that a dataset $\mathcal{D}$ consists of $M = \sum_i n_{q_i}$ instances of the form $\langle x_j^q, y_j^q \rangle$. Figure 6 shows the format of the training set.

As explained in the previous section, the elements of the feature vector are scores of simple (traditional) rankers, for example, the cosine similarity scores over tf-idf vectors for the particular query-document pair, or the BM25 score for the same pair, etc. These scores are usually normalized[20] at the query level, such that each feature value lies in the range 0 to 1 (Qin *et al.*, 2010). Thus:

Figure 6. Training Set of LtR Problem

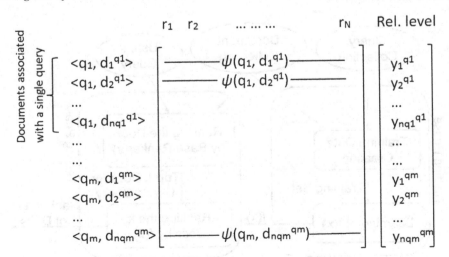

$$x_j^q = \psi(q, d_j^q) =$$

$$\left(\frac{r_1(q, d_j^q)}{\max(\{r_1(q, d_k^q)\}_{k=1}^{n_q})}, \dots, \frac{r_N(q, d_j^q)}{\max(\{r_N(q, d_k^q)\}_{k=1}^{n_q})} \right)$$

where r_i denotes the score computed by the ith base ranker.

A ranking function is then a function $f : \mathbb{R}^N \rightarrow \mathbb{R}$ that assigns a score to a feature vector. Given a query q, let

$$\vec{s}_f(q) = (f(\psi(q, d_1^q)), \dots, f(\psi(q, d_{n_q}^q)))$$

denote the vector of scores assigned by f to the documents for that query. The vector can then be sorted in decreasing order to produce a ranking:

$$sort(\vec{s}_f(q)) = (rank_f(d_1^q), \dots, rank_f(d_{n_q}^q)). \tag{5}$$

Here $rank_f(q, d_i^q)$ returns the position of document d_i^q in sorted list based on the scores generated by f.

Given a training set $\mathcal{D}$, the goal of an LtR algorithm is to find the function f amongst a set of functions $\mathcal{F}$ that minimises a loss function $\mathcal{L}$ over the training set:

$$f^* = \arg \min_{f \in \mathcal{F}} \mathcal{L}(\mathcal{D}, f). \tag{6}$$

The set of functions $\mathcal{F}$ from which a function[21] f is chosen, and the loss function $\mathcal{L}$ are defined differently in different algorithms which will be discussed in Sections 9 – 10.

Figure 7 depicts the overall scenario of an LtR-based IR system. Its task can be broadly divided into two subtasks, the training and test/evaluation phases. During the training phase, the first job is to create the training data (cf. Section 6.3.1). Then a model $f(x)$ is learnt from the training data. During test phase, a query is taken from a user, and usually some preprocessing is performed to get a better representation of the information need presented in the query[22]. Then the same base ranker(s) (which was used during training data creation process) is applied to retrieve the top k documents for the query. A feature vector (obviously the same features used in the train-

Figure 7. An LtR Based IR System

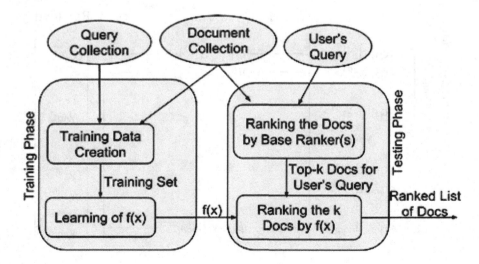

ing phase) x is then computed for each of these documents with respect to the query. Finally, the learnt function $f(x)$ is used to predict a relevance score for each of these documents. After that, the ranked list of these k documents is prepared by sorting them in decreasing order by these scores, and then the list is presented to the user. As for the other documents that are not among the top k documents by the base ranker(s), these may be ranked according to an effective raw scorer (i.e., one of the features).

It can be noted that LtR adds yet another level of approximations in addition to the existing ones (cf. Figure 3). The accuracy heavily depends on the effectiveness of supervised learning algorithm. Due to various pitfalls of the LtR framework (such as using too many uninformative features, small training set, noisy training examples, noisy labels etc.), the accuracy of an LtR system may not be as good as initially expected.

7. EVALUATION METRICS FOR RANKING

By now we know that an IR system, be it conventional or LtR based, returns a ranked list of documents for each of the queries. Now we need to measure how good a system's predicted ranked list is. As the users are the ultimate judges of the performance of an IR system, the IR metrics should be able to capture the nature of a good ranked list—good in the eyes of the users—as much as possible.

In order to decide how to design IR metrics, we should first understand what are the characteristics of a good ranked list. Those characteristics should be captured in the metrics. Understanding the nature of the metrics of IR ranking is crucial because an LtR algorithm can aim at optimizing such a metric.

From the user's point of view, she is normally interested in the top few documents (Niu *et al.*, 2012; Burges *et al.*, 2005). So the retrieval sys-

tem's goal is to provide her not only with highly relevant documents, but also presenting them in the top portion of the returned list. For this reason, IR metrics are mostly concerned with top k positions of the ranked list where the value of k depends on the application domain, for example, for web search, usually k is around 10 (Burges *et al.*, 2005).

A question may naturally arise here: why not use existing metrics of machine learning? Traditional machine learning metrics are usually not concerned with the top k results, rather with the overall accuracy (Cossock & Zhang, 2006). Also, the very nature of the ranking task is different from the general machine learning task (as will be evident in Section 8). For example, recall is a much-used machine learning metric which is defined as the percentage of relevant documents retrieved by a system. Precision is another metric which is the fraction of the retrieved documents that are relevant. But recall is not very important for IR ranking (except for a few domains like Patent Search, Legal Search etc. (Macdonald *et al.*, 2013; Geng, Liu, Qin & Li, 2007)) because the users are mostly concerned with the precision of the top k documents in the ranked list. As recall is not that important, so is the F1 measure (a combination of precision and recall).

Below we discuss some commonly used IR metrics. Some useful resources for understanding these and other metrics are Järvelin & Kekäläinen, (2000), and Chapelle, Metlzer, Zhang & Grinspan (2009).

7.1 Discounted Cumulative Gain (DCG) and Normalized DCG

DCG consists of two parts: one is the relevance labels (these can be thought of *gains*) of the documents, while the other is a discount at each position of the ranked list. The intuition is as follows. As mentioned in Section 6.3.1 that during the judgement process of the documents, numerically higher labels are assigned to the more relevant documents. Since the highly relevant documents are placed in the top portion of a ranked list, if we sum up the labels of the top k positions, it will be higher than another ranked list where top k documents are less relevant. As a concrete example, suppose the labels of the documents are 2 (highly relevant), 1 and 0 (irrelevant). If we are concerned with only top 3 positions (i.e., $k = 3$) of a ranked list, then suppose the ground truth labels of this ranked list is $\langle 2, 2, 1 \rangle$ (left to right corresponds to top to bottom), which gives us a total gain of 5; whereas another ranked list with ground truth labels $\langle 2, 1, 1 \rangle$ yields 4. However, such plain summation is not sufficient to identify better ranked list. For example, a ranked list with ground truth labels $\langle 2, 1, 2 \rangle$ should have lower score than the one with labels $\langle 2, 2, 1 \rangle$; but the sum of gains are the same in both cases. Therefore, some sort of weighting should be included along with the gains, thereby yielding a weighted sum. The weight of the top position should be the most (because the user cares about it the most), after that gradually it should decrease. A popular choice is logarithmic weight: $1/\log(1+\text{position})$ where the position starts from 1. A usual practice among the researchers is, in order to magnify the effect of the gain, $G(i)$ at position i, people use $2^{G(i)}$ ($G(i)$ is simply the relevance label at position i of the ranked list). Thus DCG@k is expressed by:

$$DCG@k = \sum_{i=1}^{k} \frac{2^{G(i)} - 1}{\log_2(i + 1)}. \tag{7}$$

DCG is good at capturing the human judgement to some extent; but it is inappropriately biased towards queries having more relevant documents. As a concrete example, suppose that query q_1 has 10 relevant documents, whereas query q_2 has only 2 relevant documents and 1 partially relevant document. Also suppose that we are interested in DCG@5 and the ground truth labels of ranked_list(q_1) = 1, 1, 2, 2, 2 and ranked_list(q_2) = 2, 2, 1, 0, 0. Then DCG(ranked_list(q_1)) =

5.48 > DCG(ranked_list(q_2)) = 5.4 even though ranked_list(q_2) is perfect whereas ranked_list(q_1) is imperfect. To mitigate this discrepancy, normalized DCG (NDCG) is used by normalizing DCG of a list by the DCG of the most accurate ranking possible for that list. Formally, if IDCG is the DCG of perfect (or ideal) ranking of the list at hand, then NDCG is expressed by:

$$NDCG@k = \frac{DCG@k}{IDCG@k}. \tag{8}$$

7.2 Precision at k (P@k)

This is the same as the one used in machine learning literature except that normally IR people use it with a small cut-off value (k), typically no more than 10. As such, this metric is less useful for assessing the very top ranks. This is because, for example, for the two ranked lists $\langle 1, 1, 1, 0, 0 \rangle$ and $\langle 0, 0, 1, 1, 1 \rangle$ the p@5 is 3/5 in both cases, but it is clear that the first list is preferable to the second. $p@k$ measures what fraction of the top k documents are relevant. Note that this measure assumes that there is only two categories of relevancy: relevant and non-relevant. If there are more than two relevance levels, some higher levels may be considered as relevant while the others as irrelevant (Mohan, 2010). If N_k is the number of relevant documents among the top k positions, then $p@k$ is expressed by:

$$p@k = \frac{N_k}{k}. \tag{9}$$

7.3 Mean Average Precision (MAP)

Like precision, this measure also assumes that there are only two levels of relevancy: relevant and non-relevant. First we define Average Precision (AP). AP is the average of the precisions at each position where a relevant document is found across the entire list of ranked documents. If the set of positions of relevant documents found in a ranked list is denoted by $rel_{positions}$, then AP is defined by:

$$AP = \frac{1}{|rel_{positions}|} \sum_{i \in rel_{positions}} p@i \,. \qquad (10)$$

We note that unlike NDCG and $p@k$, this metric is not related to any k value explicitly; but can still recognize (i.e., assign a higher value to) a ranked list which has more relevant documents in the top portion. The intuition is as follows. If the relevant documents are at the top positions, then there are very few irrelevant documents in between those top relevant documents, which in turn implies that the precision at those top positions (where the relevant documents are) will be higher (because the very few irrelevant ones are among many relevant ones). On the contrary, if the relevant documents are not clustered in the top positions of a ranked list, i.e., if the relevant documents are scattered across/positioned in the bottom part of the whole list, then this implies that there are many irrelevant documents in between/above the relevant documents, in other words, there are many irrelevant documents before many of the relevant ones. This means that the precisions at the positions of those relevant documents will be lower. So if we take the average of the precisions measured at each relevant document's position, it will tell us how well the top portion of a ranked list is. An advantage of MAP over many other metrics is that it also incorporates to some extent as to how well the recall is (Macdonal *et al.*, 2012). Recall is useful in domain-specific (also known as vertical) IR tasks such as legal search, patent search etc. (Macdonal *et al.*, 2012), because when searching in a particular domain, the users are more likely to be concerned with getting all the correct information rather than only some of them and they are more likely to spend more time in searching.

MAP is the average of APs across all test queries. MAP has been extended to capture the graded relevance (Robertson, Kanoulas & Yilmaz, 2010), but it is yet to gain as popularity as MAP enjoys[23].

Since NDCG is good at capturing how well the top portion of a ranked list is, it is heavily used for tasks where user satisfaction depends on initial documents such as web search. MAP is comparatively less biased towards top ranks, so it can be used to measure the overall accuracy of a ranked list. P@k with very low values of k (e.g. 1 or 2) is useful for tasks where only one or two documents match the query such as homepage finding.

We note here that developing metrics which are even closer to the human judgement is still an active research area (Pavlu, 2008).

8. THREE MAJOR TASKS OF SUPERVISED LEARNING

In this section we briefly discuss three major supervised learning tasks, namely, classification, regression, and ordinal regression. In order to understand the LtR problem thoroughly, it is imperative to know the similarities and dissimilarities between different tasks.

8.1 Classification

There is a finite number of distinct classes as labels of the data points. In *binary classification*, there are only two possible class labels, for example, either a patient (data point) has a disease (positive class) or not (negative class). In *multi-class classification*, a data point belongs to one of several classes, for example, if we consider the task of classifying images of triangle, rectangle and circle, then there are three classes. The error of a classification algorithm is usually measured by the total number of misclassified instances of the test data.

8.2 Regression

Here the label for a data point is a continuous value (cf. our example of house data given in Section 6.2). The error in evaluation phase is computed using the actual algebraic difference between a predicted label and corresponding ground truth label.

8.3 Ordinal Regression

This task is also called as ordinal classification by some researchers such as Li (2011). It shares the properties of both the classification and regression (Xia, Zhou, Yang & Zhang, 2007). Like classification (and unlike regression), it has a finite set of labels. Like regression (and unlike classification), there is an ordering relationship between the labels, i.e., the instances have a preference relationship with one another. For example, the weather condition may be of three categories: cold, mild, and hot. At a first glance, although it may sound like classification, it is in fact different because hot weather is "hotter" than mild, and "more hotter" than cold. In classification, there is no such ordering relationship. In regression, there does exist a relationship between the labels because, for example, the house price 2000 is *more* than the house having price 1000, and the difference between two labels is well-defined by the arithmatic difference. But in ordinal regression, the difference between labels is not defined, for example, the difference between hot and mild is not obvious. As such, ordinal regression lies somewhere in between classification and regression. More on the relationship between these tasks will be discussed in the next section.

Although the labels of ordinal regression are not numerical values, they are turned into numerical values before applying an algorithm. There can be two scenarios. (1) The labels may be, like classification, categorical numbers, with a difference that the higher value means that the instance having a higher label has a preference over another instance having a lower value as its label. For instance, the hot, mild and cold labels in our example may be assigned 2, 1 and 0 labels respectively. (2) The actual values of the labels are not important, rather their preference relationship is everything we care about (Norusis, 2008, Ch.4). So the preference relationship among each pair of instances can be given as ground truth label. If there is no preference for any pair, then those two instances can be ordered in any order.

It can be noted that ordinal regression is called by some researchers such as Li & Lin (2007) as (general) ranking. But we argue in the next section that LtR settings has some characteristics which are different from ordinal regression.

8.4 Comparison between Various Tasks

This section underlines similarities and dissimilarities between LtR problem and other supervised learning tasks.

8.4.1 Ordinal Regression, Classification, and Regression

LtR problem is closer to ordinal regression than classification or regression. Hence we first compare ordinal regression with classification and regression. A question may be raised: can we solve the ordinal regression problem using standard classification or regression algorithm? For example, can we use a regression algorithm to get the labels of the test instances, and then rank those instances in decreasing order of those labels? It turns out that there are some problems for which we should treat ordinal regression as a separate problem.

1. Problems of using classification for solving ordinal regression.
   a. The goal of ordinal regression is to learn ordering among the pairs of instances, not to learn which class they fall into.

So pairwise preferences could be incorporated in the loss function during learning phase, but the loss functions of classification algorithms do not include it.

b. In ordinal regression, the loss/cost of misclassifying an instance during the learning phase should be, unlike classification, different for different types of misclassification. For example, if, in one scenario, hot weather is misclassified as moderate weather, whereas in another scenario, hot weather is misclassified as cold weather, then it is obvious that the former error is preferable to the later in ordinal regression settings. But in classification settings, both the errors are the same. Note that this aspect is not the same as including simple pairwise preference information mentioned above—the pairwise preference information may or may not consider varying cost for different miss-ordered pairs.

c. If the classification is wrong, still ordering (or ranking) of the instances may be right. For example, if the predicted labels for three documents A, B and C are 1, 2, and 2 respectively, and if their true labels are 0, 1, and 2 respectively, then the classification error is 2/3, but ranking error is either 0 (if the ranked list is $\langle C, B, A \rangle$ where left to right corresponds to top to bottom)) or 1/3 (if the ranked list is $\langle B, C, A \rangle$)[24]. Thus we could avoid solving an unnecessarily hard problem (i.e., classification) by developing dedicated algorithms for ordinal regression.

2. Problems of using regression for solving ordinal regression.

a. In ordinal regression, the loss/cost is not well defined like regression (Herbrich, Graepel & Obermayer, 1999). Here the ranks are of different types, but the loss for misclassifying one rank to another is not well-defined. But in regression, we can specifically define the cost. For example, suppose in one scenario the predicted and true labels of an instance are 2000 and 1000, respectively. Then the algebraic difference between 2000 and 1000 is 1000. Now if in another scenario the predicted label is 1900, then an algorithm which predicts the latter is better than an algorithm which predicts the former. But in ordinal regression there is no exact notion of measuring such errors.

b. The number of labels in ordinal regression are finite and typically very few, so treating these few discrete values as continuous values may not be a good option – it reminds us about the original motivation as to why the regression algorithms should not be used for solving the classification problem.

c. As a small but concrete example, suppose doc A is preferred over doc B, and the scores predicted by the algorithm for A and B are 2.6 and 1.6 respectively, and the true labels of A and B are 2.0 and 1.0 respectively. So a regression error (in terms of absolute difference) is: $|2.0 - 2.6| + |1.0 - 1.6| = 1.2$, whereas the ranking error is 0. But if the predicted scores of A and B are 1.9 and 2.0 respectively, then the regression error is: $|2.0 - 1.9| + |1.0 - 2.0| = 1.1$, but the ranking error is 1—less than the former case. However, a regression algorithm will prefer the latter label assignment because of less regression error (in spite of having higher ranking error). So again, we could avoid solving an unnecessarily hard problem (regression), and moreover, not only that, in some cases like the above example, it might lead to a wrong ranking preference.

Due to the dissimilarities between ordinal regression and classification or regression, researchers tried to solve ordinal regression by developing algorithms dedicated to it. In fact, the problem of ranking a set of items is not something very new. Cohen, Schapire & Singer (1999) wrote a useful survey on this topic.

8.4.2 LtR and Ordinal Regression

Although LtR and ordinal regression share some common properties, the following differences do exist:

1. LtR is more concerned with the top ranks (Järvelin & Kekäläinen, 2002), whereas ordinal regression usually does not have such emphasis. This phenomenon can be utilized in LtR algorithms. For example, Cossock & Zhang (2006), Niu *et al.* (2012) and others propose LtR algorithms that are specific for IR ranking because these are focused on the top k ranks of a ranked list.
2. The LtR data set is partitioned by query. In ordinal regression, all the pairs of the items are considered during the learning phase. But in LtR, only pairs related to a particular query—not to another query—are considered. Thus the LtR problem is less constrained than the ordinal regression problem (Joachims, 2002). For example, an LtR algorithm does not need to predict any ordering relationship between documents A and B having labels 2 and 0 for two different queries, respectively, because there is no prescribed ordering. But a standard ordinal regression algorithm will pay attention to these type of preferences, i.e., it will try to put document A ahead of B—which is not

only unnecessary for IR ranking, but it may also miss some truly necessary preference(s) due to the influence of these unnecessary preferences. This is because it may happen that the number of unnecessary preferences outnumbers the number of necessary preferences in an intermediary step during learning, and the algorithm then will try to minimize the overall number of miss-ordered pairs (which is dominated by the unnecessary preferences). In fact, algorithms developed specifically for the LtR problem leverage this property (e.g. the listwise LtR algorithms discussed in Section 10). Put differently, the perfect ranking in ordinal regression is also perfect in LtR task, but not necessarily vice versa. As a concrete example, suppose documents (with labels) d_1 (label = 2), d_2 (label = 1), d_3 (label = 0) are associated with q_1, and documents d_4 (label = 2), d_5 (label = 1), d_6 (label = 0) with q_2. The ranking $\langle d1, d2, d3, d4, d5, d6 \rangle$ is perfect in LtR (for query q_1). But from the perspective of ordinal regression, this ranking has 3 miss-ordered pairs, namely, (d_2, d_4), (d_3, d_4), and (d_3, d_5).

3. A less important difference is that in LtR setting, it may happen that two feature vectors are exactly the same[25] but still have two different labels (Joachims, 2002). In ordinal regression, this is called a noise[26].

Although some papers used the terms *ordinal regression* and *rank-learning* interchangeably (for example, Shashua *et al.,* 2003), from the above arguments, we see that there are differences. Hence IR researchers later (such as Li, 2011) argued that LtR should not be treated as ordinal regression.

To sum up, in this section we have argued that (1) the ordinal regression problem should not be treated as an application of classification or regression problem, and (2) despite the fact that the ordinal regression is closer in spirit to the LtR problem, the two do have some differences.

However, initial works on LtR did address the LtR problem using standard machine learning algorithms, inspired mainly by the fact that classification and regression errors are upper bounds to the ranking error. More on this is discussed in the next section.

9. IMPORTANT ASPECTS OF AN LTR ALGORITHM

The existing surveys categorize the LtR algorithms straightforwardly into three groups: pointwise, pairwise and listwise. However, we observe that in doing so, it becomes difficult to get a global picture. That is why we, before describing any specific algorithm, discuss some general aspects pertaining to any LtR algorithm.

1. *During learning phase, does the loss function directly use an IR metric, or a surrogate metric?* It may sound natural to directly use IR metrics in a loss function which is optimized during training phase because this is expected to decrease the generalization error. However, it is important to note that almost all of the IR metrics are either flat or discontinuous with respect to the parameters of the learning algorithm (Taylor *et al.*, 2008), so it is infeasible to optimize them directly. (We elaborate this point after discussing the next aspect.) That is why some algorithms use surrogate metrics (e.g. number of miss-ordered pairs) during training.

2. *How the loss function (to be used in the learning phase) is actually defined? For example, does it take the query-document structure present in the data into account, or does it simply use the loss functions of standard classification or regression problem?* Most of the algorithms learn a function $f(x)$ from the training data (i.e., the local function mentioned in Section 6.4). The loss function is usually defined in one of three ways:

a. The loss can be defined based on the individual $f(x_i)$ (this is called the *pointwise approach* in the literature). Hence the total loss over the training set which a learning algorithm minimizes during training phase can be written as:

$$\mathcal{L}_{Training} = \sum_{j=1}^{M} loss(f(x_j), y_j). \tag{11}$$

It can also be written as:

$$\mathcal{L}_{Training} = \sum_{i=1}^{m}\sum_{j=1}^{n_{q_i}} loss(f(x_j^i), y_j^i) \tag{12}$$

where M is the total number of query-document pairs present in the training set, i.e., $M = \sum_{j=1}^{m} n_{q_j}$ (in accordance with the problem formulation described in Section 6.4), $x_j^i = \psi(q_i, d_j^{q_i})$ is a feature vector, and y_j^i is the corresponding relevance judgement (ground truth label)[27]. An example of $loss(f(x_j), y_j)$ is the algebraic difference from true label and the predicted label (used by Crammer & Singer, (2001)) of an instance.

This approach has the advantage that it can use any classification or regression method off-the-shelf. Moreover, it has theoretical foundation as it has been proven that the IR ranking error in terms of IR metrics like DCG is bounded by both classification error (Li, Burges & Wu, 2007) and regression error (Cossock & Zhang, 2006) (this is intuitive as shown in some examples of Section 8.4.1). If a classification algorithm is used, the algorithm treats distinct ranks as distinct classes (Li *et al.*, 2007). If a regression algorithm is used, the algorithm either treats distinct classes as continuous values (Geurts & Louppe, 2011) or it maps them onto a continuous scale (Burges *et al.*, 2005; Geurts & Louppe, 2011).

A drawback of pointwise approach is, as we have already discussed in Sections 8.4.1 and 8.4.2 that there are some differences between the classification/ regression and the LtR problem. Note that it is not possible to incorporate any IR metric in pointwise loss function because the IR metrics are concerned with the total ranked list whereas the pointwise loss is defined over individual instances.

b. The loss can be defined based on the pairs $f(x_i)$, $f(x_j)$ (this is called *pairwise approach*). The two instances of a pair to be considered should (1) be associated with a particular query, and (2) have different ranks as ground truth labels[28]. Thus the loss function can be written as:

$$\mathcal{L}_{Training} = \sum_{i=1}^{m}\sum_{j=1}^{n_{q_i}}\sum_{k=j+1}^{n_{q_i}} loss(f(x_j^i), f(x_k^i), y_j^i, y_k^i); y_i^j \neq y_i^k.$$

(13)

An example of such loss function (*loss*(.) in the above equation) is the number of miss-ranked pairs (used by Joachims, (2002)).

An advantage of this approach is, as this loss function is related to ordinal regression, we can use existing ordinal regression algorithms. But as there are some dissimilarities between ordinal regression and LtR problem (discussed in Section 8.4.2), modifying ordinal regression algorithms as per the characteristics of IR ranking gives better results (Joachims, 2002; Cao *et al.*, 2006). Also, we can directly apply classification algorithms because if we generate new training data from each pair of the instances by subtracting one from another, and give labels +1 or -1 depending on their preferences in the ranked list, then it turns into a standard binary classification problem. Another important merit of this approach is, this loss function is closer to the spirit of LtR problem than the pointwise loss function in the sense that it takes into account the query-document structure present in the LtR data to some extent. Hence this approach is usually said to be empirically better than the pointwise approach (Qin *et al.*, 2010; Liu, 2011; Li, 2011).

A drawback is, pairwise loss does not fully represent the IR metrics (NDCG etc.) because although it takes the query-document structure into account, it gives no emphasis on the top part of the ranked list. Another problem is, it essentially has to deal with quadratic order of the number of training instances which is computationally costly.

c. The loss can be based on scores of all documents of a query, i.e., all the $f(x_i)$ is associated with a single query (this approach is called *listwise*). It can be written as:

$$\mathcal{L}_{Training} = \sum_{i=1}^{m} loss\left(f(x_1^j), f(x_2^i), ..., f(x_{n_{q_i}}^i), y_1^i, y_2^i, ..., y_{n_{q_i}}^i\right).$$

(14)

An example of such loss is the degree of disagreement between the true ranked list of all the documents associated with a query and the predicted ranked list of the same documents using

K-L divergence measure (used by Cao, Qin, Liu, Tsai & Li, (2007)) – these two ranked lists are created by sorting the true labels $\left(y_1^i, y_2^i, ..., y_{n_{q_i}}^i \right)$ and predicted labels

$$\left(f\left(x_1^j\right), f\left(x_2^i\right), ..., f\left(x_{n_{q_i}}^i\right) \right).$$

The advantage of this approach is, it deals with the LtR problem more closely in the sense that the loss function *loss*(.) is defined over all the documents associated with a query. Note that the pairwise approach also deals with the query-document structure, but in listwise loss function we have more flexibility over how to choose the function (*loss*(.) in Equation 14). This flexibility allows us to use smooth approximations to the IR metrics (Taylor *et al.*, 2008; Quoc & Le, 2007), or to use smooth surrogate (but still listwise) loss functions (Cao *et al.*, 2007; Xia *et al.*, 2008) (more on these will come in the next section). Hence its empirical performance in general is said to be better as compared to the pointwise and pairwise approach (Qin *et al.*, 2010; Li, 2011; Liu, 2011).

One drawback of this approach is, these algorithms usually computationally expensive (Cao *et al.*, 2007), and also are conceptually more complex.

Please note that the above discussion of loss functions answer to the question 3 posed in the Section 6.3.

Why IR metrics cannot be optimized directly during learning phase. Now we explain this important aspect. Many IR metrics such as NDCG are flat or discontinuous everywhere with respect to the parameters of a model. This is because, for a particular assignment of the values of the model parameters[29], a score, $s = f(x)$ is generated (which is a real number) for each query-document pair of the training set; and the documents associated with a query are ranked in decreasing order of their scores so as to get a ranked list for each of the training queries. Now if we change model parameters, the scores of the documents change smoothly, but the order of the documents in the ranked list will not change until the score of at least one document which is below in the ranked list becomes greater than some other document which is above this document. This is because only after this incident, the first document can topple the second documents rank[30]. If we analyse NDCG, we find that it can take on only certain discrete values[31]. So if we alter parameters of a learning algorithm, either NDCG will not change, or it will make a steep (discontinuous) jump to the next possible NDCG score. Figure 8 depicts this scenario. To optimize the loss function during learning phase, many learning algorithms needs to calculate a gradient of the loss function. That is why a loss function which makes use of IR metrics directly is very difficult to optimize.

What is the underlying method being used for learning f(x)? The existing algorithms use a variety of supervised machine learning models for learning the function $f(x)$. That is, these methods usually optimize certain types of loss functions, and in LtR the loss function is defined according to our previous discussion. The prevalent models are: SVM (Herbrich *et al.*, 1999; Joachims, 2002; Nallapati, 2004; Shashua *et al.*, 2003; Cao *et al.*,

Figure 8. NDCG is Either Flat or Discontinuous with Respect to the Model Parameters

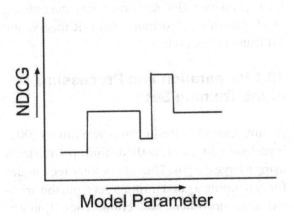

2006), neural network (Burges *et al.*, 2005; Cao *et al.*, 2006; Taylor *et al.*, 2008), boosted tree ensemble (Freund, Iyer, Schapire & Singer 2003; Li *et al.*, 2007; Wu, Burges, Svore & Gao, 2010; Xu & Li, 2007), regression (Cossock & Zhang, 2006, Zheng, Chen, Sun & Zha, 2007), random forest (Geurts & Louppe, 2011; Mohan, 2010), perceptrons (Crammer & Singer, 2001).

Please note that this discussion answers to the question 2 posed in Section 6.3

In summary, in order to design an LtR algorithm, we need:

- To decide which metric we shall be using during training phase (e.g. pairwise miss-ordered pairs).
- To design the loss function (eg., pointwise).
- To select a learning framework (e.g. SVM).

The above steps need not necessarily to be consecutive. That is, for example, the 3rd step may influence the 2nd and vice versa.

10. A BRIEF REVIEW OF LTR LITERATURE

With the knowledge of general aspects of an LtR algorithm, we now describe some research works. There is a large number of research papers on LtR; hence we discuss a representative subset of them, and we categorize them into several groups as follows: (1) preparation and processing the training set, (2) learning algorithms, (3) LtR theory, and (4) feature selection.

10.1 Preparation and Processing of the Training Set

Aslam, Kanoulas, Pavlu, Savev & Yilmaz (2009) investigate different methods for top-k retrieval using a large corpus. They study some techniques for generating a good training set from the original large document collection. Their findings include: (1) the same level of accuracy can be achieved by using much smaller set of training data, (2) the proportion of relevant documents and the similarity among the relevant and irrelevant documents in the training set have effect on the accuracy of the LtR algorithm, and the higher the number of relevant documents, the lower the MAP, (3) some LtR algorithms are more robust to the quality of the training set than others.

Geng, Qin, Liu, Cheng & Li (2011) propose an algorithm to rectify the training set found after top k retrieval. They propose a scoring function to measure the goodness of a training set. Then they try to find an optimal training set in terms of that scoring function. The down sides of this method are: (1) it is computationally very expensive (theoretically fourth order of the size of the training set, though they provide an efficient approximation to the original solution) to calculate the score, and (2) it is exclusive for pairwise LtR algorithms.

McDonald *et al.* (2013) focus on the properties of a good training set through extensive empirical study on some large data sets. They consider the size of the sample to be used in the top k retrieval stage in their experiment (i.e., different values of k), and empirically search for the optimal values of k for different tasks and data sets using some LtR algorithms. They also study the type of information need (navigational, informational etc.), document representation etc. They use a single base ranker as the initial retrieval method, and experiment with some values of k which are selected based on previous studies and rules of thumb. Their conclusions include: retrieval performance in general increases with increasing size of training sample (i.e., the values of k) up to a certain point, after which it saturates.

Dang *et al.* (2013) develop an improved initial retrieval method in the sense that it retrieves more relevant documents than existing methods like mere BM25. Their method uses some advanced features like proximity based features (Bendersky, Metzler & Croft, 2010).

Long *et al.* (2010) propose an Active Learning framework which selects the examples which minimizes expected DCG loss over a training set. The main motivation of active learning is to reduce the large cost associated with labelling documents by human. Some other works such as Donmez & Carbonell, (2008) and Yu (2005) also try to find the examples which, if added to a training set, increase the quality of the learned ranking function.

Ibrahim & Carman, (2014a) investigate the use of undersampling techinques in the context of LtR. LtR training sets are highly imbalanced because the number of relevant documents are very small. The authors use some undersampling techniques to show that similar level of performance can be achieved if only some smaller fraction of irrelevant documents are used. And additional benefit of using these techniques is that the training time is reduced because of using smaller training set.

Niu *et al.* (2014) address the issue of robustness of LtR training data in terms of label noise. The labels are usually noisy because of disagreement among human judges. They study two methods which explains the performance degradation of LtR algorithms due to label noise.

Ibrahim & Carman, (2014b) uses the sub-sampling method in congruence with an ensemble learning model (random forest) in order to reduce training time. They show that using only a small sub-sample of a training set per base learners not only reduces trainnig time significantly, but also yields sllightly better performance.

Thus we see that in the literature the following issues have been addressed in the context of training data: size (Macdonal *et al.*, 2013), quality (Dang *et al.*, 2013; Aslam *et al.*, 2009; Geng *et al.*, 2011; Long *et al.*, 2010; Donmez & Carbonell, 2008; Yu, 2005), imbalancedness (Ibrahim & Carman, 2014a), robustness (Niu *et al.*, 2014), and training time (Ibrahim & Carman, 2014b).

10.2 LtR Algorithms

In our discussion below, we roughly follow the chronological order of the publication date of the papers. This review is by no means exhaustive as it is not feasible to discuss all algorithms in a single chapter[32]. At first we summarize the important characteristics of some algorithms in Table 1 which will assist us to get an overall picture. Note that the three columns in the Table correspond to the three aspects discussed in Section 9.

10.2.1 Description of Existing LtR Algorithms

In spite of the differences between between ordinal regression and LtR problem, there are nonetheless some similarities as discussed in Section 8.4.2. So we start with a few algorithms for ordinal regression which heralded the LtR research. Herbrich *et al.* (1999) is one of such earliest works. During training phase, the algorithm learns a function f(x) which takes the feature vector of a document as input, and outputs a real number which the authors called the utility value. During training, it tries to ensure that $f(x_i) > f(x_j)$ for all pairs of x_i and x_j where x_i has an upper rank than x_j in the training set. So the loss function is number of miss-classified pairs of instances, hence it is a pairwise approach. The algorithm uses an SVM approach to learn $f(x)$. In the testing phase, it computes the $f(x)$ values for all the test instances. Then these values are used to rank the instances (the higher the value for an instance, the higher the rank). They use small amount of text data, and use the number of miss-ordered pair as evaluation metric. The positive sides of this work are: (1) It uses SVM which is very effective large margin classifier. (2) Empirically it outperforms both multi-class SVM classification and SVM regression in case of more than two ranks. One major disadvantage of this method is, it essentially operates on a much bigger training set which is in quadratic order of

Table 1. Characteristics of Some LtR Algorithms

Method/Paper and Year	Does Loss Function Use IR Metric or Surrogate?	Pointwise, Pairwise, or Listwise?	Learning Model
Herbrich *et al.* (1999)	Surrogate: # miss-ordered pairs	Pairwise	SVM
Pranking (Crammer & Singer, 2001)	Surrogate: # miss-ordered pairs	Pointwise	Perceptrons
RankSVM (Joachims, 2002)	Surrogate: Kendall's τ	Pairwise	SVM
RankBoost (Freund *et al.*, 2003)	Surrogate: # miss-ordered pairs	Pairwise	AdaBoost
Nallapati, (2004)	Surrogate: hinge loss	Pointwise	SVM
RankNet (Burges *et al.*, 2005)	Surrogate: logistic loss	Pairwise	Neural Net
Subset Ranking (Cossock & Zhang, 2006)	Surrogate: least square error	Pointwise	Linear regression
LambdaRank (Quoc & Le, 2007)	NDCG-based	Pairwise	Neural Net
McRank (Li *et al.*, 2007)	Surrogate: exponential loss	Pointwise	Gradient Boosting
LambdaMart (Wu, Burges, Svore & Gao, 2010)	NDCG-based	Listwise	Gradient Boosting
ListNet (Cao *et al.*, 2007)	Rank-based	Listwise	Neural Net
AdaRank (Xu & Li, 2007)	NDCG-based	Listwise	AdaBoost
Metzler & Croft (2007)	NDCG-based	Listwise	Coordinate Ascent
SoftRank (Taylor *et al.*, 2008)	NDCG-based	Listwise	Neural Net
Geurts & Louppe, (2011)	Surrogate: mean-squared loss	Pointwise	Random Forest

the original training set because every document must be compared with every other document during training phase. Their algorithm does not consider the group structure of LtR training set.

Crammer and Singer, (2001) treat each rank as an interval in the real line, and then try to learn the rank boundaries between each pair of adjacent ranks. The algorithm (named as *pranking*) learns $k - 1$ parallel perceptrons (i.e., hyperplanes) at the same time for a training data having k distinct labels. The algorithm tries to confine k-th group of training instances in between $(k - 1)$-th and k-th perceptron. At test time, it tests k number of perceptrons, and decide which is the first k for which $f(x_{test}) > 0$, and gives k as the label of the test instance. It used a 0-1 loss function on miss-labelling of each training instance, i.e., $\sum |y - \hat{y}|$ where y and $\hat{y}$ are integer numbers representing the of true and predicted relevance levels respec-

tively. As such, it is a pointwise approach. Unlike Herbrich *et al.*, (1999) it does not work with quadratic order of training data, rather it operates on original data thereby having a computational advantage over its competitors. This algorithm also does not consider the group structure of LtR training set.

Joachims, (2002) is thought to have used the current format of LtR data extensively for the first time. By current format we mean that the documents are partitioned by different queries with supervised learning method, and different features (scores) for a single query-document pair. The algorithm (which is now called RankSVM) he designs is similar to that of Herbrich *et al.*, (1999), i.e., an SVM approach, but the pairs are confined to each query, rather than across the whole training set. It uses Kendall's τ as evaluation metric[33] which had long been used by statisticians in the ordinal regression problem for comparing two sets of preference pairs defined over the same set of items. It inherits the advantages of Herbrich *et al.,* (1999). One additional novelty of this work is that it proposes a way to utilize click-through data as ground truth labels the documents. Additionally, he analyzes importance of some features based on the weights learnt by the SVM after training. The down sides are the same as Herbrich *et al.,* (1999) – it has to operate on a training set which quadratic order of the original training set.

Freund *et al.* (2003) propose an algorithm called RankBoost which use the AdaBoost framework with a pairwise loss function. AdaBoost (Freund & Schapire, 1995) builds an ensemble of weak learners (normally decision trees) from a weighted training set, and the final output is given as a weighted average of the predictions of all these weak learners. Now the RankBoost learns a function $f(x)$ from the training data using AdaBoost framework, but for calculating the loss over the training set after building a weak learner, it uses the $f(x_i)$ and $f(x_j)$ for every pair of the training instances instead of single instance, and determines a loss if they are miss-ordered, i.e., if $f(x_i) < f(x_j)$ but x_i has higher preference than x_j in the training set. Also, it assigns weights to pairs of instances as opposed to AdaBoost's individual weights. During testing, the instances are ranked according to $f(x)$. This work tests the algorithm with limited amount of text data, and the evaluation metric is the number of miss-ordered pairs of instances. Its positive side is, it uses Adaboost framework which is a very effective learning algorithm. One disadvantage is the same as that of all the pairwise approaches: the training set size is increased by quadratic order.

Nallapati, (2004) first discusses some motivations for using discriminative (supervised) approaches to rank documents. He then uses two models: maximum entropy model and support vector machine using a pointwise approach with classification settings. The two methods are compared with (unsupervised) language modeling approach on text data, and the evaluation metric is mean average precision. The author reports that SVM performs better in most of the cases than language model.

Burges *et al.,* (2005) propose an algorithm called RankNet which uses a pairwise probabilistic cost function using cross-entropy. The pairwise cost P_{ij} indicates that what is the probability that ith instance will be ranked higher than jth instance. From the ground truth labels, ground truth probabilities are generated. Then using this ground truth probability and the probability predicted by the model (this probability is calculated using the $f(x)$ i.e. scores of individual feature vectors output by the model) using a logistic function, a cost is calculated. The cost function is differentiable (because the cross-entropy function itself is differentiable), so its gradient is available which is essential in many learning frameworks. The underlying learning algorithm (they used neural network) can use these gradients of the cost function (which is a function of the model parameters) with respect to the model parameters to optimize the cost function thereby minimizing the differences between the predicted pairwise probabilities and the ground truth probabilities. They compare performance of their algorithms with pranking and some of its variations using text data collected from a commercial search engine.

Cossock and Zhang, (2006) prove that DCG error is bounded by regression error. Thus they justify the use of regression framework during learning. They propose a pointwise algorithm which uses a modified least square regression framework in such a way that the instances which have higher score (highly relevant) are given more importance in the learning phase. That is, they argue that since only the top few results are mostly important to the user, and those top results must be highly relevant, so the ranking algorithm should give more importance in correctly labelling these instances. Their work is theoretical in nature, so they did not give any result on experiment.

Quoc and Le, (2007) address the problem of non-smoothness of the IR metrics with respect to the model parameters (as discussed in Section 9). That is, a cost function which tries to directly optimize the IR metrics is not feasible, because in machine learning a common way to get the optimum value of a (cost) function (which is a function of the model parameters) is to get the gradient with respect to the model parameters, and then to use that gradient to update the parameters in such a way that the updated parameters are closer to their optimum setting. Since the IR metrics are either flat or discontinuous, so finding the gradient is not feasible. So this paper proposes a framework where the gradient is approximated by assuming an implicit cost function – implicit because this framework does not need to define the cost function itself, rather it only approximates the gradient of the implicit cost function with respect to the score of each training instance produced by the current model, which in turn is used (using chain rule of differentiation) to find the gradient of the implicit cost function with respect to the model parameters. In order to have high accuracy in terms of IR metrics, the gradient should have the quality that the top-ranked documents of a ranked list are more cared for during training. So the authors make sure that this property is present in the approximated gradient. The gradient at each point (instance) of the training set is found using a modified version of the probabilistic cost function used in the authors' previous algorithm RankNet discussed above which includes, importantly, NDCG metric directly into account. So the authors essentially bypass the problem of finding the gradient of non-smooth cost function directly – instead of finding the actual gradient, they analyze the properties of the actual gradient, and then they use a surrogate gradient which tries to maintain those properties. As the gradient is found, now they use neural network to train the learning model. This algorithm (called LambdaRank) actually emerged in the sequel of a fast implementation of the RankNet algorithm. Empirical result show

that their algorithm is superior to RankNet. This is mainly due to the fact that they used IR metric (NDCG) in the learning process. They test with text data from commercial search engine.

Li *et al.*, (2007) use a pointwise approach with an effective learning framework called gradient boosting for the first time in LtR. The algorithm is called McRank. Gradient boosting (Friedman, 2001) fits in the general AdaBoosting framework, but it uses a different approach for building the weak learners, i.e., trees. The author showed that this new instantiation of the general boosting framework increases the effectiveness, and its robustness to the presence of outliers (Hastie *et al.*, 2009, Ch.10). This framework is primarily designed for regression task, but there are classification versions as well. Now the LtR algorithm proposed by Li *et al.* uses this framework as it is, and then solves the LtR problem using both regression and classification settings. They evaluate their algorithms using data from commercial search engine. They compared performance of their algorithms with LambdaRank.

Metzler and Croft, (2007) use coordinate ascent method to learn a ranking function which finds a local optimum of an objective function which directly uses IR metric like NDCG or MAP. The coordinate ascent updates one parameter at a time while keeping other parameters fixed, thereby avoiding the feasibility issue of learning a grid search over a large parameter space. They report better result than a strong language model. Tan, Xia, Guo & Wang, (2013) propose another coordinate-wise ascent method.

Cao *et al.* (2007) propose a listwise algorithm called ListNet. Its loss function calculates the disagreement between the true ranked list of documents associated with a query and the predicted ranked list during the learning phase – that is why it is a listwise algorithm. As the learning algorithm outputs scores for individual documents, a measure is need to calculate the disagreement between ranked lists incurred by two sets of scores – where the true labels of documents are assumed to be scores of the target ranked list. The authors argue that given a list of scores for documents, we can think all possible ranked lists (permutations of documents) as a probability distribution – the ranked list incurred by the scores should have the highest probability, whereas the reversed ranked list should have the minimum probability, and the intermediate ranked lists should have intermediate probabilities as per their deviation from the perfect ranked list (incurred by those scores). This is because the scores themselves have uncertainty associated with them, so instead of incurring a single, *rigid* ranked list from a list of scores, they adopt a probabilistic view. Now a method is needed to assign probabilities on ranked lists. The authors adapt Luce-Plackett model which is well known for this task. Then the KL divergence model (which is differentiable) is used to compute the loss due to the disagreement between the predicted ranked list and the true ranked list. Then a neural network framework is used for learning $f(x)$ with this loss function. The authors compare performance of ListNet with that of RankSVM, RankBoost and RankNet.

Wu *et al.* (2010) propose the LambdaMart algorithm which blends the sophisticated idea of LambdaRank and the gradient boosting framework. That is, as gradient boosting framework can be utilized with any loss function which has a gradient at each training point, and as LambdaRank uses (approximated) gradient of the (implicit) loss function at each training point, these approximated gradients can be used in gradient boosting framework instead of neural network framework (which was used in LambdaRank). The authors use it successfully, and compare the performance of LambdaMart with LambdaRank and McRank. Burges, (2010) wrote a useful paper for understanding RankNet, LambdaRank and LambdaMart. Note that this algorithm uses a pairwise loss function similar to equation 11, but still gives emphasis on the top part of the ranked list. Hence we classify it into the listwise approach.

Xu and Li, (2007) propose a simple but effective algorithm called AdaRank which uses AdaBoost framework but it maintains a listwise approach. The AdaBoost framework assigns weights of the individual weak learners of the ensemble according to the classification error of individual (weighted) training instances made by the weak learner at hand, the authors modify the weighting scheme so that instead of classification error, it reflects the ranking error of all the documents associated with a query. Then it uses this error term to assign a weight to that particular tree. Also, it assigns weights to the set of documents associated with a query (instead of a single document) thereby retaining the query-document structure of the LtR problem. This way it is ensured that the later weak learners of the ensemble focus more and more on the hard queries (and associated documents) – hard to get a good NDCG. Thus it is intuitive that the AdaBoost framework produces the weak learners which are specifically built to deliver high NDCG, in contrast to delivering high classification performance. So AdaRank adapts AdaBoost to IR ranking problem in a more natural way than RankBoost. As for weak learners, they use single base rankers (features of the training set). They compare the performance of AdaRank with RankSVM and RankBoost on a number of data sets. Note that RankBoost previously used AdaBoost framework, but their approach was pairwise, and they did not include IR metrics in the loss function.

Yue, Finley, Radlinski & Joachims, (2007) proposes SVM-MAP which optimizes a relaxed and smooth version of MAP using SVM.

Taylor *et al.*, (2008) also address the issue of non-smoothness of the IR metrics. They point out that although the IR metrics like NDCG are either flat or discontinuous everywhere with respect to the model parameters, the scores are smooth with respect to the model parameters. So they argue that if the individual ranks of the instances can be mapped into a smooth distribution instead of discrete ranks, then these ranks will be changed smoothly with change of the model parameters. As NDCG changes only if the ranks of the documents change, so if the ranks themselves are smoothly changed with respect to the model parameters, it is possible to devise a *soft* version of NDCG – soft in the sense that it will change smoothly with respect to the model parameters, thereby solving the fundamental problem of non-smoothness of the IR metrics. They use neural network framework for training the algorithm. Their algorithm is called SoftRank. They compare the performance of SoftRank with RankNet and LambdaRank.

Geurts and Louppe, (2011) develop a simple pointwise but effective and efficient algorithm. They use the random forest framework (Breiman, 2001), an effective, efficient but still surprisingly simple tree ensemble framework, perhaps for the first time in LtR. The random forest builds an ensemble of decision trees, each learnt from a bootstrap sample of the training data, and each node of the tree works with only a randomly selected subset of features. The final prediction is made based on average prediction of the individual trees. The authors deal with both regression and classification pointwise approach. The results are evaluated on the *Yahoo! Learning to Rank Challenge*, (Chapelle & Chang, 2011), and the authors report good results in comparison with other more complicated and computationally costly algorithms.

10.2.2 Discussion of Existing Algorithms

We already compared the pointwise, pairwise and listwise approaches in the context of their loss functions in Section 9. Here we add more.

Initially researchers were more inclined to use pointwise and pairwise approaches for solving the LtR problem. Later they became convinced that the use of IR metrics directly was likely to yield better performance, thereby giving rise to, and gradually focusing more on, listwise ap-

proaches. In general, the empirical performance of the listwise approaches are said to be better than the two other approaches. The pointwise approach, however, enjoys the benefit of having less computational time and conceptual simplicity in comparison with pairwise and listwise approaches. Pairwise approach has one additional problem: it is biased towards queries having many associated documents – there are overwhelming number of pairs generated from the documents associated with these queries than that of queries having less number of associated documents. Both pointwise and pairwise algorithms can use existing learning algorithms, but listwise approach needs new algorithms. Complex algorithms like listwise and some pairwise approaches suffer from the high computational cost. Computational efficiency and conceptual simplicity are important factors in LtR algorithms as opined, for example, by Burges, (2010). Hence developing algorithms having conceptual simplicity and low computational cost but having favorable performance is still considered as an active research area (Wang, Lin & Metzler, 2010; Acharyya, Koyejo, & Ghosh, 2012). That is why simple pointwise approaches are still preferred if their performance is found to be comparable (Li *et al.*, 2007; Geurts & Louppe, 2011; Pavlov, Gorodilov & Brunk, 2010; Mohan, 2010). A brief theoretical discussion of these three approaches comes in the next section.

It should be mentioned here that there is no single winning algorithm which performs best in all situations. Performance varies across different datasets, evaluation metrics, tasks (like web search, offline corpus search, home page finding, topic distillation) etc.

Another point worth-mentioning is that so far mainly the discriminative models have been used as learning models. We found only one work by Gupta, (2011) which tackles the LtR problem using generative model. Use of generative models should be investigated more by the research community.

10.2.3 A Useful Taxonomy

Now that we know how LtR algorithms practically work, we present a graphical view of their categorization in Figure 9[34]. The existing categorization is based on only the first level of the tree of the figure whereas we have added one more layer for the sake of better explanation.

Let us explain the figure. First of all, if the loss function is pointwise, then any existing (multi-class) classification or regression framework can be used to optimize the loss function. If it is pairwise, then further decision needs to be taken as to whether it will use any rank-based information in it (such as LambdaRank (Quoc & Le, 2007) does) – this area is less explored in research community, and we conjecture that most of the classification and regression framework are eligible to be used. If the pairwise loss function uses no rank-based information, then any binary classification framework can be used. Finally, if the loss function is listwise, then it can be one of two types: (a) smooth approximation of the true loss function (recall that an example of a true loss function is $1 - NDCG$), or (b) non-smooth true loss function. In the former case, any standard learning framework can be used which can find a global optimum of smooth loss function. In the latter case, very few learning algorithms such as coordinate ascent can be used which does not necessarily find a global optimum, rather use heuristics which is highly likely to result in finding a local optima, but still performs well in practice.

10.3 Theory of LtR

Supervised learning framework enjoys strong theoretical underpinnings (Vapnik, 1999; Hastie *et al.*, 2009). However, unlike the prolific literature on LtR algorithms, research on their theoretical foundation is not plentiful. Herbrich *et al.* (1999) discusses the theory of ordinal regression which, as we discussed in Section 8.4, has some similarities with LtR problem. Some papers on the theory of LtR algorithms are written by Lan, Liu, Ma & Li, (2009), Xia *et al.*, (2008), Lan, Liu, Qin, Ma & & Li, (2008), Xia, Liu & Li, (2009), Calauzènes, Usunier & Gallinari, (2013). Duchi *et al.*, (2013). Another line of work deals with the theory of IR ranking (not necessarily LtR) can be found in Wang *et al.*, (2013b).

We devote Section 11 for discussion of theory of LtR.

Figure 9. A Taxonomy of LtR Algorithms

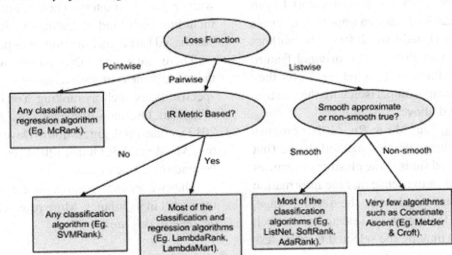

10.4 Feature Selection for LtR

In the literature of classification task, many feature selection methods are available. However, studies such as Geng *et al.*, (2007), Yu, Oh & Han, (2009) etc. suggest that specialized feature selection methods should be proposed for ranking rather than using existing methods of classification because of the differences between ranking and classification.

Geng *et al.* (2007) is perhaps the first work on feature selection in an LtR framework, the previous works on feature selection on ranking were based on bag-of-words model, i.e., each feature was a distinct term in the dictionary. The authors introduce a new feature importance score based on its ability to rank the documents correctly. They also propose a method to compute feature correlation. Then they solve an optimization problem which tries to select features with high importance scores and at the same time to decrease correlation among the selected features. The major conclusions of their study include: (1) their method outperform the feature selection methods designed for classification but used in ranking, (2) the subset of features selected by their method can even improve the performance of LtR algorithms.

Pan, Converse, Ahn, Salvetti & Donato, (2009) propose a feature selection method based on boosted trees. The boosting framework has an inherent mechanism to assign importance scores to the features (Friedman, 2001). The authors use two other variations of the original feature selection mechanism of boosted trees. But they did not provide any comparison with the existing work mentioned above.

Hua, Zhang, Liu, Ma & Ru, (2010) propose a two stage feature selection method. In the first stage, the method finds some clusters of features who are similar in the sense that the information they contain are similar. In the second stage, representative feature(s) are selected from each cluster thereby making the selected features less similar to each other. Selecting the representative feature is simple in their method: either selecting the one whose performance in terms of NDCG or MAP, is maximum when used alone, or using some linear LtR algorithm and selecting the feature having maximum weight from each cluster.

Lai, Pan, Tang, & Yu, (2013) criticises the most of the above mentioned papers in that they are two-stage processes where the first stage selects the features using some measurement (e.g. Something related to the correlation of the features) and the second stage uses those features to learn a function which is optimizes a different objective function (sucs as NDCG in some listwise algorithms). So the authors propose a single-stage algorithm which simultaneously selects features which are expected to yield better performance in terms of some ranking measure. They also note an interesting point: there is an *orthogonal* relationship between feature selection and some of the papers discussed in Section 10.1 which tries to improve the quality of a training set in that the former papers select most effective features whereas the latter papers select the most effective training examples.

Macdonal, Santos & Ounis,. (2012) studies the effectiveness of using query features, i.e., the features which depends only on queries and hence have the same value for all the documents with respect to a query. Their results show that including such kind of features within a regression based LtR algorithm improves performance.

There are some other papers which study the effectiveness of various kinds of features for specific tasks such as ranking YouTube videos (Chelaru, Orellana-Rodriguez & Altingovde, 2013), contextual suggestions (Deveaud, Albakour, Macdonald & Ounis, (2014) etc. which are beyond the scope of this chapter.

Thus we see that research on feature engineering is still in its infancy. More research should be devoted in this area.

11. THEORETICAL FRAMEWORK OF LEARNING TO RANK

As mentioned earlier, the LtR training set has a query level partitioning characteristic. That is, we can treat the query-document pairs $\langle q_i, d_j^{q_i} \rangle$ with all j as a single instance corresponding to query q_i. Pictorially, Figure 10 shows this phenomenon. The reason for this treatment is logical: the evaluation phase of LtR problem involves predicting the ranked list of a set of documents for a single query – so a single test instance means testing the performance of a single query and a set of associated documents, not a single query-document pair.

Let X and Y be random variables such that X be a query-level instance, and Y be the relevance judgements for the documents associated with the query at hand. We assume that the instances (X, Y) are i.i.d. (independent and identically distributed), and each such instance comes from an unknown probability distribution $P(X, Y)$. Our job is to learn a function $Y = F(X)$ such that some loss function $L_{per\_inst}(F(X), Y)$ is minimized across the entire population. Thus the total loss we want to minimize is:

$$\mathcal{L}_{total}^{Ideal} = \mathbb{E}_{X,Y}[L_{per\_inst}(F(X), Y)]$$
$$= \int_{X,Y} L_{per\_inst}(F(X), Y)P(X, Y)dXdY \,.$$

$$(15)$$

During learning, we want to find the function $F^*(X)$ which minimizes the total loss. Therefore,

$$F^*(X) = \underset{F(X)}{argmin}\, \mathcal{L}_{total}^{Ideal} \,.$$

$$(16)$$

In order to find the optimal function $F^*(X)$ we need to solve for Equation 15. But since the distribution $P(X, Y)$ is unknown, computing Equation 15 is not possible. Instead,, an empirical loss over the training data is computed. Using Empirical Risk Minimization framework (Vapnik, 1999), if the number of training instances is n, the empirical loss can be written as:

$$\mathcal{L}_{total}^{Emprical} = \sum_{i=1}^{n} L_{per\_inst}(F(X_i), Y_i) \,.$$

$$(17)$$

With this setting, during learning, we want to find the function $F^*(X)$ which minimizes the total empirical loss:

Figure 10. Training Set of LtR Problem is Partitioned by Query

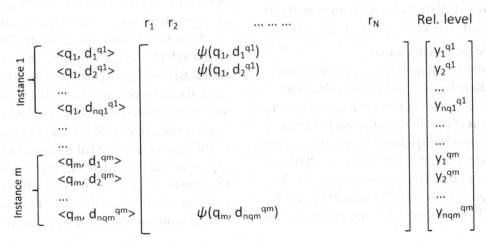

$$F^*(X) = \underset{F(X)}{argmin} \quad L_{total}^{Empirical}. \qquad (18)$$

Now we need to make two primary decisions: (1) How can we define the loss function $L_{per\_inst}(F(X_i), Y_i)$? (2) How can we learn $F^*(X)$ using the loss function?

As for the first question, an example of a perfect loss function is:

$$L_{per\_inst}(F(X_i), Y_i) = 1 - NDCG. \qquad (19)$$

If NDCG for a query is perfect (i.e., 1)[35], the loss for that instance will be 0. The more deviates the ranked list of documents from the ideal DCG, the less will be the NDCG, the more will be the loss. But as we have discussed in Section 9 that NDCG is either flat or discontinuous everywhere with respect to the parameters of the learning algorithm, so is $1 - NDCG$. That is why using Equation 19 as loss function in order to get the optimal ranking function $F^*(X)$ is not a feasible solution. Hence we need to use some surrogate loss function which is easy to optimize (for example, which is smooth so that its gradient with respect to the model parameters can easily be computed). To this end, the link between the theory and the practice is established: different approaches of LtR algorithms (pointwise, pairwise, and listwise) differ in the definition of this empirical loss function $L_{per\_inst}(F(X_i), Y_i)$. Below we describe their implications.

The listwise approach adopts the nearest approximation to the original loss function. It maintains the query-document structure present in the data (as opposed to treating each document independently) (cf. Equation 14), and then it uses some surrogate loss function (Cao *et al.*, 2007), or some form of approximation to the original loss function (Quoc & Le, 2007; Taylor *et al.*, 2008). The general superiority of listwise approaches in terms of empirical results over other approaches (Metzler & Croft, 2007) can be intuitively explained by this phenomenon.

The pairwise loss goes a bit further from the original problem. It uses a loss function which is concerned with the every pair of documents under the same query (cf. Equation 13). To some extent, it also maintains the query-document structure of the training set because it does not deal with the pairs outside a particular query. But yet it deviates from the original problem more than listwise approach, because, under the same query, it is no longer concerned with the actual IR metrics (which produce an evaluation score based on the whole list of documents associated with a single query), rather it takes a pairwise loss into account.

The pointwise approach adopts the furthest approximation to the loss function from the original problem. It treats each document independently, and calculates a loss based on that (cf. Equation 11). Its mediocre empirical performance (in general) in comparison with pairwise and listwise approaches might be attributed to this characteristics.

As for the second question mentioned a short while ago (i.e., how can we learn $F^*(X)$ using the loss function), mostly the discriminative learning models (SVM, neural network etc.) have been used so far. They are capable of learning the function effectively given a suitable loss function. Once a good $F^*(X)$ is found, this function is used to rank the documents associated with a test query.

We note here that the search for the optimal function $F^*(X)$ deviates from the original problem in at least two places: (1) the use of empirical loss instead of true loss (cf. Equation 18), and (2) the sacrifice of even the true empirical loss (because of the nature of the IR evaluation metrics). The first deviation is embedded in all supervised learning tasks like classification, regression etc. But the second deviation is special for the IR ranking problem due to, again, the non-smoothness of the IR evaluation metrics. This perhaps explains why there are so many algorithms in LtR literature, because people found that there is much room for investigating different types of loss functions with different types of learning models.

12. CURRENT TRENDS IN LTR RESEARCH

After analyzing the recent papers of the last few years, we have found the following trending topics that are currently dominating the LtR literature:

1. **Applications of LtR Algorithms in New Domains:** The overwhelming majority – over a hundred – of recent research papers on LtR fall into this category. This trend echoes our proclamation in Section 1 that any task which involves ranking a set of items based on a query is a potential application of LtR algorithms.

2. **Improving and Extending Existing LtR Algorithms:** Most of the supervised learning models (Neural Network, SVM etc.) have already been explored along with various loss functions (pointwise, pairwise, and listwise with several variants in each of these categories—cf. Sections 9 and 10). Instead of developing completely new algorithms, some researchers are motivated to fine tune the existing ones, such as, Busa-Fekete, Kégl, Éltető & Szarvas, (2013), Yu *et al.*, (2014), and Renjifo & Carmen, (2012).

3. **Efficiency Issues of Existing LtR Algorithms:** Computational efficiency is highlighted under a separate heading to signify its importance in LtR algorithms due to the inherent large size of the training data used in commercial search engines. Some noteworthy papers are Wauthier, Jordan & Jojic, (2013), Tonellotto, Macdonald & Ounis, (2013), Ibrahim & Carman, (2014b) and Asadi & Lin, (2013).

4. **Training Set Preparation and Modification:** Although this topic did not receive sufficient attention at the initial stage of LtR research, it has recently attracted significant research interests. Some papers of this category are: Niu *et al.*, (2014), Ibrahim & Carman, (2014a), and Lin, Jan & Li., (2013).

5. **Feature Engineering:** This is yet another topic which did not receive adequate research interest in the initial phase of developing LtR algorithms. Some noteworthy papers are Chelaru *et al.*, (2013), Deveaud *et al.*, (2014), and Can, Croft & Manmatha, (2014).

6. **Transfer LtR:** This task is related to the concepts of multi-task learning and model adaptation that have gained research momentum lately e.g., Duh & Fujino, (2012), Gao & Yang, (2014), and Wang *et al.*, (2013a).

Forecasting future trends is difficult, especially in a dynamic research area like LtR. A few years back, Chapelle, Chang & Liu, (2011) arranged a commercial competition on LtR (Chapelle & Chang, 2011), and thereafter utilized their experience to predict a number of future research directions on LtR. Not all of their anticipated topics, however, have drawn sufficient research attention lately, and hence left out from our list mentioned above. Some of these uncharted topics (along with the very few papers we have encountered, if any) include semi-supervised LtR, rank diversification, robustness in terms of performance fluctuation across different test queries (Wang, Bennett & Collins-Thompson, 2012), robustness in terms of irrelevant features (Lim, Lanckriet & McFee, 2013), and online LtR (Hofmann, Whiteson & de Rijke, 2013).

13. SUMMARY

The chapter opened by portraying the big picture of the ranking problem of document retrieval task.

We have explained what relevancy of a document with respect to a particular query means. Several prevalent traditional approaches used for solving the ranking problem have been briefly described. We have then explained the justification of using supervised machine learning methods and elaborated how the training data are prepared. This has been followed by a formal problem formulation of the LtR approach. We have then discussed some of the evaluation metrics heavily used for assessing the performance of a ranking method in IR. The similarities and dissimilarities between the LtR problem and three major tasks of supervised learning framework, namely, classification, regression, and ordinal regression have been demonstrated. We have then outlined some of the important aspects pertaining to any LtR algorithm, namely, the loss function used during learning phase of the algorithm (surrogate or IR metrics), the nature of the loss considered during learning phase (pointwise, or pairwise, or listwise), and the underlying learning framework (SVM, Neural Network etc.) for learning a ranking function. After that we have presented a brief technical discussion of some representative LtR algorithms, and shed some light on the theoretical underpinnings of the LtR problem. Finally, we have listed the research directions and trends of the recent years.

14. CONCLUSION

When LtR emerged as a research direction back in the early 2000's, it was not as popular as it has increasingly become. These days commercial search engines such as Microsoft and Yahoo! are thought to be using this framework[36]. Although there are some criticisms regarding the trade-off between the relatively higher computational resource requirement and the accuracy, LtR methods are now widely accepted as a standard practice in the IR community.

Research on LtR seems to be shifting from designing new algorithms to finding new applications of the existing LtR algorithms. A reason for this may be that the performance of state-of-the-art algorithms do not differ greatly, implying that research on developing new algorithms is somewhat saturated now. Instead, some peripheral issues such as feature engineering, training set analysis etc. are getting attention. This is because the accuracy of an LtR system heavily depends not only on the algorithm itself but also on the the entire supervised learning framework where many issues are needed to be addressed such as informativeness of the features, size of the training set, noisy training instances, noisy labels etc. Nevertheless, research on LtR is still young compared to other supervised machine learning tasks such as classification and regression. As more research is being focused on the out-of-the-box topics of LtR, its performance will continue to improve.

We have also identifed a gap between the IR and machine learning researchers in the context of LtR. IR researchers are somewhat skeptical about the inner machineries of the complex LtR algorithms, whereas machine learning researchers often ignore the *IR sides* of the LtR problem, for example, the intrinsic relationship between the features of LtR training set, the nature of the training set (such as, the highly skewed nature of the trainnig data, the fact that documents associated with a query are not i.i.d.) etc. Future research on LtR should focus on reducing this gap.

REFERENCES

Acharyya, S., Koyejo, O., & Ghosh, J. (2012). Learning to rank with bregman divergences and monotone retargeting. *arXiv preprint arXiv:1210.4851*.

Alpaydin, E. (2004). *Introduction to machine learning*. MIT press.

Asadi, N., & Lin, J. (2013). *Training efficient tree-based models for document ranking. Advances in Information Retrieval. 146 – 157.* Springer.

Aslam, J. A., Kanoulas, E., Pavlu, V., Savev, S., & Yilmaz, E. (2009). Document selection methodologies for efficient and effective learning-to-rank. *Proceedings of the 32nd international ACM SIGIR conference on Research and development in information retrieval* (pp. 468–475). doi:10.1145/1571941.1572022

Bendersky, M., Metzler, D., & Croft, W. B. (2010). Learning concept importance using a weighted dependence model. *Proceedings of the third ACM international conference on Web search and data mining* (pp. 31–40). doi:10.1145/1718487.1718492

Breiman, L. (2001). Random forests. *Machine Learning, 45*(1), 5–32. doi:10.1023/A:1010933404324

Burges C. (2010). From ranknet to lambdarank to lambdamart: An overview.

Burges, C., Renshaw, T. S. E., Lazier, A., Deeds, M., Hamilton, N., & Hullender, G. (2005). Learning to rank using gradient descent. *Proceedings of the 22nd international conference on Machine learning* (pp. 89–96).

Busa-Fekete, R., Kégl, B., Éltető, T., & Szarvas, G. (2013). Tune and mix: Learning to rank using ensembles of calibrated multi-class classifiers. *Machine Learning, 93*(2-3), 261–292. doi:10.1007/s10994-013-5360-9

Calauzènes, C., Usunier, N., & Gallinari, P. (2013). Calibration and regret bounds for order-preserving surrogate losses in learning to rank. *Machine Learning, 93*(2-3), 227–260. doi:10.1007/s10994-013-5382-3

Can, E. F., Croft, W. B., & Manmatha, R. (2014). Incorporating query-specific feedback into learning-to-rank models. *Proceedings of the 37th international ACM SIGIR conference on Research and development in information retrieval* (pp. 1035 – 1038).

Cao, Y., Xu, J., Liu, T., Li, H., Huang, Y., & Hon, H. (2006). Adapting ranking svm to document retrieval. *Proceedings of the 29th annual international ACM SIGIR conference on Research and development in information retrieval* (pp. 186–193).

Cao, Z., Qin, T., Liu, T., Tsai, M., & Li, H. (2007). Learning to rank: from pairwise approach to listwise approach. *Proceedings of the 24th international conference on Machine learning* (pp. 129–136). doi:10.1145/1273496.1273513

Chapelle, O., & Chang, Y. (2011). Yahoo! learning to rank challenge overview. *Journal of Machine Learning Research-Proceedings Track, 14*, 1–24.

Chapelle, O., Chang, Y., & Liu, T. (2011). Future directions in learning to rank. *Proceedings of Yahoo!* (pp. 91–100). Learning to Rank Challenge.

Chapelle, O., Metlzer, D., Zhang, Y., & Grinspan, P. (2009). Expected reciprocal rank for graded relevance. *Proceedings of the 18th ACM conference on Information and knowledge management* (pp. 621–630).

Chelaru, S., Orellana-Rodriguez, C., & Altingovde, I. S. (2013). How useful is social feedback for learning to rank YouTube videos? [WWW]. *World Wide Web (Bussum)*, 1–29.

Cohen, W. W., Schapire, R. E., & Singer, Y. (1999). Learning to order things. *Journal of Artificial Intelligence Research, 10*, 243–270.

Cossock D., & Zhang T. (2006). Subset ranking using regression. *Learning theory*, 605–619.

Crammer, K., & Singer, Y. (2001). Pranking with ranking. *Advances in Neural Information Processing Systems*, *14*, 641–647.

Craswell, N., Fetterly, D., Najork, M., Robertson, S., & Yilmaz, E. (2009). *Microsoft research at trec 2009. web and relevance feedback tracks. Technical report*. DTIC Document.

Dang, V., Bendersky, M., & Croft, W. B. (2013). Two-stage learning to rank for information retrieval. In Advances in Information Retrieval, 423–434. doi:10.1007/978-3-642-36973-5_36

Donmez, P., & Carbonell, J. G. (2008). Optimizing estimated loss reduction for active sampling in rank learning. *Proceedings of the 25th international conference on Machine learning* (pp. 248–255). doi:10.1145/1390156.1390188

Duchi, J. C., Mackey, L., & Jordan, M. I. (2013). The asymptotics of ranking algorithms. *Annals of Statistics*, *41*(5), 2292–2323. doi:10.1214/13-AOS1142

Duh, K., & Fujino, A. (2012). Flexible sample selection strategies for transfer learning in ranking. *Information Processing & Management*, *48*(3), 502–512. doi:10.1016/j.ipm.2011.05.002

Freund, Y., Iyer, R., Schapire, R. E., & Singer, Y. (2003). An efficient boosting algorithm for combining preferences. *Journal of Machine Learning Research*, *4*, 933–969.

Freund, Y., & Schapire, R. E. (1995). A desicion-theoretic generalization of on-line learning and an application to boosting. In *Computational learning theory* (pp. 23–37). Springer. doi:10.1007/3-540-59119-2_166

Friedman, J. H. (2001). Greedy function approximation: A gradient boosting machine.(english summary). *Annals of Statistics*, *29*(5), 1189–1232. doi:10.1214/aos/1013203451

Gao, W., & Yang, P. (2014). Democracy is good for ranking: Towards multi-view rank learning and adaptation in web search. *Proceedings of the 7th ACM international conference on Web search and data mining* (pp. 63—72). doi:10.1145/2556195.2556267

Geng, X., Liu, T., Qin, T., & Li, H. (2007). Feature selection for ranking. *Proceedings of the 30th annual international ACM SIGIR conference on Research and development in information retrieval* (pp. 407–414).

Geng, X., Qin, T., Liu, T., Cheng, X., & Li, H. (2011). Selecting optimal training data for learning to rank. *Information Processing & Management*, *47*(5), 730–741. doi:10.1016/j.ipm.2011.01.002

Geurts, P., & Louppe, G. (2011). Learning to rank with extremely randomized trees. *JMLR: Workshop and Conference Proceedings* (Vol. 14).

Gupta, P. (2011). Learning to rank: Using bayesian networks. *PhD Thesis*.

Harman, D. (1995). Overview of the second text retrieval conference (trec-2). *Information Processing & Management*, *31*(3), 271–289. doi:10.1016/0306-4573(94)00047-7

Hastie, T., Tibshirani, R., & Friedman, J. (2009). *The elements of statistical learning*. Berlin: Springer. doi:10.1007/978-0-387-84858-7

He, C., Wang, C., Zhong, Y., & Li, R. (2008). A survey on learning to rank. *Proceedings of International Conference on Machine Learning and Cybernetics* (pp. 1734—1739).

Herbrich, R., Graepel, T., & Obermayer, K. (1999). Large margin rank boundaries for ordinal regression. *Advances in Neural Information Processing Systems*, 115–132.

Hofmann, K., Whiteson, S., & de Rijke, M. (2013). Balancing exploration and exploitation in listwise and pairwise online learning to rank for information retrieval. *Information Retrieval*, *16*(1), 63–90. doi:10.1007/s10791-012-9197-9

Hua, G., Zhang, M., Liu, Y., Ma, S., & Ru, L. (2010). Hierarchical feature selection for ranking. *Proceedings of the 19th international conference on World Wide Web* (pp. 1113–1114). doi:10.1145/1772690.1772830

Ibrahim, M., & Carman, M. (2014a). Undersampling Techniques to Re-balance Training Data for Large Scale Learning-to-Rank. *Proceedings of the 10th Asia Information Retrieval Society Conference, Malaysia* (pp. 444-457). doi:10.1007/978-3-319-12844-3_38

Ibrahim, M., & Carman, M. (2014b). Improving Scalability and Performance of Random Forest Based Learning-to-Rank Algorithms by Aggressive Subsampling. *Proceedings of the 12th Australasian Data Mining Conference, Brisbane, Australia.*

Järvelin, K., & Kekäläinen, J. (2000). IR evaluation methods for retrieving highly relevant documents. *Proceedings of the 23rd annual international ACM SIGIR conference on Research and development in information retrieval* (pp. 41–48).

Järvelin, K., & Kekäläinen, J. (2002). Cumulated gain-based evaluation of ir techniques. [TOIS]. *ACM Transactions on Information Systems*, *20*(4), 422–446. doi:10.1145/582415.582418

Joachims, T. (2002). Optimizing search engines using clickthrough data. *Proceedings of the 8th ACM SIGKDD international conference on Knowledge discovery and data mining* (pp. 133–142).

Jones, K. S., Walker, S., & Robertson, S. E. (2000). A probabilistic model of information retrieval: development and comparative experiments: Part 1. *Information Processing & Management*, *36*(6), 779–808. doi:10.1016/S0306-4573(00)00015-7

Lai, H., Pan, Y., Tang, Y., & Yu, R. (2013). FSMRank: Feature Selection Algorithm for Learning to Rank. *IEEE Transactions on Neural Networks and Learning Systems*, *24*(6), 940–952. doi:10.1109/TNNLS.2013.2247628 PMID:24808475

Lan, Y., Liu, T., Ma, Z., & Li, H. (2009). Generalization analysis of listwise learning-to-rank algorithms. *Proceedings of the 26th Annual International Conference on Machine Learning* (pp. 577–584).

Lan, Y., Liu, T., Qin, T., Ma, Z., & Li, H. (2008). Querylevel stability and generalization in learning to rank. *Proceedings of the 25th international conference on Machine learning* (pp. 512–519).

Li, H. (2011). Learning to rank for information retrieval and natural language processing. [Morgan and Claypool Publishers.]. *Synthesis Lectures on Human Language Technologies*, *4*(1), 1–113. doi:10.2200/S00348ED1V01Y201104HLT012

Li, H., & Xu, J. (2012). Beyond bag-of-words: machine learning for query-document matching in web search. *Proceedings of the 35th international ACM SIGIR conference on Research and development in information retrieval* (pp. 1177–1177). doi:10.1145/2348283.2348528

Li, L., & Lin, H. (2007). Ordinal regression by extended binary classification. *Advances in Neural Information Processing Systems*, *19*, 865–872.

Li, P., Burges, C., & Wu, Q. (2007). Learning to rank using classification and gradient boosting. *Advances in Neural Information Processing Systems*, *19*, 897–904.

Lim, D., Lanckriet, G., & McFee, B. (2013). Robust structural metric learning. *Proceedings of The 30th International Conference on Machine Learning* (pp. 615—623).

Lin, K., Jan, T., & Lin, H. (2013). Data selection techniques for large-scale learning to rank. *Proceedings of Conference on Technologies and Applications of Artificial Intelligence. Taipei, Taiwan,* (pp. 25 – 30).

Liu, T. (2011). *Learning to rank for information retrieval.* Berlin: Springer. doi:10.1007/978-3-642-14267-3

Long, B., Chapelle, O., Zhang, Y., Chang, Y., Zheng, Z., & Tseng, B. (2010). Active learning for ranking through expected loss optimization. *Proceedings of the 33rd international ACM SIGIR conference on Research and development in information retrieval* (pp. 267–274). doi:10.1145/1835449.1835495

Macdonald, C., Santos, R. L. T., & Ounis, I. (2012). On the Usefulness of Query Features for Learning to Rank. *Proceedings of the 21st ACM international conference on Information and knowledge management* (pp. 2559–2562). doi:10.1145/2396761.2398691

Macdonald, C., Santos, R. L. T., & Ounis, I. (2013). The whens and hows of learning to rank for web search. *Information Retrieval, 16*(5), 584–628. doi:10.1007/s10791-012-9209-9

Manning, C. D., Raghavan, P., & Schütze, H. (2008). *Introduction to information retrieval* (Vol. 1). Cambridge: Cambridge University Press. doi:10.1017/CBO9780511809071

Metzler, D., & Croft, W. B. (2007). Linear feature-based models for information retrieval. *Information Retrieval, 10*(3), 257–274. doi:10.1007/s10791-006-9019-z

Metzler, D., Strohman, T., & Croft, W. B. (2006). *Indri at trec 2006: Lessons learned from three terabyte tracks. Technical report.* DTIC Document.

Mohan, A. (2010). An empirical analysis on point-wise machine learning techniques using regression trees for web-search ranking [Thesis].

Mohan, A., Chen, Z., & Weinberger, K. Q. (2011). Web-search ranking with initialized gradient boosted regression trees. *Journal of Machine Learning Research-Proceedings Track, 14,* 77–89.

Nallapati, R. (2004). Discriminative models for information retrieval. *Proceedings of the 27th annual international ACM SIGIR conference on Research and development in information retrieval* (pp. 64–71).

Ng, A. Y., & Jordan, M. I. (2001). *On discriminative vs. generative classifiers: A comparison of logistic regression and naive bayes* (pp. 841–848). NIPS.

Niu, S., Guo, J., Lan, Y., & Cheng, X. (2012). Top-k learning to rank: Labelling, ranking and evaluation. *Proceedings of the 35th international ACM SIGIR conference on Research and development in information retrieval* (pp. 751–760). doi:10.1145/2348283.2348384

Niu, S., Lan, Y., Guo, J., Cheng, X., & Geng, X. (2014). What makes data robust: A data analysis in learning to rank. *Proceedings of the 37th annual international ACM SIGIR conference on Research and development in information retrieval* (pp. 1191–1194). doi:10.1145/2600428.2609542

Norusis, M. (2008). *SPSS 17.0 statistical procedures companion.* Prentice Hall Press.

Page, L., Brin, S., Motwani, R., & Winograd, T. (1999). *The pagerank citation ranking: Bringing order to the web.* Stanford InfoLab.

Pan, F., Converse, T., Ahn, D., Salvetti, F., & Donato, G. (2009). Feature selection for ranking using boosted trees. *Proceedings of the 18th ACM conference on Information and knowledge management* (pp. 2025–2028). doi:10.1145/1645953.1646292

Pavlov, D. Y., Gorodilov, A., & Brunk, C. A. (2010). Bagboo: a scalable hybrid bagging-the-boosting model. *Proceedings of the 19th ACM international conference on Information and knowledge management* (pp. 1897–1900).

Pavlu, V. (2008). *Large scale ir evaluation*. ProQuest LLC.

Phophalia, A. (2011). A survey on learning to rank (letor) approaches in information retrieval}. Proceedings of *Nirma University International Conference on Engineering (NUiCONE)* (pp. 1—6).

Ponte, J. M., & Croft, W. B. (1998). A language modeling approach to information retrieval. *Proceedings of the 21st annual international ACM SIGIR conference on Research and development in information retrieval* (pp. 275–281). doi:10.1145/290941.291008

Qin, T., Liu, T., Xu, J., & Li, H. (2010). Letor: A benchmark collection for research on learning to rank for information retrieval. *Information Retrieval, 13*(4), 346–374. doi:10.1007/s10791-009-9123-y

Quoc, C., & Le, V. (2007). Learning to rank with nonsmooth cost functions. *Proceedings of the Advances in Neural Information Processing Systems, 19*, 193–200.

Renjifo, C., & Carmen, C. (2012). The discounted cumulative margin penalty: Rank-learning with a list-wise loss and pair-wise margins. *Proceedings of IEEE International Workshop on Machine Learning for Signal Processing (MLSP)* (pp. 1—6). doi:10.1109/MLSP.2012.6349807

Robertson, S., Zaragoza, H., & Taylor, M. (2004). Simple bm25 extension to multiple weighted fields. In *Proceedings of the thirteenth ACM international conference on Information and knowledge management*, pages 42–49. doi:10.1145/1031171.1031181

Robertson, S. E., Kanoulas, E., & Yilmaz, E. (2010). Extending average precision to graded relevance judgments. *Proceedings of the 33rd international ACM SIGIR conference on Research and development in information retrieval* (pp. 603–610). doi:10.1145/1835449.1835550

Salton, G., & Buckley, C. (1988). Term-weighting approaches in automatic text retrieval. *Information Processing & Management, 24*(5), 513–523. doi:10.1016/0306-4573(88)90021-0

Salton, G., Wong, A., & Yang, C. (1975). A vector space model for automatic indexing. *Communications of the ACM, 18*(11), 613–620. doi:10.1145/361219.361220

Schamber, L., Eisenberg, M. B., & Nilan, M. S. (1990). A re-examination of relevance: Toward a dynamic, situational definition. *Information Processing & Management, 26*(6), 755–776. doi:10.1016/0306-4573(90)90050-C

Shashua, A., & Levin, A & Others. (2003). Ranking with large margin principle: Two approaches. *Advances in Neural Information Processing Systems, 15*, 937–944.

Singhal, A., Salton, G., Mitra, M., & Buckley, C. (1996). Document length normalization. *Information Processing & Management, 32*(5), 619–633. doi:10.1016/0306-4573(96)00008-8

Tan, M., Xia, T., Guo, L., & Wang, S. (2013). Direct optimization of ranking measures for learning to rank models. *Proceedings of the 19th ACM SIGKDD international conference on Knowledge discovery and data mining* (pp. 856—864). doi:10.1145/2487575.2487630

Taylor, M., Guiver, J., Robertson, S., & Minka, T. (2008). Softrank: optimizing non-smooth rank metrics. *Proceedings of the international conference on Web search and web data mining* (pp. 77–86). doi:10.1145/1341531.1341544

Tonellotto, N., Macdonald, C., & Ounis, I. (2013). Efficient and effective retrieval using selective pruning. *Proceedings of the sixth ACM international conference on Web search and data mining* (pp 63 72. doi:10.1145/2433396.2433407

Vapnik, V. (1999). *The nature of statistical learning theory*. Berlin: Springer.

Wang, B., Tang, J., Fan, W., Chen, S., Tan, C., & Yang, Z. (2013a). Query-dependent cross-domain ranking in heterogeneous network. *Knowledge and Information Systems*, *34*(1), 109–145. doi:10.1007/s10115-011-0472-7

Wang, L., Bennett, P. N., & Collins-Thompson, K. (2012). Robust ranking models via risk-sensitive optimization. *Proceedings of the 35th international ACM SIGIR conference on Research and development in information retrieval* (pp. 761 – 770.

Wang, L., Lin, J., & Metzler, D. (2010). Learning to efficiently rank. *Proceedings of the 33rd international ACM SIGIR conference on Research and development in information retrieval* (pp. 138–145).

Wang, Y., Wang, L., Li, Y., He, D., Liu, T., & Chen, W. (2013b). A theoretical analysis of ndcg type ranking measures. *arXiv preprint arXiv:1304.6480*.

Wauthier, F., Jordan, M., & Jojic, N. (2013). Efficient ranking from pairwise comparisons. *Proceedings of the 30th International Conference on Machine Learning* (pp. 109–117).

Wu, Q., Burges, C. J. C., Svore, K. M., & Gao, J. (2010). Adapting boosting for information retrieval measures. *Information Retrieval*, *13*(3), 254–270. doi:10.1007/s10791-009-9112-1

Xia, F., Liu, T., & Li, H. (2009). Top-k consistency of learning to rank methods. *Advances in Neural Information Processing Systems*, *22*, 2098–2106.

Xia, F., Liu, T., Wang, J., Zhang, W., & Li, H. (2008). Listwise approach to learning to rank: theory and algorithm. *Proceedings of the 25th international conference on Machine learning* (pp. 1192–1199). doi:10.1145/1390156.1390306

Xia, F., Zhou, L., Yang, Y., & Zhang, W. (2007). Ordinal regression as multiclass classification. *International Journal of Intelligent Control and Systems*, *12*(3), 230–236.

Xu, J., & Li, H. (2007). Adarank: a boosting algorithm for information retrieval. *Proceedings of the 30th annual international ACM SIGIR conference on Research and development in information retrieval* (pp. 391–398). doi:10.1145/1277741.1277809

Yu, H. (2005). SVM selective sampling for ranking with application to data retrieval. *Proceedings of the eleventh ACM SIGKDD international conference on Knowledge discovery in data mining* (pp 354–363). doi:10.1145/1081870.1081911

Yu, H., Oh, J., & Han, W. (2009). Efficient feature weighting methods for ranking. *Proceedings of the 18th ACM conference on Information and knowledge management* (pp. 1157–1166).

Yu, Z., Wu, F., Zhang, Y., Tang, S., Shao, J., & Zhuang, Y. (2014). Hashing with listwise learning to rank. *Proceedings of the 37th International ACM SIGIR Conference on Research and Development in Information Retrieval* (pp. 999-1002).

Yue, Y., Finley, T., Radlinski, F., & Joachims, T. (2007). A support vector method for optimizing average precision. *Proceedings of the 30th annual international ACM SIGIR conference on Research and development in information retrieval* (pp. 271–278). doi:10.1145/1277741.1277790

Zhang, M., Kuang, D., Hua, G., Liu, Y., & Ma, S. (2009). Is learning to rank effective for web search? *Proceedings of SIGIR 2008 workshop learning to rank for information retrieval (LR4IR)* (pp. 641-647).

Zheng, Z., Chen, K., Sun, G., & Zha, H. (2007). A regression framework for learning ranking functions using relative relevance judgments. *Proceedings of the 30th annual international ACM SIGIR conference on Research and development in information retrieval* (pp. 287–294). doi:10.1145/1277741.1277792

KEY TERMS AND DEFINITIONS

Classification: A supervised learning task where the ground truth labels are integer numbers.

Information Retrieval System/Search Engine: A system which takes queries from users, and returns a list of relevant documents for a given query. The documents are usually ordered by their degree of relevance with respect to the query.

Learning-to-Rank: Supervised machine learning techniques are used to predict the degree of relevancy of a document with respect to a given query.

Rank-Based Metric: An evaluation metric that is used to measure the goodness of a ranking function. It usually gives more importance on the top part of a ranked list.

Ranking Function: Given a document representation and a query representation, a ranking function predicts a relevance score (usually real number) for the document with respect to the query.

Regression: A supervised learning task where the ground truth labels are real numbers.

Relevancy of a Document: The degree to which a document is relevant to a given query.

Supervised Machine Learning: Given some example patterns and their true labels, a supervised machine learning technique finds a function which can predict the labels of unseen examples.

ENDNOTES

[1] http://www.w3.org/History/19921103-hypertext/hypertext/DataSources/WWW/Servers.html (Retrieved on 2012-05-14).

[2] www.google.com

[3] www.yahoo.com

[4] www.microsoft.com

[5] Data source: http://www.statista.com/statistics/185966/us-customer-satisfaction-with-google/ (Retrieved on 31st July 2014).

[6] From now on, we shall use query instead of information need, because eliciting the information need from a given query using sophisticated techniques is considered to be a separate research in the IR community (known as query refinement, reduction, expansion etc.) and out-of-scope of the chapter. We assume that the query is the only piece of information we need in order to retrieve documents and a simple model, called bag-of-words (described later) on the query and documents, will be used.

[7] While this is not one of the best queries to represent this particular information need, a layman to the IR system does submit this kind of queries. Thus a smart IR system is expected to effectively handle this kind of verbose queries.

[8] There is a narrow field in IR research called Boolean retrieval back in 1970s that lacks the *degree of relevancy* concept. We do not discuss it in this chapter. Interested readers are requested to go through Manning *et al.*, (2008, Ch. 1).

[9] In IR nomenclature, the words of the documents are usually called *terms*. We use both interchangeably.

[10] For example, $idf(t, C) = log(N_t/|C|)$, N_t is the number of documents where t appears at least once, $|C|$ is the total number of documents in the collection.

[11] Some spam documents unnecessarily and intentionally repeat the keywords in order to get high position in a ranked list.

[12] We omit the subscripts if the meaning is obvious.

[13] Queries can be navigational (means one single document is wanted by the user), informational (means vast information is

needed on a topic) etc. (Manning *et al.*, 2008, Ch. 19). The nature of the collections can differ due to, among others, the lengths of the documents, the topic of the documents, the number of the documents, the ratio of relevant to non-relevant documents in the collection etc.

[14] The New York Times (2008-06-03) quoted Amit Singhal of Google as saying that Google was using over 200 various relevance judgements.

[15] Two points to note here: (1) it is straightforward to convert any reverse scoring function (such as measurement of a document being spam) by taking reciprocal, and (2) the scores may need to be normalized (Qin, Liu, Xu & Li, 2010).

[16] This is intuitive because for a query there are some relevant documents and the rest are irrelevant which are nearly infinite.

[17] For example, a document containing astronomical content is relevant to some astronomical query but irrelevant to a sports query.

[18] To see some of these features, please visit http://research.microsoft.com/en-us/projects/mslr/feature.aspx.

[19] This phenomenon may explain as to why the evaluation metrics are apparently low when the LtR algorithms are evaluated. That is, an LtR algorithm may learn many relevant documents (which are not in the top k list) as irrelevant. But in test phase, the algorithm will label many relevant documents as irrelevant (just because it learnt to do so). But evaluation metrics use the ground truth labels, so their values will be much lower. Burges *et al.*, (2005) also hint this point.

[20] The reason for normalization can be explained using the following example: the feature vector $\langle 4,3 \rangle$ corresponding to a query-document pair may be highly relevant,

while, theoretically, the same feature vector, i.e., $\langle 4,3 \rangle$ may be irrelevant for another query-document pair because in the latter case we may have another feature vector $\langle 40,30 \rangle$ corresponding to the same query but another document which is highly relevant. Hence we need to normalize the feature values on a per-query basis. During evaluation, the system applies the same normalization technique.

[21] It is called *local function* in some literature such as Li, (2011) because the authors there uses another function F which takes a set of documents (associated with a query) as input and using the local function f it outputs a ranked list of those documents.

[22] Such as query reformulation (Li & Xu, 2012).

[23] The term *MAP* is somewhat confusing because in a test phase (not in real-life usage), the system produces a separate ranked list for each of the test queries. The evaluation metric at hand gives a score for each of the ranked lists, and finally all these scores are averaged to get an overall score of the performance of the system. This process is the same for all the metrics discussed in this section. But unlike NDCG@k or p@k, AP specifically uses the term Mean AP (MAP) to represent the final (average) score.

[24] Here for the sake of simplicity we use the number of miss-ordered pairs as ranking error.

[25] If not practically, but theoretically it is possible.

[26] In order to avoid this problem, some researchers, for example, Qin *et al.*, (2010) suggest to normalize the data of LtR on a per-query basis.

[27] For the sake of simplicity we omit some subscripts/superscripts when the meaning is obvious.

28   Because two documents having the same relevance level under the same query have no ordering relationship between them, i.e., they can be ranked in both ways.

29   Here we mean that $f(x, \theta)$ is a function of x parameterized by θ. For example, $f(x, \theta) = \theta_0 x_0 + \theta_1 x_1$.

30   Moreover, these two documents must be associated with the same query and must have different relevance levels; otherwise no preference relation between them should be assumed by the learning algorithm as discussed earlier.

31   In fact, if the number of distinct levels of relevance is r, then there are r^k possible values of NDCG@k.

32   There are over a hundred research papers on LtR (http://research.microsoft.com/en-us/um/beijing/projects/letor/paper.aspx).

33   Kendall's τ counts the number of concordant and discordant pairs among the true and predicted ranked list of documents, and gives a similarity score in the range -1 to +1.

34   For brevity, in the figure we did not put the references of the algorithms, they can be found in Table 1.

35   We could write NDCG@k here and in Equation 19, but in this context the value of q is not important.

36   These companies do not disclose their exact working procedure due to business secret policy, but the academic literature published by their researchers indicate that they may be using some form of LtR methods. Researchers of Google do not publish too often, so it is hard to guess anything about Google.

Chapter 4
Prediction of International Stock Markets Based on Hybrid Intelligent Systems

Salim Lahmiri
ESCA School of Management, Morocco

ABSTRACT

This paper compares the accuracy of three hybrid intelligent systems in forecasting ten international stock market indices; namely the CAC40, DAX, FTSE, Hang Seng, KOSPI, NASDAQ, NIKKEI, S&P500, Taiwan stock market price index, and the Canadian TSE. In particular, genetic algorithms (GA) are used to optimize the topology and parameters of the adaptive time delay neural networks (ATNN) and the time delay neural networks (TDNN). The third intelligent system is the adaptive neuro-fuzzy inference system (ANFIS) that basically integrates fuzzy logic into the artificial neural network (ANN) to better model information and explain decision making process. Based on out-of-sample simulation results, it was found that contrary to the literature GA-TDNN significantly outperforms GA-ATDNN. In addition, ANFIS was found to be more effective in forecasting CAC40, FTSE, Hang Seng, NIKKEI, Taiwan, and TSE price level. In contrary, GA-TDNN and GA-ATDNN were found to be superior to ANFIS in predicting DAX, KOSPI, and NASDAQ future prices.

INTRODUCTION

Since trading financial assets is a highly risky task, investors and portfolio managers need accurate predicting systems. However, financial assets time series are nonlinear and non-stationary. Therefore, they mostly follow a noisy path. The nonlinearity implies that asset prices do not follow a linear pattern, and non-stationary implies that their dynamics change over time. As a result,

sophisticated systems were proposed to model the underlying financial time series by capturing the above patterns in order to provide accurate forecasts (Lahmiri, 2013, 2014a, 2014b, 2014c; Lahmiri & Boukadoum, 2014a, 2014b; Lahmiri, Boukadoum, & Chartier, 2014a, 2014b; Lahmiri & Boukadoum, 2015a, 2015b). In the 2000s, nonlinear and adaptive forecasting models such as artificial neural networks (ANNs) have become popular intelligent systems widely used in stock

DOI: 10.4018/978-1-4666-8833-9.ch004

market modeling and forecasting (Zimmermann, Neuneier & Grothmann, 2001; Yao & Tan, 2000; Atsalakis & Valavanis, 2009; Huang & Wu, 2010; Hsieh, Hsiaso & Yeh, 2011; Wang et al, 2011). In general, previous works (Zimmermann, Neuneier & Grothmann, 2001; Yao & Tan, 2000; Atsalakis & Valavanis, 2009a) have shown that ANNs were superior to traditional statistical models such as the well known auto-regressive integrated moving average (ARIMA) models (Box & Jenkins, 1970). Indeed, ARIMA models are based on the assumptions that the time series are stationary and that the errors of the model are normally distributed. Unfortunately, financial data do not meet those criteria and, as a result, the techniques based on statistical approaches could not provide accurate financial forecasts. However, the ANN systems suffer several disadvantages, namely dependency on network architecture, type of transfer function, parameters choice, and being considered as a black-box.

To overcome these disadvantages, hybrid soft computing systems were proposed in the literature. These systems combine synergistically ANNs and other soft computing models to obtain complementary hybrid intelligent system models. For instance, genetic algorithms (Goldberg, 1989) were proposed to automatically optimize the topology and parameters of ANNs (Yao, 1999), and fuzzy logic (Zadeh, 1965) was incorporated into ANN resulting in adaptive neuro-fuzzy inference system (ANFIS) (Jang, 1993). In particular, in one hand ANN is capable to recognize patterns and adapt to data. On the other hand, fuzzy inference systems incorporate human knowledge and expertise to make fuzzy inference and decision (Jang, 1993; Atsalakis & Valavanis, 2009b).

This study compares three artificial neural network architectures for the prediction of next day individual stock price using past values. The three soft computing models used are the ANFIS, and two types of recurrent neural networks which are genetically optimized; namely the time delay neural network (TDNN) (Kim, 1998; Saad et al,

1998) and the adaptive time delay neural network (ATDNN) (Kim, 1998; Saad et al, 1998). The ANFIS was chosen thanks to its hybridization of linguistic and numerical techniques, its fast convergence due to its hybrid learning algorithm, and its ability to generate rule-based explicative models. In addition, ANFIS can model non linear functions and has been reported to achieve higher accuracy than classical statistical models (Tan, 1997; Taha & Ghosh, 1999; Yao, 1999; Jang, 1993). The TDNN and ATNN were considered because recurrent feedback in the network is a positive factor to predict financial time series (McCluskey, 1993; Castiglione, 2001) since they have a long memory than the general feed-forward neural network. Indeed, recurrent networks possess two specific features: a rudimentary memory and capability to exhibit internal chaotic behavior (Karray & De Silva, 2004). Therefore, they may capture the chaotic behavior of financial time series and are suitable to be adopted as forecasting systems since empirical finance have found that stock returns time series are chaotic (Brock, Hsieh & LeBaron, 1991; Hsieh, 1991; Blank, 1992; Decoster, Labys & Mitchell, 1992; Frank & Stengos, 1988). Furthermore, a little attention has been given to the use TDNN and ATDNN for financial time series prediction. Indeed, most of previous works dealing with the applications of recurrent networks in finance employed the well known partially recurrent networks such as the Elman network (Elman, 1990) and the Jordan's sequential network (Jordan, 1986). In addition, a comparison with ANFIS has not been considered in the literature. Such comparison may help international investors choose the right ANN type to be used in international portfolio management.

Since choosing the architecture of a neural network is often subjective and depends on the experimenter's experience, a genetic algorithm (GA) is incorporated into the architectures of TDNN and ATDNN to optimize their respective designs. This includes finding the optimal topology in terms of the numbers of hidden layers and processing elements. In this respect, the GA tends to converge to optimal or near-optimal solutions.

All three neural systems rely on daily observations to predict stock prices. The choice of using daily observations is meant to maximize the number of observations, thereby achieving a consistent learning process. The second reason is related to the importance that the ability to predict future daily stock price has for both short term investment and tactical asset allocation. Ten international stock markets were concerned in this study to better generalize the results. They are the CAC40, DAX, FTSE, Hang Seng, KOSPI, NASDAQ, NIKKEI, S&P500, TSE, and Taiwan stock market price index. For each international financial market, the residual mean squared errors (RMSE) from forecasts are computed and compared.

The remainder of the paper is organized as follows. First, we present a brief summary of previous works dealing with hybrid intelligent systems with application in financial prediction. Second, we describe the prediction systems used in the study; namely the GA-TDNN, GA-ATDNN, and ANFIS. Third, we describe the data and discuss the experimental findings. Fourth, we present future works. Finally, conclusions are given.

BACKGROUND

According to the efficient market hypothesis (Fama, 1965; Fama, 1970; LeRoy, 1989; Lo & MacKinley, 1999), flow of information is immediately reflected in stock prices and prices fully reflect all known information. As a result, price changes are unpredictable and random. More generally speaking, the efficient market hypothesis suggests that making profits from predicting price movements is a very difficult task and is also unlikely. Empirically, there is no real answer to whether stock prices follow a random walk. However, there is increasing evidence they do not. In particular, the efficient market hypothesis

is seriously criticized within economic and financial academic community (Shiller, 2003; Malkiel, 2003). In addition, several studies demonstrated that soft computing techniques are accurate in stock market prediction; hence, one can conclude that they do not follow a random walk (Atsalakis & Valavanis, 2009a).

Indeed, in the last decade, there have been active researches on designing hybrid soft computing systems for financial forecasting purpose. Indeed, the literature is abundant, however recent significant works related to our study will be presented. For instance, Kim and Shin (2007) compared the standard ATDNN and TDNN with GA-ATNN and GA-TDNN in detecting temporal patterns for stock market prediction task of the daily Korea Stock Price Index 200 (KOSPI 200) from January 1997 to December 1999. The experimental results showed the effectiveness of the hybrid approach with ATDNN and TDNN using GA for the prediction of KOSPI. Indeed, they showed that the accuracy of GA-ATDNN and GA-TDNN is higher than that of the standard ATDNN and TDNN. Quah (2008) compared the performance of three soft computing models: the multi-layer perceptron (MLP), adaptive neuro-fuzzy inference systems (ANFIS), and the general growing and pruning radial basis function (GGAP-RBF). Using the Dow Jones Industrial Average (DJIA) data set from 1995 to 2004, the experimental results indicated that GGAP-RBF has huge time complexity as compared to MLP and ANFIS. In addition, the GGAP-RBF does not out-perform the MLP and ANFIS in terms of accuracy. Atsalakis and Valavanis (2009b) used ANFIS to predict daily prices of five stocks listed in Athens Stock Market, and four stocks listed in the New York Stock Exchange (NYSE) based on historical prices. Using data from 2 January 1986 to 31 May 2006, the experimental results indicated that ANFIS outperforms the buy and hold strategy. They concluded that accurate predictions of stock price trends are achievable using historical data and ANFIS.

Recently, Huang and Wu (2010) used the discrete wavelet transform to analyze financial time series including the NASDAQ (US), S&P500 (US), CAC40 (France), FTSE100 (UK), DAX30 (Germany), MIB40 (Italy), TSX60 (Canada), NK225 (Japan), TWSI (Taiwan) and the KOSPI (South Korea); all index data were for period from January 2004 to December 2005. Recurrent Self-Organizing Map (RSOM) neural network was used for partitioning and storing temporal context of the feature space. Finally, a multiple kernel partial least square regression was used for forecasting purpose. The simulation results indicated that the presented model achieved the lowest root mean squared forecasting errors in comparison with neural networks, pure support vector machines or the well known traditional general autoregressive conditional heteroskedasticity (GARCH) model. Hsieh et al. (2011) applied the wavelet decomposition to analyze the stock price time series of the Dow Jones Industrial Average Index (DJIA), London FTSE-100 Index (FTSE), Tokyo Nikkei-225 Index (Nikkei), and Taiwan Stock Exchange Capitalization Weighted Stock Index (TAIEX); all index data were for period from 1997 to 2008. Then, they used a recurrent neural network (RNN) to perform forecasting task. The Artificial Bee Colony algorithm (ABC) was adopted to optimize the RNN weights and biases. The authors concluded that the proposed system is highly promising based on the obtained simulation results.

In their more recent study, Kao et al. (2013) integrated wavelet transform, multivariate adaptive regression splines (MARS), and support vector regression (SVR) (called Wavelet-MARS-SVR) to improve the forecast accuracy. The performance of the proposed method was evaluated by comparing the forecasting results of Wavelet-MARS-SVR with other five competing approaches; including the Wavelet-SVR, Wavelet-MARS, ARIMA, SVR and ANFIS. In order to evaluate the performance of the proposed Wavelet-MARS-SVR forecasting model, they used two emerging daily stock market indexes; namely the Composite index of China (SSEC) (2006/4/18 to 2010/4/1) and Bovespa index of Brazil (2006/3/14 to 2010/4/1). In addition, two mature daily stock market indexes were considered for comparison purpose; including the United States Dow Jones (DJ) index (2006/4/12 to 2010/4/1) and the Nikkei 225 index of Japan (2006/3/3 to 2010/4/1). The empirical study showed that the Wavelet-MARS-SVR outperformed all the other competing models considered in the study. In general, previous works concluded that hybrid intelligent systems are effective tools in stock market modeling and forecasting.

The purpose of this study is to compare two classes of hybrid intelligent systems in stock market modeling and forecasting. The first one hybridizes genetic algorithms with ANN for architecture optimization purpose. The obtained systems are the GA-ATDNN and GA-TDNN. The second class hybridizes fuzzy logic and ANN to make the later not only adaptive to ambiguous, uncertain and imprecise information, but also to make the information processing of the ANN explainable through rules and fuzzy inference. Indeed, incorporating fuzziness allows ANN controlling decision making in uncertainty. The contributions of this comparative study follow. First, unlike (Kim, 1988; Saad et al, 1998; Kim & Shin, 2007) where only a single market was considered we use a large set of international stock markets to examine the effectiveness of GA-ATDNN and GA-TDNN in financial time series prediction. Second, the same contribution applies to ANFIS as opposed to the work done in Atsalakis and Valavanis (2009b) where single stocks were considered. In addition, we enrich the work of Kao et al, (2013) by checking the effectiveness of ANFIS on a larger and more recent data set composed of global international financial markets. Indeed, we aim to validate the effectiveness of the ANFIS, GA-ATDNN, and GA-TDNN at the international level using more recent data. Third, a comparison between recurrent models (GA-ATDNN, GA-TDNN) and ANFIS is

Figure 1. General flowchart of stock market prediction system

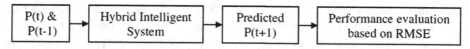

conducted to provide additional insights on the performance of these models, and to enrich the literature on the subject.

In summary, the contribution of this research is a presentation of three hybrid intelligent systems that incorporate fuzzy logic or evolutionary-based algorithms to artificial neural networks with application to different international stock markets forecasting. An obvious benefit of this study is that recurrent neural networks are examined at international level as they posses a rudimentary memory and a capability to exhibit internal chaotic behavior. These characteristics would help these intelligent systems to better capture the dynamics of global financial markets.

METHODS

In this study, each hybrid intelligent system (GA-ATDNN, GA-TDNN, ANFIS) for international stock market modeling and forecasting is trained to generate a one-step-ahead prediction of a given stock market next day's price level. The number of inputs can be a large number of past price levels. However, a large input set yields a serious computational burden with no guarantee of improvement in accuracy, unless an input selection scheme is employed. However, the optimal selection of historical inputs is out of the scope of this paper. As a result, the inputs to the hybrid intelligent systems under study are the current and previous levels of the actual stock price as it has been shown to be effective (Kim & Shin, 2007; Atsalakis & Valavanis, 2009b). In addition, this scheme is adopted because of fast convergence

of all systems, and particularly for ANFIS. The time delay neural network (TDNN), the adaptive time delay neural network (ATDNN), genetic algorithms (GA), ANFIS, and performance measure are described next.

TDNN and ATNN

Unlike the multilayer perceptron (MLP) (Rumelhart et al, 1996), recurrent neural networks are dynamic and possess a memory to perform temporal processing of the input space. In this paper, two types of recurrent neural networks are considered: the time delay neural network (TDNN) and the adaptive time delay neural network (ATDNN) (Kim, 1998; Saad et al, 1998). Like the MLP, TDNN has feed forward connections, but has multiple connections between the individual neurons: each neuron consists of the outputs of earlier neurons during both the current time epoch and fixed number of previous ones (*t-1, t-2,...,t-n*). Then, each neuron possesses a memory to remember previous layer outputs for *n* periods of time. On the other hand, the ATDNN is an extension of the TDNN where time delay values as well as weights are adapted during the training phase. Consequently, ATDNN features a better accommodation of temporal sequences and allows for flexible optimization (Yen, 1994).

Similar to the MLP, TDNN and ADNN all use the back-propagation algorithm optimized based on the gradients method. In particular, the adaptation of the weights is derived based on the gradient descent method and error back-propagation to minimize the error function E given by:

$$E = \frac{1}{2} \sum_{j=1}^{k_j} \left(d_j - y_j \right)^2 \qquad (1)$$

Here, y_j and d_j are the actual and the desired output in each node j respectively. The error is then back-propagated by the gradient descent through the network by adjusting the new weights according to this equation:

$$\Delta W(t) = -\gamma \frac{\partial E}{\partial W} + \alpha \Delta W(t-1) \qquad (2)$$

where ΔW is the weight change at time t and the parameters γ and α are respectively the learning rate and the momentum coefficient. This latter, makes the convergence faster and the training more stable.

Genetic Algorithms

The genetic algorithm (Goldberg, 1989) is used to automatically optimize the architectures of TDNN and ATDNN. In a GA, each solution to a problem is called an individual and the solutions are coded as a string of bits or real values. A set of solutions is called a population. Therefore, the GA is a population-based technique because instead of operating on a single potential solution, it uses a population of potential solutions. Thus, the larger the population, the greater the diversity of the members composing the population; but unfortunately, the larger the domain searched by the population.

The GA was chosen for three reasons. First, the architectural design is crucial to the success of a network's information processing capabilities (Yao, 1999). Second, genetic search provides an advantage over expert experience in building neural networks and also over constructive and destructive algorithms (Yao, 1999). Finally, genetic algorithms allow the convergence speed of artificial neural networks to be faster because of

the search multiple initial states and the effect of mutation operations (Goldberg, 1989).

The process of a genetic algorithm is iterative and consists of the following steps:

1. Create an initial population of genotypes which are a genetic representation of neural networks, and network architectures are randomly selected.
2. Train and test the neural networks to determine how fit they are by calculating the fitness measure of each trained network i. The fitness function is calculated as: $f_i = 1/MSE_i$, where MSE is the mean squared error.
3. Compare the fitness of the networks and keep the best top 10 for future use.
4. Select better networks from each completed population by applying the selection operator.
5. Refill the population back to the defined size.
6. Mate the genotypes by exchanging genes (features) of the networks.
7. Randomly mutate the genotypes according to a given probability.
8. Return back to step 2 and continue this process until stopping criteria (RMSE $< \varepsilon$) is reached.

The initial parameters of the neural networks to be optimized are described in Table 1.

The Adaptive Neuro-Fuzzy Inference System

The ANFIS is a hybrid system between the multilayer perceptron (MLP) neural network and a fuzzy logic inference system. This hybridization between linguistic and numerical techniques allows achieving higher accuracy (Tan, 1997; Taha & Ghosh, 1999), hence the choice of ANFIS to model daily stock prices in this work. It consists

Table 1. GA initial parameters set

Hidden layers	maximum 2
Neurons by each hidden layer	maximum 8
Activation functions	sigmoid, tanh and linear
Size of initial population	30
Selection	0.50%
Refill	cloning
Mating	tail swap
Mutations	random exchange at 0.25%
Number of passes	20 to 50
Learning rate	0.4 to 0.1
Momentum rate	0.3 to 0.1
Hidden layers	maximum 2

of a five layer feed-forward network that can automatically learn input-output fuzzy mapping rules and membership functions from training data. For instance, the ANFIS learns the input-output mapping as a set of if-then fuzzy rules of the form:

If

X_1 is A_1 and X_2 is A_2 ...and X_n is A_n,

Then

$$f = c + \sum_{i=1}^{n} p_i X_i \qquad (3)$$

where X_i are the inputs, A_i are linguistic values, f is the scalar output, and p_i and c are system parameters. The truth value of each antecedent in the previous statement is determined via a membership function. This study uses the generalized bell membership function which is specified by three parameters $\{a, b, c\}$ and defined as follows:

$$B(x; a, b, c) = \frac{1}{1 + \left| \dfrac{x - c}{a} \right|^{2b}} \qquad (4)$$

The generalized bell membership function is shown in Figure 2 where parameters a, b, and c are respectively set to 2, 4, and 6. Figure 3 shows the ANFIS architecture. Each neuron in first layer represents a given input; for instance $p(t-1)$ or $p(t)$. In the second layer, these inputs are processed with the membership function to obtain fuzzy inputs (inputmf). Then, fuzzy rules are generated to obtain the fuzzy outputs (outputmf) in the fourth layer. Finally, all fuzzy outputs are aggregated in a linear form to obtain the predicted future price $p(t+1)$.

Finally, each hybrid intelligent system is evaluated based on the popular root mean of squared errors (Atsalakis & Valavanis, 2009a, 2009b) given by:

$$RMSE = \left(N^{-1} \sum_{t=1}^{N} \left(F_t - R_t \right)^2 \right)^{0.5} \qquad (5)$$

where R_t and F_t are respectively the observed price and the forecasted price over the testing (out-of-sample) period; for example $t = 1$ to N.

DATA AND EXPERIMENTAL RESULTS

The dataset used in this paper includes ten international stock markets from January 3rd 2000 to December 31st 2012 all obtained from Yahoo finance official website. They are the CAC40 (France), DAX (Germany), FTSE (UK), Hang Seng (Hong Kong), KOSPI (South Korea), NASDAQ (USA), NIKKEI (Japan), S&P500 (USA), TSE (Canada), and Taiwan stock market price index. Figures 4, 5, and 6 exhibit respectively the price level of each international stock market. In this study, we used 80% of first observations for learning and remaining 20% for testing and computing RMSE.

Table 2 provides the obtained RMSE for each hybrid intelligent system. It is shown that the GA-TDNN outperforms GA-ATDNN in fore-

Figure 2. Bell membership function

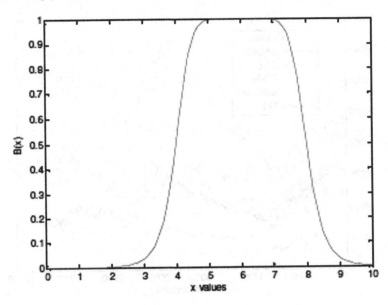

Figure 3. Structure of ANFIS with two inputs x and y

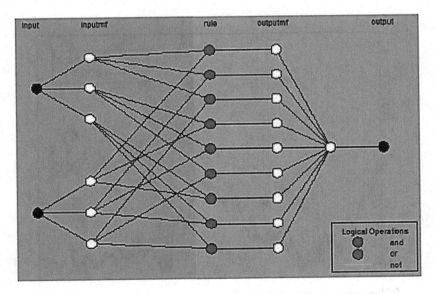

casting future value of all international markets; except in the case of S&P500 where the RMSE of GA-TDNN is slightly superior to the one of GA-ATDNN. For instance, the difference between the RMSE of each one is only 0.0399. As a result, this finding is not in accordance with Kim and Shin (2007) where GA-ATDNN was found to be superior to GA-TDNN in forecasting the KOSPI from 1997 to 1999.

In addition, the experimental results presented in Table 2 show that the ANFIS provided more accurate forecasts than GA-TDNN and

Figure 4. Taiwan, CAC40, DAX, FTSE, NASDAQ, and TSE price levels

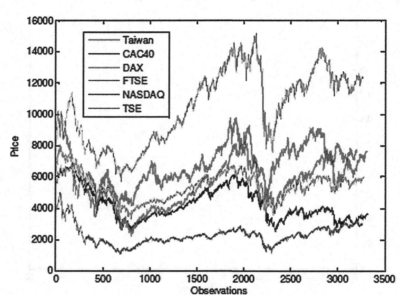

Figure 5. Hang Seng and NIKKEI price levels

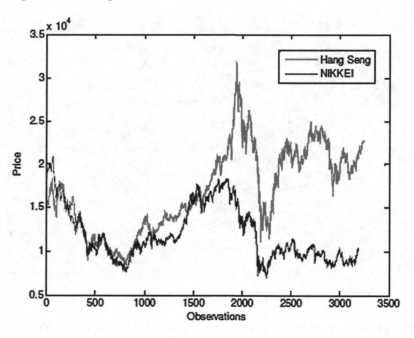

GA-ATDNN; except in the prediction of DAX, KOSPI, and NASDAQ future prices. Moreover, the difference in terms of RMSE between ANFIS and time delay based systems are large for CAC40, FTSE, Hang Seng, NIKKEI, Taiwan, and TSE. This fact suggests that input-output fuzzy mapping allows smoothing the errors; thus obtaining accurate forecasts. Indeed, Figure 7 shows how

Figure 6. KOSPI and S&P500 price levels

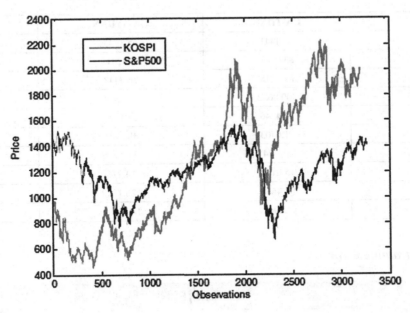

Figure 7. ANFIS fuzzy surface

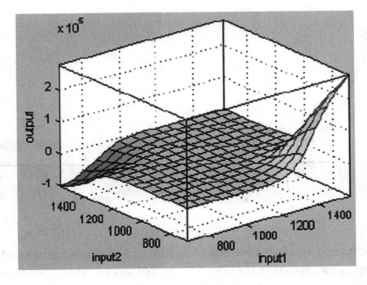

the fuzzy surface of ANFIS is smooth. In this figure, input1, input2, and output are respectively $p(t-1)$, $p(t)$, and $p(t+1)$. The computational time for training the GA-TDNN or GA-ATDNN is 24mn, and it is 2mn for the ANFIS on 1.6GHz CPU. For instance, Figure 8 exhibits the evolution of the training RMSE and the step size according to the number of epochs for ANFIS. It indicates that after 35 epochs, the lowest and stable RMSE is achieved. This illustrates how the ANFIS is fast. Finally, the large difference in terms of RMSE can be explained by the computational complexity to obtain optimal topology and parameters because of infinite number of possible combinations.

Table 2. Out-of-sample RMSE

	GA-TDNN	GA-ATDNN	ANFIS
CAC40	55.4441	65.1943	50.4768
DAX	83.0308	118.2915	91.2346
FTSE	65.1118	76.7443	61.9036
Hang Seng	309.8632	347.367	262.2504
KOSPI	19.4246	26.1095	26.0758
NASDAQ	31.6403	38.2901	33.772
NIKKEI	155.3741	194.6829	120.7484
S&P500	15.0159	14.976	14.1293
Taiwan	98.4665	126.1142	86.6865
TSE	132.0427	149.8597	115.4734

Figure 8. ANFIS training error

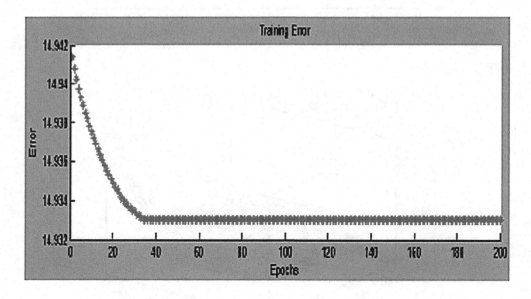

In summary, the obtained results show that GA-TDNN provides better forecasts than the GA-ATDNN. In addition, they suggest that ANFIS is a promising tool for international stock market forecasting.

FUTURE RESEARCH DIRECTIONS

Future works should deal with the following issues. The first one is about the generalization of the results by using active and poorly traded individual stocks. The second issue should consider the optimization of parameters and topology of the intelligent systems using heuristic optimization algorithms to better improve the accuracy of the predictive systems. Finally, the third issue will deal with design of other hybrid intelligent systems that combines soft computing methods and statistical models.

CONCLUSION

In recent years, a large attention has been given to the design of hybrid intelligent systems for stock market prediction. In this paper, two types of recurrent neural networks optimized with genetic algorithms and the adaptive neuro-fuzzy inference systems (ANFIS) are tested on a large set of international stock markets for better generalization of the experimental results. Contrary to the literature, it is found that GA-TDNN provides accurate forecasts than the GA-ATDNN. They were in general slow to converge mainly because of the complexity of the domain of search for optimal solution. In addition, ANFIS is found to be superior to both GA-TDNN and GA-ATDNN in forecasting most of the international stock markets considered in this study. Hence, it is concluded that ANFIS could be a promising system for financial markets modeling and prediction.

REFERENCES

Atsalakis, G. S., & Valavanis, K. P. (2009a). Surveying stock market forecasting techniques – Part II: Soft computing methods. *Expert Systems with Applications*, *36*(3), 5932–5941. doi:10.1016/j.eswa.2008.07.006

Atsalakis, G. S., & Valavanis, K. P. (2009b). Forecasting stock market short-term trends using a neuro-fuzzy based methodology. *Expert Systems with Applications*, *36*(7), 10696–10707. doi:10.1016/j.eswa.2009.02.043

Blank, S. C. (1992). Chaos in futures markets? a nonlinear dynamical analysis. *Journal of Futures Markets*, *11*(6), 711–728. doi:10.1002/fut.3990110606

Box, G., & Jenkins, G. (1970). *Time Series Analysis: Forecasting and Control*. Holden-Day.

Brock, W. A., Hsieh, D., & LeBaron, B. (1991). *Nonlinear Dynamics, Chaos, and Instability: Statistical Theory and Economic Evidence*. Cambridge, MA: MIT Press.

Castiglione, F. (2001). Forecasting Price Increments Using an Artificial Neural Network. *Advances in Complex Systems*, *3*(01), 45–56. doi:10.1142/S0219525901000097

Decoster, G. P., Labys, W. C., & Mitchell, D. W. (1992). Evidence of chaos in commodity futures prices. *Journal of Futures Markets*, *12*(3), 291–305. doi:10.1002/fut.3990120305

Elman, J. L. (1990). Finding structure in time. *Cognitive Science*, *14*(2), 179–211. doi:10.1207/s15516709cog1402_1

Fama, E. F. (1965). The behaviour of stock market prices. *The Journal of Business*, *38*(1), 34–106. doi:10.1086/294743

Fama, E. F. (1970). Efficient capital markets: A review of theory and empirical work. *The Journal of Finance*, *25*(2), 383–417. doi:10.2307/2325486

Frank, M. Z., & Stengos, T. (1988). Some evidence concerning macroeconomic chaos. *Journal of Monetary Economics*, *22*(3), 423–438. doi:10.1016/0304-3932(88)90006-2

Goldberg, D. E. (1989). *Genetic Algorithm in Search, Optimization, and Machine Learning*. Addison Wesley.

Hsieh, D. (1991). Chaos and nonlinear dynamics: Applications to financial markets. *The Journal of Finance*, *46*(5), 1839–1878. doi:10.1111/j.1540-6261.1991.tb04646.x

Hsieh, T.-J., Hsiaso, H.-F., & Yeh, W.-C. (2011). Forecasting stock markets using wavelet transforms and recurrent neural networks: An integrated system based on artificial bee colony algorithm. *Applied Soft Computing*, *11*(2), 2510–2525. doi:10.1016/j.asoc.2010.09.007

Huang, S.-C., & Wu, T.-K. (2010). Integrating recurrent SOM with wavelet-based kernel partial least square regressions for financial forecasting. *Expert Systems with Applications, 37*(8), 5698–5705. doi:10.1016/j.eswa.2010.02.040

Jang, J. S. R. (1993). ANFIS: Adaptive-network-based fuzzy inference system. *IEEE Transactions on Systems, Man, and Cybernetics, 23*(3), 665–685. doi:10.1109/21.256541

Jordan, M. I. (1986). Attractor dynamics and parallelism in a connectionist sequential machine, *Proceedings of the Eighth Annual IEEE Conference of the Cognitive Science Society*, New York, 53, 1-520.

Kao, L.-J., Chiu, C.-C., Lu, C.-J., & Chang, C.-H. (2013). A hybrid approach by integrating wavelet-based feature extraction with MARS and SVR for stock index forecasting. *Decision Support Systems, 54*(3), 1228–1244. doi:10.1016/j.dss.2012.11.012

Karray, F. O., & De Silva, C. (2004). *Soft Computing and Intelligent Systems Design: Theory, Tools and Applications*. Pearson Education.

Kim, H.-J., & Shin, K.-S. (2007). A hybrid approach based on neural networks and genetic algorithms for detecting temporal patterns in stock markets. *Applied Soft Computing, 7*(2), 569–576. doi:10.1016/j.asoc.2006.03.004

Kim, S. S. (1998). Time-delay recurrent neural network for temporal correlations and prediction. *Neurocomputing, 20*(1-3), 253–263. doi:10.1016/S0925-2312(98)00018-6

Lahmiri, S. (2013). Forecasting S&P500 Directions using Wavelets and Support Vector Machines. *International Journal of Strategic Decision Sciences, 4*, 78–88. doi:10.4018/jsds.2013010105

Lahmiri, S. (2014a). Entropy-based technical analysis indicators selection for CAC40 fluctuations prediction using support vector machines. *Fluctuation and Noise Letters, 13*. doi:10.1142/S0219477514500138

Lahmiri, S. (2014b). Improving forecasting accuracy of the S&P500 intra-day price direction using both wavelet low and high frequency coefficients. *Fluctuation and Noise Letters, 13*(01), 1450008. doi:10.1142/S0219477514500084

Lahmiri, S. (2014c). Wavelet low and high frequency components as features to predict stock prices with backpropagation neural networks. *Journal of King Saud University - Computer and Information Sciences, 26*, 218-227.

Lahmiri, S., & Boukadoum, M. (2015a). An Ensemble System Based on hybrid EGARCH-ANN with Different Distributional Assumptions to Predict S&P500 Intraday Volatility. *Fluctuation and Noise Letters, 14*(01), 1550001. doi:10.1142/S0219477515500017

Lahmiri, S., & Boukadoum, M. (2015b). Intelligent ensemble forecasting system of stock market fluctuations based on symmetric and asymmetric wavelet functions. *Fluctuation and Noise Letters*, 1550033. doi:10.1142/S0219477515500339

Lahmiri, S., Boukadoum, M., & Chartier, S. (2014a). A supervised classification system of financial data based on wavelet packet and neural networks. *International Journal of Strategic Decision Sciences, 4*(4), 72–84. doi:10.4018/ijsds.2013100105

Lahmiri, S., Boukadoum, M., & Chartier, S. (2014b). Exploring Information Categories and Artificial Neural Networks Numerical Algorithms in S&P500 Trend Prediction: A Comparative Study. *International Journal of Strategic Decision Sciences, 5*(1), 76–94. doi:10.4018/IJSDS.2014010105

LeRoy, S. F. (1989). Efficient capital markets and martingales. *Journal of Economic Literature*, *27*, 1538–1621.

Lo, A. W., & MacKinley, A. C. (1999). *A nonrandom walk down Wall Street*. Princeton: Princeton University Press.

Malkiel, B. G. (2003). The Efficient Market Hypothesis and Its Critics. *The Journal of Economic Perspectives*, *17*(1), 59–82. doi:10.1257/089533003321164958

McCluskey, P. C. (1993). *Feedforward and Recurrent Neural Networks and Genetic Programs for Stock Market and Time Series Forecasting* [Master's thesis]. Brown University, USA.

Quah, T.-S. (2008). DJIA stock selection assisted by neural network. *Expert Systems with Applications*, *35*(1-2), 50–58. doi:10.1016/j.eswa.2007.06.039

Rumelhart, D. E., Hinton, G. E., & Williams, R. J. (1996). Learning representations by back-propagating errors. *Nature*, *323*(6088), 533–536. doi:10.1038/323533a0

Saad, E., Prokhorov, D., & Wunsch, D. (1998). Comparative study of stock trend prediction using time delay, recurrent and probabilistic neural networks. *IEEE Transactions on Neural Networks*, *9*(6), 1456–1470. doi:10.1109/72.728395 PMID:18255823

Shiller, R. J. (2003). From Efficient Markets Theory to Behavioral Finance. *The Journal of Economic Perspectives*, *17*(1), 83–104. doi:10.1257/089533003321164967

Taha, T. A., & Ghosh, J. (1999). Symbolic interpretation of artificial neural networks. *IEEE Transactions on Knowledge and Data Engineering*, *11*(3), 448–468. doi:10.1109/69.774103

Tan, H. (1997). Cascade ARTMAP: Integrating neural computation and symbolic knowledge processing. *IEEE Transactions on Neural Networks*, *8*(2), 237–250. doi:10.1109/72.557661 PMID:18255628

Wang, J.-Z., Wang, J.-J., Zhang, Z.-G., & Guo, S.-P. (2011). Forecasting stock indices with back propagation neural network. *Expert Systems with Applications*, *38*, 14346–14355.

Yao, J., & Tan, C. L. (2000). A case study on using neural networks to perform technical forecasting of Forex. *Neurocomputing*, *34*(1-4), 79–98. doi:10.1016/S0925-2312(00)00300-3

Yao, X. (1999). Evolving Artificial Neural Networks. *Proceedings of the IEEE*, *87*(9), 1423–1447. doi:10.1109/5.784219

Yen, G. (1994). Adaptive time-delay neural control in space structural platforms. Proceedings of *IEEE World Congress on Computational Intelligence* (Vol. 4, pp. 2622-2627). doi:10.1109/ICNN.1994.374635

Zadeh, L. A. (1965). Fuzzy sets. *Information and Control*, *8*(3), 338–353. doi:10.1016/S0019-9958(65)90241-X

Zimmermann, H., Neuneier, R., & Grothmann, R. (2001). Multi-agent modeling of multiple FX-markets by neural networks. *IEEE Transactions on Neural Networks*, *12*(4), 35–743. doi:10.1109/72.935087 PMID:18249909

ADDITIONAL READING

Adhikari, R., & Agrawal, R. K. (2014). A combination of artificial neural network and random walk models for financial time series forecasting. *Neural Computing & Applications*, *24*(6), 1441–1449. doi:10.1007/s00521-013-1386-y

Alpaydin, E. (2004). *Introduction to machine learning*. MIT press.

Chen, M.-Y., Chen, D.-R., Fan, M.-H., & Huang, T.-Y. (2013). International transmission of stock market movements: An adaptive neuro-fuzzy inference system for analysis of TAIEX forecasting. *Neural Computing & Applications*, 23(S1Suppl 1), S369–S378. doi:10.1007/s00521-013-1461-4

Dunis, C. L., Rosillo, R., de la Fuente, D., & Pino, R. (2013). Forecasting IBEX-35 moves using support vector machines. *Neural Computing & Applications*, 23(1), 229–236. doi:10.1007/s00521-012-0821-9

Haykin, S. (1999). *Neural networks, a comprehensive foundation*. Prentice Hall.

Jones, M. T. (2008). *Artificial intelligence: A systems approach*. Jones & Bartlett Learning.

Lahmiri, S. (2013). Do MENA stock market returns follow a random walk process? *International Journal of Industrial Engineering Computations*, 4(1), 165–172. doi:10.5267/j.ijiec.2012.11.005

Lahmiri, S. (2014). Multi-scaling analysis of the S&P500 under different regimes in wavelet domain. *International Journal of Strategic Decision Sciences*, 5(2), 43–55. doi:10.4018/ijsds.2014040104

Lu, S. (2013). Hybridizing nonlinear independent component analysis and support vector regression with particle swarm optimization for stock index forecasting. *Neural Computing & Applications*, 23(7-8), 2417–2427. doi:10.1007/s00521-012-1198-5

Negnvitsky, M. (2004). *Artificial intelligence, a guide to intelligent systems*. USA: Addison Wesley.

Rosillo, R., Giner, J., & de la Fuente, D. (2014). *The effectiveness of the combined use of VIX and Support Vector Machines on the prediction of S* (p. 500). Neural Comput & Applic; doi:10.1007/s00521-013-1487-7

KEY TERMS AND DEFINITIONS

Artificial Neural Network: An artificial neural network is an information processing system which is inspired by the human nervous system for information processing. It can be trained to simulate a number of outputs in response to provided inputs.

Backpropagation Algorithm: It is a training algorithm for artificial neural network based on calculation of the gradient of a loss function to optimize weights in neural network.

Fuzzy Logic: It is a type of reasoning designed to mathematically represent uncertainty and vagueness where logical statements are not only true or false. Fuzzy logic is a formalized mathematical tool which is useful to deal with imprecise problems.

Genetic Algorithm: It is a stochastic but not random method of search used for optimization or learning. Genetic algorithm is basically a search technique that simulates biological evolution during optimization process.

Learning Algorithm: A learning algorithm is a method used to process data to extract patterns appropriate for application in a new situation. In particular, the goal is to adapt a system to a specific input-output transformation task.

Stock Market: It is a particular market where stocks and bonds are issued by companies and are publically traded.

Chapter 5
Data System–Embedded Guidance Significantly Improves Data Analyses:
When Data Is Made 'Over-the-Counter' for Users

Jenny Grant Rankin
Northcentral University, USA

ABSTRACT

In the field of Education, computerized data systems are used to manage, retrieve, and analyze information. Educators view this information in the form of data reports, which educators use to inform decisions that impact students. These decisions are frequently undermined by misunderstandings concerning the data and its implications. Yet data systems and their reports typically display data without any guidance concerning the data's proper analysis. In a quantitative study, medicine labeling conventions were applied to data systems to embed guidance in the proper use of contents. Among 211 educators of varied backgrounds and roles, data analyses were found to be 307% more accurate when a report label/footer was present, 205% more accurate when a 1-page reference sheet was present, and 273% more accurate when a reference guide was present. Findings hold implications for those who provide or use tools for high-stakes information retrieval, analysis, and/or management, particularly in Education.

INTRODUCTION

Pharmaceutical companies are required by such agencies as the Food and Drug Administration (FDA) to embed usage guidance in the packaging of over-the-counter medication to reduce errors when the medicine is used (DeWalt, 2010). Thus consumers can read the medicine's purpose, ingredients, dosage instructions, and dangers in order to better understand these important details (Kuehn, 2009). Considering how a mistake in medicine use can impact a person's wellbeing, one might expect similar usage guidance on other products that – if used incorrectly – could harm people.

DOI: 10.4018/978-1-4666-8833-9.ch005

In the field of Education, computerized data systems are used to manage, retrieve, and analyze student, educator, and school information. These systems display this data in the form of data reports, which educators view and analyze to make data-informed decisions that impact stakeholders. Essentially, educators use the data to impact students' wellbeing, whether that wellbeing is academic, emotional, behavioral, social, or otherwise. Yet, unlike common over-the-counter products, data systems do not typically embed usage guidance to ensure each data report's content is understood and used appropriately. In fact, many data systems display data for educators without sufficient support to use the systems' contents – data – wisely (Coburn, Honig, & Stein, 2009; Data Quality Campaign [DQC], 2009, 2011; Goodman & Hambleton, 2004; National Forum on Education Statistics [NFES], 2011).

This chapter profiles a quantitative study by Rankin (2013a) in which the concept of making data "over-the-counter" was explored, meaning usage guidance was embedded within the environment in which the data content was viewed and used. The researcher tested the impact on 211 educators and identified formats through which data systems can embed report-specific data usage guidance in order to significantly improve educators' data analysis accuracy. The chapter will provide background on current problems when data systems are used for data analyses, summarize the focus and scope of previous studies conducted, and share the purpose of the Rankin (2013a) study conducted in response. The study's details and findings will then be provided, as well as implications for future research. The chapter's main objective is to provide readers with an understanding of why data systems should offer over-the-counter data, and how this can best be achieved in order to best help students or other stakeholders affected by data-informed decisions facilitated by the data systems.

BACKGROUND

Given the many complexities of education data, particularly assessment data, educators' data-informed decisions are frequently undermined by misunderstandings concerning the data and its implications. Yet data systems and their reports typically display data without any guidance concerning the data's proper analysis. Pharmaceutical label conventions can result in improved understanding on non-medication products, as well (Hampton, 2007; Qin et al., 2011). Thus, in the way over-the-counter medicine's proper use is communicated with a thorough label and sometimes with added documentation, the researcher hypothesized a data system used to analyze student performance could include components to help users better comprehend the data it contains.

A data system, also referred to in education as a student data system, is software that provides student data to educators in a digestible, report-based format (Wayman, 2005), and educators use data systems to make decisions that impact students (VanWinkle, Vezzu, & Zapata-Rivera, 2011). No or poor medication labels have resulted in many tragic errors (Brown-Brumfield & DeLeon, 2010), and the researcher hypothesized that data systems' lack of proper labeling for educators was similarly contributing to poor data understanding and use. Feedback is one of the most powerful influences on student learning and achievement, but this impact can be negative if the performance feedback is not provided in the best way (Hattie & Timperley, 2007).

Although data systems are commonly used to generate data reports, research on aspects of report format and system support that could enhance analysis accuracy is scarce (Goodman & Hambleton, 2004). Previous research that was devoted to ways in which data systems and reports communicate data to educators limited this exploration to participants' preferences and participants' perceived value of supports. However, user preference can be the opposite of the reporting format that actually renders the more accurate interpretation (Hattie, 2010).

The Rankin (2013a) study was used to examine how effective varied analysis supports were in improving data analysis accuracy, and it did not rely on participants' preferences or perceived value of supports. Rather, the research questions were designed to facilitate more specific determinations than previous studies. The study and research questions were thus structured to determine the specific extent to which each form of analysis guidance improves educators' data analysis accuracy, and rendered examples and templates for real-world implementation. The findings of this study filled a gap in education field literature by containing evidence that can be used to identify whether, how, and to what extent data systems can help increase educators' data analysis accuracy by providing analysis support within data systems and their reports. Improvements data system and report providers make in light of this study have the potential to improve the accuracy with which educators analyze the data generated by their data systems. Though study findings cannot automatically be generalized to non-educator populations, applications to non-education data systems used to manage, retrieve, and analyze data should also be considered, as there are likely benefits. More accurate data analyses will likely result in more accurate data-informed decision-making for the benefit of students and other stakeholders.

INNOVATION IN EDUCATION INFORMATION MANAGEMENT AND ANALYSIS

A History of Problems to Remedy

Most teachers and other educators are highly skilled (American Institutes for Research, 2013), well-educated (Papay, Harvard Graduate School of Education, 2007), and intelligent (Hurley, 2012).

Despite this, educators frequently misunderstand and misuse data from data system reports (Hattie, 2010; Wayman, Snodgrass Rangel, Jimerson, & Cho, 2010; Zwick et al., 2008). Educators' data use failures should not be mistaken as primarily the fault of educators, and this chapter will explain the likelier culprit. Nonetheless, in order to better understand the scope of the problem, consider the following timeline of findings concerning educators' data use:

1996:

- In 59 interviews, many of the high-level educators and policymakers who expressed medium to high interest in national student achievement demonstrated limited statistical knowledge, and analysis errors and misunderstandings concerning the data were common (Hambleton & Slater, 1996).

2002:

- Many educators have problems understanding and interpreting assessment report data (Hambleton, 2002).
- Few teacher preparation programs cover topics like state data literacy (Stiggins, 2002).

2004:

- There is clear evidence that many users of assessment reports, such as a large number of teachers, have trouble understanding and interpreting the data these reports contain (Goodman, & Hambleton, 2004).
- Research reveals many educators have difficulty understanding the terminology and ways in which results are displayed in assessment reports (Lukin, Bandalos, Eckhout, & Mickelson, 2004).

- Online data systems reduce time needed to generate data reports, but they still require educators' time in order to know how to act on the data, and lack of such time is limiting the data's use at many sites, as few sites offer this critical component of data-informed decision-making (Ingram, Louis, & Schroeder, 2004).

2006:

- School staff often lacks the ability to interpret data; not all educators have the skills and time needed to successfully use data to inform decisions, and educators' incomplete understanding of statistics can lead them to draw false conclusions from data; in addition, educators often lack the ability and support needed to interpret data and translate it into next steps (Marsh, Pane, & Hamilton, 2006).
- Teachers do not often know how to translate data into action, and this could become the biggest challenge facing effective data use once educators are accessing technology otherwise deemed adequate; also, teachers have very little time for data analysis, and this problem worsens as assessment frequency and complexity increases (Rennie Center for Education Research and Policy, 2006).

2007:

- In a report by the Center on Education Policy (CEP), an examination of CEP survey data of officials in all 50 United States (U.S.), as well as interviews with 15 prominent state education officials from 11 U.S. states, found state-level staff are at varying stages of being able to actually analyze the data their data systems generate (Minnici & Hill, 2007).

2008:

- Only 23%-43% of teachers, depending on the district, reported feeling moderately or very prepared to interpret and use student data (Ikemoto & Marsh, 2008).
- Teachers do not understand or value some data included in data system reports, and teachers have difficulty using data systems to interpret student data, even amongst teachers who serve as assessment coaches to their peers (Underwood, Zapata-Rivera, & VanWinkle, 2008).
- In a mixed-methods Canadian study of over 40 school boards, involving 14,000 student and educator survey responses and several hundred in-depth interviews, challenges to data use was the most frequently mentioned challenge noted by respondents (45%), with many educators noting they had access to data but lacked the knowledge and ability to use the data to drive improvement (Ungerleider, 2008).
- Teachers and administrators must be skilled at using data daily to improve student learning, yet many teachers and administrators do not know fundamental analysis concepts, and 70% have never taken a college or post graduate course in educational measurement (Zwick et al., 2008).

2009:

- Few educators automatically know how to use available data effectively; the majority of stakeholders who need to use data to comprehend and raise student achievement are not trained statisticians, and the vast majority of educators need guidance in order to understand and use data, including how to apply it to decision-making that can help students succeed (DQC, 2009).

- In a study involving districts known for *strong* data use, teachers had difficulty posing questions prompted by data (48%), did not comprehend given data (36%), and incorrectly interpreted data (52%) (U.S. Department of Education Office of Planning, Evaluation and Policy Development [USDEOPEPD], 2009).
- Many educators struggle to understand how to translate data into specific actions (Cho & Wayman, 2009; Wayman & Cho, 2009).
- Educators in many districts have difficulty using data, and misunderstandings when using a data system can cripple data use in a school district (Wayman, Cho, & Shaw, 2009).

2010:

- Increasing accountability demands have led to the use of more reports, yet not all users of these reports are as test-sophisticated as they need to be (Hattie, 2010).
- One of the main problems with using assessment data is that stakeholders at all levels have trouble interpreting the data; for example, administrators misunderstand the meanings of symbols and terms used in assessment reports and are often confused by the reports' complexity (Underwood, Zapata-Rivera, & VanWinkle, 2010).
- Teachers have frequent difficulties using data (Wayman, Snodgrass Rangel, Jimerson, & Cho, 2010).
- Teachers express a need for easier ways to use data, are overwhelmed by data, and have to work longer hours to use data (Wayman, Snodgrass Rangel, Jimerson, & Cho, 2010).
- Educators' have a propensity for misinterpretation when using data reports (NFES, 2010).

2011:

- If data system users do not understand how to properly analyze data, the data will be used incorrectly if it is used at all (NFES, 2011).
- States are not using student data effectively, and few teacher preparation programs cover topics like state data literacy (Halpin & Cauthen, 2011).
- Few school stakeholders use data to which they have access (Sabbah, 2011).
- Different understandings districts and teachers have concerning the goals of interim assessments may limit teachers' use of assessment data (Shepard, Davidson, & Bowman, 2011).
- In a study of teachers at 13 school districts considered exemplars of active data use, where teachers have access to student data systems and receive support in data-informed decision-making, most teachers struggled when trying to pose questions that could be investigated within the data system; only 37% of teachers demonstrated an understanding of multiple measures; only 18% of teachers studied recognized the impact outliers had on data, which can lead to misinterpretations; many teachers made inaccurate inferences when trying to frame data system queries, make sense of differences, or make sense of trends; and teachers achieved only 48% correct when making data inferences involving basic statistical concepts (USDEOPEPD, 2011).
- Stakeholders including state politicians, superintendents, and education reporters frequently misunderstand and misinterpret national assessment score reports; although administrators are increasingly asked to make data-informed decisions, they also have trouble understanding data presented in score reports (VanWinkle, Vezzu, & Zapata-Rivera, 2011).

2012:

- Teachers often underutilize data systems, finding available data to be unsatisfactory or late, having a hard time locating needed data, not being familiar with the data and how to use it, and finding the system to be hard to use (Cho & Wayman, 2012).
- In some districts, teachers' awareness or perceptions about a data system's available infrastructure and capabilities is not in line with the actual available infrastructure, and a study by the U.S. Department of Education found data systems are frequently of limited use in informing instruction because of limitations in terms of the system's interface or tools (Faria, et al., 2012).
- Three phases of work with Australian teachers' data use rendered findings that data displays can be misunderstood, which can be despairing to staff (Glasswell, 2012).
- States have a long way to go in terms of data system use; only three U.S. states have implemented policies and practices ensuring educators know how to analyze and use data appropriately, and only six states share data on teacher performance with the preparation programs through which they became educators (National Association of States Boards of Education, 2012).

2013:

- School district staff can reject data systems, use them for unintended purposes, or use them for only a small portion of tasks the data systems are capable of performing (Cho & Wayman, 2013).
- According to Vera Turner of The School Superintendents Association, the problem with the many school districts collecting data is they do not understand how to use

the information strategically to increase student achievement (Davis, 2013).

- Through a national survey of 511 educator leaders (51% principals and 49% district administrators) relating to data-informed instruction, it was found that (a) 60% deem district-level support to be "not enough" in all areas of data use, and this perception has worsened when compared to 2 years prior; (b) only 36% believe over 60% of their own district's teachers are actively using data to drive instruction, and this perception has worsened when compared to 2 years prior; and (c) only 16% of teachers are believed to be proficient in data use, and administrators are believed to be about 3 times more proficient, but this is still less than half (Ed Tech Ticker, 2013).
- Most education professionals are not data savvy and they need help understanding and interpreting data before they can make correctly informed decisions; for example, researchers found most of the ways National Assessment of Educational Progress (NAEP) data were used for cause-and-effect claims about policies and interventions were speculative and/or inaccurate (Sawchuk, 2013).
- One problem contributing to New Zealand's historic underachievement of indigenous and ethnic minorities could be lack of data expertise amongst those supporting schools in data use (Schildkamp, Lai, & Earl, 2013).
- The American Association of School Administrators (AASA) reports teachers know data can help them but are overwhelmed by the data and need help using it (Stansbury, 2013).

A review of literature reveals educators are clearly struggling with using data provided by their data systems, and they have been struggling for a long time. Given these problems, many efforts have been devoted to improving educators' abilities to use data. These efforts commonly fall into the categories of professional development (PD) or staff supports, such as site leaders, data teams, data experts, and/or instructional coaches. There is an abundance of evidence these interventions can be implemented effectively and render improvements in educators' data analyses. However, neither approach renders *absolute* success in educators' data use. PD has clear limitations (Lock, 2006; Kidron, 2012; O'Hanlon, 2013; USDEOPEPD, 2011), and staff supports are not foolproof (McDonald, Andal, Brown, & Schneider, 2007; Underwood et al., 2008; Wayman et al., 2010). Even educator preparation programs cannot be counted on for complete data literacy. For example, in a study involving teachers who had taken at least one course in measurement, *all* teachers struggled afterwards with statistical terms and measurement concepts and 60% of teachers had difficulty explaining a term used in a score report (Zapata-Rivera & VanWinkle, 2010). Even in districts where these approaches are utilized, more support is needed for educators using data.

Students are impacted by educators' data-informed decisions, which can improve learning (Sabbah, 2011; Underwood et al., 2010; Wohlstetter, Datnow, & Park, 2008). Likewise, data-*mis*informed decisions can hurt these children and young adults. Yet labeling and tools within data systems to assist analysis are uncommon, even though most educators analyze data alone (USDEOPEPD, 2009). There is clearly a need for research identifying how data reports can better facilitate correct interpretations by their users (Goodman & Hambleton, 2004; Hattie, 2010). The Rankin (2013a) study research questions and findings addressed this need. The power of data systems that generate these reports will not be realized until researchers

contribute to improving data system design to improve analysis (DQC, 2011).

Study on Embedding Usage Guidance within Reporting Environment

The purpose of the experimental, quantitative Rankin (2013a) study was to facilitate causal inferences concerning how different forms of data usage guidance embedded within a data system reporting environment can improve educators' understanding of the data contents. This arrangement of accompanying data system data reports with embedded data analysis guidance was termed *over-the-counter data*. The study was inspired by the way in which different forms of usage guidance embedded within over-the-counter packaging actively facilitate *appropriate* understanding and use of the over-the-counter content.

Variables and Research Questions

Independent variables included three different forms of embedded data analysis guidance, with which only *some* study participants were provided:

- A concise footer was featured at the bottom of the data report to help users understand the report's data.
- A reference sheet accompanied the data report to help users understand the report's data. This single page contained the report's title, description, image, focus (content reported), and warning (vital, cautionary information an educator would need to avoid the most common analysis errors made when analyzing the particular data being displayed). It also communicated the report's purpose (key questions the report will help answer) and additional focus information (intended audience, and format in which data is reported).

- A reference guide accompanied the data report to help users understand and use the report's data. The report's reference sheet (described above) functioned as the guide's first page, and subsequent pages contained the report's instructions (how to read the report), essential questions (showing the user where to look on this report – and what to look for – to answer each question listed in the purpose area of the guide's 1st page), and a "more info" section (offering where to get additional information on related topics).

All three of these data analysis supports held potential to improve educators' data-based conclusions, yet their prospective impact had not yet been measured. Thus research questions, with null and alternative hypotheses for each, were designed to measure the supports' precise impact on educators' data analysis accuracy. An additional research question, with null and alternative hypotheses, was designed to measure the precise impact of any tested support on educators' data analysis accuracy, in terms of exposure to or use of any one of the supports. These questions, and the data analysis performed in conjunction with them, also addressed educators' likelihood of using each of these supports.

Q1: What impact does data analysis guidance accompanying a data system report in the form of footer, reference sheet, or reference guide have on how frequently educators draw accurate conclusions concerning student achievement data?

Q2a: What impact does a footer with analysis guidelines on a data system report have on how frequently educators draw accurate conclusions concerning student achievement data?

Q3a: What impact does providing a report reference sheet, such as a one-page reference sheet with report purpose and data use warnings specific to the report it accompanies, with a data system report have on how frequently educators draw accurate conclusions concerning student achievement data?

Q4a: What impact does providing a reference guide, such as a two-sided reference sheet with analysis guidance and examples specific to the report it accompanies, with a data system report have on how frequently educators draw accurate conclusions concerning student achievement data?

In order to thoroughly adhere to the study's theoretical framework involving behavioral economics, research questions also addressed framing, which was another reason behind the necessity of this study. Thus each of the three data analysis supports investigated in the study were framed in two different formats within the handouts given to participants in the study. This helped the researcher to identify the best way in which to frame analysis support within a data system to specifically improve educators' analyses, which had not yet been determined. Thus research questions, with null and alternative hypotheses for each, were designed to measure the precise impact the supports' framing had on educators' data analysis accuracy. Again, these questions, and the data analysis performed in conjunction with them, also addressed educators' likelihood of using each of these supports.

Q2b: What impact does the manner in which a footer is framed, in terms of moderate differences in length and text color, have on its ability to impact the frequency with which educators draw accurate conclusions concerning student achievement data?

Q3b: What impact does the manner in which a reference sheet is framed, in terms of moderate differences in density and header color, have on its ability to impact the frequency with which educators draw accurate conclusions concerning student achievement data?

Q4b: What impact does the manner in which a reference guide is framed, in terms of moderate differences in length and information quantity, have on its ability to impact the frequency with which educators draw accurate conclusions concerning student achievement data?

The study also featured additional variables that could possibly have impacted educators' likelihood of using the investigated supports and/or educators' data analyses. These were used to help better understand the implications of findings in regards to all the research questions discussed above. These questions, and the data analysis performed in conjunction with them, also addressed educators' likelihood of using each data analysis support. Half of these questions concerned school site demographics:

Q5a: What impact does an educator's school site level type (i.e., elementary or secondary) have on the frequency with which he or she draws accurate conclusions concerning student achievement data?

Q5b: What impact does an educator's school site level (i.e., elementary, middle/junior high, or high school) have on the frequency with which he or she draws accurate conclusions concerning student achievement data?

Q5c: What impact does an educator's school site academic performance, as measured by the 2012 Growth Academic Performance Index (API), which is the California state accountability measure, have on the frequency with which he or she draws accurate conclusions concerning student achievement data?

Q5d: What impact does an educator's school site English Learner (EL) population have on the frequency with which he or she draws accurate conclusions concerning student achievement data?

Q5e: What impact does an educator's school site Socioeconomically Disadvantaged population have on the frequency with which he or she draws accurate conclusions concerning student achievement data?

Q5f: What impact does an educators' school site Students with Disabilities population have on the frequency with which he or she draws accurate conclusions concerning student achievement data?

The other half of these questions concerned educator demographics:

Q6a: What impact does an educator's veteran status have on the frequency with which he or she draws accurate conclusions concerning student achievement data?

Q6b: What impact does an educator's current professional role (e.g., teacher, site/school administrator, etc.) have on the frequency with which he or she draws accurate conclusions concerning student achievement data?

Q6c: What impact does an educator's perception of his or her own data analysis proficiency impact the frequency with which he or she draws accurate conclusions concerning student achievement data?

Q6d: What impact does an educator's professional development over the past year, devoted specifically to how to analyze student data, have on the frequency with which he or she draws accurate conclusions concerning student achievement data?

Q6e: What impact does the number of graduate-level educational measurement courses an educator has taken have on the frequency with which he or she draws accurate conclusions concerning student achievement data?

The study's single dependent variable was accuracy of educators' data analysis-based responses. This accuracy took the form of a percent correct score, which was based on the percent of questions answered correctly when those questions required analysis of given data. Findings from this research can be used to identify how data systems used by educators can help prevent common analysis mistakes by providing analysis support within the interface and the reports they are used to generate. Though study findings cannot automatically be generalized to non-educator populations, findings can likely inspire similar innovations in non-education data systems used to manage, retrieve, and analyze data.

Research Method and Design

The experimental, quantitative study was arranged to examine multiple reporting environments that could be replicated by a data system. It had to show whether educators make analysis errors when using typical data system reports, which do not contain embedded analysis guidance. The researcher also had to compare those results to results for educators using data system reports embedded with data analysis guidance in the varied formats described. The research design also had to allow for framing influences by presenting each of the three data analysis supports in two different formats. This combination of conditions allowed the study to measure the extent to which each embedded analysis support can increase analysis accuracy, as well as the more effective way in which to frame each support.

In addition to regression analyses, the G*Power 3.1 statistical analysis tool was used to conduct a priori analysis in which the necessary sample size was calculated by specifying values for the required significance level α, the desired statistical power 12β, and the population effect size that has yet to be determined (Faul, Erdfelder, Buchner, & Lang, 2009). The researcher conducted a two-tailed t-test to determine the difference between two independent means utilizing the G*Power 3.1 statistical analysis tool. The priori two-tailed t-test resulted in a recommended sample size of

at least 210 educators. The researcher also used G*Power 3.1 to conduct an F-test linear multiple regression analysis, fixed model, R2 deviation from zero. The priori F-test resulted in a recommended sample size of at least 153 educators. Since the 210 sample size from the two-tailed t-test was greater than 153, responses from 211 participants were collected for the study in order to exceed the more rigorous recommendation.

The study employed a random, cross-sectional sampling procedure. The researcher prevented interaction of selection and treatment to avoid threats to external validity by including educators of varied roles and from varied school sites. For example, educators were based at the elementary and secondary levels, veterans and non-veterans, teachers and administrators, etc. The 211-participant size lent itself well to establishing a reliable data sampling, the mix assisted in the stratification of the population, and the randomization provided an appropriately mixed sample that could be generalized to the education population at large.

The quantitative survey method was an appropriate fit for measuring performance on data questions with clear answers, as are regularly encountered by teachers seeking to understand student data. A web-based, self-administered Google Docs survey form was used to collect response data. This allowed for efficient collection without initial interpretation and thus with minimal risk of misunderstanding or accidental alteration by the researcher. However, the researcher was present with participants as they completed the survey in case clarification was needed on how to proceed.

Many educators are intimidated by technology (Combs, 2004; Rodriguez, 2008) or do not use technology as much as others do. For example, only 44% of educators who have access to data systems use these systems directly rather than only reading printed versions of reports others use the data systems to generate for them (Underwood et al., 2008). Thus study participants interacted with printed versions of reports rather than online versions that require use of technology during analysis. Also, technology can prevent someone from demonstrating a skill when he or she lacks computer familiarity (Bennett & Gitomer, 2009; Horkay, Bennett, Allen, Kaplan, & Yan, 2006). Thus the printed reports also allowed for better isolation of study variables considering users' varied technical skills. Since some educators are also intimidated by data (Underwood et al., 2010), reports used in the study also conformed to research-based recommendations concerning the exclusion of intimidating features like jargon and statistical terms that could have a negative priming effect.

An initial pilot test with five educators was used to garner feedback through the survey instrument, as well as verbal feedback from participants on the instrument and completion time. This was done to identify any problems prior to the survey's official administration, though no adjustments were necessary. Pilot test participants were representative of the varied roles and backgrounds of the educators who ultimately served as participants in the study, and the materials they were given varied in order to test all variable types. No participant took longer than 15 minutes to complete the survey, and no part of the survey was deemed confusing or to require change.

Population

The population for which the study was specifically designed consists of public educators of all TK-12 school levels in the U.S.. However, findings can be extended to other populations with a similar makeup. The sample was aligned to many population characteristics, some of which include:

- Highly skilled; for example, 95% of teachers are considered "highly qualified" by No Child Left Behind (NCLB) standards (American Institutes for Research [AIR], 2013), though there is debate concerning this label's merit.

- Well-educated; for example, 99% of American teachers have bachelor's degrees, 48% have master's degrees, and over 7% have more advanced graduate degrees (Papay, Harvard Graduate School of Education, 2007).

- Embracing data use; for example most educators are eager to analyze and then act on the data they see (Hattie, 2010; van der Meij, 2008).

Sample

The sampling procedure for study participants was random and cross-sectional, and responses from 211 educators of all TK-12 school levels were collected to allow for the inclusion of all veteran levels, working in varied roles, and at schools with a range of demographics, such as high versus low performing and varied student populations. All demographic variables were included in the study's multiple regression analysis. Though varied school sites were selected, the procedure for sampling these individuals at those sites was random in order to generalize results to educator populations. The survey session for each group of participants was set up by a school administrator at the school site, but participation at each site was voluntary and thoroughly communicated as such.

The inclusion of varied participants from varied school sites allowed the sample drawn from the population to appropriately match the actual educator population. For example, the sample represented all veteran levels, all credentialed educator roles, all perceived data analysis proficiency levels, all data analysis professional development categories, and all graduate-level educational measurement course categories. Likewise, sites where sample participants worked represented the varied demographics of those nationwide. Data was collected at one point in time for each participant within a 32-day research window of April 8 through May 10, 2013.

Materials and Procedures

Survey questions were designed to measure the accuracy with which educators draw inferences when viewing student performance data contained in report formats typical of most data systems versus reports containing or accompanied by some level of embedded data analysis guidance. The survey was administered in 10 separate sessions in computer labs at nine school sites, as one school site was visited twice to administer the survey to two separate groups.

Each participant reviewed and signed a copy of the Informed Consent Form, which was approved by Northcentral University's Institutional Review Board (IRB), upon arriving at the computer lab. Next, the researcher introduced the study so participants knew key facts such as the nature of the study, anonymity of responses, voluntary nature of participation, lack of penalties if any attendees wished not to participate, and lack of benefits to participating other than contributing to field literature in a way that was hoped to eventually help educators and students. All attendees in all cases opted to participate.

The researcher then handed each participant a different folder containing reports and handouts to view in conjunction with survey questions. There were seven different folder types, each in a different color, and each of these contained a different form of reports and handouts. Folders were stacked ahead of time in the alternating format of white, yellow, green, blue, purple, red, black, then white again, etc. so they were distributed evenly with participants seated as far as possible from participants with the same folder contents.

- White Folders (Control Group with No Added Analysis Supports) Respondents received two plain reports with no footers. Respondents received no reference sheets and no reference guides.

- Green Folders (Footer, Format A): Respondents received two reports with footers that were shorter and slightly less wordy (1st report footer: 39 words, 186 characters without spaces, 224 characters with spaces; 2nd report footer: 34 words, 156 characters without spaces, 228 characters with spaces) than the alternatively-framed footers (given to participants with yellow folders) and contained headings that utilized text color with meaning. Respondents received no reference sheets and no reference guides.

- Yellow Folders (Footer, Format B): Respondents received two footers on their reports that were longer and slightly wordier (1st report footer: 58 words, 269 characters without spaces, 324 characters with spaces; 2nd report footer: 42 words, 199 characters without spaces, 237 characters with spaces) than the alternatively-framed footers (given to participants with green folders) and contained no headings or colored text. Respondents received no reference sheets and no reference guides.

- Purple Folders (Reference Sheet, Format A): Respondents received two plain reports with no footers. They also received two report-specific reference sheets: one for each report. These sheets were less dense and contained less information than the alternatively-framed reference sheets (given to participants with blue folders) and utilized heading color with meaning. Respondents received no reference guides.

- Blue Folders (Reference Sheet, Format B): Respondents received two plain reports with no footers. They also received two report-specific reference sheets: one for each report. These sheets were more dense and contained more information than the alternatively-framed reference sheets (given to participants with purple folders) and did not utilize heading color with meaning. Respondents received no reference guides.

- Black Folders (Reference Guide, Format A): Respondents received two plain reports with no footers. They also received two report-specific reference guides: one for each report. These guides were shorter and contained less information (two pages) than the alternatively-framed guides (three pages, given to participants with red folders) and utilized heading color with meaning. Respondents received no reference sheets.

- Red Folders (Reference Guide, Format B): Respondents received two plain reports with no footers. They also received two report-specific reference guides: one for each report. These guides were longer and contained more information (three pages) than the alternatively-framed guides (two pages, given to participants with black folders) and did not utilize heading color with meaning. Respondents received no reference sheets.

The report sets participants received *all contained the same data*; they merely contained different degrees of embedded data analysis guidance to *accompany* that data, with the control group participants receiving no such added supports. In other words, the graph of data looked identical on every participant's version of Report 1, and the table of data looked identical on every participant's version of Report 2. Keeping the data the same was vital in order to:

- Allow the measurement of each participant's data analysis accuracy to be compared to that of the other participants with parity.
- Ensure the most common incorrect approaches to analyzing the data from each particular assessment on which the data was based did not result in the same an-

swers as the correct approaches to analyzing the data. This prevented educators who were making the most common faulty analyses from being mistaken for educators making correct analyses, and thus the data could remain as indicative as possible of the nature of educators' data analyses.

The researcher called participants' attention to the sticker on the cover of each folder that stated the folder's color in order to accommodate color blind participants. This was important since folder color was used to determine which version of a handout-specific question each participant automatically answered on the survey (Question 8). The researcher also directed participants to two stickers on each folder's two inside pockets, which indicated which materials related to Report 1 and which materials related to Report 2, as this helped participants understand which reports to use when answering particular survey questions. In addition, "Report 1" was also displayed directly on Report 1, and "Report 2" was also displayed directly on Report 2.

The researcher prompted participants to begin the online survey on the computer, which was set to a web address that could not be accessed by anyone who did not have the exact uniform resource locator (URL). This URL was changed after each survey administration.

Survey questions participants answered were as shown in Box 1. The web-based survey used to collect responses was administered in Google Docs, employing the Google Form feature. Since an appropriate survey did not already exist, one was created specifically for this study that included 10 numbered questions. The Google Docs Form tool automatically assigned an anonymous ID to each respondent's data, and this number was used in complete absence of participant names or employee numbers, maintaining respondent anonymity. As soon as it was entered, the data was automatically and securely stored, as well as password-protected, online, and it was removed

Box 1. Survey questions

1. How long have you worked as an educator (e.g., teacher or administrator) for students under 19 years of age? *Select the highest option applicable.*
   - □ less than 1 year
   - □ 5 years
   - □ 10 years
   - □ 15 years
   - □ 20 or more years
2. Which of the following roles best describes your current position? *If your role is mixed, select the role requiring most of your time.*
   - □ Teacher
   - □ Colleague Coach (e.g., Teacher on Special Assignment)
   - □ Site/School Administrator
   - □ District Administrator
3. How proficient are you at analyzing student performance data? *In your opinion:*
   - □ Very proficient
   - □ Somewhat proficient
   - □ Not proficient
   - □ Far from proficient
4. Which content cluster is most likely the School's strength? *Base your answer on the folder's Report 1.*
   - □ Word Analysis and Vocabulary Development
   - □ Reading Comprehension
   - □ Literary Response and Analysis
   - □ Written Conventions
   - □ Writing Strategies [*this was the correct answer*]
   - □ Writing Applications
5. Which content cluster is most likely the School's weakness? *Base your answer on the folder's Report 1.*
   - □ Word Analysis and Vocabulary Development
   - □ Reading Comprehension
   - □ Literary Response and Analysis
   - □ Written Conventions [*this was the correct answer*]
   - □ Writing Strategies
   - □ Writing Applications
6. Which student(s) did NOT score Proficient on the CELDT? Check all that apply. *Base your answer on the folder's Report 2.* CHECK ALL THAT APPLY.
   - □ Student A
   - □ Student B [*a combination of this* – Student B – *and* Student D *was the correct answer*]
   - □ Student C
   - □ Student D [*a combination of this* – Student D – *and* Student B *was the correct answer*]
7. In which area(s) did at least 1 student earn a score that PREVENTED him/her from scoring Proficient on the CELDT? *Base your answer on the folder's Report 2.* CHECK ALL THAT APPLY.
   - □ Listening
   - □ Speaking [*a combination of this* – Speaking – *and* Overall *was the correct answer*]
   - □ Reading
   - □ Writing
   - □ Overall [*a combination of this* – Overall – *and* Speaking *was the correct answer*]

[*Not Numbered*] What color is your folder? *The cover of your report materials folder features the name of its color.* [*folders were also colored in entirety to match their color names*]
   - □ White
   - □ Yellow
   - □ Green
   - □ Blue
   - □ Purple
   - □ Red
   - □ Black

continued on following page

Box 1. Continued

[*Question 8 varied based on the data analysis support each respondent received (i.e., participants automatically received the appropriate version of Question 8 – meaning only Question 8a, 8b, 8c, or 8d – based on how they answered the above question regarding folder color). The four different versions of Question 8 are listed below as Question 8a for respondents with no data analysis supports, Question 8b for respondents with footers, Question 8c for respondents with abstracts (as reference sheets were called in the survey), and Question 8d for respondents with interpretation guides (as reference guides were called in the survey):*]

8a. The 2 reports you just used did not offer any special assistance in analyzing the data. If they had been accompanied by text (e.g., a footer, guide, or abstract) designed to help you interpret the data, would you likely have used the added support?

    □ Yes – I probably would use the support.

    □ No – I probably would not use the support.

8b. The 2 reports you just used contained footers with analysis guidelines designed to help you. Did you read these footers *before* answering questions related to the reports?

    □ Yes – I referred to both reports' footers.

    □ I referred to Report 1's footer but not Report 2's footer.

    □ I referred to Report 2's footer but not Report 1's footer.

    □ No – I did not refer to either footer.

8c. The 2 reports you just used were each accompanied by a 1-page abstract (like a reference sheet) with analysis guidelines designed to help you. Did you read these abstracts/sheets before answering questions related to the reports?

    □ Yes – I referred to both reports' abstracts/sheets.

    □ I referred to Report 1's abstract/sheet but not Report 2's abstract/sheet.

    □ I referred to Report 2's abstract/sheet but not Report 1's abstract/sheet.

    □ No – I did not refer to either abstract/sheet.

8d. The 2 reports you just used were each accompanied by an interpretation guide (a packet) with analysis guidelines designed to help you. Did you read these guides before answering questions related to the reports?

    □ Yes – I referred to both reports' guides.

    □ I referred to Report 1's guide but not Report 2's guide.

    □ I referred to Report 2's guide but not Report 1's guide.

    □ No – I did not refer to either guide.

11. Lots of professional development happens at school sites: for example, demonstrations to accompany textbook adoptions, meetings with colleagues to share differentiation strategies, training on how to use new software, etc. Only some professional development specifically focuses on how to analyze student data. Within the last 12 months, how many hours of professional development have you had that specifically focused on teaching you how to correctly interpret student data? *Select the highest option applicable. Time spent analyzing student data without guidance should not be counted, nor should time spent learning technology to generate student data.*

    □ 0 hours

    □ 1 hour

    □ 2 hours

    □ 5 hours

    □ 8 or more

12. *Educational Measurement* refers to the analysis of student assessment data to draw conclusions about abilities. How many graduate-level courses have you taken that were *specifically dedicated* to educational measurement (e.g., student performance data analysis, measurement theory, or psychometrics)? *Select the highest option applicable.*

    □ 0 courses

    □ 1 course

    □ 2 courses

    □ 3 courses

    □ 4 or more

Questions the researcher answered for each participant based on his or her school site's demographics, as provided by the California Department of Education, were as follows:

6. What was the educators' school site level type?

7. What was the educators' school site level?

8. What was the Growth API of the school site?

9. What was the population of English Learners attending the school site?

10. What was the population of Socioeconomically Disadvantaged students attending the school site?

    What was the population of Students with Disabilities attending the school site?

Table 1. Key Findings for Embedded Data Analysis Support in each Reporting Environment

Report Environment	% Use	Data Analysis Accuracy (% of Qs Correct)				
7 Different Report Environments Were Used in the Study, Each with a Different Level of Embedded Data Analysis Support (None, Footer A or B, Reference Sheet A or B, or Reference Guide A or B)	Wanted/ Used Support	Would Not Have Used Support	Would Have Used Support	Did Not Use Available Support	Regardless of Support Use	Used Available Support
No Support (Control Group) 31 (15% of) participants got: - 2 plain reports with no footers - no reference sheets - no reference guides	87%	13%	11%	n/a	11%	n/a
Footer A (Shorter) 30 (14% of) participants got: - 2 reports with footers that were shorter with some color - no reference sheets - no reference guides	75%	n/a	n/a	27%	36%	33%
Footer B (Longer) 30 (14% of) participants got: - 2 reports with footers that were longer with no color - no reference sheets - no reference guides	70%	n/a	n/a	6%	32%	40%
Either Footer Format This data combines the 2 rows above & is for 60 (28% of) participants	73%	n/a	n/a	15%	34%	37%
Reference Sheet A (Less Dense) 30 (14% of) participants got: - 2 plain reports with no footers - 2 reference sheets (1 for each report) that were less dense - no reference guides	53%	n/a	n/a	11%	21%	31%
Reference Sheet B (Denser) 30 (14% of) participants got: - 2 plain reports with no footers - 2 reference sheets (1 for each report) that were denser - no reference guides	47%	n/a	n/a	9%	24%	36%
Either Reference Sheet Format This data combines the 2 rows above & is for 60 (28% of) participants	50%	n/a	n/a	10%	23%	33%
Reference Guide A (2-Page) 30 (14% of) participants got: - 2 plain reports with no footers - no reference sheets - 2 reference guides (1 for each report) that were each 2 pages	52%	n/a	n/a	0%	32%	48%
Reference Guide A (3-Page) 30 (14% of) participants got: - 2 plain reports with no footers - no reference sheets - 2 reference guides (1 for each report) that were each 3 pages	52%	n/a	n/a	3%	28%	48%
Either Reference Guide Format This data combines the 2 rows above & is for 60 (28% of) participants	52%	n/a	n/a	2%	30%	48%
Any Form of Embedded Support This data combines the data for the 180 (85% of) participants who received some form of support (i.e., all except Control Group)	58%	n/a	n/a	8%	29%	39%

from this online location after the survey. The survey prompted participants to hold their folders in the air as they finished, allowing the researcher to check each computer screen to ensure the survey was successfully submitted, which was only possible if all questions were answered, and participants were exited from the online survey environment.

The researcher used straightforward categorical scales in the form of correct/incorrect for data analysis questions, as the answers were clearly right or wrong based on the guidelines from the performance data's governing body (California Department of Education), as stipulated in the guides that were regularly released in order to explain appropriate analysis of data from the California Standards Test (CST) and California English Language Development Test (CELDT), as these were the assessments on which the study's data report handouts reported.

These state assessments were those with which the Californian study participants were most likely to be familiar with analyzing. At the time this study was conducted, the CST constituted the largest component of California's Standardized Testing and Reporting (STAR) Program and was considered the participants' highest stakes test for both state and federal accountability, and all Californian educators were supposed to consider a student's CELDT results when determining whether or not to recommend the English Learner (EL) for reclassification. Because there was a single, objective correct answer for each data analysis question and the study was quantitative, the need to scale respondents' analysis responses further was circumvented and the percent of analysis-related questions participants answered correctly was used.

Response data was coded in Microsoft Excel® and used with the Microsoft 2010 Data Analysis feature, and also used with Predictive Analytics Software (PASW) Version 18 with the Statistical Package for the Social Sciences (SPSS) Data Ac-

cess Pack. The researcher analyzed results in order to (a) answer the study's seven primary research questions with related hypothesis strands, (b) answer the study's 11 secondary research questions with related hypothesis strands that served the sole role of informing implications addressed by the primary research questions, and (c) identify themes, patterns, relationships, and implications.

The researcher used SPSS for Independent Samples T-Tests for analyses of nominal and scale data and investigated the relationship between data analysis support *use* and data analysis accuracy, as well as data analysis support *presence* and data analysis accuracy. Each of these tests was run for every data analysis support used in the study. The researcher also conducted Independent Samples T-Tests to determine if each embedded data analysis support's format had a significant impact on its effectiveness. Crosstabulations with Chi-square were also used to analyze data. The SPSS Analyze: Descriptive Statistics: Crosstabs function was used to conduct Chi-square analyses to investigate relationships between the independent variables and respondents' data analysis accuracy, as well as respondents' likelihood of using embedded data analysis supports.

Findings

Every form of embedded data analysis guidance investigated in the study had a significant, positive impact on the participating educators' data analysis accuracy. Table 1 features key findings from the study. In terms of relative and absolute differences, participants' data analyses were:

- 264% more accurate (with an 18 percentage point difference) when any one of the three forms of embedded data analysis guidance was present and 355% more accurate (with a 28 percentage point difference) when respondents specifically indicated having used the support,

- 307% more accurate (with a 23 percentage point difference) when a report footer was present and 336% more accurate (with a 26 percentage point difference) when respondents specifically indicated having used the footer,
- 205% more accurate (with a 12 percentage point difference) when a report-specific reference sheet was present and 300% more accurate (with a 22 percentage point difference) when respondents specifically indicated having used the sheet, and
- 273% more accurate (with a 19 percentage point difference) when a report-specific reference guide was present and 436% more accurate (with a 37 percentage point difference) when respondents specifically indicated having used the guide.

The substantial rate at which all embedded supports were utilized rendered their value significant for all educators as a whole, even when respondents' use of the supports was not considered. However, respondents' data analyses were even higher when they specifically indicated having used the available support. The minor modifications in format, mainly in terms of length and color usage, had no significant impact on the participating educators' data analysis accuracy. It was thus concluded such minor variations are also minor in their impact on educators' data analyses.

Educators' school site demographics were found to have no significant impact on their data analysis accuracy that might impact the primary research questions. In other words, an educator's school level type, school level, academic performance, EL population, Socioeconomically Disadvantaged population, or Students with Disabilities population had an insignificant impact on data analysis accuracy and on use of embedded data analysis guidance. Likewise, educators' demographics had no significant impact on their data analysis accuracy that might impact the primary research questions. In other words, an educator's

veteran status, current professional role, perception of his or her own data analysis proficiency, data analysis PD time, and number of graduate-level educational measurement courses had an insignificant impact on data analysis accuracy and on use of embedded data analysis guidance. Thus it is concluded the supports will be equally used and equally effective regardless of educator demographics or school site demographics.

Solutions and Recommendations

In reviewing literature for and after the Rankin (2013a) study, the researcher identified recurring themes and best practices for effective data reporting. The researcher has organized these best practices as Over-the-Counter Data Standards for the effective reporting of data to educators and other stakeholders. These standards (see Rankin, 2013b) represent a synthesis of over 300 studies and texts from experts in then field. The standards involve implementation of effective labels, supplemental documentation, help system, package/display, and content when reporting data to educators. Templates are also available to allow anyone to create his or her own reference sheets and reference guides that are modeled after those found to be effective in the study: http://overthecounterdata. com/templates/. Though Rankin (2013a) study findings cannot automatically be generalized to non-educator populations, it is recommended applications of Over-the-Counter Data Standards and templates in non-education information systems be explored, as the discovery of benefits is likely, particularly if users match characteristics of the study's educator population.

Education Data System and Report Providers

Data system and report providers, such as data system vendors but also including district staff who maintain in-house data systems, are encouraged to:

- Create a report-specific footer for each of the data reports they provide.
- Use the study-based templates at http://overthecounterdata.com/templates/ to create a reference sheet and reference guide for each of the data reports they provide.
- Review the reporting standards (see Rankin, 2013b), which were based on the study's literature review and findings, and modify their data systems and reports as necessary to adhere to the standards.

Data system and report providers should also remain well-versed in new research concerning educator data use, effective data visualization, best user interface practices, and other ways in which they can better support educators accurate use of data.

Educators

Educators who use data systems and reports – particularly educators in leadership positions who impact data system selection, support, and replacement – are encouraged to advocate for their data system and report providers to:

- Create a report-specific footer for each of the data reports they provide.
- Use the study-based templates at http://overthecounterdata.com/templates/ to create a reference sheet and reference guide for each of the data reports they provide.
- Review the reporting standards at (see Rankin, 2013b), which were based on the study's literature review and findings, and modify their data systems and reports as necessary to adhere to the standards.

Over-the-counter data is not meant to replace PD or other interventions that educators employ to improve data use. Thus educators should consider such efforts while *also* advocating for over-the-counter data and its significant benefits.

Outside of Education

Most of the research shared in this chapter pertains to educators and education information systems. Thus many of the studies' limitations concern not assuming findings can be generalized to non-educator populations and tools in order to maintain external validity. However, it is likely many of the findings, including the over-the-counter data standards based on such findings, can be used to improve data systems for non-educator populations to great effect. Such applications should thus be explored, measured, and utilized when appropriate.

FUTURE RESEARCH DIRECTIONS

There is a division drawn in most dialogue, research, and literature within the field of Education that concerns topics covered by this chapter:

- Most dialogue, research, and literature concerning data systems are focused on data storage, data security, data privacy, data access, and standards for interoperability. The topic of improving educators' data analysis accuracy is not usually presented as a data system issue.
- Most dialogue, research, and literature concerning the improvement of educators' data analyses are focused on matters within the educators' power and responsibility, such as improved PD, added staffing, and improved teacher preparation programs. Again, the topic of improving educators' data analysis accuracy is not usually presented as a data system issue.

Although historically it has not been adequately acknowledged, there is much that data systems and reports can do to better support educators' accurate use of data. Fortunately, this blind spot for data system's role in data analysis accuracy is slowly being diminished. Goodman and Hambleton (2014) established one of the most cited and comprehensive examinations of education data reporting, followed by Underwood et al. (2010), Sabbah (2011), VanWinkle et al. (2011), Rankin (2013a), and others.

This research on innovations in the computer data systems used for education information retrieval, analysis, and management represents great strides for students affected by educators' otherwise-commonly-flawed data-informed decision-making. This research is also a relief to many educators, as their flawed data use is commonly treated as primarily an educator problem, which is a dubious placement of blame considering educators' higher-than-average intellect and academic accomplishments. In addition, when findings can be appropriately applied to improve data systems for non-educator populations, the innovation-derived benefits will multiply.

Research community members are encouraged to fill remaining gaps in field literature on over-the-counter data. Investigating various data system and reporting aspects in relation to specific impact on educators' data analysis accuracy, as opposed to which supports and formats participants prefer, is recommended. As mentioned earlier, user preference can be the opposite of the reporting format that actually renders the more accurate interpretation (Hattie, 2010).

Researchers can also explore the impact of varied OTCD Standards (see Rankin, 2013b) in concert, on respondents' data analyses in both laboratory and real world environments. In addition, researchers can also explore different formats for reference sheets and reference guides in case the format and templates available at http://over-thecounterdata.com/templates/ can be improved.

CONCLUSION

Education information retrieval, analysis, and management involves the use of computerized data systems by educator stakeholders such as teachers and administrators. However, there is clear evidence many users of data system reports have trouble understanding the data (Wayman et al., 2010; Zwick et al., 2008). Despite these struggles, labeling and tools within data systems to assist analysis are uncommon (USDEOPEPD, 2009).

The lack of adequate data usage guidance embedded within data systems and reports is surprising considering the success with which embedded usage guidance is employed within the pharmaceutical industry. In fact, a lack of such guidance on over-the-counter medicine is deemed negligent (DeWalt, 2010). Labeling conventions can result in improved understanding on non-medication products, as well (Hampton, 2007; Qin et al., 2011). As evidenced in the Rankin (2013a) study, data can be made over-the-counter by the accompaniment of embedded usage guidance to help users better understand, analyze, and use the data being communicated. It is likely over-the-counter data can benefit data systems and their users outside the field of Education, as well.

The Rankin (2013a) study rendered findings that data system-embedded data analysis support in the forms of footers, reference sheets, and reference guides all have a significant, positive impact on the accuracy of educators' data analyses. Key findings include:

- 87% of educators desire embedded data analysis support from their data systems and reports.
- 58% of educators use embedded data analysis support when it is available.
- Data systems and the report environments they generate can significantly increase data analysis accuracy when they feature embedded data analysis support in one of the formats featured in this study (covered by the next three bullets); educators' data analyses are 264% more accurate (with an 18 percentage point difference) when any one of the three forms of embedded data

analysis guidance is present and 355% more accurate (with a 28 percentage point difference) when respondents specifically indicate having used the support.

- Educators' data analyses are 307% more accurate (with a 23 percentage point difference) when a report footer is present and 336% more accurate (with a 26 percentage point difference) when respondents specifically indicate having used the footer,

- Educators' data analyses are 205% more accurate (with a 12 percentage point difference) when a report-specific reference sheet is present and 300% more accurate (with a 22 percentage point difference) when respondents specifically indicate having used the sheet, and

- Educators' data analyses are 273% more accurate (with a 19 percentage point difference) when a report-specific reference guide is present and 436% more accurate (with a 37 percentage point difference) when respondents specifically indicate having used the guide.

- Educators' personal and school site demographics have no significant bearing on any of the embedded data analysis supports' use or success, and thus the supports can be implemented with expected success at varied locations and for varied users.

- Very minor modifications in support format, mainly in terms of length and color usage, do not significantly impact educators' data analysis accuracy. This should not be mistaken to mean the supports' *format* does not matter, but rather that *minor* format differences do not seem to matter. Best practices for footers, as were followed in the study, should be followed.

- There is evidence (as produced by the study and referenced in its literature review) to support the use of Over-the-Counter Data Standards (see Rankin, 2013b), to which

data systems and reports can adhere when reporting data to educators and other education stakeholders in order to improve their understanding and use of the data.

Innovations made to education information retrieval, analysis, and management systems in light of this study have the potential to improve the accuracy with which educators analyze the data generated by their data systems. For example:

- Data systems and reports can be made to adhere to Over-the-Counter Data Standards (see Rankin, 2013b) for the effective reporting of data to educators and other stakeholders. These standards represent a synthesis of over 300 studies and texts from experts in the field, as profiled in the Rankin (2013a) literature review.

- Data systems and reports providers can utilize the open source templates anyone can use to create reference sheets and reference guides modeled after those found to be significantly effective in the Rankin (2013a) study. These templates are available at http://overthecounterdata.com/templates/.

Benefits are likely for non-educator populations and systems, as well. More accurate data analyses will likely result in more accurate data-informed decision-making for the benefit of stakeholders. Students and other populations affected by decisions made using high-stakes data deserve for the systems used to manage, retrieve, and analyze this information to make the data over-the-counter for users. To provide less is deemed by this chapter's author to be as negligent as it would be for a bottle of medicine to be sold without a label, directions, warnings, or other usage guidance. Like medicine, data affects lives and should be disseminated responsibly and with the utmost care to ensure its content is understood and used correctly.

REFERENCES

American Institutes for Research (AIR). *Most teachers "highly qualified" under NCLB standards, but teacher qualifications lag in many high poverty and high minority schools.* (2013). Retrieved from http://www.air.org/reports-products/index.cfm?fa=viewContent&content_id=417

Bennett, R. E., & Gitomer, D. H. (2009). Transforming K-12 assessment: Integrating accountability testing, formative assessment and professional support. In C. Wyatt-Smith & J. J. Cumming (Eds.), Educational assessment in the 21st century, 43-61. New York, NY: Springer.

Brown-Brumfield, D., & DeLeon, A. (2010). Adherence to a medication safety protocol: Current practice for labeling medications and solutions on the sterile field. *Association of Operating Room Nurses*. AORN Journal, 91(5), 610-610-7. doi:10.1016/j.aorn.2010.03.002

Cho, V., & Wayman, J. C. (2009, April). *Knowledge management and educational data use.* Paper presented at the 2009 Annual Meeting of the American Educational Research Association, San Diego, CA.

Cho, V., & Wayman, J. C. (2012). Districts' efforts for data use and computer data systems: The role of sensemaking in system use and implementation. Proceedings of the *2012 Annual Meeting of the American Educational Research Association, Vancouver, British Columbia, Canada*. Retrieved from http://www.vincentcho.com/uploads/9/6/5/2/9652180/cho__wayman_aera_2012_final.pdf

Cho, V., & Wayman, J. C. (2013). District leadership for computer data systems: Technical, social, and organizational challenges in implementation. Proceedings of the *UCEA Convention*, Indianapolis, IN. Retrieved from http://www.vincentcho.com/uploads/9/6/5/2/9652180/ucea_2013_co_data_systems_final.pdf

Coburn, C. E., Honig, M. I., & Stein, M. K. (2009). What's the evidence on districts' use of evidence? In J. Bransford, D. J. Stipek, N. J. Vye, L. Gomez, & D. Lam (Eds.), The role of research in educational improvement, 67-88. Cambridge, MA: Harvard Education Press.

Combs, G. (2004). Why teachers hate tech training... and what to do about it. *MultiMedia & Internet@Schools, 11*(1), 8-8.

Davis, M. R. (2013, October 1). Managing the digital district: Intelligent data analysis helps predict needs. [Bethesda, MD: Editorial Projects in Education.]. *Education Week, 33*(06), 20–21.

DeWalt, D. A. (2010). Ensuring safe and effective use of medication and health care: Perfecting the dismount. *Journal of the American Medical Association, 304*(23), 2641–2642. doi:10.1001/jama.2010.1844 PMID:21119075

Ed Tech Ticker. (2011, March 18). Data-driven instruction survey released. *Tech & Learning: Ideas and Tools for Ed Tech Leaders*. Retrieved from http://www.techlearning.com/default.aspx?tabid=67&entryid=5837

Faria, A., Heppen, J., Li, Y., Stachel, S., Jones, W., & Sawyer, K. ... Palacios, M. (2012, Summer). *Charting success: Data use and student achievement in urban schools.* Council of the Great City Schools and the American Institutes for Research. Retrieved from http://www.cgcs.org/cms/lib/DC00001581/Centricity/Domain/87/Charting_Success.pdf

Faul, F., Erdfelder, E., Buchner, A., & Lang, A.-G. (2009). Statistical power analyses using G*Power 3.1: Tests for correlation and regression analyses. *Behavior Research Methods, 41*(4), 1149–1160. Statistical power analyses using G*Power 3.1: Tests for correlation and regression analyses doi:10.3758/BRM.41.4.1149 PMID:19897823

Glasswell, K. (2012). Building teacher capacity and raising reading achievement. *Australian Council Educational Research Conference 2012, Session R, 112-115*. Queensland, Australia: Australian Council Educational Research.

Goodman, D. P., & Hambleton, R. K. (2004). Student test score reports and interpretive guides: Review of current practices and suggestions for future research. *Applied Measurement in Education, 17*(2), 145–220. doi:10.1207/s15324818ame1702_3

Halpin, J., & Cauthen, L. (2011, July 31). The education dashboard. *Center for Digital Education's Converge Special Report, 2*(3), 2–36.

Hambleton, R. K. (2002). How can we make NAEP and state test score reporting scales and reports more understandable? In R. W. Lissitz & W. D. Schafer (Eds.), Assessment in educational reform (pp. 192-205). Boston, MA: Allyn & Bacon.

Hambleton, R. K., & Slater, S. C. (1996). *Are NAEP executive summary reports understandable to policymakers and educators?* Paper presented at the annual meeting of the National Council on Measurement in Education, New York.

Hampton, T. (2007). Groups urge warning label for medical devices containing toxic chemical. [JAMA]. *Journal of the American Medical Association, 298*(11), 1267. doi:10.1001/jama.298.11.1267 PMID:17878415

Hattie, J. (2010). Visibly learning from reports: The validity of score reports. *Online Educational Research Journal*. Also: Paper presented at the annual meeting of the National Council for Measurement in Education (NCME), San Diego, CA. Retrieved from http://www.oerj.org/View?action=viewPaper&paper=6 Hattie, J., & Timperley, H. (2007, March). The power of feedback. *Review of Educational Research, 77*(1), 81-112. doi: 10.3102/003465430298487

Horkay, N., Bennett, R. E., Allen, N., Kaplan, B., & Yan, F. (2006, November). Does it matter if I take my writing test on computer? An empirical study of mode effects in NAEP. *The Journal of Technology, Learning, and Assessment, 5*(2), 1–50. Retrieved from http://ejournals.bc.edu/ojs/index.php/jtla/article/view/1641/

Ikemoto, G. S., & Marsh, J. A. (2008). Chapter 5: Cutting through the "data-driven" mantra: different conceptions of data-driven decision making. Evidence and Decision Making: Yearbook of the National Society for the Study of Education, 106(1), 105-131. Santa Monica, CA: RAND Corporation and National Society for the Study of Education.

Ingram, D., Louis, K. S., & Schroeder, R. G. (2004). Accountability policies and teacher decision making: Barriers to the use of data to improve practice. *Teachers College Record, 106*(6), 1258–1287. doi:10.1111/j.1467-9620.2004.00379.x

Knapp, M. S., Swinnerton, J. A., Copland, M. A., & Monpas-Hubar, J. (2006). *Data-informed leadership in education*. Seattle, WA: Center for the Study of Teaching and Policy.

Kuehn, B. M. (2009). FDA focuses on drugs and liver damage: Labeling and other changes for acetaminophen. [JAMA]. *Journal of the American Medical Association, 302*(4), 369–371. doi:10.1001/jama.2009.1019 PMID:19622807

Leveraging the power of state longitudinal data systems: Building capacity to turn data into useful information. (2011). *Data Quality Campaign*. Retrieved from http://www.dataqualitycampaign.org/files/DQC-Research%20capacity%20May17.pdf

Lukin, L. E., Bandalos, D. L., Eckhout, T. J., & Mickelson, K. (2004). Facilitating the development of assessment literacy. *Educational Measurement: Issues and Practice, 23*(2), 26–32. doi:10.1111/j.1745-3992.2004.tb00156.x

Marsh, J. A., Pane, J. F., & Hamilton, L. S. (2006). *Making sense of data-driven decision making in education: Evidence from recent RAND research.* Santa Monica, CA: RAND Corporation.

McDonald, S., Andal, J., Brown, K., & Schneider, B. (2007). *Getting the evidence for evidence-based initiatives: How the Midwest states use data systems to improve education processes and outcomes (Issues & Answers Report, REL 2007–No. 016).* Washington, DC: U.S. Department of Education, Institute of Education Sciences, National Center for Education Evaluation and Assistance, Regional Educational Laboratory Midwest.

Minnici, A., & Hill, D. D. (May 9, 2007). Educational architects: Do state education agencies have the tools necessary to implement NCLB? Washington, D.C.: Center on Education Policy.

Born in another time: Ensuring educational technology meets the needs of students today – and tomorrow. (2012, December). *National Association of States Boards of Education.* Arlington, VA: Author.

Traveling through time: The forum guide to longitudinal data systems. Book Two of Four: Planning and Developing an LDS (NFES 2011–804). (2010). *National Forum on Education Statistics.* Washington, DC: National Center for Education Statistics, Institute of Education Sciences, U.S. Department of Education.

Papay, J. Harvard Graduate School of Education. (2007). *Aspen Institute datasheet: The teaching workforce.* Washington, DC: The Aspen Institute.

Qin, Y., Wu, M., Pan, X., Xiang, Q., Huang, J., & Gu, Z. et al. (2011, February 25). Reactions of Chinese adults to warning labels on cigarette packages: A survey in Jiangsu Province. *BMC Public Health*, *133*(11), doi:10.1186/1471-2458-11-133 PMID:21349205

Rankin, J. G. (2011). *Over-the-Counter Data Standards.* Retrieved from www.overthecounterdata.com/s/OTCDStandards.pdf

Rankin, J. G. (2013). *Over-the-counter data's impact on educators' data analysis accuracy.* ProQuest Dissertations and Theses, 3575082. Retrieved from http://pqdtopen.proquest.com/doc/1459258514.html?FMT=ABS

Rennie Center for Education Research and Policy. (2006, February). *Data-driven teaching: Tools and trends.* Cambridge, MA: Rennie Center for Education Research and Policy.

Rodriguez, M. (2008, May 01). Learning how to incorporate technology in classrooms. *Inland Valley Daily Bulletin.* Retrieved from http://www.highbeam.com/doc/1P2-16433823.html

Sabbah, F. M. (2011). Designing more effective accountability report cards. *ProQuest Dissertations and Theses, AAT 3469488.* Retrieved from http://search.proquest.com/docview/893068662?accountid=28180

Sawchuk, S. (2013, July 14). When bad things happen to good NAEP data. *Education Week*, *32*(37), 1–22. Retrieved from http://www.edweek.org/ew/articles/2013/07/24/37naep.h32.html?tkn=XWSFjintSc1tarwBowLttmHfKt77SXIkUIav&cmp=ENL-EU-NEWS1

Schildkamp, K., Lai, M. K., & Earl, L. (2013). Data-based decision making in education: Challenges and opportunities. Dordrecht, Netherlands: Springer Science+Business Media

Shepard, L., Davidson, K., & Bowman, R. (2011). How middle school mathematics teachers use interim and benchmark assessment data. Los Angeles, CA: University of California, Los Angeles (UCLA), Center for Research on Evaluation, Standards, and Student Testing (CRESST), CRESST Report 807.

Stansbury, M. (2013, July). More training is key to better school data use: States have continued to make progress in building robust data systems—but stakeholders must know how to use student data effectively. *eSchool News*. Retrieved from http://www.eschoolnews.com/2012/11/16/more-training-is-key-to-better-school-data-use/?ast=104&astc=9990

Stiggins, R. (2002). Assessment for learning. *Education Week*, *21*(26), 30, 32–33.

The next step: Using longitudinal data systems to improve student success. (2009). *Data Quality Campaign*. Retrieved from http://www.dataqualitycampaign.org/find-resources/the-next-step/

Traveling through time: The forum guide to longitudinal data systems. Book Four of Four: Advanced LDS Usage (NFES 2011–802). (2011). *Education Statistics*. Washington, DC: National Center for Education Statistics, Institute of Education Sciences, U.S. Department of Education.

Underwood, J. S., Zapata-Rivera, D., & VanWinkle, W. (2008) Growing Pains: Teachers Using and Learning to Use IDMS®. *ETS Research Memorandum. RM-08-07*. Princeton, NJ: ETS.

Underwood, J. S., Zapata-Rivera, D., & VanWinkle, W. (2010). *An evidence-centered approach to using assessment data for policymakers (ETS Research Rep. No. RR-10-03)*. Princeton, NJ: ETS.

Ungerleider, C. (2008, September). *Evaluation of the Ontario Ministry of Education's student success / learning to 18 strategy: Final report.* Canadian Council on Learning (CCL). Retrieved from http://www.edu.gov.on.ca/eng/teachers/studentsuccess/ccl_sse_report.pdf

United States Department of Education Office of Planning, Evaluation and Policy Development. (2009). Implementing data-informed decision making in schools: Teacher access, supports and use. United States Department of Education (ERIC Document Reproduction Service No. ED504191)

United States Department of Education Office of Planning, Evaluation and Policy Development. (2011). Teachers' ability to use data to inform instruction: Challenges and supports. United States Department of Education (ERIC Document Reproduction Service No. ED516494)

Van der Meij, H. (2008). Designing for user cognition and affect in a manual. Should there be special support for the latter? *Learning and Instruction*, *18*(1), 18–29.

VanWinkle, W., Vezzu, M., & Zapata-Rivera, D. (2011). *Question-based reports for policymakers* (ETS Research Memorandum No. RM-11-16). Princeton, NJ: ETS.

Wayman, J. C. (2005). Involving teachers in data-driven decision making: Using computer data systems to support teacher inquiry and reflection. *Journal of Education for Students Placed at Risk*, *10*(3), 295–308. doi:10.1207/s15327671espr1003_5

Wayman, J. C., & Cho, V. (2009). Preparing educators to effectively use student data systems. In T. J. Kowalski & T. J. Lasley II (Eds.), Handbook of data-based decision making in education (pp. 89-104). New York, NY: Routledge.

Wayman, J. C., Cho, V., & Shaw, S. M. (2009, December). *First-year results from an efficacy study of the Acuity data system.* Paper presented at the Twenty-fourth Annual Texas Assessment Conference, Austin, TX.

Wayman, J. C., Snodgrass Rangel, V. W., Jimerson, J. B., & Cho, V. (2010). *Improving data use in NISD: Becoming a data-informed district.* Austin, TX: The University of Texas at Austin.

Wohlstetter, P., Datnow, A., & Park, V. (2008). Creating a system for data-driven decision-making: Applying the principal-agent framework. *School Effectiveness and School Improvement*, *19*(3), 239–259. doi:10.1080/09243450802246376

Zapata-Rivera, D., & VanWinkle, W. (2010). A research-based approach to designing and evaluating score reports for teachers (*ETS Research Memorandum No. RM-10-01*). Princeton, NJ: ETS.

Zwick, R., Sklar, J., Wakefield, G., Hamilton, C., Norman, A., & Folsom, D. (2008). Instructional tools in educational measurement and statistics (ITEMS) for school personnel: Evaluation of three web-based training modules. *Educational Measurement: Issues and Practice*, 27(2), 14–27. doi:10.1111/j.1745-3992.2008.00119.x

KEY TERMS AND DEFINITIONS

Data System (within the Context of Education): A computerized system, often accessible online, that houses and displays student, educator, and school information and allows users to retrieve, manage, and analyze the data. Data systems go by many names and there is much overlap in terms of what different systems do. Examples include the assessment system, data and assessment management system, data mart, data warehouse, decision support system (DSS), information system, instructional management system (IMS), learning management system (LMS), special education system (SES), student information system (SIS), and other educational technology product types that contains a significant feedback component.

Data-Informed Decision-Making: The process of using data to guide decisions. In the field of Education, these decisions ultimately impact students and often impact other stakeholders, such as teachers and administrators. While data-*driven* decision-making is a more common term, data-*informed* decision-making is a preferable term since decisions should not be based solely on quantitative data (Knapp, Swinnerton, Copland, & Monpas-Hubar, 2006; USDEOPEPD, 2009).

Footer: A means for labeling a data report with data usage guidance, involving brief (such as one to three lines of) text at the bottom of a data report.

Help System: A computer-based, online collection of task-based lessons that walk data system users through sequential steps to accomplish tasks within the data system, as well as topic-based lessons that help users understand and use the data housed in the data system.

Over-the-Counter Data: Data that is accompanied by embedded usage guidance just as over-the-counter products are accompanied by embedded usage guidance. Data systems and reports can feature over-the-counter data by adhering to Over-the-Counter Data Standards (www.overthecounterdata.com/s/OTCDStandards.pdf) when reporting data to educators and other education stakeholders in order to improve their understanding and use of the data. The standards involve implementation of effective labels, supplemental documentation, a help system, package/display, and content.

Professional Development (PD): Educators' recommended continual process of learning, which can involve a range of improvement strategies such as online networks, embedded videos, on-the-job training, traditional workshops, weekly collaboration sessions, and more.

Reference Guide: Accompanies each report to help users understand and use that specific report's data. It is often called a data guide, interpretation guide, or interpretive guide. The report's reference sheet (described below) functions as the guide's first page, and subsequent pages contain the report's instructions (how to read the report), essential questions (showing the user where to look on this report – and what to look for – to answer each question listed in the purpose area of the guide's 1st page), and a "more info" section (offering where to get additional information on related topics).

Reference Sheet: Accompanies each report to help users understand that specific report's data. It is often called an abstract or summary. This single page contains the report's title, description, image, focus (content reported), and warning (vital, cautionary information an educator would need to avoid the most common analysis errors made when analyzing the particular data being displayed). It can also communicate the report's purpose (key questions the report will help answer) and additional focus information (intended audience, and format in which data is reported).

Report: An arrangement of data around a particular topic and purpose in order to communicate the data to a particular audience through graphs/ graphics, tables, text, and/or other means. Reports can take online forms such as data dashboards or can appear as traditional printed pages.

User: Any person using a data system. In the field of Education, this is likely an educator (including classified staff), but in some cases can also be a student, parent, or other stakeholder.

Chapter 6
The New "ABC" of ICTs (Analytics + Big Data + Cloud Computing):
A Complex Trade–Off between IT and CT Costs

José Carlos Cavalcanti
Universidade Federal de Pernambuco, Brazil

ABSTRACT

Analytics (discover and communication of patterns, with significance, in data) of Big Data (basically characterized by large structured and unstructured data volumes, from a variety of sources, at high velocity - i.e., real-time data capture, storage, and analysis), through the use of Cloud Computing (a model of network computing) is becoming the new "ABC" of information and communication technologies (ICTs), with important effects for the generation of new firms and for the restructuring of those ones already established. However, as this chapter argues, successful application of these new ABC technologies and tools depends on two interrelated policy aspects: 1) the use of a proper model which could help one to approach the structure and dynamics of the firm, and, 2) how the complex trade-off between information technology (IT) and communication technology (CT) costs is handled within, between and beyond firms, organizations and institutions.

INTRODUCTION

As described by *The Global Information Technology Report 2014* (World Economic Forum- WEF, 2014), data have always had strategic value, but with the magnitude of data available today – and our capability to process them – they have become a new form of asset class. The report stresses that

in a very real sense, data are now the equivalent of oil and gold:

And today we are seeing a data boom rivaling the Texas oil boom of the 20th century and San Francisco gold rush of the 1800s. It has spawned an entire support industry and has attracted a great deal of business press in recent years (WEF, 2014).

DOI: 10.4018/978-1-4666-8833-9.ch006

Data growth is skyrocketing. Over 2.5 quintillion bytes of data are created each day; 90 percent of the world's stored data was created in the last two years alone (Pepper and Garrity, 2014). However, current estimates suggest that only half a percent of all data is being analyzed for insights; furthermore, the vast majority of existing data are unstructured and machine-generated. Applying analytics to a greater share of all data can lead to productivity increases, economic growth, and societal development through the creation of actionable insights (Pepper and Garrity, 2014).

No doubt that applying analytics to a greater share of all data can lead to great economic and social improvements; the important issue, however, is *how*, and *when*, this can be achieved, and at *what* costs. In this way, the main argument advanced in this chapter is that successful application of *Analytics* (which can be described as the discover and communication of patterns, with significance, in data) to *Big Data* (basically characterized by large structured and unstructured data volumes, from a variety of sources, at high velocity - i.e., real-time data capture, storage, and analysis), through the use of *Cloud Computing* (a model of network computing), what is called here as the new "*ABC*" of information and communication technologies (ICTs), depends on depends on two interrelated policy aspects: 1) the use of a proper model which could help one to approach the structure and dynamics of the firm, and, 2) how the complex trade-off between information technology (IT) and communication technology (CT) costs is handled within, between and beyond firms, organizations and institutions.

In this way, this chapter is organized as follows. Section 1 briefly presents the main aspects of the concepts of Analytics, Big Data and Cloud Computing. Section 2 shows a brief discussion of the evolution, applications and emerging research connected to these new *ABC* technologies and tools. Section 3 describes the main players of the support industry created by the *ABC* technologies and tools. In section 4 some of the main aspects of a novel model, called the *Architecture-Governance-Growth Model* (or the *AGG Model*) are shown, taking into account the relevant contributions and limitations of the knowledge-based hierarchy view of the firm to the understanding of the complex trade-off between information technology (IT) and communication technology (CT) costs when firms apply and manage new *ABC* technologies and tools, and offers a way to deal with such a trade-off. Finally, section 5 presents the final conclusions.

BACKGROUND

The modern enterprise is a complex system and is evolving dramatically in recent years. In a world where the digital revolution is accelerating innovation, driving productivity, and irreversibly transforming employment and the economy, as expressed by the 2011 book titled "*Race Against the Machine*", written by Erik Brynjolfsson and Andrew McAffe, the enterprise also is being transformed in a radical way.

In order to deal with such complexity, Cavalcanti (2014) introduced a novel model for dealing with the structure and dynamics of the firm: the *Architecture-Governance-Growth* (*AGG*) model. The main thesis of this model is that *the firm's observable architectural characteristics determine its governance issues, and that the governance agenda of the firm determines its measurable growth conditions*. The observable architectural characteristics of the firm are those related to its design, structure, functioning and management. In the AGG model they constitute the *architecture* realm of the model, which is comprised by both its *corporate* and its *information and communication technology (ICT)* domains. The *governance* realm is also comprised by both its *corporate* and its *information and communication technology (ICT)* domains.

When a firm decides to make use of *ABC* technologies and tools, either in isolation or through combined solutions, it has to take into consideration the distinct effects of information technology (IT) and communication technology (CT) on the firm architecture (effects with deep implications for the governance and growth of the firm). These distinct effects have been pointed out by Bloom, Garicano, Sadun and Van Reenen (2013).

These authors observe that, on the one side, through the spread of cheap storage and processing of data (aspects related to IT), information is becoming cheaper to access and, on the other side, through the spread of cheap wired and wireless communications (aspects related to CT), agents find it easier to communicate with each other (e.g. e-mail and mobile devices). Reductions in the cost of accessing information stored in databases and of communicating information among agents can be expected to have a very different impact on firm organization. While cheaper information access has an empowering effect, allowing agents to handle more of the problems they face autonomously, cheaper communication technology facilitates specialization: since agents can easily rely on others to solve tasks outside their immediate area of expertise, they ultimately perform a more limited variety of tasks. This difference matters not just for firm's organization, but also for productivity and in the labor market.

The starting point of their analysis is the work conducted by Garicano (2000) on the hierarchical organization of expertise, also known as the *knowledge-based hierarchy* view of the firm. According to this view, decisions involve solving problems and thus acquiring the relevant knowledge for the decision. When matching problems with solutions is cheap, expertise is organized horizontally. But when matching problems and solutions is expensive, the organization of knowledge is hierarchical: those below deal with the routine problems, and those "above" deal with the exceptions.

Although this knowledge-based hierarchy view seems to represent, at first sight, the key aspects of the trade-off between information technology (IT) and communication technology (CT) costs in the architecture of the firm, it does not reflect the broad complexity inherent to the application and management of the new *ABC* technologies and tools within the firm and across its business relations.

Therefore, the main objective of this chapter is to present, through the use of the AGG model, a sound way to deal with such a trade-off when firms apply and manage new *ABC* technologies and tools. In sum, it is hope that this chapter can offer some understanding of the implications of the adoption of these new ABC technologies to the generation of new firms and to the restructuring of those ones already established.

THE NEW "ABC" OF ICTS: (A)NALYTICS + (B)IG DATA + (C)LOUD COMPUTING

In the beginning of their path-breaking book entitled "*The Second Machine Age: Work, Progress and Prosperity in a Time of Brilliant Technologies*", Brynjolfsson and McAfee (2014) ask: *What have been the most important developments in human history?* Although recognizing that this is a question difficult to answer, these authors provide a graph in which anyone can observe that for many thousands of years, humanity was a very gradual upward trajectory. Progress was achingly slow, almost invisible.

But, as these authors stress, just over two hundred years ago, something sudden and profound arrived and bent the curve of human history - of population and social development – almost ninety degrees. This sudden change in the graph corresponds to the development of the Industrial Revolution, a "*sum of several simultaneous developments in mechanical engineering, chemistry, metallurgy, and other disciplines that underlie* the sudden, sharp, and sustained jump in human progress" (Brynjolfsson and McAfee, 2014), which is commonly characterized as humanity's first machine age.

Now comes *"the second machine age"*, as Brynjolfsson and McAfee (2014) brilliantly argue. These authors state that computers and other digital advances are doing for *mental power* – the ability to use our brains to understand and shape our environments – what the steam engine and its descendants did for *muscle power*. The main conclusions of their book are:

1. *We're living in a time of astonishing progress with digital technologies – those that have computer hardware, software, and networks at their core;*
2. *The transformations brought about by digital technology will be profoundly beneficial ones;*
3. *And, digitalization is going to bring with it some thorny challenges.*

Analytics, Big Data and Cloud Computing can be understood as technologies, as well as business models, that are at the very center of the digital technologies that Brynjolfsson and McAfee are writing about. They can also be seen as *general purpose technologies* (GPTs), since they are technologies that can affect an entire economy (usually at a national or global level). Lipsey, Carlaw and Bekar (2006) call GPTs as the pervasive technologies that occasionally transform a society's entire set of economic, social and political structures. They treat GPTs as one of the main forces that sustain economic growth in the long run.

But, what do Analytics, Big Data and Cloud Computing really mean, and how are they affecting our economy and our society? Let's begin a brief description without concerns of which of the topics came first in terms of historical development, starting with Analytics. There are several definitions for this term, but all of them seem to converge to this one: Analytics is *the discovery,*

and communication, of patterns, with significance, in data.

In a book entitled *"Competing on Analytics: The New Science of Winning"*, Davenport and Harris (2007) consider Analytics as the extensive use of data, statistical and quantitative analysis, explanatory and predictive models, and fact-based management to drive decisions and actions. They treat this topic as a subset of what has come to be called as *Business Intelligence*: a set of technologies and processes that use data to understand and analyze business performance. According to these authors, business intelligence includes both data access and reporting, and analytics (Figure 1). Each of these approaches addresses a range of questions about an organization's business activities. The questions that analytics can answer represent the higher-value and more proactive end of this spectrum.

These authors also inform that although in principle analytics could be performed in a simple manner (using paper, pencil, or a slide rule), today anyone employs information technology. The range of analytical software goes from relatively simple statistical and optimization tools in spreadsheets, to statistical software packages, to complex business intelligence suites, predictive industry applications and the reporting and analytical modules of major enterprise systems. Additionally, good analytical capabilities also require good information management capabilities to integrate, extract, transform, and access business transaction data (Davenport and Harris, 2007).

In a brief historical account of how analytics came into being, these authors also state that the use of this technique began as a small, out-of-the-way activity performed in a few data-intensive business functions. As early as the late 1960s, practitioners and researchers began to experiment with the use of computer systems to analyze data and support decision making. Called *decision support systems (DSS)*, these applications were used for analytical, repetitive, and somewhat narrow

Figure 1. Business intelligence and analytics
Source: Davenport & Harris (2007)

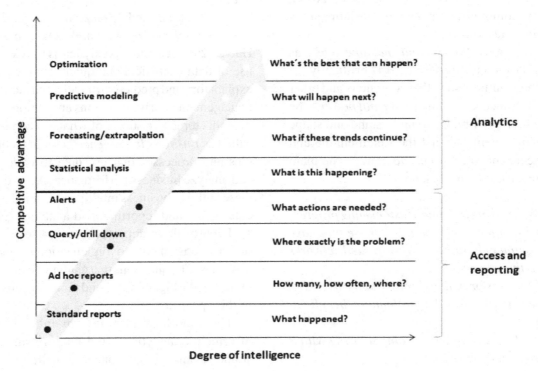

activities such as production planning, investment portfolio management, and transportation routing (Davenport and Harris, 2007).

However, statistical analysis on computers became a much more mainstream activity in the 1970s, as companies such as SAS Institute and SPSS introduced packaged computer applications that made statistics accessible to many researchers and businesspeople. Today the entire field of Analytics is often referred to with the term business intelligence and incorporates the collection, management, and reporting of decision-oriented data as well as the analytical techniques and computing approaches that are performed on the data (Davenport and Harris, 2007).

After the success of their book "*Competing on Analytics*", in their book entitled "*Analytics at Work: Smart Decisions Better Results*", Davenport, Harris and Morison (2010) reveal that

they saw a need for more structure around the topic of how to build analytical capabilities. They note that the first book was about the earliest and most aggressive adopters of analytics, but many other companies and organizations just wanted to know how analytical they were already, and how to become more so over time. Therefore, they (the companies and organizations) wanted frameworks, assessment tools, examples, and further insights. And this is the set of materials that the authors provided in their second book on analytics.

By reading this second book one can look at two key aspects that the authors address in dealing with analytics: a) the kinds of questions analytics can answer; and b) what sort of framework can help companies and organizations to improve their analytical maturity. In respect to the first aspect, Davenport, Harris and Morison (2010) observe that every organization needs to answer some fundamental questions about its business. Taking an analytical approach, as the authors suggest, begins with anticipating how information will be used to address common questions (Figure 2) that can be organized across two dimensions: i) *Time frame*: Are we looking at the past, present, or future?; and ii) *Innovation*: Are we working with known information or gaining new insight?

In relation to the second aspect, in order to put analytics to work in a business, the authors develop what they call as the *Analytical DELTA*. To describe what capabilities and assets one needs to succeed with analytics initiatives, the authors prescribe five success factors grouped under the acronym DELTA- the Greek letter (depicted as Δ or δ) that signifies "change" in an equation. For them these factors change the business equation. Therefore, DELTA represents:

D: For accessible, high-quality *data*;

E: For *enterprise orientation;*

L: For analytical *leadership;*

T: For strategic *targets*; and,

A: For *analysts*.

Although these steps in Analytics are relevant to companies and organizations, they appear to become traditional in the face of the emergence of the phenomenon of *Big Data*. As presented in Cavalcanti (2014), Big Data does not imply that pre-existent data were "small" (what are not) or that its only challenge is its size (size is only one of them). The term Big Data applies to information that cannot be processed or analyzed using traditional processes or tools.

Figure 2. Key Questions addressed by analytics
Source: Davenport, Harris and Morison (2010)

	Past	Present	Future
Information	What happened? (Reporting)	What is happening now? (Alerts)	What will happen? (Extrapolation)
Insight	How and why did it happen? (Modeling, experimental design)	What's the next best action? (Recommendation)	What's the best/worst that can happen? (Prediction, optimization, simulation)

Big Data is important due to some key principles:

- Big Data solutions are ideal for analyzing not only structured raw data but also semi-structured data and non-structured data from a wide variety of sources;
- Big Data solutions are ideal for interactive and exploratory analyzes when business measures with data are not pre-determined;
- Big Data is an appropriate technology to solve challenges of information that cannot be treated by traditional approaches of relational data bases usual in the marketplace.

Three characteristics define Big Data: *volume*, *variety* and *velocity* (known as 3 Vs). Some authors add another characteristic (another V): veracity. Approaches for Big Data require new tools such for *Analytics*, which allow the analysis of new (*quantities/volume*) of different sources of information, for example, social networks, search engines, payment transactions, or all categories of ecommerce (*variety*). The success of Big Data is inevitably related to an intelligent management of selection and use of data, as well as joint efforts towards clear cut rules related to (*quality*) of data. A clear governance of data and a clear policy for data are inevitable to enable a significant use of data (*veracity*).

In order to deal with this phenomenon of Big Data (for a glimpse on the recent growing and forecasted worldwide production of data, see Figure 3, from the International Data Corporation – IDC – www.idc.com) the traditional concept of *Analysis* (which is the process of breaking a complex topic or substance into smaller parts to gain a better understanding of it) continues to be necessary, but such a concept is not sufficient to take into account the growing use of complex computerized methods and tools that are emerging

in the context of the new information technologies and Big Data environments.

As discussed in Cavalcanti (2014), the advent of Big Data turns the field of Analytics even more specialized. In terms of the steps in which Analytics can be used one can look at Figure 4. In the first step organizations gain skills and competences for *Descriptive Analytics*, by using methods, techniques and computational tools for discovering what happened in their common activities. In a second step, called *Diagnostic Analytics*, organizations begin to develop capabilities for discovering and evaluating why determined events had happen. In these two steps what is realized is that organizations are making use of *hindsight* mechanisms, that is, the perception of the significance and nature of events after they have occurred. When these two steps are understood, organizations advance in their skills and competences in order to anticipate events, and they become to utilize *insight* mechanisms, i.e., capacities to discern the nature of a situation.

Then, organizations can be able to initiate the third step, which is the *Predictive Analytics* as a way to predict what can happen in their activities. From that step organizations can acquire skills and competences for the fourth step, which is called *Prescriptive Analytics*, where they can foresee (and act) in order to direct facts and events as they find them suitable. In this step organizations are already making use of foresight mechanisms, that is, the perception of the significance and nature of events before they have occurred.

As shown in Figure 4, as long as organizations advance in their analytical steps, they will be optimizing the use of information, which means, by its turn, an aggregation of value to business (that can lead to obtaining sustainable competitive advantages), not without an increment of difficulty in advancing in those steps.

The changing role in Analytics led by Big Data has also been observed by Thomas Davenport in his recent 2014 book entitled "*big data @ work: Dispelling the Myths, Uncovering the*

Figure 3. Recent and forecasted global production of data

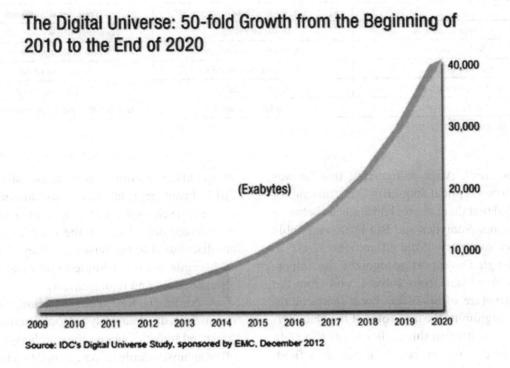

Figure 4. Improving business performance
Source: Edjalali (2011)

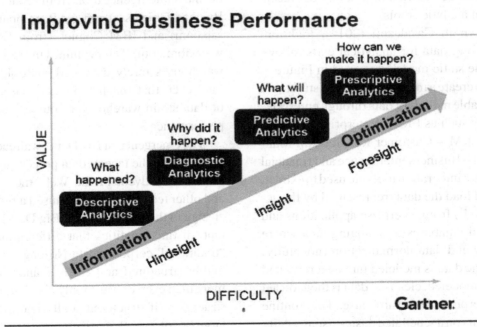

Table 1. Big data and traditional analytics

	Big Data	**Traditional Analytics**
Type of data	Unstructured data	Formatted in rows and columns
Volume of data	100 terabytes to petabytes	Tens of terabytes or less
Flow of data	Constant flow of data	Static pool of data
Analysis methods	Machine learning	Hypothesis-based
Primary purpose	Data-based products	Internal decision support and services

Source: Davenport (2014)

Opportunities". After recognizing that he was wrong to be skeptical about Big Data, this author concluded that there are real differences between conventional Analytics and Big Data, and Table 1 shows a summary of the differences.

Although Davenport recognizes the importance of Big Data, from Table 1, and from the whole structure of his recent book (particularly when he highlights the new roles of the Data Scientists), it seems that this author treats Big Data as a trend that overcomes *Analytics* as a field. The perspective of this chapter, however, is that Big Data demands a distinct kind of Analytics, which is called here as *Big Data Analytics*. Such a position can be justified in terms of the recent evolution in analytics tools.

As shown in Cavalcanti (2014), traditionally processing data for analytical ends follows basically the static model presented in Figure 5. Enterprises create a modest quantity of structured data with stable models of data through enterprise applications such as ERP – Enterprise Resource Planning, CRM – Customer Relationship Management, BI – Business Intelligence and financial systems. Data integration tools are used to extract, transfer and load the data (represented by the acronym of ETL) from enterprise applications and transactional databases to a staging area where data quality and data normalization (hopefully) occur and the data is modeled into neat rows and tables. The modeled, cleansed data is then loaded into an enterprise data warehouse. This routine usually occurs on a scheduled basis – usually daily or weekly, sometimes more frequently (Kelly, 2013). From there, data warehouse administrators create and schedule regular reports to run against normalized data stored in the warehouse, which are distributed to the business. They also create dashboards and other limited visualization tools for executives and management.

According to Kelly (2013) business analysts, meanwhile, use data analytics tools/engines to run advanced analytics against the warehouse, or more often against sample data migrated to a local data mart due to size limitations. Non-expert business users perform basic data visualization and limited analytics against the data warehouse via front-end business intelligence tools from vendors like SAP BusinessObjects (from SAP company: www.sap.com) and IBM Cognos (from IBM Corp.: www.ibm.com). Data volumes in traditional data warehouses rarely exceeded multiple terabytes (and even that much is rare) as large volumes of data strain warehouse resources and degrade performance.

The emergence of Big Data, as already argued, has changed the face of data processing for Analytics. The advent of the Web, mobile devices and other technologies has caused a fundamental change to the nature of data. Big Data has important, distinct qualities that differentiate it from "traditional" corporate data. No longer centralized, highly structured and easily manageable, now, more than ever, data is highly distributed, loosely structured (if structured at all), and increasingly large in volume. Specifically in terms of:

Figure 5. Traditional way of processing data for Analytics
Source: Kelly (2013)

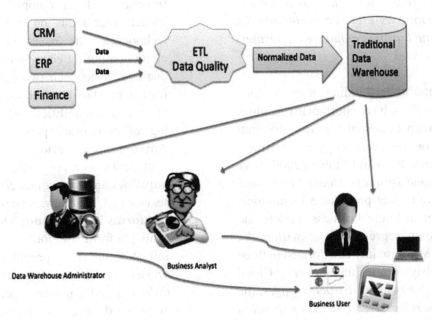

- **Volume:** The amount of data created both inside corporations and outside the firewall via the web, mobile devices, IT infrastructure, and other sources is increasing exponentially each year;
- **Type:** The variety of data types is increasing, namely unstructured text-based data and semi-structured data like social media data, location-based data, and log-file data;
- **Speed:** The speed at which new data is being created – and the need for real-time analytics to derive business value from it -- is increasing thanks to digitization of transactions, mobile computing and the sheer number of internet and mobile device users.

But, in order to understand how Big Data Analytics (or Analytics of Big Data) is gaining prominence, and is fast, and deeply, becoming a general purpose technology, one has to recognize the importance of a third concept (and the last element of our "ABC" acronym): *Cloud Comput-*

ing. There are several denominations for cloud computing. The one chosen here (which also reveals its main goal) is that which was presented at the 2012 Institute of Electrical and Electronics Engineers- IEEE 5th International Conference on Cloud Computing:

Cloud computing has become an elastic pay-as-you-go service creation, delivery, consumption, and management platform in services computing. The technical foundations of cloud computing include a service-oriented architecture (SOA), virtualization of hardware and software, process and workflow optimization, and usage-based accounting and billing. The goal of cloud computing is to cost effectively manage the life cycle of quality-assured services and to share resources among service consumers, partners, and vendors in the cloud value chain. The resource sharing at various levels results in various cloud offerings, such as infrastructure clouds (e.g., hardware, IT infrastructure management), software clouds (e.g., software as a service focusing on middleware as a service, or traditional CRM as a service), application clouds (e.g., application as a service, UML modeling tools as a service, social network as a service), and business clouds (e.g., business process as a service).

To clarify the understanding of what cloud computing comprises, it is important to recognize what are the main pillars of this new computing paradigm, or new technology and business model. Weinhardt, Blau and Stober (2009) have developed a *Cloud Business Model Framework* (CBMF) (Figure 6) that provides a hierarchical classification of different business models and some well-known representatives within the Cloud. The CBMF is mainly categorized in three layers, analogously to the technical layers in Cloud realizations, such as the *infrastructure layer*, the *platform-as-a-service layer* and the *application layer* on top. These layers are described by the authors as follows:

- **Infrastructures in the Cloud:** The infrastructure layer comprehends business models that focus on providing enabler technologies as basic components for cloud computing ecosystems. The authors distinguish between two categories of infrastructure business models: the provision of storage capabilities and the provisioning of computing power. For example, Amazon offers services based on their infrastructure as a computing service (EC2, http://aws.amazon.com/ec2/) and a storage service (S3, http://aws.amazon.com/s3/);

- **Platforms in the Cloud:** This layer represents platform solutions on top of a cloud infrastructure that provides value-added services (platform-as-a-service) from a technical and a business perspective. The authors distinguish between *development platforms* and *business platforms*. Development platforms enable developers

Figure 6. Cloud Business Model Framework
Source: Weinhardt, Blau and Stober (2009)

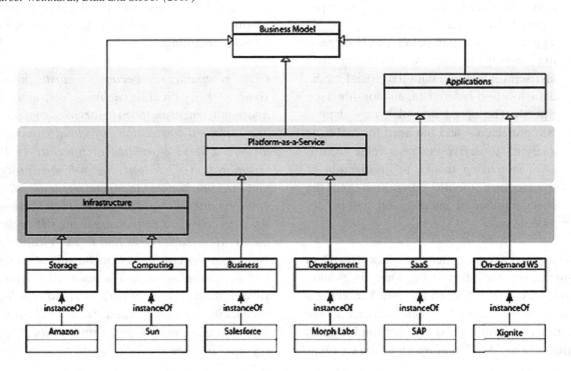

to write their applications and upload their code into the cloud where the application is accessible and can be run in a web-based manner. Developers do not have to care about issues like system scalability as the usage of their applications grows. Prominent examples are Morph Labs (http://www.mor.ph/) and Google App Engine (http://appengine.google.com/), which provide platforms for the deployment and management of Grails, Ruby on Rails and Java applications in the cloud. Business platforms such as Salesforce (http://www.salesforce.com/platform/) with their programming language Apex, and *Microsoft Azure* have also gained strong attention and enable the development, deployment and management of tailored business applications in the cloud;

- **Applications in the Cloud:** The application layer is what most people get to know from Cloud Computing as it represents the actual interface for the customer. Applications are delivered through the Cloud facilitating the platform and infrastructure layer below which are opaque for the user. The authors distinguish between *Software-as-a-Service (SaaS)* applications and the provisioning of rudimentary *Web services on-demand*. Most prominent examples in the SaaS area are Google Apps with their broad catalogue of office applications such as word and spreadsheet processing as well as mail and calendar applications that are entirely accessible through a web browser (http://www.google.com/a/). An example from the B2B sector is SAP that delivers their service-oriented business solution BusinessByDesign over the web for a monthly fee per user (http://www.sap.com/solutions/sme/businessbydesign/index.epx). In the field of Web service on-demand provisioning well-established examples are Xignite (http://www.

xignite.com) and StrikeIron (http://www.strikeiron.com) that offer Web services hosted on a Cloud on a pay-per-use basis.

THE EVOLUTION, APPLICATIONS AND EMERGING RESEARCH RELATED TO THE NEW "ABC' OF ICTS

Having briefly presented what the concepts of Analytics, Big Data and Cloud Computing mean, this section shows a brief account of the evolution, applications, and emerging research areas of this new "ABC" of ICTs. In this respect, the section benefits initially from the research conducted by Chen, Chiang and Storey (2012).

In this research, whose results have been published as the introduction article to a Special Issue of the journal *Management of Information Systems- MIS Quarterly* on Business Intelligence, the authors deal with the areas of Business Intelligence and Analytics (BI&A) and the related field of Big Data Analytics. Figure 7 shows the key sections of the article, including BI&A evolution, applications, and emergent analytics research opportunities.

According to the authors, *BI&A 1.0* (seen in the evolution stack of Figure 7), as a data-centric approach, has its roots in the long-standing database management field. It relies heavily on various data collection, extraction, and analysis technologies. The BI&A technologies and applications currently adopted in industry can be considered as BI&A 1.0, where data are mostly structured, collected by companies through various legacy systems, and often stored in commercial relational database management systems (RDBMS). The analytical techniques commonly used in these systems, popularized in the 1990s, are grounded mainly in statistical methods developed in the 1970s and data mining techniques developed in the 1980s.

The next stage in evolution of BI&A is called by the authors as *BI&A 2.0*. As they state, since

Figure 7. BI&A Overview: Evolution, Applications, and Emerging Research
Source: Chen et. al. (2012)

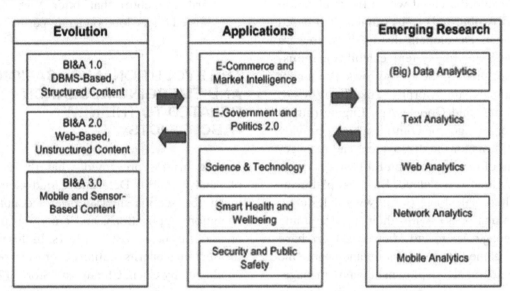

the early 2000s, the Internet and the Web began to offer unique data collection and analytical research and development opportunities. The http-based Web 1.0 systems, characterized by Web search engines such as Google and Yahoo and e-commerce businesses such as Amazon and eBay, allow organizations to present their businesses online and interact with their customers directly. In addition to porting their traditional RDBMS-based product information and business contents online, detailed and IP-specific user search and interaction logs that are collected seamlessly through cookies and server logs have become a new gold mine for understanding customers' needs and identifying new business opportunities. Web intelligence, web analytics, and the user-generated content collected through Web 2.0-based social and crowd-sourcing systems have ushered in a new and exciting era of BI&A 2.0 research in the 2000s, centered on text and web analytics for unstructured web contents (Chen et. al., 2012).

The final stage pointed out by Chen et. al. (2012) is *BI&A 3.0*. To provide a better understanding of what this new stage is about, the main

justification of the authors for labelling this stage as BI&A 3.0 is reproduced here as follows:

Whereas web-based BI&A 2.0 has attracted active research from academia and industry, a new research opportunity in BI&A 3.0 is emerging. As reported prominently in an October 2011 article in The Economist (2011), the number of mobile phones and tablets (about 480 million units) surpassed the number of laptops and PCs (about 380 million units) for the first time in 2011. Although the number of PCs in use surpassed 1 billion in 2008, the same article projected that the number of mobile connected devices would reach 10 billion in 2020. Mobile devices such as the iPad, iPhone, and other smart phones and their complete ecosystems of downloadable applications, from travel advisories to multi-player games, are transforming different facets of society, from education to healthcare and from entertainment to governments. Other sensor-based Internet-enabled devices equipped with RFID, barcodes, and radio tags (the "Internet of Things") are opening up exciting new steams of innovative applications.

The ability of such mobile and Internet-enabled devices to support highly mobile, location-aware, person-centered, and context-relevant operations and transactions will continue to offer unique research challenges and opportunities throughout the 2010s. Mobile interface, visualization, and HCI (human–computer interaction) design are also promising research areas. Although the coming of the Web 3.0 (mobile and sensor-based) era seems certain, the underlying mobile analytics and location and context-aware techniques for collecting, processing, analyzing and visualizing such large scale and fluid mobile and sensor data are still unknown.

The authors observe that in addition to being data driven, BI&A is highly applied and can leverage opportunities presented by the abundant data and domain-specific analytics needed in many critical and high impact application areas. Several of these promising and high-impact BI&A applications are presented in their article, with a discussion of the data and analytics characteristics, potential impacts, and selected illustrative examples or studies in areas such as: (1) ecommerce and market intelligence, (2) e-government and politics 2.0, (3) science and technology, (4) smart health and well-being, and (5) security and public safety. In Table 2 the authors summarize the promising BI&A applications, data characteristics, analytics techniques, and potential impacts by each of these five areas.

An important aspect highlighted by the authors is that the opportunities with the above mentioned emerging and high-impact applications have generated a great deal of excitement within both the BI&A industry and the research community. Whereas industry focuses on scalable and integrated systems and implementations for applications in different organizations, the academic community needs to continue to advance the key technologies in analytics.

Emerging analytics research opportunities can be classified, according to the authors, into 05

(five) critical technical areas - (big) data analytics, text analytics, web analytics, network analytics, and mobile analytics - all of which can contribute to BI&A 1.0, 2.0, and 3.0. The classification of these five topic areas is intended to highlight the key characteristics of each area; however, a few of these areas may leverage similar underlying technologies. In each analytics area we present the foundational technologies that are mature and well developed and suggest selected emerging research areas (see Table 3)(Chen et. al., 2012).

From the point of view of Cloud Computing, this new computing technology, or business model, can be considered as an evolution from the term Grid Computing. As pointed out by Weinhardt, Blau and Stößer. (2009), in the mid 1990s, the term "Grid Computing" was derived from the electrical power grid to emphasize its characteristics like pervasiveness, simplicity and reliability. The upcoming demand for large-scale scientific applications required more computing power than a cluster within a single domain (e. g. an institute) could provide. Due to the fast interconnectedness via the Internet, scientific institutes were able to share and aggregate geographically distributed resources including cluster systems, data storage facilities and data sources owned by different organizations.

However, resource sharing among distributed systems by applying standard protocols and standard software was rarely commercially realized (Weinhardt et. al., 2009). Nevertheless, the combination of cheaper, flexible, scalable and reliable ICT infrastructure demands from businesses with the interconnectedness via the Internet, led to the recognition that Clouds are not limited to Grid environments, but also support "*interactive, user-facing applications*" such as Web applications and three-tier architectures.

In such way, Clouds became to be known as "pools of virtualized computer resources". As observed by Boss, Malladi, Quan, Legregni and Hall (2007), Clouds complement Grid Environments by supporting the management of Grid resources. In

Table 2. BI&A Applications: From Big Data to Big Impact (Source: Chen et. al. (2012))

	E-Commerce and Market Intelligence	E-Government and Politics 2.0	Science and Technology	Smart Health and Wellbeing	Security and Public Safety
Applications	Recommender systems • Social media monitoring and analysis • Crowd-sourcing systems • Social and virtual games	• Ubiquitous government services • Equal access and public services • Citizen engagement and participation • Political campaign and e-polling	• S&T innovation • Hypothesis testing • Knowledge discovery	• Human and plant genomics • Healthcare decision support • Patient community analysis	• Crime analysis • Computational criminology • Terrorism informatics • Open-source intelligence • Cyber security
Data	• Search and user logs • Customer transaction records • Customer generated content	• Government information and services • Rules and regulations • Citizen feedback and comments	• S&T instruments and system generated data • Sensor and network content	• Genomics and sequence data • Electronic health records (EHR) • Health and patient social media	• Criminal records • Crime maps • Criminal networks • News and web contents • Terrorism incident databases • Viruses, cyber attacks, and
	Characteristics: Structured webbased, usergenerated content, rich network information, unstructured informal customer opinions	Characteristics: Fragmented information sources and legacy systems, rich textual content, unstructured informal citizen conversations	Characteristics: High-throughput instrument-based data collection, finegrained multiple modality and large scale records, S&T specific data formats	Characteristics: Disparate but highly linked content, person-specific content, HIPAA, IRB and ethics issues	Characteristics: Personal identity information, incomplete and deceptive content, rich group and network information, multilingual content
Analytics	• Association rule mining • Database segmentation and clustering • Anomaly detection • Graph mining • Social network analysis • Text and web analytics • Sentiment and affect analysis	• Information integration • Content and text analytics • Government information semantic services and ontologies • Social media monitoring and analysis • Social network analysis • Sentiment and affect analysis	S&T based domain-specific mathematical and analytical models	• Genomics and sequence analysis and visualization • EHR association mining and clustering • Health social media monitoring and analysis • Health text analytics • Health ontologies • Patient network analysis • Adverse drug side-effect analysis • Privacy-preserving data mining	• Criminal association rule mining and clustering • Criminal network analysis • Spatial-temporal analysis and visualization • Multilingual text analytics • Sentiment and affect analysis • Cyber attacks analysis and attribution
Impacts	Long-tail marketing, targeted and personalized recommendation, increased sale and customer satisfaction	Transforming governments, empowering citizens, improving transparency, participation, and equality	S&T advances, scientific impact	Improved healthcare quality, improved long-term care, patient empowerment	Improved public safety and security

Table 3. BI&A Research Framework: Foundational Technologies and Emerging Research in Analytics

	(Big) Data Analytics	Text Analytics	Web Analytics	Network Analytics	Mobile Analytics
Foundational Technologies	• RDBMS • data warehousing • ETL • OLAP • BPM • data mining • clustering • regression • classification • association analysis • anomaly detection • neural networks • genetic algorithms • multivariate statistical analysis • optimization • heuristic search	• information retrieval • document representation • query processing • relevance feedback • user models • search engines • enterprise search systems	• information retrieval • computational linguistics • search engines • web crawling • web site ranking • search log analysis • recommender systems • web services • mashups	• bibliometric analysis • citation network • coauthorship network • social network theories • network metrics and topology • mathematical network models • network visualization	• web services • smartphone platforms
Emerging Research	• statistical machine learning • sequential and temporal mining • spatial mining • mining high-speed data streams and sensor data • process mining • privacy-preserving data mining • network mining • web mining • column-based DBMS • in-memory DBMS • parallel DBMS • cloud computing • Hadoop • MapReduce	• statistical NLP • information extraction • topic models • question-answering systems • opinion mining • sentiment/affect analysis • web stylometric analysis • multilingual analysis • text visualization • multimedia IR • mobile IR • Hadoop • MapReduce	• cloud services • cloud computing • social search and mining • reputation systems • social media analytics • web visualization • web-based auctions • internet monetization • social marketing • web privacy/ security	• link mining • community detection • dynamic network modeling • agent-based modeling • social influence and information diffusion models • ERGMs • virtual communities • criminal/dark networks • social/political analysis • trust and reputation	• mobile web services • mobile pervasive apps • mobile sensing apps • mobile social innovation • mobile social networking • mobile visualization/HCI • personalization and behavioral modeling • gamification • mobile advertising and marketing

Source: Chen, Chiang and Storey (2012)

particular, Clouds allow: (i) the dynamic scale-in and scale-out of applications by the provisioning and de-provisioning of resources, e. g. by means of virtualization; and (ii) the monitoring of resource utilization to support dynamic load-balancing and re-allocations of applications and resources.

In terms of deployment models, a computing cloud can evolve as one, or more, of the three types: private, public or hybrid (NIST, 2014)(see Figure 8). A *private cloud* is cloud infrastructure operated solely for a single organization, whether managed internally or by a third-party, and hosted either internally or externally. A cloud is called a *"public cloud"* when the services are rendered over a network that is open for public use. Public cloud services may be free or offered on a pay-per-usage model. Technically there may be little or no difference between public and private cloud architecture, however, security consideration may be substantially different for services (applications, storage, and other resources) that are made available by a service provider for a public audience and when communication is effected over a non-trusted network. Finally, *hybrid cloud* is a composition of two or more clouds (private, community or public) that remain distinct entities but are bound together, offering the benefits of multiple deployment models. Hybrid cloud can also mean the ability to connect collocation, managed and/or dedicated services with cloud resources.

As with any computing model, the technological landscape is rapidly evolving in cloud computing. As stressed by Marston, Li, Bandyopadhyay, Zhang and Ghalsasi (2011), even though it might be impossible to conjecture all the technological changes in future (for one to get an impression of what went on at the 2014 IEEE annual conferences on Cloud, Big Data, Mobile and Services – Web Services, Computing Services and Mobile Ser-

vices – just have a look at this site: http://www. thecloudcomputing.org/2014/AdvanceProgram-ICWS-SCC-CLOUD-MS-BigDataCongress-SERVICES-2014.pdf), and even, as the authors indicate, that the economic forces shaping this phenomenon, in contrast, are very logical and almost inexorable in nature, these authors suggest several potential streams of research for, at least, Information Systems (IS) researchers.

They do not concentrate on the core technological issues in cloud computing, since that is outside the purview of IS research. The broad IS research agenda in cloud computing can be divided into six categories: (1) Cloud computing economics; (3) Cloud computing and IT strategy/policy issues (including security); (4) Technology adoption and implementation issues; (5) Cloud computing and green IT; and (6) Regulatory issues.

Figure 8. Cloud Computing types
Source: http://www.salesforcetutorial.com/introduction-to-cloud-computing/

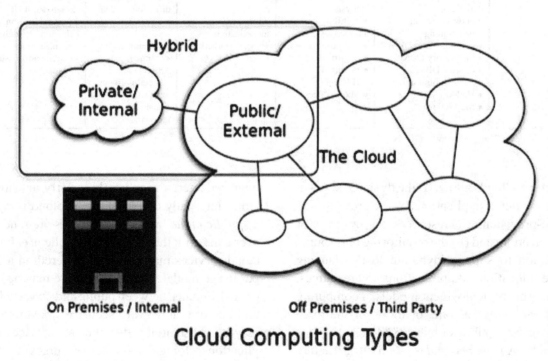

Figure 9. Cloud computing business-technology framework

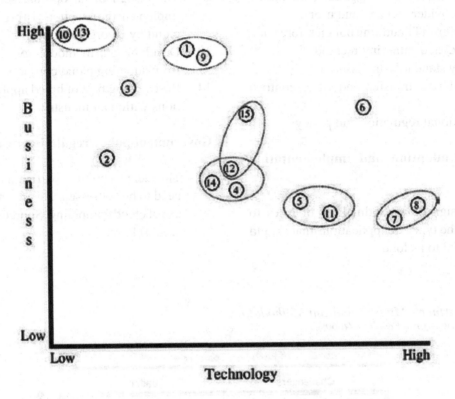

The authors observe that there are two fundamental dimensions under which these topics could also be classified. Some of the research topics, such as cloud computing pricing strategy can be thought of to be more of a *"business"* issue, while a topic like security standards is more of a *"technology"* issue. Figure 9 summarizes some of the specific research topics they identified and places them in a "business-technology" framework (Marston et. al., 2011).

Obs: The circled numbers in the business-technology framework shown in Figure 9 refer to the research topics indicated below (the topics are grouped under the six main research categories that we mention in the main text, and the dashed figures indicate the linkages between the various topics):

Research Agenda

Cloud computing economics research:

1. Cloud service pricing strategy
2. The role of enablers effect on the cloud computing provider economic value and the entire value chain

Strategy research in cloud computing:

3. Corporate culture impact
4. Partnership/3rd party relational impact

IS policy research:

5. Managing and implementing consistent IS policy across the usage of multiple cloud providers

6. Optimal software management for both a cloud provider and a Cloud user
7. The design of IT auditing policies, forensics, and evidence gathering methods
8. Security standards and issues
9. Optimal risk transfer and SLA contract design
10. International regulation and policy

Technology adoption and implementation research:

11. The design of an optimal set of rules to decide the types of applications that should be moved to a cloud

12. The design of an optimal set of rules to implement the adoption of a private or public cloud by an organization
13. Developing a methodology to assess risk from adopting cloud computing
14. Researching best of breed application solutions within an industry

Government policy/regulation research:

15. The identification of pertinent issues which need to be addressed that are created by the use of cloud computing. Source: Marston et. al., 2011

Figure 10. Gartner's Magic Quadrant Methodology
Source: https://www.gartner.com/doc/486094

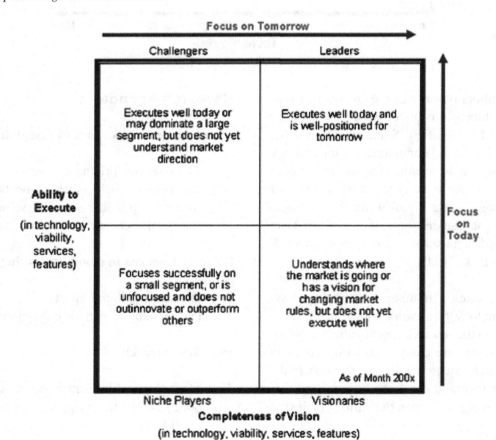

THE MAIN PLAYERS IN THE INDUSTRY CREATED BY THE NEW "ABC" OF ICTS

The best way to describe the main players in the industry created by the new "ABC" of ICTs is to present briefly one of the internationally known business/commercial surveys developed by one of the research companies that conduct researches and analyses about the ICT industry. The one chosen here is that of the Gartner Group (www.gartner.com). Since 2006, Gartner has published a Magic Quadrant survey, which is a culmination of research in a specific market, providing a wide-angle view of the relative positions of the market's competitors. By applying a graphical treatment and a uniform set of evaluation criteria, a Gartner Magic Quadrant quickly helps one digest how well technology providers are executing against their stated vision.

A Magic Quadrant provides a graphical competitive positioning of four types of technology providers, in markets where growth is high and provider differentiation is distinct, according two dimensions: Ability to Execute and Completeness of Vision (see Figure 10). The types are:

- **Leaders:** Execute well against their current vision and are well positioned for tomorrow;
- **Visionaries:** Understand where the market is going or have a vision for changing market rules, but do not yet execute well;
- **Niche Players:** Focus successfully on a small segment, or are unfocused and do not out-innovate or outperform others;
- **Challengers:** Execute well today or may dominate a large segment, but do not demonstrate an understanding of market direction.

Since 2006 Gartner has published a *Magic Quadrant on Business Intelligence - BI and Analyt-ics* (the name has changed slightly over the years) to evaluate vendors across the entire spectrum of BI and analytic capabilities but focused on their ability to provide traditional query and reporting (descriptive) capabilities. During the past few years, interactive visualization (diagnostic), predictive and prescriptive analysis has become more important to organizations, and this has been reflected in the vendors evaluated in the Magic Quadrant and their positions therein (Gartner, 20 February 2014).

In 2013, Gartner's analysts research team decided that the scope of the Magic Quadrant had grown to cover multiple markets. Although the decisions were sometimes connected, the evaluation process that most clients followed for "traditional" BI capabilities had become separate form that used to evaluate "advanced" analytic capabilities. Hence the team decided it was time to introduce an additional Magic Quadrant on advanced analytics platforms (Gartner, 20 February 2014).

In this way, the new *"Magic Quadrant for Advanced Analytics Platforms"* covers the diagnostic, predictive and prescriptive components, but assigns most weight to the predictive (see Figure 11 included in this survey). The *"Magic Quadrant for Business Intelligence and Analytics Platforms"* encompasses all four components – descriptive, diagnostic, predictive and prescriptive – but allocates more weight to the descriptive and diagnostic (see Figure 12).

In terms of Cloud Computing, although it is possible to find many surveys and researches produced by Gartner related to this subject area, it is only possible to find two published Magic Quadrant reports in the company's web site: one for *Cloud Infrastructure as a Service* and another for *Cloud-Based IT Project and Portfolio Management Services*. Hence, here it is presented the main players of the Magic Quadrant report for Cloud Infrastructure as a Service: Amazon Web Services (see Figure 13).

Figure 11. Magic Quadrant for Advanced Analytics Platforms
Source: Gartner (2014)

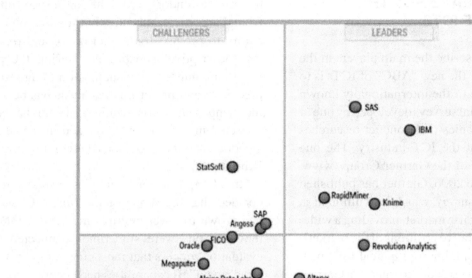

THE NEW "ABC" TECHNOLOGIES, THE AGG MODEL, AND THE IMPACT OF THE TRADE-OFF BETWEEN INFORMATION TECHNOLOGY (IT) AND COMMUNICATION TECHNOLOGY (CT) COSTS ON THE FIRM'S ORGANIZATION

As it was possible to infer from the previous sections, the emergence of new Analytics, Big Data and Cloud Computing technologies, tools and business models, is changing radically and deeply the way in which we deal with data, information,

and knowledge, and, as a consequence, it is transforming the way our economy and our society are being organized.

A question that still remains to be properly answered is: How do these new "ABC" technologies, tools and business models affect the way firms are structured, managed, and, as a result, perform? Although this is not a simple question to answer, there are, in the academic and professional literature, several attempts to move in such a direction. Some of the works already referred to in this chapter can be described as representative of this move: Davenport and Harris (2007),

Figure 12. Magic Quadrant for Business Intelligence and Analytics Platforms
Source: Gartner (2014)

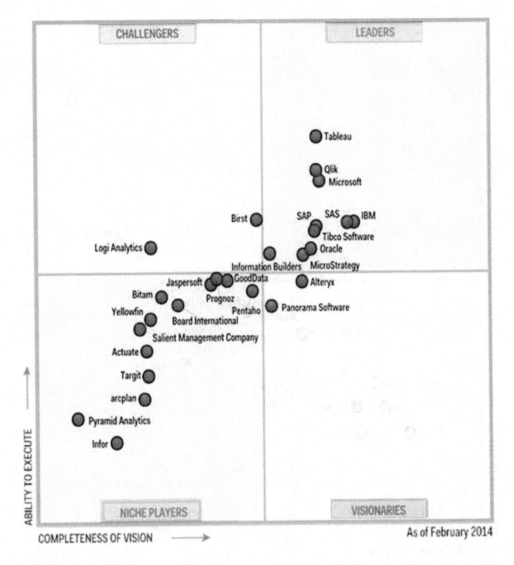

Davenport, Harris and Morison (2010), Davenport (2014). It is also possible to point out Vitalari and Shaughnessy (2012), with their concept of "The Elastic Enterprise", Hamel (2012) with his argument for a new kind of Management in "What Matters Now", Brynjolfsson and McAffe (2011) with their fascinating "Race Against the Machine", and so many others.

However, in Cavalcanti (2014) one can find a comprehensive model that can address three interconnected realms of the firm and helps to understand how these realms affect each other. This model is called the *"Architecture-Governance-Growth - AGG Model"*. The central thesis of the AGG framework (represented here by Figure 14 as a typical firm dynamics comprising the *corpo-*

Figure 13. Magic Quadrant for Cloud Infrastructure as a Service
Source: Gartner (2014)

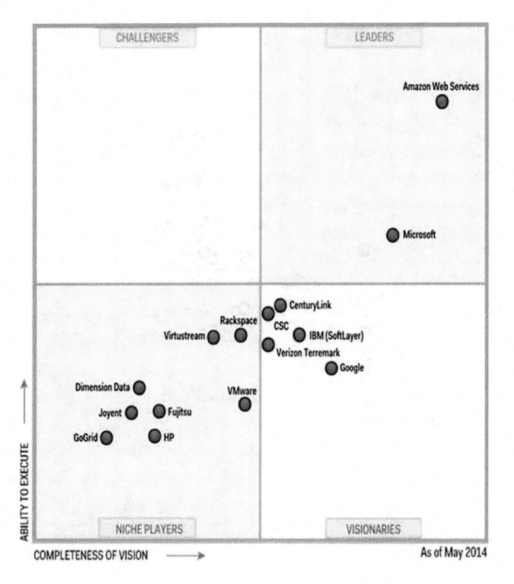

rate and the *information technology-IT* domains) is that "*observable architectural characteristics of a firm determine the governance issues of the firm, and that the governance agenda of the firm determines its measurable growth conditions*".

The basic idea of the AGG Model rests upon the concept of the *Firm or Enterprise Architecture*. The observable architectural characteristics of the firm are those related to its design, structure,

functioning and management. In the AGG model they constitute the *architecture* realm of the model, which is comprised by both its *corporate* and its *information and communication technology (ICT)* domains. But, where does this concept of firm/enterprise architecture come from?

As indicated in Cavalcanti (2014), perhaps no one in the information systems academic and professional literature is more cited, and referred,

Figure 14. The AGG- Architecture-Governance-Growth Model

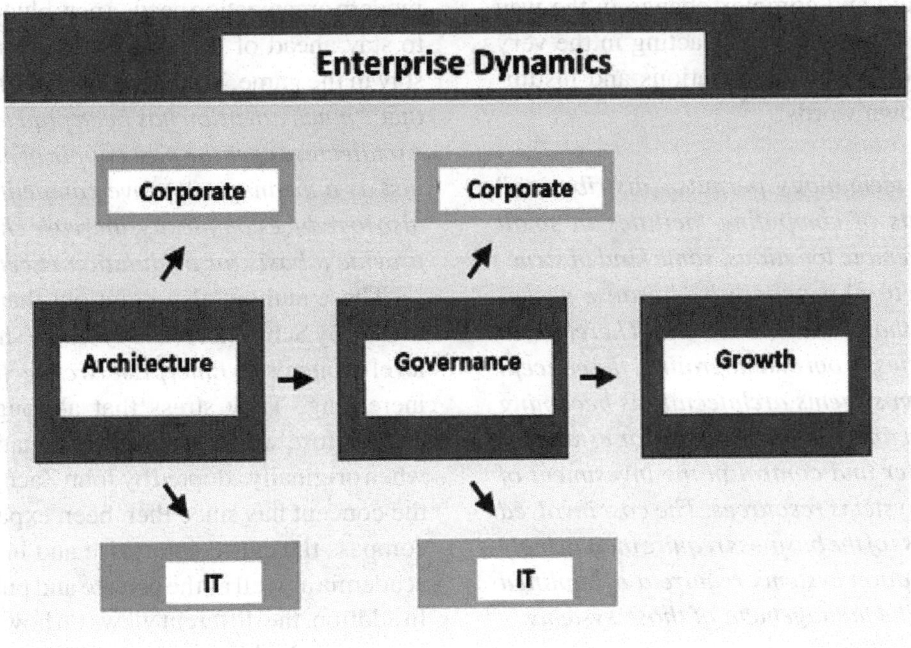

Source: The Author

in relation to the subject matter of firm architecture, than J. A. Zachman. In his acclaimed article of 1987, entitled "*A framework for information systems architecture*", published at the IBM Systems Journal, Zachman presents the following abstract of his famous article:

With increasing size and complexity of the implementation of information systems, it is necessary to use some logical construct (or architecture) for defining and controlling the interfaces and the integration of all of the components of the system. This paper defines information systems architecture by creating a descriptive framework from disciplines quite independent of information systems, then by analogy specifies information systems architecture based upon the neutral, objective framework. Also, some preliminary conclusions about the implications of the resultant descriptive framework are drawn. The discussion is limited to architecture and does not include a strategic planning methodology.

What Zachman was observing more than a quarter of a century ago was an important fact that was affecting firms, organizations and institutions alike: '*the subject of information systems architecture is beginning to receiving considerable attention*' (Zachman, 1987). He observed that the increased scope of design and levels of complexity of information systems implementations were forcing the use of some '*logical construct (architecture)*' for defining and controlling the interfaces and the integration of all of the components of the system. In his opinion: '*Thirty years ago this issue was not at all significant because the technology itself did not provide for either breadth in scope or depth in complexity in information systems*'.

In fact what Zachman (1987) was anticipating was a profound and complex change in the way information systems were impacting in the very constitution of firms, organizations and institutions. In his own words:

… since the technology permits "distributing" large amounts of computing facilities in small packages to remote locations, some kind of structure (architecture) is imperative because decentralization without structure is chaos. Therefore, to keep the business from disintegrating, the concept of information systems architecture is becoming less an option and more a necessity for establishing some order and control in the investment of information systems resources. The cost involved and the success of the business require increasingly on its information systems require a disciplined approach to the management of those systems.

At the time he was proposing and supporting the concept of *information systems architecture* there was little consistency in concepts or in specifications of 'architecture'. Therefore, he observed that it would be necessary to develop some kind of framework for rationalizing the various architectural concepts and specifications in order to provide for clarity of professional communication, to allow for improving and integrating development methodologies and tools, and to establish credibility and confidence in the investment of systems resources.

Although the term architecture has been used in some aspects of the information and comunication technology industry, and although the term was mostly limited to information systems when originally adopted by John Zachman (1987), the concept has since then expanded to encompass the entire firm/enterprise.

In a 2012 article entitled '*Alignment in Enterprise Architecture: A Comparative Analysis of Four Architectural Approaches*', Thanos Magoulas, Ainda Hadzic, Ted Saarikko and Kalevi Pessi, from the Department of Applied IT of the University of Gothenburg, Sweden, argue that the modern organization needs a new blueprint in order to stay ahead of the game – or at the very least stay in the game. To this end, the authors observe that: "*much attention has been paid to Enterprise Architecture over the past couple of decades – not just as a means to improve competitiveness, but also to reduce complexity, increase changeability, provide a basis for evalutation et cetera*".

These authors also point out that a literature review by Sch enherr (2009) cleary shows that the level of interest in *Enterprise Architecture* is indeed increasing. They stress that although the term architecture was limited to information systems when originally adopted by John Zachman (1987), the concept has since then been expanded to encompass the entire enterprise and interpreted by academia as well as the private and public sectors. In addtion, the different views on how to approach Enterprise Architecture are often documented and compiled into 'guides' or 'frameworks' which are intended to instruct practitioners in how to apply this concept to their organization.

After presenting how the concept of architecture came into being in the information systems academic and professional literature, and after reporting some aspects of its evolution from an information systems architecture concept into the enterprise architecture concept, Cavalcanti (2014) observes that another aspect related to the understanding of the structure and dynamics of the modern digital (or digitalized) enterprise concerns to its relation to the market where it belongs or to the market it contributed to generate.

However, moving the discussion from the firm/enterprise to the market (and vice-versa) is not a simple journey, and one has to have a clear understanding of how to deal with these two realms of the business environment. That is why Cavalcanti (2014) works with the concept of "*market architecture*", or simply put, the way by which markets are designed, structured, and, as a result, function. The propositon advanced in his book is that:

To be properly designed, to function adequately, and to sustain its activities, an enterprise's architecture should be aligned to the market architecture of its main business environment, and also to the market architectures of its subsidiary business environments.

Besides its architectural dimension, the AGG Model incorporates the governance and the growth dimensions (which are presented in a very brief fashion). Cavalcanti (2014) argues that the *governance* dimension of the AGG Model in general, and the *corporate governance* plus the *information technology governance* in particular, are key tools connecting the *architecture of firms/enterprises* and the *architecture of markets* to the *growth of firm/enterprises* and to the *growth of markets*. The important issue to be addressed is how such connections are established.

In this respect, Cavalcanti (2014) rescues the literature on corporate finance. He observes that in one of the most downloaded and most cited article of the Journal of Corporate Finance, entitled '*Corporate governance and firm performance*', published by Snajai Bhagat and Brian Bolton in 2008, these authors begin by asking two important questions: '*How is corporate governance measured?*' and, '*What is the relationship between corporate governance and performance?*'.

The above mentioned article sheds light on these questions while taking into account the endogeneity of the relationships among corporate governance, corporate performance, corporate capital structure, and corporate ownership structure. Without commenting on the details of the expanded introduction of the Bhagat and Bolton (2008) article, it is important to highlight here the most salient aspects of the brief review these authors made concerning the literature on the relationship among corporate ownership structure, governance, performance and capital structure.

Bhagat and Bolton (2008) begin their review by stating that some governance features of the firm may be motivated by incentive-based economic models of managerial behavior. In their view these models fall into two categories. In *agency models*, a divergence in the interests of managers and shareholders causes managers to take actions that are costly to shareholders. Contracts cannot preclude this activity if shareholders are unable to observe managerial behavior directly, but *ownership* by the manager may be used to induce managers to act in a manner that is consistent with the interest of shareholders.

This first category can be understood as revealing one of the first channels through which *corporate governance* can be described: the connection between *ownership structure* and *corporate governance*. And this can also be understood as a first explanation for the connection between the *corporate governance* and the *enterprise architecture* dimensions of the AGG Model (see Figure 15).

The second category presented by Bhagat and Bolton (2008) is *adverse selection models*. Adverse selection models are motivated by the hypothesis of differential ability that cannot be observed by shareholders. In this setting, ownership may be used to induce revelation of the manager's private information about cash flow or her ability to generate cash flow, which cannot be observed directly by shareholders.

Bhagat and Bolton (2008) also add that in the above scenarios, some features of corporate governance may be interpreted as a characteristic of the contract that governs relations between shareholders and managers. Governance is affected by the same unobservable features of managerial behavior or ability that are linked to ownership and performance.

These authors also observe that since Berle and Means (1932), economists have emphasized the costs of diffused share-ownership; that is, the impact of ownership structure on performance. However, Demsetz (1983) argues that since we observe many successful public companies with diffused share-ownership, clearly there must be offsetting benefits, for example, better risk-

Figure 15. Ownership structure as a connection between the enterprise architecture and corporate governance dimensions relations
Source: The author

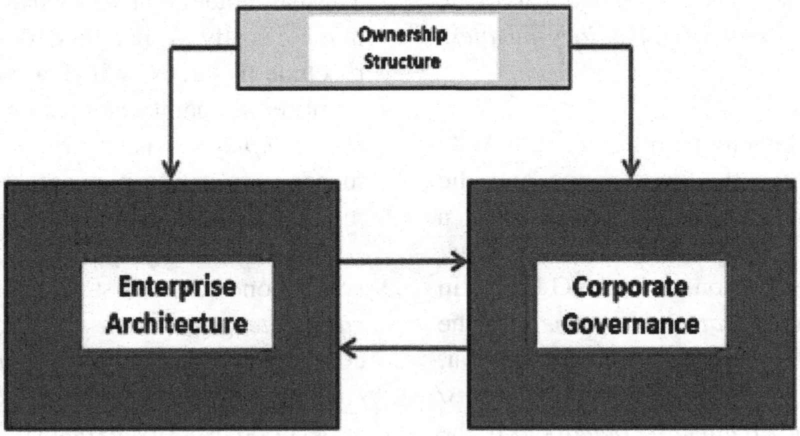

bearing. Also, for reasons related to performance-based compensation and insider information, firm performance could be a determinant of ownership. For example, superior firm performance leads to an increase in the value of stock options owned by management which, if exercised, would increase their share ownership. Also, if there are serious divergences between insider and market expectations of future firm performance then insiders have an incentive to adjust their ownership in relation to the expected future performance.

This can be interpreted as another channel connecting *corporate governance*: through *ownership* and *firm performance*. In this way, this channel can also be understood as the connection to the third dimension of the AGG Model, by assuming that the firm's growth is the result of the enterprise performance (see Figure 16).

Finally, Bhagat and Bolton (2008) point out that in a seminal paper Grossman & Hart (1983) considered the *ex ante* efficiency perspective to derive predictions about a firm's financing deci-

Figure 16. Ownership structure and enterprise growth
Source: The author

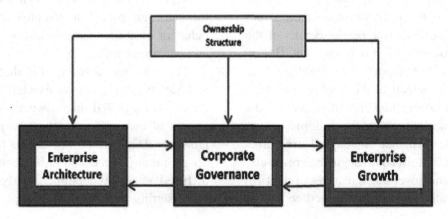

sions in an agency setting. Novaes and Zingales (1999) show that the optimal choice of debt (from the viewpoint of shareholders), differs from the optimal choice of debt from the viewpoint of managers. While the above focuses on capital structures and managerial entrenchment, a different strand of the literature has focused on the relation between capital structure and ownership structure; for example, see Grossman and Hart (1986) and Hart and Moore (1990).

These observations lead to two other channels through which corporate governance can be analyzed: one is the connection between *corporate governance* and *capital structure*, and the other is *capital structure* and *ownership structure*. These two additional channels can be visualized in Figure 17. By extension, one can infer that the connections presented in this Figure 17 can be generalized for the understanding of the necessary alignment of the firm to the architecture, operation and growth of its own market and to other related or non-related markets.

The governance dimension of the AGG Model is completed with the information technology (IT) domain. Cavalcanti (2014) observes that information technology is an increasingly important element of organizational products and services and the foundation of enterprisewide processes. The tight linkage between IT and organizational processes means that the IT unit cannot bear sole responsibility for the effective use of information and IT. As a result, *getting more value from IT is an increasingly important organizational competency, and leaders throughout an enterprise must develop this competence*" (Weill & Ross, 2004). This message is a strong evidence for the necessity of a better understanding of the mechanisms that govern the information life cycle, and, consequently, the correspondent information technologies inside and across firms. Therefore, aside corporate governance, the *IT governance* is becoming a crucial activity in modern firms.

The last component of the AGG Model is the growth realm, which recognizes the relevance of

Figure 17. The AGG Model and its defining connections
Source: The author

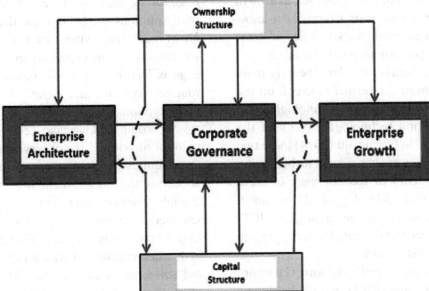

technology and innovation to this subject. Without going into extensive details that Cavalcanti (2014) uses to justify this component within the AGG Model, for the interest of this chapter it is important to stress that the growth of the firm has been one of the most widely researched topics in economic literature, and several arguments highlight the crucial importance of this field. And there is no shortage of arguments for that: a) First, firm growth is related to firm survival; b) Second, firm growth has consequences for employment; c) Third, associated to importance of firm growth is its effect on economic growth; d) Fourth, firm growth is a way to introduce innovation and is a leitmotiv of technological change; and, e) The evolution of the size of incumbents and new entrants determines market concentration; and, f) Moreover, a study of firm's growth can shed light on the importance of the selection process after an firm has entered the market (Carrizosa, 2006).

Another important characteristic of this topic, as stressed by Carrizosa (2006) is that firm's growth has practical consequences for policy makers' decisions. Firm's growth can increase employment and economic activity and policy makers can control these macroeconomic variables using firm's growth policies. However, as growth is heterogeneous across firms, it is crucial to know the internal and external characteristics of firms that affect their performance in the market.

This last statement is considered here the main reason for the need for further research on the distinct effects of information technologies (IT) and communication technologies (CT) on the firm architecture. In Cavalcanti (2014) these two sets of technologies are considered as belonging to the same category of technologies; in order words, information technologies –IT or information and communication technologies – ICT, used interchangeably, are treated as an aggregate homogeneous capital stock.

However, as pointed out by Bloom, Garicano, Sadun and Van Reenen (2013), these technologies have two distinct components. First, through the spread of cheap storage and processing of data information (aspects related to IT) is becoming cheaper to access. Second, through the spread of cheap wired and wireless communications (aspects related to CT), agents find it easier to communicate with each other (e.g. e-mail and mobile devices). For these authors, reductions in the cost of accessing information stored in databases and of communicating information among agents can be expected to have a very different impact on firm organization. While cheaper information access has an *"empowering"* effect, allowing agents to handle more of the problems they face autonomously, cheaper communication technology facilitates *specialization*: since agents can easily rely on others to solve tasks outside their immediate area of expertise, they ultimately perform a more limited variety of tasks. This difference matters not just for firms' organization, but also for productivity and in the labor market.

The starting point of their analysis is the work conducted by Garicano (2000) on the hierarchical organization of expertise, also known as the *knowledge-based hierarchy* view of the firm. According to this view, *decisions* involve solving problems and thus acquiring the relevant knowledge for the decision. When matching problems with solutions is cheap, expertise is organized *horizontally*. But when matching problems and solutions is expensive, the organization of knowledge is *hierarchical*: those below deal with the routine problems, and those "above" deal with the exceptions.

According to Garicano (2000), the starting point of his view is the observation that production requires physical resources and knowledge about how to combine them. If communication is available, workers do not need to acquire all the knowledge necessary to produce. Instead, they may acquire only the most relevant knowledge and, when confronted with a problem they cannot solve, ask someone else. The organization must then decide who must learn what and whom each worker should ask when confronted with an unknown problem. When classifying knowledge is cheap, figuring out where to turn when a problem solution is unknown is straightforward. Production know-how is, however, often tacit and thus is "embodied" in individuals. Knowing if someone knows the solution to a problem inevitably involves asking that person.

As a result, Garicano (2000) stresses that it is natural to organize the acquisition of knowledge as a *"knowledge-based hierarchy."* In such a structure, knowledge of solutions to the most common or easiest problems is located in the production floor, whereas knowledge about more exceptional or harder problems is located in higher layers of the hierarchy. Production workers who confront problems they cannot solve refer them to the next layer of the organization, formed by specialist problem solvers. Problems are then passed on until someone can solve them or until the conditional probability of finding the solution is too low to justify continuing the search.

This distinctive approach to the organization of the firm, also called the *"design of knowledge'"* or *"skill hierarchies"* within organizations, has been expanded by other researchers, such as those represented by the papers of Beggs (2001), Garicano and Rossi-Hansberg (2006), Antràs, Garicano and Rossi-Hansberg (2006), Garicano and Rossi-Hansberg (2012), and Garicano and Prat (2013).

Despite its distinctive appeal and elegance, this approach does not seem to represent, at first sight, key aspects related to the trade-off between information technology (IT) and communication technology (CT) costs in the architecture of the firm, and it does not seem to reflect the complexity inherent to the application and usage of the new ABC technologies and tools (treated in this chapter) within the firm and across its business relations. And this can be justified in two grounds: one theoretical and one practical.

From a theoretical view point, it is possible to refer to a recent research in the field of *crowd innovation*. In an attempt to distinguish their work

from that of the above mentioned papers in the "skill hierarchies" approach, Acemoglu, Mostagir and Ozdaglar (2014) observe that in those papers *workers* belong to the same firm and can cooperate on solving problems in order to increase output, and workers in different levels of the hierarchy specialize in solving only certain kinds of problems that complement other existing skills. The decision of which skills to obtain is a decision that is endogenous to the workers and the organization, and can be based, as in Garicano (2000), on the difficulty distribution that the firm faces. This ensures that the skills in the pool of workers and difficulties in the task pool are aligned.

But, as Acemoglu et. al. (2014) note, this feature, though it makes these models elegantly tractable, does not provide an adequate description of *crowd innovation environments*, where a mismatch between task difficulties and skills is commonplace, where skills are often very dispersed and unknown, and where voluntary participation of workers is a central issue.

In their work, Acemoglu et. al. (2014) state that *crowdsourcing* is an emerging technology where innovation and production are sourced out to the public through an open call. As the authors perceive, at the center of crowdsourcing is a *"resource allocation problem"*: there is an abundance of workers but a scarcity of high skills, and an easy task assigned to a high-skill worker is a waste of resources. This problem is complicated by the fact that the exact difficulties of innovation tasks may not be known in advance, so tasks that require high-skill labor cannot be identified and allocated ahead of time.

Therefore, the authors show that the solution to this problem takes the form of a *"skill hierarchy"*, where tasks are first attempted by low-skill labor, and high-skill workers only engage with a task if less skilled workers are unable to finish it. This hierarchy can be constructed and implemented in a decentralized manner even though neither the difficulties of the tasks nor the skills of the candidate workers are known. In this way, the authors provide a dynamic pricing mechanism that achieves this implementation by inducing workers to *self select* into different layers. The mechanism is simple: each time a task is attempted and not finished, its price (reward upon completion) goes up.

From a practical view point, when deploying ABC technologies and tools firms face a complex set of decisions concerning what could be the most reliable and economic solutions for their problems, and this implies a planned of specification (and choice) of information technologies (IT) and communication technologies (CT), and the consideration of their associated costs. The trade-off between these costs is dealt by managers when they decide what kind of assets of the firm they intend to mobilize to achieve their intended goals. These decisions, as a result, have serious implications for the firm architecture and for its governance and growth domains, as highlighted by the AGG Model.

In terms of IT and CT assets, Weil (1998) provides a framework (Figure 18) for the analysis of these assets that can be a good starting point for when the firm decides to make use of ABC

technologies and tools, and chooses to use them in terms of the functions to which those assets were designed and implemented. The classes of assets are:

- **Transactional IT:** Automates processes, cuts costs or increases the volume of business a firm can conduct per unit cost, e.g., order processing, bank cash withdrawal, billing, accounting and other repetitive transaction processing functions;
- **Informational IT:** Provides information for managing, accounting, reporting and communicating internally and with customers, suppliers and regulators, e.g., decision, support, accounting, planning, control, sales analysis, customer relationship and Sarbanes-Oxley reporting systems;
- **Strategic IT:** supports entry into a new market, development of new products or capabilities, and innovative implementations of IT. Example: ATMs;
- **Infrastructure IT:** provides the foundation of shared IT services (both technical

Figure 18. Rethinking IT as an Investment Portfolio: Four Different Classes of Assets
Source: Weil (1998)

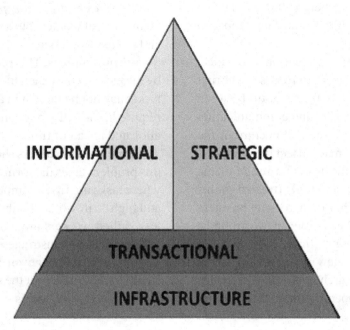

and human) used by multiple applications, e.g., servers, networks, laptops, shared customer databases, help desk, application development. A project may be any combination of all four.

In the end, the successful application of the new *ABC* technologies and tools treated in this chapter depends on two interrelated policy aspects: 1) the use of a proper model which could help one to approach the structure and dynamics of the firm, and, 2) how the complex trade-off between information technology (IT) and communication technology (CT) costs is handled within, between and beyond firms, organizations and institutions.

FINAL CONCLUSION

As it was possible to see in this chapter, *Analytics* (discover and communication of patterns, with significance, in data) of *Big Data* (basically characterized by large structured and unstructured data volumes, from a variety of sources, at high velocity - i.e., real-time data capture, storage, and analysis), through the use of *Cloud Computing* (a model of network computing), which was called here the new *"ABC"* of information and communication technologies (ICTs), is changing radically and deeply the way in which we deal with data, information, and knowledge, and, as a consequence, it is transforming the way our firms, our economy and our society are being organized.

In an attempt to answer how these new "ABC" technologies, tools and business models affect the way firms are structured, managed, and, as a result, perform, this chapter showed briefly a comprehensive model (the AGG Model) that can address three realms of the firm (its architecture, its governance, and its growth) and can help to understand how these realms affect each other, as well as may be affected by the introduction of new ABC technologies. After considering that ICT technologies have two distinct components,

the chapter attempted to introduce the question of how the trade-off between information technologies (IT) and communication technologies (CT) costs may affect the architecture of the firm, and as a result, affect also the governance and growth domains of the firm.

As presented in the chapter, the introduction of new ABC technologies can be very important for considerations of firm's gains in productivity and efficiency. However, such an introduction must be balanced with other relevant questions such as the hierarchical organization of expertise inside the firm, also known as the *knowledge-based hierarchy* view of the firm, as well as with the supply of expertise through new technologies and tools of crowdsourcing of skills and expertise from outside the firm.

It is too early to assert definite conclusions in this new research area, but for sure it is reasonable to argue that a successful application of the new *ABC* technologies and tools depends on two interrelated policy aspects: 1) the use of a proper model which could help one to approach the structure and dynamics of the firm, and, 2) how the complex trade-off between information technology (IT) and communication technology (CT) costs is handled within, between and beyond firms, organizations and institutions.

REFERENCES

Acemoglu, D., Mostagir, M., & Ozdaglar, A. (2014, January). Managing Innovation in a Crowd. *National Bureau of Economic Research* [Working Paper 19852].

Antràs, P., Garicano, L., & Rossi-Hansberg, E. (2006). Offshoring in a knowledge economy. *The Quarterly Journal of Economics, 121*, 31–77.

Baghat, S., & Bolton, B. (2008). Corporate governance and firm performance. *Journal of Corporate Finance, 14*(3), 257–273. doi:10.1016/j.jcorpfin.2008.03.006

Beggs, A. W. (2001). Queues and hierarquies. *The Review of Economic Studies*, 68(2), 297–322. doi:10.1111/1467-937X.00170

Berle, A., & Means, G. (1932). *The Modern Corporation and Private Property*. Chicago: Commerce Clearing House.

Bloom, N., Garicano, L., Sadun, R., & Van Reenen, J. (2013). The distinct effects of Information Technology and Communication Technology on firm organization [Unpublished paper]. Retrieved from http://www.stanford.edu/~nbloom

Boss, G, P. Malladi, S. Quan, L. Legregni, and H. Hall (2007). Cloud computing [Technical Report]. *IBM high performance on demand solutions*.

Brynjolfsson, Erik and Andrew McAfee (2014). *The Second Machine Age*. W. W. Norton & Company. Kindle edition.

Brynjolfsson, E., & McAffe, A. (2011). *Race against the Machine*. Digital Frontier Press.

Carrizosa, M. T. (2006). *Firm growth, persistence and multiplicity of equilibria: An analysis of Spanish manufacturing and service industries* [Unpublished PhD Dissertation]. University Rovira I Virgili, Spain.

Cavalcanti, J. C. (2014). *Effects of IT on Enterprise Architecture, Governance and Growth*. Pensylvannia, USA: IGI-Global.

Chen, H., Chiang, R. H. L., & Storey, V. C. (2012, December). Business Intelligence and Analytics: From Big Data to Big Impact. *Management Information Systems Quarterly*, 36(4), 1165–1188.

Davenport, T. (2014). *big data @ work: Dispelling the Myths, Uncovering the Opportunities*. Harvard Business Press. doi:10.15358/9783800648153

Davenport, T., Harris, J. G., & Morison, R. (2010). *Analytics at Work: Smart Decisions Better Results*. Harvard Business Press.

Davenport, T. H., & Harris, J. G. (2007). *Competing on Analytics: The New Science of Winning*. Harvard Business Press.

Demsetz, H. (1983). The structure of ownership and the theory of the firm. *Journal of Law and Economics, No, 26*(June).

Edjalali, R. (2011). *Information 20/20: Focus, Connect and Lead with Information*. Gartner.

Garicano, L. (2000). Hierarchies and the Organization of Knowledge in Production. *Journal of Political Economy*, 108(5), 874–904. doi:10.1086/317671

Garicano, L., & Prat, A. (2013). Organizational economics with cognitive costs. Proceedings of *Advances in Economics and Econometrics: Tenth World Congress* (Volume 1, 342), Cambridge University Press.

Garicano, Luis and Esteban Rossi-Hansberg (2006). The Knowledge Economy at the Turn of the Twentieth Century: The Emergence of Hierarchies. *Journal of the European Economic Association*. April-May. 4(2-3): 393-403.

Garicano, L., & Rossi-Hansberg, E. (2012). Organizing growth. *Journal of Economic Theory*, 147(2), 623–656. doi:10.1016/j.jet.2009.11.007

Gartner Magic Quadrant. (2014). *Gartner*. Retrieved from http://www.gartner.com/technology/research/methodologies/magicQuadrants.jsp

Grossman, S. J., & Hart, O. D. (1986). The Costs and Benefits of Ownership: A Theory of Vertical and Lateral Integration. *Journal of Political Economy*, 94(4), 691–719. doi:10.1086/261404

Hamel, G. (2012). *What Matters Now: How to Win in a World of Relentless Change, Ferocious Competition, and Unstoppable Innovation*. Jossey-Bass.

Hart, O. D., & Moore, J. (1990). Property rights and the theory of the firm. *Journal of Political Economy*, *48*(6), 1119–1158. doi:10.1086/261729

International Data Corporation. (2012). *Digital Universe Study*.

Kelly, J. (2013, December 14). *Big data: Hadoop, Business Analytics and Beyond: A Big Data manifesto from the Wikibon Community*. Retrieved from http://wikibon.org/wiki/v/Big_Data:_Hadoop,_Business_Analytics_and_Beyond

Lipsey, R. G., Carlaw, K. I., & Bekar, C. T. (2006). *Economic Transformations: General Purpose Technologies and Long Term Economic Growth*. Oxford University Press.

Magoulas, Thanos, Ainda Hadzic, Ted Saarikko & Kalevi Pessi (2012). Alignment in Enterprise Architecture: A Comparative Analysis of Four Architectural Approaches. *The Electronic Journal of Information Systems Evaluation*, 15(1), 88-101.

Marston, S., Li, Z., Bandyopadhyay, S., Zhang, J., & Ghalsasi, A. (2011). Cloud computing- The business perspective. *Decision Support Systems*, *51*(1), 176–189. doi:10.1016/j.dss.2010.12.006

National Institute of Standard and Technology. (2014). Retrieved from http://www.nist.gov/itl/csd/cloud-102511.cfm

Novaes, W., & Zingales, L. (1999). Capital structure choice under a takeover threat [University of Chicago working paper].

Pepper, R., & Garrity, J. (2014). The Internet of Everything: How the Network Unleashes the Benefits of Big Data. In B. Bilbao-Osorio, S. Dutta, & B. Lanvin (Eds), *The Global Technology Report: Rewards and Risks of Big Data*. World Economic Forum.

Schnherr, M. (2009). Towards a Common Terminology in the Discipline of Enterprise Architecture. In G. Feuerlicht, & W. Lamersdorf (Eds.), Service-Oriented Computing - ICSOC 2008 Workshops, *Lecture Notes in Computer Science* (Vol. 5472, pp. 400-413). Springer-Verlag, Berlin.

Vitalari, N., & Shaughnessy, H. (2012). *The Elastic Enterprise: The New Manifesto for Business Revolution*. Telemachus Press, LLC.

Weill, P., & Broadbent, M. (1998). *Leveraging the New Infrastructure: How market leaders capitalize on IT*. Harvard Business School Press.

Weill, P., & Ross, J. W. (2004). *IT Governance: How Top Performers Manage IT Decision Rights for Superior Results. Center for Information Systems Research – CISR/MIT*. Harvard Business School Press.

Weinhardt, C., Blau, B., & Stößer, J. (2009). Cloud Computing – A Classification, Business Models, and Research Directions. *Business and Information Systems Engineering*. 5.

World Economic Forum- WEF. (2014). *The Global Technology Report: Rewards and Risks of Big Data*. Beñat Bilbao-Osorio, Soumitra Dutta, and Bruno Lanvin (editors).

Zachman, J. A. (1987). A framework for information systems architecture. *IBM Systems Journal*, *26*(3), 276–292. doi:10.1147/sj.263.0276

KEY TERMS AND DEFINITIONS

Analytics: The discovery and communication of patterns – with significance – in data.

Big Data: Applies to information that cannot be processed or analyzed using traditional processes or tools.

Capital Structure: In finance, *capital structure* refers to the way a corporation finances its assets through some combination of equity, debt, or hybrid securities.

Cloud Computing: Is computing in which large groups of remote servers are networked to allow centralized data storage and online access to computer services or resources.

Communication Technology: The activity of designing and constructing and maintaining communication systems.

Corporate Governance: Relates to the ways in which the suppliers of finance to corporations assure themselves of getting a return on their investment.

Enterprise Architecture: A well-defined practice for conducting enterprise analysis, design, planning, and implementation, using a holistic approach at all times, for the successful development and execution of strategy.

Information Technology: It refers to anything related to computing technology, such as networking, hardware, software, the Internet, or the people that work with these technologies.

Ownership Structure: The relative amounts of ownership claims held by insiders (management) and outsiders (investors with no direct role in the management of the firm).

Chapter 7
The Human Side of Information Systems:
Capitalizing on People as a Basis for OD and Holistic Change

Telmo Antonio Henriques
ISCTE-IUL, Portugal

Henrique O'Neill
ISCTE-IUL, Portugal

ABSTRACT

In this chapter the authors explore the relationship between Information Systems and Organization Development, highlighting the value that Holistic Change Interventions can introduce when applied to IS/IT areas, mobilizing Individuals, Groups and the whole Organization to promote Organizational Effectiveness. A "soft" approach to Organizational Change is proposed, focusing on main internal aspects which are determinant for Organizational Performance, including Organizational Culture and Values, Leadership, Work Teams, and Employee Engagement. The approach is illustrated by a successful "real-world" Transformational Change Program which has been developed, within an IT Unit of a major financial organization, following an Action Research paradigm. The intervention has integrated two main cycles – a first one covering the strategy determination and behavioral preparation for further action, and a second one devoted to a coordinated implementation of strategic actions which have emerged from the first cycle – where communication, engagement, action and improvement have been the most relevant attributes of the whole process. From a Research perspective this successful Change intervention has served to develop and test, within context, a Framework of Critical Success Factors for Holistic Change, which is described on its management implications, and covering distinct areas and dimensions. Also, the high potential of Action Research, to promote Holistic Change within real organizational settings, and, simultaneously, to address complex research issues, questions, objectives, and test hypothesis, is deeply illustrated within this chapter.

DOI: 10.4018/978-1-4666-8833-9.ch007

INTRODUCTION

Contextualization

The relationship between Information Systems and Organizational Change is, often, explored along the path's direction from Information Systems to Organizational Change. This includes two main typical perspectives: (1) the integration of the organizational side of change as a non-negligible dimension within IS/IT Programs (strategic, preventive view); and (2) the appraisal of the impact of IS/IT changes over Organizational effectiveness (evaluative view).

However, the reverse direction – highlighting the value that Organizational Development and Change can introduce when applied to IS/IT areas, through People – is a rich research domain, not so often explored within this context.

In fact, Individuals, Groups, the Organization as a whole, and its interactions, form the basis of the traditional "People, Process & Technology" triangle, having a special impact over Organizational Effectiveness.

So, this reverse direction, promoting IT Organizational Development, should be considered, as a forward path towards the preparation of IS/IT People, in context, to face their responsibilities of serving the whole organization.

Also, within these technical areas, "hard" dimensions (product, process, risk, control and service) are, often, overemphasized by best practices' (e.g., COBIT, ITIL, CMMI and PMBOK) adoption projects, minimizing the critical importance of the human factor as a base ingredient of any comprehensive approach to Organizational Effectiveness.

As a consequence of this restrict vision some important Organizational Development and Change aspects, including Organizational Culture and Values, Leadership, Work Teams and Employee Engagement, are relegated to a minor dimension.

The current chapter, based from a Strategic Management perspective on a Resources-based View (Hitt, Ireland, & Hoskinsson, 2009) and focusing on main internal aspects which are determinant for Organizational Performance (Burke & Litwin, 1992) highlights the relevance of key concepts, relationships, processes and critical success factors of organizational improvement.

It illustrates these aspects with a successful "real-world" Transformational Change Program which has been developed, within an IT Unit of a major financial organization, following an Action Research paradigm (Shani & Pasmore, 1982).

From a change perspective, the organizational intervention configures a 2nd order planned change, thus, transformational (Porras & Robertson, 1992), built at the level of a single entity, with development induction through a cycle of goal formulation, implementation, evaluation and modification of goals based on what was learned (Van de Ven & Poole, 1995) and materializes a double-loop (Argyris, 2002), generative (Senge, 2006), organizational learning and development process. These concepts (allowing us to typify the kind of envisaged change and the associated approach) will be further clarified by the literature review.

The intervention has integrated two main cycles:

1. Strategy determination and behavioral preparation for further action, and
2. Coordinated implementation of strategic actions, which have emerged from the first cycle.

The first cycle has targeted the enhancement of a Service Culture, the development of harmonized Leadership practices, and the promotion of Employee Engagement and Participation, through an integrated set of highly participative actions.

Communication, engagement, action and improvement were the most relevant attributes of the process.

The second cycle, covering a set of coordinated actions (setting new policies, structures and procedures, and targeting structural improvement) has addressed main areas of Employee Training and Development, Communication, Leadership Practices, IT Best Practices' adoption, Process Improvement and Tools' Implementation.

Chapter Outline

Following an Organizational Development approach to Information Systems Management, on a Holistic blueprint to Transformational Change, and using Action Research, this Chapter intends to highlight some of its most relevant aspects, including:

- To provide an overview of the main substantive areas which within real organizational settings can (must) be addressed to promote an effective and holistic transformational change focused on the role of people, as a seeding basis for organizational effectiveness;
- To address relevant knowledge associated with targeted areas of organizational improvement and learning, including Organizational Behavior, Organizational Development and Transformational Change;
- To give evidence of the importance of Organizational Research, in particular of the Action Research paradigm, balancing rigor and relevance and promoting sustained Organizational Effectiveness;
- To illustrate the application of such knowledge sources, through a specific Transformation Program case which has been successfully implemented within a "real world" IT Organization, and;
- To highlight, under the form of critical success factors and management implications, the emergent knowledge which reflects what can be learned from the case.

Being Action Research a participatory postmodern interpretive paradigm deeply associated with meaning and reflection, special emphasis must be given to these two distinctive aspects.

So, the traditional organization of chapters has been changed in order to, explicitly, evidence these essential characteristics. They cover the following main topics:

- **Research Meaning and Directions:** An introductory note concerning (1) motivation and commitment, (2) problem definition, (3) change and research questions, (4) change and research objectives, and (5) main research hypothesis;
- **Literature Review:** Relevant results of a comprehensive review of underlying theories, covering (1) the strategic positioning; (2) the intervention domains; a special reference to (3) Quality and Organizational Excellence; and (4) the foundational aspects of change and research.

Being the research intimately associated with Transformational Change, this last topic covers, by its relevance, the essential aspects of (a) Organizational Development, (b) paradigmatic approaches to Planned Change, (c) Change related attitudes and behaviors, (d) main types of Organizational Change, (e) Organizational Research approaches and paradigms, and (f) the Action Research paradigm;

- **Change Design and Development:** Covering the essential aspects associated with the specific change program which has been developed, including (1) the organizational context and Change characterization, (2) the first OD Cycle of behavioral preparation and strategy determination, and (2) the second OD Cycle of a coordinated strategy implementation.

For each cycle, main relevance is given to its main stages and actions, evaluation methodology, and interventions' results;

- **Reflection and Main Results:** Drawn on the whole program outcomes, it integrates a (1) Reflection on Organizational Change Results and a systematic presentation of the (2) Research Results.

These results represent the knowledge which has been acquired along the process and evidence relevant implications and recommendations for possible transposition to other contexts.

Being the associated Organizational Transformation Program just a real-case illustration of the essential aspects addressed within this Chapter, major detail and relevance will be given to the "knowledge" aspects (base and emergent) associated with the subject.

Research Meaning and Directions

In order to make sense of the change and research dimensions of the intervention there is a need to give a previous perspective concerning its meaning and directions.

This implies to provide, for both dimensions, some chained essential aspects on motivation and commitment, problems, questions, objectives, and hypothesis.

Motivation and Commitment

Impetus to engage on a wide, complex, transformational research and change program, needs, at least, the confluence of two major forces: researcher's motivation and organization's commitment.

Being responsible for an IT Quality Improvement and Organizational Development unit, (1) having a past experience of Management Consultancy, (2) a special interest on Organizational Change, and (3) a specific Organizational

Transformation Program on hands, has been the main triangle to *ignite* this action research project.

Coghlan (2006), focused on Insider Action Research Doctorates, reflects on the executive action research doctorate in terms of:

Engagement of the individual manager–researcher in first person inquiry, the collaborative activities with others in second person inquiry and the third person contribution of actionable knowledge to the practitioner and academic communities.

He describes quite well the characteristics associated with this kind of research process, highlighting some bullet points which, for a researcher interested in the development of its own organization and knowledge, can shape a strong motivational decision's path (Table 1).

No better set of arguments could be found to seduce and illustrate the researcher's motivation to embrace this challenge.

From a humanistic perspective, there is only a simple personal statement to add:

To work with persons, for persons, on behalf of persons, simultaneously developing the researcher's personal skills, engagement with people, and changing the way they look and feel their organizational world.

However, as evidenced by Buchanan & Bryman (2011) when detailing the "*system of influences for the choice of organizational research methods*", there are some important organizational issues which must be considered when facing this kind of collaborative research.

Particularly, they refer some aspects related to "*political properties*", highlighting that:

Researchers are routinely engaged in political actions in at least four ways, when negotiating research objectives, obtaining permissions to access respondents, aligning with stakeholder groups, and when attempting to publish findings.

Table 1. Action Research Doctorates – Insiders' participation

- Participants undertake a research project *as insiders of their own organizations*, frequently through an action-oriented approach such as action learning and action research;
- Such research aims at *generating actionable knowledge*, which can be defined as knowledge that is useful to both the academic and practitioner communities;
- They also foster the *development of the executives as practitioner–researchers*;
- The context for insider research, particularly insider action research is the strategic and operational setting that executives *confront in their managerial working lives*;
- *Issues of organizational concern, such as systems improvement, organizational learning, the management of change and so on are suitable subjects for action research*, since (a) they are real events which must be managed in real time, (b) they provide opportunities for both effective action and learning, and (c) they can contribute to the development of theory of what really goes on in organizations;
- Executives who undertake an action research project in and on their own organization *do so while a complete permanent member*, by which is meant, that they want to remain a member within their desired career path when the research is completed;
- *The researchers are already immersed in the organization and have built up knowledge of the organization from being an actor in the processes being studied*. This knowledge comes from the actor engaging in the experiential learning cycles of experiencing, reflecting, conceptualizing and experimenting in real life situations;
- *The primary purpose of action research is to produce practical knowing which is embodied in daily actions by the manager–researcher and the development of learning organizations* and which aims to guide inquiry and action in the present.

Coghlan (2006)

Using the term *"gatekeeper"*, as *"anyone in a position to decide whether or not a research project can proceed at a given site"*, they explicitly advice that:

Researchers often find themselves negotiating their objectives with the 'gatekeepers' who can sanction or block their work.

These are important potential change restraining aspects, which must be balanced with change enablers in order to make change happen.

Following a positive path to organizational change several authors (e.g., Armenakis et al., 1993; Miller, Johnson, & Grau, 1994) refer readiness, openness, sponsorship and commitment to change as favorable conditions to create active engagement and involvement to lead and participate on challenging change programs, modifying the status quo and solving important organizational problems.

Often, the existence of relevant organizational problems combined with a strong concern and willingness to solve them can act as a major organizational driver to trigger major change initiatives.

In the current case there was a strong motivation to engage on a major transformational change, solving primary problems on Leadership and Customer orientation. This need had been clearly evidenced by the regular Customer and Employee's Satisfaction Surveys, which have highlighted these issues.

Also, a newly appointed IT Top Manager has got strong awareness of the fact. He had already promoted organizational structure changes and created a new Customer's Support unit, but he had also a clear vision (sense of urgency) that much more should be done within the people and process dimensions to sustain future improvements.

IT Employees and Managers were also aware of the situation, evidencing some discomfort with the status quo. Some improvement proposals were latent.

This confluence of factors has created the proper conditions to trigger the program, with a supportive environment to facilitate the process.

Problem Definition

Gummesson (2000) considers that action research *"is about research in action and does not postulate a distinction between theory and action"*, involving *"two goals: solve a problem and contribute to science"*, and putting a double challenge on the researcher: "*to engage in making the action happen and to stand back from the action and reflect on it as it happens in order to contribute to the body of knowledge*".

Referring to this "*dual imperatives of action research*", McKay & Marshall (2007) highlight "*its interest in, and commitment to, organisational problem solving, and its interest in, and commitment to, research, and the production of new insights and knowledge*".

This implies a double formulation concerning the Action Research Problem's definition, covering its "organizational" and "research" dimensions. This also applies to Questions and Objectives.

Concerning the current case in terms of organizational problems, the situation has evidenced that, despite the previously implemented organizational changes, some relevant issues still persisted. This has been clearly confirmed by the results of IT Internal Customers' Satisfaction surveys, as well as by Employee Satisfaction surveys. They've clearly pointed out to the need to address Customer orientation, Leadership practices and Employee Engagement problems.

Also, within IT management structures there was a wide consensus on the need to improve Internal Communication, Project Management, Process Management, Tools and Workforce Development practices.

At IT Top Management level, there was the deep conviction that the process should go deeper: involving the participation of all IT Employees along an integrative and multidimensional approach.

It should not address only isolated areas, functions or processes. It must involve a participative, planned and coordinated process to deal with all these problems on a structured way, addressing all issues and identifying, on a wide systemic view, other relevant problems, involving Employees, Managers and Internal Customers.

The complexity of the interrelated problems and the nature of Change to be addressed was a fertile field to formulate research problems and associated questions.

In fact, being the required dynamics completely new within these settings, it would be necessary to find am adequate way to:

- Address a complex, transformational, planned change;
- Using a multidimensional and integrative approach based on an holistic, open, systemic vision;
- Target IT Quality Improvement and Organizational Development actions, on a wide and integrated form (using TQM-like and Organizational Excellence visions);
- Involve the empowerment and the use of parallel structures (networking, as a complement to the traditional hierarchical structures) to support participative problem solving;
- Obtain sustained sponsorship from all management levels.

Also, the approach should consider that:

- There is no "best unique process or solution" for a complex set of problems; thus adopting an open and participative view, within context, and searching for a combination between new and existing approaches;
- There is a set of interconnected critical success factors for the process, to be identified and addressed;
- The process should not only deliver direct solutions for the identified problems, but also produce structural results in terms of a "toolkit" emerging from the process itself;
- Organizational double-loop learning should result from the program;
- The outcomes should be reflectively evaluated in order to highlight emergent knowledge (1) for the organization and (2) for a more global community.

These essential aspects, concerning the process and the approach, configure themselves the main characteristics of the research problem to be addressed within the specific organizational context.

In terms of the choice of the research and change paradigm, its nature clearly pointed to Action Research.

It would involve a Transformational Change program (multidimensional, multi-level, radical and discontinuous, with an organizational paradigm's rupture); in order to develop, anticipatively, a new strategic vision, for relevant IT organizational unit's vital functions and processes (double-loop learning).

Change and Research Questions

For some research approaches (where the researcher puts himself outside the research context, maintaining only the control over the experiment, but neither influencing nor changing the observed reality, and using a positivist position) research questions, models and hypothesis are clearly formulated in advance. Tests are done in order to confirm hypotheses, and, often, the objective of the research consists of filling a theoretical gap.

The process develops new theories associated with the emerging knowledge; which, in turn, aim to be further applied, on a generalized way, and used for subsequent research on the field.

A theoretical self-feeding process is subjacent to this kind of research.

Not being the strict objective of the current research to fill, explicitly, any theoretical gap, but, mainly, to address an empirical gap (solving problems within its context and, as a result, introducing direct improvements, with evident results), and a methodological gap (developing a set of methods and procedures within the organizational settings, which induce learning, with capability for future application), the Action Research paradigm was, in fact, the most adequate for the purpose.

Due to its participative, iterative, longitudinal and exploratory nature, particularly when involving holistic change, the associated questions are not completely formulated in advance; being, frequently, chained along the research cycles. Often, the response to these questions influences the subsequent steps, driving the researcher to other chained questions.

This is a consequence of a non-deterministic approach to change, involving participative processes.

It is, undoubtedly, the current case, where the organizational change cycles of the Program must be seen as a two-stage major transformational process, including:

- **Strategy Determination:** Including organizational diagnosis, change definition and planning, training, communication, engagement, action identification and decision; with a double-target of (1) preparing Employees for participation attitudes and, simultaneous, (2) identifying and deciding on strategic actions;
- **Strategy Implementation:** Covering the coordinated planning, development and implementation of a group of strategic actions.

So, although targeting pre-identified problem-areas, the only possible organizational change questions, which could be formulated in advance without any preconception regarding its answers, were some initial Diagnostic and planning questions (Coghlan & Brannick, 2010:p. 9).

This set of high-level questions (Table 2, questions CQ00-CQ04) aligns with the essence of the work undertaken during the diagnostic stage of the first cycle of intervention.

Based on a joint analysis and decision (consensual between the researcher, the consultants, the management structure and the navigation team) the intervention has been planned.

Table 2. Organizational Change related Questions – formulated along the intervention

#	Step	Most Relevant Questions
1	Current Culture versus Desired Culture Diagnosis	CQ00 – What is the context and the main associated problematic areas, issues, and change objectives? Within this context, what is a feasible structure of approach to the intervention? CQ01 – What are the current organizational culture characteristics and its associated main problems? CQ02 – What are the desired culture characteristics and its associated nuclear values? CQ03 – What is the gap between the current and the desired organizational culture? CQ04 – What are the next stages, steps, and essential characteristics to enhance within the program?
2	Service's Culture Workshop	CQ05 – What is the level of Employees adherence to the new Services' Culture? CQ06 – How to implement the Values of the new Culture, through Employee Attitudes and Behaviors?
3	Change Agents Team Preparation	CQ07 – What is the role of the Change Agents? CQ08 – What is its required Profile for selection? CQ09 – What is the training to be provided to them?? CQ10 – What are the relevant Case Studies to be discussed by the Employees?
4	Preparation of the Communication Plan and launching of the Program's Site	CQ11 – What is the target population, its subgroups, and specific positioning? CQ12 – What are the key communication events and associated specific communication needs (messages)? CQ13 – What are the most appropriates communication channels to be used for each circumstance? CQ14 – How to guarantee feedback along the process and to evaluate the respective results?
5,9	Leadership Training (Modules I and II)	CQ15 – What are the essential aspects for training the Team Leaders on its individual relationship with each team Member? CQ16 – What are the critical leadership competencies to train the Leaders on their relationship with his work Team?
6	Conduction of 5 Cycles of *Learning Meetings*	CQ17 – What is Employees' perception concerning the problematic situations and issues illustrated by the cases? CQ18 – What is their participation level (engagement) on its debate? CQ19 – What are their action proposals to solve the problems identified during the meetings?
7	Presentation of Improvement Proposals to Top-Management	CQ20 – What is the form of systematization / structure to present the conclusions for each learning meeting outcomes? CQ21 – What are the perceptions of situation / suggestions / proposals (constructive feedback) to enhance?
8	Proposal Selection and Implementation	CQ22 – What is the perception of Top Management of Employees' proposal presented by Change Agents? CQ23 – What are the inherit Decisions and underlying Structural Actions?
10	Results Evaluation	CQ24 – What is the level of attained results, against the objectives (measured in terms of the pre-defined evaluation parameters)? CQ25 – What are the positive outcomes to be retained, reused and to be developed in the future? CQ26 – What is the external contribute, in terms of results which can be transposed to other contexts and organizations? CQ27 – What is the emergent Knowledge? CQ28 – What are the next steps, in order to promote future Quality Improvement and Organizational Development?

Further questions have emerged along the program, benefiting from wide employee participation.

As it can be recognized over the list, some of the questions issued along the change process are, by themselves, also important research questions.

However, on a wider perspective, (re)searching for emergent knowledge (applicable outside this context) requires a set of precise research questions (summarized in Table 3).

Naturally, these two sets, of change oriented and research related questions, overlap; due to the interleaving objectives of action research; or, as previously referred (McKay and Marshall, 2007), its "dual imperatives".

Table 3. Research Questions

RQ01. How to *successfully address a complex change with these characteristics* (planed, multidimensional, integrative, participative, and transformational)? What are the main *dimensions and characteristics* to be considered?
RQ02. What *structures / functions must be put in place* in order to sponsor, manage, and actively support the change process?
RQ03. How to *engage people, developing positive attitudes* towards change (and its objectives), and promoting *active cooperative behaviors*?
RQ04. How to *involve people on positive problem-solving activities*, in order to obtain structured contributes to strategic action identification?
RQ05. How can *group networking be conciliated with hierarchy*, and used as a complement of traditional structures, in order to cross organizational boundaries, promoting change, cooperation, learning and development?
RQ06. How can *organizational values* contribute to this?

Change and Research Objectives

A good set of meaningful and relevant questions is, in fact, a necessary basis to challenge the organizational status quo, as well as to query about new ways of doing action and to promote new research insights. However, it is not sufficient to proceed with action and research.

Adequate objectives' formulation is an essential step to create commitment. Furthermore, a good balance between organizational and research targets is essential to grant feasibility to the research proposal, and, simultaneously, to keep the action viable along the project's lifecycle. Otherwise it can compromise, either the necessary organizational relevance (responding to stakeholders expectations), or research rigour (providing right answers to the right questions).

Concerning intra-organizational research, although the main forces emerge from organizational relevance (goals, objectives, participation, learning and achievements), research rigour (formalism) combined with relevant theoretical knowledge integration is also crucial to imprint a sound basis to the approach.

This combination should facilitate organizational transformation, promote innovation and produce emergent knowledge. The integration of both dimensions, of organizational and research objectives, should produce a synergistic effect, between relevance and rigour; and, simultaneously, sustain the change momentum, facilitating its outcomes.

Table 4 summarizes the Organizational Objectives for both cycles of the intervention.

In strict alignment with the pre-identified research questions and in consonance with the change approach and objectives, Table 5 summarizes the Research Objectives.

As it can be observed, change objectives are directly linked with the kind of problems faced by the organization, and change questions are mainly connected with the main steps which, on a chained sequence, have been identified as necessary to solve them.

On the research front, it can also be seen that the research questions are tied together with the need to face an adequate approach to the complex nature of a transformational and non-deterministic change, querying on its main dimensions, characteristics, structures, functions, processes, agents, and attributes, and pointing out to specific research objectives.

Main Research Hypothesis

Finally, in strict alignment with these research questions and objectives, a set of main hypothesis has been formulated, as summarized in Table 6.

How These Elements Fit Together

In summary, these main elements integrate what we have called the "research meaning and directions".

Table 4. Organizational Objectives

1st Cycle – Strategy Definition and Organizational Preparation	• To develop a *Service Culture* – customer oriented and based on a more open and flexible internal communication structure; • To develop and harmonize more effective *Leadership practices* – valuating employee's coaching, leadership skills development and team's attitude alignment towards values and principles; • To promote the *Engagement and Participation* of all employees on the definition and implementation of service and internal functioning improvements.
2nd Cycle – Coordinated Strategy Implementation	• To implement coordinated structural actions targeting Employee Satisfaction, Motivation and Teams Effectiveness.

Table 5. Research Objectives

RO01. Develop a process to support a complex planned change intervention, which, simultaneously, address the specific change objectives, and incorporate the role of engagement and participation
RO02. Develop adequate supportive groups, roles, and actions to manage and enforce change along all the process
RO03. Develop base anchors, and engaging processes to promote change through active people involvement
RO04. Design specific environments, and processes to engage people on positive problem-solving, decision, and strategic actions' determination
RO05. Design a structured process, and a set of working principles, teams, rules and procedures to provide added value to existent organizational structures, in order to implement organizational values, promoting engaged generative learning
R006. Highlight the role of organizational values alignment and implementation as catalytic drivers of change

Table 6. Research Hypothesis

RH01. A holistic Process, involving People, through Meaning creation, and using an Ethical basis, will create appropriate conditions to facilitate change objectives, and increase satisfaction levels
RH02. Top Management Sponsorship, a Coordination Team, and an active / independent Change Agents' Team, together with Leadership Training and Group Learning Sessions, will promote Leadership practices development, and Employee Engagement and Participation
RH03. A strong focus on Values and Participation, along group open discussions concerning organizational life, will facilitate active cooperative behaviors and outcomes
RH04. Small-group thematic (case-based) Learning Meetings, focusing on problems' solutions, within an open, positive and participative discussion, crossing organizational boundaries and supported by independent Change Agents, will produce internal learning and knowledge, as well as objective structured contributes for strategic actions
RH05. Using a bottom-up mechanism - based on inclusive, open, and participative group discussions, and its transparent presentation to Top Management - will increase cross-organizational communication, cooperation, and change-related significant outcomes
RH06. Meaningful values shall be a good basis to promote cross-organizational engagement. Participative definition and discussion of those values, across all the organization, will enforce its sharing / alignment, promote positive attitudes around them, and stimulate congruent behaviors

They've started from a strong statement of individual motivation and organizational commitment to trigger such a deep initiative, targeting, simultaneously, to solve specific organizational problems and to research on new processes and approaches to solve them (the research problem).

Being the necessary approach non-deterministic, some change and research interrelated questions have been formulated in order to address these problems.

Also, they have associated objectives – either for the change as well as for the research dimensions of the intervention – which must fit together.

Along the intervention it is supposed that both set of objectives are reached.

Also it is supposed that the emergent knowledge confirms (or discards) the research hypothesis which had been formulated (in strict alignment with the research questions and objectives).

LITERATURE REVIEW

A pre-condition for the success of large-scale holistic change, using Action Research and covering a wide set of Organizational Disciplines, is a deep understanding of the:

1. Theories and scientific foundations of these material intervention domains,
2. Main aspects related with the proper dynamics of organizational transformation, and
3. Formal aspects directly associated with the research paradigm.

Although not having here a specific objective on promoting a theoretical debate within these areas, it is, however, important to emphasize its most relevant aspects, as significant knowledge to be applied along the intervention.

Also, because the Action Research process is not as usual, well-understood and accepted as other traditional approaches (having its specific characteristics and evaluation criteria), special topics, concerning this research paradigm and focusing on insider research, must be addressed.

So, the literature review will cover essential aspects related with (1) the strategic positioning which is behind this approach, (2) the theoretical domains which have been worked out along the intervention, (3) a special reference to Quality and Organizational Excellence, and (4) some foundational aspects of Change and Research.

All of them are observed here from an Organizational Development perspective and targeting an Action Research intervention.

Strategic Positioning

Before developing all these aspects a special reference must be done concerning our strategic positioning and approach.

As stated, as global contextualization:

1. Within the IS/IT areas, Quality and Organizational Excellence are often reduced to some visions strongly influenced by operational and tactical instruments (e.g., COBIT, ITIL, CMMI and PMBOK) overestimating the product, process, risk, control and service dimensions;
2. A consequence of this restrictive view is, often, the underestimation of important Organizational Development aspects which are crucial to any Quality and Innovation's Strategy;
3. These include not addressing important areas like Organizational Culture and Values, Leadership, Work Team and Employee Engagement.

So, consistently, the approach here developed is deeply rooted on an Organizational Development (OD) perspective of the organization, rather than on a simple project or process view of organizational change.

Particularly, it aligns with a Positive Organizational Scholarship (POS) perspective, as introduced by Cameron, Dutton, & Quinn (2003) when highlighting that it is "*concerned primarily with the study of especially positive outcomes, processes, and attributes of organizations and their members*".

From a Strategic Management perspective the fact that distinct (and divergent) approaches to organizational effectiveness coexist implies an advanced clarification of our positioning on the light of existing literature.

Hitt, Ireland, & Hoskinsson (2009) defining Strategic Management as "*the full set of commitments, decisions, and actions required for a firm to achieve strategic competitiveness and earn above-average returns*"; highlight two theoretical models, with different orientations and assumptions, to achieve firm's financial performance.

One of these, the old "Industrial Organization Model", considers the external environment as a primary determinant for the strategies adopted by organizations to succeed.

The other, the "Resource-based Model", is rooted on the assumption that "each organization is a collection of unique resources and capabilities" where people play a major role, highlighting the importance of "firm's capabilities" as "competitive advantages" to formulate adequate strategies for reaching above-average returns.

These approaches to strategy have also some parallelism with two distinct approaches to change (Beer & Nohria, 2000):

1. Theory E, associating change with "economic value" (as for the I/O model), and
2. Theory O, basing change on "organizational capability" (in consonance with the resource-based view).

Theory O, considered as a "soft" approach, enhances the goal of developing "corporate culture and human capability through individual and organizational learning", where the human dimension of change (considering "employee behaviours, attitudes, capabilities and commitment") is combined with "organizational ability to learn from its experience", as a main route to organizational success.

Focusing on Human Resources Management, Truss et al. (1997) also refer these soft and hard forms, as quite distinct approaches, respectively aligned with the "developmental-humanistic" or with the "utilitarian-instrumentalist" principles, and emphasizing, respectively, the human or the resources dimensions.

Focused on Ethical aspects of leaders' practices, Vargas (2005) enhances the importance of integrating the "material" (strategy, structure, processes, and competencies) and "immaterial" (values, beliefs, norms, and attitudes) dimensions of organizational life, in order to effectively implement its Mission and Vision. He stresses the major relevance of considering these last determinant aspects of Organizational Culture.

This strategic vision (inherit to the Resource-based Model, congruent with Theory O, and putting the focus on the "soft", "immaterial", and "human" dimension of the organization) is, clearly, our line of thought. It invests on the role of people, along the internal value chain, to promote the development of the organization.

Heskett et al.'s (2000) "service-profit chain" (establishing "relationships between profitability, customer loyalty, and employee satisfaction, loyalty and productivity") also confirms this major employees' role.

Finally, focusing on an internal perspective, Burke & Litwin's (1992) Causal Model of Organizational Performance and Change highlights its main areas of concern: Leadership, Management Practices, Work Unit Climate, Motivation, Organizational Culture and Individual Values and Needs.

Together, these models integrate the vision which supports both cycles of this organizational development intervention centered on people and its participation on a Strategic Process, being, thus, our main strategic references.

An important note must be given at this point concerning the strategic direction here developed: the fact that no special relevance is given to literature on IT Strategy. This is intentional.

In fact, the scope and objectives of the intervention do not depend of any specific technical approach to IS/IT Strategy; on the contrary, any IT strategy implementation relies on people, groups, and organizational culture to be successful.

Also, a second note must be done concerning the aspects related with IT specific Organizational Structures and Policies other than the ones related with Leadership, People, and Group management, and the targeted functions and processes. In fact, they have been considered as not having any major relevance for the analysis and evaluation of the current case.

So, intentionally these aspects have been omitted, in order to give the adequate relevance to the "soft" dimensions of Organizational Development and Learning.

According to Argyris (2002) organizational learning may be defined as the "*detection and correction of error*"; with a clear distinction between single-loop learning (which "*occurs when errors are corrected without altering the underlying governing values*") and double-loop learning (which "*occurs when errors are corrected by changing the governing values and then the actions*").

Together, both cycles of this large organizational transformation configure a double-loop organizational development and learning process.

Both exhibit, as a common characteristic, a strong investment on peoples' involvement along its preparation, action and subsequent initiatives.

Intervention Domains

Focusing now on the main theories and scientific foundations of the material domains of the intervention, a special reference must be made to the main areas of Organizational Culture and Values, Leadership and Team Effectiveness, and Employee Engagement, which have covered along its first OD cycle.

It has prepared the ground to face, on a second OD cycle, a set of interrelated projects, developing Support Structures for Workforce Development, targeting Process Improvement and Tool Implementation, enhancing Organizational Communication, and promoting Quality and Organizational Excellence.

So, relevance must be given to all this areas in terms of research and change fundamental bedrocks.

On a broad vision of Organizational Culture, Cameron & Quinn (1998) detail essential aspects of their approach: the Competitive Values Framework. It supports a diagnostic stage, on the understanding of the existent culture and determination of the essential aspects of the desired culture. For the purpose they have designed a process and a proper questionnaire (Organizational Culture Assessment Instrument).

Concerning Leadership and Team Effectiveness, several publications highlight the leader's influence on team performance and its determinant role on transformational change (Hackman, 1987; Marks, Mathieu, & Zaccaro, 2001; Zaccaro, Ritman, & Marks, 2001; Burke et al., 2006; Salas et al., 2007, 2009; Kolowski et al., 2009; Zaccaro, Heinen, & Shuffler, 2009).

Important theories give relevance for multiple approaches to Leadership, including the Treat's approach, Charismatic and Visionary leadership, Skills, Styles, Functional leadership, Leader-Member Exchange and Transformational leadership (Northouse 2007).

Associated with Employee Engagement, multiple constructs (Values, Attitudes, Behaviors, Organizational Identification, Engagement, Empowerment and Extra-Role Behavior) form a critical, "intangible", basis for organizational effectiveness; supporting the "soft" dimension of organizational strategy.

Studies on values, attitudes, norms and behaviors (Allport, 1954; Fishbein & Ajzen, 1975, 1980; Alcobia, 2001) enhance its relevance and strong implications on organizational performance.

Organizational identity and identification, being "positively connected with cohesion and cooperation, motivation, performance and extra-role behavior" (Tavares, 2007), are critical to promote individual well-being and organizational effectiveness.

The alignment of organizational values (espoused, attributed, shared and aspirational) is a major vehicle to promote and sustain change (Bourne & Jenkins, 2013).

Espoused Values, mediating Artifacts and Assumptions on Schein's (2009) model of Organizational Culture, play a major role; explaining "why the members of the organization are behaving as they do and why each organization is constructed as it is".

Commitment, and particularly affective commitment (with its main antecedents on need's fulfillment and individual-organizational values' matching) has "the strongest and most favorable correlations with organization-relevant (attendance, performance and organizational citizenship behavior) and employee-relevant (stress and work–family conflict) outcomes" (Meyer & Allen, 1991; Meyer et al., 2002).

Psychological Sense of Community (recently transposed to the field of management by Boyd & Nowell, 2014) aggregates several dimensions (membership, influence, integration and fulfillment of needs, shared emotional connection and responsibility) with relevance to "rebuild companies as communities for the long-term success of the firm" (Mintzberg, 2009).

Extra-role discretionary behaviors, namely Organizational Citizenship Behavior, are essential to "promote the effective functioning of the organization" (Organ, 1988).

Communication, participation and facilitation are key strategic drivers to "positively influence specific individuals and groups during a change process" (Kotter & Schlesinger, 1979).

Individual engagement is an essential ingredient of active participation in self-assessment processes; on the basis of several approaches to organizational excellence (e.g., EFQM-B, 2013). It facilitates more realistic views on improvement opportunities' identification; driving to higher levels of self-identification with solutions; increasing individual's adherence to implementation and sustainability.

These were the main theoretical references associated with the work which has been developed along the 1st cycle of the intervention.

Concerning its 2nd cycle, the focus has been set on Employee Training and Development, Organizational Communication, Best Practices' Adoption, Work Process Optimization and Supporting Tools Implementation.

According to Meister (1998:22), Employee Training and Development has evolved to a new paradigm, "from training to learning", with new characteristics:

Anywhere, any place, building core workplace competencies, incorporating action learning, shifting from individual to team, developing corporate universities, facing learning as a continuous process and focusing on real problem solving.

The Corporate University, "as a metaphor for learning", represents a cohesive structure, with proactive focus, strategic scope, enrolling on just-in-time learning and increasing on-the-job performance.

It should not only cover "traditional" training, but address (p. 90) new areas:

- *Corporate Citizenship: Culture, values, traditions and vision,*
- *Contextual Framework: Grounding employees on an appreciative vision of the company, its customers, competitors and best practices, and*
- *Development of "Core Workplace Competencies": Learning to learn communication and collaboration, creative thinking & problem-solving, technological & global business literacy, leadership development and career self-management skills.*

Organizational communication plays a central role on organizational development and change.

This is vastly evidenced by OD & Change literature, as well as, by Communication's scholarship.

Krone, Kramer & Sias (2010) refer that:

... although it began to emerge as an identifiable academic field around a set of practical questions concerning what makes managerial communication in organizations effective", it has expanded to "address the effects of small group networks, superior-subordinate communication, and communication climate on employee satisfaction and performance ...

highlighting that it has, since then, grown to include:

... a concern for non-managerial voices, the technical rationality that underlies most organizational decision making, understanding the very nature of 'organization' and the role of organizations in democratic societies.

Jones et al. (2004) emphasize, as research challenges, the need to *"understand the communication of organizational change"* and *"explore diversity and the intergroup aspects of communication"*.

Eisenberg & Riley (2001:293), considering the relevance of Organizational Culture for Communication studies, highlight the *"constitutive role of communication in creating organizational culture"*, and refer that *"from the early 1980s forward, communication processes were recast as the way organizations were constructed, maintained and transformed"*.

Concerning participative processes, Seibold and Shea (2001:665) underline the role of communication as "an integral part" of them, highlighting that it *"may moderate the effects of various types of participation or involvement programs"*.

Referring to software process improvement (SPI), Muller, Mathiassen & Balshoj (2010) emphasize that a significant number of publications on the subject address SPI with a primary focus on organizational change. They refer strong evidence that *"effective management of change during SPI requires serious consideration of context and underpinning values"*, highlighting some critical success factors:

Alignment with business goals, communicating clear SPI goals and managing expectations amongst employees, ensuring that senior management is committed and allocates the resources needed for SPI, making sure that employees feel well equipped for SPI participation (informed, trained and motivated), getting all levels of the organization engaged in SPI through participation, having well-defined process descriptions of what to do and plans for how to do it, measuring progress towards the SPI goals, and enlisting support from within and outside the organization.

One of the most used frameworks for assessing software development process maturity is the Capability Maturity Model Integration (CMMI) from the Software Engineering Institute. It integrates a set of "best practices that help organizations to improve their processes" (CMMI Product Team, 2010; Chrissis, Konrad, & Shrum, 2011) and specific orientations for a formal appraisal process (SCAMPI Upgrade Team, 2011) conducting to a certification.

Its staged "CMMI for development" representation considers, for maturity level 2, seven main practice areas, namely *"requirements management, project planning, project monitoring and control, supplier agreement management, measurement and analysis, process and product quality assurance and configuration management"*.

Essentially, they focus on project management, as an initial basis to, along further levels, promote best practices' institutionalization.

So, project management best practices' adoption (e.g., as prescribed in PMI, 2013) should also be considered as important to support a software improvement process for this level of maturity.

The implementation of a flexible and extensible project management tool, covering most of these practice areas with the necessary process and data, is essential to sustain a controlled environment, facilitating the progression to upper maturity levels.

These are, in broad terms, the most relevant references which represent the knowledge to be considered, and incorporated as fundamental bedrocks, for the whole OD intervention.

Quality and Organizational Excellence

Considering that the whole set of interventions which have been developed aim to produce a significant organization development impulse, targeting further incursions on organizational excellence, it is important to approach the subject of Quality and Organizational Excellence on its most relevant aspects.

This includes (1) a brief historical perspective of quality, some (2) essential visions of quality and its main dimensions, and (3) the relevant roles of people and participation which are integrated in organizational excellence models.

A Brief Historical Perspective of Quality

Quality as a field for research and practice has significantly evolved along time on visions, concepts, processes, practices, and tools. This is mainly due to a synergistic improvement helix, resulting from practitioners' needs and improvement efforts, allied with academic researchers' support and knowledge contributes. Often, within this area both roles have been performed by the same actors (e.g., Deming, Juran, Crosby, Ishikawa, Tagushi, and Feigenbaum) aggregated in specialized consulting firms, normative agencies, and professional associations. In fact, Quality has emerged from practice and from the need to introduce rigor within relevant practices.

Since the middle age, the concept of quality has emerged within craftsmanship – with simple product requirements, professionalism, and professional associations (guilds) – on the basis of skills, processes, and products' control. It was then a matter of professionals' survival and affirmation; often on an individual basis, and competing on local markets, with minimal products' quality

basis. These "quality roots" have evolved on a continuous improvement cycling paradigm, creating, progressively, some structures and informal standards, without significant disruptions and according to evolutionary needs.

At the beginning of the last century, theoretical streams of thought associated with industrial work organization (such as Scientific Management, General Theory of Business Administration, and Theory of Bureaucracy) have developed new paradigmatic visions over the productive process, its planning, and organization. They have triggered process-centred approaches to quality, including inspective and quality assurance activities supported by quality control departments, in order to guarantee the needs of large consumer markets through mass production and minimal defect products.

During World War II the need for statistical process control (as well as standards' impositions, in order to control productive steps and cycles, and adequate input supplies) has conducted to more formalized quality functions and structures (including quality professional's development, quality research, key publications, and professional body associations).

After the war, Juran and Deming intervening in Japan's reconstruction efforts have developed new strong quality theories, approaches, and techniques, and started focusing on top management awareness and training on quality. These new emerging visions have been more welcome in Japan rather than in the United States and Western Europe. In 1951 the Union of Japanese Scientists and Engineers (JUSE) created the Deming Prize for quality. During two decades Japanese products (although considered as inferior products) have been accepted by its quality standards ("made in Japan" label) and low-price across the American market.

Along the decade of 70 (due to a rising on products' quality in the north-American market) the consumer increased its preferences and attention to high-quality products.

On the next decade, publications like Consumer Reports appear in the market supporting product benchmark and evaluation, and introducing the usability concept dimension. The focus shifts from supplier and production to consumer. Governmental institutions develop normalization processes, and the media support the diffusion of a new quality movement.

Total Quality Management movement progressed, and, in 1987, an American Congress act institutes the Malcolm Baldrige National Quality Award. One year later the European Foundation for Quality Management (EFQM) is created, and, in 1991, the European Commission instituted the European Quality Award. These new prize approaches have enlarged the traditional product-process-service Quality concept along several dimensions; towards an effective Organizational Excellence holistic view.

Essential Views of Quality and Its Main Dimensions

As evidenced by this historical narrative there has been a cumulative progression on the main visions and concept of Quality. In fact, concerning their main targets, they can be viewed and classified through the following integrative staged categorization:

1. **Product Orientation:** Strongly connoted with the concept of quality control and, in earlier stages, with the process of inspection; focusing on verifying product conformity with its specifications in order to minimize defects, rejections, and rework activities;

2. **Production Process Orientation:** Targeting the creation of preventive quality assurance processes; introducing quality systems and norms; and regulating the execution of all the process and product activities necessary to ensure full compliance with conformity and security requirements;

3. **Customer Orientation:** Integrating into the former perspectives (product-process) the customer and employee dimensions; in order to guarantee and manage quality across of all areas of activity; producing, without defects, usage adequate products; satisfying internal and external customers; exceeding their expectations; engaging all managers and employees; at a minimal cost;

4. **Culture and Organizational Excellence Orientation:** Considering total quality management as a path to organizational effectiveness; thus intervening not only on product, process, customer, and results dimensions, but, mainly, on mobilizing all the organization and transforming the culture to respond to organizational excellence challenges; thus assimilating and evidencing continuous improvement, organizational learning, innovation, stakeholders' involvement, and sustainability attitudes across all organizational principles and practices.

Organizational Excellence Models

As already focused, since 1951 that Organizational Excellence regional awards have been institutionalized in order to incentive and recognize best practices related to Total Quality Management.

As the most significant ones, three major awards must be quoted:

- Deming Prize, from Japan;
- Malcolm Baldrige National Quality Award, from USA and
- European Foundation for Quality Management Award, from Europe.

All of them have underlying reference models which envision a total, holistic, approach to Quality as a path to organizational effectiveness, promoting dynamic change initiatives, within a large spectrum of areas, and being evaluated according to high-standards' criteria.

This is visible for the Deming Prize (JUSE, 2013) grouping its evaluation criteria within the main categories of

Management policies and their deployment regarding quality management; New product development and/or work process innovation; Maintenance and improvement of product and operational qualities; Establishment of systems for managing quality, quantity, delivery, costs, safety, environment; Collection and analysis of quality information and utilization of information technology and Human resources development.

Also, the Malcolm Baldrige National Quality Award model (NIST, 2013) incorporates those essential areas into its criteria for performance excellence, considering, as major evaluation categories, the areas of "*Leadership; Strategic Planning; Customer focus; Measurement, Analysis, and Knowledge Management; Workforce Focus; Operations Focus; and Results*".

The European Foundation for Quality Management Model (EFQM-A, 2013) on its nine base evaluation criteria also highly emphasizes, either on enablers ("*Leadership; Strategy; People; Partnerships & Resources; and Processes, Products, and Services*") as well as on results ("*People; Customer; Society; and Business*") the relevance of these wide set of areas congregated within a holistic approach to organizational excellence.

These visions – which integrate into the traditional "hard" technical and management view of quality all the necessary "soft" dimensions of organizational life – are, undoubtedly, the ones that align with the targeted stage for quality promotion. They advocate a holistic, systemic organization development and change strategy to approach quality, encompassing culture, values, people, and process on the path to organizational effectiveness.

Particularly, the aspects of leadership, engagement, and participation in self-assessment processes – as highlighted by EFQM Model (EFQM-B, 2013) – are of special interest. In fact, these dynamics and processes can be considered as strategic determinants of organizational effectiveness improvement by promoting an objective identification of strong supporting points and opportunities and the participative development of the associated actions and plans.

Focusing on self-assessment, Conti (1997) emphasizes two differentiated approaches to TQM: (1) award-like, focused on formal evaluation for recognition awards; and (2) diagnostic, more participative and oriented by diagnosis and improvement objectives.

According to this author, this second kind of approach, by definition, assumes only the form of an internal evaluation serving organizational diagnostic needs; while the first one consists mainly on an external evaluation conducted by a certified evaluator, and a self-audit lead by management.

Both are interesting opportunities which can be explored on the route to Organizational Excellence, and based on internal organizational dynamics congregation individuals, groups, and the whole organization around common learning and improvement goals.

Foundational Aspects of Change and Research

Besides covering specific knowledge on change targets' disciplines, also adequate relevance must be given to essential aspects of Organizational Development, Paradigmatic Approaches to Planned Change, Change related Attitudes and Behaviors, Main Types of Organizational Change, Organizational Research Approaches and Paradigms, and the Action Research paradigm.

Organizational Development

Along many years of research and practice, the concept of Organizational Development (OD) has been, progressively, viewed and defined with quite differentiated emphasis; denoting a strong evolution over multiple perspectives. Egan (2002) has reported this multiplicity of definitions and of associated outcomes.

This confirms OD as an evolving field, with a multiplicity of approaches, definitions, affinities and outcomes to be explored, making it a dynamic theoretical and practical discipline to be explored by academic and practitioner's communities.

As an applied field, there is an evident, interesting, mutual reinforcement spiral dynamics: new theories inform new practices and new practices' developments introduce new experimental knowledge to produce theories.

Cummings and Worley (2009, pp.1-2), considering the essential aspects of the concept's evolution, propose a wide OD definition:

A system wide application and transfer of behavioural science knowledge to the planned development, improvement, and reinforcement of the strategies, structures, and processes that lead to organizational effectiveness.

McLean (2006), aggregating the practitioners' perspective of the Organizational Development Network where academics, consultants and practitioners put efforts together on "advancing the practice and theory of OD" highlights their statement of principles (Table 7).

Considering their complementarities, integrating the most relevant dimensions, issues and concerns associated with a living OD concept, these definitions constitute the main reference adopted here.

Planned Change: Paradigmatic Approaches

Despite the traditional discussions between researchers and practitioners either on Organizational Development or on Organizational Change (in terms of distinction, intersection and inclusion), a brief review of the most relevant literature on the field (theoretical and applied) evidences a strong relationship between these two areas.

Table 7. Organizational Development Network – OD definition and Principles of Practice

Definition	**Organization Development** is a dynamic values-based approach to systems change in organizations and communities; it strives to build the capacity to achieve and sustain a new desired state that benefits the organization or community and the world around them.
Principles of Practice	• **Values-Based:** The practice of OD is grounded in a distinctive set of core values and principles that guide behaviour and actions - including respect and inclusion, collaboration, authenticity, self-awareness, and empowerment, • **Supported by Theory:** Draws from multiple disciplines that inform an understanding of human systems, including applied behavioural and physical sciences, • **Systems Focused:** Approaches communities and organizations as open systems; that is, acts with the knowledge that change in one area of a system always results in changes in other areas; and change in one area cannot be sustained without supporting changes in other areas of the system, • **Action Research:** Continuously re-examines, reflects and integrates discoveries throughout the process of change in order to achieve desired outcomes. In this way, the client members are involved both in doing their work, and in dialogue about their reflection and learning in order to apply them to achieve shared results, • **Process Focused:** Intervenes in organizational or community processes to help bring about positive change and help the client work toward desired outcomes, • **Informed by Data:** Involves proactive inquiry and assessment of the internal environment in order to discover and create a compelling need for change and the achievement of a desired future state of the organization or community. Some methods include survey feedback, assessment tools, interviewing, focus groups, storytelling, process consultation and observation, • **Client Centred:** Focuses on the needs of the client in order to continually promote client ownership of all phases of the work and support the client's ability to sustain change after the consultant engagement ends, • **Focused on Effectiveness and Health:** Helps to create and sustain a healthy effective human system as an interdependent part of its larger environment.

It is almost impossible, even in mere theoretical terms, to study one discipline without refer the other.

As Cummings & Worley (2009:p.13) highlight:

OD is directed at bringing about planned change to increase an organization's effectiveness and capability to change itself", being these processes "generally initiated and implemented by managers, often with the help of an organizational development practitioner from either inside or outside of the organization", which can "use Planned Change to solve problems, to learn from experience, to reframe shared perceptions, to adapt to external environmental changes, to improve performance, and to influence future changes.

This clearly evidences that:

1. Planned Change must be understood as a critical way to promote Organizational Development, and, reciprocally,
2. The process of Organizational Development, using Change as an instrument, produces positive effects over Organizational preparedness (through action development) and individual preparedness (through values/attitudinal assimilation) to face continuous improvement challenges between transformational change periods.

Concerning the typical Planned Change paradigms, these authors consider three major theoretical approaches (Figure 1) which aggregate to the most widely-applied and well-tested organizational transformation processes.

The first one, corresponding to the traditional Lewin's (1951) approach, conceives change as *"an effect of modification on forces' equilibrium"*, between those that tend to keep the systems stable (the status quo) and those pushing for change, where the resultant force determines change or maintenance.

According to this approach, the change process involves three main steps:

- **Unfreezing:** A process of "psychological disconfirmation", reducing forces that sustain the status quo, "surfacing" them, and creating "discomfort" with the current situation;
- **Moving:** Engaging on an individual, group and organizational behaviour, shifting to a new level, intervening in order to develop new behaviours, values and attitude changes;
- **Refreezing:** Stabilizing the organization at a new state of equilibrium.

Several intervention methods and frameworks of planned change still follow the base of this paradigm, including the seven-step Lippit, Watson, & Westley's (1958) approach and Kotter's (1996) eight steps to change. They have been widely applied, with success, during the last decades.

A second paradigmatic approach corresponds to the classical Action Research model, based on eight-step iteration (Table 8).

By its relevance to the current intervention it will be further analysed from a research methods' angle.

A third approach, widely applied for social change, corresponds to the Positive Model.

One of its most prominent variants is Appreciative Inquiry (Cooperrider & Whitney, 2005), which proposes (pp.25-35) a specific approach, either to transform an existing organization or to create Appreciative Organizations, integrating four essential stages: "Discovery, Dream, Design, and Destiny".

It has been born in rupture with the previous models, considering them as representing a deficit based approach to OD with excessive focus on problem solving.

Notwithstanding, some of their proponents start now to consider any potential for comple-

Figure 1. Major Planned Change Approach Paradigms
(Cummings & Worley, 2009)

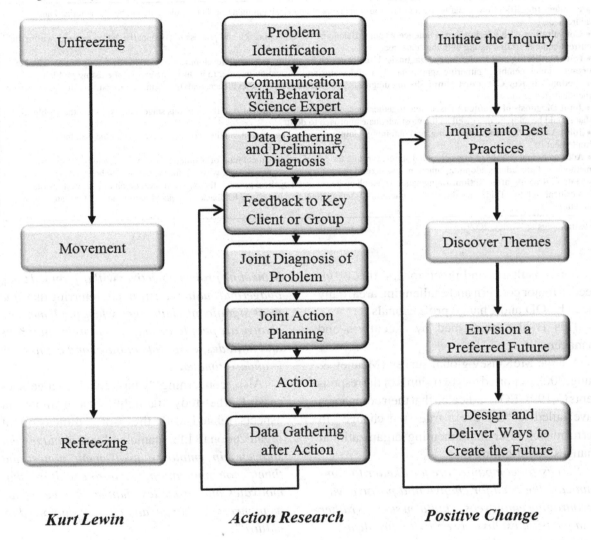

mentarities, in some cases valuing a new "Positive Problem Solving" approach.

Change Related Attitudes and Behaviors

Playing the human dimension a relevant role on Organizational Change, change related behaviours must be carefully considered.

In particular, its positive and negative potential impacts on change progression and success.

Beer & Nohria (2000) highlight:

Although large-scale organizational change efforts occur with increasing regularity, all too frequently these efforts fail to achieve their intended aims.

Table 8. An OD perspective of Action Research – Main Steps

- **Problem Identification:** Usually triggered by top-management and establishing a relevant problem area to be characterized and addressed;
- **Consultation with a Behavioural Science Expert:** Balancing the best approach and process to conduct the action research within the current context, in fine tuning with the "customer";
- **Data Gathering and Preliminary Diagnosis:** Usually driven by an organizational development expert, in strict cooperation with key organizational members, gathering appropriate data, and analysing information in order to identify the causes of existing problems;
- **Feedback to Key Client or Group:** Sharing diagnostic's objective results and evidence, and discussing, cooperatively, its relevance for the identified problem area;
- **Joint Diagnosis of Problem:** Discussing together the feedback elements provided in the previous stage, and exploring the problems that should be addressed, as well as the most adequate approach to do it;
- **Joint Action Planning:** Identifying, and obtaining a joint consensual agreement, on the actions to develop and the best form to implement it;
- **Action:** Actual change of organizational status, through the effective implementation of planned action, which may include, new methods and procedures adoption, functional, structural reorganization, work redesign, with reinforcement of new behaviours;
- **Data Gathering after Action:** Being action research an incremental cyclical process, the objective evaluation of achieved results is a critical step to: (1) identify the effects of action, (2) report them as a necessary feedback to engaged parties, and (3) initiate a new iteration.

(Cummings & Worley, 2009)

For consultants and practitioners' this is, indeed, a major concern and challenging area, daily faced by OD and Change professionals.

This is also confirmed by executives and managers.

A large McKinsey global survey (Meaney & Pung, 2008) reported that two-thirds of the respondents (3,199 CEOs) indicated that their companies have failed to "achieve a true step change" in performance after implementing organizational changes, highlighting that

Successful companies are far likelier to communicate the need for change in a positive way, encouraging employees to build on success rather than focusing exclusively on fixing problems.

This confirms the need for communication and engagement, minimizing resistances and developing change readiness at all levels.

Another study developed by IBM (Jorgensen, Owen & Neus, 2008) and based on a survey and interviews with more than 1,500 practitioners, reported that "m*ost CEOs consider themselves and their organizations to be executing change poorly; but some practitioners have begun to learn how to improve their outcomes*".

Among other aspects, the study evidences that "*only 41% of projects were considered successful in meeting project objectives within planned time, budget and quality constraints*", referring that "*the most significant challenges when implementing change are people-oriented: "changing mindsets and attitudes, corporate culture, and complexity is underestimated*".

Also, concerning "what makes change successful", the study highlights a set of important aspects related with the "soft" dimension of organizational life, namely: "*top management sponsorship, employee involvement, honest and timely communication, corporate culture that motivates and promotes change, change agents as pioneers of change, and change supported by culture*".

Revealing strong perceptions from the community of practice, these results are also in deep alignment with the relevance that the academic community gives to conceptual work on change attitudes, in particular to "*change readiness*" and "*resistance to change*".

These are important aspects, by its impact on programs' success and, therefore, on organizational development and effectiveness.

As any coin, the human side of change has also two faces. As Armenakis et al. (1993) refer:

While some name resistance to change as a major problem in organisations, others have focused on readiness for change and the role that it plays in facilitating organisational change.

In congruence with Lewin's (1951) focus on Force Field Analysis, both aspects must be considered, balancing change restraining and change facilitating forces in order to promote change.

Considering Resistance to Change many studies focus on it as a primary source of organizational change failure (Waldersee & Griffiths, 1996; Erwin & Garman, 2010), identifying many variety of ways of resistance (Oreg, 2006).

However, some authors advocate the use of resistance as a positive influencer (Downs, 2012), where others (Maurer, 1996) as something that may be used to build support to change.

So, resistance can be interpreted, either as "*any attitudes or behaviours that thwart organisational change goals*" (Chawla & Kelloway, 2004: p. 485), or as "*any conduct that serves to maintain the status quo in the face of pressure to alter the status quo*" (Zaltman & Duncan, 1977:p. 63).

Other authors use the construct of openness to change to refer to "*the positive affect towards change and willingness to support it*" (Miller, Johnson, & Grau, 1994; Wanberg & Banas, 2000).

Armenakis et al. (1993: pp. 681-682) use a wider concept of readiness to change as

The cognitive precursor to the behaviours of either resistance to, or support for, a change effort; a process where employees' beliefs and attitudes about an organizational change are altered to perceiving the change as necessary and achievable.

For them, "*resistance and readiness have been used interchangeably, often causing confusion and thus not providing a clear classification for determining what the antecedents and consequences of these constructs are*".

Furthermore, they enhance that, "*past research has suggested that change readiness attitudes pre-empt change resistance*", highlighting the relevance for using "*strategies for combating resistance to change (such as communication and participation) which are described as actually creating readiness*".

McKay, Kuntz, & Naswall (2013), based on an exhaustive literature review, highlight the correlation between important variables like "affective commitment", "communication adequacy", "participation", "readiness for change", and "resistance to change", which confirms that the promotion of successful conditions to make change happen is not a trivial task.

Concerning resistance to change, many authors consider that one of the most of its important aspects are related to prevention and minimization.

As a first prominent contribute on the area, Coch & French (1948) have investigated the effect of group consultation on the amount of resistance evidenced and have concluded that "*participation in group meetings decrease resistance and increase team members' commitment to change*".

Also, Lawrence (1969), enhancing employee participation and involvement as a strategy to overcome resistance, assert that "*maintaining the quality of social relationships would help to keep resistance to a minimum*".

Elaborating more on the subject, Kotter & Schlesinger (1979) argue that "*many managers underestimate not only the variety of ways people can react to organizational change, but also the ways they can positively influence specific individuals and groups during a change*", describing several causes for resistance and proposing a systematized way to select a strategy to address it. Based on an analysis of "*successful and unsuccessful organizational changes*", they propose six essential management strategies.

The first three – communication, participation and facilitation – are considered as positive, people-oriented approaches to deal with resistance, understanding and responding, working with resistance.

The remaining – negotiation, manipulation and coercion – are considered as negative, structure-oriented approaches, fighting against resistance.

Positive approaches understand resistance as legitimate, avoidable reactions, and opportunities to behavioral change and development, while negative approaches face resistance as undesirable, unavoidable, and harmful reaction to change which must be fought.

All these aspects are relevant and must be considered as impacting issues.

Main Types of Organizational Change

Having previously elaborated on aspects related with organizational development, organizational change and some critical issues associated with people reactions to change, it is now important to highlight some key aspects concerning the distinct types, paradigms and approaches to organizational change.

One of the first associated debates involves the kind of envisioned organizational change, its characterization, and dynamics along organizational life.

Greiner (1972) on his evolution-revolution framework concerning organizational change dynamics has described the typical life cycle of an organization as consisting of "*extended evolutionary periods of incremental change interspersed with short revolutionary periods*", setting the foundations for new change theories involving *strategic redirection and transformation*, and highlighting that:

During reorientations large and important parts of the organization (strategy, structure, control systems, and sometimes basic beliefs and values) change almost simultaneously in a way that leads to very different organizational emphases.

This theory have been further elaborated at the "punctuated equilibrium" model (Tushman and Romanelli, 1985) emphasizing the combination of the "life cycle motor" with the "teleological motor".

The concept of "motor", developed by Van de Ven & Poole (1995) within his Process Theories of OD and Change, has been used to refer to distinct underlying mechanisms associated with four ideal theories of change: "life cycle", "teleology", "dialectics" and "evolution". It suggests that most change theories could be understood within one motor or in a combination of them.

This classification is based on a two dimensional view, considering the mode of change (prescribed versus episodic) and the unit of change (single entity or multiple entities).

Weick & Quinn (1999) identified four distinct types of changes:

- **Incremental:** Planned, first order changes; corresponding to intentional changes on the normal organizational functioning;
- **Transformational:** Planned, second order changes; such as deep changes targeting organizational culture and climate, involving a previous plan of structured actions, with a wide impact on management processes, structures and work design;
- **Evolutionary:** Unplanned, first order changes; reacting to environmental changes, just like customer needs or competitive pressure, and
- **Revolutionary:** Unplanned, second order changes; when the organization is forced by extreme external conditions to drastically change their principles, involving radical changes on strategy, policies, structure, operative, or resources.

For these authors the terms "first order" and "second order" are related with the extent to which organizational conditions are changed. So, "first-order changes" means that they "do not involve a change on organizational functioning core assumptions"; while "second-order changes" means that "they imply a radical rupture".

On a strategic purpose perspective Beer & Nohria (2000) suggest a dichotomy: "economic-driven transformations" versus "changes to support organizational capabilities". For them economic-driven changes target directly the creation of economic value (focusing on structure and systems in order to reduce costs), while changes directed at the development of the organizations' capabilities, usually focus on culture, behaviour and attitudes.

Another relevant perspective concerning organizational change highlights its learning levels and is evidenced on the works of Argyris (Argyris & Schön, 1974; Argyris, Putnam, & McClain Smith, 1985; Argyris, 2002) it introduces the concepts of Model I versus Model II theories of action; and single-loop versus double-loop learning.

Argyris & Schon's (1974) Model II learning and Argyris, Putnam, & Smith's (1985) action science model provide a common base for dialectic action science methods. For them, change is triggered by calling attention to discrepancies between action and espoused values; where the difference between "theories in use" and "espoused theories" generates the impetus for change.

Argyris has focused on the relevance over organizational change of the processes which enable double-loop learning. He defines (2002) learning as the "*detection and correction of error*" and makes a clear distinction between single-loop learning, which "*occurs when errors are corrected without altering the underlying governing values*" and double-loop learning, which "*occurs when errors are corrected by changing the governing values and then the actions*".

Senge (2006:p. 766), rooted on these concepts and developing the theme of the Leaders' role on building Learning Organizations, refers a clear distinction between the notions of generative learning, "which is about creating" and adaptive learning, "which is about coping".

These theoretical foundations, used to typify change dynamics, motors and main purposes, as well as some important guiding principles and orientations on double-loop and generative learning which are on the basis of Learning Organizations, will help us to contextualize the current intervention.

Organizational Research Approaches and Paradigms

Having previously declared our strategic positioning, and covered the most relevant knowledge items related to the theoretical domains to be worked out along the intervention, as well as some foundational aspects of Change and Research, it is now important to make a small incursion on organizational research methods.

In fact, as any professional activity, doing Organization Research requires deep knowledge of the Organization (context), of the areas being worked (substance), and of the method to do it (form).

So, although not playing a role of "research methods' researcher", attention must be given to these aspects. Particularly it is important to proceed here to a brief contextualization of our positioning within a research methods' panoply of approaches before progressing to the details of Action Research's specific characteristics and main principles.

Researching inside organizations – with change and about change – implies a constant balance between research objectives and organization's objectives, research methods and organizational ways of "doing things".

Deviance to a pure research interest and method can generate extra, reactive, phenomena, which may interfere with those which are object of study; compromise its focus, observation and results; and organizational expectations and commitment. In extreme situations, research inflexibility and 'fundamentalism' can compromise the viability / continuity of the research.

Deviance to the organizational side of interests, capitulating to agendas, power and influence, can compromise research independence and rigour.

In extreme situations, pressure on time, economics, or vested interests, can drastically affect the research objectives, model, ethics and validity; even abort the process.

So, tensions are always present and must be continuously managed between two distinct communities of academics and practitioners, for the sake of cooperative research within organizational settings.

Robson (2011: p.11) illustrates this problematic with a caricature which highlights a set of distinct researcher's interests, work nature and typical approaches, contrasting (Table 9) "real world" versus "traditional academic" researchers.

It enhances a "researcher-versus-practitioner dilemma", contrasting and antagonising two classical dominant views over research practices.

Also, the so called, last century "paradigms' war", based on a dichotomy of approaches, has radicalized positions between quantitative (claiming that their number and facts approach was the only way to conduct scientific research) and qualitative researchers (arguing that numbers and statistics are no way to understand anything worthwhile about people and their problems).

Robson (2011: pp.18-19) also evidences this dichotomy in terms of competing values associated with extremes: (1) numerical vs. non-numerical; (2) hypothetic-deductive vs. inductive; (3) fixed design vs. flexible design; (4) generalization (de-contextualized) vs. particularization (contextualized); (5) objectivity vs. subjectivity; and (6) value-free vs. value-laden. The quantitative approach is connoted with positivism and the qualitative with social-constructionism.

Considering the "alternative inquiry paradigms", Lincoln, Lynham, & Guba (2011) go substantially deeper, detailing the "axiomatic nature of research paradigms" and its "practical issues", and providing a clear systematization based on these distinctive characteristics. Considering the substantial changes which have emerged on the "legitimacy" and "hegemony" aspects of the most significant research paradigms, they emphasize an increasing relevance for postmodern paradigms and a strong evolution on the participatory paradigm (Heron & Reason, 1997).

Their taxonomy considers five main research categories: Positivism (realists, "hard science" researchers), Post-positivism (a modified form of positivism), Critical theory (creating change to the benefit of those oppressed by power), Constructivism (or Interpretivism; gaining understanding by interpreting subject perceptions) and Participatory research (transformation based on democratic participation between researcher and subject).

Beside these contrasting differences, they highlight that:

Table 9. Real World versus Traditional Academic Researchers characteristics

Real World Researcher	Traditional Academic Researcher
• Interest is in solving problems, getting large effects (robust results) and concern for actionable factors (where changes are feasible); • Almost always working in the 'field', with strict time constraints; • Often with little consistency of topic from one study to the next; • As a generalist researcher (which need for familiarity with range of methods and approaches); • Oriented to client needs; • Currently viewed as dubious by many academic researchers; • With a high need for well-developed social skills	• Interest is in gaining knowledge and advancing the discipline, • Establishing relationships and developing theory; • In some discipline, working mainly in laboratories, • Using time as the topic needs, with as much finance as the topic needs; • Exhibiting high consistency of topic from one study to the next; • Highly specialized on his discipline and oriented to academic peers; • Carrying high academic prestige, • With limited needs for social skills

(Robson, 2011)

The various paradigms are beginning to inter-breed" and that "inquiry methodology can no longer be treated as a set of universally applicable rules or abstractions.

Action Research – with its Ontological, Epistemological and Methodological "basic believes", Inquiry Aims, Nature of Knowledge, Values, Ethics, Voice and Inquirer posture – fits clearly within their classification of Participatory Research.

The Action Research Paradigm

Combining Research with Change (or, as Coghlan & Brannick (2010) stress, "*doing research in action, rather than research about action*") Action Research can be seen by two complementary lenses:

1. A paradigmatic approach to Organizational Change (for Organizational Development and Change theorists and practitioners), and
2. A specific Research paradigm (from the point of view of research method's scholars).

In fact, this approach conciliates both aspects by combining research and action within organizational settings, based on solid theoretical knowledge, applying it in congruence with organizational objectives, promoting change, and getting new knowledge.

It is, indeed, "*driven by two masters, serving both*" (McKay & Marshall, 2007).

As a "*form of self-reflective problem solving which enables practitioners to better understand and solve pressing problems in social settings*" (McKernan, 1988), it promotes a "*systematic inquiry that is collective, collaborative, self-reflective, critical, and undertaken by the participants of the inquiry*" (McCutcheon & Jung, 1990).

It "*builds descriptions and theories within the practice context itself, and tests them there through intervention experiments – that is, through experiments that bear the double burden of testing*

hypotheses and effecting some (putatively) desired change in the situation" (Argyris & Schon, 1989).

It integrates a "*spiral in which each cycle increases the researchers' knowledge of the original question, puzzle, or problem and, it is hoped, leads to its solution*" (Kemmis, 1982).

Although exhibiting a set of common characteristics, there still persists a large spectrum of "*distinct intellectual traditions*" under a global denomination of Action Research (Herr & Anderson, 2005):

Participatory action research (PAR); practitioner research; action science; collaborative action research; cooperative inquiry; educative research; appreciative inquiry; emancipator praxis; community-based participatory research; teacher research; participatory rural appraisal; feminist action research; feminist, antiracist participatory action research; and advocacy activist, or militant research.

Within this panoply it is important to define the set of characteristics associated to the kind of Action Research being undertaken. This is done by here by appealing to a set of main authors' specific references which form the bedrock of our methodological approach.

One of these foundations is provided by Shani & Pasmore (1982), which have proposed a widely accepted definition for this research paradigm, considering it an "*evolving change process which is undertaken in a spirit of collaboration and co-inquiry*", and have detailed a set of key characteristics for a process to be considered as Action Research (Figure 2).

Another main reference is the one provided by Gummesson (2000) which evidences some of its most relevant characteristics (Table 10).

Together, these references (Shani & Pasmore, 1982; Gummesson, 2000) provide a clear definition and characterization of the Action Research process that we adhere to.

Figure 2. Action Research – Definition and key characteristics
Adapted from Shani & Pasmore (1982)

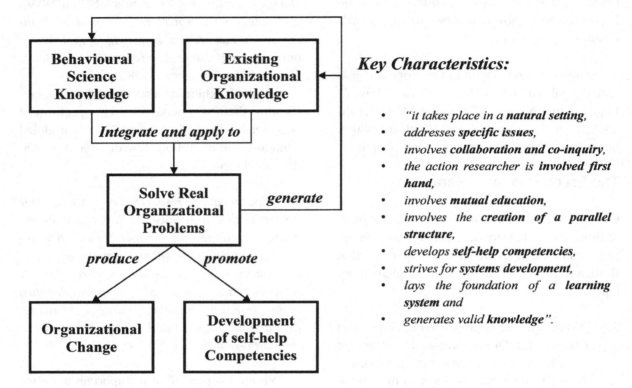

Key Characteristics:

- *"it takes place in a **natural setting**,*
- *addresses **specific issues**,*
- *involves **collaboration and co-inquiry**,*
- *the action researcher is **involved first hand**,*
- *involves **mutual education**,*
- *involves the **creation of a parallel structure**,*
- *develops **self-help competencies**,*
- *strives for **systems development**,*
- *lays the foundation of a **learning system** and*
- *generates valid **knowledge**".*

"emergent inquiry process in which behavioural science knowledge is integrated with existing organizational knowledge and applied to solve real organizational problems", "simultaneously concerned with bringing about change in organizations, in developing self-help competencies in organizational members, and in adding to scientific knowledge"

To complement them – making explicit our principles and ethics approach to Action Research – a third element is essential to complete this bedrock.

It is provided by Stringer (1996), which refers to community-based action research as "*a collaborative approach to inquiry or investigation that provides people with the means to take systematic action to resolve specific problems*" and enhances that it "*favours consensual and participatory procedures that enable people (a) to investigate systematically their problems and issues, (b) to formulate powerful and sophisticated accounts of their situations, and (c) to devise plans to deal with the problems at hand*".

From a values / ethics perspective, he highlights that it "*focuses on methods and techniques of inquiry that take into account people's history, culture, interactional practices, and emotional lives*", being "*a more user-friendly approach to investigation than most*".

Concerning the "*cultural style of action research*" he argues that traditional approaches (including the "scientific method") often "*involve an adversarial or authoritarian style that reflects the cultural ethos of competition and achievement endemic in modern societies*", contrasting with community-based action research which "*seeks to change the social and personal dynamics of the research situation so that it is non-competitive*

Table 10. Major characteristics of Action Research

Action researchers take action. Action researchers are not merely observing something happening; they are actively working at making it happen.
Action research always involves two goals: solve a problem and contribute to science. Action research is about research in action and does not postulate a distinction between theory and action. Hence the challenge for action researchers is both to engage in making the action happen and to stand back from the action and reflect on it as it happens in order to contribute theory to the body of knowledge.
Action research is interactive. Action research requires cooperation between the researchers and the client personnel, and continuous adjustment to new information and new events. In action research, the members of the client system are co-researchers as the action researcher is working with them on their issue so that the issue may be resolved or improved for their system and a contribution be made to the body of knowledge. As action research is a series of unfolding and unpredictable events, the actors need to work together and be able to adapt to the contingencies of the unfolding story.
Action research aims at developing holistic understanding during a project and recognizing complexity. As organizations are dynamic socio-technical systems, action researchers need to have a broad view of how the system works and be able to move between formal structural and technical and informal people subsystems. Working with organizational systems requires an ability to work with dynamic complexity, which describes how a system is complex not because of a lot of detail (detail complexity) but because of multiple causes and effects over time.
Action research is fundamentally about change. Action research is applicable to the understanding, planning and implementation of change in groups, organizations and communities. As action research is fundamentally about change, knowledge of and skill in the dynamics of organizational change are necessary.
Action research requires an understanding of the ethical Framework, values and norms within which it is used in a particular context. In action research, ethics involves authentic relationships between the action researcher and the members of the client system as to how they understand the process and take significant action. Values and norms that flow from such ethical principles typically focus on how the action researcher works with the members of the organization.
Action research can include all types of data gathering methods. Action research does not preclude the use of data gathering methods from traditional research. Qualitative and quantitative tools, such as interviews and surveys, are commonly used. What is important in action research is that the planning and use of these tools be well thought out with the members of the organization and be clearly integrated into the action research process.
Action research requires a breadth of pre-understanding of the corporate or organizational environment, the conditions of business or service delivery, the structure and dynamics of operating systems and the theoretical underpinnings of such systems. Pre-understanding refers to the knowledge that the action researcher brings to the research project. Such a need for pre-understanding signals that an action research approach is inappropriate for researchers who, for example, think that all they have to do to develop grounded theory is just to go out into the field.
Action research should be conducted in real time, though retrospective action research is also acceptable. While action research is a live case study being written as it unfolds, it can also take the form of a traditional case study written in retrospect, when the written case is used as an intervention into the organization in the present. In such a situation the case performs the function of a 'learning history' and is used as an intervention to promote reflection and learning in the organization.
The action research paradigm requires its own quality criteria. Action research should be judged not by the criteria of positivist science, but rather within the criteria of its own terms.

(Gummesson, 2000)

and non-exploitative and enhances the lives of all those who participate", building "*positive working relationships and productive interactional and communicative styles*".

Considering organizations as communities of persons, these principles are of most relevance for organizational research, in order to create open collaborative environments where people's well-being is a major foundation to reach sustained improvements.

For Stringer (1996) "*the role of the researcher is not that of an expert who does research, but that of a resource person*". He becomes "*a facilitator or consultant who acts as a catalyst to assist stakeholders in defining their problems clearly and to support them as they work toward effective solutions to the issues that concern them*".

Asserting that "*community-based research seeks to develop and maintain social and personal interactions that are non-exploitative and enhance*

Table 11. Community-based Action Research – Working Principles

Dimension	Essential Characteristics	Key Concepts
Relationships	Should: • Promote feelings of *equality* for all people involved • Maintain *harmony* • *Avoid conflicts,* where possible • *Resolve conflicts* that arise, openly and dialogically • *Accept* people as they are, not as some people think they ought to be • Encourage *personal, cooperative relationships,* rather than impersonal, competitive, conflictual, or authoritarian relationships • Be *sensitive* to people's feelings	equality, harmony, acceptance, cooperation, sensitivity
Communication	In effective communication, one: • Listens *attentively* to people • *Accepts* and acts upon what they say • Can be *understood* by everyone • Is *truthful and sincere* • Acts in socially and *culturally appropriate* ways • Regularly *advises* others about what is happening	attentiveness, acceptance, understanding, truth, sincerity, appropriateness, openness
Participation	Is most effective when it: • Enables significant levels of active *involvement* • Enables people to *perform* significant tasks • Provides *support for* people as they learn to act for themselves • Encourages plans and activities that people are able to *accomplish* themselves • Deals *personally* with people rather than with their representatives or agents	involvement, performance, support, accomplishment, personalization
Inclusion	Involves: • Maximization of the involvement of *all* relevant *individuals* • Inclusion of *all groups* affected • Inclusion of *all* relevant *issues - social,* economic, cultural, political – rather than a focus on narrow administrative or political agendas • Ensuring *cooperation* with other groups, agencies, and organizations • Ensuring that all relevant groups *benefit* from activities	individuals, groups, issues, cooperation, benefit

(Stringer, 1996)

the social and emotional lives of all people who participate" he strongly advocates a set of working principles for the community (Table 11).

Citing Habermas (1979), who suggested that "*positive change originates from communicative action – the capacity for people to work through disagreements to achieve effective solutions to problems*", he enhances that:

Where people feel acknowledged, accepted, and treated with respect, their feelings of worth are enhanced and the possibility that they will contribute actively to the work of the group is maximized.

As a final message on these principles, deeply rooted on ethics and values, it is important to highlight Stringer's (1996) strong beliefs:

At every stage of their work, research facilitators should ensure that procedures are in harmony with these guidelines, constantly checking that their actions promote and support peoples' ability to be active agents in the processes of inquiry. The underlying principle here is that human purposes are at least as important as technical considerations.

These were the base guidelines for Action Research which has been followed along the current research in action program: in line with the perspectives of Shani & Pasmore (1982), Gummesson (2000), Coghlan & Brannick (2010), and Stringer (1996).

CHANGE DESIGN AND DEVELOPMENT

Having previously detailed the essential foundations of the intervention – in terms of Research Meaning and Directions and of Literature Review – well will cover now the essential aspects associated with its design and development.

Organizational Context, Diagnosis, and Change Characterization

Before proceeding to the presentation of the main characteristics and details associated with the two cycles of the whole intervention, it is important to contextualize it.

So, as it has targeted the "soft" dimension of "organizational life", major relevance will be given to these characteristics in terms of background information.

The intervention has been developed and implemented within the IT Unit of a major Portuguese Bank which provides application development and infrastructure management services to all the organization, and, on a cultural point of view, it is important to refer some historical perspectives.

In the past, the Bank had been subject of a major merger between two main financial institutions, both very relevant to the Portuguese Banking System, and with very different historical background and progressions. Their original orientations concerning the market's approach, services, and employee management were also quite different.

Within the context of the IT areas the merge has occurred through a progressive departmental integration of teams from the original institutions, resulting into a new IT structure.

However, although some socialization training actions have been conducted at institutional level, there have not been developed any formal and visible socialization's strategy and plan emerging from a structured actions' definition towards a new global organizational culture.

The integration of hardware, software, and base services platforms, as well as of operational processes, had been planned and quickly implemented with a significant success, but the individual, group, and organizational dimensions had took a long time and an informal path till its integration. Working practices were quite different, with one organization (older) being routine process oriented and the other (younger) project and innovation oriented.

Concerning people management orientations, including leadership and individual employee management processes, both institutions had also quite different practices.

The policies and processes of people management from the acquiring institution had been prevalent, as a standard for the whole institution. They pointed out to a global principle of direct hierarchy responsibilities, with a decentralized role, controlled along all the hierarchical chain and with a common set of centrally defined management support processes.

Along time, these common management processes, practices, and instruments have been adopted and, progressively, accommodated within the new organization by all its members.

When the program has started the IT Unit had, internally, about 500 employees, providing application development, global services, and infrastructure management to the entire Bank.

On the specific domain of infrastructures' operation and control a structured outsourcing contract with a main international IT provider was hold. The external company which delivers these services has been set-up, under the management of this contractor, on the basis of former employees of the Bank which have been temporarily transferred to the firm. Despite being subject to a proper independent management these former employees still feel some organizational affinity link with the Bank.

Concerning application development (including its conception, design, and maintenance) and internal customer's support services (involving relationship management, help desk, and global IT services' support) most products and services were, mainly, internally developed and controlled.

Common processes and instruments have been set-up in order to measure and improve internal and external quality and satisfaction, in line with the standard organizational policies and practices, and including Customer surveys and Employee's surveys. These instruments have demonstrated to be good sources to identify and implement, specific, regular, and isolated actions concerning product, service, and process improvement.

Based on specific internal customers' and employees' perceptions about organizational functioning and service levels, these instruments have also allowed the IT Unit to identify the specific need for a more "soft", cultural, improvement approach.

Among others aspects, it has been clearly identified a special need for leadership training within the IT Unit in order to harmonize and align distinct organizational practices, and also some improvement requirements targeting customer orientation and employee engagement. In fact, the setting of common artefacts – mostly visible by a global organizational structure, standard rule's definition, and associated processes – was not sufficient to promote the necessary organizational integration and development.

In particular, within an organization which should engage on common objectives – communicating across organizational silos and with their customers and external providers in order to provide critical business support products and services – the establishment, and continuous improvement, of common values, attitudes, behaviours, and effective practices' alignment was a critical factor.

This has been the main decisional trigger for the intervention.

The program has started with a Diagnostic stage, where through a proper questionnaire (OCAI, Cameron & Quinn, 1998), a set of focus group sessions and customer oriented semi-structured interviews it has been possible to obtain a "picture" of the current culture and an image of the desired culture. The process has involved all employees and its leaders, as well as top-representatives from the main internal customers. It has allowed for a proper identification of existing gaps and associated problems, providing the basis to tailor the intervention. Concerning the type of cultural change, the study evidenced a strong hierarchical culture and a convergent desire to evolve to a market one.

The first cycle of the intervention, named as Changing IT, was developed along 2009, involving all IT Employees. Communication, engagement, action and improvement were the most relevant attributes of the process. As previously mentioned, it has integrated a set of structured actions targeting the areas of Organizational Culture and Values, Leadership and Employee Engagement, which are in line with the pre-defined Organizational Objectives for the 1st OD Cycle (see Table 4).

It has been set-up, managed and implemented by an internal team, supported by external consultants, coordinated with the IT management team, facilitated by a Change Agent's Team and sponsored by IT top-level management.

Concerning the kind of change promoted (Porras & Robertson, 1992) it can be classified as a 2nd order planned change (multidimensional, multi-level, radical and discontinuous, involving an organizational paradigm's rupture), this is, transformational. It has targeted "changes in organizational climate and culture, with significant changes on working processes, organization structure, conception and management, according to a previous plan" (Caetano, 2001).

It configures a scenario of planed change (Van de Ven & Poole, 1995) built at the level of a single entity, with development induction through a cycle of goal formulation, implementation, evaluation and modification of goals based on what was learned.

According to Weick & Quinn's (1999) classification it can be characterized as episodic change (infrequent, discontinuous and intentional) occurring during divergence periods where organizations are moving away from their equilibrium conditions (Punctuated equilibrium model; Tushman & Romanelli, 1985).

Both cycles of the intervention configure a typical double-loop (Argyris, 2002), generative (Senge, 2006) development and learning process.

First OD Cycle: Behavioral Preparation and Strategy Determination

As previously referred (Table 4) the first Organizational Development cycle of the intervention has targeted the development of a Service Culture,

of Leadership Practices, promoting an active Employee Engagement on the identification and proposal of strategic actions to improve IT Unit's effectiveness.

Main Stages

This first OD cycle, named as the "Changing" IT program, has involved a wide and complex set of structured organizational transformation actions, as depicted by Figure 3.

It has followed, along a year-and-half period, a typical diagnosis-intervention-evaluation structure, and has benefited from a wide participation of all IT employees.

Figure 3. Changing IT Program – Main Stages

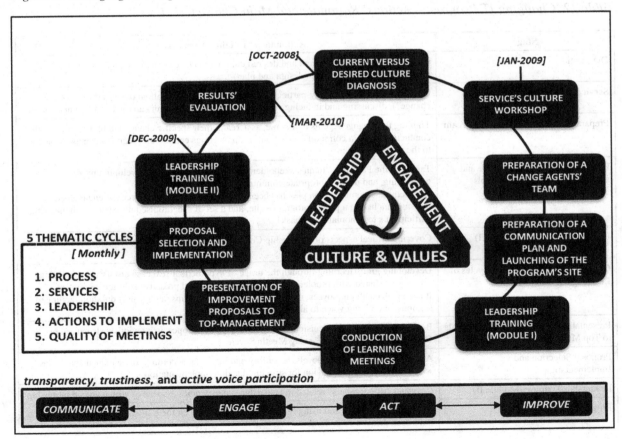

Preparing Employees for participation, triggering new attitudes, discussing together the main IT problems, and proposing strategic actions to implement a more service oriented culture, has been a major challenge.

So, a strong investment has been made on discussing "the Values of IT" as an inspiring step to change, preparing an independent Change Agents' Team to facilitate learning sessions, continuously communicating with the distinct stakeholders, getting employees' contributes to solve major problems, and preparing IT managers to lead and engage on a new IT Culture.

These were the major landmarks of the program, involving a specific set of actions, whose rationale and main characteristics are summarized at Table 12.

Evaluation Methodology

The program's evaluation has involved the previous identification and selection of a set of specific indicators (Table 13) measured along the intervention and evaluated at the end of it.

As it can be observed, the Evaluation Methodology has integrated a significant set of complementary indicators. Most of them can be considered as "soft" indicators, being measured through perceptive information collected via semi-structured interviews, surveys, focus group sessions, testimonials and implementation reports.

On a complex intervention (developed within a "real world" context and targeting a multitude of actions) evaluation parameters are, often, conditioned by several kinds of reasons.

Table 12. Changing IT Program – Actions' Rationale and Main Characteristics

Stage	Rationale and Main Characteristics
Diagnostic	Characterization of the current and desired culture, inherit gap analysis, and action determination (intervention's design and plan)
Services' Culture Workshop	Half-day small group highly-participative sessions, integrating all employees ("inspiring for change"), discussing and inducing values, attitudes and behaviours aligned with the new culture
Preparation of a Change Agents' Team	Training the Change Agents to assume, as a Team, their specific change facilitation role on the conduction of open communication bottom-up meetings centred on specific subjects associated to the desired change
Launching of the Project's Site and associated communication tools	Targeting the Programs' main stakeholders, segmenting messages, developing proper positioning, and using appropriate communication channels. A structured communication plan has been developed in order to enforce the engagement message, including a proper program's site, and a set of synchronised newsletters emphasizing participant's testimonials (feedback)
Leadership Training (Module I)	Covering critical aspects of Leadership Competence's development, concerning the individual action toward employees
Conduction of five thematic cycles of Learning Meetings	Developing group learning through the usage of hypothetical-real case discussion, analysing aspects associated with problem identification, causes, and proactive solution's proposal. It has involved all employees, on small heterogeneous groups, along short duration facilitated sessions, and giving voice to all participants
Presentation of improvement proposals to Top Management	Bottom-up feedback for decision, based on employees' proposals, previously structured by Change Agents for each Learning Meeting cycle
Proposal Selection and Implementation	Attribution of importance levels, feasibility and meaning, according to the planed change, as well as the associated decision for structured action implementation
Leadership Training (Module II)	Covering critical aspects related to leadership competencies associated with team's relationship
Program Evaluation	Against its objectives and using the instruments included on the evaluation methodology which have been previously defined

Table 13. Changing IT Program – Evaluation parameters

Scope	Instrument	Evaluation Moments
Workshop and Training Actions Effectiveness	1. Culture Workshop Satisfaction Survey 2. Leadership Training Satisfaction Survey 3. Change Agent Training Satisfaction Survey 4. Methodologies Implementation narrative reports	At the end of each training action At the follow-up session

Internal Perception of IT Culture	5. Culture Survey
	   5.1. Dimension Values
	   5.2. Dimension Leadership
	   5.3. Dimension Information
	6. Self-evaluation Questionnaire on Leadership Practices
	7. Focus groups with employees
		Before and after the Program
		At the end of the Program
		Before and after the Program

Customer Satisfaction with IT Services	8. Annual IT Internal Customers Satisfaction Survey 9. Structured Interviews with Major IT Customers (top-level managers)	During the Program Before and after the Program
IT Improvement Actions Implemented	10. Characterization of the validated proposals and analysis of its implementation level	At the end of the Program

In fact, not being Firms the best models for Experimental Labs (where the context, the research subjects, objects and instruments are within a highly-controlled environment), all these aspects have to be conform to real organizational settings.

The wide scope, complexity and changing nature of the intervention, constraint these measurements; not allowing either for (1) fine tuning the effects of its multiple dimensions, or (2) isolation from effects of parallel actions implemented inside the organization (e.g., a new individual performance appraisal process).

Also, due to the universal scope of the intervention, covering all IT areas and employees, it was not possible to set-up any kind of quasi-experimental process (Campbell & Stanley, 1963) using control groups.

Main Results

Covering the three fundamental dimensions of the intervention (Service Culture and Values, Leadership Practices, and Employee Engagement and Participation), Figures 4, 5 and 6 depict, for each one, its stages, objectives, evaluation instruments and results.

Second OD Cycle: Coordinated Strategy Implementation

As it emerges from the results evaluated at program closure, service quality has improved and several actions have been decided, to be implemented during the second OD cycle and potentiating future improvements.

The internal and external program's recognition (namely through the attribution of APCE 2010 Great Award from Portuguese Association for Organizational Communication) has set a prominent milestone on the recognition of organizational ability. It has incremented collective self-confidence, acting as an incentive for new OD initiatives towards organizational excellence.

Several important actions (Figure 7) have been developed targeting Employee Satisfaction, Motivation and Teams Effectiveness, and covering Training, Development and Communication; Leadership practices; Best Practices Adoption; Work Process Optimization and Tools Implementation.

This set of structural initiatives, evidencing new strategic directions, as an organizational learning effect from the 1st OD cycle reflected on the sec-

Figure 4. Service Culture and Values – Stages, Objectives, Evaluation Instruments and Results

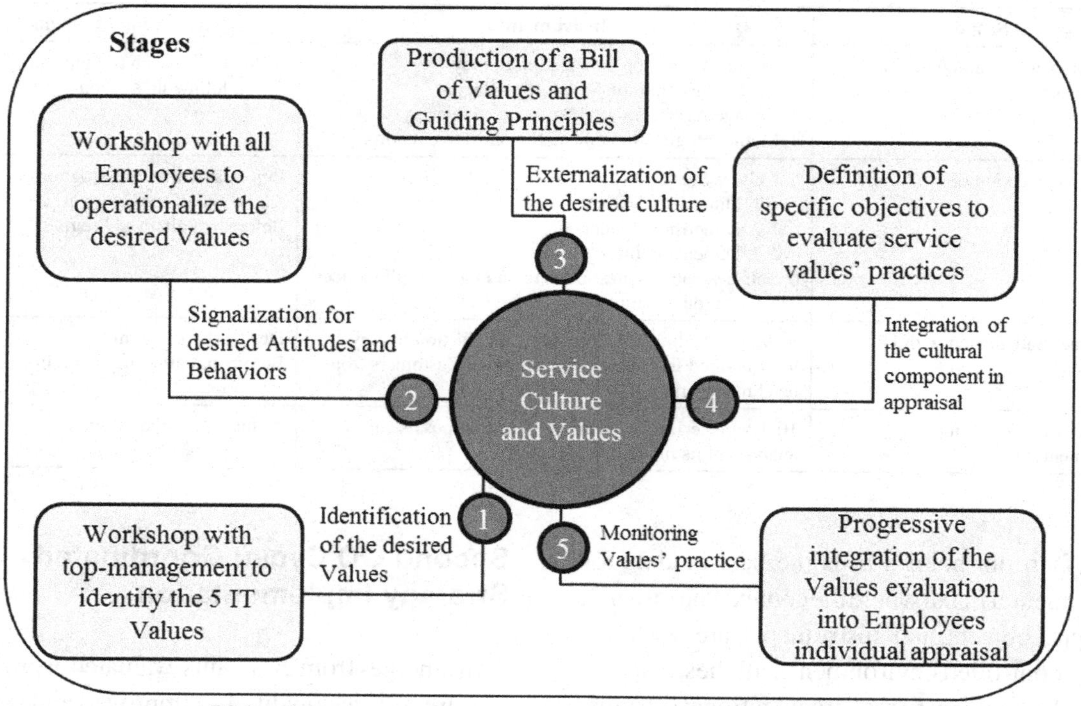

Objectives

- To promote internal service practices aligned with the desired values and principles
- To enforce performance management through Culture
- To improve internal and external service levels

Evaluation Instruments

[EM1]   Culture Workshop Satisfaction Survey
[EM4.1] Culture Survey - dimension Values
[EM7]   Annual IT Internal Customers Satisfaction Survey
[EM8]   Structured Interviews with Major IT Customers

Main Results:

- The results from the regular Internal Customer's Satisfaction Survey, evidenced an immediate services' quality improvement – very clear on items related to behavioural elements, pointing to new attitudes within the IT area (increased availability for customer attendance and more effective support on problem resolution). Considering that the Culture Workshops have been focused on these variables, it is valid to assert that there is an effective congruence between the investment and the perceived outcomes.

- Based on the interviews' results, it is possible to assert that the improvement effort, at internal processes' level and on service quality, has been visible for the customers' top-management structures. Most of them have made explicit references to the teams' customer proximity and perceived the program, and its communication strategy, as an explicit evidence of a strong commitment to improvement – thus recognizing *ChangingIT* as a structuring element for the new IT unit's positioning (next to its internal customers).

- The internal Culture Survey results also denoted a great congruency between Employees' and Internal Customers' perceptions – in the sense they perceive the IT Unit's culture positioning: a typical Market Culture, focused on results, with major attention on service delivery's quality monitoring. Although, within the Culture's Value dimension it has been denoted some enforcement on items related to a hierarchical culture – control, rule accomplishment, maintenance and stability. In fact, besides the evident greater concern with customer's satisfaction, employees still perceive the IT Unit as somewhat focused on internal processes.

Figure 5. Leadership Practices – Stages, Objectives, Evaluation Instruments and Results

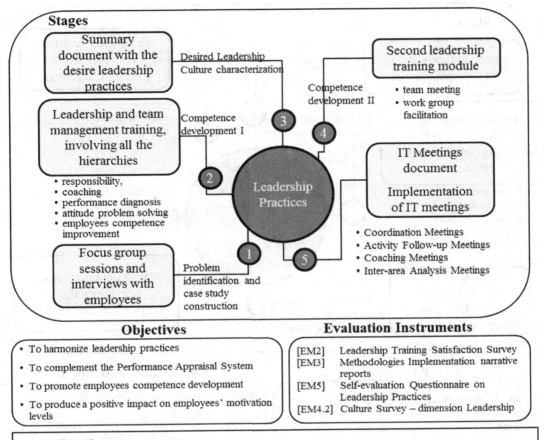

Objectives

- To harmonize leadership practices
- To complement the Performance Appraisal System
- To promote employees competence development
- To produce a positive impact on employees' motivation levels

Evaluation Instruments

[EM2]	Leadership Training Satisfaction Survey
[EM3]	Methodologies Implementation narrative reports
[EM5]	Self-evaluation Questionnaire on Leadership Practices
[EM4.2]	Culture Survey – dimension Leadership

Main Results:

- The satisfaction levels' with leadership training have been very high.
- Also, the volume and quality of associated methodologies' implementation has been quite remarkable, evidencing a change on the current perception that employees have about leadership practices. It has been observed a shift on employees' perception towards the desired leadership culture. Now, they evaluate their direct hierarchies' leadership style and practices as more close to them, more objective and focused on results.
- The leaders, themselves, became more exigent concerning their own practices. On most situations, employees are more satisfied with the individual objectives definition process, the way they receive feedback and the form how leaders deal with attitude problems.
- Practices which have been assumed as mandatory (e.g., individual performance appraisal meetings and team coordination meetings), has evidenced more expressive implementation levels. It is also visible a growing attention to the development of employees' technical, business and behavioural competencies.
- Coaching is done mainly at direct hierarchies' level, but still in a poorly structured way and more focused on supporting short term tasks. There is still a low frequency on medium-large term employees' support. This heterogeneity on the coaching process implementation is perceived by the team leaders, which consider it as an opportunity for improvement.
- It is also visible some difficulty to delegate – with its impact on the growing volume of operational work done by intermediary leaders, and its implications on their lower availability to carry on some leadership tasks directly related to employees follow-up and support. The results of employees' focus group sessions evidence the existence of a significant volume of work still being carried out at a hierarchical level upper than recommended.
- Globally, the results evidence a very positive impact of the leadership training component of this program – which, jointly with the reformulation on the institutional performance appraisal process, has implied a shift, towards the desired direction on the leadership style perceived by employees.

Figure 6. Engagement and Participation – Stages, Objectives, Evaluation Instruments and Results

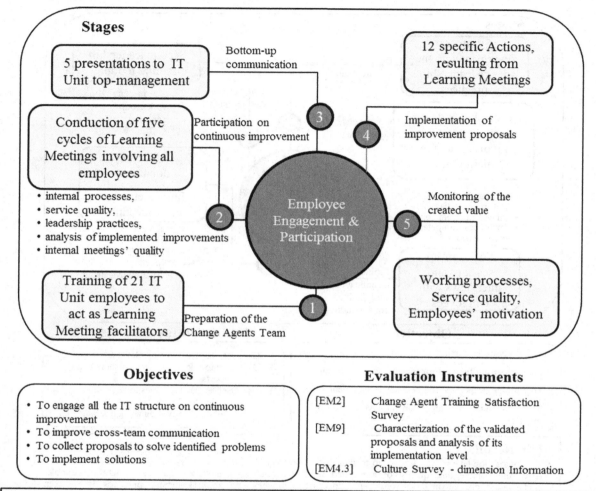

Objectives

- To engage all the IT structure on continuous improvement
- To improve cross-team communication
- To collect proposals to solve identified problems
- To implement solutions

Evaluation Instruments

[EM2]   Change Agent Training Satisfaction Survey

[EM9]   Characterization of the validated proposals and analysis of its implementation level

[EM4.3]   Culture Survey - dimension Information

Main Results:

- All the critical tasks of this dimension have been completed with success, being evident all intervenient satisfaction – either from oral feedback or from recorded employees' testimonial (available at the program's site).
- The bottom-up communication mechanism, created by all employees and reciprocated by top-management, has generated an effective dynamic towards improvement action's implementation.
- Twelve important actions were developed – with distinct impacts at internal organization, processes and service quality levels.
- IT Academy and IT Portal were some the most important, emerging from them a significant change on the perceptions about internal forms of IT communication.
- Undoubtedly, the results measured on the internal culture survey evidenced a global shift towards more flexibility in information / communication within the IT Unit.

Figure 7. Second OD Cycle - Main Initiatives subsequent to the Changing IT Program

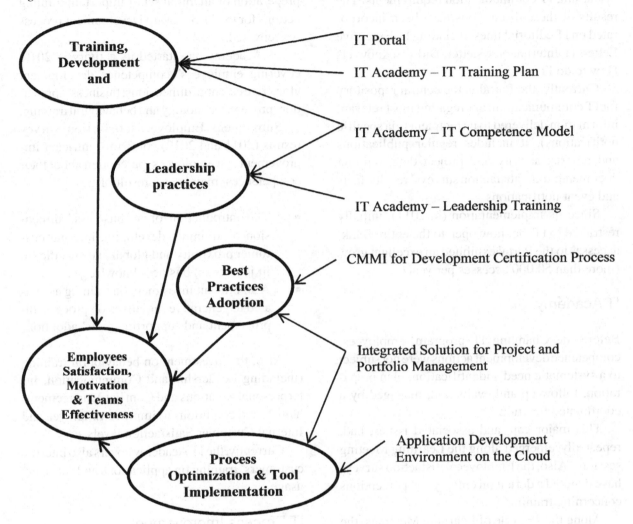

ond one, has been implemented by project teams, sponsored by IT top-management, controlled by Steering Committees; benefiting from an engaged cooperation of employees.

The next topics provide a brief description of those initiatives and its major achievements.

IT Communication and IT Portal

The IT Communication Unit had been already created in 2008, on the sequence of a major restructuring.

It has played a major role along the Changing IT program, being actively involved in planning, joint-decisions and implementation, cooperating on the set-up of an integrated communication plan, program's Site, periodical newsletters, specific communications and testimonials' collection. Some of these new formats were, further, reused for the regular IT Communication process.

Along the 4th cycle of Learning Meetings (September, 2009) its support instruments, in particular the IT Portal, have been subject to important discussions and proposals, as well as on discussing IT communication requirements. The results of these discussions have been incorporated on IT editorial lines, including IT Executive Letter, IT Internal Newsletter, Did you know IT, How to do IT.

Currently, the Portal is the central repository for IT communication, aggregating most relevant information delivered to its recipient (via specific notifications). It includes regular publications and reports, activity and project data, training documentation, satisfaction surveys' results, facts and event notifications.

Since its implementation (in 2011), initially restricted to IT, but now open to the entire Bank, accesses to the Portal exhibited an excellent grow (more than 50.000 accesses per year).

IT Academy

Before the Changing IT program, employees' competence development actions were not subject to a systematic need's identification, plan preparation, follow-up and evaluation, managed by a coordinated function.

This major gap, and associated issues, had, repeatedly, emerged along the Learning Meeting sessions. Also, the Employee Satisfaction surveys have denoted a deficit on employees' perceptions concerning training.

Along the 4th cycle of Learning Meetings, the topic has been subject of deep discussion, exploring employees' perception on the situation and problems and stimulating their contributions to develop the high potential idea of IT Academy.

In 2009 (4th quarter) a project has been triggered in order to set-up this new IT organizational unit. It has covered the definition of its working models: (1) strategic (vision, mission, strategy, orientation principles and objectives); (2) governance (structures, processes, KPIs, operational procedures, stakeholders and partnerships, logistics and resources); and (3) operational. Also, the

preparation of an initial set of important training actions for the IT Software Development process was covered.

IT Academy has started its activity in 2010, covering employees' competence development along five essential dimensions: business, application, process, technology and behavioural training.

Subsequent Employee satisfaction survey results (2011 and 2012) confirm significant improvements on employees' perception about their competences, mainly as a result of:

- The introduction of a "business" dimension on training; developing internal customer proximity and global and specific (to fit job needs) business knowledge;
- A significant investment on training associated to generative initiatives on process improvement and supporting tools' adoption.

Also, the investment on behavioural training (including Leadership and Communication, Interpersonal Relations and Conflict Management) has created conditions to improve Employee and Internal Customer Satisfaction levels.

Currently, the IT Academy covers also internal customers' training on applications and services' usage.

IT Process Improvement and CMMI Certification

On the sequence of a complex project developed in 2002 and targeting the IT infrastructure externalization, a great effort had been put into the development of IT internal processes.

Concerning service management and delivery (service desk, incident, problem, configuration, change, release, service level, capacity, availability, continuity, and security management) a significant investment had been made in the past towards best practices' application (ITIL aligned) and associated tools. These practices were considered as quite satisfactory, aligned and stabilized, and did not constitute a concern for transformational programs. So, any associated certification (ISO20000 or CMMI for Services) was not a priority.

On the Software Development practices front, the IT Division had already (2001) set-up an internal unit devoted to standardization and continuous improvement.

In 2006, a first attempt was made to identify practices and improvement needs', through an assessment supported by external consultants and following a CMMI for Development ML2 referential. Its results had evidenced a need for significant improvements to be achieved before trying to reach any formal certification. Since then, process improvement activities have been developed on a continuous mode, mainly following COBIT, PMBOK and CMMI orientations.

Along 2009, the Changing IT Program has evidenced the opportunity, willingness, and self-confidence to face more transformational initiatives. This was quite evident, and has triggered a top-management decision to initiate a strategic project targeting a SEI CMMI for Development formal certification.

The project, initiated in October 2010, has been lead by the IT Software Improvement Unit, sponsored by a Steering Committee, supported by an external consultant, and has integrated members from IT Development and Project Management Office.

It has started with an assessment stage, contrasting current practices against CMMI guidelines. A formal report, identifying the associated gaps and main improvements needs, has been produced.

A second stage – engaging all IT Development project managers and focusing on the improvement and redesign of the Development Process in order to cope (at least) with CMMI ML2 orientations – has been completed. All IT Business Relationship Management, Development and Quality Control units' members have been extensively trained and involved in the implementation of the associated changes. Also, IT Software Process Improvement Unit activities have been redesigned to cope with the new support, control, audit, and quality assurance requirements.

The effective Appraisal Process has been conducted in June 2011. It has integrated a regular SEI sample from all Projects, involved 30 appraisal interview sessions, with 60 employees, being driven by a team of 10 independent appraisal members, led by an authorized Lead Appraisal.

At 12 July 2011, the IT Division has been awarded with a SEI CMMI for Development ML2 Certification, with full implementation, being all generic and specific goals satisfied, for all practice areas, without any weakness.

IT Tools: Project Management Integrated Solution

Although the IT Division already had in place a set of instruments to support Project and Portfolio Management (PPM) and covering all development stages (feasibility study, requirements' definition, decision, analysis, software development and test) these tools exhibit a great lack of integration and low flexibility to evolve. The Learning Meetings' sessions have clearly evidenced the problem, pointing out to a desirable tools' replacement.

Due to its negative impacts on efficiency, effectiveness and quality, and strong obstacle to agile process improvement, this imperative has been quite recognized IT top-management. So, along 2010, a PPM project had been started in order to select and implement a proper support tool to address, primary, needs on Project Planning and Project Management and Control.

The selection stage, highly participative, has integrated a wide group of representatives from IT Business Relationship Management, Development and Quality Control units.

A core team has been set-up to support the whole project, including product's customization. It has been leaded by the IT Quality Improvement

& Organizational Development unit, in strict cooperation with Project Management Office. All employees from interested parties (including management structures and customers) have been trained on the new tool.

Implementation has been successfully completed by the end of 2012.

REFLECTION AND MAIN RESULTS

Reflection on Organizational Change Results

Despite some IS/IT areas' tradition of addressing Quality Improvement and Organizational Excellence on a reductionist perspective, overestimating the sole power of technical / tactical instruments and underestimating the role of People, the current intervention evidences that an OD approach can produce effective and deep transformations.

In fact, a direct reflection on the light of the existing literature and considering the most significant organizational change outcomes clearly evidences the following main relevant aspects:

1. **Common Set of Meaningful Values:** Changing the governing values as a preliminary basis to change the course of action (Argyris, 2002), aligning espoused, attributed, shared, and aspirational values (Bourne & Jenkins, 2013), considering them on the critical path from believes, norms, and attitudes to promote desired behaviours (Ajzen & Fishbein, 1980), and following a specific Value-Based Management process (Vargas, 2005) has proved to be a successful strategy to enforce organizational identity and identification, organizational commitment, and employee engagement, developing a psychological sense of community within the IT organizational unit;

2. **New Positive Problem Solving Practices:** The usage of participative meetings involving all employees on small heterogeneous groups in short duration facilitated sessions as a form to decrease resistance to change (Coch & French, 1948), promoting employee participation and involvement (Lawrence, 1969), using education and communication, participation and involvement, facilitation and support as proper strategies to decrease resistance and increase commitment (Kotter & Schlesinger, 1979), and using positive problem solving techniques, has introduced a process which has proved (as the learning meetings' results evidence) to be effective to promote peer interaction on problem identification, discussion, positive contributions, mutual enrichment, and solutions' proposal;

3. **Enforced Organizational Commitment and Employee Engagement:** Creating the necessary bounds of engagement in terms of motivation and incentive to bound, organization identification, internalization, and psychological ownership resulting in promotion of change, using values' congruence to promote affective commitment to the organization (Burne & Jenkins, 2013) has demonstrated to be an excellent strategy to promote individual and group engagement on change.

This has been made particularly evident by observation of individual behaviours contributing to group performance during learning meetings, video, and written testimonials, as well as through the narratives of the sessions and its high relevant outcomes;

4. **Enhanced Psychological Sense of Community:** As a consequence of the active employee involvement and internal open communication strategies which have been put in place around the program (Dessler, 1999) a multiple sense of membership, influence, integration and fulfilment of needs, shared emotional connection, and responsibility configuring the base dimensions of Psychological Sense of Community (Boyd

& Nowell, 2014) has emerged, turning the organization into a real living community (Mintzberg, 2009), and progressively creating the proper conditions to a strong, active, and visible employee engagement on change;

5. **Significant Improvement of Leadership Practices:** As a consequence of specific leadership training, involving all employees with management responsibilities, the volume and quality of associated methodologies' implementation has been quite remarkable, evidencing a positive change on the current perception that employees have about leadership practices.

The leaders became more exigent concerning their own practices and employees evaluate their direct hierarchies' leadership style and practices as more close to them, more objective, and focused on results (as evidenced by the leadership survey conducted after the program).

Employee surveys, conducted before and after the program, give strong evidence of a relevant increase on satisfaction levels, particularly those related to their direct managers;

6. **Strong Enforcement of Internal Communication:** Being communication, participation, and facilitation key strategic drivers to positively influence individuals and groups towards change (Kotter & Schlesinger, 1979), considering its expanded role to "address the effects of small group networks, superior-subordinate communication, and communication climate on employee satisfaction and performance" (Krone, Kramer, & Sias, 2010), moving from micro-level interpersonal issues to more macro-level ones (Jones et al., 2004), and being "an integral part" of participative processes (Seibold & Shea, 2001), a special emphasis has been given to the communication process along the whole program.

In fact, communication, engagement, action, and improvement were the most relevant attributes of the program, benefiting from a strong engagement of the IT Communication Unit.

Communication has been a focal strategic tool to leverage the process, but also a focal area of discussion within the program. In fact, IT Communication and its main instrument (the IT Portal) have been deeply discussed by all employees along "learning meetings". As a result of these discussions new communication processes, tools, practices, editorial lines, and publications have been incorporated within IT Communication regular activity. The Program itself has been externally recognized as a winner of a Portuguese Association of Organizational Communication Award in 2010;

7. **Relevant Strategic Initiatives:** Using Employee Commitment (Meyer & Allen, 1991; Meyer et al., 2002), creating a Psychological Sense of Community and acting on its components (to improve psychological well-being and motivate pro-social-behaviour during a change event), using its positive relationship with collaborative learning to influence a group's ability to generate alternative ideas and solutions to problems (Boyd & Nowell, 2014), the "Learning Meeting" sessions, involving all employees, have played a major role on the identification of strategic initiatives, configuring extra-role behaviours on the basis of contextual performance.

The pragmatic strategic outcomes, in terms of the employee-proposed structural actions approved by IT top-management give clear evidence of this;

8. **New Organization Development Structures:** Based on the success of the first cycle of the program, which has created

within the IT organization a sense of urgency to implement new structural actions and functions as well as a strong spirit of self-confidence on organizational capabilities to drive the whole process, new organizational structures have been created to support the several organization development initiatives.

IT communication activity has been enlarged and improved, and three major units have been created within an IT management support office: a Software Process Improvement Unit, the IT Academy Unit, and a specific IT Quality and Organization Development Unit. Together these four Units have coordinated the second cycle's main projects, which have been sponsored by IT top-management, benefiting from the creation of specific Steering Committees, involving relevant organizational units and employees, external providers, and specialized consultants; and

9. **Improved Processes, Tools, and Practices:** As a result of the main projects which have been developed during the second OD cycle of the intervention, several processes have been aligned and improved (employee development processes; internal and external communication; application portfolio and project management; software development; and application documentation process).

Also, more flexible and integrated tools have been implemented to support those processes (IT Portal to support IT communication, IT Project and Portfolio management tools have been integrated and enhanced to support software development projects).

New IT practices have been developed in strict alignment with these new set of processes and tools; being more mature; aligned with international standards; and certified by independent entities (CMMI for Development).

This set of strategically coordinated improvement actions have been implemented using high-participation mechanisms and wide-communication processes, which have been developed, learned, and tested along the first cycle of the intervention, thus engaging relevant stakeholders along all the process.

In summary, this means that holistic change can promote values' consistency, potentiate new behavioral patterns, create engagement, and drive the organization, as a whole team, to new strategic initiatives which sustain organizational learning and improvement.

Some of these initiatives can include the use of the same traditional instruments within a totally new environment and approach where individuals, teams and their leaders are synchronized, face common organizational challenges, share their commitment, actively communicate, and produce effective results (e.g., IT Process Improvement and CMMI Certification). Some other ones can promote new tools implementation potentiating and supporting new ways of doing things (e.g., IT Tools – Project Management Integrated Solution). Some could target new ways for internal communication, sustaining cohesion through information and knowledge sharing (e.g., IT Communication and IT Portal). Some other can target Employee Development on a wider perspective; promoting traditional training; corporate citizenship and core workplace competencies (e.g., IT Academy). All these actions together can contribute to increase Organizational Excellence.

As a main result of such dynamics where individuals learn in group, act together and get strongly motivated, customers are served and, both increase their satisfaction levels.

In fact, the specific outcomes of the program evidence a remarkable evolution on satisfaction levels. These results, measured through the regular institutional Satisfaction Surveys, give clear evidence of a significant sustained improvement, progressing along subsequent years (Figure 8).

As it can be observed, being sustained by employee engagement on continuous improvement the Internal Customers' satisfaction levels have

Figure 8. Sustained evolution of Employees and Internal Customers' Satisfaction Levels

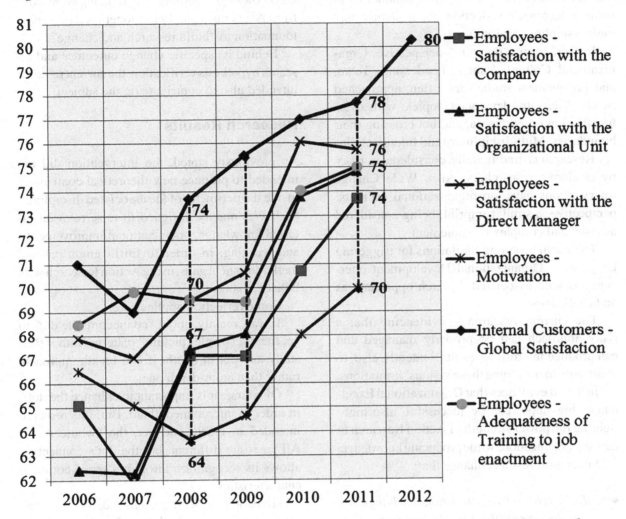

End year values

evidenced a significant progression, projecting the index to higher levels, above the institutional scores.

Also, as a result of Leadership development actions, the levels of Employee Satisfaction, namely those directly related with the Organizational Unit and Direct Manager, have evidenced a remarkable evolution.

Furthermore, as a consequence of the communication and engagement dynamics which

had been set up, the Motivation levels exhibit an evident progress. Also, the positive impact of IT Academy is clearly reflected on employees' evaluation of "adequateness of training to job enactment".

As previously detailed, from an organizational perspective, many others intermediary achievements have been reached.

These high-level achievements – emerging from a holistic, multidisciplinary, and complex transformational program – must conduct us to some researcher's reflection about change and multidisciplinary initiatives.

In fact, from a domains' perspective, Organizational Culture, Values, Leadership, Team, and Engagement studies are, often, approached as specific, intra-developed, topics, with over-focalization on each area, and not crossing their boundaries. Multidisciplinary and Interdisciplinary Research is, traditionally, considered as risky by academic researchers. Also, Wide Change Interventions have, on organizational deciders' perspective, a similar imprint, being considered as risky and complex to implement.

These can be strong limitations for triggering Large-scale Organizational Development interventions with associated research opportunities and challenges.

The current research – evidencing that a risky approach can be properly managed and can produce interesting results – intends, also, to contribute to overcome these visions' limitations.

In fact, it evidences that Organizational Excellence "big-steps" can be successful, also highlighting the power strength of Action Research to develop organizations while producing knowledge.

Successful results enhance that:

- *Research and Organizational Change are not incompatible*. On the contrary, they can produce synergistic results, combining theoretical rigor with organizational relevance;
- *Holistic and Systemic approaches are possible, being precious instruments*. Where "the whole" can produce more effective results than the "sum of the parts", creating structures, systems and behaviors for the future.

So, more applications within organizational settings must be conducted, producing new results, developing the body of knowledge, and, "loop it again", with subsequent application, reflection and knowledge accumulation. Existing knowledge from Academics and Practitioners is an essential foundation to "build research and change".

Behind its specific change outcomes and research hypothesis verification, the current research intended also to contribute on the subject.

Research Results

As previously stated, the intervention did not intended to produce new theoretical contributes inside the perimeter of the associated disciplines.

It was mainly designed to raise relevant internal knowledge, organizational improvements, and learning, in order to fulfill empirical and methodological gaps, using Action Research with holistic change.

Some reflection applies here.

It was, mainly, about "connecting the dots to get the big (whole) picture" patterns, rather than study any dot in depth. It is a breath approach, rather than an in-depth one.

Of course, it is important to enhance the dots, in order to interconnect them. But, this research intended to reach, and get, the "whole face". All faces are different, but the dot's connection allows its recognition through a set of common characteristics.

Here, it has been recognized, by its characteristics, a new whole face for change: more communicative, participative, value based and people-friendly. So, less tense, less deterministic, less bureau-made.

It is a new holistic, people-based approach to change.

Although these aspects cannot be entirely reproduced and generalized "as-is and outside context" it is important to highlight its characteristics which, undoubtedly, can be successfully adapted and adopted by other organizations.

So, on a management utility perspective, relevance must be given to some key emergent knowledge which represents the essence of the approach and the basis of its success.

Figure 9 evidences those aspects, under the form of a framework, integrating key critical areas and dimensions which group a set of critical success factors which are detailed at Table 14.

A straightforward reading of this Framework can be done as follows:

- On the Ethics dimension, it is important to highlight that the success of such a process requires transparency and trustiness and an active voice process. It forms the bedrock of the action process and can be summarized by a strong sequence of verbs: communicate, engage, act and improve.

- Another crucial dimension involves the Creation of Meaning across organizational boundaries. This involves: definition of an Inspiring Set of Organizational Values, use of Study Cases, Transparent Decisions, Testimonial and Constructive

Figure 9. Management Implications – Critical Areas and Dimensions

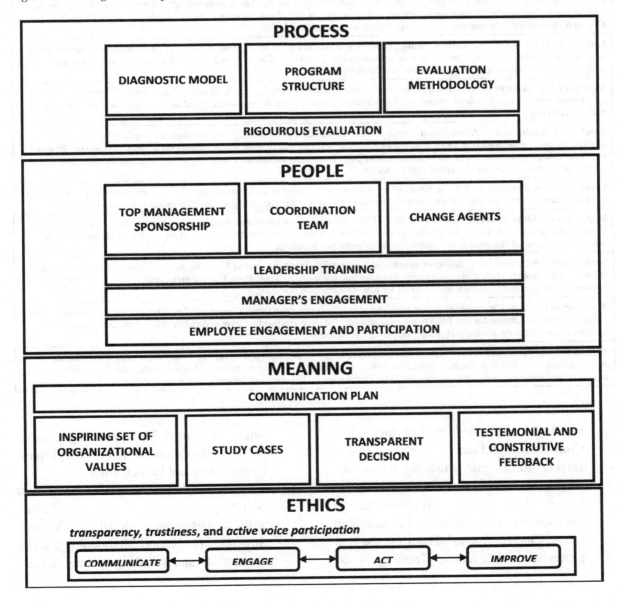

Table 14. Management Implications – Critical Success Factors

Diagnostic Model: Use of a *solid, well-tested and extensive model* for organizational diagnosis, facilitating the identification of *current states,* change's *gap analysis,* and providing adequate information to *draw the intervention's plan.*
Program Structure: Essential to proceed to a *clear and adapted design,* including *diagnosis, intervention* and *evaluation,* ensuring a proper program management, accurate decisions, and adequate stakeholder's management.
Evaluation Methodology: Previous definition of a *set of evaluation instruments and parameters,* including *longitudinal* dimensions, *hard* and *soft* measurements.
Rigorous Evaluation: Clear reporting on the developed actions along the program, its objective evaluation, and the production of adequate improvement recommendations for future action.
Top Management Sponsorship: *Strong, active* and *visible* top-management engagement, both for the *launching* of the program, and for its future *sustainability,* continuously supporting all the subsequent transformational initiatives.
Coordination Team: Set-up of a coordination team to guarantee, along all the intervention, the *engagement* of the main stakeholders, ensuring balanced and differentiated knowledge *competencies* (theoretical and professional).
Change Agents: An *"inspired to change",* active and committed Change Agents' Team, representing all the organizational sub-units, with a clear definition of roles and responsibilities, well-trained and with full autonomy to assume their mission within the process. Crucial for the success of a catalytic action along change implementation.
Leadership Training: Direct classroom training, concerning essential aspects of the leader's roles. Crucial to develop influential skills, authenticity, and the mutual trust, necessary to potentiate results, within the spirit of desired change. Participation, use of role-play and simulation, are desirable ingredients to create a positive change dynamics.
Manager's Engagement: Guarantee of a perfect, visible and continuous identification of all management levels with the transformational process. Absolutely necessary to guarantee employees' trust on the process, based on the congruence between change massages and day-to-day practices' behavioural evidence.
Employee Engagement and Participation: Direct involvement of all employees, using empowerment mechanisms, and contributing to positive, specific problem solving, along joint learning meeting sessions, and crossing organizational boundaries and barriers. Essential to remove change restraining forces. Motivation; creative participation; organizational values' alignment; inspiring attitudes, and behavioural stimulation are on the critical path to change.
Communication Plan: Set-up of a *structured and extensive* communication plan, synchronizing all the *actions* with the appropriate key communication *events* – segmenting stakeholders, targeting messages, developing adequate positioning and using proper channels.
Inspiring set of Organizational Values: Definition of referential values for the organization, with strong meaning for each employee, aligned with the transformational change objectives. Critical to promote an effective development of organizational identification, to assimilate the value of change, and to stimulate sustained extra-role behaviour.
Study Cases: Set-up of an integrated set of meaningful hypothetical cases to be worked on during group learning meetings, stimulating employee participation, producing creative open solutions and action oriented initiatives. Using it on facilitated positive problem solving sessions, is a major asset to address real solutions for real organizational problems.
Transparent Decision: Clear structuration of non-filtered proposals emerging from the employees' collaborative process; its independent presentation by the Change Agents' Team to top management, and the corresponding level of deciders' adherence. Determinant to guarantee trust within the process and enforce employees' participation.
Testimonial and Constructive Feedback: Continuous communication of results and achievements. A central process to eliminate cognitive dissonance and to propagate a pro-active climate. Continuous publishing of meaningful testimonials, enforcing positive messages, and reporting strong involvement should be a focal strategic link with and between employees.

Feedback, supported by an integrative Communication Plan.

- Having Ethics and Meaning as an engaging basis, People must be actively involved. This requires Top-Management Sponsorship, a Coordination Team, and an active Change Agents' Team on the real groundwork. Leadership Training is essential to promote Managers' Engagement, as a precondition to ignite Employees' Engagement and Participation.
- On the top of this, an adequate Process must be set-up to promote the desired change, with a Diagnostic Model, a Program Structure, Evaluation Methodology, and a Rigorous Evaluation along the intervention.

Table 14 summarizes the set of main critical success factors associated with these Critical Areas and Dimensions.

As a whole, this framework, which emerged from the research, answers to the research questions initially set (Table 4), achieves the research objectives (Table 5) and confirms the hypothesis previously formulated (Table 6).

FUTURE WORK AND RESEARCH DIRECTIONS

The intervention has prepared people, structures and systems to address new levels of Organizational Excellence, including a mobilizing dynamics, reframed values and behavioral systems, increased self-confidence and trust, organization-wide skills and competencies, and participation mechanisms. They have been assimilated and became effective within the organization.

This represents a significant increase on organizational preparedness to face the challenge of an Organizational Excellence certification process, following the EFQM model (EFQM-A, 2013) and using the extreme potentialities of self-assessment (EFQM-B, 2013).

As previously referred, concerning self-assessment Conti (1997) emphasizes two differentiated paths to TQM, including award-like approaches (focused on formal evaluation for recognition awards) and diagnostic approaches (oriented by diagnosis and improvement objectives).

The researchers believe that beside their distinct orientation these two approaches can be combined for Organizational Excellence and Recognition purposes.

Also, the "learning, creativity and innovation" loop which is depicted over the EFQM Model as a link between "results" and "enablers" is a path not yet sufficiently explored. It can be successfully researched using an OD route.

So, further investigation will focus on interdisciplinary research combining these approaches, with confluent use of OD & Change and TQM knowledge, and using Action Research.

A FINAL REFLECTION

People within organizations tend to overestimate the power of technical work tools and methods, often using them in isolated forms and expecting them to be the sole predictors of organizational effectiveness.

This is particularly accurate for IS/IT organizations where specialized task-oriented tools, best practices, frameworks, models and methods are intensively used to facilitate the activity.

However, underestimating the importance of other powerful instruments which must be used to promote Organizational Development inhibits the raising of important people-centered capabilities which are also key determinants of effectiveness.

The current intervention has put the primary focus on this human dimension as the bedrock of the traditional "people-process-tools" triangle. Subsequently it has integrated the other two dimensions of performance within a new, dynamic, and strategically improved working environment.

In fact, Organizational Culture and Values, Leadership and Team Effectiveness, and Employee Engagement have been the primary areas which had been addressed to prepare people to engage on a set of interrelated strategic projects covering Process Improvement, Tool Implementation, Organizational Communication, Employee Training and Development.

Although a holistic transformational change is traditionally considered by organizational deciders as a high-risk activity the institution has deeply engaged on it and significant results have been achieved.

Also, multidisciplinary and interdisciplinary research in action with such a wide scope is, by similar reasons, often avoided by academic researchers. However, research outcomes have emerged and have confirmed the hypothesis which have been formulated, evidencing that this kind of approach can be properly managed and can produce emergent knowledge.

A new organizational change process was designed to cover those Organizational Development and Change areas which can be adopted with contextual adaptations by other organizations.

Also, external knowledge has emerged in the form of a set of critical areas, dimensions and success factors which are applicable to such kind of interventions.

The outcomes – at organizational and research level – reveal a new face of change: communicative, participative, value based and people-friendly, as opposed to tense, deterministic, and bureau-made.

So, a final reflection (and main conclusion) should tautologically apply:

- IT Areas are, by the nature of its activity, focused on Resources and Artifacts;
- People have capacity to, autonomously, appreciate/depreciate and change their self and behaviors;
- So, People are neither Resources, nor Artifacts;
- A People-driven change approach to IT Strategy is welcome and produces effective results;
- Results evidence Value for Organizations and, simultaneously, a Contribute to Knowledge;
- So, People-driven approaches to IT Development must be researched and implemented more often.

Also, considering that the Research Community's mission (particularly in social sciences) includes also a desirable Contribute to Society, and that researchers are often criticized by "being very far from Real-World Problems", this kind of research is a good opportunity to contribute to this mission and to strengthen the links between academic and practitioners' communities.

REFERENCES

A guide to the project management body of knowledge (PMBOK Guide) (5th ed.). (2013PMI. USA: Project Management Institute.

Ajzen, I., & Fishbein, M. (1980). *Understanding Attitudes and Predicting Social Behavior* (2nd ed.). New Jersey: Prentice Hall.

Alcobia, P. (2001). Atitudes e Satisfação no Trabalho. In J. M. C. Ferreira, J. Neves, & A. Caetano (Eds.), *Manual de Psicossociologia das Organizações* (pp. 531–565). Lisbon: McGraw-Hill.

Allport, G. (1954). Attitudes in the History of Social Psychology. In G. Lindsey & A. Aronson (Eds.), *Handbook of Social Psychology*. Reading: Addison-Wesley.

Argyris, C. (2002). Double-Loop Learning, Teaching and Research. *Academy of Management Learning & Education*, *1*(2), 206–218. doi:10.5465/AMLE.2002.8509400

Argyris, C., Putnam, R., & Smith, D. (1985). *Action Science: Concepts, Methods, and Skills for Research and Intervention*. San Francisco, CA: Jossey-Bass.

Argyris, C., & Schon, D. (1974). *Theory in practice: increasing professional effectiveness*. San Francisco, CA: Jossey-Bass.

Argyris, C., & Schon, D. A. (1989). Participatory Action Research and Action Science Compared: A Commentary. *The American Behavioral Scientist*, *32*(5), 612–623. doi:10.1177/0002764289032005008

Armenakis, A. A., Harris, S. G., & Mossholder, K. W. (1993). Creating readiness for organizational change. *Human Relations*, *46*(6), 681–703. doi:10.1177/001872679304600601

Beer, M., & Nohria, N. (2000). Cracking the code of change. *Harvard Business Review*, *78*(3), 133–141. PMID:11183975

Bourne, H., & Jenkins, M. (2013). Organizational Values: A Dynamic Perspective. *Organization Studies, 34*(4), 495–514. doi:10.1177/0170840612467155

Boyd, N. M., & Nowell, B. (2014). Psychological Sense of Community: A New Construct for the Field of Management. *Journal of Management Inquiry, 23*(2), 107–122. doi:10.1177/1056492613491433

Buchanan, D., & Bryman, A. (Eds.). (2011). *The organizational research context: properties and implications in Sage handbook of organizational research methods.* Thousand Oaks, CA: SAGE Publications.

Burke, C., Stagl, K., Klein, C., Goodwin, G., Salas, E., & Halpin, S. (2006). What types of leadership behaviors are functional in teams? A meta-analysis. *The Leadership Quarterly, 17*(3), 288–307. doi:10.1016/j.leaqua.2006.02.007

Burke, W., & Litwin, G. (1992). A causal model of organizational performance and change. *Journal of Management, 18*(3), 523–545. doi:10.1177/014920639201800306

Caetano, A. (2001). Mudança e Intervenção Organizacional. In J. M. C. Ferreira, J. Neves, & A. Caetano (Eds.), *Manual de Psicossociologia das Organizações* (pp. 531–565). Lisbon: McGraw-Hill.

Cameron, K., Dutton, J., & Quinn, R. (2003). An Introduction to Positive Organizational Scholarship. In K. Cameron, J. Dutton, & R. Quinn (Eds.), *Positive Organizational Scholarship* (pp. 3–13). San Francisco, CA: Berrett-Koehler.

Cameron, K., & Quinn, R. (1998). *Diagnosing and changing organizational culture: based on the competing values framework.* Reading: Addison-Wesley.

Campbell, D. T., & Stanley, J. C. (1963). Experimental and quasi-experimental designs for research on teaching. In N. L. Gage (Ed.), *Handbook of research on teaching* (pp. 171–246). Chicago, IL: Rand McNally.

Chawla, A., & Kelloway, E. K. (2004). Predicting openness and commitment to change. *Leadership and Organization Development Journal, 25*(5/6), 485–498. doi:10.1108/01437730410556734

Chrissis, M., Konrad, M., & Shrum, S. (2011). CMMI for development: guidelines for process integration and product improvement, 3rd Ed. SEI Series in Software Engineering. Boston: Pearson Education.

CMMI for Development, Version 1.3 [Technical Report]. (2010). *CMMI Product Team.*

Coch, L., & French, J. R. P. (1948). Overcoming resistance to change. *Human Relations, 2*(4), 512–532. doi:10.1177/001872674800100408

Coghlan, D. (2006). Insider action research doctorates: Generating actionable knowledge. *Higher Education, 54*(2), 293–306. doi:10.1007/s10734-005-5450-0

Coghlan, D., & Brannick, T. (2010). *Doing action research in your own organization* (3rd ed.). Thousand Oaks, CA: Sage Publications.

Conti, T. (1997). *Organizational Self-assessment.* London: Chapman & Hall.

Cooperrider, D., & Whitney, D. (2005). *Appreciative Inquiry: a Positive Revolution in Change.* San Francisco: Berrett-Koehler Publishers.

Cummings, T., & Worley, C. (2009). Organizational Development & Change, 9th Edition. Mason: South-Western Cengage Learning.

Downs, A. (2012). Resistance to change as a positive influencer: An introduction. *Journal of Organizational Change Management*, 25(6), 784. doi:10.1108/jocm.2012.02325faa.001

EFQM-A. (2013). *EFQM Excellence Model*. Brussels: European Foundation for Quality Management.

Egan, T. M. (2002). Organization development: An examination of definitions and dependent variables. *Organization Development Journal*, 20(2), 59–71.

Eisenberg, E., & Riley, P. (2001). Organizational Culture. In F. Jablin & L. Putnam (Eds.), *The New Handbook of Organizational Communication* (pp. 291–323). Thousand Oaks, CA: SAGE Publications.

Erwin, D. G., & Garman, A. N. (2010). Resistance to organizational change: Linking research and practice. *Leadership and Organization Development Journal*, 31(1), 39–56. doi:10.1108/01437731011010371

Fishbein, M., & Ajzen, I. (1975). *Belief, Attitude, Intention and Behavior: An Introduction to Theory and Research*. Reading: Addison-Wesley.

Greiner, L. E. (1972). Evolution and Revolution as Organizations Grow. *Harvard Business Review*, 50(4), 37–46. PMID:10179654

Gummesson, E. (2000). *Qualitative Methods in Management Research* (2nd ed.). Thousand Oaks, CA: Sage Publications.

Habermas, J. (1979). *Communication and the evolution of society* (T. McCarthy, Trans.). Boston: Beacon.

Hackman, J. (1987). The design of work teams. In J. W. Lorsch (Ed.), *Handbook of organizational behavior* (pp. 315–342). Englewood Cliffs, NJ: Prentice-Hall.

Heron, J., & Reason, P. (1997). A participatory inquiry paradigm. *Qualitative Inquiry*, 3(3), 274–294. doi:10.1177/107780049700300302

Herr, K., & Anderson, G. (2005). *The Action Research Dissertation – a guide for students and faculty*. Thousand Oaks, CA: SAGE Publications, Inc.

Heskett, J. L., Jones, T. O., Loveman, G. W., Sasser, W. E. Jr, & Schlesinger, L. A. (2000). *Putting the service-profit chain to work. (Product No. 4460, HBR On Point)*. Cambridge, MA: Harvard Business School Publishing Corporation.

Hitt, M., Ireland, R., & Hoskinsson, R. (2009). Strategic Management: Competitiveness and Globalization (Concepts and Cases) (8th ed.). Mason: South-Western Cengage Learning.

Jones, L., Watson, B., Gardner, J., & Gallois, C. (2004). Organizational Communication: Challenges for the new century. *Journal of Communication*, 54(4), 722–750. doi:10.1111/j.1460-2466.2004.tb02652.x

Jorgensen, H., Owen, L., & Neus, A. (2008). *IBM Global Making change work study report*. USA: IBM Global Services.

JUSE. (2013). *The Application Guide for The Deming Prize 2013, For Companies and Organizations Overseas*. Japan: The Deming Prize Committee, Union of Japanese Scientists and Engineers.

Kemmis, S. (1982). Action research. In T. Husen, Postlethwaite (Eds.), International Encyclopedia of Education: Research & Studies. Oxford: Pergamon Press.

Kolowski, S., Watola, D., Jensen, J., Kim, B., & Botero, I. (2009). Developing adaptative teams: a theory of dynamic team leadership. In E. Salas, G. Goodwin, & C. Burke (Eds.), *Team effectiveness in complex organizations: cross-disciplinary perspectives and approaches* (pp. 113–154). USA: Psychology Press, Taylor & Francis Group.

Kotter, J. P. (1996). *Leading Change*. Boston, Massachusetts: Harvard Business School Press.

Kotter, J. P., & Schlesinger, L. A. (1979). Choosing strategies for change. *Harvard Business Review*, (March-April): 106–114. PMID:10240501

Krone, K., Kramer, M., & Sias, P. (2010). Theoretical developments in organizational communication research. In *The Handbook of communication science* (2nd ed.). Thousand Oaks, CA: SAGE Publications. doi:10.4135/9781412982818.n10

Lawrence, P. R. (1969). *How to deal with resistance to change*. Harvard Business Review, January - February.

Lewin, K. (1951). *Field theory in Social Science*. New York: Harper & Row.

Lincoln, Y. S., Lynham, S. A., & Guba, E. G. (2011). Paradigmatic controversies, contradictions, and emerging confluences revisited. In N. K. Denzin & Y. S. Lincoln (Eds.), *The SAGE Handbook of Qualitative Research*. Thousand Oaks, CA: SAGE Publications, Inc.

Lippit, R., Watson, J., & Westley, B. (1958). *The Dynamics of Planned Change*. New York: Harcourt, Brace and World.

Marks, M., Mathieu, J., & Zaccaro, S. (2001). A temporally based framework and taxonomy of team processes. *Academy of Management Review*, *26*, 356–376.

Maurer, R. (1996). Using resistance to build support for change. *Journal for Quality and Participation*, 56–63.

McCutcheon, G., & Jung, B. (1990). Alternative perspectives on action research. *Theory into Practice*, *29*(3), 144–151. doi:10.1080/00405849009543447

McKay, J., & Marshall, P. (2007). Driven by two masters, serving both - The Interplay of Problem Solving and Research in Information Systems Action Research Projects. In N. Kock (Ed.), Information Systems Action Research: An Applied View of Emerging Concepts and Methods.

McKay, K., Kuntz, J., & Naswall, K. (2013). The Effect of Affective Commitment, Communication and Participation on Resistance to Change: The Role of Change Readiness. *New Zealand Journal of Psychology*, *42*(2).

McKernan, J. (1988). The countenance of curriculum action research: Traditional, collaborative, and emancipatory-critical conceptions. *Journal of Curriculum and Supervision*, *3*(3), 173–200.

McLean, G. (2006). Organization development: An examination of definitions and dependent variables. *Organization Development Journal*, *20*(2).

Meaney, M., & Pung, C. (2008). McKinsey global results: Creating organizational transformations. *The McKinsey Quarterly*, (August), 1–7.

Meister, J. C. (1998). *Corporate Universities – lessons in building a world-class workforce. Revised and updated edition*. New York: McGraw-Hill.

Meyer, J. P., & Allen, N. J. (1991). A three-component conceptualization of organizational commitment. *Human Resource Management Review*, *1*(1), 61–89. doi:10.1016/1053-4822(91)90011-Z

Meyer, J. P., Stanley, D. J., Herscovitch, L., & Topolnytsky, L. (2002). Affective, Continuance, and Normative Commitment to the Organization: A Meta-analysis of Antecedents, Correlates, and Consequences. *Journal of Vocational Behavior*, *61*(1), 20–52. doi:10.1006/jvbe.2001.1842

Miller, V. D., Johnson, J. R., & Grau, J. (1994). Antecedents to willingness to participate in a planned organizational change. *Journal of Applied Communication Research*, 22(1), 59–80. doi:10.1080/00909889409365387

Mintzberg, H. (2009). Rebuilding companies as communities. *Harvard Business Review*, (July-August): 1–7.

Müller, S., Mathiassen, L., & Balshøj, H. (2010). Software Process Improvement as organizational change: A metaphorical analysis of the literature. *Journal of Systems and Software*, 83(11), 2128–2146. doi:10.1016/j.jss.2010.06.017

NIST. (2013). *Malcolm Baldrige National Quality Award 2013-2014 Criteria for Performance Excellence*. USA: National Institute of Standards and Technology.

Northouse, P. (2007). *Leadership: Theory and Practice* (4th ed.). Thousand Oaks, CA: SAGE Publications, Inc.

Oreg, S. (2006). Personality, context, and resistance to organizational change. *European Journal of Work and Organizational Psychology*, 15(1), 73–101. doi:10.1080/13594320500451247

Organ, D. W. (1988). Organizational Citizenship Behavior: The good soldier syndrome. Lexington, MA.

Porras, J. I., & Robertson, P. J. (1992). Organization development: Theory, practice, and research. In M. Dunnette & L. Hough (Eds.), *Handbook of industrial and organizational psychology* (2nd ed., Vol. 3, pp. 719–822). Palo Alto: Consulting Psychologists Press.

Robson, C. (2011). *Real world research: a resource for users of social research methods in applied settings* (3rd ed.). USA: John Wiley & Sons, Ltd.

Salas, E., Goodwin, G., & Burke, C. (2009). Team Effectiveness in Complex Organizations: an Overview. In E. Salas, G. Goodwin, & C. Burke (Eds.), *Team effectiveness in complex organizations: cross-disciplinary perspectives and approaches* (pp. 3–16). USA: Psychology Press, Taylor & Francis Group.

Salas, E., Stagl, K., Burke, C., & Goodwin, G. (2007). Modeling complex systems: Motivation, cognition and social processes. In *Nebraska Symposium on Motivation* (pp. 185–243).

SCAMPI Upgrade Team. (2011). *Standard CMMI Appraisal Method for Process Improvement A, Version 1.3 Model Definition Document. Handbook CMU/SEI-2011-HB-001*. USA: Carnegie Mellon University/Software Engineering Institute.

Schein, E. (2009). *The Corporate Culture Survival Guide - New and* (Revised Edition). San Francisco, CA: Jossey Bass.

Seibold, D., & Shea, C. (2001). Participation and Decision Making. In F. Jablin & L. Putnam (Eds.), *The New Handbook of Organizational Communication* (pp. 664–704). Thousand Oaks, CA: SAGE Publications.

Senge, P. (2006). The Leader's New Work - Building Learning Organizations. In J. V. Gallos (Ed.), *Organization development: a Jossey-Bass reader* (pp. 765–792). San Francisco, CA: Jossey Bass.

Shani, A. R., & Pasmore, W. (1982, August). Towards a New Model of the Action Research Process. Academy of Management Proceedings.

Stringer, E. T. (1996). *Action research: A handbook for practitioners*. Thousand Oaks, CA: SAGE Publications, Inc.

Tavares, S. (2007). *O fenómeno da identificação organizacional: contributos para a sua explicação* [Unpublished Doctoral Dissertation]. ISCTE-IUL, Lisbon.

Truss, C., Gratton, L., Hope-Hailey, V., McGovern, P., & Stiles, P. (1997). Soft and hard models of human resource management: A reappraisal. *Journal of Management Studies*, *34*(1), 53–73. doi:10.1111/1467-6486.00042

Tushman, M. L., & Romanelli, E. (1985). Organizational evolution: A metamorphosis model of convergence and reorientation. In B. M. Staw & L. L. Cummings (Eds.), *Research in organizational behavior* (Vol. 7, pp. 171–222). Greenwich: JAI Press.

Van de Ven, A. H., & Poole, M. S. (1995). Explaining Development and Change in Organizations. *Academy of Management Review*, *20*(3), 510–540. doi:10.2307/258786

Vargas, R. (2005). *Os meios justificam os fins – a gestão baseada em valores: da ética individual à ética Empresarial*. Lisbon: Gradiva.

Waldersee, R., & Griffiths, A. (1996). *The changing face of organizational change*. Australia: Center for Corporate Change, Australian Graduate School of Management University of New South Wales.

Wanberg, C. R., & Banas, J. T. (2000). Predictors and outcomes of openness to changes in a reorganizing workplace. *The Journal of Applied Psychology*, *85*(1), 132–132. doi:10.1037/0021-9010.85.1.132 PMID:10740964

Weick, K. E., & Quinn, R. E. (1999). Organizational Change and Development. *Annual Review of Psychology*, *50*(1), 361–386. doi:10.1146/annurev.psych.50.1.361 PMID:15012461

Zaccaro, S., Heinen, B., & Shuffler, M. (2009). Team Leadership and Team Effectiveness. In E. Salas, G. Goodwin, & C. Burke (Eds.), *Team effectiveness in complex organizations: cross-disciplinary perspectives and approaches* (pp. 83–111). USA: Psychology Press, Taylor & Francis Group.

Zaccaro, S., Rittman, A., & Marks, M. (2001). Team leadership. *The Leadership Quarterly*, *12*(4), 451–483. doi:10.1016/S1048-9843(01)00093-5

Zaltman, G., & Duncan, R. (1977). *Strategies for planned change*. New York: Wiley.

KEY TERMS AND DEFINITIONS

Action Research: Simultaneously a *Planned Change approach* paradigm and a *Research Method*, which is about *research in action*, involving, simultaneously, two *goals*: solving an organizational problem and contributing to knowledge. The *process* is based on existing behavioral science knowledge, integrated with organizational knowledge; applied to solve real organizational problems; promoting organizational change and learning and generating new (internal and external) knowledge. As *main characteristics*, it is developed within natural settings, addressing specific issues, within a spirit of collaboration and co-inquiry, involving the researcher and organizational stakeholders, promoting organizational learning, systems' improvement, and generating valid knowledge. It *requires an ethical positioning*, based on a deep understanding of *values* and *norms* regarding the cooperation between the researcher and organizational members; preserving special *working principles* on relationships, communication, participation and inclusion.

Employee Engagement: A concept which can be seen from two different perspectives: as a *result* (an *emotional commitment* that an employee has to the organization and its goals) or, from an *organizational process* perspective (as a *workplace approach* designed to ensure that employees are committed to their organization and goals and motivated to contribute to organizational success). Being change an essential ingredient for sustaining organizational success, engagement and its associated constructs are determinant. Values, Norms, Beliefs, Attitudes, Behaviors, Organizational Identity and Identification, Participation, Communication, Empowerment, Affective Commitment and Psychological Sense of Community are major dimensions which must be worked in order to promote engagement, individual well-being and organizational effectiveness.

Leadership: A set of *processes of influence*, within a *group* of *individuals*, in order to reach *common goals*; being the influencer "the *leader*" and the influenced "the *followers*". Several approaches exist: some centered on the *influencer's* characteristics and behaviors; others, focused on the *relationship*, considering the tasks, the individuals, the group, the exchange interactions and the influence process. All have been successfully applied to political, social and organizational contexts. Although some criticism (outdated or incomplete phenomena explanations) they still include valid and complementary aspects. As any model, they are simplified representations of reality, with a limited, set of variables and processes. Specific understanding of actors, context, process and goals is a necessary condition to recognize situations and improve effectiveness on the ground.

Organizational Culture: The basic *pattern* of *shared beliefs*, *behaviors* and *assumptions*, acquired over time by members of an organization, as a result of a *common learning process*, which *endure organizational behavior*. Interpreted as integrating several *layers:* some more visible (external manifestations, commonly denominated as *artifacts*); some others invisible (*underlying assumptions*); mediated by *espoused values*. As a product of organizational history, it strongly contributes to identity. Often presented to new organizational members as "the way we do things around here" and referred as "our collective mental programming".

Organizational Excellence: A *comprehensive approach to Quality*, integrating, into the traditional "*hard*" technical and management views of quality, all the necessary "*soft*" dimensions of organizational life: encompassing the traditional "product, process, customer and results" dimensions with an organizational development perspective. Mobilizing the organization; transforming the culture to respond to organizational excellence challenges; engaging people on self-assessment and implementation; promoting continuous improvement, organizational learning, innovation and stakeholders' management, are main basis of modern Organizational Excellence Models targeting organizational effectiveness. They incorporate a set of congruent primary values, concepts, principles, areas, evaluation criteria and improvement logics.

Transformational Change: A planned change process, targeting, in a systemic approach, organizational culture and climate, people, groups, strategies and processes; actively communicating, involving and engaging stakeholders; with primary focus on changing attitudes, beliefs and values, and a secondary concern for processes, structures and systems; promoting double-loop, generative, learning.

Values: A double concept, including *Personal values* as beliefs that guide individual behaviors, and *Organizational values* as norms transmitted to employees who guide decisions and behavior in the workplace. Its *alignment* plays a major role on *organizational commitment*. So, *espoused* (sanctioned by senior managers and located at the level of top management), *attributed* (those that members attribute to the organization and located at the collective level), *shared* (reflections of members' personal values located at the level of individual members) and *aspirational* (members' ideas of what ought to be the values and located at the level of individuals and groups) values should *overlap*. Values' mismatch can be a good opportunity to promote participative transformational changes, through a *values-based approach:* identifying and solving existing *gaps;* promoting values' *congruence* and *assimilation*; thus (re)addressing the basis of culture.

Chapter 8
Creativity in the Information Systems Planning Process

Vitor M. Santos
New University of Lisbon, Portugal

Luis Amaral
University of Minho, Portugal

Henrique S. Mamede
University Aberta, INESC TEC, Portugal

Ramiro Gonçalves
University of Trás-os-Montes and Alto Douro, Portugal

ABSTRACT

In face of growing global competition, the ability of organizations to effectively use information technologies to deliver innovation and creativity is widely recognized as an important competitive advantage. In this context, knowledge of how to apply creativity techniques to information systems planning becomes particularly relevant. This chapter presents a framework for the introduction of creativity in Information Systems Planning. The framework aims at promoting the development of innovative Information Systems, which traditional methods of requirements elicitation fail to address. Finally, we discuss how the framework was implemented at a public organization to identify information systems opportunities.

INTRODUCTION

Information Systems Planning (ISP) is a vital activity for the success and competitive edge of companies (Amaral, 2007) and (Ravishankar, 2010). The diversity of corporate activity sectors, the different contexts and organizational structures along with the growing complexity of the global-

ized business world are a huge challenge for this project to become effective.

The ability of companies to efficiently use information technologies with respect to innovation and creativity are recognized as important factors for the competitive edge and agility of companies. Organizations naturally take benefit, through creativity and innovation, to reorganize their processes and products in a more effective way (Cooper 2000).

DOI: 10.4018/978-1-4666-8833-9.ch008

In this context, the opportunity to apply creativity techniques to the generation of ideas that may have an impact in the Information Systems Planning process holds an immense generative potential. In response to this challenge, this chapter advances a framework for the introduction of creativity and innovation techniques in Information Systems Planning. Ultimately the framework aims at facilitating the development of Information Systems that are more agile and effective, thus enhancing the competitive advantage of organizations.

CREATIVITY IN INFORMATION SYSTEMS PLANNING

The role of Information Systems Planning has become crucial for the development of effective strategic plans in organizations (Lederer, 1991) and (Chen, 2010). The increasing uncertainty in the markets has encouraged organizations to be more proactive. On the one hand, information technology provides a set of opportunities for gaining competitive advantage. This requires strategic alignment and a fit of Information Systems with the strategies, goals and operations of organizations. On the other hand, organizations acknowledge that the ability to provide a quick response to unforeseeable events is paramount for their survival (Alleire, 1989).

Although the importance of creativity in Information Systems Planning is recognized and even a key component in the main ISP approaches – such as the three-stage model of Bowman (1983) and the multi-dimensional approach of Earl (1989) - research in this area has been scarce.

In another respect, Ruohonen & Higgins analyzed the potential of activity theory in ISP (Ruohonen, 1998). Their analysis was divided into three distinct time frames that followed an ISP evolutionary perspective and the relationship of creativity and Information Systems Planning in each time frame was discussed.

Horton & Dewar (2001) proposed the use of formalized Alexandrine patterns to encapsulate the creative aspects of strategic Information Systems formation (Horton, 2001). They used a United Kingdom police force as a case study, which allowed them to derive two patterns that show the uses of creative practice in a political micro-organism.

Indeed for the purposes of this paper the relevant theoretical contributions are those that highlight the ISP stages and the embedding of creativity in those stages as a means to ensure that the resulting information system are competitive, responsive and adaptive to environmental changes. As far as the review of creativity and creative techniques is concerned, it is possible to assert that this is a well-defined area that comprises some two hundred different creativity techniques that can be grouped and used in different situations. However, in the study of creativity techniques, there are different proposals for the grouping of the different creativity techniques. In this article we adopt the classification proposed by Zusman (1988), shown in Figure 1. This scheme classifies creativity techniques into seven distinct groups, where each one has its own characteristics and a preferential applicability scenario.

Of these techniques that allow for support, stimulation and acceleration of creative production, we selected - for use in different methodological stages - those that presented themselves as more adequate depending upon the different types of problem in each case.

Through cross referencing the two themes of Information Systems and Creative Thinking, we were able to identify relevant areas of inquiry: the generation of ideas mediated by computer, creativity in Information Systems development, support tools for Information Systems creativity and Creativity in Information Systems Planning. The work presented in this chapters focuses on the latter, more specifically on the convergence between ISP activity and creative processes.

Figure 1. Applicability of creativity techniques and different ISP problems

Categories (Zusman)		Type of ISP Problem			
		Current System			New business
		No Coverage	Improvement	Integration	New business
	Conditioning/Motivating/Organizing techniques	X	X	X	X
	Randomization	X		X	X
	Focusing techniques		X	X	
	Systems	X	X		X
	Pointed techniques		X	X	
	Evolutionary directed techniques		X		X
	Innovation knowledge-base techniques		X	X	X

RESEARCH ON CREATIVITY AND INFORMATION SYSTEMS PLANNING

In the last 60 years research on creativity has been vast. Creativity and creative processes are the object of case studies in many fields of knowledge, namely in psychology, cognitive sciences, neuro-biology, education, philosophy, theology, technologies, sociology, linguistics, management, innovation, sciences, economy, among others (Tarrida, 2008).

Psychology and cognitive sciences have focused their attention on the study of mental representations and the underlying creative thinking. According to Candeias (2008) the main focus until the 1970s was on approaches related to creativity based on personality studies in order to identify the creativity features in different domains. From then on the main focus of research changed to the components of creative thinking and the resolution of problems (Candeias, 2008).

The study of creativity in neuro-biology has had - in the last few years - a reasonable success

with, for example, the appearance of works that attempt to link individual creativity to communication between areas of the brain that are not normally linked together (Heilman, 2003). Also in epistemology and theology is research that attempts to shed light on creativity. Philosophy tries to answer questions such as What is creativity? How does it come to be? How does creativity manifest itself in findings, inventions, science and art? What is the role that creativity has in the construction of the subject? Theologians debate the connection between creativity and holy and divine inspiration, attempting to solve the tension between human creation vs new creation as an expression of God's work.

Also in the fields of Sociology and Education it is possible to identify a renewed interest in the issue of creativity. Recently, researchers have turned their attention to the introduction of strategies in the classroom that would allow for the stimulation and development of creativity among students. Creativity is also growingly encouraged as a means to promote both autonomous learning and increased interaction between teachers and students (Moraes, 2008).

In the fields of management, innovation, entrepreneurship, economics and technologies the importance of creativity, as a first step for the birth of inventions and innovation has had a strong and diversified focus in virtually every domain. This is particularly the case of information systems and technology. The activity of information systems planning faces great challenges, since, on the one hand, fast technological developments make it hard to judge what the future holds. On the other hand determining the best way to place technologies at the service of organizations is a difficult task, as environmental and contextual changes may make previous decisions rapidly obsolete.

Managers are pressed, as never before. They must have the ability to perceive the multiplicity of changes that are taking place and the ramifications that these changes might have. As managers, they must predict the future and follow a course that leads a team or organization to a position where they can compete in an effective way and reach sustainability. Thus, planning is considered to be one of the main activities of managers and its success is fundamental for the good performance of organizations (Amaral, 2007). In a similar vein, Amaral (1994) posits that considering information systems planning is "to approach an activity with a higher complexity order, where any generalization or conceptualization effort becomes even more difficult".

This complexity originates in the fact that information systems combine human and technological resources and - in a transverse way - they involve human activities, organizations, politics, markets, environment, industry, etc. ISP, as a planning activity, adds to the difficulty of trying to anticipate the constraints and also the opportunities that may occur in the future. A major problem in ISP is therefore the absence of a sufficiently broad strategy to allow for an easy, flexible and effective way. The introduction of creative processes in different ISP approaches may hold the key for

several of these constraints, as it stimulates the development of ideas, new answers and new solutions. The search for a solution to this problem determined the main motivation and purpose of the research reported in this chapter: the possibility to propose a framework that facilitates the introduction of creative processes in ISP processes.

A RATIONALE FOR AN ACTION RESEARCH APPROACH

In any research endeavor it is fundamental to adopt an adequate methodology, which will allow the rigorous identification of answers to the question under investigation by supplying guidance for its execution and validation (Wazlawick, 2009).

The same question can be approached from different rational perspectives and processes. The specificity of each research theme - being different from all others - determines in the minds of those who are conducting reserarch, the necessary prudence for not using research processes that may be too costly or lead to inadequate or unreliable results (Sousa, 1998).

Defining a research methodology to tackle all possibilities inherent to the ISP stages and all the characteristics of creative processes proved to a challenge. However, the fact that creativity resorts mostly to cognitive process, where human participation is paramount lead to the choice of action research. Action research may be described as a family of methodologies that includes "action" (change) and "research" (understanding) simultaneously, through the use of a cyclical or spiral process that switches between action and critical reflection. In further cycles the methods, data and interpretation in the light of experience (knowledge), which are obtained in the previous cycle, are perfected in a continuous way.

Furthermore, action research allows the intervention in an entity under investigation, making use the results of the analysis undertaken. It allows an open approach in the field of investigation, which makes it possible to capture information that cannot usually be predetermined. This strategy leads the investigator to actively take part in whatever change occurs in a system (Myers, 1997) The researcher can examine the change in the system, as well as the change in the investigator him- or herself. In this way, a change can be caused by the investigator and then the result of the change can be examined. Habemass (1983) defended that any investigation must always incorporate the intention to cause change. Both the researcher and the system learn through the change that occurs (Coutinho, 2011). Throughout time, the constitution of cycles has evolved, through changes that vary according to different authors. For Susman et al. (1978) the more consensual composition is the cycle comprising five phases. According to Kock (1997) the steps involved in action research are: diagnosis, planning an action, execution of the action, evaluation and specific learning

The first phase is to make a diagnosis, followed by planning the action, executing the action, assessing and learning from it and/or documenting the action. Following the learning/documenting phase one can start a new cycle going back to the diagnosis phase. This cycle is presented in Figure 2.

The action research cycle repeats itself several times, through all of the sequences of the methodological phases. The first phase, "diagnosis", aims at identifying an opportunity for the solution or improvement of a previously identified problem. During this stage it is important to have a global view in an attempt to understand the problem, as a whole. At the end of this phase, there are often assumptions made about the nature and domain of the problem.

The second phase consists of planning the set of actions to take in the investigation and to identify the approach and objectives of the investigation. In planning, we should consider the different

Figure 2. "Investigation-Action" cycle

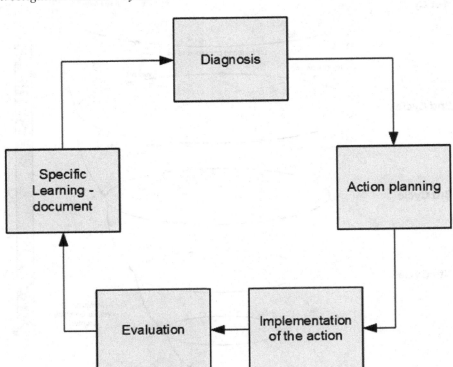

alternative actions to take and proceed with the more adequate alternative.

In the third phase one proceeds to the execution of the actions planned in the earlier phase by executing the actions selected in the planning phase.

Once the action phase is over, the assessment phase follows. This phase aims at verifying whether the actions carried out had the expected outcome and if they were useful in solving the initial problem(s). It is very useful to include in this assessment a critical analysis that judges in which way the actions undertaken were the only originators of the results. We justify this screening by the possibility of detecting the existence of interferences originated by actions that are inherent to the environment that is being studied.

Finally, in the fifth and final phase, "specific learning", one proceeds to the identification and recording of the conclusions about the outcome of the process.

Each time a cycle is repeated a set of improvements is introduced, which aim at obtaining the results initially stated. Once stabilization is considered significant, one may conclude the intervention or redefine new objectives and then begin another cycle.

The greatest virtue of this model resides in that it requires the fulfillment of a determined set of stages, which assure that - once a cycle is implemented - a new implementation is prepared, which takes advantage of the knowledge acquired in the previous implementation. Figure 3 presents

Figure 3. Lewinian auto-reflective spiral
Source: E. Santos, C Morais & J. Paiva (2004)

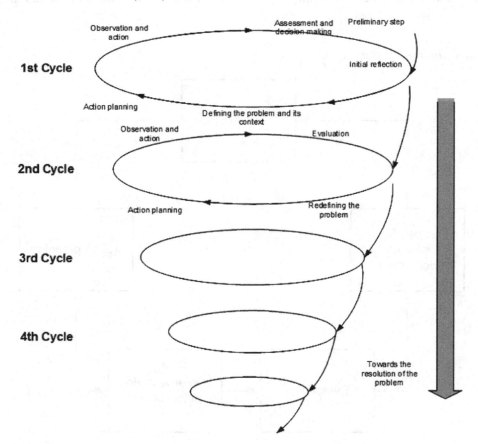

the Lewinian (1946) auto-reflective spiral – a synthesis of the cyclical processes contained in the action research approach,

Action research is a dynamic method that can be understood as a planning and action spiral, as well as a research of facts about the results of the previously taken actions in which the descent stream of the spiral comes closer to the resolution of the problem. In each downward step there is a new cycle of analysis, where one proceeds to a redefinition of the problem, through the planning and implementing of an intervention and an assessment of its efficacy.

In the course of our investigation two action research implementation cycles were performed. The two cycles were of a different nature: the first being focused on design, learning and reflection, while the second was on implementation, testing and documentation.

The first cycle focused on designing the strategy and the method for introducing creativity in the ISP process. Apart from the support of literature; namely the analysis of other existing methods, the design process was essentially experimental and operated through a series of workshops bringing together researchers and practitioners. The following workshops on creativity and the generation of ideas took place:

1. **Creativity and Generation of Ideas for Information Systems:** ANJE Porto (Portugal), 2009.
2. **Creativity and Generation of Ideas for Information Systems:** Instituto Politécnico da Guarda (Portugal), 2010.
3. **Creativity and Generation of Ideas for Innovative IT Companies:** The Importance of the Brand in the position of PMEs-Associação Industrial da Região do Oeste. Auditório da Expoeste, Caldas da Rainha (Portugal), 2010.
4. **Creativity and Generation of Ideas:** Instituto Politécnico Autónomo, Lisbon (Portugal), 2010.

5. **Creativity and Generation of Ideas on IT for the Wine Industry:** Universidade de Trás os Montes e Alto Douro (Portugal), 2010.

The workshops were essentially practical and each had a total duration of six hours. They were divided into four parts, as envisioned in the method designed prior to the experience, namely: constitution of the team, focus on the problem, finding the solution and implementation. In each workshop the method was corrected and adjusted until a first stable version was arrived at. In the second cycle of action research we resorted to the knowledge acquired through the previous cycle and to methodological development work in order to implement the execution of validation tests. The main goals was the validation and improvement of the methodology by trying to promote the convergence of creative processes with Information Systems Planning.

The method for introducing creativity was tested and validated with using Lisbon's City Council's (LCC) Information Systems Strategic Planning project as a case study. The main activities performed in the second cycle were:

1. Applying the methodology in an Information Systems Planning project within a large public organization;
2. Conducting the methodology validation and evaluation process;
3. Implementing the second phase of *workshops* on creativity and idea generation;
4. Executing corrections/changes to the methodology;
5. Publishing the methodology in scientific outlets to ensure formal validation by "peers".

The results and the feedback obtained in the process of execution and evaluation of the methodology in the LCC were relevant and meaningful, as they allowed us to perform further improvement and refining. Based on these, it was also possible to continue publishing on the methodology's applicability (Santos et al., 2001a), (Santos et al., 2001b), (Santos et al. 2011c), (Santos et al., 2012a) and (Santos et al., 2012b).

During this phase a number of workshops on creativity and idea generation allowed us to continue the process of refining the methodology:

1. Rethinking the positioning on the IT market- Creativity and generation of Ideas-Tecnidata, 2011.
2. Creativity and generation of Ideas", Semana Aberta, Instituto Politécnico Autónomo, Lisbon (Portugal), 2011.
3. How to generate an IT business idea in 60 minutes - Job initiatives today, Citeforma, 2011.

The knowledge obtained from the second cycle of action research culminated with the construction of the final strategy and proposed methodology for the introduction of creativity in Information Systems Planning. Figure 4 presents diagrammatically the two action research cycles explained in detail in this section.

STRATEGY FOR THE INTRODUCTION OF CREATIVITY IN INFORMATION SYSTEMS PLANNING

Considering the existence of several ISP approaches, namely the alignment and impact approaches, it was necessary to better understand the mechanisms that could facilitate the embedding of creativity. This has lead us to review a several ISP approaches, namely Bowman's three-stage model of (1983), Earl's (1989) multi-dimensional approach, and the PRAXIS model proposed by Amaral (1994), which proposes a conflation of the three-stage method and multi-dimensional approach.

The "3 Stages Model" is one of the most relevant ISP approaches. It is based on the search for IS alignment within the organization, which aims at analyzing the needs and requirements in information, as well as the rationalization of resources. It is followed by a top-down strategy and points to a set of activities and tasks that are well ordered and clearly defined. The model is depicted in Figure 5.

Figure 4. Main activities performed in each cycle of Investigation Action

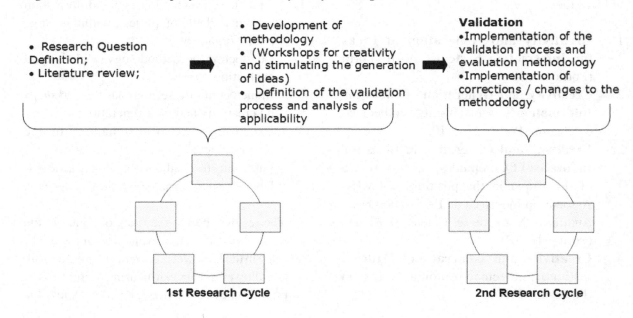

Figure 5. "3 Stages Model"

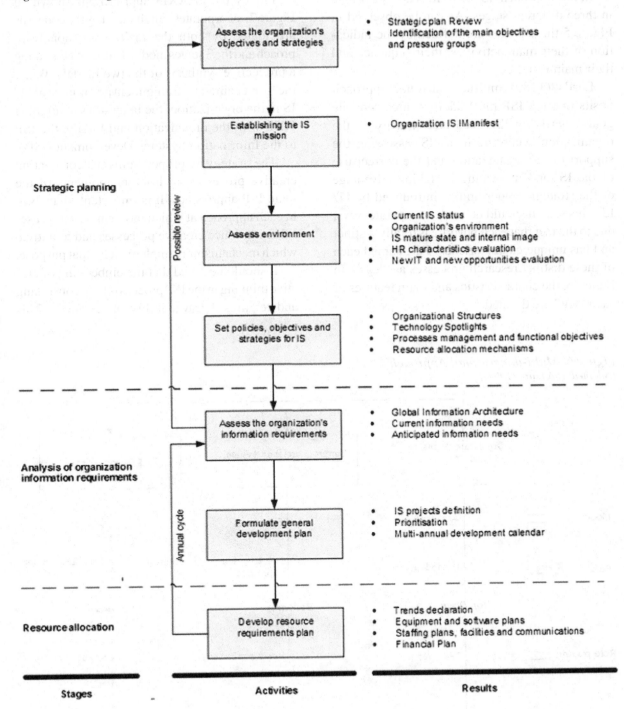

In this approach, ISP activities are performed in three different stages. As can be observed in Figure 5 these stages are defined by the indication of their main activities, their sequence and their main results.

Earl's (1989) multidimensional approach posits that the ISP must address three separate goals: clarifying the need and strategy of the organization according to its IS, assessing the support to the organization and the correct use of the IS, and innovating by taking advantage of the strategic opportunities introduced by IT/IS. This search should be made in separate ways, due to the fact that each purpose is totally distinct and has unique characteristics. Earl named each of these distinct research processes as "legs". In Figure 6, the characteristics and main features of each "leg" are defined.

Finally the PRAXIS approach, as shown on Figure 7, incorporates simultaneously the concerns articulated by both the multi-dimensional approach and the 3 stages model. It aims at generating a productive synthesis of the two models. While the former aims at the alignment and impact of IT/IS in the organization, the latter aims at aligning IT/IS with the organization and linking the ISP to the Information Systems Development (ISD).

The strategy we propose aims at incorporating creative processes at different moments of the main ISP approaches. It is important to analyze in each approach at which moment will it be useful to introduce creative processes and to outline which mechanisms to implement for that purpose.

It should be noted that the embedding of creative thinking in the ISP process is time consuming and requires the availability of resources. This

Figure 6. Multi-dimensional Approach
[Adapted by Amaral (1994)]

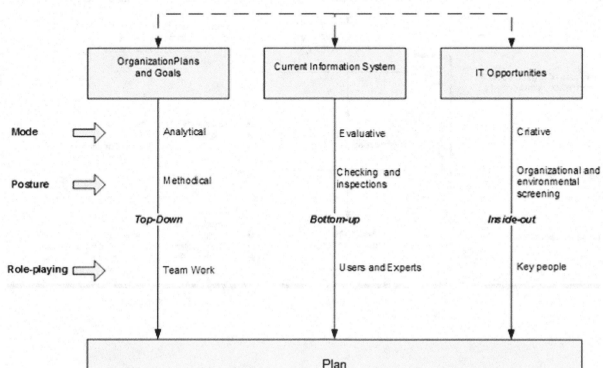

Figure 7. PRAXIS/a approach with relative positioning of the Three-stage Model and Multi-dimensional Approach
[Adapted by Amaral (1994)]

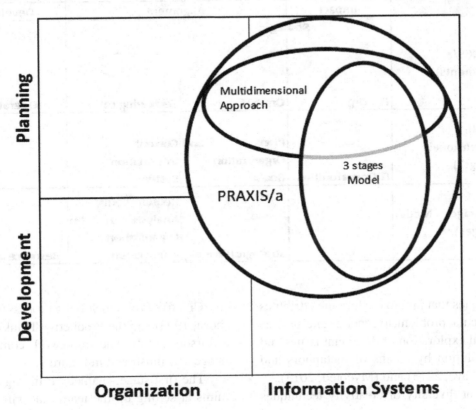

makes the case for defining a precise moment when it is more sensible to embed creative thinking techniques in the planning process. Figure 8 outlines the moment – in all three models - where we suggest creativity should be embedded in ISP. The letter "C" indicates it more clearly.

Taking a simplistic view one could assume that introduction of creative thinking at each of these moments could be achieve through the direct application of creativity techniques. However, the ISP activity is contingent and complex, as it has multiple variables and perspectives. In many cases, in order that creative processes may be of real use for the ISP, they themselves are complex. They must be able to frame the internal and external environments of the organization, the contributions stemming from the variety of collaborators,

the business opportunities, and opportunities accrued from the information systems themselves.

Such a complexity implies that the introduction of creative processes should be supported by a structured framework, able on the one hand to frame and accommodate all of the dimensions referred to above, and on the other hand able to originate viable solutions. In response to this challenge, in the subsequent section we propose a generic framework to embed creativity in ISP.

THE ISP CREATIVE POTENTIALIZATION FRAMEWORK

Information systems planning techniques have been traditionally classified into problem defini-

Figure 8. Creativity in ISP approaches

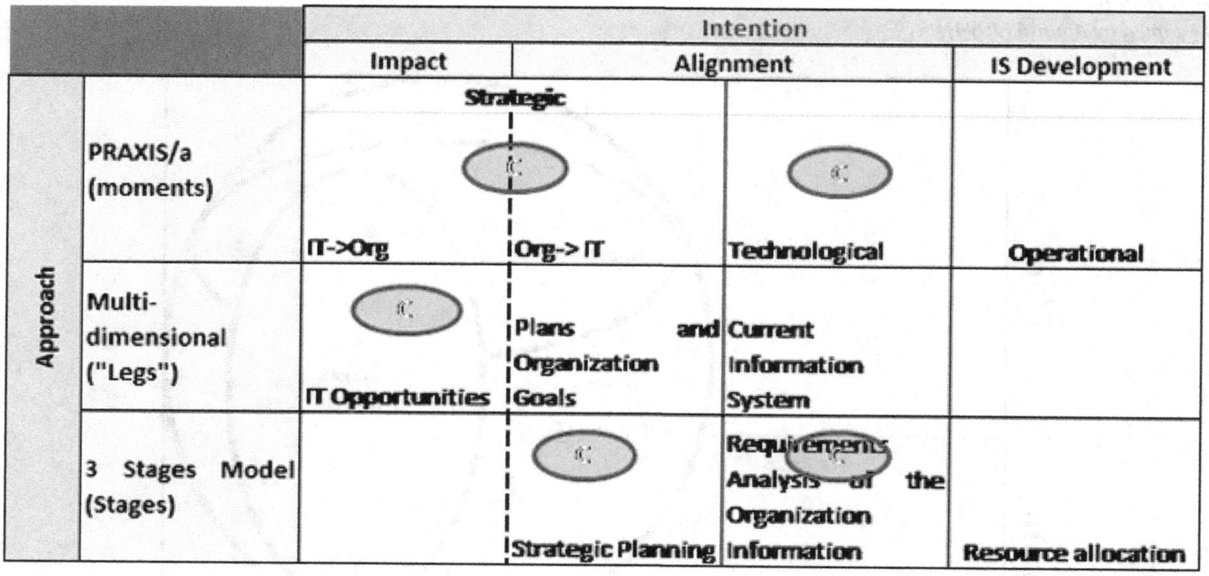

		Intention			
		Impact	**Alignment**		**IS Development**
Approach	**PRAXIS/a (moments)**	Strategic			
		IT->Org	IOrg-> IT	Technological	Operational
	Multi-dimensional ("Legs")		Plans and Organization Goals	Current Information System	
		IT Opportunities			
	3 Stages Model (Stages)		Strategic Planning	Requirements Analysis of the Organization Information	Resource allocation

tion techniques that aim to explore the attributes of one particular problem, to generate alternatives or the visual exploration of dominant issues and potential solution by means of metaphors and analogies (Cave, 2013) and (Mycoted, 2013).

This great diversity of creativity techniques is promising for the goals of the work described in this chapter, since ISP is typically part of a vaster context comprising organizations, their environment, people, activities and technology. In practical terms this means that multiple tools may be available and the difficulty resides in choosing the most adequate solution for each specific problem.

On the other hand, we tend to assume that complexity is inherent to the ISP process, and that creative processes applied to ISP should be governed by a structured method that is powerful enough to originate relevant results yet flexible enough to allow transferability.

The ISP creative potentialization framework (Santos, 2012) proposed in this chapter and further described in the remainder of this section is inspired by methods and techniques for the creative resolution of existing problems, mainly

the Creative Problem Solving Process (CPS) (Osborn, 1993) and the Productive Thinking Model (Hurson, 2007). The framework comprises six stages, as illustrated in Figure 9.

The first stage - named "Building a team" – aims at setting up the team that will apply the framework. It is important to nominate a team leader and to identify the competences and personal experience of each member that composes the team. Preferably the members should hold different personal and professional profiles. This stage is not to be overlooked, since the composition of the group may determine the overall success of the process.

In the second stage- "Clarifying the objective" - we aim at formulating a specific objective. Multiple objectives or vagueness in the formulation of objectives may lead the application of the framework to fail. In this stage, starting from a generic business need (typically a new challenge, opportunity, lack or improvement), the team must clearly identify the specific outcome to be achieved with the development of the Information System. The outcome must be defined in a clear, precise and measurable manner.

Figure 9. Vision of the Generic Method for PSI problem solving

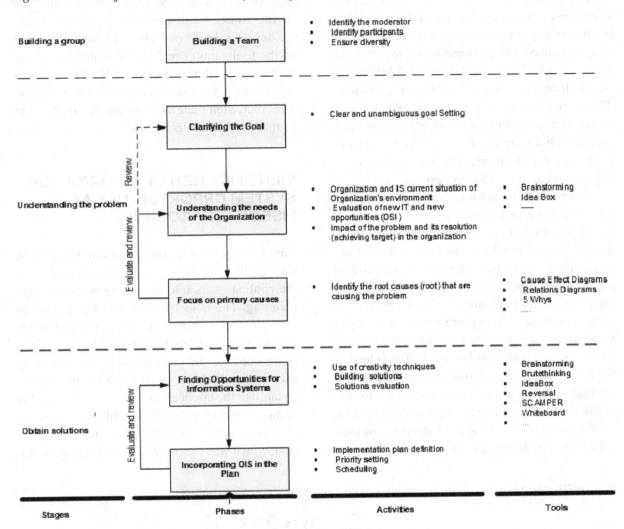

The third step - "Understanding the needs of the organization" - structures the process around the search for a creative solution, maximizing strategic alignment with the organization's goals. This analysis aims at understanding the criteria that condition success and explaining what the ideal situation is. The use of brainstorming techniques is particularly helpful at this stage.

The fourth stage - "Focusing on primary causes" – aims at identifying the primary (root) causes that underlie the problem to be approached. This is a fundamental issue, as it is only possible to think about new approaches and solutions, if one has established the real causes behind the needs of the business. Again, the use of brainstorming techniques is useful for the identification of underlying causes.

During the fifth stage - "Finding solutions" - the needs of the organization and the problem's primary causes are considered in an attempt to find innovative solutions that will tackle the challenges identified. The type of creative thinking technique to be employed at this stage can vary according to the type of organization. Amongst the several creativity techniques listed in the classification proposed by Zusman (1998), we select brainstorming, brute thinking, and whiteboard (all of which are considered randomizer techniques), as well as idea box, reversal and SCAMPER (all of which are considered focalization techniques. This choice was based on three criteria: the ease of use of each technique, its creative power and the predicted adaption to the different types of problems, organizations and people, which we expect to find in the ISP process.

As a result of our ongoing experimentation with this framework and its practical implementation in various workshops, we were able to extract a number of general recommendations that are of practical use for this interested in embedding creativity in ISP. These recommendations are represented diagrammatically in Figure 10.

In this stage it is important to keep an open mind, so that it is possible to generate the greatest number of alternative solutions, before selecting the best fit. In face of a high number of possible alternative solutions, one must consider a formal evaluation method in order to choose the best fit.

Finally, in the sixth stage - "Incorporating plan solutions" - we proceed to incorporate PSI-based solutions. As a support for the implementation of the strategy and methods explained above, we developed a set of tools and templates. Some of the tools aim at realizing the analysis of the problems and data retrieval, while others aim to support the production of documentation. Figure 11 depicts a template that supports the application of the SCAMPER technique.

IDENTIFICATION OF INFORMATION SYSTEM OPPORTUNITIES AT LISBON CITY COUNCIL

The ISP creative potentialization framework was applied at Lisbon City Council (LCC), in the context of its information systems strategic planning. The objective was to develop a series of work sessions aimed at identifying innovative Information Systems Opportunities (ISO). The framework for the embedding of innovation in ISP was applied across all sessions. In order to instantiate the application of the framework, this section of the chapter will describe the sequence of activities undertaken during the first work session, which was specifically aimed at identifying

Figure 10. Applying creativity techniques according to the type of problem

		Type of Problem			
		Current System			
		No Coverage	Improvement	Integration	New business
Creativity Techniques	Brainstorming	X		X	X
	Brute Thinking				X
	Idea Box		X	X	
	Reversal	X	X		
	SCAMPER		X	X	
	Whiteboard				X

Figure 11. Template for the application of the SCAMPER technique

SCAMPER

Purpose: SCAMPER is a technique for looking at possible transformations that you could apply to a product or process. Looking at these transformations can help you identify "out-of-the-box" approaches by looking at the problem from different perspectives. It is particularly useful where conventional approaches to the problem may already have been tried unsuccessfully

Process/product reviewed:			
	Transformation	**Typical questions**	**Solution ideas**
S	**SUBSTITUTE**	What can I substitute to make an improvement? What happens if I swap X for Y? How can I substitute the place, time, materials or people?	
C	**COMBINE**	What materials, features, processes, people, products or components can I combine within the problem area? Where can I build synergy with other products/processes?	
A	**ADAPT**	What other products/processes are similar to the one at root cause of our problem? What if we adapted them? What could we change to make them fit our purpose?	
M	**MODIFY/ MAGNIFY/ MINIFY**	What ways can we completely change the product/process? Can it be improved by making it stronger, larger, higher, longer, exaggerated or more frequent? Can it be improved by making it smaller, lighter, shorter, less prominent or less frequent?	
P	**PUT TO OTHER USES**	What other products/processes could do what we need to do? What other things are going on that we could make use of?	
E	**ELIMINATE**	What would happen if we remove a component of the product/process? What would happen if we remove the whole thing? How could we achieve the same objective if we weren't able to do it this way?	
R	**REARRANGE/ REVERSE**	What if we reversed the process? What if we did step B before step A? What if we moved step A & did it last or put step Z first? What if we did these two steps together?	

innovative ISOs for the LCC's Directorate for Culture (DC). The framework was applied following the subsequent steps:

1. Constitution of a heterogeneous team at LCC, combining cultural specialists and non-specialists to allow out of the box thinking. The team comprised professional service staff, informatics department staff and staff working directly under the DC.
2. The DC put forward the following business need:

It is necessary to enhance communication with citizens about cultural activities, and to reach out for new audiences. The tradi-tional media are not interested but there is a variety of channels available and abundant information.

The problem was tackled jointly by producing a briefing document and collectively deciding on an ideal scenario solution.

3. Debate ensued focused on the production of a diagram that could help identify causal relationships and the primary sources of the problem. The emergent diagram of relationships is presented in Figure 12.
4. Based on the ideal solution (i.e. the objective identified at the center of the diagram) we proceeded to outline the key actions that would help delivering it.

5. In order to approach the problem in terms of primary causes identified, we selected and applied two creative thinking techniques, namely brute thinking and reversal. Brute thinking as proposed by Michalko (2006) is a technique that aids lateral thinking, as well as creativity. It can be used to conceive alternative solutions but may also be useful for identifying the causes of problems. This technique is based on a very simple process that is developed in four steps, which are referred to as: choosing a random word, choosing associated elements for that word, forcing links between the word and the problem and the associations and the problem, then listing and analyzing the resulting ideas. On the other hand, and following principles that draw from Osborn's (1993) brainstorming process, the reversal technique challenges participants to list assumptions about the subject area and then to reverse those assumptions to try and make them work.

Figure 12. Diagram of Relationships

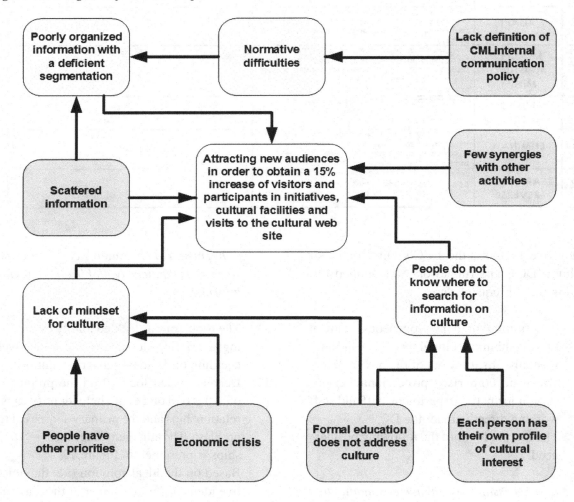

6. The application the two techniques contributed to the identification of seven ISOs that DC specialists deemed promising:
   a. Customer relationship management system for DC;
   b. Publication management system designed for the collection, audit, and reporting of DC's publication output. In particular the system should assist with the process of magazine publishing, namely document management, workflow management, copyright controls, copyediting support, illustration management, etc.;
   c. Knowledge management system to promote the sharing of knowledge between Culture and Engineering departments. This would be the base for the development of portal aggregating information about the city's cultural scene;
   d. Virtual reality applications such as an electronic passport for visitors to personalize and manage the collection of art collections and heritage sites they engage with.

CONCLUSION

Information Systems Planning is one of the most challenging activities in Information Systems management. In a market environment characterized by rapid technological development and the intensification of global competition, the introduction of creativity in Information Systems Planning, can impact highly in the success of organizations. The need to creatively approach the design of new systems is both an opportunity and a challenge for Information Systems managers (Cooper, 2000). In this chapter we presented a framework for the embedding of creativity into Information Systems Planning by describing the process in detail and by presenting a case study where the framework was successfully applied

to identify ISO in a large public sector organization. Future work will necessarily involve further iterations and the refinement of the framework to ensure it effectively supports the design and development of innovative IS strategies in other organizational contexts.

ACKNOWLEDGMENT

This work is funded by FEDER funds through the Operational Program for Competitiveness Factors - COMPETE and National Funds through FCT - Foundation for Science and Technology under the Project: FCOMP-01-0124-FEDER-022674."

REFERENCES

Amaral, L. (1994). PRAXIS: Um referencial para o planeamento de sistemas de informação.

Amaral, L., & Varajão, J. (2007). Planeamento de sistemas de informação, FCA - Editora de Informática, Lda, Lisboa, 4ª ed, p. 247.

Bowman, B., G. Davis & J. Wetherbe (1993). Three stage of MIS planning. *Information and Management*, 6, 1, 1983.

Candeias, A. A. (2008). Criatividade: Perspectiva integrativa sobre o conceito e a sua avaliação. In M. F. M. S. Bahia (Ed.), *Criatividade: conceito, necessidades e intervenção*. Braga: Psiquilibrios.

Cave, C. (2013). Creativity Web - Resources for Creativity and Innovation.

Chen, D. Q., Mocker, M., Preston, D. S., & Teubner, A. (2010). Information systems strategy: Reconceptualization, measurement, and implications. *Quarterly*, *34*(2), 233–259.

Cooper, R. B. (2000). Information technology development creativity: A case study of attempted radical change. *Management Information Systems Quarterly*, *24*(2), 245–275. doi:10.2307/3250938

Coutinho, C. P. (2011). *Metodologia da Investigação em ciências sociais e humanas – Theory and Practice*. Coimbra: Almedina.

Earl, M. (1989). *Management strategies for information technologies*. London: Prentice Hall.

Heilman, K.M., Nadeau, S.E., & Beversdorf, D.Q. (2003). Creative innovation: possible brain mechanisms. *Neurocase*, 9(5), 369-379.

Horton, K. S., & Dewar, R. G. (2001). Evaluating creative practice in information systems strategy formation: the application of Alexandrian patterns. Proceedings of the 34th Hawaii International Conference on System Sciences. doi:10.1109/HICSS.2001.927123

Hurson, T. (2007). *Think Better: An innovator's guide to productive thinking*. New York: McGraw-Hill.

Kock, N.F., McQueen, R.J., & Scott., J.L. (1997). Can action research be made more rigorous in a positivist sense? The contribution of an iterative approach. *Journal of Systems & Information Technology*, 1(1), 1-24.

Lederer, A. L., & Sethi, V. (1991). Critical dimensions of strategic information systems planning. *Decision Sciences*, 22(1), 104–119. doi:10.1111/j.1540-5915.1991.tb01265.x

Lewin, K. (1946). Action research and minority problems. *The Journal of Social Issues*, 2.

Michalko, M. (2006). *Thinkertoys: A handbook of creative-thinking techniques* (2nd ed.). Toronto: Ten Speed Press.

Morais, M. F., & Bahia, S. (2008). *Criatividade*. Braga: Psiquilibrios.

Mycoted (2013). Creativity, Innovation, Tools, Techniques, Books, Discussions, Puzzles, Brain Teasers, Training ...

Myers, M.D. (1997). Qualitative research in information systems. *MIS Quarterly*, 21(2), 241-242.

Osborn, A. F. (1993). *Applied imagination: principles and procedures of creative problem-solving* (3rd ed.). Creative Education Foundation.

Ravishankar, M. N., Pan, S. L., & Leidner, D. E. (2010). (forthcoming). Examining the strategic alignment and implementation success of a KMS: A Subculture-Based Multilevel Analysis. *Information Systems Research*.

Ruohonen, M., & Higgins, L. F. (1998). Application of creativity principles to IS planning. In Hugh J. Watson (Ed.), Proceedings of the Thirty-First Hawaii International Conference on System Sciences (*Vol. VI*), Los Alamitos, California. doi:10.1109/HICSS.1998.654798

Santos, E., Morais, C., & Paiva, J. (2004). Formação de professores para a integração das TIC no ensino da matemática – a study of the Autonomous Region of Madeira. Proceedings of the 6th International Symposium on Computers in Education, Cáceres.

Santos, V., & Amaral, L. (2012a). Introdução de criatividade no processo de identificação de estratégias de qualidade de dados. Proceedings of the Creativity and Innovation in Information Systems and Engineering Workshop CRIISE2012, Madrid, Spain.

Santos, V., & Amaral, L. (2012b). Estratégias para a introdução de criatividade em diferentes abordagens de planeamento de sistemas de informação. Proceedings of the 11th Conference of the Portuguese Association of Information Systems, Guimarães, Portugal.

Santos, V., Amaral, L., & Mamede, H. (2011a). A methodology for creativity introduction in the information systems planning. Proceedings of the 8th International Conference on Information Systems and Technology Management - CONTECSI, São Paulo

Santos, V., Amaral, L., & Mamede, H. (2011b). Método para a introdução de criatividade no processo de planeamento de sistemas de informação. Proceedings of the 6th Iberian Conference on Information Systems and Technologies (CISTI) Chaves

Santos, V., Amaral, L., & Mamede, H. (2011c). Information systems planning - How to enhance creativity? Proceedings of the CENTERIS'2011 Conference on ENTERprise Information Systems, Vilamoura.

Santos, V., & Mamede, H. (2007). Creative information systems. In M. Freire & M. Pereira (Eds.), *Encyclopedia of Internet Technologies and Applications* (pp. 126–131). USA: IGI Global. doi:10.4018/978-1-59140-993-9.ch019

Sousa, G. V. e. (1998). *Metodologia da investigação. Redacção e apresentação de trabalhos científicos*. Livraria Civilização.

Susman, G. I., & Evered, R. D. (1978). An assessment of the scientific merits of action research. *Administrative Science Quarterly, 23*(4), 582–603. doi:10.2307/2392581

Tarrida, A. C., & Femenia, D. C. (2008). Dirigir la creatividad: Una aproximación al funcionamiento intelectual de los directores de cine. In M.d.F. Morais & S. Bahia (Eds.) Criatividade: conceito, necessidades e intervenção. Psiquilibrios Braga.

Wazlawick, R. S. (2009). *Metodologia de pesquisa para ciência da computação Elsevier*. São Paulo.

Zusman, A. (1998). *Overview of creative methods*. Southfield, Michigan, USA: Ideation International Inc.

Chapter 9
IT Alignment:
Stakeholder Dynamics Perspective

Taghred Alghaith
Lancaster University, UK

ABSTRACT

This chapter seeks a deeper understanding of stakeholder dynamics as a critical social component influencing IT strategy alignment. Perez-Batres et al. (2012) recognized the paucity of research on alignment dynamics, mainly stakeholder dynamics. Stakeholder theory, primarily Mitchell et al. (1997) identification model, is used to determine stakeholders' saliency throughout an ICT strategic project in a Saudi public hospital. However, stakeholder theory is static and does not help in tracing how saliency is gained and lost through time, and hence interpreting the influence on the alignment process. Therefore, this research utilizes the appreciative systems concepts of Geoffrey Vickers as dynamizing instrument to understand saliency dynamics and their influence. Results show that stakeholder dynamics resides in the nature of the relationship they pursue with each other.

INTRODUCTION

Contemporary organizations, whether public or private, are investing hugely in Information and Communication Technologies (ICTs) (Moghaddasi, Asadi, Hosseini, & Ebnehoseini, 2012). However, senior managers and IT directors are concerned that investing in sophisticated ICTs is not enough. They are aware that they need to leverage ICT infrastructure and processes in a certain way to meet the desired needs and capabilities of their organizations. This process is referred to as IT strategic alignment. Therefore, to achieve a sustainable alignment between IT and business

strategy it is imperative that IT strategy considers the needs of the organization. Yet, despite the realization of how eminent IT alignment is, practitioners as well as researcher are still finding it problematic (Iveroth, Fryk, & Rapp, 2013), and they feel that IT alignment happens in a complex social context that has to be addressed for the alignment process to succeed (Reich & Benbasat, 2000). One approach that can result in a high level of alignment is having a better understanding of stakeholder dynamics, which is the main objective of this chapter. It seeks understanding 'how' stakeholder dynamics develop in a complex IT project context, and how these dynamics impact alignment process.

DOI: 10.4018/978-1-4666-8833-9.ch009

The Ministry Of Health (MOH), which is the main provider of healthcare services in Saudi Arabia, is investing a large amount of money and effort in developing the information technology infrastructure and information systems in its hospitals (Alghaith, Brown, & Worthington, 2013). The reason behind this huge investment is the national ICT-based schemes. Almalki, Fitzgerald, and Clark (2011) described that among the future challenges that the Saudi healthcare system encounters are the implementation of strategies such as the e-health strategy, the national HIS scheme and the cooperative health insurance plan. However, the MOH is having misgivings about the outcome of such investments, as it does not have a clear strategy on how to improve and follow-up the ICT strategies already applied in some MOH automated hospitals. Therefore, the MOH supported this case study and provided the researcher with an access to three public hospitals to carry out a pilot study. The pilot study showed that the ICT strategic projects seemed to be facing serious barriers in relation to the dynamics of internal and external stakeholders, for example the MOH, ICT main providers and subcontractors, top management, staff of the ICT departments, and key-users. Hence, this research is concerned about understanding how stakeholder dynamics develop and influence throughout time on IT strategy alignment over time.

Based on that, exploring stakeholder dynamics—mainly the emergence of stakeholder saliency dynamics and their influence over time on IT strategy alignment—is broadly shaped by three premises (Alghaith et al., 2013). The first premise is the significant strategic role that Information and Communication Technologies (ICTs) play in various industries. The potential benefits that ICTs can offer to organizations to improve their performance in the long-term are immense, and therefore have become of central interest to both academics and practitioners. The second premise is the criticality of grasping the contexts of ICT strategic projects through which IT strategies

are translated. A report for the Council of Health Services (CHS) in Saudi Arabia (CHS, 2009) — which is a national council responsible for healthcare strategies — stated that ICT strategies are experiencing substantial obstacles related to the social context, and thus encouraged researching such intricate context. The final premise stems from IT project management literature, mainly the social process perspective. Nelson (2007) described that ICT strategic projects are generally considered as being challenging not only because of the technical factors but also because of stakeholder-oriented and social processes factors, which are both important when aligning IT projects to business strategy and needs.

The remainder of this chapter is divided into four sections. The first section is the literature review. It covers two aspects of the literature, which are the contextual and the interpretive. In terms of the contextual literature, the IT project studied in this research is strategic and approached through an IT alignment lens. Consequently, it is important to visit the literature of the IT strategy, IT alignment and IT project management. On the other hand, the interpretive framework discusses stakeholder theory and the appreciative systems concepts.

The second section addresses the methodological philosophy of this study. In particular, it explains the single case study approach that is adopted to collect and analyze data in order to answer the main research questions. The third section discusses the research findings and proposes a base for an IT alignment mechanism in relation to stakeholder dynamics. Finally, the fourth section provides a conclusion that sums up this study.

LITERATURE REVIEW

This section is divided into two main subsections. The first subsection contextually reviews the literature of IT strategy, IT alignment and IT project management respectively in relation to the social process perspective, with a focus on stakeholder dynamics. Then, the second subsection discusses the interpretative framework used to make sense of the stakeholder dynamics phenomenon.

Contextual Literature

IT Strategy

Dubey (2011) argued that for businesses to improve and develop using information technologies there is a need to have a long-term perspective of ITs, which is known as IT strategy. He highlighted that IT strategy assists organizations in not only competing and surviving in an industry, but also realizing a competitive advantage, granting them a more powerful position compared to their competitors. In broader terms, Gallier (1993) indicated that IT strategy refers to information systems (IS) strategy formulation and implantation. However, researchers such as Earl (1989, cited in Sabherwal & Chan, 2001) explained that that there is a difference between IS strategy and IT strategy. The first refers to what is required, while the latter indicates how to produce it. Hence, whilst the IS strategy delineates the organization's needs the IT strategy defines what technologies (i.e. computer systems, communication systems, data and databases, and applications) can be utilized to meet these needs. Gottschalk (1999) provided a more operational definition of IT strategy. He defined it as a plan, including projects to apply information technologies that help businesses meet their goals. On a slightly different perspective of IT strategy, Ward and Peppard (2002) considered the term IT strategy as a wide umbrella term comprised of two dimensions: the IS and the IT. Gottschalk (1999), nevertheless, claimed that IT strategy implementation is proven to be critical to IS strategy success. He explained that failing to deliver the IS strategy leads to waste of strategic resources and opportunities, unrealized needs of the organization and hesitancy in continuing IS strategy. That, as he described, leaves organiza-

tions in a state of uncertainty when it comes to any future IT investment. Similarly, Galliers (1993) stated that continuously evaluating and reviewing IT strategy implementation increases the possibility of IS strategy delivering its goals and significantly increasing the IS strategy adaptation to a changing environment.

The IT strategy literature not only focuses on the concept of IT strategy, but it also endeavors to explain the potential of ICTs in considerably improving organizational performance. Lucas (1999) argues that strategically using IT has a greater impact on performance. Moreover, ICTs, when utilized strategically, lead to efficient performance and facilitate the managing of organizations (Galliers & Leidner, 2003). Other researchers, such as Zahra and George (2002), stressed how IT strategy increases the ability of organizations in creating a sustainable competitive advantage.

However, despite this recognition of the importance of IT strategy for organizational success and survival, researchers are becoming increasingly concerned about the social factors inhibiting IT strategy implementation. Zhang, Dawes, and Sarkis (2005) claimed that designing, developing, evaluating and implementing ICTs differ depending on the stakeholders involved in these processes and the roles they handle. They highlighted that although it has long been acknowledged that social context and social processes can either inhibit or enable IT strategy implementation, it is still overlooked in practice. Furthermore, Ballantine and Cunningham (1999, 2002) pointed out that organizations, especially in the public sector, have multiple stakeholder individuals and groups with diverse interests and expectations, and different goals of information technologies. According to them, that makes implementing IT strategies problematic. Heeks and Bhatnagar (1999), also, argued that overlooking the complex social and political environment of the public sector can lead to a failure of IT strategy implementation. Therefore, Ballantine and Cunningham (1999) urged managers to increase their awareness of the complex dynamic reality of implementing ICT strategy: " Little attention has been paid in planning literature to the way in which managers make sense of the world within which they interact and the manner in which shared conceptions affect what they do" (p.308).

The next paragraphs shed light on IT alignment literature, which is an approach striving to explain how to best align different dimensions of IT strategy.

IT Alignment

One of the main approaches advocated by researchers to tackle the problematic context of IT strategy is IT alignment. Avison, Jones, Powell, and Wilson (2004) described that for organizations to be competitive and realize their strategy they need to align it to IT strategy. Therefore, in IT strategy literature IT alignment is being viewed as the extent to which the IT plan supports and is supported by the organization plan (Reich & Benbasat, 2000). Yet, Reich and Benbasat (2000) criticized this definition for considering alignment an outcome rather than a process. Likewise, Henderson and Venkatraman (1993) commented that aligning IT plans to business plans is a process of constant change and adjustment and not an event. Similarly, Luffman, Papp, and Brier (1999, cited in Kashanchi & Toland, 2008) emphasized that alignment is dynamic and changing. Ballantine and Cunningham (1999, 2002) also stressed that aligning IT strategy to an organization's strategic needs while paying attention to the dynamic social reality is significant. As a result, the literature offered different alignment models for practitioners to carry out the alignment process effectively.

Henderson and Venkatraman (1993) developed a widely cited Strategic Alignment Model (SAM). They theorized their model based on two substantial aspects of strategic management, which are strategic fit and functional integration (Al-Hatmi, 2014). Al-Hatmi (2014) explained that strategic fit refers to identifying the ways in which external

and internal dimensions are interrelated, while functional integration indicates to aligning organizational and technological dimensions. SAM demonstrates that the strategic alignment process has to involve business strategy, infrastructure, processes and skills, as well as IT strategy and its infrastructure and processes (Henderson & Venkatraman, 1993). In other words, the alignment process has to include the internal and external domains of IT and business strategies. In order to apply the SAM model properly, Henderson and Venkatraman (1993) emphasized that utilizing sophisticated technologies to meet organizational needs is not enough. Rather, practitioners should change how they view IT functions in organizations and understand the critical dimensions of IT strategy.

Nevertheless, Avison, Jones, Powell, and Wilson (2004) criticized the SAM model as not being practically helpful to managers when aligning their IT and business strategies. Moreover, Al-Hatmi (2014) described that the SAM model fails to recognize the political, cultural, financial, and social dimensions of alignment. Therefore, he calls for reviewing the model in the light of these dimensions to effectively improve the alignment process. Reich and Benbasat (2000) also particularly stressed the impact of the social factor when aligning IT and business strategies. They described that generally strategic alignment has two main domains, which are the intellectual and the social. The intellectual domain deals with the plan contents and methodologies used in planning. The social dimension, however, concentrates on stakeholders involved in alignment. According to them, while both domains are critical in effectively carrying out the alignment process, the social domain has not yet been sufficiently studied by researchers. However, they pointed out that the literature calls for more attention to be paid to the social dimension of alignment: "The social dimension…has not been accorded the same degree of attention by IT researchers …we are aware that there is no well-accepted theory of the social aspects of alignment."(pp. 82-83)

Researchers' concern about offering insights, models and recommendations to better the alignment process is incited by how beneficial alignment can be if carried out efficiently to businesses (Avison et al., 2004). Alignment, as they explained, helps in gaining the support of senior management for IS strategy, creating a competitive advantage for the organization, enhancing performance efficiency and leading to the development of systems important for the business.

Finally, it is important to note that in practice IT strategy is often translated into IT strategic projects. Kearns and Sabherwal (2007) indicated that IT projects represent IT strategies, i.e., IT projects are middling between IT and business strategies. Therefore, it is necessary to visit the IT project management literature with regard to the social processes, which is what the following few paragraphs is focusing on.

IT Project Management

The case study explored in this research is an IT project, which is strategic, in a Saudi public hospital. It was implemented to meet the hospital's strategic needs, as the methodology section explains. Hence, this subsection sheds light on what an IT project means and covers the social process aspect of IT projects.

Janvrin, Bierstaker, and Lowe (2008) explained that information technology refers to the means through which technology originates, processes, stores and communicates information, and that IT is comprised of communication and computer systems (both hardware and software). Ward and Peppard (2002) clarified that technology refers to hardware, software and telecommunications, which are utilized in processing, storing, delivering and circulating information. This information technology comes in the form of IT projects in modern organizations.

An IT project, therefore, is defined as a temporary activity carried out by a team to improve and/or support organizational systems using technologies within an identified budget project and with a final goal of meeting organizational objectives (Wutyi, 2012). Project management literature, however, provided a generic definition for the term 'project' as a concept. Schwalbe (2010) argued that a project is a short-term activity undertaken to achieve certain goals, create products or deliver services. Nevertheless, researchers such as Engwall (2003) proposed that there is a need to change the temporal view of projects. He claimed that a project takes place in an open system, not a closed one, and called for a new theorization of project nature. Soderlund, Vaagaasar, and Andersen (2008) agreed with Engwall's (2003) argument and stressed that a project must be looked at as "a complex web of connections…a process that is undergoing continuous development and change" (p.7). The noted change in thinking about projects is echoed in a study by Winter, Smith, Morris, and Cicmil (2006). They called for a new perspective reflecting the complex and dynamic realities of projects, in particular the social processes aspects:

Future research in this area needs to concentrate on developing new ways of thinking which relate to the actual complexity of projects, at all levels, focusing on aspects such as: the ever-changing flux of events, the complexity of social interaction and human action, and the framing and reframing of projects and programs within an evolving array of social agenda, practices, stakeholder relations, politics and power. (p. 644)

Researchers in IT project management, such as Sauer and Reich (2009), responded to this call and carried out research that emphasized the criticality of the social process influence in effectively managing IT projects. They explained that a shift from the traditional view of IT projects is a necessity in modern organizations. Chong and Tan (2012) considered several social factors like organizational culture, commitment and knowledge sharing to be fundamental when establishing effective IT project governance. Similarly, Kappelman, Mckeeman, and Zhang (2006) explained that postmortem studies show that the social aspects, primarily stakeholder-related issues, represent a critical risk factor for IT projects. They added that technical failures could actually be traced back to the people involved. Likewise, Winter et al. (2006) argued that a broader view of IT projects, not the traditional narrow one, is needed. To facilitate that, they presented a number of lenses through which projects can be viewed. They refer to these lenses as 'images' and explained that each image has its own impact on the resulting actions. For example, viewing a project as an IT system development can result in actions that are different from those stemming from viewing it as an IT intervention project. Therefore, Winter and Szczepanek (2009) indicated that changing from the production image of IT projects to a broader image, like a social or political image, leads to different actions: "how people initially perceive and think about projects, or situations involving projects, is hugely important, simply because it determines the subsequent thinking and action that is carried out" (p.19) Finally, the IT strategic project examined here echoes this argument. Approaching it as a temporary activity carried out to achieve certain goals can lead to failure in understanding its complex context. Asrilhant, Dyson, and Meadows (2004) explained that strategic projects have a long-term impact on the firm and its implementation can take several years. Also, they stated that a project is considered strategic when it attempts to meet the overall strategy of the business and hence resembles high-risk as the firm tries to allocate their top resources and capabilities to implement it.

Evidence from practice-based research such as Lee (2013) shows that in strategic IT project environment aligning stakeholder dynamics remains challenging. Weiss and Anderson (2004) conducted a research in seven companies investigating IT alignment context. They concluded that there is a need to manage business "while orchestrating cultural and political interests of multiple stakeholders" in order to efficiently complete projects. They, also, added that despite the long line of research on IT alignment know-how, gap still exists on how to effectively achieve it. However, it is important to note that stakeholder behaviors are not only driven by interests, but also by psychological factors such as values (Nota & Aiello, 2014) and needs and expectations (Thiry, 2002).

To conclude, this review of IT project management, IT strategy and IT alignment provides a substantial contextual frame for understanding stakeholder saliency dynamics and their influence on the alignment process. The next part of the literature covers the interpretive framework utilized to make sense of stakeholder saliency dynamics and the resulting influence.

Interpretive Literature

Stakeholder Theory

During the ICT strategic project initiation and implementation, complexity appears to be emerging from certain social dynamics. Therefore, it is imperative to understand 'who matters' among the internal and external stakeholders and how their dynamics develop over time and influence the IT alignment process. To have such understanding, this subsection describes stakeholder theory concepts relevant to the research problem.

Freeman, Harrison and Wicks (2007) stated that during the 1980s there was a shift in organizational approaches from economical to social contexts. This, according to them, is clear in stakeholder theory, as theorists started viewing organizations as needing to consider the interests of stakeholders involved. Eden and Ackermann (1998) explained that in order to survive and achieve equilibrium, an organization has to take into account the different interests of stakeholders and their interactions.

As the theory about the concept of the stakeholder was developing concepts were to some extent blurred (Donaldson & Preston, 1995; Brummer, 1991). Therefore, in their milestone paper Donaldson and Preston (1995) classified these concepts into three central connected approaches, which are: descriptive/empirical, instrumental and normative. They consider stakeholder theory as being unarguably descriptive. It introduces descriptive models focusing on what a firm is and views it as a constellation of competing interests. It, moreover, shows what managing is to managers and senior management and how they think of rivaling interests within the organization. For instance, the model of Mitchell, Agle, and Wood (1997), which is the model adopted in this research, is descriptive because it tries to identify salient stakeholders using certain attributes. The instrumental approach, which is the second approach Donaldson and Preston (1995) included, is usually used along with descriptive data to define the relation between the applying of stakeholder management notions and the accomplishment of the organizational needs. For example, Simmons and Lovegrove (2005) used in their study a descriptive stakeholder model to explore the organizational performance in UK academic institutions. The final approach of Donaldson and Preston (1995) is the normative one. Stakeholder theory thinks of organizations in terms of moral values. They contended that whilst the descriptive and instrumental approaches are significant, they fully accept that stakeholder individuals and groups have varying legitimate interests that firms have to respond to. Put simply, the normative approach is believed to be the central part of stakeholder theory.

Freeman et al. (2007) stressed that a balanced attention to internal and external stakeholder interests helps organizations make value and create a favorable organizational environment. In his effort to establish a theory to help manage stakeholders,

Freeman (1984) introduced an acknowledged definition of the term stakeholder, and an instrumental model to determine the organization stakeholders and their relationships within organizational boundaries. He explained that a stakeholder is "any group or individual who can affect or is affected by the achievement of an organization's purpose" (p.25). The definition involves anyone with a stake in the firm, and that is the reason it is accepted by many researchers (Mitchell et al., 1997; Andriof et al., 2002). Additionally, Freeman (1984) demonstrated, in a two-tier map, the internal and external stakeholders that the organization has to include when strategically viewing their interactions and relationships. His model is comprised of three levels that need to be analyzed. The first level includes determining who the stakeholders are and what stakes they hold. The second level is about identifying the processes applied to manage stakeholders strategically and address their relationships, and then deciding whether these processes 'fit' with the mapping of stakeholders in the first level. The final level tries to understand the transactions taking place between the organization and its stakeholders, and whether the transactions 'fit' with the stakeholder analysis and processes used, i.e. whether there is a fit with the results of the first and second levels. Freeman's (1984) model is not only descriptive and instrumental but also built on normative ground. Donaldson and Preston (1995) argued that Freeman's (1984) model gives organizations a way to include the moral norms of stakeholder individuals and groups.

Nevertheless, stakeholder theory faces fundamental criticism by many researchers. Post, Lawrence, and Weber (1996) indicated that Freeman's (1984) model is too comprehensive to be used in analyzing stakeholder-related issues. Friedman and Miles (2002) highlighted the lack of dynamism in stakeholder theory. They explained that it does not provide a technique to help in tracking stakeholder dynamics and identifying their interests over time. Friedman and Miles (2002) pointed out that the degree to which stakeholder relationships can alter through time, alongside the exploration of how and why such alteration happens, has also been overlooked. Similarly, Beaulieu and Pasquero (2002) argued that stakeholder theory is static and unilateral, as it concentrates on managers' perspectives only. Therefore, a number of conceptual models emerged to support the dynamizing of stakeholder theory. For instance, Mitchell, Agle, and Wood (1997) presented their identification model as an attempt to tackle some of the weaknesses found in stakeholder theory. The next paragraphs describe this model, as it is the model utilized in this study.

Mitchell et al. (1997) pointed out that Freeman's (1984) model does not help in determining the exact attributes needed to map salient stakeholders:

Yet...there is no agreement on what Freeman (1994) calls "The Principle of Who or What Really Counts." That is, who (or what) are the stakeholders of the firm? ...although Freeman's (1984) definition is widely cited in the literature, it is not accepted universally among scholars working in the stakeholder minefields. Narrowing the range of stakeholders requires applying some acceptable and justifiable sorting criteria...(p.853)

Therefore, Mitchell et al. (1997) developed a theoretical framework to define stakeholder saliency. The identification model includes three main attributes for mapping stakeholders, based on the perception of managers: power, legitimacy and urgency. Power, as they described, refers to "the ability of those who possess power to bring about the outcomes they desire" (p. 865) and they classified it into: coercive power (i.e. physical abilities), utilitarian power (i.e. stemming from resources) and normative power (i.e. coming from a certain prestige or esteem owned by a stakeholder). Regarding legitimacy, they accepted Suchman's (1995) definition of legitimacy, which stated that legitimacy is "a generalized perception or assumption that the actions of an entity are desirable, proper or appropriate within some socially constructed system of norms, values, beliefs and definitions"(p. 866). Finally, by urgency they meant "the degree to which stakeholder claims call for immediate attention" (p.867). Urgency, according to Mitchell et al. (1997), is recognized by two elements: time-sensitivity and criticality. Time-sensitivity refers to the degree to which the delay in the response to a claim or a relationship is unacceptable to stakeholders. Criticality, however, means the importance of a claim or a relationship to stakeholders.

Furthermore, they built the model on one main assumption, which is that stakeholder saliency is determined by the number of attributes (power, legitimacy, urgency) a stakeholder owns; see Figure 1 below. Then they labeled stakeholder categories as the following: (a) stakeholders with one attribute are called latent, therefore of low salience (1,2,3 in Figure 1); (b) stakeholders with two attributes are called expectant, therefore of moderate salience (4,5,6 in Figure 1); (c) stakeholders with all three attributes are called definitive, therefore highly salient (7 in Figure 1).

Mitchell et al. (1997) further outlined the attributes to have a clearer identification of salient stakeholders (Frooman, 1999). If a latent stakeholder holds power, but with no legitimacy or urgency to act upon his or her claims then he/she is labeled as a dormant stakeholder. If a stakeholder possesses legitimacy only, with no power or urgency, then he/she is discretionary. Yet, if a stakeholder has urgent claims but no power or legitimacy to pursue them, then he/she is labeled as a demanding stakeholder.

Secondly, if an expectant stakeholder, who possesses two attributes, has legitimate claims and power to pursue them but these claims are not urgent, then he/she is dominant expectant. If a stakeholder owns legitimate and urgent claims with no power to pursue them, then he/she is considered dependent expectant. That is, they depend on other stakeholders to pursue their claims. Lastly,

Figure 1. Qualitative classification of stakeholder attributes (Mitchell et al, 1997)

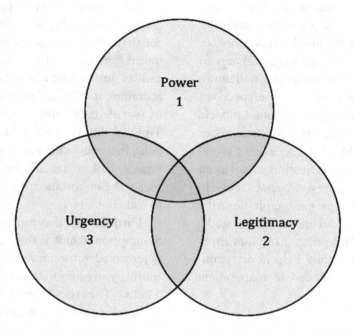

if a stakeholder has urgent claims and power to carry them out but with no legitimacy, then he/she is called dangerous expectant, as Mitchell et al. (1997) explained. Finally, as described earlier, if a stakeholder holds all three attributes then he/she has power to pursue their legitimate urgent claims, which makes managers pay attention immediately to such claims and their relationships with the stakeholder.

However, several researchers have criticized the identification model of Mitchell et al. (1997) alongside stakeholder theory. For example, Simmons and Lovegrove (2005) contended, after applying the model in their study of organization performance, that there are a number of issues, mainly the inability to explain how stakeholder individuals and groups gain and lose saliency through time: "we...identify [five] issues...explaining how stakeholder groups acquire or lose saliency" (p.498) Likewise, Beaulieu and Pasquero (2002) highlighted the same issue and argued that stakeholder dynamics as a concept is, relatively, not yet well-researched. They, additionally, ex-

plained that determining stakeholder saliency only from the manager's perception is insufficient and that stakeholders should be the focus of the whole theory. Mitchell et al. (1997) realized that their model provides a base for future research on stakeholder dynamics. Hence, this research aims at extending the model of Mitchell et al. (1997) by challenging its staticity. The appreciative system concepts are used to instrumentally dynamize the model in order to understand 'who matters' through time and what influence it has. In the next paragraphs, appreciative systems will be explained.

Appreciative Systems Concepts

In the late 1950s, Sir Geoffrey Vickers, after he had officially retired, established the appreciative systems concepts. He endeavored to uncover the complexity of human behaviors at individual, group, or society levels (Checkland, 2005). Therefore, with such a practical background he guided theorists in his field. He was, at the same time, aware of the prominent behavioral approaches that were used to understand human actions in firms (Blackmore, 2005); thus he called for a move to phenomenology (Blunden, 1984). Phenomenology makes sense of a certain phenomenon by exploring how individuals perceive it, i.e., it studies the experience as perceived by individuals (Lester, 1999). Thus, Blunden (1984) pointed out that Vickers was calling for a better model, explaining the process through which a human brain appreciates reality in a way that produces an action and even identifies the future experiences that the brain pays attention to. According to Vickers, the appreciative concept is founded on the idea that the appreciated everyday life exists because that is what we select to pay attention to (Murrell, 1999).

Vickers (1965), additionally, contended that human action is not based on a goal-seeking principle as the psychological approaches describe. Rather, he claimed that human action stems from the 'continual maintenance of relationships'. Vickers (1965) described that our appreciation of reality is guided by what relationships we pursue. He assumed that human goals take their meaning from the type of relationship he/she seeks. He illustrated this notion by an example of wanting an apple: if one desires an apple (a goal) then he/she, essentially, wishes eating it, selling it, or drawing it, i.e., he/she is establishing or changing relations with it. Accordingly, Vickers (1968, 1973) argued against the problem-solving techniques that assume that reality remains steady while choosing an optimal action. Vickers (1965, 1968) elucidated that the goal-led models fail to make sense of social issues because they cannot offer an explanation of the norms and standards that a person bases his/her action on.

Throughout his corpus, Vickers formed his concepts about reality and appreciation, led by his argument that human behaviors are based on relationship-seeking, and introduced a cognitive dynamic concept which he referred to as 'the appreciative system' (Alghaith et al., 2013). The appreciative system includes two main components, which are the appreciative process and the appreciative setting. The appreciative process, as Vickers (1965) described, is a cognitive process triggered as an individual observes a certain event or idea because of an inner interest or responsibility, which is called a 'set of readinesses'. Then, the individual subconsciously forms two inseparable judgments. The first judgment is made about realities, internal and external, related to the event or idea observed. The realities/facts might be present, future, or past. Then, he/she value-judges the significance of these facts as being good and satisfactory, or bad and improper, in accordance with certain norms and standards, which leads to making a decision on the relationships to be maintained, eluded, or modified. This process, at the end of the appreciative cycle, results in an action influencing the present reality and shaping experiences in the future. This appreciative process and the subsequent action are together referred to as 'the appreciative setting' (Checkland, 2005).

In 1986, Checkland and Casar (1986) produced an operational model of Vickers' concepts in order to facilitate using the appreciative systems to understand human behavior. Figure 2 shows their model, which is slightly adapted for the purpose of this research. The model demonstrates how the appreciation process (i.e. observing certain events or ideas, judging their realities and valuing them compared to norms and standards, choosing relationships, and producing a subsequent action), through time, feeds into the everyday experienced life and is generated by it (Checkland & Casar, 1986).

To conclude, Checkland and Casar (1986) defined five key themes elicited from Vickers' corpus (1965, 1968, 1970, 1983), which according to them humanized 'system' as a notion. The first theme is the day-to-day experienced life as a flux of events and ideas, which Vickers also referred to as the 'lebenswelt'. Secondly, the judgments of reality (what the situation is/was/will be) and what is good, bad, accepted, rejected. The third

Figure 2. The appreciative system recursive loop
Adapted from Checkland and Casar (1986)

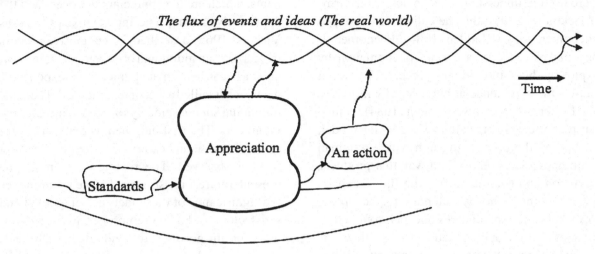

theme is the relationship-driven, not goal-led, actions. The fourth is that actions are produced by subconscious judgments. Fifth and finally, the appreciative process elements, including reality and value judgments and the subsequent actions, are ordered and interconnected as a system because a change in one element affects another.

METHODOLOGY

Research Philosophy

Easterby-Smith, Thorpe, and Lowe (2002) described that there are philosophical propositions behind any research, which range from positivism to social constructionism. The positivism approach views social reality as existing externally and that a researcher has to examine it objectively through experimentation. However, social constructionism views reality in a subjective way, i.e. it tends to interpret complex phenomena and how people react and assign meaning to them. Therefore, since this research is trying to make sense out of the complex context of an ICT strategic project in terms of its stakeholders, then social constructionism is adopted as an appropriate philosophical approach.

In the same vein, Hirschhiem (1992) explained that the context of IT projects is socially constructed. Myers and Avison (1997), also, pointed out that an in-depth case study is among the most popular and relevant qualitative methods when trying to understand complex contexts. Thus, case study was chosen as the research design to explore stakeholder dynamics and their influence within the ICT strategic project context. Nevertheless, it is important to note that case study approach might be criticized for not enabling generalizability of results. Flyvbjerg (2006) argued against this criticism and explained that if researchers cannot generalize results then this "does not mean that it cannot enter into the collective process of knowledge accumulation in a given field... [a] phenomenological case study without any attempt to generalize can certainly be of value in this process and has often helped cut a path toward scientific innovation" (p.227).

The next section explains the logic behind using case study methodology in this research.

Case Study

A case study is a mechanism that is used to explore a phenomenon in practice-or a theory- by following specific measures (Knight & Ruddock, 2008). Yin (2003), also, highlighted that it enables making sense of complex phenomena, especially those related to social contexts and everyday events. Similarly, Eisenhardt (1989) described that single or multiple case studies are significant in exploring dynamics happening in everyday life, in particular micro-level dynamics within a specific context (Corbin & Strauss, 2008).

To further guide researchers into properly utilizing case study approach, Yin (2003) explained that if the research focus is on understanding a particular context and the key question to be answered is how and why, then case study is the appropriate methodology to be used. Furthermore, he stated that case study supports researchers in building theories and challenging existing ones, due to the rich data it generates. Therefore, despite the limitations mentioned in the previous section this research adopted case study as the most apposite methodology to be utilized. The main purpose of this study is to understand 'how' stakeholder dynamics emerge in a complex context of an ICT strategic project, and how such dynamics influence the alignment process. Moreover, this study challenges the staticity inherent in an existing theory, which is stakeholder theory.

The following subsections cover case study type, case selection, unit of analysis and data collection methods, which are the four practical case study criteria provided by Benbasat, Goldstein, and Mead (1987) for researchers to apply when choosing case research.

Case Study Type

This criterion indicates the number of cases to be incorporated in the research design in order to tackle the main research focus. Yin (2003) described that case study can be either multiple cases or a single case. A multiple case study design allows the repeating of cases and conducting cross-analysis in order to get the evidence required (Ulkuniemi, 2003). Nevertheless, Ulkuniemi

(2003) pointed out that multiple case studies normally require enormous resources and along time, which are not feasible for a researcher with limited time and resources. Yin (2003) also argued that despite the strong evidence provided by multiple case studies, they demand strenuous efforts to be carried out. However, Ulkuniemi (2003) and Yin (2003) stressed that when choosing a single case study design then a rationale must be provided by the researcher. Hence, as this research is a single case study, a rationale justifying adopting it is presented in the following paragraphs.

Yin (2003) emphasized that the choice between a single or multiple case design needs to be kept open throughout the research course. He argued that this is beneficial for two reasons: (1) The chosen single case may appear to be a misrepresentation of the phenomenon examined by the researcher; or (2) the case gets hindered by some obstacles, which is also a reason indicated by Stake (1995). Accordingly, while executing this case study, the option of incorporating a second case was taken into consideration. However, throughout the research process the single case design proved to be the most suitable one, given the goal and complex context of the research.

Secondly, external factors might influence the process of conducting the case markedly. Therefore, a multiple-case design, which entails replicating the design, might be problematic Yin (2003). In this study, making sense of the emergence of salient stakeholder dynamics and their influence over time on the IT alignment process in a complex context makes it more reasonable to select a single case design. It not only facilitates having a holistic understanding of the case but also allows contemplating it more exhaustively. Thirdly, Yin (2003) explained that if a research is to challenge and extend a well-established theory, like this study, then an in-depth single-case study is advised. Vaughan (1992) emphasized Yin's point and added that the unique details that a researcher can get from an in-depth single case study increase his/her theoretical insights.

Case Selection

If a single case design is adopted then the selection of the specific case needs to be based on a specific rationale. Silverman (2000) indicated that a case has to be purposively chosen; particularly the researcher must consider the time available and the accessibility to data. Moreover, Stake (2005) indicated that a researcher can randomly choose a case. However, the case from which the researcher will mostly learn from must be selected. Therefore, the ICT strategic project examined here was selected for three reasons. First, regarding accessibility, the researcher had permission from the Ministry of Health (MOH) to explore ICT project stakeholder context in one of its major specialized hospitals, which is King Khalid Eye Specialist Hospital (KKESH). It is a 250-bed hospital, opened in 1983 and considered to be the largest ophthalmic tertiary referral center in Saudi Arabia (Mufti, 2000). KKESH allowed the researcher to access archived emails, plans, charts, evaluation forms for the IT project, surveys and flyers, i.e. rich documentary resources. Second, this research is based on the researcher's PhD dissertation, therefore the time available for accomplishing it was limited. The researcher had the opportunity to allocate 5 months at the project site. Finally, the nature of the IT project chosen here is complex. It is strategic in a public system and has been running for a long time. It facilitated examining past and present dynamics in an extremely intricate context and learning from it.

Unit of Analysis

Yin (2003) described that a unit of analysis can be systems, events, relationships, or more concrete entities like individuals and programs. He also highlighted that researchers need to derive the unit of analysis from the main research objective. Patton (2002), also, noted that the identification of the unit of analysis must stem from not only

the research purpose but also theory the underlying the case study. Therefore, as the key purpose of this study is to understand how stakeholder saliency dynamics emerge over time and influence IT alignment, and based on the interpretive framework adopted, events generating change in saliency dynamics and resulting in the influence represent the unit of analysis. *The changing events* targeted are not only current events but also historical events that occurred when the ICT project was initiated. Such a holistic perspective provides whole, rather than partial, insights into the stakeholder saliency dynamics phenomenon.

Data Collection Method

Myers (1997) explained that in order to understand a phenomenon from the viewpoint of individuals experiencing it, then qualitative sources of data should be used. Yin (2003), also, described that in qualitative case studies the semi-structured interview technique is suitable to help researchers answer how question, as well as why. Therefore, in 2009 the empirical data gathering began and lasted for five months. 40 semi-structured in-depth interviews were carried out and ranged between 20 to over 140 minutes. Additionally, secondary data were gathered from a number of documentary sources, such as archived emails, project plans and charters, evaluation forms, surveys and flyers.

Furthermore, the interview themes and questions were piloted as the researcher carried out a preliminary analysis using primary and secondary resources, which were collected at the early phases of data collection. George and Bennett (2005) indicated that conducting a preliminary analysis is important as it assists the researcher in avoiding any difficulties that might occur during the following main analysis. Finally, data were analyzed exhaustively using a time-series analysis and Atlas.ti, which is Qualitative Data Analysis Software, to support the researcher in managing the extensive data analysis.

Findings

This section presents the results of the case analysis. In general, the researcher identified 9 changing events that were categorized into 3 key phases: Phase 1-i.e. project antecedents-included two events, Phase 2-i.e. project emergence-consisted of four events, and Phase 3-i.e. project implementation-had three events.

The following subsections intend to demonstrate the applicability of the interpretive framework developed to understand stakeholder saliency dynamics and the resulting influence on IT alignment process. However, it does not intend to present a thorough explanation of the stakeholder dynamics and influences that happened throughout the ICT project. Therefore, for the purpose of this chapter, one changing event from Phase 3 is chosen, which is the 'submission of audit committee's report to the MOH', to demonstrate the conceptual framework of this study. This event is selected as it includes three different statuses of saliency attributes (i.e. lost, gained, and maintained), which eventually reveals the saliency dynamics of stakeholders in this event and hence the influence it makes on alignment.

A BRIEF INTRODUCTION TO THE EVENT

During the implementation phase (i.e. phase 3) three changing events happened. In the first event, which is the 'failure of HIS data migration by the ICT provider team', the key-user salient group declined to go live with the HIS system, delaying the project's progress. As a result, senior management requested a project progress report from the ICT project teams (i.e. both the hospital and the IT provider teams). That led to the second changing event, which is the 'submission of the specially commissioned project progress report'. Senior management appreciated this event and formally vetoed going live with the HIS system. That

again hindered the project progress. Both events resulted in gained and lost saliency to stakeholder individuals and groups involved.

To tackle the situation, senior management employed an external audit committee to evaluate the situation and decide the future of the IT project. In 2009, the report of the audit committee was submitted to the MOH. This event, i.e. the 'submission of audit committee's report', immediately triggered the attention of the MOH, as it is the entity that is financing and responsible for this ICT strategic progress. Thus the MOH came to play a significant role in this event. An MOH senior described: "... the minister's office called and asked me to visit the hospital first thing in the morning as the ICT project there was facing problems and the Supervisor General was crying for help..." As a definitive player with power, legitimacy and urgent claims, the MOH appreciated the event in a way that influenced the saliency of other involved stakeholders and hence influenced the project and its alignment process.

The next subsection provides an overview of salient stakeholder groups involved, mainly the ICT provider team, the ICT hospital teams, the hospital senior management, the MOH, and external auditors.

Stakeholder Saliency Analysis

Using Mitchell et al.'s model, Table 1 represents a tabulation of stakeholder groups who played vital roles in this event and the status of their saliency attributes. Further explanation is provided in the following paragraphs.

During this event, senior management continued to maintain the power and legal legitimacy that it had throughout the previous events. However, what changed was the urgency that senior management had for its claims during the audit event. Their claims concerning the ICT situation were time-sensitive and their relationship was critical to other stakeholder groups. The Supervisor General commented on the situation: "...We have reached

Table 1. Stakeholder groups' tabulation during the event of the submission of the specially commissioned project progress report

Stakeholder Group	Stake	Status
Senior management (Definitive stakeholder group)	*Power*	
	- Utilitarian	Maintained
	Legitimacy	
	- Legal	Maintained
	Urgency	
	Criticality and time sensitivity of claims/relationships	Gained
Audit committee (Definitive stakeholder group)	*Power*	
	- Utilitarian	Gained
	Legitimacy	
	- Legal	Gained
	- Moral	Gained
	Urgency	
	Criticality and time sensitivity of claims/relationships	Gained
MOH (Definitive stakeholder group)	*Power*	
	- Utilitarian	Maintained
	Legitimacy	
	- Legal	Maintained
	- Moral	Gained
	Urgency	
	Criticality and time sensitivity of claims/relationships	Gained
Hospital ICT team (Expectant dependent stakeholder group)	*Legitimacy*	
	- Legal	Maintained
	- Moral	Maintained
	Urgency	
	Criticality and time sensitivity of claims/relationships	Gained
Provider ICT team (Expectant dependent stakeholder group)	*Power*	
	- Utilitarian	Lost
	Legitimacy	
	- Legal	Lost
	- Moral	Maintained
	Urgency	
	Criticality and time sensitivity of claims/relationships	Gained

an end... the company cannot finish the project, not at all...." Moreover, in describing the criticality of having a relationship with senior management, the hospital ICT project manager said: "...[We will do] anything to create a common language between us and senior management..." Hence, senior management maintained its definitiveness during this event.

Having a temporary contract with the hospital, the audit committee gained power and legal legitimacy, as Table 1 shows. Furthermore, the committee's interest in assessing and saving the project conferred a moral legitimacy on the group. The chief auditor indicated: "… they contacted me, told me about the situation … they wanted my opinion, so I worked there…I told them, when I started working, I don't care about you, I care about the project…" Additionally, the committee's claims concerning the ICT project status were urgent. In other words, their claims were time-sensitive and critical, which made other salient stakeholder groups respond to them immediately. The chief auditor stated:

… *The contract duration was about to end, the company was asking for a 6-month extension, senior management was not sure whether to go on or seize it. Maintenance bidding was about to start and the project itself hadn't finished yet…if the project had finished I would have approved that [the maintenance bidding start]…*

The supervisor general explained his relationship with the audit committee: "I am not an IT expert, I am a physician, so to be fair I hired an auditing team of consultants…"

Senior management, when the audit report was completed, submitted it to the MOH. The Supervisor General clarified: "…to be legal we informed the MOH [about the report]…" Therefore, the MOH started to play a definitive role in this event. The MOH continued possessing power and legal legitimacy as the entity that owns the hospital and the project. A senior from the MOH stated: "… the minister sent me to investigate the project situation…" Additionally, the MOH was interested in keeping the project, as it is an indication of the MOH's ability to automate other hospitals. That made MOH a morally legitimate stakeholder group. One MOH senior commented: "…the result will be having hospitals with electronic systems to enable us (the MOH) to link hospitals together according to the strategic plan…" Moreover, the MOH gained time-sensitive claims

regarding the project. An MOH senior described: "…the minister's office called and asked me to visit the hospital first thing in the morning as the ICT project there was facing problems…" Furthermore, the MOH relationship with other stakeholders, primarily senior management, was critical. One MOH senior pointed out: "…the Supervisor General was crying for help…" Hence, time sensitivity of MOH claims and criticality of its relationship to stakeholders called for immediate attention from salient stakeholders. The MOH, then, was a definitive stakeholder group with power, legitimacy and urgency during the audit event.

The last two stakeholder groups – which are the company and the hospital project teams – also played a role in this event. The hospital ICT project team had already lost its definitive role during the previous event when senior management had seized its power over the project, and that continued throughout this event. However, the hospital ICT project team maintained its legal and moral legitimacy- legally, because of their ongoing contract with the hospital itself, and morally because the team was still interested in making the project succeed. Yet, when the audit report was issued the team gained urgent claims regarding the audit report. Furthermore, their relationship with senior management continued being critical to them. The hospital ICT project manager indicated: "…we have gone too far in this, it's disastrous now… I was willing to have an external audit or [do] anything to create a common language between us [hospital team and senior management]…" Consequently, this group was an expectant dependent stakeholder group with legitimacy and urgent claims and critical relationships, but with no power to act on them.

The company project team, on the other hand, lost its power and legal legitimacy due to the MOH appreciative process that will be explained in the next subsection. One MOH senior stated: "I suggested…they start with another company" Therefore, the contract with the ICT provider was not extended. Nevertheless, the team maintained their moral legitimacy due to the long-term benefits expected from the ICT project. The Healthcare Unit manager stated: "… we have a reputation to care about… we do not leave projects behind…" and the company project manager commented: "… we intended to gain them back, they are a potential reference for the company in the future…"The company team, additionally, gained urgent claims in the audit event. Such claims were time-sensitive to the company team and their relationship to other stakeholders, as well, was critical. These time-sensitive claims and critical relationships called for urgent attention by other stakeholders, mainly the MOH and senior management. The Healthcare unit manager clarified: "I was literally living in the hospital at that time, everyday! We wanted the project to succeed… when the clash [the audit event] happened we admitted the delay, but we wanted from senior management a free extension…" The chief auditor described the company's demands: "… the company was asking for a 6-month extension…" Consequently, the ICT provider stakeholder group was an expectant dependent stakeholder group with legitimacy and urgency, but without power to pursue its agenda.

The next subsection will explain the appreciative process of MOH that produced these stakeholder saliency dynamics and the influence on the strategic alignment process.

Appreciative Process Model Application

When senior management submitted the audit committee's report to the MOH, it paid immediate attention to this report and started appreciating it motivated by its responsibility and obligations towards the ICT program. That is, their set of readinesses had been triggered, see Figure 3. One MOH member indicated: "… the minister sent me to investigate the project situation…" The immediacy in paying attention to the event by the MOH, as a definitive stakeholder group,

was due to the time-sensitivity of the ICT project situation and criticality of the relationship with senior management during this event. The MOH information systems consultant explained: "… the minister's office called and asked me to visit the hospital first thing in the morning as the ICT project there was facing problems and the Supervisor General was crying for help…" Mitchell et al. (1997) described that urgency attribute is not only a measure of stakeholder saliency, but also it accounts for the speed with which a stakeholder individual or group responds to an event.

Once the urgent attention of the MOH was paid to the submission of the audit report it started judging certain internal and external realities, valuing them, considering relationships involved in this event, deciding upon one and, based on all that, producing a decision that led to a ultimate action. The MOH team judged internal realities that were related to the hospital context. The first fact they observed was that the IT department was not performing satisfactorily and failed to keep its staff. Second, they noticed that senior management was not intending to make the project continue until it delivered its goals. Furthermore, the MOH team appreciated the fact that its job was to find a way of saving the project. The MOH team, finally, perceived the results of the audit committee report. An MOH senior explained:

… The IT was not doing well…in a huge project like that they lost a medical informatics and chair leader…the hospital leadership wanted to end the project…the report estimated [that the company finished] 25% [of the project]…senior management started telling me about how they thought that the IT staff were incapable, how the company wasn't delivering the applications, and how the reports were not true…the MOH work is not to find whose fault, but to see if we can save it or not…

Externally, the MOH team observed a number of related realities. The first external reality they noticed was that the HIS subcontractor started

Figure 3. Appreciative process of the MOH stakeholder group during the Submission of Audit Committee Report event
(Alghaith et al., 2013)

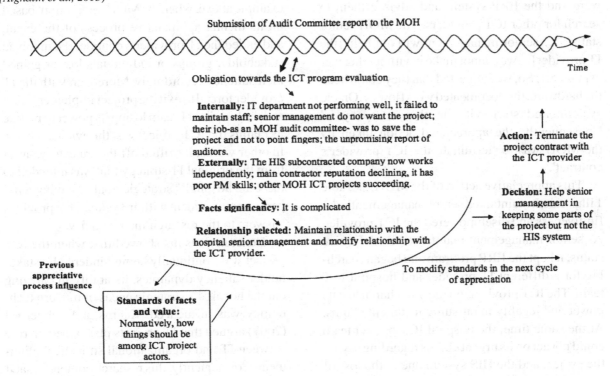

working independently, i.e. it was no longer in a contractual relationship with the main provider. The second fact they appreciated was that the reputation of the main contractor was deteriorating. It started assigning its project to less qualified project managers. The MOH team, also, noted that a partial implementation of the HIS system was succeeding in another MOH hospital, although this other hospital was not as advanced and specialized as the hospital studied here. The MOH senior commented:

... The HIS provider ended its subcontract with the main contractor... another MOH hospital partially implemented this HIS system and it worked and the users' satisfaction was high, although it is not advanced... the company's problem was that it neglects projects and hands them to inexpert project managers...

These realities were value-judged by the MOH team as being complicated and problematic. The MOH senior stated: "...they have lots of problems... and complications..." The MOH team value judgment was a result of comparing the realities to standards of how things should be normatively among any ICT project teams. An MOH senior explained: "... if senior management does not like the IT people, does not believe in the project anymore, and it started lobbying with [other] seniors against the project, then things are not going to work, it is lots of complications... people should change [the way they think]..." The standards stemmed from the MOH's previous experiences (i.e. previous appreciative systems) in other MOH hospitals. As the MOH team appreciated the audit report and the factual realities, it chose to *maintain* its relationship with senior management and *elude* its relationship with the

ICT provider. Therefore, the MOH team decided to help senior management in keeping the hardware and the ERP system and advised them to search for other ICT providers. The MOH senior stated: "...senior management will not help [the IT provider]...we cannot make it without their acceptance... So, we suggested that they could keep the hardware, the documented workflows...Oracle system...and start with another company..." Consequently, the appreciated action taken by the MOH was to 'terminate the ICT provider's contract'.

This appreciative action of the MOH, as Table 1 illustrated, maintained senior management's definitiveness and disempowered the ICT provider. As senior management maintained its definitive status, it kept the ERP program and began searching for a different IT provider and hospital ICT team. The ICT provider, on the other hand, lost its power and legality in pursuing its urgent claims. At the same time, the hospital ICT project team could not act on its urgent claims regarding saving the project and the HIS system due to the loss of power in the previous event. Thus, the project was suspended and thrown into a chaotic, uncertain situation.

DISCUSSION

The literature review has discussed the nature of IT strategy and IT strategic projects, their vital role in both public and private sectors, and the significance of continuously aligning IT strategy to the organizational needs and strategic objectives. Based on such arguments and the analysis findings, this section explains how saliency dynamics, as a critical social component of IT strategy, can inform the alignment process concept.

The findings presented above illustrated that stakeholders' saliency dynamics reside in the nature of the relationship they pursue with each other. Stakeholders continually appreciate the changing events in a way causing involved stakeholders to lose or gain saliency and influence the ICT project's strategic direction. In the example above, when the MOH took action, based on its mental appreciative process of the event, and ended the IT provider's contract the involved stakeholder groups or individuals lost or gained their saliency accordingly. Moreover, with the IT provider forced to exit the project implementation and the hospital IT team losing its power to pursue its claims the ICT project was thrown into chaos. In other words, it drifted off the trajectory, away from the original IT strategy that was intended to meet the hospital's strategic goal of having a paperless environment within 3 years. That provides answers to the research main enquiry.

Generally, results showed that when the ICT project was continually being hindered by stakeholder saliency dynamics, its ability in carrying out the hospital's strategic needs of modern technology was influenced. Kearns and Sabherwal (2007) argued that IT projects play a median role between IT and organizational strategies' alignment. Consequently, this research contends that it is significant to understand how salient stakeholders think while acting, in order to successfully align IT and organizational strategies. Cicmil Williams, Thomas, and Hodgson (2006) argued that understanding "the actuality of projects means focusing on social process and how practitioners think in action, in the local situation of a living present" (p.676). Using these research terms, it is vital to understand that stakeholders' lost/gained saliency and the resulting actions are embedded in the subconscious appreciative processes experienced within the consecutive changing events setting. The appreciative processes through which they mentally negotiate certain relationships to be modified, eluded, or maintained, eventually influence the project trajectory.

Despite the relationship-driven dynamics, the ICT project salient stakeholders endeavored to align the project's strategic plan with the hospital's overall strategic needs during the first two phases, i.e. the antecedents and the project emergence.

However, when the actual implementation process was embarked upon and more salient stakeholders got involved a gradual drift from the alignment process occurred as a result of continual stakeholder saliency dynamics emerging in response to events. The strategic project was adapting to its stakeholder saliency dynamics, as Artto, Kujala, Dietrich, and Martinsuo (2008) explained: "The project adapts to its stakeholders' goals and objectives set for the project, to stakeholders' standards of practice, and potentially to the industry practice that the stakeholders represent" (p.10). Such adaptation resulted in an unintended deviation from the alignment of the IT strategic project to the hospital's substantial needs. The hospital ICT project manager referred to his failing efforts in achieving the ICT project objectives and in meeting the hospital's needs: "I was giving them choices and solutions … I was willing to have an external auditing or anything to create a common language between us and senior management…I was trying to protect the project…" Furthermore, the hospital HIS team leader described the project status at that stage: "… this is a project that must work out…it is for the hospital not for any particular person…" Thus failing to realize the very dynamic, interpretive and evolving nature of the ICT project, as it was 'strategic', led to the misalignment being witnessed as happening gradually.

Artto et al. (2008) argued that project strategy and strategy literature assume that a project strategy includes a static plan or certain 'plan-like descriptions', while ignoring the project multistakeholder environment, how it fits in, and the dynamic nature of strategies. Cheah and Garvin (2004) contended that despite the IT strategy, IT implementation appears to follow 'vague goals', leading to a lack of linkage between IT and firms' strategies. Therefore, Artto et al. (2008) called for a stakeholder perspective - to help in "understanding how project strategy…evolves across a network of several stakeholders, each with different and even conflicting objectives concerning the project at hand" (p.11). Hence, this research provides a response to the call of Artto et al. (2008) for a new thinking of project strategy, in particular the approaches through which stakeholders shape and influence the project strategy. Inspired by the work of Winter and Szczepanek (2009), Figure 4 sums up and illustrates the insights provided in this chapter about stakeholder saliency dynamics in order to inform the alignment literature. It shows saliency dynamics as a critical factor to be considered and monitored alongside the traditional production image of projects by practitioners, and academics, if they aim to achieve better IT alignment results.

Figure 4. IT strategy critical components to be aligned to organizational strategy

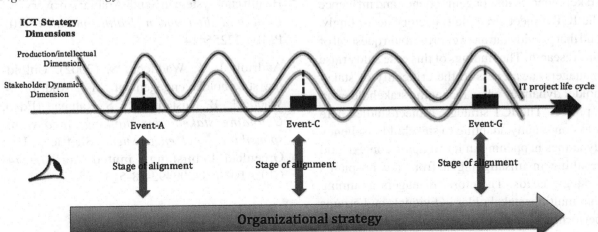

CONCLUSION

The single case study presented in this chapter focuses on understanding the emergence of stakeholder saliency dynamics and the resulting influence on the IT alignment process. To address this enquiry the researcher developed a theoretical framework to help make sense of such dynamics and their influence.

The literature review section shed light on the contextual literature to which this research contributes. Mainly, it covered the IT strategy, IT alignment, and IT project management literature. Moreover, it visited the literary texts in stakeholder theory and appreciative systems concepts, which form the basis of the theoretical framework used to interpret stakeholder dynamics and hence understand the influence. Appreciative systems concepts were used as a dynamizing instrument challenging the staticity of stakeholder theory. Appreciative systems proved to be helpful not only in tracking stakeholder dynamics over time but also in making sense of how they emerge and leave an influence on project reality.

The findings sections explained that stakeholder saliency dynamics stem from the nature of the relationship they pursue with each other. Continual appreciation of changing events in the ICT project context results in stakeholders subconsciously selecting to maintain, elude, or modify certain relationships. That causes involved stakeholders to lose or gain saliency and influence the ICT project strategic trajectory accordingly, and that provides an answer to the main question of this research. The findings of this case study raise managers' awareness to the criticality of stakeholder dynamics when managing stakeholders in a project. The ICT strategic project studied here was continually adapting to stakeholder saliency dynamics happening in its complex context, and resulting in misaligning it from the hospital's strategic needs. Therefore, managers assuming that multiple stakeholder individuals and groups perform according to plans might face challenges in accomplishing IT projects. Furthermore, findings inform IT alignment literature about the approaches through which stakeholders shape and influence the alignment process between IT and organization strategies. IT strategy, normally translated into IT strategic projects in businesses, exists in dynamic social systems where stakeholders influentially interact making it critical for both academics and practitioners/managers to be aware of it.

To conclude, the approach for understanding stakeholder dynamics laid out in this research aspires to provide a base for future researchers aiming to produce an IT alignment mechanism in which the stakeholder dynamics perspective is to be incorporated and managed.

REFERENCES

Al-Hatmi, B. (2013). *Public IT Investment: The Success of IT Projects*. Singapore: Partridge Publishing.

Alghaith, T., Brown, D., & Worthington, D. (2013). *Stakeholder saliency dynamics in strategic ICT projects in the Saudi public healthcare system: appreciative systems perspective. (Doctor of Philosphy)*. United Kingdom: Lancaster University Management School.

Almalki, M., Fitzgerald, G., & Clark, M. (2011). Health care system in Saudi Arabia: An overview. *Eastern Mediterranean Health Journal, 17*(10). PMID:22256414

Andriof, J., & Waddock, S. (2002). Unfolding stakeholder engagement. In J. Andriof, S. Waddock, B. Husted, & S. S. Rahman (Eds.), *Unfolding stakeholder thinking: theory, responsibility, and engagement*. Sheffield, UK: Greenleaf Publishing Limited. doi:10.9774/GLEAF.978-1-909493-28-5_3

Artto, K., Kujala, J., Dietrich, P., & Martinsuo, M. (2008). What is project strategy? *International Journal of Project Management*, *26*(1), 4–12. doi:10.1016/j.ijproman.2007.07.006

Asrilhant, B., Dyson, R. G., & Meadows, M. (2004). Strategic projects on the sector of oil exploration and production. *Revista de Administração de Empresas*, *44*(1), 82–95. doi:10.1590/S0034-75902004000100006

Avison, D., Jones, J., Powell, P., & Wilson, D. (2004a). Using and validating the strategic alignment model. *The Journal of Strategic Information Systems*, *13*(3), 223–246. doi:10.1016/j.jsis.2004.08.002

Avison, D., Jones, J., Powell, P., & Wilson, D. (2004b). Using and validating the strategic alignment model. *The Journal of Strategic Information Systems*, *13*(3), 223–246. doi:10.1016/j.jsis.2004.08.002

Ballantine, J. A., & Cunningham, N. (Eds.). (1999). *Strategic information systems planning: applying private sector frameworks in UK public healthcare.*

Ballantine, J. A., & Cunningham, N. (Eds.). (2002). *Strategic information systems planning: applying private sector frameworks in UK public healthcare.*

Beaulieu, S., & Pasquero, J. (2002). Reintroducing stakeholder dynamics in stakeholder thinking: A negotiated-order perspective. *Journal of Corporate Citizenship*, *6*(6), 53–69. doi:10.9774/GLEAF.4700.2002.su.00007

Benbasat, I., Goldstein, D. K., & Mead, M. (1987). The case research strategy in studies of information systems. *Management Information Systems Quarterly*, *11*(3), 369–386. doi:10.2307/248684

Blackmore, C. (2005). Learning to appreciate learning systems for environmental decision making: A 'work-in-progress' perspective. *Systems Research and Behavioral Science*, *22*(4), 329–341. doi:10.1002/sres.697

Blunden, M. (1984). Geoffrey Vickers—an intellectual journey. Open Systems Group (Ed.), The Vickers papers, 3-42.

Brummer, J. J. (1991). *Corporate responsibility and legitimacy: An interdisciplinary analysis.* Greenwood Press New York.

Chan, Y. E., & Reich, B. H. (2007). IT alignment: What have we learned? *Journal of Information Technology*, *22*(4), 297–315. doi:10.1057/palgrave.jit.2000109

Cheah, C. Y. J., & Garvin, M. J. (2004). An open framework for corporate strategy in construction. *Engineering, Construction, and Architectural Management*, *11*(3), 176–188. doi:10.1108/09699980410535787

Checkland, P. (2005). Webs of significance: The work of Geoffrey Vickers. *Systems Research and Behavioral Science*, *22*(4), 285–290. doi:10.1002/sres.692

Checkland, P., & Casar, A. (1986). Vickers' concept of an appreciative system: A systemic account. *Journal of Applied Systems Analysis*, (13): 3–17.

20. Chong, J. L., Tan, F. B., & Felix, B. (2012). IT governance in collaborative networks: A sociotechnical perspective. *Pacific Asia Journal of the Association for Information Systems*, *4*(2), 31–48.

Cicmil, S., Williams, T., Thomas, J., & Hodgson, D. (2006). Rethinking project management: Researching the actuality of projects. *International Journal of Project Management*, *24*(8), 675–686. doi:10.1016/j.ijproman.2006.08.006

Corbin, J. M., & Strauss, A. L. (2008). *Basics of qualitative research: Techniques and procedures for developing grounded theory*. Los Angeles, Calif.: Sage Publications, Inc.

Council of Health Services. (2009). Healthcare Strategies in the Kingdom of Saudi Arabia. (B/39175). Saudi Arabia.

Donaldson, T., & Preston, L. E. (1995). The stakeholder theory of the corporation: Concepts, evidence, and implications. *Academy of Management Review*, 65–91.

Dubey, S., & Hefley, W. E. (2011). *Greening ITIL: Expanding the ITIL lifecycle for Green IT*. Paper presented at the Technology Management in the Energy Smart World (PICMET), 2011 Proceedings of PICMET'11.

Easterby-Smith, M., Thorpe, R., & Lowe, A. (2002). *Management research: An introduction*. London, Thousand Oaks: Sage Publications Ltd.

Eden, C., & Ackermann, F. (1998). *Making strategy: The journey of strategic management*. Sage Publications Ltd.

Eisenhardt, K. M. (1989). Building theories from case study research. *Academy of Management Review*, 532–550.

Engwall, M. (2003). No project is an island: Linking projects to history and context. *Research Policy*, *32*(5), 789–808. doi:10.1016/S0048-7333(02)00088-4

Flyvbjerg, B. (2006). Five misunderstandings about case-study research. *Qualitative Inquiry*, *12*(2), 219–245. doi:10.1177/1077800405284363

Freeman, R. E. (1984). Strategic management: A stakeholder approach. *Analysis*, *38*(01).

Freeman, R. E., Harrison, J. S., & Wicks, A. C. (2007). *Managing for stakeholders: Survival, reputation, and success*. Yale University Press.

Friedman, A. L., & Miles, S. (2002). Developing stakeholder theory. *Journal of Management Studies*, *39*(1), 1–21. doi:10.1111/1467-6486.00280

Frooman, J. (1999). Stakeholder influence strategies. *Academy of Management Review*, 191–205.

Galliers, R., & Leidner, D. (Eds.). (2003). *Strategic Information Management: Challenges and Strategies in Managing Information Systems*. Oxford, Great Britain: Butterworth-Heinemann.

Galliers, R. D. (1993). IT strategies: Beyond competitive advantage. *The Journal of Strategic Information Systems*, *2*(4), 283–291. doi:10.1016/0963-8687(93)90007-W

George, A. L., & Bennett, A. (2005). *Case studies and theory development in the social sciences*. The MIT Press.

Gottschalk, P. (1999a). Strategic information systems planning: The IT strategy implementation matrix. *European Journal of Information Systems*, *8*(2), 107–118. doi:10.1057/palgrave.ejis.3000324

Gottschalk, P. (1999b). Strategic information systems planning: The IT strategy implementation matrix. *European Journal of Information Systems*, *8*(2), 107–118. doi:10.1057/palgrave.ejis.3000324

Heeks, R., & Bhatnagar, S. (Eds.). (1999). *Understanding success and failure in information age reform*.

Henderson, J. C., & Venkatraman, N. (1993). Strategic alignment: Leveraging information technology for transforming organizations. *IBM Systems Journal*, *32*(1), 4–16. doi:10.1147/sj.382.0472

Hirschheim, R. (1992). Information systems epistemology: An historical perspective. In R. Galliers (Ed.), *Information Systems Research: Issues, Methods and Practical Guidelines* (pp. 28–60). London: Blackweel Scientific Publications.

Iveroth, E., Fryk, P., & Rapp, B. (2013). Information technology strategy and alignment issues in health care organizations. *Health Care Management Review*, *38*(3), 188–200. doi:10.1097/HMR.0b013e31826119d7 PMID:22722318

Janvrin, D., Bierstaker, J., & Lowe, D. J. (2008). An examination of audit information technology use and perceived importance. *Accounting Horizons*, *22*(1), 1–21. doi:10.2308/acch.2008.22.1.1

Kappelman, L. A., McKeeman, R., & Zhang, L. (2006). Early warning signs of IT project failure: The dominant dozen. *Information Systems Management*, *23*(4), 31–36. doi:10.1201/1078.10580530/46352.23.4.20060901/95110.4

Kashanchi, R., &Toland, J. (2008). Investigating the social dimension of alignment: Focusing on communication and knowledge sharing. Proceedings of *ACIS 2008 (Vol. 2)*.

Kearns, G. S., & Sabherwal, R. (2007). Strategic alignment between business and information technology: A knowledge-based view of behaviors, outcome, and consequences. *Journal of Management Information Systems*, *23*(3), 129–162. doi:10.2753/MIS0742-1222230306

Knight, A., & Ruddock, L. (2008). *Advanced research methods in the built environment*. Blackwell Pub.

Lee, S. (2013). IT Governance Issues in Korean Government Integrated Data Center. *International Journal of Advancement in Computing Technology*, *5*(11), 438–444. doi:10.4156/ijact.vol5.issue11.54

Lester, S. (1999). An introduction to phenomenological research.

Lucas, H. (1999). *Information Technology and the Productivity Paradox: Assessing the Value of Investing in IT: Assessing the Value of Investing in IT*. New York: Oxford University Press.

Mitchell, R. K., Agle, B. R., & Wood, D. J. (1997). Toward a theory of stakeholder identification and salience: Defining the principle of who and what really counts. *Academy of Management Review*, 853–886.

Moghaddasi, H., Asadi, F., Hosseini, A., & Ebnehoseini, Z. (2012). E-health: A global approach with extensive semantic variation. *Journal of Medical Systems*, *36*(5), 3173–3176. doi:10.1007/s10916-011-9805-z PMID:22113437

Mufti, M. H. (2000). *Healthcare Development Strategies in the Kingdom of Saudi Arabia*. New York: Kluwer Academic.

Murrell, K. (1999). International and intellectual roots of appreciative inquiry. *Organization Development Journal*, *17*, 49–62.

Myers, M. D., & Avison, D. (1997). Qualitative research in information systems. *Management Information Systems Quarterly*, *21*(2), 241–242. doi:10.2307/249422

Nelson, R. R. (2007). IT project management: Infamous failures, classic mistakes, and best practices. *MIS Quarterly Executive*, *6*(2), 67–78.

Nota, G., & Aiello, R. (2014). Managing Uncertainty in Complex Projects. In M. Faggini & A. Parziale (Eds.), Complexity in Economics: Cutting Edge Research (pp. 81-97). Switzerland: Springer International Publishing. doi:10.1007/978-3-319-05185-7_5

Patton, M. Q. (2002). *Qualitative research & evaluation methods*. Thousand Oaks, CA. USA: Sage publication.

Perez-Batres, L. A., Doh, J. P., Miller, V. V., & Pisani, M. J. (2012). Stakeholder pressures as determinants of CSR strategic choice: Why do firms choose symbolic versus substantive self-regulatory codes of conduct? *Journal of Business Ethics*, *110*(2), 157–172. doi:10.1007/s10551-012-1419-y

Post, J. E., Lawrence, A. T., & Weber, J. (1996). *Business and society: Corporate strategy, public policy, ethics*. McGraw-Hill New York.

Reich, B. H., & Benbasat, I. (2000). Factors that influence the social dimension of alignment between business and information technology objectives. *Management Information Systems Quarterly*, *24*(1), 81–113. doi:10.2307/3250980

Sabherwal, R., & Chan, Y. E. (2001). Alignment between business and IS strategies: A study of prospectors, analyzers, and defenders. *Information Systems Research*, *12*(1), 11–33. doi:10.1287/isre.12.1.11.9714

Sauer, C., & Reich, B. H. (2009). Rethinking IT project management: Evidence of a new mindset and its implications. *International Journal of Project Management*, *27*(2), 182–193. doi:10.1016/j.ijproman.2008.08.003

Schwalbe, K. (2010). *Information technology project management*. Course Technology Ptr.

Silverman, D. (2000). *Doing qualitative research: a practical handbook*. London: Sage.

Simmons, J., & Lovegrove, I. (2005). Bridging the conceptual divide: Lessons from stakeholder analysis. *Journal of Organizational Change Management*, *18*(5), 495–513. doi:10.1108/09534810510614977

Söderlund, J., Vaagaasar, A. L., & Andersen, E. S. (2008). Relating, reflecting and routinizing: Developing project competence in cooperation with others. *International Journal of Project Management*, *26*(5), 517–526. doi:10.1016/j.ijproman.2008.06.002

Stake, R. E. (1995). *The art of case study research*. Sage Publications, Inc.

Stake, R. E. (2005). Qualitative case studies. In N. Denzin & Y. Lincoln (Eds.), *The Sage handbook of qualitative research* (pp. 443–466). Thousand Oaks, CA: Sage Publications Ltd.

Suchman, M. C. (1995). Managing legitimacy: Strategic and institutional approaches. *Academy of Management Review*, 571–610.

Teubner, R. (2007). Strategic information systems planning: A case study from the financial services industry. *The Journal of Strategic Information Systems*, *16*(1), 105–125. doi:10.1016/j.jsis.2007.01.002

Thiry, M. (2002). Combining value and project management into an effective programme management model. *International Journal of Project Management*, *20*(3), 221–227. doi:10.1016/S0263-7863(01)00072-2

Ulkuniemi, P. (2003). *Purchasing software components at the dawn of market*. University of Oulu.

Vaughan, D. (1992). Theory elaboration: The heuristics of case analysis. In C. Ragin & B. H. (Eds.), What is a Case? Exploring the foundations of social inquiry (pp. 173-202): Cambridge University Press.

Vickers, G. (1968). Value systems and social process. London, Sydney etc.: Tavistock Publications.

Vickers, G. (1970). *Freedom in a rocking boat: changing values in an unstable society*. London: Allen Lane.

Vickers, G. (1973). *Making institutions work*. London: Associated Business Programmes Ltd.

Vickers, G. (1983). *Human systems are different*. London, New York: Harper & Row.

Vickers, S. G. (1965). *The art of judgement: a study of policy making*. Chapman & Hall.

Ward, J., & Peppard, J. (2002). *Strategic planning for information systems* (Vol. 28). Wiley.

Weiss, J. W., & Anderson, D. Jr. (2004). CIOs and IT professionals as change agents, risk and stakeholder managers: A field study. *Engineering Management Journal*, *16*(2), 13–18. doi:10.1080/10429247.2004.11415244

Winter, M., Smith, C., Morris, P., & Cicmil, S. (2006). Directions for future research in project management: The main findings of a UK government-funded research network. *International Journal of Project Management*, *24*(8), 638–649. doi:10.1016/j.ijproman.2006.08.009

Winter, M., & Szczepanek, T. (2009). *Images of projects*. Gower Publishing, Ltd.

Wutyi, H. (2012). *An exploratory Study of Factor Influencing IT Project Initiation Decision*. Auckland University of Information Technology.

Yin, R. K. (2003). *Case Study Research: Design and Methods* (Vol. 5). Thousand Oaks, CA: Sage Publications.

Zahra, S. A., & George, G. (2002). The net-enabled business innovation cycle and the evolution of dynamic capabilities. *Information Systems Research*, *13*(2), 147–150. doi:10.1287/isre.13.2.147.90

Zhang, J., Dawes, S. S., & Sarkis, J. (2005). Exploring stakeholders' expectations of the benefits and barriers of e-government knowledge sharing. *Journal of Enterprise Information Management*, *18*(5), 548–567. doi:10.1108/17410390510624007

KEY TERMS AND DEFINITIONS

Appreciative Process: A cognitive process through which stakeholders make sense of events happening around them in the real world.

Event: An occurrence triggering the attention of stakeholders involved and leading to changing actions.

IT Alignment: A continuous process undertaken by an IT project team in order to ensure that the IT strategy and its resources are leveraged to achieve the overall organization's objectives.

Operational Model: An abstract representation of how a conceptual process occurs systematically.

Saliency: The level of importance a stakeholder individual or group obtains during a particular event.

Stakeholder Dynamics: Refer to the changing attributes, roles and perceptions of stakeholder individuals and groups throughout a project life cycle.

Strategic Project: A project to which strategic financial, human and physical resources are allocated and managed to realize strategic goals.

Chapter 10
Developing an E‑Learning Platform:
A Reflective Practitioner Perspective

Maria Potes Barbas
University of Aveiro, Portugal

ABSTRACT

This chapter applies the principle of reflective practice - as the capacity to reflect on action - so as to engage in a process of continuous learning about the implementation of an e-learning platform at the Polytechnic Institute of Santarem, Portugal. The chapter begins with an introduction to the role of reflective practice, a discussion of fundamental e-learning principles and an overview of the e-learning platform's information architecture. In addition, two methodological tools support the reflective thinking process and the extraction of recommendations: social network analysis and visualization of structured discussion forum activity, and an inductive thematic analysis of the postings to the platform's unstructured fora.

INTRODUCTION

Using a reflective practice angle, this chapter describes the stages that led to the implementation on an e-learning platform at a Portuguese Higher Education Institution, notably the use of the e-learning platform to promote the development of a community of practice, in the context of an MA in Education and Multimedia Communication. Since the author was involved in the development of the e-learning platform described in this chapter, reflective practice is understood here as a process of learning through and from experience towards developing new insights of individual professional practice (Mezirow, 1981; Boyd & Fales, 1983; Jarvis, 1992).

The reflections contained in this chapter are presented from the perspective of the instructor as facilitator, which implies embracing pedagogical roles, but also the roles of the technologist, researcher and administrator (Gilbert and Dabbagh, 2004; Bawane & Spector, 2009). Two methodological tools have supported the analysis of data that sustains the reflections contained in the chapter: real-time social network analysis and visualization of structured discussion forum activity using the Social Networks Adapting Pedagogical Practice (SNAPP) tool (Dawson,

DOI: 10.4018/978-1-4666-8833-9.ch010

2009), and an inductive thematic analysis (Braun & Clarke, 2006) of the postings to the platform's unstructured fora with a view to understand and categorize participants' perceptions of motivations, activities, and community-orientation.

BACKGROUND

Reflective Practice

John Dewey was a pioneer in the development of theory about reflection, more specifically theory that focused on how to extract meaning from experience and subsequently apply it to educational practice. Dewey's definition of reflective practice refers to a 'conscious and voluntary effort to establish belief upon a firm basis of evidence and rationality' (Dewey, 1933, p. 9), which includes action, extraction of meaning from experience and a personal desire for intellectual development (Rodgers, 2002). Indeed Dewey (1938) called for the amalgamation of human experience as a privileged means to understanding experience. This requires an integrative effort, a process of connecting experience.

Similar understandings of the role played by experience in the shaping of knowledge were later put forward by Lewin (1951) and his 'cycle of action'. This model of learning described the process of knowledge as moving across a process of experience, reflection on experience, extracting meaning from experience and experimenting with new emerging concepts.

Different theoretical orientations concerning reflection have followed since Dewey's original formulation. Mezirow (1997), for instance, emphasised the importance of achieving a deeper level of understanding through moving from a descriptive level to a fuller comprehension of the impact and significance of experiences and how they influence individuals' behaviour and learning.

Further theoretical orientations include Schön's (1983) reflection-in-action; Boyd & Fales'

(1983) reflective learning; Mezirow's (1990) critical self-reflection; Fogarty's (1994) metacognitive reflection; Loughran's (2002) critical reflective practice; Fisher's (2003) critical reflection.

Debates surrounding the concept are ongoing but there seems to agreement around the importance of deeply interrogating experienced as opposed to merely thinking about events. In this sense this chapter adheres to the definition offered by Eyler et al. (1996, p. 13), who define reflective practice as 'a process specifically structured to help examine the frameworks we use to interpret experience: critical reflection pushes us to step outside of the old and familiar and to reframe our questions and our conclusions in innovative and more effective terms'.

The process of reflection entails an examination of the experience, an analysis of its significant and an honest appreciation of its implications for the future. Biggs (1999) describes this process as an example of abstract higher order learning that compels individuals to questioning existing assumptions, and challenging our prevailing frames of reference (Brookfield, 1995). This challenging of established frames of reference is what promotes and enables change, and critical reflection allows the transformation of meaning structure – admittedly not without friction and trepidation (Mezirow, 1997).

There is a vast body of literature illustrating the role of reflective practice in specific professional contexts such as medical education (e.g. Glynn et al., 2006; Lachman & Pawlina, 2006; Mann et al., 2009), nursing training (e.g. Hyde, 2009; Issitt, 2003), and teacher training and professional development (e.g. Farrell, 2004; Flanagan, 2007; Generett & Hicks, 2004; Husu et al., 2008; Lyons, 2010; Ottesen, 2007; Palmer, 2007; York-Barr et al., 2006; Yost et al., 2000), but fewer examples of reflection on e-learning development and implementation (e.g. Carroll, 2013; Cochrane, 2013).

In that sense, what this chapter aims to achieve is a depth of understanding and the ability to see beyond the e-learning instructors' own presuppositions and therefore deconstruct the positions of role, belief and culture that typically shape the experience (Hart, 2008) of practitioners (in this case an instructor engaged in the development of an e-learning platform). This aim is also future-oriented in the sense that reflection on past experience feeds into the development of future professional practices (Silcock, 1994).

Higher Education Institutions and E-Learning

Over the last decades, Higher Education Institutions have adopted a variety of e-learning tools into their educational delivery processes. Although the literature alerts for the difficulty to find a universally accepted definition of e-learning several umbrella-like definitions have gained traction in the field, notably the European Commission's (2001) understanding of e-learning as the use of 'new multimedia technologies and the Internet to improve the quality of learning by facilitating access to facilities and services as remote exchanges and collaboration'; and HEFCE's (2005, p. 4) emphasis on the 'confident use of the full range of pedagogic opportunities provided by ICT', which in Higher Education Institutions encompasses 'flexible learning as well as distance learning, and the use of ICT as a communication and delivery tool between individuals and groups, to support and improve the management of learning'.

Across institutions different models of e-learning implementation have developed, although an evolutionary, incremental and bottom-up process in which new educational technologies integrate into existing practices is generally acknowledged to be the most common (Collis & Van der Wende, 2002).

Similarly, the most widespread adoption of educational technology is that of virtual learning environments (Smith, 2005). The implementation of virtual learning environments progressively leads to processes of strategic implementation and institutionalisation, which reflect the acknowl-edgement of e-learning as an integral part of the core processes of Higher Education Institutions.

This chapter focuses on a case where the Higher Education Institution was making steps towards the implementation and institutionalization stage. This required, as identified by Collis & Van der Wende (2002, p. 8): 'establish[ing] an institution-wide technological infrastructure, mak[ing] rich pedagogical use of this infrastructure and develop[ing] strategic plans to use ICT with a view to different target groups'. It also required a fundamental shift towards responding to changing students' needs and expectations, particularly allowing technology to fit a more flexible vision for teaching and learning (Bates, 2000).

Developing the E-Learning Platform

The starting point in the development of the e-learning platform was an international review of successful online learning environments to identify concepts, methodologies, pedagogical practices and interaction tools. In this process we highlight Spain's National University of Distance Education (UNED) – the distance learning and research university founded in 1972 - and the University of the People, an international non-profit, accredited online institution of higher education.

UNED's e-learning platform is aLFanet (IST-2001-33288), an adaptive intelligent Learning Management System that provides personalized e-learning based on learning routes, interactions in services, peer-to-peer collaboration, and presentation. It follows the main standards in the educational field (IMS-LD, IMS-CP, IEEE-LOM, IMS-LIP, IMS-QTI) (Santos, Barrera and Boticario, 2004).

The University of the People uses instructor support and a variety of innovative methods that include learning by teaching and peer-to-peer learning. It uses online discussion forums and online communities that allow students to cover readings, share resources and ideas and discuss assigned questions. Many of the pedagogical materials used are also open educational resources. Therefore its pedagogical model emphasizes openness as a fundamental value, which Wiley and Hilton (2009) recognize as a distinctive feature of higher education institutions that wish to remain relevant to society.

The principles outlined above and contained in the practices of both UNED and The University of the People inspired the creation of e.raízes_redes, the e-learning platform of the Polytechnic Institute of Santarém. Furthermore, a review of the literature in technology-enhanced learning contributed to identifying requirements that the platform to be developed should meet, namely:

1. Respect for each individual's learning rhythm (Woolf, 2010);
2. Flexible and personalized structure, allowing users to compose and define the sections they intend to interact with in the first place (Schiaffino and Amandi, 2008);
3. Possibility of interaction with facilitators and other students (Bates, 2005);
4. Opportunity to reflect on a specific course of learning/learning path (Stefani, Mason & Pegler, 2007);
5. Opportunity to co-create knowledge (Lewis and Pea, 2010);
6. Flexibility that allows the learner to choose the time, place, and preferred method of learning (Bates, 2005).

These requirements are complemented by a series of core defining values that institutions promoting the development and implementation of e-learning commonly share:

1. **Opportunity:** The principle that citizens have the right to access knowledge (Garrison, 2011);
2. **Accessibility:** Creation of a learning environment that is accessible to all citizens (Park, 2009);

3. **Inclusive Community:** Promotion of interaction with the wider community including participants from other academic institutions, business and the wider society (Palloff and Pratt, 2010);
4. **Integrity:** Promotion of a culture of openness and transparency, where diversity is an asset (Weller, 2007);
5. **Quality:** Keeping to the fundamental principles of clearly-defined learning activities, instruction excellence and facilitator responsiveness (Laurillard, 2013).

The identification of these principles has contributed to the operational definition of e-learning proposed in this chapter. E-learning is understood here as an opportunity for anyone to flexibly access online quality contents, based on a mixed learning model that combines collaboration in peer to peer teaching (students share resources; exchange ideas, discuss topics, undergo competence-based assessment) with access to open contents mediated by multiple digital spaces (e.g. WEBct, Blackboard, Moodle with additional modules, ALF, SL, Ning, LinkdeIn, SLOODLE, Facebook, etc.).

As in other educational technology venture, the operationalization of the e.raízes_redes platform required the constitution of a multidisciplinary team of instructors, programmers, researchers and technicians. Indeed, the successful implementation of e-learning requires the close collaboration of interaction strategists, content specialists, administrators and technologists (McPherson and Nunes, 2008). In the specific case of the e.raízes_redes platform, this was paramount to objectively define which courses or modules could be adapted for online delivery, and also for designing the learning environment: http://eraizes.ipsantarem.pt/.

The platform was conceived to be experience as a flexible and open environment, respecting the profile of individual learners. This aspect in particular determined several decisions concerning specific functionalities: the platform is accessible via mobile devices; activities can be moved around by drag and drop; users can be given different roles and attributes at the file level; copyrights of the files uploaded into the platform can be managed; files can be exported into Google Drive and the e-Portfolio Mahara.

Other important design decisions revolved around the creation of a hybrid learning space where contact with instructor and specialist guest instructors would be both synchronous and asynchronous, although the former would be favored. Contact with tutors was conceived as a longer, meeting-like interaction (Salmon, 2000).

DEVELOPING THE E-LEARNING PLATFORM'S PORTAL

The development of the e-learning platform's portal was a priority, and work began with the identification of a information architecture (Morville & Rosenfeld, 2006). Figure 1 illustrates the architecture, presenting its rhizomatic structure where the major nodes correspond to navigation tabs (e.g. "Percurso" stands for Pathways; "Colabore!" gives users access to collaboration tools and spaces).

This architecture is effectively a navigation map, as the project team was aware of the significance of the portal to ensure navigability and retrievability of information users would need in their first encounter with the platform. In this sense, the portal also operates as a hub from where learners can visit the different Schools of the Polytechnic Institute of Santarem, access a dedicated FAQs section, learn about active users who may be using the platform simultaneously, and share information using any of the social media outlets available such as Twitter, Facebook and LinkedIn.

Figure 2 illustrates the contents displayed by the page "Inicio - Start" that users access from the portal. Here, users can learn about the latest news

related to the project and consult the calendar and synchronize dates for the hand-in of assignments.

As also shown in Figure 2, users can navigate to four additional pages, namely "Apresentacao – Introduction"; "Saiba Tudo – About us"; "Percurso – Pathway"; and "Login" where finally users gain access to the e-learning platform proper.

The page "Apresentacao – Introduction" is where the e-learning platform is introduced through short narratives and video clips. A wider contextualization of the e-learning platform in terms of its relevance and fit with national and international policy is offered to learners when visiting this page. This includes familiarizing learners with the Europe 2020 strategy (Oprean, Brumar, Canţer & Bărbat, 2011) and with Portugal's governmental strategy for the mainstreaming of e-learning across Higher Education Institutions.

Figure 3 shows in greater detail what learners find on the page "Saiba Tudo – About us". This is where learners are acquainted to the key pedagogical principles underlying the development of the e-learning platform: opportunity, accessibility, community, quality and diversity. The operational definition used by the project is also shared with learners with the purpose of setting clear mutual expectations concerning effort and commitment by all members in the community of learners. Finally, the page features profiles and contact details of permanent and invited instructors, and facilitates access to their key research.

Figure 4 illustrates the contents contained in "Percurso – Pathway". This page features academic guidelines and an overview of the curriculum with modules descriptions, alongside quality indicators, evaluation results, and an area dedicated to learning administration procedures (e.g. registration, course requirements, and modes of assessment).

Finally, Figure 5 presents the structure of the e-learning platform proper, that learners can access after inserting their credentials in the portal's login area. Moodle was adopted in order to provide a convenient resource to consolidate

Figure 1. Architecture of the E-learning platform portal

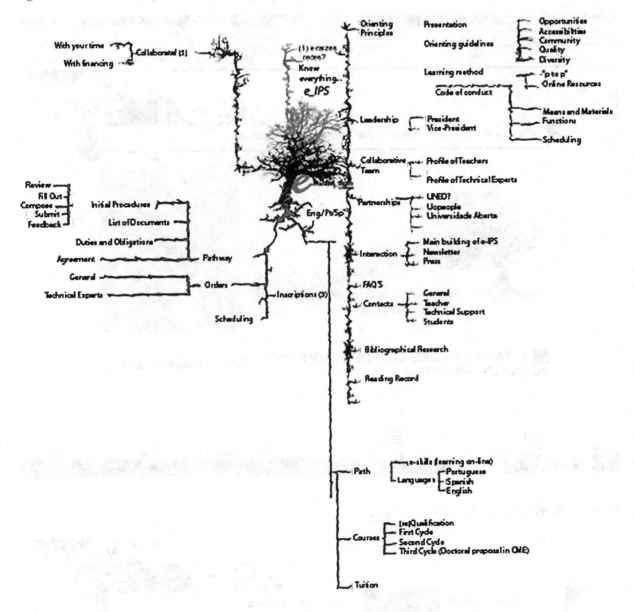

all educational resources, to which a number of plugins and modules were added to increase functionality and enhance the level of customization (e.g. videoconferencing tool via Colibri; access to virtual world via Second Life).

At a finer grained level of analysis, the proposed structure for each module typically comprises a Guide, News and Forum areas. Figure 6 illustrates the introductory session of a module designed to introduce students to the practice of professional development reporting. The module further included sessions on interaction in technology enhanced learning environments, online research,

Figure 2. Screenshot of the "Start" page

Figure 3. Screenshot of the "About us" page

Figure 4. Screenshot of the "Pathway" page

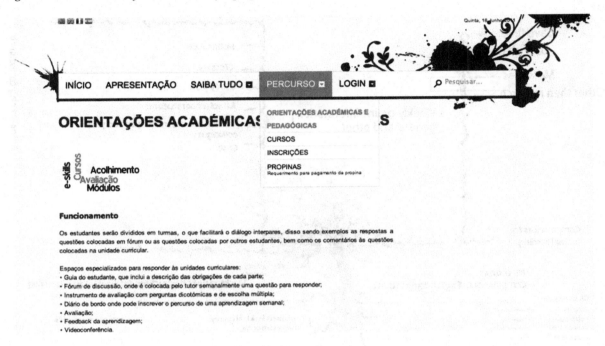

social networks, virtual worlds, and inquiry and reflection methods.

Throughout the development of the module a number of features remain accessible to the community of learners:

1. The student guide includes a detailed description of the module, including objectives and expected learning outcomes, aligned with a range of competences that learners must develop. The guide also contains suggestions of activities learners can undertake in order to personalize their learning experience, and an indication of which tools could potentially be used to operationalize the creation of individual learning pathways through different modes of engagement with the core content of the module.

2. The discussion forum is the place where structured and unstructured discussion takes place. Structured moments of discussion are coordinated weekly by the forum facilitator who defines a topic. The community of learn-

ers must in turn demonstrate engagement with the discussion taking place by replying to at least three original posts.

3. The learning journal as a tool for reflection. Writing the learning journal supports' learning while students handle current topics in the module.

4. The glossary as a tool constructed by the community of learners to collectively negotiate the meaning of key concepts.

5. An evaluation questionnaire aimed at collecting learners' views on highlights and lowlights, with a view to improving practice.

In addition to these features, the community of learners can also access the profiles of participants, a record of individual performance, and a calendar that is particularly helpful for keeping track of dates and relevant events.

Figure 5. Architecture of the E-learning platform

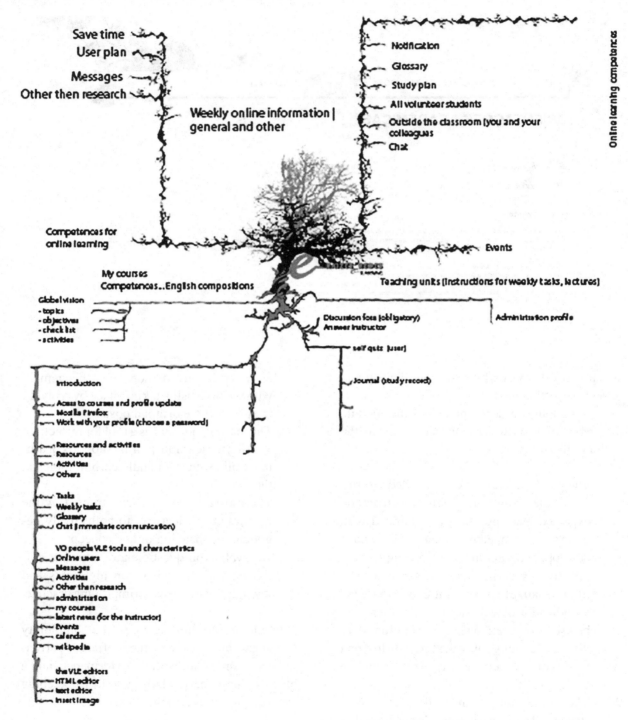

Figure 6. Screenshot of an introductory session

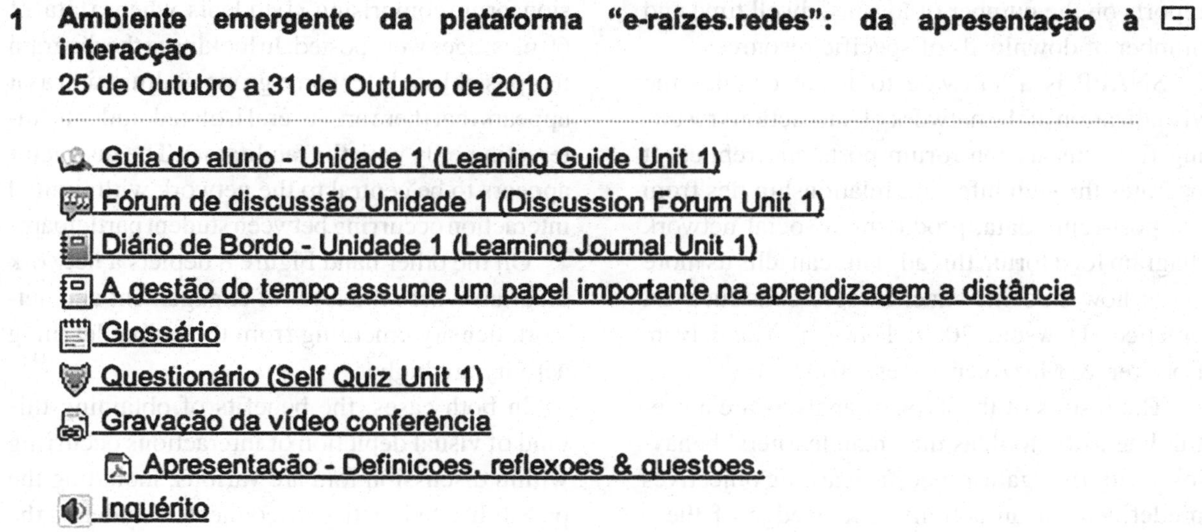

1 Ambiente emergente da plataforma "e-raízes.redes": da apresentação à ☐ interacção
25 de Outubro a 31 de Outubro de 2010

··

  📖 Guia do aluno - Unidade 1 (Learning Guide Unit 1)

  📝 Fórum de discussão Unidade 1 (Discussion Forum Unit 1)

  📓 Diário de Bordo - Unidade 1 (Learning Journal Unit 1)

  📋 A gestão do tempo assume um papel importante na aprendizagem a distância

  📑 Glossário

  🏅 Questionário (Self Quiz Unit 1)

  🎞 Gravação da vídeo conferência

      📄 Apresentação - Definicoes, reflexoes & questoes.

  🔊 Inquérito

MAKING SENSE OF THE DEVELOPING INTERACTIONS

In face of technology enhanced learning environments such as the platform described in the sections above, there is a strong emerging field of research concerned with the study of online constructivist pedagogies (e.g. McConnell, 2005; Laurillard, 2013). A particularly important aspect is determining how people learn in communities that are formed in e-learning platforms. Lave and Wenger's (1990) concept of community of practice is a useful theoretical construct for study of the pedagogical design of online courses.

Communities of practice are defined as "a set of relations among persons, activity and world, over time and in relation with other tangential and overlapping communities of practice" (Lave and Wenger, 1990). However, when applied to the pedagogical design of online courses, the definition is not free from problems, as it can be questioned whether the mechanisms of identity construction and knowledge creation can be found in formal online learning environments (Kimble, Hildreth & Boudron, 2008).

Therefore, in order to better understand how learners within e.raízes_redes were able to develop key elements of communities of practice such as mutual engagement, joint enterprise and shared repertoire (Wenger, 1998), a two-fold investigation was conducted. First, the Social Networks Adapting Pedagogical Practice (SNAPP) tool was used to perform a social network analysis and visualization of structured discussion forum activity. Secondly, an inductive thematic analysis of the postings to the platform's unstructured fora took place. The two approaches are presented in the subsequent subsections.

Social Network Analysis as a Diagnosis Tool

The Social Networks Adapting Pedagogical Practice (SNAPP) tool performs social network analysis and visualization of the activities that take place within discussion fora typically found in Learning Management Systems (LMS). However, it is difficult to infer the level and direction of activity between participants from the simple observation of messages displayed in a common thread. The same applies to the kind of analytics automatically gathered by LMS, which include reports on the number of log-ins, dwell time and number of downloads of specific resources.

SNAPP is a software tool that enables the visualization of the network of interactions resulting from discussion forum posts and replies. It operates through inferring relationship ties from the post-reply data, producing a social network diagram for a forum thread. This can tells us more about how students enact a socio-constructivist practice (Dawson, 2009; Dawson, Macfadyen, Lockyer, & Mazzochi-Jones, 2011).

The results of this type of analysis are a useful diagnostic tool, as they map learners' behavioral patterns against specific learning objectives predefined for an activity. Knowledge of these trends and patterns gives facilitators the ability to intervene and redirect the learning efforts of the community. The following figures illustrate how SNAPP re-interpreted discussion forum postings into a network diagram. Participants' names have been removed from the diagram to protect their identities.

Figure 7 is the diagram produced for a discussion forum comprising 21 students, where a total of 60 messages were posted. In looking at the diagram it is possible to infer some group malfunction as it appears that there are several isolated students (interacting only with the facilitator). The instructor appears to be central to the network with limited interaction occurring between student participants

On the other hand Figure 8 depicts a network diagram where the level of engagement and network density emerging from the online learning activity are higher.

In both cases, the benefits of obtaining this kind of visual depiction of interactions occurring within discussion fora are various, including the possibility to identify disconnected students, the possibility to identify key knowledge brokers, and on a longitudinal perspective the possibility to map the extent to which a learning community is developing.

Figure 7. Network diagram for discussion forum (21 participants, 60 posts)

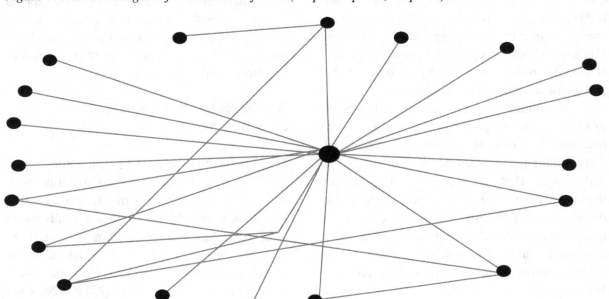

Figure 8. Network diagram for discussion forum (21 participants, 81 posts)

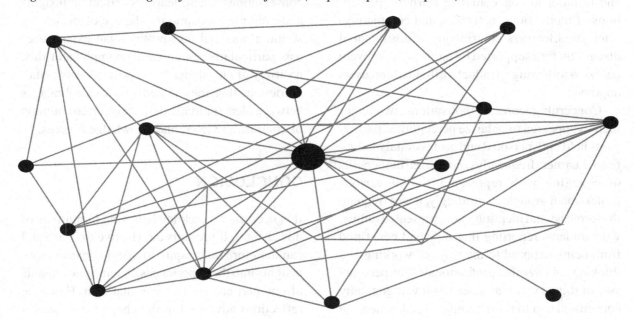

Inductive Thematic Analysis of Learners' Perceptions of Motivations, Activities, and Community-Orientation

The existence of infrastructure does not form a community of practice alone. A community of practice requires more than the transmission of contents and learning objects, it must be grounded in "a collective narrative which is the support for the conception of community as an organic and functional whole" (Dias, 2008).

Furthermore, as purported by Siemens (2004), learning in a digital and connected age does not depend on "individual knowledge acquisition, storage and retrieval; rather, it relies on the connected learning that occurs through interaction with various sources of knowledge (including the Internet and learning management systems) and participation in communities of common interest, social networks and group tasks" (Siemens, 2004). Individuals must develop certain skills and competences, that are a requirement to active participation in the knowledge society as co-creators, and not simply as consumers.

Within a networked society (Castells, 2005) the demand for digital skills is crucial to boost competitiveness, productivity and innovation as well as the professionalism and employability of the workforce (McCormack, 2010). The realisation of a truly collaborative community of practice in a digital context requires individuals who are committed to creating and sharing knowledge in a open perspective (Surowiecki, 2005; Tapscott & Williams, 2008). These individuals create their own personal networks, engaging in different services, communities, groups and networks, according to their needs, interests, preferences and motivations. This leads us into a novel approach to learning approach - connectivism - described as the learning theory for the digital age. According to connectivism, "knowledge – and therefore the learning of knowledge – is distributive, that is, not located in any given place (and therefore not 'transferred' or 'transacted' per se) but rather consists of the network of connections formed from experience and interactions with knowing community" (Downes, 2009).

In order to understand the extent to which e.raízes_redes created a community of practice, and in order to conceptualize learners' perceptions of motivations, activities, and community-orientation, learners' contributions to unstructured discussion fora supported by e.raízes_redes were analysed following an inductive thematic analysis approach.

Concerning learners' motivations, two major themes appeared to polarize perceptions: participants held both personal and professional motivations. Learners frequently emphasized the benefits of engaging with representatives of various professional groups. Accordingly, it was frequent that professional identities were presented online, with students reporting that they had benefitted from being exposed to the ways of working and thinking held by other professionals. The personal side of things was manifested as it was generally consensual that the community these learners are part of is composed of individuals with unique identities and personalities. This diversity was expected to impact on the variety of contributions to the community, based on members' backgrounds and interests.

Participants in the unstructured forum tended to perceive activities in the e-learning platform as being placed along a continuum where the extremes are localized activities and collaborative activities. Localized activities denote learners' perception that as they are completing a module with clearly defined outcomes and assessment criteria, their enterprise, personal initiative and collective negotiation of meaning is somehow predetermined. Collaborative activities, on the other hand, denote the dynamic negotiation of meaning within the community, and the opportunity to develop new ideas from common interpretations. Although a number of students appears to value autonomous learning, data in the fora reveals abundant examples of negotiation, including the development of a common approaches for assignments.

Finally, the main directions in participants' community-orientation reveal a concern with sharing knowledge or being a mediator. Knowledge sharing took place mostly through online informal

conversations where learners articulate insights and even misconceptions. The use of stories describing personal and professional experiences was particularly common. To complement this, a variety of knowledge brokers acted as intermediaries, in that they aimed to provide linkages between ideas, individuals that displayed common or contrasting views, and knowledge sources.

CONCLUSION

It is necessary to acknowledge the limitations of this chapter. It presents a reflective exercise and can therefore only aspire to offering exploratory insights into the experiences of some participants of one particular e-learning platform. From the reflections advanced in the chapter, it is apparent that participants were exposed to some of the tensions created by taking part in a community of practice that came to existence because of a structured programme of studies. That fact in itself points to the need to assert the fundamental difference between spontaneous communities of practice and learning communities that emergence within academic programmes (Kimble, Hildreth & Bourdon, 2008). The fundamental tension is that communities of practice are a spontaneous aggregate of individuals who share a common passions, and who engage in an interaction regime that assumes a distribution of power relations (Anderson, 2008). On the other hand, learning communities of practice are time-bounded and are somehow constrained by the power relations that are artificially established between tutors and students (Bitterman, 2008).

Based on the above discussion some recommendations are advanced. These recommendations stem from a single case study and cannot therefore be generalizable. However, they can be transferrable and potentially applicable to other contexts and communities.

The first recommendation is an explicit encouragement to members in the community to more actively share personal and professional knowledge. This is paramount to avoid members potentially feeling isolated from the discussion or unable to claim their voice with sufficient confidence. This recommendation is clearly aligned with what Henri and Pudelko (2003) identify as the major challenge of a community of practice: "to develop and enrich professional practice by sharing and pooling complementary knowledge among its members".

Similarly, a final recommendation is concerned with time as an enabling condition for the successful integration of members into the community of learners. It takes time for individuals to identify with common practice and to gain or improve competencies, and more efforts should be made to ensure that the community will evolve spontaneously over time.

FUTURE RESEARCH DIRECTIONS

A natural follow up for this study is the engagement of a group of instructors in wider reflection processes focused on collaborative course design. This is all the more important given the role played by collaborative design teams as a professional developed strategy to prepare instructors for online delivery, as reported in a series of studies philosophically-rooted in social constructivist theory (e.g. Clarke & Hollingsworth, 2002; Garet, 2001; Penuel et al, 2007; Porter et al, 2003).

Design teams can positively impact instructors' professional development (Mishra & Yahya; 2007; Penuel et al., 2007) through a number of features that allow instructors in a team to collaborate and support each other towards realizing common teaching and learning goals: sharing experiences of technology integration, redesigning courses, forming a cohesive community (Waddoups et al., 2004), storytelling (Little, 1997), etc.

Accordingly a future avenue of research is the study of the diverse patterns and dynamics by which instructors work in design teams.

ACKNOWLEDGMENT

The author wishes to acknowledge FCT / MEC who funded this research through National funds (PIDDAC) and FEDER through COMPETE -Competitiveness Factors Operational Program under the project PEst-C/CED/UI0194/2013.

REFERENCES

Anderson, V. (2008). Communities of practice and part-time lecturers: opportunities and challenges in Higher Education. In C. Kimble, P. Hildreth, & I. Bourdon (Eds.), *Communities of practice. Creating learning environments for educators* (pp. 83–103). North Carolina: Information Age Publishing.

Bates, T. (2000). *Managing technological change. Strategies for college and university leaders*. San Francisco: Jossey-Bass.

Bates, T. (2005). *Technology, e-learning and Distance Education*. London: Routledge. doi:10.4324/9780203463772

Bawane, J., & Spector, J. M. (2009). Prioritization of online instructor roles: Implications for competency-based teacher education programs. *Distance Education*, *30*(3), 383–397. doi:10.1080/01587910903236536

Biggs, J. (1999). What the student does: Teaching for enhanced learning. *Higher Education Research & Development*, *18*(1), 57–75. doi:10.1080/0729436990180105

Bitterman, J. E. (2008). Concepts in adult education doctoral study. In *Communities of Practice*. In C. Kimble, P. Hildreth, & I. Bourdon (Eds.), *Communities of practice. Creating learning environments for educators* (pp. 311–333). North Carolina: Information Age Publishing.

Boyd, E. M., & Fales, A. W. (1983). Reflective learning: Key to learning from experience. *Journal of Humanistic Psychology*, *23*(2), 99–117. doi:10.1177/0022167883232011

Braun, V., & Clarke, V. (2006). Using thematic analysis in psychology. *Qualitative Research in Psychology*, *3*(2), 77–101. doi:10.1191/1478088706qp063oa

Brookfield, S. D. (1995). *Becoming a critically reflective teacher*. San Francisco, CA: Jossey-Bass.

Carroll, N. (2013). E-learning – the McDonaldization of education. *European Journal of Higher Education*, *3*(4), 342–356. doi:10.1080/21568235.2013.833405

Castells, M. (2005). *The Network Society: A Cross-cultural Perspective*. Northampton, MA: Edward Elgar Publishing.

Clarke, D., & Hollingsworth, H. (2002). Elaborating a model of teacher professional growth. *Teaching and Teacher Education*, *18*(8), 947–967. doi:10.1016/S0742-051X(02)00053-7

Cochrane, T., Black, B., Lee, M., Narayan, V., & Verswijvelen, M. (2013). Rethinking e-learning supporting strategies. *The International Journal for Academic Development*, *18*(3), 276–293. doi:10.1080/1360144X.2012.733884

Collis, B. A., & Wende, M.C. van der (Eds.) (2002). *Models of Technology and future use of ICT in Higher Education*. Enschede: University of Twente

Dawson, S. (2009). 'Seeing' the learning community: An exploration of the development of a resource for monitoring online student networking. *British Journal of Educational Technology*, *41*(5), 736–752. doi:10.1111/j.1467-8535.2009.00970.x

Dawson, S., Macfadyen, L., Lockyer, L., & Mazzochi-Jones, D. (2011). Using Social Network Metrics to Assess the Effectiveness of Broad-Based Admission Practices. *Australasian Journal of Educational Technology*, *27*(1), 16–27.

Dewey, J. (1933). *How we think: a restatement of the relation of reflective thinking to the educative process*. Boston, MA: Heath.

Dewey, J. (1938). *Experience and Education*. New York: Touchstone.

Dias, P. (2008). *E-Conteúdos para E-Formadores. TecMinho/ Gabinete de Formação Contínua*. Braga: Universidade do Minho.

Downes, S. (2009). Learning Networks and Connective Knowledge. Retrieved from http://www.downes.ca/post/36031

The eLearning Action Plan: Designing tomorrow's education. (2001). European Commission. Retrieved from http://www.uni-mannheim.de/edz/pdf/sek/2002/sek-2002-0236(01)-en.pdf

Farrell, T. S. C. (2004). *Reflective practice in action: 80 reflection breaks for busy teachers*. Thousand Oaks, CA: Corwin Press.

Fisher, K. (2003). Demystifying critical reflection: Defining criteria for assessment. *Higher Education Research & Development*, *22*(3), 313–325. doi:10.1080/0729436032000145167

Flanagan, N. (2007). Teacher in a strange land: yet more reflections on reflecting. Retrieved from http://teacherleaders.typepad.com/teacher_in_a_strange_land/2007/01/yet_more_reflec.html

Fogarty, R. (1994). *The mindful school: how to teach for metacognitive reflection*. Palatine, IL: IRI/Skylight Publishing.

Garet, M., Porter, A., Desimone, L., Birman, B., & Yoon, K. (2001). What makes professional development effective? Results from a national sample of teachers. *American Educational Research Journal*, *38*(4), 915–945. doi:10.3102/00028312038004915

Garrison, D. R. (2011). *E-Learning in the 21st Century: A Framework for Research and Practice*. London: Routledge.

Generett, G. G., & Hicks, M. A. (2004). Beyond reflective competency: Teaching for audacious hope-in-action. *Journal of Transformative Education*, *2*(3), 187–203. doi:10.1177/1541344604265169

Gilbert, P. K., & Dabbagh, N. (2005). How to structure online discussions for meaningful discourse: A case study. *British Journal of Educational Technology*, *36*(1), 5–18. doi:10.1111/j.1467-8535.2005.00434.x

Glynn, L. G., MacFarlane, A., Kelly, M., Cantillon, P., & Murphy, A. W. (2006). Helping each other to learn - a process evaluation of peer assisted learning. *BMC Medical Education*, *6*(18), 1–9. PMID:16524464

Hart, T. (2008). Interiority and education. Exploring the neurophenomenology of contemplation and its potential role in learning. *Journal of Transformative Education*, *6*(4), 235–250. doi:10.1177/1541344608329393

HEFCE. *HEFCE strategy for e-learning.* (2005). London: HEFCE.

Henri, F., & Pudelko, B. (2003). Understanding and analysing activity and learning in virtual communities. *Journal of Computer Assisted Learning*, *19*(4), 472–487. doi:10.1046/j.0266-4909.2003.00051.x

Husu, J., Toom, A., & Patrikainen, S. (2008). Guided reflection as a means to demonstrate and develop student teachers' reflective competencies. *Reflective Practice*, *9*(1), 37–51. doi:10.1080/14623940701816642

Hyde, A. (2009). Thought piece: reflective endeavours and evidence-based practice: directions in health sciences theory and practice. *Reflective Practice*, *10*(1), 117–120. doi:10.1080/14623940802652938

Issitt, M. (2003). Reflecting on reflective practice for professional education and development in health promotion. *Health Education Journal*, *62*(2), 173–188. doi:10.1177/001789690306200210

Jarvis, P. (1992). Reflective practice and nursing. *Nurse Education Today*, *12*(3), 174–181. doi:10.1016/0260-6917(92)90059-W PMID:1625667

Kimble, C., Hildreth, P., & Bourdon, I. (2008). Communities of Practice. Creating Learning Environments for Educators (Vol. 1 & 2). North Carolina: Information Age Publishing.

Lachman, N., & Pawlina, W. (2006). Integrating professionalism in early medical education: The theory and application of reflective practice in the anatomy curriculum. *Clinical Anatomy (New York, N.Y.)*, *19*(5), 456–460. doi:10.1002/ca.20344 PMID:16683241

Laurillard, D. (2013). *Rethinking university teaching: a conversational framework for the effective use of learning technologies.* London: Routledge.

Lave, J., & Wenger, E. (1990). *Situated learning: legitimate peripheral participation.* Cambridge, MA: University of Cambridge Press.

Lewin, K. (1951). *Field theory in social sciences.* New York: Harper Torchbooks.

Lewis, S., Pea, R., & Rosen, J. (2010). Beyond participation to co-creation of meaning: Mobile social media in generative learning communities. *Social Sciences Information. Information Sur les Sciences Sociales*, *49*(3), 351–369. doi:10.1177/0539018410370726

Little, J. W. (1997). The persistence of privacy: Autonomy and initiative in teachers' professional relations. *Teachers College Record*, *91*, 509–536.

Loughran, J. J. (2002). Effective reflective practice: In search of meaning in learning about teaching. *Journal of Teacher Education*, *53*(1), 33–43. doi:10.1177/0022487102053001004

Lyons, N. (Ed.). (2010). *Handbook of reflection and reflective inquiry: mapping a way of knowing for professional reflective inquiry.* New York: Springer. doi:10.1007/978-0-387-85744-2

Mann, K., Gordon, J., & MacLeod, A. (2009). Reflection and reflective practice in health professions education: A systematic review. *Advances in Health Sciences Education: Theory and Practice*, *14*(4), 595–621. doi:10.1007/s10459-007-9090-2 PMID:18034364

McConnell, D. (2005). Examining the dynamics of networked e-learning groups and communities. *Studies in Higher Education*, *30*(1), 25–42. doi:10.1080/0307507052000307777

McCormac, A. (2010). *The e-Skills manifesto*. Brussels: European Schoolnet.

McPherson, M., & Nunes, J. M. (2008). Critical issues for e-learning delivery: What may seem obvious is not always put into practice. *Journal of Computer Assisted Learning*, *24*(5), 433–445. doi:10.1111/j.1365-2729.2008.00281.x

Mezirow, J. (1981). A critical theory of adult learning and education. *Adult Education*, *32*(1), 3–24. doi:10.1177/074171368103200101

Mezirow, J. (1990). How critical reflection triggers transformative learning. In J. Mezirow (Ed.), *Fostering critical reflection in adulthood: a guide to transformative and emancipatory learning* (pp. 1–20). San Francisco, CA: Jossy-Bass.

Mezirow, J. (1997). Transformative learning: Theory to practice. *New Directions for Adult and Continuing Education*, *1997*(74), 5–12. doi:10.1002/ace.7401

Mishra, P., Koehler, M. J., & Zhao, Y. (2007). *Faculty development by design: integrating technology in higher education*. Charlotte, NC: Information Age Publishing.

Morville, P., & Rosenfeld, L. (2006). *Information architecture for the World Wide Web*. Sebastopol, CA: O'Reilly.

Oprean, C., Brumar, C. I., Cater, M., & Barbat, B. E. (2011). Sustainable development: E-teaching (now) for lifelong e-learning. *Procedia: Social and Behavioral Sciences*, *30*, 988–992. doi:10.1016/j.sbspro.2011.10.192

Ottesen, E. (2007). Reflection in teacher education. *Reflective Practice*, *8*(1), 31–46. doi:10.1080/14623940601138899

Palloff, R. M., & Pratt, K. (2004). *Collaborating online: learning together in community*. San Franscico, CA: Jossey-Bass.

Palmer, P. (2007). *The courage to teach guide for reflection and renewal*. San Francisco, CA: Jossey-Bass.

Park, S. Y. (2009). An analysis of the technology acceptance model in understanding university students' behavioral intention to use e-learning. *Journal of Educational Technology & Society*, *12*(3), 150–162.

Penuel, W. R., Fishman, B. J., Yamaguchi, R., & Ghallagher, L. P. (2007). What makes professional development effective? Strategies that foster curriculum implementation. *American Educational Research Journal*, *44*(4), 921–958. doi:10.3102/0002831207308221

Porter, A., Garet, M. S., Desimone, L. M., & Birman, F. (2003). Providing effective professional development: Lessons from the Eisenhower program. *Science Educator*, *12*(1), 23–40.

Salmon, G. (2000). *E-moderating: the key to teaching and learning online*. London: Kogan Page. doi:10.4324/9780203465424

Santos, O. C., Barrera, C., & Boticario, J. G. (2004). An overview of aLFanet: An adaptive iLMS based on standards. *Adaptive Hypermedia and Adaptive Web-based Systems. Lecture Notes in Computer Science*, *3137*, 429–432. doi:10.1007/978-3-540-27780-4_67

Schiaffino, S., Garcia, P., & Amandi, A. (2008). eTeacher: Providing personalized assistance to e-learning students. *Computers & Education*, *51*(4), 1744–1754. doi:10.1016/j.compedu.2008.05.008

Schön, D. (1983). *The reflective practitioner: how professionals think in action*. New York: Basic Books.

Siemens, G. (2004). Connectivism: A Learning Theory for the Digital Age. Retrieved from http://www.elearnspace.org/Articles/connectivism.htm

Smith, P. (2005). From flowers to palms: 40 years of policy for online learning. *ALT-J. Research in Learning Technology*, *13*(2), 93–108. doi:10.1080/09687760500104054

Stephani, L., Mason, R., & Pegler, C. (2007). *The Educational Potential of e-Portfolios: Supporting Personal Development and Reflective Learning*. New York: Routledge.

Surowiecki, J. (2005). *The Wisdom of Crowds*. New York: Anchor Books.

Tapscott, D., & Williams, A. (2008). *Wikinomics: How Mass Collaboration Changes Everything*. New York: Penguin Group.

Waddoups, G. L., Wentworth, N., & Earle, R. (2004). Principles of technology integration and curriculum development: A faculty design team approach. *Computers in the Schools*, *21*(1/2), 15–23. doi:10.1300/J025v21n01_02

Weller, M. (2007). The distance from isolation: Why communities are the logical conclusion in e-learning. *Computers & Education*, *49*(2), 148–159. doi:10.1016/j.compedu.2005.04.015

Wenger, E. (1998). *Communities of practice: learning, meaning, and identity*. Cambridge: Cambridge University Press. doi:10.1017/CBO9780511803932

Wiley, D., & Hilton, J. (2009). Openness, dynamic specialization, and the disaggregated future of Higher Education. *International Review of Research in Open and Distance Learning*, *10*(5).

Woolf, B. P. (2008). *Building intelligent interactive tutors: student-centered strategies for revolutionizing e-Learning*. Burlington, CA: Morgan Kaufmann.

York-Barr, J. et al. (2006). *Reflective practice to improve schools: an action guide for educators*. Thousand Oaks, CA: Corwin Press.

Yost, D. S., Sentner, S. M., & Forlenza-Bailey, A. (2000). An examination of the construct of critical reflection: Implications for teacher education programming in the 21st century. *Journal of Teacher Education*, *51*(1), 39–49. doi:10.1177/002248710005100105

ADDITIONAL READING

1. Ashwin, P. (2015). *Reflective Teaching in Higher Education*. London: Bloomsbury Academic.

2. Bean, C. (2014). *The Accidental Instructional Designer: Learning Design for the Digital Age*. Aleksandria, VA: ASTD Press.

3. Major, C. M. (2015). *Teaching Online: a Guide to Theory, Research, and Practice*. Baltimore: Johns Hopkins University Press.

4. Pelet, J.-E. (Ed.). (2013). *E-Learning 2.0 Technologies and Web Applications in Higher Education*. Hershey, PA: IGI Global.

5. Ritzhaupt, A., & Kumar, S. (Eds.). (2013). *Cases on Educational Technology Implementation for Facilitating Learning*. Hershey, PA: IGI Global. doi:10.4018/978-1-4666-3676-7

KEY TERMS AND DEFINITIONS

Community of Practice: A network of peers with diverse levels of skills and experience that engages in a process of sensemaking and collective learning.

Connectivism: A theory of learning that argues knowledge is distributed across a network of connections, and therefore that learning consists of individuals' ability to construct, curate and extract value from those networks.

E-Learning Institutionalization: The stages of strategic implementation by which e-learning becomes fully acknowledged as an integral part of the core processes of Higher Education Institutions.

E-Learning Platform: An integrated set of interactive online services that provide a community of learners and facilitators with information, tools and resources to support the delivery and management of teaching and learning activities.

Information Architecture: The structural design of information environments such as websites, intranets and online communities to support usability and findability.

Reflective Practice: A process whereby individuals engage in critical analysis of practice and decision making, drawing on theory and personal and professional experience to improve the way they work.

Social Networks Adapting Pedagogical Practice (SNAPP): A software tool that performs real-time social network analysis and visualization of discussion forum activity within a Learning Management System.

Chapter 11
Formulating a Framework for Desktop Research in Chinese Information Systems

Lihong Zhou
Wuhan University, China

Miguel Baptista Nunes
The University of Sheffield, UK

ABSTRACT

The investigation of information systems (IS) development usually relies on two different research approaches, namely, quantitative approach and qualitative approach. Both approaches are equally important and useful to the development of IS theories. No research approach should be considered to be superior or inferior to the other. However, the mainstream of Chinese IS research mainly follows the quantitative approach, whereas the qualitative approach is generally viewed as "too soft" or not scientific enough. As a qualitative approach, desk case-study research approach has been widely accepted and applied in a number of IS research in the West. However, in China, this approach is merely considered as an effective approach for teaching, but not valid for scientific research investigations. Thus, Chinese IS research have neglected a number of important experiences, viewpoints and lessons, which can be elicited from IS case-studies occurred in the past. This chapter generally aims at introducing and discussing the desk case-study approach in IS research. Specifically, this chapter discusses this approach through four incremental research stages, namely, defining the research question, establishing theoretical framework from literature review, case-study selection, and theory formulation through case-study analysis. Furthermore, two exemplary research projects are presented in this chapter to further clarify and substantiate the research methods, tools and processes. It is expected that by formulating a rigorous research framework and specifying incremental processes of theory development, this research approach could be accepted and used by Chinese IS scholars in the future.

DOI: 10.4018/978-1-4666-8833-9.ch011

1. INTRODUCTION

It is universally accepted that IS research predominantly adopt two research approaches, namely, quantitative approach and qualitative approach (Myers, 1997). The quantitative approach mainly adopts objectivist ontological and positivist epistemological position, attempts to understand a social phenomenon by interpreting numbers (Bryman, 2001). This approach emphasises on quantification in the processes of data collection and analysis and is usually used to test a theory and to draw conclusions (Bryman, 2001). On the other hand, the qualitative approach usually employs constructivist ontological and interpretivist epistemological positions, depends on the use of words and is usually used to generate or extend a theory (Bryman, 2001). The two approaches adopt two very different philosophical stances, consist of different sets of methods and techniques, and are used in IS research for very different purposes.

In any case, both approaches are scientific and one cannot be considered as superior or inferior than the other. Nonetheless, in the field of Chinese IS research, there is a generally accepted presumption, which believes that the quantitative research methods and the extensive use of statistics and mathematics are the symbols of good and high quality scientific research. Moreover, it is almost public knowledge that Chinese IS and management academic journals are more willing to accept quantitative research articles, particularly those embody complex mathematical algorithms, even though in some cases the algorithms probably have very limited relevance to the contents of the article (Zhang, 2007). For instance, the Journal of the China Society for Scientific and Technical Information is well accepted as the top IS journal in China. It is well-known in the field that this particular journal only accept articles, which report quantitative analysis and statistical research works. One should always include some kind of mathematical components in an article. On the other hand, qualitative research approach is generally disregarded as "too soft" and not scientific enough (Zheng et al., 2006). The negligence and bias against qualitative approach have resulted in a heavy reliance on the concepts and theories developed in the West and in a significant lack of locally developed knowledge and theories.

This chapter, instead of campaigning for qualitative methods and providing a general debate on pros and cons, aims at introducing and describing a specific IS research approach, namely, a desk case-study IS research approach. This approach not only is a very useful and effective approach in the study of IS, but also is internationally accepted and widely applied. It is hoped that by presenting and discussing technical details of this research approach in this book and on an international stage could significantly increase the perceived credibility of this approach and hence can be accepted and used by Chinese scholars.

This chapter aims to explain the desk case-study approach in great details. Specifically, this chapter is structured as follows. Section 2 attempts to provide a definition to the desk case-study approach. Section 3 explains the research processes when performing this type of research. Specifically, four main research steps are defined, explained and discussed in this section. Section 4 aims to discuss advantages and disadvantages of this approach. Finally, in Section 5, two completed research projects are presented and discussed in order to exhibit how this approach is operationalised in practice.

2. DEFINING THE DESK CASE-STUDY APPROACH

Desk research is generally accepted as equate to literature review and is very concisely defined by Jackson (1994, p. 21) as "the process of accessing published secondary data". This definition points to two distinct characteristics of desk research. Firstly, desk research exclusively relies on published secondary data. The term "published" is very broadly used here and includes books, journals, articles indexed in many databases, and business and research reports (Jackson, 1994, pp. 21-22). The "secondary data" refers to a type of data, which "already exists and has been collected in the past for some purpose quite unconnected to our project" (Jackson, 1994, p. 20). Secondly, all processes of desk research are exercised "in-house" (Jackson, 1994, p. 11).

Nonetheless, the definition provided by Jackson (1994) is extremely poor and reductionist, since merely assessing and synthesising secondary sources does not necessarily add to the existing body of knowledge in the field of IS (Zhou et al., 2008). This notion is clearly stressed by Remenyi et al. (1998), who argues that this type of study must be a critical evaluation of the thoughts of other academics, rather than merely accepting secondary sources on face value. However, the processes of traditional critical literature are aiming at demonstrating a critical awareness of background studies and usually take place early in research projects for construct validity purposes (Gill & Johnson, 1991).

In truth, desk research approach can be adopted as the main method of research, not just as a construct validity vehicle (Zhou et al., 2008). In IS research, it is not uncommon to adopt a desk research strategy to achieve the purpose of inductive theory development, by exploring claims of different organisations, through the analysis of published and publicly available case-studies.

Case-study is a very common research methodology used to explore and understand complex and localised human activity systems and social environments (Zhou et al., 2008). In the study of IS, some of the classic studies have been derived from such detailed investigations (Bryman, 2001). The term "case-study" has multiple meanings. It can be used to describe a unit of analysis (for example, a case study of an organisation, a location, a person or an event) or to describe a research method (Bryman & Bell, 2003).

Furthermore, a case-study approach is generally accepted as inductive in nature, as it is believed that it is possible to infer general truths from the particular, that is induce theoretical conclusions from specific cases (Zhou et al., 2008; Walliman, 2001). Moreover, research using this approach is particularly concerned with the research context; therefore, the study of a reasonably small sample of cases may be more appropriate than a large number (Easterby-Smith, 2002). Thus, it is expected that the selection of a meaningful and representative sample of case-studies may provide a good basis for a good critical analysis that may result in generalisable understandings.

Nevertheless, the research approach discussed in this chapter is not a traditional case-study research approach, but rather the surveying and cross case critique of the findings of case-study analysis undertaken by others. It uses case-study findings as secondary data because of the contextualised and applied nature of that type of research.

3. RESEARCH PROCESSES

The desk research approach is inductive in nature, as it is believed that it is possible to infer general truths from the particular, that is induce theoretical conclusions from a set of case-studies (Zhou et al., 2008). An inductive approach starts with a question or "problem statement" (Glesne & Peshkin, 1992) followed by conclusions that are generated from the existing data. Specifically, a survey of case-studies consists of seven inductive stages, as shown in the framework in Figure 1.

On the basis of this framework, Zhou et al. (2008) further point out four main stages of theory induction, namely: the definition of research question, the establishment of a tentative theoretical framework from the review of existing literature, the selection of case-studies, and, finally, the establishment of theory through the analysis of case-studies. These four stages are described and discussed in the following sections.

Figure 1. Framework of case-study survey
Adopted from Zhou et al.(2008)

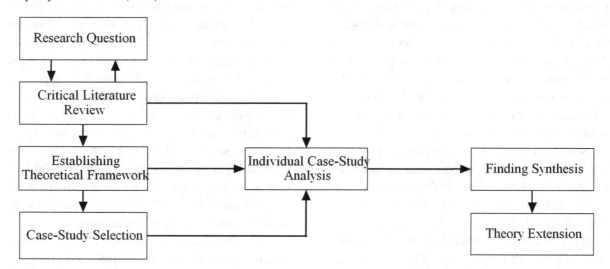

3.1 Defining Research Question

When performing a desk case-study research, like in nearly all IS research projects, the formulation of research question could be regarded as the starting point for a research project. Bryman and Bell (2003) stress that research questions are extremely important, since "no research questions or poorly formulated research questions will lead to poor research" (Bryman & Bell, 2003, p. 36). More specifically, these authors claim that an appropriately defined research question guides the review of literature, drives the selection of research methodology and the establishment of research design, provides a guiding light for the collection and analysis of data, and prevents potential diversions into unnecessary directions.

Moreover, as discussed by Collis and Hussey (2003), inductive research studies usually starts with relatively general research questions, which progressively evolve and narrow down during research progress. Very often, research questions established at the beginning of a study may need to be refined or modified when performing literature review.

3.2 Establishing Theoretical Framework from Critical Literature Review

At early stages of an IS research, a review of prior, relevant literature is a crucial stage. Creswell (2003) highlights that it provides a lens to identify issues that are pertinent to be examined and needed to be investigated. In addition, Bryman and Bell (2003, p. 557) claims that it prevents mistakes made before from happening again. Furthermore, reviewing literature can provide important indications to the selection of research methodology and research design (Bryman & Bell, 2003, p. 557). Moreover, literature review can enhance researchers' contextual and theoretical sensitivities, both of which are crucial to the analysis of data and theory development (Strauss & Corbin, 1998).

More importantly, from the critical review of literature, it is critical to establish a tentative theoretical framework, which needs to be adopted as a base structure that leads the analysis of case-studies (Eisenhardt, 1989). This theoretical framework could be seen as an aggregation of concepts, insights and issues, which are identified through the critical literature review and which could be considered as tentative constructs to the final theory. Yin (1994, p. 21) proposes that these tentative constructs are essential to the development of theory, since each construct reflects an important theoretical issue that deserves attentions to examine. Even, some tentative constructs could suggest researchers to consider theoretical propositions and concepts that might not otherwise have thought about (Bryman & Bell, 2003). Moreover, relevant constructs need to be connected and categorised in order to form a theoretical framework, presenting an initial categorisation of key themes and sub-themes (Yin, 1994).

Nonetheless, it does not mean that a tentative theoretical framework must be prepared as comprehensive and complete as possible. In fact, King (2008) warns that if invest too much time and effort in creating an elaborate initial framework, "you may be reluctant to make substantial changes to it later". More seriously, Strauss and Corbin (1998) claim that a rigid set of predefined theoretical constructs may "constrain", "stifle", or even "paralyze" researcher's analytical senses, and may possibly bring strong biases to theory building.

Therefore, Eisenhardt (1989) points out that it is fundamental to acknowledge the framework is only tentative. No theoretical proposition at this stage is guaranteed a place in the final theory. Thus, King (2008) advises that, when generating an a tentative theoretical framework, it is not necessary to be "too concerned with fine distinctions at third, fourth or even lower levels of the coding hierarchy", but should at least cover the main thematic areas as emerged from the literature review.

Furthermore, it is important to note that this framework, apart from its importance in the analysis of case-studies, should be employed to assess the appropriateness of individual case-studies and to guide the selection of case-study.

3.3 Case-Study Selection

Due to the inductive nature, this research approach is particularly concerned with the context; therefore, the study of a small sample of subjects may be more appropriate than a large number (Easterby-Smith et al., 2002). Thus, it is expected that a careful selection of a meaningful and representative sample of case-studies may provide a good basis for a good critical analysis that may result in generalisable understandings.

In general, two strategies are normally used in the case-studies selection, according to Eisenhardt (1989). Firstly, a research study can choose case-studies with heterogeneous characteristics or even at polar positions, in order to fill diverse theoretical categories and increase the generalisability of the emergent theory. Very differently, case-studies having similar characteristics can be selected in purposes of reconfirmation, revalidation, controlling extraneous variation, and helping to define the limits for generalising the findings. In any case, both strategies should be performed under the light of research questions. Also, a tentative theoretical framework is an effective tool to evaluate the relevancy and appropriateness of a case-study.

In addition, when surveying case-studies using a desk research approach, the selection of case-studies has an additional role. The main concern here is that, as claimed by Jackson (1994, p. 37), all that is published is not necessarily accurate and some may even be quite untrue. Consequently, researchers must assess the authenticity and quality of case-study reports obtained from secondary sources. To assist this assessment, Bryman and Bell (2003) propose a set of evaluation criteria, which include four characteristics, namely: authenticity, credibility, representativeness and meaning. To perform an evaluation, the four characteristics of a case-study report are evaluated by asking four questions:

- **Authenticity:** Is the evidence genuine and of unquestionable origin?
- **Credibility:** Is the evidence free from error and distortion?
- **Representativeness:** Is the evidence typical of its kind, and if not, is the extent of its untypicality known?
- **Meaning:** Is the evidence clear and comprehensible?

Finally, at the end of a case-study selection, researchers should have an organised collection of case-study reports, which are then set up ready for analysis.

3.4 Theory Formulation through Case-Study Analysis

As an end product of an inductive research, the final theory needs to be formulated on basis of close examination and analysis of individual case-study reports. The case-study analysis adopts a thematic analysis approach, which, according to King and Horrocks (2010, pp. 166-169), can be simply understood as a way of coding and representing qualitative data. Data here mean individual case-study reports. Coding means the identification and interpretation of themes and sub-themes in the reports. Representation means the production of a theoretical narrative which summarises the themes identified by the researchers and organises them in a meaningful and useful manner. In other words, individual reports are examined and interpreted, coded and constantly compared against themes and theoretical constructs that emerged from a tentative theoretical framework (Chen et al., 2011). Finally, at the end of the analysis stage, the findings of each case-study are merged and aggregated in order to form a final theory. The analysis of case-studies can be shown in the framework presented in Figure 2.

The framework shown in Figure 2 provides a holistic view and detailed information demonstrating the process of data analysis. Adopting this framework allows a sustained and consistent analysis of the different case-studies surveyed and for constant verification and internal validity checks throughout the analysis.

Figure 2. Case-study analysis framework

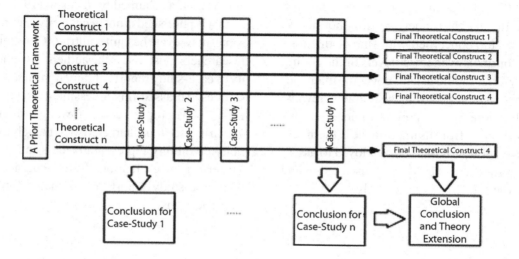

4. ADVANTAGES AND DISADVANTAGES

Surveying case-studies by using desk research approach has three main advantages:

1. Surveying case-studies obtained from secondary data resources is an enormous saving in resource, in particular time and money (Saunders et al., 2009) and can be accomplished by a lone researcher (Jackson, 1994).
2. Secondary sources are likely to provide high quality case-study and research reports, which sometimes could have higher quality than collecting first-hand data (Saunders et al., 2009).
3. Case-study reports offer unobtrusive measures allowing researchers to conduct close investigations into case-studies (Yin, 1994). Also, case-study reports could provide rich description and insights about those case sites, which are very difficult to gain entry access.

Therefore, Jackson (1994) claims that if more and better desk research could be performed, it is very likely that less field research would be needed. However, this research approach is not perfect and has several disadvantages. Saunders et al. (2009, pp. 269-271) point out three disadvantages. Firstly, case-study reports are usually generated for purposes that do not match your needs. Secondly, access to those reports could be difficult and costly. Thirdly, the definitions of "data variables" used in the case-study reports selected may be unusable to your research questions and objectives. Additionally, Yin (1994) raises another concern that case-study reports could contain biases of authors and thus could compromise the validity and reliability of the final theory. Nevertheless, these criticisms and potential problems could be mitigated, or even be minimised by carefully selecting case-studies,

evaluating the authenticity and credibility of individual reports, and rigorously and systematically perform the analysis of case-studies, as presented and discussed in this chapter.

5. EXAMPLE RESEARCH PROJECTS

This section presents two research projects, both of which adopted the desk case-study approach proposed in this chapter, and both of which have developed useful contributions and indications to the body of knowledge as well as to the practice. The first project is originally published in an academic journal, namely, Information Management and Computer Security, as Zhou et al. (2008). The second project focuses on KS in Chinese healthcare environment. A full-length reporting on this project is accepted by the iConference 2015, as Zhou et al. (2015). Although both projects used the desk case-study approach, the two projects have distinctive merits to be presented in this section. The first project focuses on the IS development and risk management in the social context in Western countries, whereas the second project focuses specifically on Chinese social and healthcare environment. The two research projects are presented here to exemplify, further clarify and substantiate methods, tools and processes that are described and discussed in previous sections.

5.1 Project 1: Establishing Information Systems Project Risk Checklist

5.1.1 Research Rationale and Questions

The design, development and implementation of IS in the Public Sector have been plagued by failure caused by lacking of effective and sufficient risk identification, assessment and decision making. After an indicative literature review, it was noted that it is in the risk analysis processes that contributions for practitioners are in actual need. Namely, in clear checklists that can be used at the planning phase and as the basis for risk assessment. Checklists are valuable planning and assessment devices when carefully developed, regularly updated, validated and applied. A sound checklist specifies and clarifies the criteria that should be considered when assessing a phenomenon in particular context and supports the evaluator not to forget important criteria (Stufflebeam, 2000). In terms of risk assessment, a checklist enhances the objectivity and credibility of the evaluation process and guides practitioners in planning for the outcomes of the evaluation. As Stufflebeam (2000) puts it, in the quality vernacular, "checklists are useful for both formative and summative evaluations."

Therefore, this research project aimed at identifying a risk ontology and checklist that will enable decision making and mitigation strategy planning in IS development. Specifically, the following overarching research questions were formulated:

RQ1: What constitutes a good IS project risk identification checklist?

RQ2: How can a risk identification checklist be created?

RQ3: What should be the content of such a checklist?

In responding to these research questions, this project then aimed at producing an extensive risk identification checklist that could be used by both practitioners and IS risk researchers.

5.1.2 Research Methodology

In order to respond the above research questions, this research project employed an inductive qualitative research methodology through a process of case-study survey. Specifically, this research employed a desk case-study approach, exclusively using case-study reports obtained from secondary sources.

Moreover, the development of risk ontology followed the research steps presented in Figure 1 and encompassed the following four main inductive stages:

- Performing a critical literature review on IS risk management and risk assessment, in order to provide a theoretical background to the study and establishing an initial proposition of main categories of risks (a tentative theoretical framework) in IS development for further exploration and critical analysis;
- Selecting an appropriate set of case-studies, which was selected on the basis of its validity and descriptive value;
- Performing an analysis of individual case studies by using the tentative theoretical framework as guides;
- Producing a synthesis of the different case-studies to provide a response to the research questions and to establish the risk identification ontology.

5.1.3 Establishing a Tentative Theoretical Framework from a Critical Literature Review

There is a vast and rich amount of both professional and academic publications addressing IS design and development and their associate risks (Charette, 1989; Keil et al., 1998). The urgent necessity of risk management is recognised to be not only obvious and inevitable, but also complex and difficult to implement. From a distillation of this literature, it emerged that most project management authors focus on procedural aspects of the management process such as estimation, planning, monitoring, team building and change management (Chapman & Ward, 1997; Kliem & Ludin, 2000; Mantel et al., 2001; Pritchard, 2004). Conversely, most software (SW) engineers and computer science authors focus on technical problems of the design and development process that is requirement specification, abstract representation of human activity systems and information environments, programming, testing and installation (Drori, 1997; Jalote, 2002; Taylor, 2003; Tsui, 2004). However, practitioners require a more integrative and holistic approach in order to be able to think about risk in context and take decisions on avoidance and mitigation of these risks (Brown, 2000). Therefore, this study developed such a holistic conceptual model shown in Figure 3, based on the five main dimensions of an IS project: pre-project, customer, project management, technological issues, and design and development methodology.

This holistic theoretical model aimed at establishing a manageable set of key risk categories in order to proceed with the analysis of the case-studies, as shown in the framework in both Figure 1 and 2. The model itself is resulted from the critical literature review and is a synthesis of a number of existing holistic models. In particular, the theoretical model proposed was strongly influenced by propositions by Hughes and Cotterell (2002) and Cadle and Yates (2001).

5.1.4 The Selection of Case-Studies

In order to identify risks existing in IS projects, this research project decided that it is a natural strategy to study cases of failure of this type of project. Past failure causes and events, can be interpreted as risks in future projects. Furthermore, due to IS project failure has different degrees of visibility, this research project focuses on failure cases occurred in the public sector, which could be seen as an ideal research field in risk management practices, due to the relatively high visibility that failure of IS projects has acquired as a consequence of the duty of accountability that characterises it. Therefore, 10 case-studies from an Anglo-Saxon tradition Public Sector, as shown in Table 1, specifically from the UK, US and New Zealand, were selected. This choice was rooted on to very high levels of transparency, detail, trustworthiness and credibility of the information disclosed about these failures. In addition, the following characteristics were adopted as quality criteria for the selection of case-studies:

Figure 3. Holistic theoretical risk model

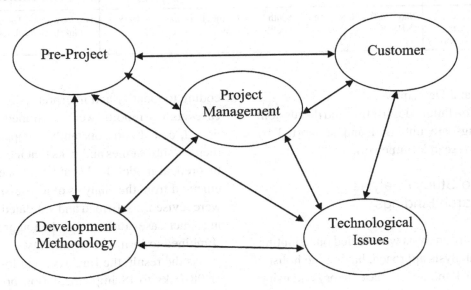

Table 1. List of case-studies from an Anglo-Saxon tradition Public Sector

ID.	Title	Organisation	Reporting Organization	Year	URL
1.	Enterprise Resource Planning in Public School District	The San Diego Public School District	Kellogg School of Management Northwestern University	2002	http://www.kellogg.northwestern.edu/faculty/jeffery/htm/cases/SDSU%20Case%20wm.pdf
2.	Integrated Financial Management Program (IFMP)	NASA	United States General Accounting Office	2003	http://www.gao.gov/new.items/d03507.pdf
3.	The National Program for IT in the NHS	Department of Health, UK	National Audit Office, UK	2006	http://www.nao.org.uk/publications/nao_reports/05-06/05061173.pdf
4.	Navy ERP	Department of Defense, US	United States General Accounting Office	2005	http://www.gao.gov/new.items/d05858.pdf
5.	Defense Travel System (DTS)	Department of Defense, US	United States General Accounting Office	2006	http://www.gao.gov/new.items/d0618.pdf
6.	IT Investment Management (ITIM)	Bureau of Land Management	United States General Accounting Office	2003	http://www.gao.gov/new.items/d031025.pdf
7.	Information Technology Management	Small Business Administration	United States General Accounting Office	2000	http://www.gao.gov/archive/2000/ai00170.pdf
8.	Identity and Passport Service: Introduction of ePassports	The Identity and Passport Service; the Foreign & Commonwealth Office and the Immigration and Nationality Directorate	National Audit Office, UK	2007	http://www.nao.org.uk/publications/nao_reports/06-07/0607152.pdf
9.	Integrated National Crime Information System (INCIS)	New Zealand Police	Ministry of Justice	2000	http://www.justice.govt.nz/pubs/reports/2000/incis_rpt/INCIS%20inquiry.pdf
10.	London Ambulance Service (LAS)	National Health Service (NHS)	South West Thames Regional Health Authority	1995	http://www.cs.ucl.ac.uk/staff/A.Finkelstein/las/lascase0.9.pdf

- Clear and Descriptive;
- Focus on failure description and discussion;
- Findings are unbiased and supported by sound research framework.

5.1.5 Case-Study Analysis and Research Findings

The case-study analysis was carried out adopting a thematic analysis approach, having the holistic theoretical risk model as a base theory and using coding to identify and interpret risks. Individual case-studies reports were examined and interpreted, coded and constantly compared against themes, sub-themes and risks that included in the theoretical model. Risks and risk categorisation emerged from the analysis of a case-study report were revised, confirmed and validated by analysing other case-studies, and then aggregated and combined to form a risk ontology.

As the result, the final risk ontology consists of 98 risks to IS implementation projects. According to the case-study analysis, these risks were categorised into 18 sub-themes and 5 main themes, as shown in Table 2.

Moreover, it is concluded that a considerable amount of risk factors are clearly incurred even before the start of the formal project. All these risks, identified in the pre-project dimension, severely pre-determine the future of the project and create very predictable risks that could be avoided if given due consideration. In fact, this research found evidence that risk thinking should start very early as part of pre-project and not, as most of the modern design and development methodologies propose, solely as part of the development process itself.

5.2 Project 2: Identifying Knowledge Sharing Barriers in Chinese Healthcare Referral Services

5.2.1 Research Rationale and Questions

In April 2009, the Central Committee of the Communist Party of China and the State Council jointly announced a new wave of health reform, which ambitiously aims to achieve universal provision of free or low-cost healthcare to the entire population by 2020 (Growth Policy Analysis, 2013; Le Deu et al., 2012). One of the key objectives of healthcare reform is to implement and opera-

Table 2. A presentation of themes, sub-themes and examples of risk

Themes	Sub-Themes	Examples of Risk
Pre-Project	Requirement specification and project scoping	Requirement specifications are ill-defined.
	Contractual relationships	Disagreement between involved partners.
	Project planning	Lack of a quality control system before project.
	Organisational environment	Inappropriate business plan and IS vision.
Customer	Internal and external environment	Conflicts between user departments.
	End-user	End user reluctance in changing or even accepting the new system.
	Management	Lack of information and IT skills by management.
Project Management	Human resource	Inappropriate staffing and/or personnel shortfalls.
	Project planning	Lack of effective processes of estimation.
	Project monitoring and reporting	Unrealistic monitoring of timeliness and budgets.
Technological Issues	IS infrastructure and base technologies	Incompatible technologies with project constraints and/or requirements.
	Development Technologies	Unfamiliar development environment to the project team.
Development Methodology	General methodological issues	Use of inadequate or reductionist methodologies.
	System analysis	Misunderstanding of user requirements.
	System design	Poor dialogue between designers and end-users.
	System development and testing	System testing without final user involvement.
	System Installation	Lack of planned and agreed systems installation and cutover processes.
	System maintenance	Lack of a clear and agreed maintenance plan.

tionalise a nationwide referral service to connect local healthcare organisations with mainstream hospitals (Le Deu et al., 2012). Ideally, the referral service system would not only create efficient and seamless pathways to transfer patients to the most suitable healthcare facilities and specialists in a timely manner, but these pathways would also become effective knowledge sharing (KS) channels to connect individual healthcare professionals in primary, secondary and tertiary healthcare services (Yuan, 2012). According to recent reports, the development of the referral system can be generally considered as rapid and steady (Zhao et al., 2010; Xu et al., 2012; Ma, 2013). In some major cities, such as Beijing, Shanghai, Guangzhou, Wuhan, Nanjing and Shenzhen, the referral system has been successfully implemented (Zhao, 2011; Ma, 2013).

In any case, healthcare referral services, as with all healthcare activities and procedures, must be practiced under a patient-centred healthcare framework, which the Chinese central government has defined and repetitively emphasised as the most essential principle for all healthcare professionals and organisations (Zhong, 2009). This framework demands that the patient's rights, benefits and requirements must be constantly ensured throughout patient referral processes. Therefore, in the healthcare referral services, it is of paramount importance that professionals communicate and share knowledge with each other to look after patients' needs and benefits (Steward, 2001; Maizes et al., 2009). In truth, without effective and rich knowledge sharing (KS), healthcare referrals would merely be procedures for handing over patients from hospital to hospital, and this procedural approach would thus contradict the principles of patient-centred healthcare (Xie et al., 2011; Zhou and Nunes, 2012).

Nevertheless, it has been reported that KS might be largely neglected in practice (Ouyang, 2010; Zhang et al., 2011). For instance, Zhang et al. (2011) investigated healthcare referral services in four Chinese cities: Wuhan, Enshi, Nanchang and Shenzhen. According to their findings, 56% of hospital doctors have never had any work-related communication with GPs, whilst 57% of GPs have never communicated with hospital doctors. Moreover, 61% of hospital doctors and 86% of GPs evaluated patient-centred communication as very poor (Zhang et al., 2011). Ouyang (2010) explains that hospitals and clinics are almost entirely isolated and have become individual information islands, on which the generation, storage and utilisation of knowledge are completely independent.

This project aimed to identify KS barriers in the newly implemented referral system in the Chinese Healthcare System and devise strategies to mitigate these barriers. Thus, to achieve the main research aim, the following research questions have been formulated:

RQ1: What barriers hinder and prevent patient-centred KS between healthcare professionals in Chinese healthcare referral services?

RQ2: What are the relationships between the individual KS barriers?

RQ3: What practical and actionable strategies can be formulated based on the identification and analysis of the barriers to KS?

5.2.2 Research Methodology

According to an initial indicative literature review, it was informed that a number of research studies have been performed investigating the Chinese healthcare referral services. These research studies have been widely reported and discussed in Chinese newspapers, academic journals and dissertations. Therefore, a set of theory was likely to be developed based on the analysis of existing case-study reports obtained from secondary sources. In this case, a desk case-study approach was considered as both suitable and plausible to achieve the research aim and to respond the research questions.

In this project, the case-studies included are relevant research publications and study reports, which present and discuss complete empirical investigations performed in Chinese hospitals. In this sense, individual research projects were systematically retrieved, selected and analysed using the research framework presented in Figure 1. Specifically, the analysis encompassed the following four main inductive stages:

- Performing a critical literature review on patient-centred KS and on healthcare referral services. The literature review aims to provide a theoretical basis and background to the study. Also, the review aims to establish a tentative theoretical framework, which consists of potential main categories of KS barriers in healthcare settings for further exploration and critical analysis;
- Selecting an appropriate set of case-studies. The case-studies are systematically retrieved from three major Chinese academic databases and carefully selected on the basis of its validity and descriptive value;
- Analysing individual case-studies by using a tentative theoretical framework as lenses;
- Synthesizing the findings from different case-studies to provide a response to the research questions and to establish KS barriers model.

5.2.3 Establishing a Tentative Theoretical Framework from a Critical Literature Review

The critical review of literature performed at the beginning of this project informed that, despite a wide recognition of the importance and value of KS, the implementation and practice of KS in healthcare organisations is not as easy and as successful as it appears. A number of studies have investigated into the KS implementation in healthcare and have identified a number of pertinent issues and barriers (e.g. Van Beveren, 2003; De Brún, 2007; Nicolini et al., 2008; Lin et al., 2008; Zhou and Nunes, 2012).

Among existing theories, a KS barrier framework, developed by Lin et al. (2008), was considered as suitable and relevant to this project. Moreover, Lin et al. (2008)'s framework was finally decided to be included in this project for two additional reasons: (1) this framework was developed in Taiwan, where has a very similar social structure and culture to mainland China; and (2) this framework has been used in a number of healthcare KS research studies in different countries and has been proven as valid and effective.

Lin et al. (2008)'s framework consists of 15 barriers in five categories:

- Knowledge source barriers, which include the knowledge source wanting to maintain his prestige, the knowledge source wanting to maintain his competence, and a lack of trust in the knowledge source.
- Knowledge receiver barriers, which include the knowledge receiver lacking absorptive capacity, the knowledge receiver lacking a positive attitude, and the NIH syndrome.
- Knowledge transfer barriers, which include the tacit nature of medical knowledge, the complex nature of medical knowledge, the difficulty of standardizing medical knowledge, and knowledge that lacks evidence.
- Organisational context barriers, which include the lack of rewards and incentives toward knowledge sharing and the lack of leadership to promote knowledge sharing.
- Knowledge flow context barriers, which include the lack of sufficient knowledge-sharing mechanisms and knowledge sources/knowledge receivers not knowing the other end of knowledge sharing.

5.2.4 The Selection of Case-Studies

The selection of case-studies was carried out in three stages. In the first stage, three major Chinese academic databases, namely, CNKI, Wanfang and CQVIP, were systematically searched in February 2014, using the search strategy presented below:

1. Referra*
2. Knowledge
3. Information
4. Management
5. Communicat*
6. Sharing
7. Transfer
8. #2 OR #3
9. #4 OR #5 OR #6 OR #7
10. #8 AND #9
11. #1 AND #10
12. TIME=2000-2014

It is necessary to highlight that the search was performed in Chinese. The search terms were translated into English to be report them in this chapter. Overall, the database search retrieved 948 articles: 693 articles from CNKI, 95 from Wanfang and 160 from CQVIP.

In the second stage, after manually excluding repetitive articles retrieved from different databases, the titles and abstracts of the retrieved articles were reviewed and screened for relevance and meaningfulness to this study. As a result, 207 articles were included for stage three.

The final stage aimed at assessing the quality of the individual articles included. Specifically, the assessment was performed according to two criteria. Firstly, the articles included should be published on core Chinese journals as certified by Peking University Library. Secondly, the articles should provide clear description of the research context, clear justification of research methods applied and unbiased discussion of research findings. Finally, 97 articles were included for the literature analysis.

5.2.5 Case-Study Analysis and Research Findings

A computer assisted qualitative data analysis software, namely, Nvivo 10, was employed for the case-study analysis. Specifically, the framework of Lin et al. (2008) has been used to drive coding practices. Individual KS barriers in this framework were transformed into codes, which were then used to examine, label and categorise valuable text segments that were identified in the review articles. However, instead of just deductively verifying the original KS barriers, the codes were only used at the beginning of the literature analysis and then were inducted, re-contextualised and adapted throughout the analysis.

For instance, the "knowledge source wants to maintain his prestige" barrier was not represented in the analysis and was thus discarded. In contrast, the "tacit nature of medical knowledge" barrier was identified as a KS barrier, but it had a different definition. According to the analysis, tacit knowledge was almost entirely neglected in practice. Therefore, this barrier was redefined as the "neglect of tacit patient knowledge in current practice". In addition, several new KS barriers emerged and were open coded in the analysis, such as "financial conflicts between healthcare organisations" and "patient records as ineffective KS tools".

The case-study analysis pointed to 13 barriers to KS in Chinese healthcare referral services. Moreover, the barriers emerged in five themes, as shown in Table 3.

The research findings were further conceptualised to identify cause-consequence relationships between individual KS barriers. Thus, the research findings were synthesized and represented through the conceptual model presented in Figure 4. This model represents not only the barriers identified above, but also relationships among these barriers.

In Figure 4, there are three types of relationships. First, the solid single-arrow lines represent the cause-consequence relationships between

Table 3. Barriers to KS in Chinese Healthcare Referral Services

Themes	KS Barrier
Knowledge Source Barriers	Difficulties in sharing knowledge to meet receiving professionals' needs.
	Overwhelmingly high workload
Knowledge Receiver Barriers	Inability to absorb knowledge received (lack of absorptive capacity)
	Lack of mutual trust
Communication Barriers	Perceptions of patient records as ineffective KS tools
	Perceptions of referral notes as ineffective KS tools
	Absence of communicating HIS between hospitals and community health clinics
	Lack of mutual acquaintance between healthcare professionals
	Absence of referral information systems
KS Context Barriers	Financial conflicts between healthcare organisations.
	Lack of explicit and pragmatic KS requirements.
Knowledge Transfer Barriers	Neglect of tacit patient knowledge in current practices.
	Absence of managerial attention

Figure 4. A Model of Emerging KS Barriers, Relationships and Themes

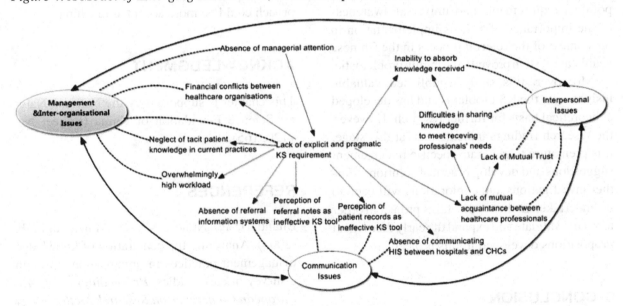

individual KS barriers. Secondly, the dotted lines demonstrate the relationships between the barriers and the emerging categories. Finally, the bold double-headed arrows show the relationships between three emerging categories, which are presented in oval shapes.

As shown in Figure 4, the identified KS barriers are interconnected, and some of them are mutually influential. It is important to note that two barriers emerged as central in the cause-consequence networks: lack of explicit and pragmatic KS requirements and lack of mutual acquaintance between healthcare professionals. It is also important to note that these two barriers are very specifically representative of the cultural context of the Chinese Healthcare system. This finding indicates that these two barriers need to be particularly addressed and resolved if KS is to be improved in practice.

Moreover, three main theoretical themes emerged through the conceptualisation: management and inter-organisational issues, communication issues, and interpersonal issues. The research findings indicate that these three categories are mutually influential. Moreover, management and inter-organisational issues also emerged as central themes in the emerging theory.

This project established and defined the process of referral in China and the used academic literature to anticipate and identify potential barriers in this referral process. Findings show that despite clear political requirements and universal awareness of the importance of KS, its implementation in the context of the referral process in the Chinese healthcare system proved to be highly problematic.

Moreover, this study established valuable insights into the KS problems and has developed a theoretical basis for further research. However, the research findings indicate that, at this stage, it is premature to generate specific management suggestions and develop practical solutions. Further investigations and explorations will need to be undertaken in the scope of this project in order to verify, validate and expand the early theoretical propositions developed in this project.

6. CONCLUSION

This chapter argues that the desk case-study approach should be valued as a scientific, valid and useful methodology for IS investigations. Published and publicly available case-studies could be a valuable source of information for inductive theory development. If these case-studies can be carefully selected, examined and analysed system-atically following a rigorous desk research process consists of defining research question, developing theoretical framework based on reviewing existing literature, selecting case-studies, and establishing theory through the analysis of individual case-studies, they could make substantial contributions to both the existing body of knowledge and the practice of IS in reality.

The desk case-study research approach reported in this chapter challenges a common bias against qualitative research approaches in Chinese academia, where the use of quantitative methods and positivist epistemological stance represent high quality, scientific IS research, whereas inductive qualitative approaches are generally seen as subjective and not scientific. It is expected that through developing a rigorous research framework, robustly defining and discussing individual research processes, this qualitative research approach could be more accepted in China.

ACKNOWLEDGMENT

This chapter is supported by the National Natural Science Foundation of China (Project No. 71203165).

REFERENCES

Bhandari, P., Nunes, M., & Annansingh, F. (2005). Analysing the penetration of knowledge management practices in organisations through a survey of case studies. *Proceedings of the 4th European Conference on Research Methodology for Business and Management Studies (ECRM 2005)*. Université Paris Dauphine, Paris, France.

Bryman, A. (2001). *Social research methods*. Bath, England: Oxford University Press.

Bryman, A., & Bell, E. (2003). *Business research methods*. Oxford, England: Oxford University Press.

Cadle, J., & Yeate, D. (2001). *Project management for information systems*. Harlow, Essex, England: Financial Times/Prentice Hall.

Chapman, C., & Ward, S. (1997). *Project risk: management processes, techniques and insights*. New York, NY: Wiley.

Charette, R. (1989). *Software engineering risk analysis and management*. New York, NY: McGraw-Hill.

Chen, H., Nunes, M., Zhou, L., & Peng, G. (2011). The role of electronic records management in information systems development: Gathering, recording and managing evidence of crucial communication and negotiations with customers. *Aslib Proceedings*, *63*(2/3), 168–187. doi:10.1108/00012531111135646

Clegg, C., Axtell, C., Damadoran, L., Farbey, B., Hull, R., Lloyd-Jones, R., & Tomlinson, C. (1997). Information technology: A study of performance and the role of human and organizational factors. *Ergonomics Journal*, *40*(9), 851–871. doi:10.1080/001401397187694

Collis, J., & Hussey, R. (2003). *Business research: A practical guide for undergraduates and postgraduate students*. Hampshire, England: Palgrave McMillan.

Creswell, J. (2003). *Research design: Qualitative, quantitative, and mixed methods approaches*. London: Sage.

De Brún, C. (2007). Knowledge management and the national health service in England. In R. Bali & A. Dwivedi (Eds.), *Healthcare knowledge management: Issues, advances, and successes* (pp. 179–188). New York: Springer New York. doi:10.1007/978-0-387-49009-0_13

Drori, O. (1997). From theory to practice or how not to fail in developing information systems. *Software Engineering Notes*, *22*(1), 85–87. doi:10.1145/251759.251875

Easterby-Smith, M., Thorpe, R., & Lowe, A. (2002). *Management research*. London: Sage.

Eisenhardt, K. (1989). Building theories from case study research. *Academy of Management Review*, *14*(4), 532–550.

Gill, J., & Johnson, P. (1991). *Research methods for managers*. London: Paul Chapman.

Glesne, C., & Peshkin, A. (1992). *Becoming qualitative researchers*. New York, NY: Longman.

Growth Policy Analysis. (2013). *China's healthcare system-overview and quality improvements*. Sweden: Swedish Agency for Growth Policy Analysis.

Hughes, B., & Cotterell, M. (2002). *Software project management*. London: McGraw-Hill.

Jackson, P. (1994). *Desk research*. London: Kogan Page.

Jalote, P. (2002). *Software project management in practice*. Boston, MA: Addison-Wesley Professional.

Keil, M., Cule, P., Lyytinen, K., & Schmidt, R. (1998). A framework for identifying software project risks. *Communications of the ACM*, *20*(11), 76–83. doi:10.1145/287831.287843

King, N. (2008). *Template analysis*. Retrieved from http://www2.hud.ac.uk/hhs/research/template_analysis

King, N., & Horrocks, C. (2010). *Interviews in qualitative research*. London: Sage.

Kliem, R., & Ludin, I. (2000). *Reducing project risk*. Aldershot, England: Gower Publishing Limited.

Lawrence, M. (2003). Are you up to it? *The Computer Bulletin for Information Systems Professionals*, *45*(2), 22.

Le Deu, F., Parekh, R., Zhang, F., & Zhou, G. (2012). *Health care in China: Entering 'uncharted waters*. Shanghai, China: McKinsey & Company.

Lin, C., Tan, B., & Chang, S. (2008). An exploratory model of knowledge flow barriers within Healthcare Organisations. *Information & Management, 45*(5), 331–339. doi:10.1016/j.im.2008.03.003

Ma, C. (2013). Research on two-way referral schema of information systems in Beijing. [in Chinese]. *Chinese Hospital Management, 33*(1), 73–74.

Maizes, V., Rakel, D., & Niemiec, C. (2009). Integrative medicine and patient-centred care. *Explore (New York, N.Y.), 5*(5), 277–289. doi:10.1016/j.explore.2009.06.008 PMID:19733814

Mantel, S., Meredith, J., Shafer, S., & Sutton, M. (2001). *Project management in practice*. New York, NY: Wiley.

Myers, M. (1997). Qualitative research in information systems. *Management Information Systems Quarterly, 21*(2), 241–242. doi:10.2307/249422

Nicolini, D., Powell, J., Conville, P., & Martinez-Solano, L. (2008). Managing knowledge in the healthcare sector: A review. *International Journal of Management Reviews, 10*(3), 245–263. doi:10.1111/j.1468-2370.2007.00219.x

Ouyang, T. (2010). *Research on the sharing of medical information resource on the basis of bidirectional referral medical care in community health service and tertiary hospital* [Unpublished master's dissertation]. Hefei Industrial University, Hefei.

Pritchard, C. (2004). *The project management Communications*. London: Toolkit Artech House.

Remenyi, D., Williams, B., Money, A., & Swartz, E. (1998). *Doing research in business and Management: An introduction to process and method*. London: Sage. doi:10.4135/9781446280416

Saunders, M., Lewis, P., & Thornhill, A. (2009). *Research methods for business students*. New York: Prentice Hall.

Steward, M. (2001). Towards a global definition of patient centred care: The patient should be the judge of patient centred care. *British Medical Journal, 322*(7284), 444–445. doi:10.1136/bmj.322.7284.444

Strauss, A., & Corbin, J. (1998). *Basic of qualitative research: Techniques and procedures for developing grounded theory* (2nd ed.). London: Sage Publications.

Stufflebeam, D. (2000). *Guidelines for developing evaluation checklists: the checklists development checklist (CDC)*. Retrieved from http://www.wmich.edu/evalctr/archive_checklists/guidelines_cdc.pdf

Taylor, J. (2003). *Managing information technology projects: Applying project management strategies to software, hardware and integration initiatives*. New York, NY: American Management Association.

Tsui, F. (2004). Managing software projects. Sudbury, Massachusetts, America: Jones and Bartlett Publishers.

Van Beveren, J. (2003). Does health care for knowledge management? *Journal of Knowledge Management, 7*(1), 90–95. doi:10.1108/13673270310463644

Whittaker, B. (1999). What went wrong? Unsuccessful information technology projects. *Information Management & Computer Security, 7*(1), 23–29. doi:10.1108/09685229910255160

Xie, M., Xie, G., & Zhang, Y. (2011). Construction of regional medical service mode of cooperation. [in Chinese]. *Modem Hospital Management, 42*(3), 18–20.

Xu, Q., Zhou, Y., Zhou, L., & Geng, Q. (2012). Study and implementation of cooperation for dual referral based on integrating healthcare enterprise cross-enterprise document sharing techniques. [in Chinese]. *Chinese Journal of Tissue Engineering Research, 16*(22), 4112–4116.

Yin, R. (1994). *Case study research, design and methods*. Newbury Park, CA: Sage Publications.

Yuan, B. (2012). Referral Anxiety. *China Health Human Resources, 2012*(5), 29-31.

Zhang, J. (2007). Case study method in information system research. *Journal of Information, 5*, 88-89, 92.

Zhang, L., Pan, L., Guo, X., & Jiang, L. (2012). Study on measurement of workload for pharmaceutical service in clinician. [in Chinese]. *Journal of Clinical and Experimental Medicine, 11*(14), 99–1101. PMID:23086188

Zhao, R. (2011). *Research on sharing electronic medical record* [Unpublished masters dissertation]. Zhengzhou University, Henan, China.

Zheng, D., He, Y., Chu, Y., & Huang, L. (2006). Compared research of information systems research trend between mainland China and international. *Journal of Fudan University, 45*(5), 577–583.

Zhong, H. (2009). The patient-centred care and hospital marketing strategies. *Management Observation (in Chinese), 2009*(10), 234-235.

Zhou, L., & Nunes, M. (2012). Identifying knowledge sharing barriers in the collaboration of traditional and western medicine professionals in Chinese hospitals: A case study. *Journal of Librarianship and Information Science, 44*(4), 238–248. doi:10.1177/0961000611434758

Zhou, L., Vasconcelos, A., & Nunes, M. (2008). Supporting decision making in risk management through an evidence-based information systems project risk checklist. *Information Management & Computer Security, 16*(2), 166–186. doi:10.1108/09685220810879636

KEY TERMS AND DEFINITIONS

Case Study: A very common research methodology for qualitative studies, which aim to explore and understand complex and localised human activity systems and social environments.

Desk Research: A research approach used for critically evaluating and analysing secondary data and existing literature.

Inductive Approach: A "bottom up" approach for research investigations, which aim at theory development. An inductive study begins with specific observation and evaluation in order to identify patterns and regularities, which are then articulated into tentative hypotheses. Finally, based on these hypotheses, general conclusions or theories are developed.

Qualitative Research: A systematic research methodology, which depends on the use of words. Qualitative research studies attempt to analyse data collected from the research context in which events occur, as well as from the perspectives of those participating in the events.

Quantitative Research: Attempts to understand a social phenomenon by interpreting numbers. This paradigm emphasises quantification in the processes of data collection and analysis.

Secondary Data: A type of data gathered by someone in the past, for some purposes very different from the research project at hand.

Thematic Analysis: Can be simply understood as a systematic approach to coding, categorising and representing qualitative data.

Chapter 12
Multidimensional and Interrelated Barriers and Risks Affecting Long–Term ERP Success in Chinese State–Owned Enterprises

Guo Chao Peng
The University of Sheffield, UK

Miguel Baptista Nunes
The University of Sheffield, UK

ABSTRACT

The research reported in this paper aimed to identify and explore potential cultural, operational, managerial, organisational and technical barriers and risks that can affect successful long-term exploitation of Enterprise Resource Planning (ERP) systems in Chinese SOEs. The study adopted a mixed-methods research design, which consisted of a questionnaire survey and a follow-up multiple case study. Business-oriented and human-related challenges associated with management deficiencies in Chinese SOEs were found to be the main triggers of the complicated network of ERP exploitation barriers and risks. The importance of these crucial business and organisational barriers however are often underestimated by SOE managers. This study thus concluded by suggesting that Chinese SOEs need to become more aware of the critical importance and the networked nature of the organisational barriers identified. Properly managing this type of ERP obstacles can help Chinese SOEs to mitigate and remove other ERP challenges and risks and thus ensuring long-term success in ERP post-implementation.

1. INTRODUCTION AND BACKGROUND OF STUDY

With the remarkable economic growth at an annual rate of around 10% during the last quarter century, China has now emerged as one of the world's economic superpower. Information Technology (IT) is certainly one of the most important driving forces in supporting this rapid economic development in the country. In fact, and ever since

DOI: 10.4018/978-1-4666-8833-9.ch012

the beginning of the 21st century, China has constructed a nationwide IT network that covers more than 2000 cities across the whole country (China Economic Yearbook Editing Committee, 2004). With this well-established national information infrastructure, IT has been increasingly embedded into the everyday life of Chinese citizens. This is evident from the increasing number of China's internet users, which has grown dramatically from only 0.62 million in 1997 to more than 420 million in 2010 (China Internet Network Information Center, 2011). Apart from its impacts on social life, IT has also become an essential part of the organisational structure of most contemporary Chinese companies. According to CCW Research (a well-known Chinese IT consulting firm), IT investments of China's manufacturing sector had increased from RMB 24.5 billion in 2004 to RMB 52.9 billion in 2010 (CCW Research, 2010). A very substantial part of these IT investments of Chinese companies was made to implement Enterprise Resource Planning (ERP) systems.

ERP systems are cross-functional enterprise information system (IS) packages, which consist of a number of software modules that aim at supporting and integrating all key business processes across the various functional divisions of an organization by using a single data repository (Peng & Nunes, 2012). It is arguably the most important development in the corporate use of IT in the 1990s (Davenport, 1998). Many previous IS research (e.g. Oliver et al, 2005; Bergstrom & Stehn, 2005; Shang & Seddon, 2002) indicated that successful adoption and use of ERPs can potentially bring companies with a wide range of benefits at operational (e.g. reduce operational and inventory cost), managerial (e.g. improve resources planning and control), and strategic levels (e.g. increase global operation power). These features and potential benefits of ERPs have resulted in a continuing high implementation rate of such integrated systems in Western companies (Buonanno et al., 2005). In China, both private companies and state-owned enterprises (SOEs)

have also frequently set ERP implementation as a top priority in their IS development agendas (Pan et al., 2011). Consequently, data provided by a prominent Chinese consulting firm (CCID Consulting) shows that, the Chinese ERP market has expanded rapidly from only RMB 560 million in 2000 to RMB 6,956 million in 2010.

However, as ERPs become an integral part of the organisational infrastructure, it is increasingly recognised by IS researchers and practitioners that, successful implementation of the system is only an important first step toward achieving ERP success (Peng & Nunes, 2009; Yu, 2005; Willis & Willis-Brown, 2002). In fact, long-term viability and success of ERP depend on its continued operation, use, maintenance and enhancement during the system post-implementation or exploitation phase (Bhattacherjee, 2001; Willis & Willis-Brown, 2002; Peng & Nunes, 2009). Please note that, for the purpose of this paper, the terms 'ERP post-implementation' and 'ERP exploitation' are used interchangeably. It can however be expected that a range of factors and barriers embedded in the local business context (e.g. lack of continuous top management support and poor cross-functional cooperation), and the system itself (e.g. poor system integration and poor data quality), may affect long-term success in ERP usage and exploitation (Peng & Nunes, 2010; Desai et al., 1998). Moreover, the existence of these barriers may in turn lead to the occurrence of a variety of risks during ERP post-implementation, e.g. staff may be resistant to use the implemented system (Pan et al., 2011; Peng & Nunes, 2009; Bhattacherjee, 2001). Disregarding these multidimensional and interrelated barriers and risks can turn initial ERP success into a failure, and thus contributing to critical business disasters (Bhattacherjee, 2001).

Although many researchers recognise the importance of ERP post-implementation and even stated it is the direction of the second wave ERP research (Yu, 2005), current studies on ERPs focused mostly on system implementation and project management aspects (e.g. Avison &

Malaurent, 2007; Oliver et al., 2005; Huang et al., 2004; Umble et al., 2003; Sumner, 2000). In contrast, research studies focused on ERP post-implementation have only begun to appear in mainstream IS journals until recently. As one of the significant examples, the study about 'how interdependence and differentiation among sub-units of an organization' can affect ERP performance after implementation, appears in MIS Quarterly (Gattiker & Goodhue, 2005). Moreover, Chou & Chang (2008) draw upon the study of Gattiker and Goodhue to explore how customisation and organisational mechanism can affect ERP benefits and performance in the post-adoption phase. Nevertheless, and as acknowledged by these authors, their studies emphasised on a very limited number of variables and factors that may affect the realisation of ERP benefits. No extensive studies on ERP post-implementation barriers/ risks in general, or in the Chinese context in particular, were identified from the literature reviewed. The research presented in this paper thus contributed to this increasingly significant research gap.

This study aimed to identify, explore and assess potential barriers and risks associated with the post-implementation of ERP systems in the context of Chinese SOEs, and more importantly to explore potential causal relationships between the identified barrier and risk items. In order to frame the study, the researchers conducted a critical literature review at the early stage of the research. This extensive review resulted in the establishment of two theoretical ontologies which respectively contained a set of barriers and a list of risks that companies may encounter during ERP exploitation. Subsequently, a mixed-methods research design, which consisted of a questionnaire survey and a follow-up case study, was adopted to examine the suitability of the established barrier and risk ontologies in Chinese SOEs. This paper is organised as follows. The next section provides a further discussion on the importance of SOEs to the Chinese economy, and thus justifies the selection of this type of company in this study.

Subsequently, the theoretical ERP exploitation barrier and risk ontology is presented. This is followed by a discussion of the research methodology. Finally, the results of the study are discussed and interpreted and the implications of these findings are discussed, with conclusions drawn.

2. THE IMPORTANCE OF SOE TO THE CHINESE ECONOMY

Between the period of 1949 and 1978, China adopted the Soviet-style central planning economic system, which allowed the government to own and control the majority of resources of the country (Shirk, 1994:9). However, this feature of planning economy determined that economic activities were controlled by the state and were not influenced by market conditions, and thus resulting in a set of crucial economic deficiencies and problems (e.g. low production efficiency, laggard technologies, and unmotivated work force, etc) to China in the 1970s (Shirk, 1994:10; Perkins, 1997:34). In order to establish a stronger and more competitive economy, China has gradually reformed its economic system from the traditional planning economy to a more competitive market-oriented economy since the late 1970s. This crucial economic transformation has allowed China to achieve rapid and continuous economic growth during the last three decades.

On the other hand, and aligned with the central control purposes, the vast majority of Chinese enterprises in the planning economy were owned and supervised by the state, and are therefore denominated as State-Owned Enterprises (SOEs). Traditionally, these SOEs were not required to be responsible for any business losses, because they operated as social-economic entities, rather than profit making units, and mainly aimed to fulfil production quotas assigned by the government and to provide lifelong employment to urban citizens (Sun et al, 2005). Consequently, these features resulted in very poor performance of

SOEs, which were often loss-making companies in the planning economy era (Yusuf et al., 2006). In order to prevent SOEs from loss making and enable SOEs to compete in the new market economic environment, reforming SOEs has been an essential part of China's economic reform since the early 1980s. Since then, thousands of SOEs have been reformed and restructured through selling or leasing to the public or employees, declaring bankruptcy, or merging with other companies (Garnaut et al., 2005:3).

Consequently, the number of SOEs has decreased rapidly and continuously, especially since the 21st century. As shown in Table 1, the number of SOEs has reduced sharply since 2000 and they accounted for only 4.5% of all industrial enterprises in China in 2010. In contrast, the number of non-SOEs (e.g. privately owned companies, self-employed businesses, foreign-invested companies, and Sino-foreign joint ventures) has been continuously increasing, and has accounted for over 95% of all industrial enterprises in the country since 2008. However, and despite the significant reduction in numbers, Chinese SOEs still continue to absorb more than 41% of the total industrial assets (which reached RMB 59288.2 billion in 2010). When this enormous amount of industrial assets is concentrated in an ever smaller number of companies, the average asset value of SOEs has been dramatically increasing year by year. In 2010, the assets held by SOEs were in average valued at RMB 1223 million, which was more than 15 times higher than the average asset value of non-SOEs (RMB 80 million in the same year). This statistics clearly demonstrates that in spite of the national reform, contemporary SOEs still play a crucial role in sustaining the continuous development of China's industry and the whole national economy. Given their average asset size, SOEs are arguably more important than other types of companies currently coexisted in the country.

Although the state is still the owner or largest shareholder of the company, reformed SOEs are run by their internal management organs (i.e. the board of directors) rather than by the state (Garnaut et al., 2005:46). They now also need to be responsible for their own losses and have to fight hard in order to survive in the new market conditions. These new features and changes result in an imperative need for SOEs to improve their traditionally inefficient management mechanism, hierarchical structure and work processes. Consequently, thousands of Chinese SOEs have implemented and used ERP systems as a strategic tool for replacing their legacy management systems and work practices, and thus hoping to enhance their core competitiveness. However, given a long history of bureaucratic control, it is questionable to what extent senior managers and employees in SOEs are ready and willing to accept the fundamental changes and a more open operating environment entailed by ERP systems. In fact, and despite the very effort of organisational reforms, a number of hitherto management issues (e.g. power centralisation, low staff empowerment, lack of in-house experts, and short-term behaviour) still seem to remain in contemporary SOEs (Sun, 2000; Martinsons, 2004; Tylecote & Cai, 2004; Peng & Nunes, 2010). These organisational and business problems will inevitably cause severe ERP challenges during the system post-implementation stage (Martinsons, 2004; Peng & Nunes, 2010). Consequently, an in-depth study on ERP exploitation barriers and risks in Chinese SOEs is not just timely but also significant for these companies to achieve effective transformation and sustain business competitiveness through their ERP systems.

3. SYNTHESIS OF THE CRITICAL LITERATURE REVIEW

In order to construct adequate theoretical foundation to base the study on, a critical literature review was conducted. The original attempt of this critical review was to identify and retrieve articles that are directly related to ERP exploitation barriers and risks. However, and as discussed above, this

Table 1. The changing status of SOEs and non-SOEs in the industrial sector between 2000 and 2010

Year	SOEs as % of All Industrial Enterprises	Non-SOEs as % of All Industrial Enterprises	SOE Assets as % of Total Industrial Assets	Average Asset Size of SOEs (RMB mn)	Average Asset Size of Non-SOEs (RMB mn)
2000	34	66	67	155	39
2001	28	72	65	184	39
2002	24	76	62	210	40
2003	19	81	57	260	46
2004	15	85	53	317	50
2005	10	90	48	428	52
2006	8	92	46	541	56
2007	6	94	44.8	765	62
2008	5	95	43.8	886	60
2009	4.7	95.3	43.7	1052	67
2010	4.5	95.5	41.8	1223	80

(Source: Data from 2000 to 2004 are obtained from Table 1, Garnaut et al., 2005:8; data from 2005 to 2010 are obtained from the China Statistics Yearbook in various years).

endeavour did not return any extensive studies on ERP post-implementation challenges. Nevertheless, a large amount of valuable literature, which addressed issues related to ERP implementation and general IS usage and deployment, were identified from this critical review. By critically analysing, comparing and synthesising these retrieved materials, the researchers identified and proposed a wide range of potential barriers and risks that may be encountered by Chinese SOEs during ERP exploitation. The following sections present a summary of the results of this extensive review.

3.1 Potential Barriers to ERP Exploitation

The literature gives a number of relatively different definitions on the concept of barrier, as shown in the two examples below:

A barrier is, generally speaking, an obstacle, an obstruction, or a hindrance that may...prevent an event from taking place ... (Hollnagel, 2004).

[From the business perspective] barrier is an obstacle within the business context that prevents business objectives from being realized (Polikoff et al., 2005).

Despite the different phrases being used, these definitions generally point out the fact that a barrier is an existing obstacle that prevents an action or event from being carried out successfully. Keeping this fundamental feature in mind, this paper defines a barrier to ERP exploitation as:

Any obstacle or factor that is inherent to the business context or the system itself, and can prevent companies from efficiently using, maintaining and improving their implemented ERP systems.

It was identified from the critical review that, IS researchers have continued to stress a variety of organisational and system factors and barriers that can prevent user companies from achieving long-term IS success. For instance, Rucks & Ginter (1982) and Reich & Benbasat (2000) argue that potential benefits associated with the use of MIS may not be achieved, due to issues such as inappropriate organizational structure, poor internal communication, and inefficient strategic planning. Other IS researchers (e.g. DeLone, 1988; Roepke et al., 2000; Shehab et al., 2004; Pan et al., 2011) reinforce that user satisfaction and acceptance toward the implemented system can be reduced, owing to barriers including insufficient user training, deficient system design, lack of top management commitment, fear of loss of job, low data quality, and poor integration of systems. Moreover, the studies of Raymond et al. (1995), Desai et al. (1998), Wright & Donaldson (2002) and Namjae & Kiho (2003) identified a further set of organisational and technical barriers to successful IS innovation, such as lack of efficient IS planning, inappropriate system upgrade, low system flexibility and compatibility, and high IS enhancement cost, etc.

Apart from these organisational and technical barriers, the Chinese culture can also raise substantial obstacles for IS and ERP usage and exploitation. For instance, high power distance is one of the features embedded in the traditional Chinese culture (Hofstede, 2001). This cultural characteristic has resulted in very centralised, directive and hierarchical management systems in traditional Chinese companies, such as SOEs (Martinsons & Westwood, 1997; Tylecote & Cai, 2004). Top managers in these Chinese firms may often tend to hold strong control on many organisational aspects, and are inclined to make centrally decisions (Martinsons & Westwood, 1997; Martinsons & Hempel, 1998). Reimers (2002) argues that such centralised management system may sometimes enable Chinese top managers to make important IS decisions without collecting and considering alternative ideas from a wider group of stakeholders (e.g. IT experts and system users). Martinsons & Westwood (1997) reinforce that Chinese leaders may symbolically consult their subordinates, but will rarely let them make a meaningful contribution to the decision-making

process. However, because top managers are very often neither IS experts nor daily users of ERPs, they may lack experience of operational situations and have insufficient technical knowledge to make appropriate ERP maintenance or enhancement decisions on their own (Peng & Nunes, 2010). Therefore, this type of centralised decision making style can threaten the long-term success of ERP post-implementation.

By systematically reviewing and synthesising these prior IS/ERP studies, the researchers established and proposed an extensive list of 25 barriers that may affect successful exploitation of ERP systems in the Chinese context, including 7 cultural barriers, 9 organisational barriers and 9 system barriers. Subsequently, a barrier ontology was developed to highlight the established ERP exploitation barriers, as presented in Figure 1. This ontology consists of two hierarchical levels ranging from general barrier categories (e.g. cultural barrier) to specific barrier items (e.g. power centralization of top managers). Moreover, it emerged from the critical review that, an ERP barrier may often be the cause or consequence of other barriers. For instance, "lack of long-term ERP plan", which can be a result of "short-term thinking of top managers", may lead to "insufficient fund to be allocated to ERP maintenance and enhancement". The established barrier ontology thus also highlights a number of potential ERP barrier relationships emerged from the literature review. A full discussion of the items involved in this barrier ontology can be seen in another journal article published by the same research team (Peng & Nunes, 2010).

3.2 Potential Risks to ERP Exploitation

On the other hand, a risk as defined by Kleim & Ludin (2000) is "the occurrence of an event that has consequences for, or impacts on" a particular business process. In fact, the terms 'barrier' and 'risk' were often misused by authors. In

Figure 1. Theoretical ontology of the 25 established ERP barriers

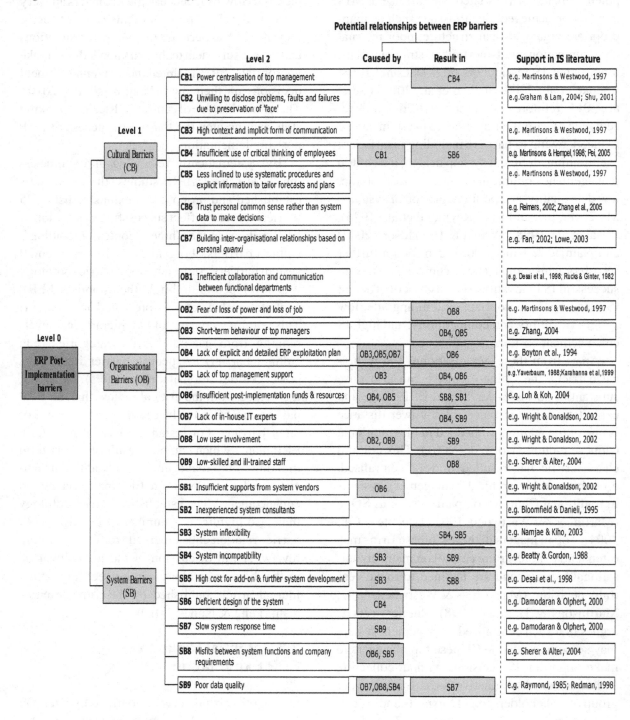

particular, some non-scientists (e.g. The Alaska Department of Natural Resources, 2003) and less careful researchers (e.g. Söderlind & Kidby, 2005) may use these two terms interchangeably. Nevertheless, these two concepts are in reality substantially different from each other. Specifically, a risk is associated with uncertainty. That is, there is a probability that the risk event may occur and thus lead to an impact on the business processes and may imply substantial losses. In contrast, a barrier is a factor that is inherent to a given context. Therefore, a barrier, unlike a risk, has no uncertainty associated to it, and has 100% probability of occurrence. Due to this characteristic, a barrier is fundamentally different from a risk. These two terms must therefore be clearly distinguished. For the purpose of this study, the researchers modified the above definition given by Kleim & Ludin, and defined an ERP post-implementation risk as:

The occurrence of an event that has consequences or impacts on the use, maintenance and enhancement of the implemented ERP system.

Given the size and complexity of an ERP system, identification of risk in ERP post-implementation was a very time-consuming and complicated task. In order to frame the study and generate meaningful outcomes, the researchers particularly looked at ERP risks in four main categories:

- **Operational Risk (OR):** ERP systems are mainly designed to integrate and automate transaction processing activities of companies (Chou et al., 2005). Operational risks refer to risks that may occur as operational staff use ERP systems to perform daily business activities.

- **Analytical Risk (AR):** Apart from daily transactional functions, ERP systems are also embedded with a set of analytical tools to facilitate planning and forecasting (e.g.

production plans, sales forecasts, financial budgets, etc) (Marnewick & Labuschagne, 2005). Analytical risks refer to risk events that may occur as managers and business analysts use ERPs to carry out analytical tasks.

- **Organization-Wide Risk (OWR):** When using and maintaining ERPs in the post-implementation stage, companies may encounter a set of risk events in relation to various internal (e.g. system users, in-house IT experts) and external factors (e.g. system vendor, system consultants). Such risks may have impact on the entire company (Lientz & Larssen, 2006), and thus are referred to as organization-wide risks.

- **Technical Risk (TR):** A set of technical (e.g. hardware and software) issues may result in risk events that can hinder the implemented system from meeting its intended functions and performance requirements (Namjae & Kiho, 2003). These risk events are identified as technical risks.

Furthermore, it was considered that operational and analytical risks occur in different functional areas and processes in a company, and are therefore very different in nature. Their study needs to take into account diverse aspects and sometimes very disparate triggers. Moreover, it emerges in the survey studies of Reimers (2001) and Tsai et al. (2005) that ERP systems are most frequently used in three business areas, namely sales and marketing area, production and purchasing area, and financial and accounting area. Based on these considerations, the researchers specifically selected and focused on these three essential business areas for identification of operational and analytical risks.

On the other hand, the literature review identified a range of organisation-wide risks that can frequently occur during the IS and ERP implementation project, such as top managers fail to provide sufficient support to IS/ERP, lose qualified

IT experts, and cannot receive sufficient support from system vendors, etc (Gargeya & Brady, 2005; Huang et al., 2004; Scott & Vessey, 2002; Sumner, 2000; Barki et al., 1993). It is reasonable to argue that such organisation-wide risks may not just affect ERP implementation but can also occur during the system exploitation stage. Moreover, IS researchers (e.g. Sherer, 2004; Loh & Koh, 2004) also highlighted a number of common technical risks that can occur during the use of IT systems, e.g. hardware and software crash, invalid data of the system is not properly managed, and system is not continually modified to meet new business requirements.

Consequently, by critically analyzing and synthesizing these IS and ERP studies, the researchers identified a comprehensive set of 40 risk events that may occur during ERP exploitation, including 9 operational risks, 8 analytical risks, 16 organization-wide risks and 7 technical risks. Subsequently, a risk ontology was developed to highlight these 40 established ERP risks. As shown in Figure 2, this established ontology for ERP post-implementation risks consists of three hierarchical levels ranging from main risk categories (e.g. operational risks), to risk sub-categories (e.g. production and purchasing risks), and then to specific risk events (e.g. ERP system contains inaccurate supplier records). In addition, it clearly emerged from the findings of the critical literature review that, the occurrence of an ERP risk may often be related to the occurrence of other risks. In other words, an identified ERP risk may be the cause or consequence of a set of other risks. For instance, 'users are not provided with sufficient training' is a common risk that can significantly reduce user satisfaction (Gargeya & Brady, 2005). The occurrence of this risk event can trigger a set of other ERP risks, e.g. 'operational staff are reluctant to use the implemented system' or 'users may input incorrect data into ERP' (Gargeya & Brady, 2005). These potential causal relationships between ERP risks, as identified from the critical review, were also summarised and highlighted in the risk ontology. Further discussion of the contents and items included in this risk ontology can be found in our other publications (Peng & Nunes, 2009; 2009b; 2012).

3.3 Potential Correlations between ERP Exploitation Barriers and Risks

Finally, by further examining the above definitions of barrier and risk, it emerges that a barrier existing in the organisational context may lead to the occurrence of a set of undesirable risk events. Our review and synthesis of prior IS and ERP literature suggested that this would be particularly true for ERP post-implementation. For instance, 'short-term behaviour' refers to the phenomenon that companies act to achieve short-term benefits, while neglecting the associated impacts and problems that may arise in the long-term (Liu, 2004). Short-term behaviour of top managers has been reported as a common problem in Chinese firms (Zhang, 2004; Tylecote & Cai, 2004). This issue is expected as a barrier to long-term ERP usage and exploitation in China's companies. Owing to short term thinking, Chinese managers may perceive the end of the implementation of ERPs, as the end of their involvement with the system. This may result in the risk that Chinese leaders may not be willing to provide continuous support to ERP exploitation in the long term. Lack of continued support by top management may in turn discourage the actual use of the system and prevent users and IT experts to proactively contribute to continuous system planning, review and improvement. Consequently, based on these results of the critical review, Figure 3 summaries and highlights a set of potential causal relationships between the identified ERP exploitation barriers and risks.

Figure 2. Theoretical ontology of the 40 established ERP risks

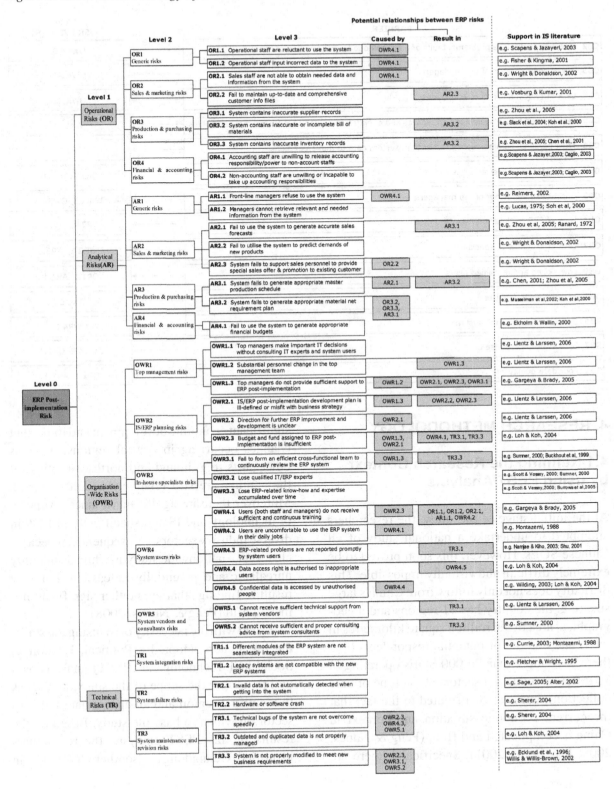

Figure 3. Potential relationships between ERP exploitation barriers and risks

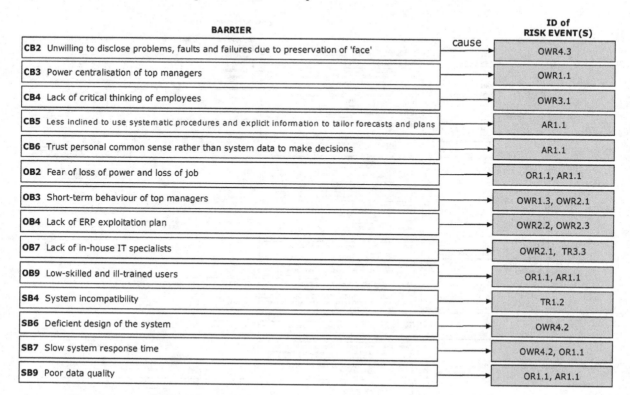

4. RESEARCH METHODOLOGY

4.1 Refining the Research Context by using PEST Analysis

At the initial stage of the study, the researchers attempted to undertake a national study of all Chinese SOEs. However, this soon proved to be extremely difficult and virtually impossible. This difficulty does not only follow from China's large size (e.g. the country has 31 regions and a geographical area of 9.6 million square kilometres in total) and number of potential respondents (e.g. there were more than 24,000 SOEs operating in 31 different industrial sectors at the time of data collection), but is also attributed to the fact that the current economic situation and context in China is complicated and fluid (Peng & Nunes, 2008; Roy et al., 2001). Specifically, there are

significant economic development and important changes occurring in coastal regions, whereas other parts (e.g. inland and northwest cities) of the country are still relatively underdeveloped. Moreover, there are significant variances in uptake of technology and IS and specifically of ERP in diverse industry sectors. Consequently, it became clear that a nationwide study in China is not only unrealistic and potentially unfeasible, but may result in findings that are neither significant nor meaningful (Peng & Nunes, 2008).

Faced with the necessity of focusing the study, the researchers adopted a Political, Economic, Social and Technological (PEST) analysis as a tool to narrow the scope of the study, as well as to identify a region and an appropriate industry sector on which to base the study. Based on the results of this PEST analysis, the researchers identified Guangdong (a southern province in

China) as an ideal context for the study of ERP post-implementation. Guangdong is one of the pioneer regions of China's economic reform and one of the most important and fast-growing economic regions in the country. Consequently, the region has achieved high levels of ICT and IS uptake and presents itself as a suitable context where to study a phenomenon such as post-implementation of ERPs. Moreover, a second important conclusion of the PEST analysis was the realisation that the ICT manufacturing industry is arguably the most important manufacturing sector in China, since it continuously contributes to the highest percentage of the national industrial output among the 31 industrial sectors of the country. Companies in the ICT manufacturing sector have also achieved high level of IS utilisation and ERP innovation, and will thus provide the prerequisite and an ideal context to investigate ERP post-implementation. Overall, as a result of the PEST analysis, the researchers identified and selected a reasonable and feasible set of Chinese SOEs for carrying out the research, namely SOEs in the ICT Manufacturing Sector in the Guangdong province of China.

4.2 Mixed-Methods Research Design

In order to examine and explore the extensive list of barrier and risk items identified from the critical literature review in the context of selected Chinese SOEs, a questionnaire survey was used as the main method of data collection. In addition, due to a lack of study in ERP post-implementation in general and in the Chinese context in particular, IS and ERP literature used to develop the above barrier and risk ontology was published mainly in the West. It was anticipated that some findings derived from the Western context may not be entirely applicable to the Chinese one. Therefore, it was expected that some findings of the questionnaire might be different from the original theory. In order to explore and further verify the findings derived from the quantitative

component, a follow-up case study was carried out at the second stage of the research. Consequently, these considerations led to the selection and use of a two-phase mixed-methods research design in this study. The first phase of the design involved a cross-sectional questionnaire survey and took the predominant position of the entire research. Subsequently, a follow-up case study was carried out to explore further the quantitative findings and thus achieve triangulation.

4.2.1 Questionnaire Design and Data Collection

The questionnaire survey was developed by using the above ERP exploitation barrier and risk ontology as the theoretical basis. From the barrier ontology, it became apparent that of the 25 predefined barriers, some were related with core business and organisational aspects, while the remainder focused on system issues. Similarly, among the 40 predefined events in the risk ontology, some were related with business issues, while the rest focused on technical aspects. This clearly indicated that two different questionnaires needed to be designed to obtain perspectives of both business managers and ICT experts.

In the first section of the questionnaires, respondents were asked to which extent they agree or disagree with the 25 listed barrier statements. Each item was scored using a 5-point Likert scale ranging from strongly disagree (1) to strongly agree (5). All barrier items were thus scaled, so that the greater the score, the greater the extent that a barrier exists in the company. Subsequently, the researchers attempted to identify which of the 40 predefined risk events would be perceived by SOE respondents as risks for ERP exploitation, as well as, to assess the importance of each identified risk according to its likelihood, impact and frequency of occurrence. In order to achieve these objectives, each of the 40 risk events was examined in the questionnaire through four questions:

1. Whether this event could be perceived as a risk to ERP exploitation (1 = yes, 2 = no).
2. What the probability of occurrence of this risk event could be (measured on a 3-point Likert scale, ranging from high [3] to low [1]).
3. What level of impact this risk could result in (measured on a 3-point Likert scale, ranging from high [3] to low [1]).
4. What the frequency of occurrence of this risk event could be (measured on a 5-point Likert scale, ranging from very often [5] to very rarely [1]).

Both questionnaire scripts were originally developed in English and then translated into Chinese. The questionnaire could actually have been directly designed in Chinese, but since the literature review was undertaken in English as based mostly (90%) on English sources, the initial script was written in that language using its terminology. Nonetheless, substantial attention had been paid during the translation process in order to ensure that both the English and Chinese versions of the questionnaire were conceptually equivalent, and thereby ensure high internal validity. In order to further improve its validity, the Chinese version of questionnaire was pilot tested with a group of Chinese postgraduate students and researchers in the authors' department, as well as with 5 Chinese managers working in one Chinese SOE. A number of corrections to the questionnaires were made according to the feedback received from the pilot test.

According to statistics provided by the Guangdong Statistical Bureau, there are 118 SOEs operating in the local ICT manufacturing sector. The two designed questionnaires were thus mailed to the operation managers and IT managers of these 118 Chinese firms. In order to increase the response rate, a web-based version of the questionnaires was also developed. Respondents could thus either fill in the questionnaire and return it by using the pre-paid envelope, or complete the online version and submit it electronically. One month after the original questionnaire, a reminder was sent out. Personal relationships and contacts were used wherever possible in the study in order to gain access to more companies, secure response and increase reliability and quality of the answers provided. Consequently, 42 out of the 118 selected SOEs responded to the questionnaire, which resulted in a response rate of 35.6%. The collected quantitative data were then carefully and systematically analysed by using a number of statistical techniques, as further discussed in section 5.

4.2.2 Data Collection of the Follow-Up Case Study

As discussed above, the follow-up case study is a supplement component that aimed to collect in-depth human insights in order to further explore and validate the questionnaire findings. At the end of the questionnaire survey, respondents were asked whether or not they would be willing to participate in the follow-up case study to discuss further ERP-related risks and issues in their companies. Two volunteer companies were thus identified to participate in the second phase of the research.

As discussed by Saunders et al. (2003:246), semi-structured interview is a very efficient tool to collect in-depth human insights to explore a list of themes and questions that are predefined prior to the collection of data (e.g. the questionnaire findings derived from the first phase). Moreover, researchers can extend and change the predetermined questions flexibly during semi-structured interviews, in order to fully explore the views of interviewees (Saunders et al., 2003:246). Given these features, semi-structured interview was used as the most suitable data collection method of this case-study component.

The interview instrument was designed based on a set of refined and selected questionnaire findings (i.e. the top 10 ERP barriers and

Table 2. Positions of interviewees in the two volunteer SOEs

	Company A	Company B
CEO	1	1
IT manager	1	2
Departmental Manager		
Sales	1	1
Financial	1	1
Production	1	1
Purchasing	1	1
System User		
Sales	1	1
Financial	1	2
Production	2	2
Purchasing	2	1
Total	**12**	**13**

risks, correlations between barriers/risks, and unexpected outcomes related to certain risks, as further discussed in section 5). Consequently, 25 semi-structured interviews were carried out with the CEOs, IT managers, and departmental managers and system users in diverse business areas (i.e. sales, financial, production, and purchasing department) of the two case companies (as shown in Table 2). These interviews, which involved managers and system users at various levels and in all major functional divisions, allow the researcher to develop a holistic understanding about current ERP usage in these SOEs.

Moreover, all interviews were digitally recorded with prior permission, and lasted for 40 minutes to 1 hour. In order to enhance the trustworthiness of the data, written transcription was done on the same day that the interview had taken place. In addition, the transcription of each interview was sent to the interviewee to read through, and thus allowing the researcher to identify and remove any potential bias or inappropriate interpretation. Consequently, a very rich set of qualitative data was collected from the two case companies, and

was then systematically analysed, as discussed in section 6 below.

5. QUANTITATIVE DATA ANALYSIS AND FINDINGS

As mentioned earlier, 42 of the 118 selected SOEs completed and returned the questionnaire. Moreover, 2 different stakeholders from each of the 42 respondent companies respectively completed Questionnaire A and B. As shown in Figure 4, the majority of the 42 respondents of Questionnaire A (which covered business-related barriers and risks) held managerial positions in the company. On the other side, most respondents of Questionnaire B (which contained technical items) held IT-related positions in the firm. These respondents thus prove to be suitable stakeholders to participate in the survey.

5.1 Top Ten ERP Exploitation Barriers

As highlighted by Bryman & Cramer (2005), the mean is often considered the most efficient method for summarising a distribution of values. Therefore, the mean was used to provide a summary of responses for each of the 25 barrier items. Table 3 shows the top ten ERP barriers ranked by their means. The standard deviation was also used and shown in the table to reflect the degree to which the values of each barrier variable differed from the mean.

It is clear from Table 3 that, the most highly-ranked ERP barriers were found around one category, namely the system category. Therefore, it emerged from these results that the respondents of the survey identified organisational and cultural barriers as less important in their companies. However, Fletcher & Wright (1995) point out that in IS studies, despite other types of barriers (e.g. organisational barriers) are in fact more important than system ones, respondents

Figure 4. Positions of respondents of both questionnaires

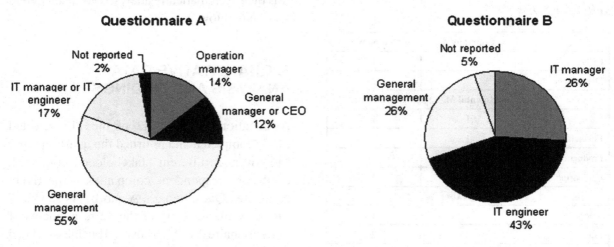

Table 3. Top ten ERP exploitation barriers in Chinese SOEs

Rank		Barrier (N = 42)	Mean	S.D.
1	SB1	Insufficient vendor support	2.95	1.081
2	SB4	System incompatibility	2.86	.977
3	SB7	Slow system response time	2.81	.862
3	SB3	System inflexibility	2.81	.969
5	SB6	Deficient design of the system	2.76	1.008
6	SB2	Inexperienced system consultants	2.69	.950
7	CB3	Power centralisation of top managers	2.55	1.31
8	OB7	Lack of in-house specialists	2.50	1.174
8	SB5	High cost for ERP add-ons	2.50	1.018
10	SB8	Misfits between ERP and user needs	2.36	.759

CB = Cultural Barriers; OB = Organizational Barriers; SB = System Barriers

may not often perceive this to be the case. These other types of barriers may often be understated by respondents, who may not fully recognise the existence and importance of these barriers (Fletcher & Wright, 1995). It is therefore possible that the cultural and organisational barriers studied in this questionnaire may be, to a certain degree, underestimated by respondents due to a lack of understanding and awareness. In fact, the findings presented in the following sections confirm that organisational and business-related barriers are in fact more important than technical problems in Chinese SOEs.

5.2 Top Ten ERP Exploitation Risks

On the other hand, the ranking of the established ERP risks was not as straightforward as the barrier one. As discussed above, the questionnaire also asked respondents to assess the importance of each risk item from three aspects, namely probability of occurrence, level of impact, and frequency of occurrence. The need for all this information lies in the fact that from a risk management perspective, a risk event that has a high probability of occurrence may not have a high impact, and vice versa. As a typical example, system crash is a risk event that often has high impact but low probability of occurrence. Moreover, while probability refers to 'how likely' a risk event may occur, frequency refers to 'how often' this event may happen. Therefore, when evaluating the importance of a risk event, it was considered necessary and vital to take into account all these three risk aspects. Consequently, and in order to facilitate risk assessment, the following formula was developed:

Risk score of each ERP risk = Σ [W *(Probability + Impact + Frequency)]

The structure of this formula is consistent with and clearly reflects the design of the questionnaire. Based on this formula, the calculation of the risk score for each identified ERP risk event should go through the following 3 steps:

Step 1: *(Probability + Impact + Frequency)*. Sum up the values given by each respondent for the three independent dimensions of a risk event, namely probability of occurrence (i.e. 3, 2 or 1), level of impact (i.e. 3, 2 or 1) and frequency of occurrence (i.e. 5 to 1).

Step 2: *W*(Probability + Impact + Frequency)*. 'W' refers to whether or not the respondent perceived this risk event as an ERP risk, with

'1' stands for 'yes' and '0' means 'no'. In case that the respondent did not perceive the given risk event as an ERP risk, the formula will turn the value generated from Step 1 into 0: W*(Probability + Impact + Frequency) = 0*(Probability + Impact + Frequency) = 0.

Step 1 and 2 thus generate the individual score that each respondent gave for a specific risk event.

Step 3: *Σ [W*(Probability + Impact + Frequency)]*. Sum up the individual score that each of the 42 respondents of the survey gave for a particular risk event, and thus generate the total risk score that this risk event received.

By using this formula, the researchers calculated the risk scores for all of the 40 ERP risk events examined, and then prioritised these risks based on their risk scores. The top 10 ERP risks were thus identified as shown in Table 4.

It is clear from Table 4 that, unlike the top barriers presented above, the top ten ERP exploitation risks seem to be found across the organizational processes and not conveniently localised around one category, namely not around the technical category. In fact, since only 2 of the top ten risks are related to technical aspects, these findings seem

Table 4. Top 10 ERP exploitation risks in Chinese SOEs

Category		The Top 10 ERP Exploitation Risks	Rank	Risk Score
Operational risks	OR2.2	Customer files contained in ERP are out-of-date or incomplete	6	246
	OR3.2	ERP system contains inaccurate or incomplete bill of materials	8	243
	OR3.3	ERP system contains inaccurate inventory records	1	263
Analytical risks	AR1.2	Managers cannot retrieve needed information from ERP	4	247
	AR2.1	Sales forecast generated by ERP is inaccurate or inappropriate	3	250
	AR4.1	Fail to use ERP to generate appropriate financial budgets	4	247
Organization - wide risks	OWR1.3	Support from top managers to ERP exploitation is insufficient	10	242
	OWR3.3	Lose ERP-related know-how accumulated over time	2	252
Technical risks	TR1.1	Seamless integration is not achieved between modules of ERP	8	243
	TR1.2	ERP is not able to seamlessly integrate with other IS application	7	233

to suggest that potential ERP post-implementation failure in Chinese SOEs may be owing to business-oriented risks rather than technical problems. In order to seek further statistical evidence to explore and support these findings, a bivariate analysis of the data was carried out.

5.3 Correlations between ERP Barriers and Risks

A bivariate analysis is a statistical technique that aims at identifying the correlation between two variables. This study used bivariate analysis to examine potential correlations between the identified ERP barriers and risks in the context

of Chinese SOEs. In particular, the researchers used bivariate analysis to explore:

- If the existence of a particular ERP barrier was related to the existence of other barriers;
- If the probability of occurrence of a particular risk event was related to the increase of the probability of occurrence of other risks;
- If the existence of a particular barrier was related to the increase of the probability of occurrence of certain ERP risks.

Figure 5. Conceptual map of correlations between ERP barriers and risks

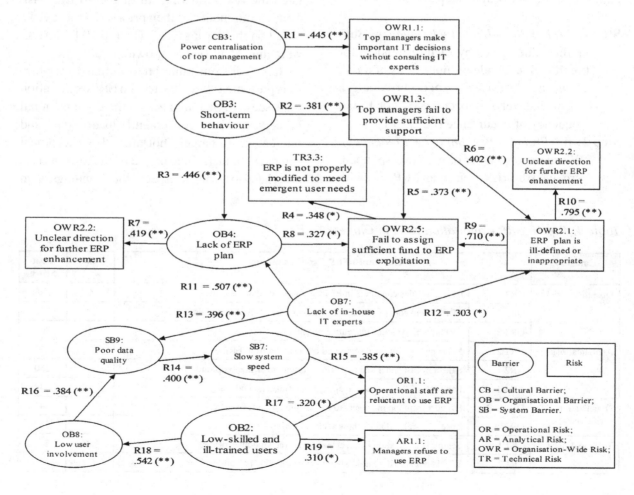

As illustrated earlier, Likert scales were used in the survey to find out to what extent each barrier existed in a respondent's company, as well as to examine the likelihood of each identified risk. Therefore, the data variables generated were ordinal data sets. According to Field (2005:130-131) and Bryman & Cramer (2005:225), Spearman's rho (r_s) is the most suitable approach to measure bivariate correlations between ordinal variables. As a consequence, Spearman's rho was adopted for this study. Moreover, one-tailed test was used to test the statistical significance (P value) of each directional correlation identified. By following these principles, the researchers identified and confirmed 19 statistically significant correlations between all of the identified ERP barriers and risks, as shown in the conceptual map in Figure 5. A full description of each of these correlations is presented in Table 5.

The findings of the bivariate analysis were very illuminating. In particular, the above conceptual map clearly shows that many identified ERP post-implementation barriers and risks are interwoven and closely correlated with each other. Further investigation of this conceptual map and the list of significant correlations identified that, organisational barriers (e.g. lack of in-house IT experts), which are mainly located at the centre of the map, can originate a number of other ERP barriers, including the system ones (e.g. poor data quality). Moreover, the existence of these organisational obstacles can also increase the probability of occurrence of a number of crucial ERP risks (e.g. ERP plan is ill-defined or inadequately developed). In contrast, system barriers, which were perceived as crucial by the respondents, do not prove to be the main triggers of other ERP exploitation barriers and risks. As a consequence,

Table 5. Description of the identified correlations

	Correlation	r_s
R1	Higher extent of power centralization can lead to higher chance for top managers to make centralized IS decisions	.445(**)
R2	The greater the extent of short-term thinking, the higher the probability to lack top management support for ERP	.381(**)
R3	Short-term behaviour of top managers can have negative effect on the establishment of long-term ERP plan	.446(**)
R4	The higher the possibility to have insufficient ERP fund, the greater the chance for ERP to be poorly enhanced	.348(*)
R5	The higher the chance to lack top management support, the higher the chance to have insufficient ERP fund.	.373(**)
R6	The higher the chance to lack top management support, the higher the chance to have ill-defined ERP plan	.402(**)
R7	Lack of ERP exploitation plan can result in unclear direction for long-term ERP development	.419(**)
R8	Lack of ERP plan can increase the probability for the firm to assign insufficient fund to ERP exploitation	.327(*)
R9	The higher the chance to have ill-defined ERP plan, the greater the possibility to have insufficient ERP fund	.710(**)
R10	A firm that is likely to have an ill-defined ERP plan, will also be likely to have unclear ERP exploitation direction	.795(**)
R11	Lack of IT experts can have negative impact on the establishment of ERP plan	.507(**)
R12	Lack of IT experts can increase the probability for the firm to have inappropriate ERP plan	.303(*)
R13	Lack of in-house IT experts can negatively affect the quality of system data`	.396(**)
R14	When data quality of ERP is poor, speed of the ERP system will be correspondingly slow	.400(**)
R15	Slow system speed can increase the probability for having user resistance	.385(**)
R16	Low user involvement can negatively affect the quality of system data	.384(**)
R17	Staff are more likely to be resistant to use ERP, when they have low skill levels and insufficient training	.320(*)
R18	Users with low skill levels and insufficient training will have low involvement in ERP-related activities	.542(**)
R19	Managers, who have lower skill levels and insufficient training, are more likely to be reluctant to use ERP	.310(*)

* Correlation is significant at the 0.05 level; ** Correlation is significant at the 0.01 level.

it can be concluded from these questionnaire findings that organisational barriers should in reality be more dangerous than the system ones, although the significance of these organisational issues seems to be overlooked by the Chinese SOE respondents. This conclusion is also supported by the qualitative results as presented below.

6. QUALITATIVE DATA ANALYSIS AND FINDINGS

As discussed above, a set of follow-up interviews were carried out in two volunteer case companies with the aim to further explore and validate the questionnaire findings. The qualitative data collected from this second phase was analysed by using a thematic analysis approach with a priori coding. Thematic analysis is a process of searching, identifying and exploring codes and themes that emerged from the data as "important to the description of the phenomenon" (Daly et al., 1997). This data-driven inductive approach can often be used together with a deductive priori coding (Fereday & Muir-Cochrane, 2006). In this study, the set of questionnaire findings used to construct the interview questions were also used as a set of priori codes, while a wide range of codes were also identified from the collected data. Following guidelines given by prior researchers (Braun & Clarke, 2006; Rice & Ezzy, 1999), the thematic analysis conducted in this study consisted of the following five stages:

Step 1: Getting familiar with the interview data (get known the data by reading and re-reading the data set);

Step 2: Coding the data (develop the coding scheme, and code the textual data in a systematic fashion across the entire data set by using NVivo);

Step 3: Connecting codes with themes (identify a number of central themes, collate codes into the identified themes, and gather all data relevant to each theme);

Step 4: Reviewing themes (check and verify if the themes work in relation to the coded quotes and the entire data set);

Step 5: Reporting findings (final analysis of selected quotes, relate results back to the research question the questionnaire findings and the literature, and then present the interview findings).

This thematic analysis process resulted in a very rich and interesting set of qualitative findings. Given the limited length of this paper, we are not able to discuss these findings in full here. However, we selected to report in the following sections the most important part of the qualitative findings, which can complement the early questionnaire results and thus allow us to draw a very significant final conclusion at the end of the article.

In particular, the follow-up case study confirmed and validated that all the 19 statistical correlations identified from the questionnaire were crucial to the two volunteer SOEs. Moreover, the analysis of the interview data also indicated and explored an additional set of casual relationships between the identified ERP barriers and risks in Chinese SOEs. Consequently, an extended conceptual map (Figure 6) was developed to highlight the original correlations identified from the questionnaire, together with the additional casual relationships emerged from the interview findings.

By carefully examining this extended conceptual map, it was identified that the entire complicated network of ERP exploitation barriers and risks in Chinese SOEs is actually originated by four critical barriers, namely *Power centralisation of top management, Short-term behaviour of top*

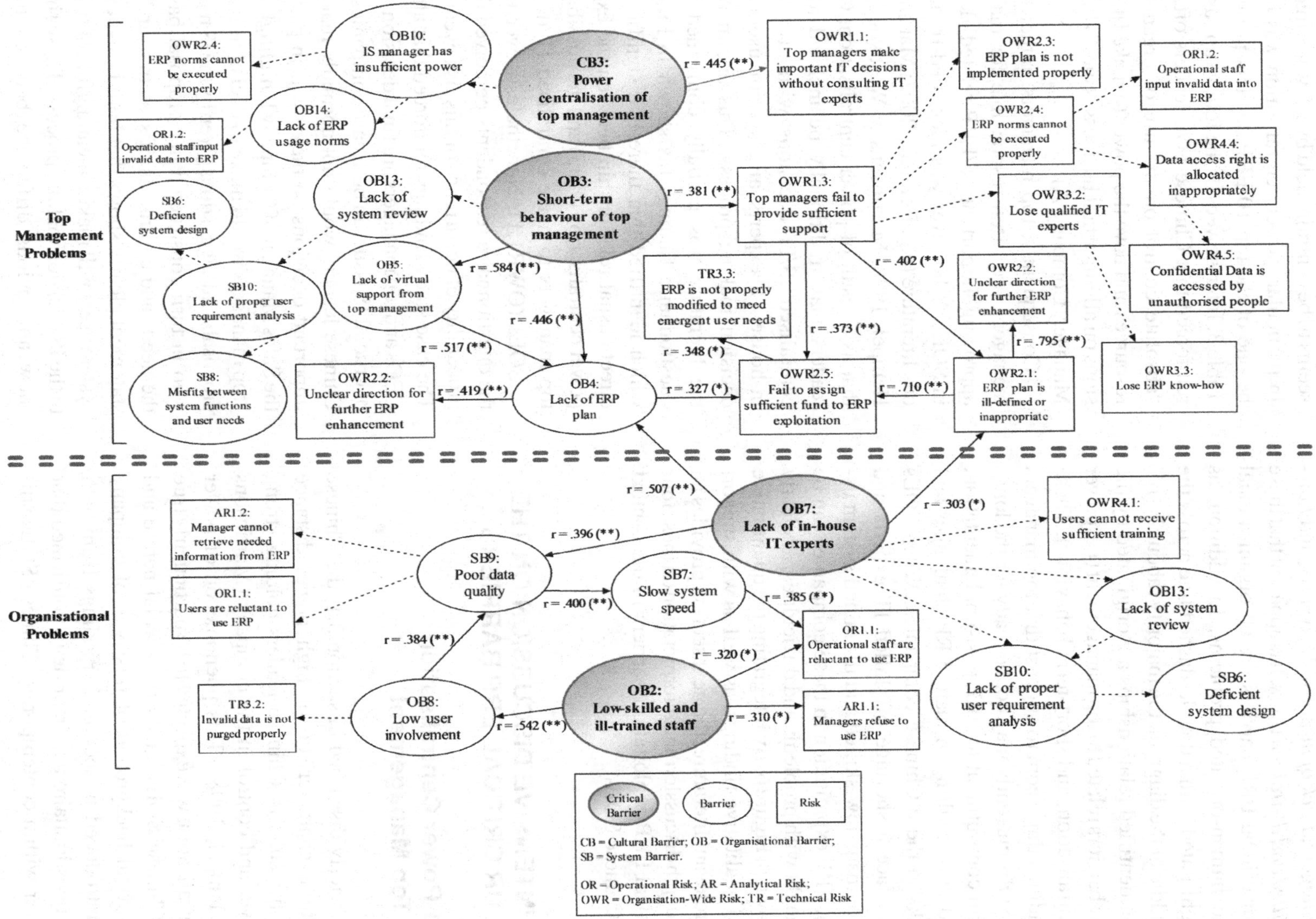

Figure 6. Full conceptual map of relationships between ERP barriers and risks in Chinese SOEs

managers, *Lack of in-house IT experts*, and *Low-skilled and ill-trained users*. It is apparent that these four critical ERP barriers are all organisational and human-oriented problems. In addition, as highlighted with a double-dashed line across the middle of the diagram, the majority (about 2/3) of the identified relationships are originated by the two barriers related to top management (i.e. power centralisation, and short-term behaviour). These findings thus seem to suggest that top managers in SOEs currently may not be ready for the long-term commitment to ERP post-implementation, and thus resulting in many ERP challenges and risks in these Chinese companies. When SOEs also face a shortage of skilled IT experts and have many low-skilled and ill-trained system users, ERP exploitation in these companies can be fraught with problems and difficulties, as clearly shown in Figure 6. By integrating the quantitative and qualitative findings, as well as with support of relevant literature, the next section provides an in-depth discussion and interpretation on these four critical ERP exploitation barriers in the context of Chinese SOEs.

7. INTENSIVE DISCUSSION ON THE FOUR CRITICAL ERP BARRIERS

7.1 Power Centralisation of Top Management

As briefly discussed in section 3.1, the Chinese cultural characteristic of high power distance often results in Chinese leaders holding strong power and control in the company (Martinsons & Hempel, 1998). This phenomenon of power centralisation was expected to be particularly true in Chinese SOEs, given the special nature and historical background of this type of company as introduced in section 2. Findings from both the questionnaire and interviews confirmed that power within contemporary Chinese SOEs still

seems to be centrally held by a few top managers. In particular, power centralisation was found to be one of the top 10 ERP barriers presented in Table 3. Interviewees of the follow-up case study reinforced that Chinese SOE leaders often have "absolute control on the use of organisational resources and have the power to make final decisions on all important business issues" (Financial Manager, Company A).

Consequently, top managers, rather than IS managers, are often responsible for making or approving important IS/ERP-related decisions in SOEs. It however was identified from previous literature (e.g. Reimers, 2002; Martinsons & Hempel, 1998; Martinsons & Westwood, 1997) that as a result of power centralisation, Chinese leaders may traditionally be inclined to make centralised IS/IT decisions without involving in-house IT experts and system users in the decision making process. This argument from the literature was partially confirmed by the questionnaire findings (as shown in Figure 6), which identified that there is a significant and direct casual relationship between the extent of power centralisation (CB3) and the possibility for top managers to make centralised IT decisions in SOEs (OWR1.1). Nonetheless, over 60% of the questionnaire respondents perceived that the probability of occurrence of this risk event is low. The case study findings reinforced that although CEOs and top managers are final decision makers of crucial IS issues in both case companies, these Chinese leaders would not normally make such important decisions on their own. In particular, the Sales Manager of Company B highlighted that "top managers would make IS decisions based on proposals and suggestions given by the IS manager, who in turn constructed her proposal based on the needs and comments of system users". This statement clearly shows that both IT experts and system users will make a meaningful contribution to the IS decision making process. These findings show an obvious difference between modern

SOEs and traditional Chinese firms reported in the literature. This positive change on decision making style of SOE leaders is certainly a result of the continuous SOE reform, and is arguably also attributed to China's increasingly competitive business environment, which requires Chinese senior managers to adopt a more cautious and systematic approach to strategic planning and decision making.

On the other hand, and despite this improvement on decision making process, staff empowerment was found to be a more severe ERP challenge caused by power centralisation in Chinese SOEs. In particular, in order to retain high level control and authority in the company, SOE leaders may not always be fully ready to empower their middle-level managers, including IS managers. As a consequence, IS managers in Chinese SOEs may not always be assigned with sufficient power and authority, and will therefore face substantial difficulties "when trying to seek cooperation from different departments, deal with user resistance and implement the fundamental business changes entailed by ERPs" (IT Manager Company A). Faced with these problems, top management support and commitment become particularly crucial to enable successful ERP use and exploitation in SOEs in the long-term. Unfortunately, owing to a short-term view, top management teams of Chinese SOEs may not always provide sufficient and continuous support to ERP exploitation, as discussed below.

7.2 Short-Term Behaviour of Top Managers

China is currently at its rapid development stage towards industrialism and modernisation. As a result, economic and market environments of the country have been changing quickly and constantly. In order to survive and compete in such fluid business environment, Chinese managers have to react fast to emergent market needs and changes. They may also often need to achieve short-term results and immediate benefits desperately, in order to secure the company's market position under the current economic pressure and the very hard business environments (Zhang, 2004). As also discussed in section 3.3, short-term thinking has thus become a prevalent phenomenon in Chinese firms (Tylecote & Cai, 2004; Zhang, 2004). Nevertheless, it is widely recognised that short-term behaviour can actually lead to crucial organisational problems to companies (Zhang, 2004; Liu, 2004). In particular, when managers act to achieve short-term benefits, they may overlook potential risks and negative impacts that may be caused to the company in the long-run (Liu, 2004).

From an IS perspective, short-term behaviour can be a substantial barrier to successful ERP exploitation in SOEs. In particular, due to short-term thinking, and also because of a lack of ERP understanding, SOE leaders may sometimes perceive ERP innovation as a one-off investment. As a consequence, they may not be willing to "assign sufficient fund to maintain, improve or upgrade the installed ERP system in the post-implementation phase" (IT Manager, Company B). The same IT Manager concluded that "this is one of the major reasons why so many technical pitfalls of ERP have not been modified after a number of years, and why the system has not been properly enhanced to meet emergent user needs". Furthermore, ERP exploitation, as a long-term endeavour, requires continuous support and engagement of top management. Nevertheless, when Chinese top managers are blinded by their short-term view, they may often not be ready to provide long-term commitment and support to ERP post-implementation. This was found to be particularly true in Chinese SOEs. The IT managers of both case companies stated that top managers of SOEs would often make verbal contributions by declaring the importance of ERP and encouraging staff to get involved in ERP exploitation. However, these senior managers in fact had very limited direct involvement in ERP exploitation, and would rarely take actual actions (e.g. lead or engage in the development of internal ERP usage norms, establish reward/punishment scheme to recognise good/poor ERP practices) to facilitate ERP usage and enhancement. As discussed above, top managers have very high status and authority in SOEs. Their attitudes and supports will not just affect the flow of fund to ERP but can also significantly affect the view of employees towards ERP usage. Therefore, when top managers fail to provide actual and continuous support to ERP due to short-term thinking, the system exploitation stage will inevitably be fraught with challenges and difficulties in Chinese SOEs. This is exactly what has been shown in Figure 6. More than 2/3 of ERP problems shown in this diagram are originated by the two critical barriers related to top management. These findings show an imperative need for top managers of Chinese SOEs to become more aware of their crucial roles to the success of ERP exploitation and provide essential support to this long-term process.

7.3 Lack of In-House IT Experts

IT staff can develop a wide range of skills and expertise (e.g. project management, system requirement analysis, business process redesign, etc) through the ERP implementation project (Scott & Vessey, 2000). In other words, the process of ERP implementation is in fact also an invaluable learning process for all in-house IT experts. Nevertheless, the better the skills in-house IT staff acquire, the higher the probability for them to seek for better jobs (Pan et al, 2011). On the other hand, as China is currently at its rapid development stage, market demands for various types of highly qualified experts have been extremely high in the country. This certainly provides the prerequisite and perfect conditions for high-skilled IT experts to hunt for better careers. In addition, under the new market-oriented environment, SOEs, although are still a key employer, are no longer the only option available to the Chinese workforce (Lee & Warner, 2002). Many attractive job opportunities are now also provided by foreign-invested and private companies, which can generally offer higher salary and better reward schemes than those in SOEs (Goodall & Warner, 1997; Ding et al., 2000). Highly qualified experts may therefore consider these other types of companies as better options to advance their careers. As a consequence of these reasons, the turnover rate of qualified IT professional was found to be particularly high in Chinese SOEs. 77% of the questionnaire respondents perceived that there is a high to medium possibility for their companies to loss high-skilled IT experts during ERP exploitation.

It is obvious that efficient ERP maintenance and enhancement require continuous effort and contribution of a large amount of IT experts. Lack of in-house IT experts thus proved to be the cause of a range of crucial ERP exploitation issues in SOEs (as shown in Figure 6). In particular, the Sales Manager of Company B highlighted that due to a severe shortage of in-house IT experts, "the implemented ERP system was often not properly maintained, e.g. redundant data of the system was not regularly purged, and technical bugs were not speedily identified and resolved. These problems in turn significantly affect system performance and reduce user satisfaction". Furthermore, the case study findings also identified that due to a lack of IT experts, SOEs would rarely carry out system audit, review or evaluation during ERP post-implementation. It is however obvious that business and user requirements of SOEs may be constantly changing under the current highly dynamic and competitive market conditions. It is therefore fundamental for SOEs to continuously review the installed ERPs in order to identify any misfits between the system and user needs. Otherwise, the installed ERP system may gradually become inefficient in supporting emergent user requirements and business goals in the long-term.

7.4 Low-Skilled and Ill-Trained System Users

As introduced in section 2, SOEs in the planning economic era were obliged to provide lifelong employment to urban citizens, who were also offered a wide range of cradle-to-grave social welfare, including housing, health, pension, children's schooling, and even transportation to and from work (Cooke, 2000; Sun et al, 2005). This type of lifelong employment system is colloquially called as the 'iron rice-bowl' (tie fan wan). However, when this employment system allowed SOEs to fulfil their social obligations by ensuring lifelong job security, it also resulted in the recruitment of a large number of workers that were typically low skilled with little education qualification and had little incentive to work hard (Cooke, 2000). It also led to significant over-manning and low productivity in most traditional SOEs (Ding et al., 2000). Consequently, and accompanied with the economic and SOE reform started in the 1980s, the state has also attempted to break the 'iron rice-bowl' system in SOEs, by introducing performance-related reward systems, as well as allowing enterprises to hire workers on contracts and dismiss redundant workers to reduce employment number (Ding et al., 2000; Giles et al., 2005). By the early 2000s, this reform process led to the layoffs of more than 36 million SOE employees (Giles et al., 2005). However, and despite these very efforts of reform, the manpower-restructuring initiative in SOEs has in fact not been implemented easily. In particular, by the late 1990s many SOE employees, who were considered redundant, were normally over 35 years old, had low levels of skills and education qualification, and were previously engaged in low-value-added jobs (Cooke, 2000). These workers therefore have very little competitiveness in the external labour market. As a result, dismissing an enormous amount of such SOE workers can lead to a substantial increase

in unemployment rate (Giles et al., 2005), which can potentially affect social security and stability in China. Moreover, the manpower reduction process can often raise a moral dilemma to SOE managers – "how can we fire an honest and humble worker who has been working for us for the last twenty-five years? His wife is laid-off already, his children are still in school and his aged parents need to be provided for" (Cooke, 2000). Furthermore, many SOE workers were not initially recruited on their merits but because their parents or relatives held a managerial position in the firm – so "how can a junior manager remove a senior manager's nephew from a desired post to a less favourable one?" (Cooke, 2000).

As a consequence, a considerable number of low-skilled workers still remain in SOEs even after the substantial reform. This phenomenon was found to be particularly true in the two volunteer SOEs involved in the follow-up case study. In particular, around 1/3 of the employees in both companies were older and low-skilled workers. These SOE employees are normally engaged in operational-level jobs, where ERP systems are used most extensively to support the daily work. However, it is obvious that these older and low-skilled workers will generally have very low level of computer literacy skills. Moreover, because they have been working in the firm for a few decades, they are normally not inclined to change their current way for doing the job. Consequently, both the questionnaire and interview findings confirmed that these low-skilled workers would have very little incentive to accept and use the implemented ERP system (as shown in Figure 6). Substantial and continuous ERP training must therefore be provided to this type of system users in order to enable ERP to be efficiently used and operated in the long-term. Unfortunately, and as also highlighted by Cooke (2000), SOE workers who get too used to the traditional 'iron rice-bowl' system, may often have little motivation to improve their skills for the sake of potential promotion or rise in pay. In light of this discussion, system users in both volunteer SOEs were found to be less engaged in the ERP training provided by the IS managers. On the other hand, further analysis of the interview data also identified a number of problems related to the quality and suitability of the internal ERP training offered by these SOEs. Specifically, it was found that although some basic ERP training was provided to system users in ERP implementation, both volunteer SOEs had not provided any follow-up training to users during the system exploitation phase. Moreover, the training sessions were designed to suit only general user needs, but failed to consider the variance in age and skill levels of different groups of users. The training materials were also not properly established to show the customised features of the implemented ERP. There was also no formal feedback route to enable system trainees to comment on the quality of the training and on the training provider. As a result, the worker trainees in the volunteer SOEs were not feeling satisfied about the ERP training that they received.

Consequently, these low-skilled and ill-trained users were found to have significant resistance for promoting ERP usage and related business changes in Chinese SOEs. When IS managers of the firm lacked sufficient power and top managers of the company also failed to provide sufficient support to ERP exploitation (as discussed in above sections), this severe user resistance in SOEs could become extremely difficult to solve and manage. Due to such substantial resistance and unwillingness to use the system, users in both volunteer SOEs became increasingly indifferent and careless when operating and using ERP. A lot of user mistakes were often made during data entry. This inappropriate system usage in turn resulted in severe data quality problems (e.g. incomplete, duplicate and inadequate data) in both case companies. The Financial Manager of Company A concluded

that: "data in ERPs can therefore often become fragmented and unusable. Since ERPs require very high data accuracy in order to work efficiently, poor data quality can make the implemented ERP system fail substantially in the exploitation phase".

8. FURTHER DISCUSSION, CONCLUSION, AND IMPLICATIONS

By adopting a mixed-methods research design, the study reported in this paper identified and explored empirically a wide range of ERP exploitation barriers and risks in the context of Chinese SOEs. The study confirms that successful implementation of the ERP system is not the end of the story. In fact, Chinese companies can often experience a large number of barriers and risks during organisational exploitation of ERPs. These ERP barriers and risks can localise in diverse operational, managerial, organisational, and technical aspects. Moreover, it was found that many identified ERP barriers and risks are closely interrelated with each other in Chinese SOEs. These ERP post-implementation challenges thus prove to be very difficult to manage and mitigate. Most importantly, the integrated findings identified that the complicated network of ERP barriers and risks is in fact originated by four human and business-related barriers, which are associated with the inherent organisational and management deficiencies in Chinese SOEs, namely Power centralisation of top management, Short-term behaviour of top managers, Lack of in-house IT experts, and Low-skilled and ill-trained system users. On the other hand, technical barriers, which are traditionally perceived as the key reasons led to ERP failure, were found to be neither interwoven with each other nor the causes of other identified ERP barriers and risks. Consequently, based on the quantitative and qualitative findings derived from the study, an overall conclusion is drawn in the form of the following root definition:

Potential failure of ERP cannot be conveniently attributed to system problems (e.g. software packages and ICT infrastructure), but more importantly should be attributed to business-oriented and organisational barriers, in particular human problems that are related to top managers, IT experts and system users, in the context of Chinese SOEs.

However, and despite their importance, organisational factors and barriers have traditionally been given less attention and even been underestimated by business managers and IT practitioners, probably due to a lack of understanding and awareness of the existence and impact of these issues (Fletcher & Wright, 1995). This understatement of organisational issues is obvious in Chinese SOEs, by examining the top ERP barriers presented in section 5.1 (7 of the top 10 barriers are technical ones) and the complicated relationships identified between ERP barriers/risks as shown in Figure 6 (organisational barriers, rather than technical problems, are actually the main triggers of a wide range of ERP challenges). In fact, this underestimation in Chinese SOEs may also be caused by an unwillingness of Chinese managers to talk about their organisational and management shortcomings. Many researchers (e.g. Graham & Lam, 2004; Xue et al., 2005) stress that, Chinese managers are traditionally less willing to disclose internal problems and failures to external bodies, in order to preserve their own and/or their firms' images. In addition, given the hitherto bureaucratic environment in SOEs, it can be argued that Chinese managers may often be reluctant to address problems embedded in their organisational and management mechanism in order to avoid potential personal risks (e.g. job loss). These attitudes however may blind Chinese practitioners to the complexity and importance of organisational barriers, which might be less obvious but proved in this study to be more difficult to resolve and more critical to long-term ERP success in the Chinese

context. Therefore, it is highly recommended that Chinese SOE managers shall become more aware of the complexity and networked nature of these organisational barriers, rather than conventionally and merely focusing on technical aspects. In fact, properly handling the identified human-related problems (especially the four core barriers triggered the complicated network of ERP risks and barriers) can help Chinese SOEs to address and overcome the other types of risks and barriers identified, including the technical ones.

The results of this study have important implications in both practical and theoretical terms. In terms of practice, the list of top ERP barriers and risks identified can be immediately used as a strategic tool and checklist by Chinese practitioners to identify, prevent and manage ERP post-implementation challenges in their workplaces. The exploration and identification of a set of barrier and risk relationships also enable Chinese SOE managers to gain a more in-depth insight into possible triggers of the severe difficulties that they are facing in ERP exploitation. More importantly, it is hoped that the findings of this study can make practitioners in Chinese SOEs become more conscious of the importance and critical impacts of organisational barriers, and thus taking proper actions to address these critical ERP obstacles to prevent potential ERP exploitation failure. As some of the important first steps to improve the current situation, it clearly emerged from the findings that top managers of Chinese SOEs need to have real engagement and provide actual support to the long-term ERP exploitation. These Chinese leaders will also need to be ready and willing to empower their IS managers, who can thus have sufficient power and authority to deal with the high-level user resistance caused by the considerable number of low-skilled SOE workers. Furthermore, current ERP training methods and contents adopted by SOEs need to be reviewed and possibly modified to ensure different groups of users can be trained properly and continuously. Overall, simply improving the technical aspects of the system may not be the solution for Chinese SOEs to address current ERP exploitation challenges. The study suggests that long-term ERP success relies more on the continuous effort of every single member, from the top management team to operational staff, of the whole company.

On the other hand, and in terms of research, the study added to the knowledge of ERP in general, and contributed to the research gap of ERP post-implementation barriers and risks in the Chinese context in particular. It represented a first attempt in producing a comprehensive study in its research area. The process of literature search could not return any other such studies. However, it should be stressed that the very effort of narrowing and focusing the research by using the PEST analysis, means that generalisation of findings is now only possible for similar company types, sectors, and regions as the ones studied (i.e. SOEs in the ICT manufacturing sector in Guangdong). Although this is a limitation of this research, it is deemed particularly appropriate due to the complexity that characterises the Chinese economy at the moment. A study that focuses on producing generalisable statements about a specific regional context is more likely to result in meaningful and significant findings than one that focuses on China as a whole (Peng & Nunes, 2008). Moreover, Manion (1994) reinforces that findings derived from a regional sample may not be applied to the entire country, but can often be used as the basis for social scientists to carry out further research on contemporary China. Nonetheless, more study on ERP post-implementation in general and in the Chinese context in particular will certainly be needed. Fellow researchers can use the established ERP exploitation barrier and risk ontologies, as well as the integrated findings derived from this study, as a knowledge foundation to carry out further research in this increasingly important research area.

REFERENCES

Avison, D., & Malaurent, J. (2007). Impact of cultural differences: A case study of ERP introduction in China. *International Journal of Information Management*, 27(5), 368–374. doi:10.1016/j.ijinfomgt.2007.06.004

Barki, H., Rivard, S., & Talbot, J. (1993). Toward an assessment of software development risk. *Journal of Management Information Systems*, 10(2), 203–225.

Bergstrom, M., & Stehn, L. (2005). Matching industrialised timber frame housing needs and enterprise resource planning: A change process. *International Journal of Production Economics*, 97(2), 172–184. doi:10.1016/j.ijpe.2004.06.052

Bhattacherjee, A. (2001). Understanding information systems continuance: An expectation-confirmation model. *Management Information Systems Quarterly*, 25(3), 351–370. doi:10.2307/3250921

Braun, V., & Clarke, V. (2006). Using thematic analysis in psychology. *Qualitative Research in Psychology*, 3(2), 77–101. doi:10.1191/1478088706qp063oa

Bryman, A., & Cramer, D. (2005). *Quantitative data analysis with SPSS 12 and 13: a guide for social scientists*. East Sussex: Routledge.

Buonanno, G., Faverio, P., Pigni, F., Ravarini, A., Sciuto, D., & Tagliavini, M. (2005). Factors affecting ERP system adoption: A comparative analysis between SMEs and large companies. *Journal of Enterprise Information Management*, 18(4), 384–426. doi:10.1108/17410390510609572

China economic yearbook. (2004). Beijing, China: China Economic Yearbook Editing Committee.

Chou, D. C., Tripuramallu, H. B., & Chou, A. Y. (2005). BI and ERP integration. *Information Management & Computer Security*, 13(5), 340–349. doi:10.1108/09685220510627241

Chou, S. W., & Chang, Y. C. (2008). The implementation factors that influence the ERP (enterprise resource planning) benefits. *Decision Support Systems, 46*(1), 149–157. doi:10.1016/j.dss.2008.06.003

Cooke, F. L. (2000). Manpower restructuring in the state-owned railway industry of China: The role of the state in human resource strategy. *International Journal of Human Resource Management, 11*(5), 904–924. doi:10.1080/095851900422348

Daly, J., Kellehear, A., & Gliksman, M. (1997). *The public health researcher: a methodological approach*. Melbourne: Oxford University Press.

Davenport, T. H. (1998). Putting the enterprise into the enterprise system. *Harvard Business Review, 76*(4), 121–131. PMID:10181586

DeLone, W. H. (1988). Determinants of success for computer usage in small business. *Management Information Systems Quarterly, 12*(1), 51–61. doi:10.2307/248803

Desai, C., Wright, G., & Fletcher, K. (1998). Barriers to successful implementation of database marketing: A cross-industry study. *International Journal of Information Management, 18*(4), 265–276. doi:10.1016/S0268-4012(98)00015-2

Ding, D. Z., Goodall, K., & Warner, M. (2000). The end of the 'iron rice-bowl': Whither Chinese human resource management? *International Journal of Human Resource Management, 11*(2), 217–236. doi:10.1080/095851900339837

Fereday, J., & Muir-Cochrane, E. (2006). Demonstrating rigor using thematic analysis: A hybrid approach of inductive and deductive coding and theme development. *International Journal of Qualitative Methods, 5*(1), 1–11.

Field, A. (2005). *Discovering statistics using SPSS: and sex, drugs and rock'n'roll* (2nd ed.). London: SAGE.

Fletcher, K., & Wright, G. (1995). Organisational, strategic and technical barriers to successful implementation of database marketing. *International Journal of Information Management, 15*(2), 115–126. doi:10.1016/0268-4012(95)00005-R

Gargeya, V. B., & Brady, C. (2005). Success and failure factors of adopting SAP in ERP system implementation. *Business Process Management Journal, 11*(5), 501–516. doi:10.1108/14637150510619858

Garnaut, R., Song, L., Tenev, S., & Yao, Y. (2005). China's ownership transformation: process, outcomes and prospects. Washington, D.C: International Finance Corporation (World Bank Group).

Gattiker, T. F., & Goodhue, D. L. (2005). What happens after ERP implementation: Understanding the impact of interdependence and differentiation on plant-level outcomes. *Management Information Systems Quarterly, 29*(3), 559–585.

Giles, J., Park, A., & Zhang, J. (2005). What is China's true unemployment rate? *China Economic Review, 16*(2), 149–170. doi:10.1016/j.chieco.2004.11.002

Goodall, K., & Warner, M. (1997). Human resources in Sino-foreign joint ventures: Selected case studies in Shanghai, compared with Beijing. *International Journal of Human Resource Management, 8*(5), 569–594. doi:10.1080/095851997341397

Graham, J. L., & Lam, N. M. (2004). The Chinese negotiation. In Harvard business review on doing business in China, 31-56. Boston: Harvard Business School Publishing.

Hofstede, G. (2001). *Culture's consequences: comparing values, behaviours, institutions, and organizations across nations* (2nd ed.). London: Sage.

Hollnagel, E. (2000). Barrier analysis and accident prevention. Retrieved from http://human-factors.arc.nasa.gov/ april01-workshop/EH_barrier_analysis.pdf

Huang, S., Chang, I., Li, S., & Lin, M. (2004). Assessing risk in ERP projects: Identify and prioritize the factors. *Industrial Management & Data Systems, 104*(8), 681–688. doi:10.1108/02635570410561672

Kleim, R. L., & Ludin, I. S. (2000). *Reducing project risks.* Hampshire: Gower Publishing Ltd.

Lee, G. O. M., & Warner, M. (2002). Labour-market policies in Shanghai and Hong Kong: A study of "one country, two systems" in Greater China. *International Journal of Manpower, 23*(6), 505–526. doi:10.1108/01437720210446379

Lientz, B. P., & Larssen, L. (2006). *Risk management for IT projects: how to deal with 150 issues and risks.* Oxford: Butterworth-Heinemann Ltd.

Liu, C. B. (2004). "私营企业短期行为与青年需求" (Short-term behaviour of private enterprises and the needs of teenagers) [In Chinese]. Retrieved from http://www.cysol.org/cnarticle_detail.asp?id=568

Loh, T. C., & Koh, S. C. L. (2004). Critical elements for a successful enterprise resource planning implementation in small-and medium-sized enterprises. *International Journal of Production Research, 42*(17), 3433–3455. doi:10.1080/00207540410001671679

Manion, M. (1994). Survey research in the study of contemporary China: Learning from local samples. *The China Quarterly, 139*, 741–765. doi:10.1017/S0305741000043149

Marnewick, C., & Labuschagne, L. (2005). A conceptual model for enterprise resource planning (ERP). *Information Management & Computer Security, 13*(2), 144–155. doi:10.1108/09685220510589325

Martinsons, M. G., & Hempel, P. S. (1998). Chinese business process re-engineering. *International Journal of Information Management, 18*(6), 393–407. doi:10.1016/S0268-4012(98)00031-0

Martinsons, M. G., & Westwood, R. I. (1997). Management information system in the Chinese business culture: An explanatory theory. *Information & Management, 32*(5), 215–228. doi:10.1016/S0378-7206(96)00009-2

Namjae, C., & Kiho, P. (2003). Exploring a priori and posteriori IS Valuation Distortion: Comparing cases in SCM, ERP, and CRM. *International Journal of Digital Management.* Retrieved from http://digital.re.kr/ijdm/past.html

Oliver, D., Whymark, G., & Romm, C. (2005). Researching ERP adoption: An internet-based grounded theory approach. *Online Information Review, 29*(6), 585–603. doi:10.1108/14684520510638052

Pan, K., Nunes, J. M. B., & Peng, G. C. (2011). Risks affecting ERP viability: Insights from a very large Chinese manufacturing group. *Journal of Manufacturing Technology Management, 22*(1), 107–130. doi:10.1108/17410381111099833

Peng, G. C., & Nunes, J. M. B. (2008, June 19-20). Issues and difficulties in doing participative research in China: lessons learned from a survey in information systems research. *Proceedings of the 7th European Conference on Research Methodology (ECRM) for Business and Management Studies*, London, UK (pp. 245-252).

Peng, G. C., & Nunes, J. M. B. (2009). Identification and assessment of risks associated with ERP post-implementation in China. *Journal of Enterprise Information Management*, 22(5), 587–614. doi:10.1108/17410390910993554

Peng, G. C., & Nunes, J. M. B. (2009b). Surfacing ERP exploitation risks through a risk ontology. *Industrial Management & Data Systems*, 109(7), 926–942. doi:10.1108/02635570910982283

Peng, G. C., & Nunes, J. M. B. (2010). Barriers to the successful exploitation of ERP systems in Chinese State-Owned Enterprises. *International Journal of Business and Systems Research*, 4(5/6), 596–620. doi:10.1504/IJBSR.2010.035077

Peng, G. C., & Nunes, J. M. B. (2012). Establishing and verifying a risk ontology for ERP post-implementation. In M. Ahmad, R. M. Colomb, & M. S. Abdullah (Eds.), *Ontology-based Applications for Enterprise Systems and Knowledge Management*. Hershey, USA: IGI Global.

Perkins, D. H. (1997). History, politics, and the sources of economic growth: China and the East Asian way of growth. In F. Itoh (Ed.), *China in the twenty-first century: politics, economy, and society* (pp. 25–47). Tokyo: United Nations University Press.

Polikoff, I., Coyne, R., & Hodgson, R. (2005). *Capability cases: a solution envisioning approach*. California: Wesley.

Raymond, L., Pare, G., & Bergeron, F. (1995). Matching information technology and organizational structure: An empirical study with implications for performance. *European Journal of Information Systems*, 4(1), 3–16. doi:10.1057/ejis.1995.2

Reich, B. H., & Benbasat, I. (2000). Factors that influence the social dimension of alignment between business and information technology objectives. *Management Information Systems Quarterly*, 24(1), 81–113. doi:10.2307/3250980

Reimers, K. (2002). Implementing ERP systems in China. *Proceedings of the 35th Annual Hawaii International Conference on System Sciences*. Hawaii, USA. doi:10.1109/HICSS.2002.994311

Research, C. C. W. (2010). IT investments of the manufacturing sector reached RMB 52.9 billion in 2010. Retrieved from http://www.donews.com/it/201102/371478.shtm

Rice, P., & Ezzy, D. (1999). *Qualitative research methods: a health focus*. Melbourne: Oxford University Press.

Roepke, R., Agarwal, R., & Ferratt, T. W. (2000). Aligning the IT human resource with business vision: The leadership initiative at 3M. *Management Information Systems Quarterly*, 24(2), 327–353. doi:10.2307/3250941

Rucks, A., & Ginter, P. (1982). Strategic MIS: Promises unfulfilled. *Journal of Systems Management*, 8, 16–19.

Saunders, M., Lewis, P., & Thornhill, A. (2003). *Research methods for business students* (3rd ed.). Essex: Pearson Education.

Scott, J. E., & Vessey, I. (2000). Implementing enterprise resource planning systems: The role of learning from failure. *Information Systems Frontiers*, 2(2), 213–232. doi:10.1023/A:1026504325010

Shang, S., & Seddon, P. B. (2002). Assessing and managing the benefits of enterprise systems: The business manager's perspective. *Information Systems Journal*, 12(4), 271–299. doi:10.1046/j.1365-2575.2002.00132.x

Shehab, E. M., Sharp, M. W., Supramaniam, L., & Spedding, T. A. (2004). Enterprise resource planning: An integrative review. *Business Process Management Journal*, 10(4), 359–386. doi:10.1108/14637150410548056

Sherer, S. A. (2004, Jan 5-8). Managing risk beyond the control of IS managers: the role of business management. *Proceedings of the 37th Hawaii International Conference on System Sciences*, 2004, Hawaii, USA. doi:10.1109/HICSS.2004.1265509

Shirk, S. L. (1994). *How China opened its door: the political success of the PRC's foreign trade and investment reform*. Washington, D.C.: Brookings Institution.

Söderlind, E., & Kidby, S. (2005). Cross cultural cooperation – a field study about India and Sweden. Retrieved from http://www.diva-portal.org/sh/abstract.xsql?dbid=300

Statistical Reports on the Internet Development in China. (2011). Economic Yearbook Press Office China Internet Network Information Center. Retrieved from http://www.cnnic.net.cn/en/index/0O/02/index.htm

Sumner, M. (2000). Risk factors in enterprise-wide/ERP projects. *Journal of Information Technology*, *15*(4), 317–327. doi:10.1080/02683960010009079

Sun, J. (2000). Organization development and change in Chinese state-owned enterprises: A human resource perspective. *Leadership and Organization Development Journal*, *21*(8), 379–389. doi:10.1108/01437730010379267

Sun, Q., Zhang, A., & Li, J. (2005). A study of optimal state shares in mixed oligopoly: Implications for SOE reform and foreign competition. *China Economic Review*, *16*(1), 1–27. doi:10.1016/j.chieco.2004.06.009

The Alaska Department of Natural Resources. (2003). RAPS feasibility study – technical assessment. Retrieved from http://www.dnr.state.ak.us/lup/Technical _Assessment_5.2.pdf

Tsai, W., Lin, T. W., Chen, S., & Hung, S. (2007). Users' service quality satisfaction and performance improvement of ERP consultant selections. *International Journal of Business and Systems Research*, *1*(3), 280–301. doi:10.1504/IJBSR.2007.015830

Tylecote, A., & Cai, J. (2004). China's SOE reform and technological change: A corporate governance perspective. *Asian Business & Management*, *3*(1), 57–84. doi:10.1057/palgrave.abm.9200070

Umble, E., Haft, R., & Umble, M. M. (2003). Enterprise Resource Planning: Implementation procedures and Critical Success Factors. *European Journal of Operational Research*, *146*(2), 246–257. doi:10.1016/S0377-2217(02)00547-7

Willis, T. H., & Willis-Brown, A. H. (2002). Extending the value of ERP. *Industrial Management & Data Systems*, *102*(1), 35–38. doi:10.1108/02635570210414640

Wright, G., & Donaldson, B. (2002). Sales information systems in the UK financial services industry: An analysis of sophistication of use and perceived barriers to adoption. *International Journal of Information Management*, *22*(6), 405–419. doi:10.1016/S0268-4012(02)00032-4

Xue, Y., Liang, H., Boulton, W. R., & Snyder, C. A. (2005). ERP implementation failures in China: Case studies with implications for ERP vendors. *International Journal of Production Economics*, *97*(3), 279–295. doi:10.1016/j.ijpe.2004.07.008

Yu, C. S. (2005). Causes influencing the effectiveness of the post-implementation ERP system. *Industrial Management & Data Systems*, *105*(1), 115–132. doi:10.1108/02635570510575225

Yusuf, S., Nabeshima, K., & Perkins, D. H. (2006). Under new ownership: privatizing China's state-owned enterprises. California: Stanford University Press and Washington: The World Bank.

Zhang, H. S. (2004). 国有及国有控股企业短期行为的制度经济学分析" (Economics analysis on the short-term behaviours of state-owned and state-holding enterprises) [In Chinese]. MSc. Political Economy, Shandong University. *China*.

KEY TERMS AND DEFINITIONS

ERP: Cross-functional enterprise information system (IS) packages, which consist of a number of software modules that aim at supporting and integrating all key business processes across the various functional divisions of an organization by using a single data repository.

ERP Barriers: An obstacle existed in the context of the company and can affect the success of ERP.

ERP Exploitation: A term that can be used interchangeably with 'ERP post-implementation'.

ERP Post-Implementation: The stage after the ERP system is implemented, and is concerned with the usage, maintenance and continuous improvement of ERP.

ERP Risk: An event that may or may or may not happen, but its occurrence can cause potential loss and ERP problems.

Mixed-Methods Research: A study that mixes the usage of both quantitative and qualitative research methods.

State-Owned Enterprises: A company that is owned and so can be influenced by the state.

Chapter 13
Developing a Multi-Agency E-Participation Strategy for Disadvantaged City Communities:
A Case Study

John N Walsh
University of Limerick, Ireland

Fergal McGrath
University of Limerick, Ireland

ABSTRACT

The objective of this chapter is to present a case study of the development of a strategy to increase eParticipation among a number of disadvantaged communities in the city of Limerick in Ireland. The chapter's authors' acted as facilitators for the strategy development process. The strategy group consisted of multiple educational, developmental and community and local government representatives. Given the participants' differing perspectives and interpretations the strategy development attempted to be as inclusive and transparent as possible and information technology was used that provided shared spaces using a wiki and allowing the sharing of the information (strategy document) as it emerged through various iterations.

INTRODUCTION

The objective of this chapter is to present a case study of the development of a strategy to increase e-Participation among a number of disadvantaged communities in the city of Limerick, Ireland. The chapter's authors' acted as facilitators for the strategy development process. The strategy group consisted of multiple educational, developmental and community and local government representatives. Given the participants' differing perspectives and interpretations the strategy development attempted to be as inclusive and transparent as possible and information technology

DOI: 10.4018/978-1-4666-8833-9.ch013

(IT) was used that provided shared spaces using a wiki and allowing the sharing of the information (strategy document) as it emerged through various iterations.

The chapter begins by examining the development of the literature from that of a digital divide to eParticipation. The perspectives outlined in previous research were found to be mirrored in the views of the strategy groups members. Next the case study will be presented as a series of stages that were used to develop the Limerick Community Connect (LCC) e-Participation Strategy. Where appropriate at each stage key issues and lessons learned will be highlighted. Finally the implications of the findings for both management and information management practice are identified along with the limitations and directions for future research.

BACKGROUND

While eParticipation is emerging as a research area it is lacking a clear research approach or literature base (Sandford & Rose, 2007). Therefore this chapter also considers the wider and longer established literature on the digital divide because this literature strongly influenced research addressing broader issues (Meneses & Momino, 2010). As will be highlighted in this chapter the development of the digital divide and changes in emphasis to eParticipation had parallels in the strategy development process itself.

Similarly the digital divide concept is elusive so that even after a decade of research there was no consensus on its definition, extent or impact (Dewan & Riggins, 2005). This may be because it is difficult to define its boundaries because it is a dynamic phenomenon that evolves and interacts with other social changes (Salvador et al., 2010). In a similar vein eInclusion is different from other types of policy making because of the speed of changes in the 'state of the art' of the digital activities from which people are excluded

(Guyader, 2009). Nonetheless how these terms are defined are important because (1) how they are used has implications for the rationale for investment as well as the outcomes expected by funding organisations (Graham, 2011) and (2) the way the problem is defined affects the policy solutions that are developed (Servon, 2002).

The divides and exclusions examined by various authors are examined at a number of different levels. Concentration is often on national comparisons to identify leader/follower countries etc. (Ayanso et al., 2010). It may also occur at a sub-national level considering particular regions, rural versus urban areas, businesses, households or at the individual level in terms of income, ethnicity or education (Graham, 2011; Borgida et al., 2002; Srinuan & Bohlin, 2011;OECD, 2001; Attewell, 2001).

Initially solutions to the digital divide, once established at a particular level, related to access (Attewell, 2001) terming this the 'first' digital divide. Garcia-Jimenez and Gomez-Barroso (2009) view this in terms of haves and have-nots and the factors that distinguish these two groups. This view leads to the separation of people into 'haves' and 'have-nots' making access to technology the problem (Ferro et al., 2011; Dewan & Riggins, 2005). The term also divides people into what Belanger & Carter (2009) refer to the information have and have-nots: those who are computer literate or illiterate. Ferro et al. (2011) argues that the conceptualisation of the digital divide has moved on from a dichotomous model based on access to a multidimensional model that considers various characteristics. Warschauer (2003a) goes on to argue that underlying the digital divide terminology is 'technological determinism' that suggests that the availability, or indeed lack of availability, of technology determines effects on behaviour and social development.

The digital divide concept has been criticised as a poor framework for policy development and social analysis: one criticism is that it created a 'pi-polar' division rather than a continuum

(Warschauer, 2003a). It has been argued by Meneses and Momino (2010) that there is no advantage to retaining a binary definition to operationalize the digital divide in terms of a purely technological solution. Authors such as Adriani and Becchetti (2003) and Compaine (2001) frame it as a delay in diffusion of a technology among geographic areas and social groups. This suggests that inequality could be overcome by providing access to internet, e-mail etc. (Warschauer, 2003a). The digital divide identified those with access as occupying the same virtual space that separates them from those without access (Graham, 2011). Warschauer (2003a) goes on to argue that there is not one type of online access but many and that the value and meaning attributed to access exists along a continuum. This means that access does not provide an automatic benefit so that getting access is not just about education and culture but also about power (Warschauer, 2003a).

There are a number of problems with the initial position of viewing the digital divide in terms of access. Stephenson (2009) sees the digital divide term as a 'rhetorical trope' used to advance a neo-liberal ideology by placing responsibility at the individual rather than system level. This viewpoint, coupled with the argument by Attewell (2001) that the access divide in the US is decreasing with PC prices decreasing as well as computers being used more in homes by disadvantaged groups as evidenced by the work of Coley et al., (1997) and Wenglinsky (1998) as well as the rapid diffusion of ICT, bringing about a belief that the digital divide may not be as large a danger than originally feared, (Ferlander and Timms, 2006). Thus by defining the issue of the digital divide solely in terms of access means that the problem will diminish as access becomes more ubiquitous.

The (OECD, 2001, p.5) define the digital divide as "the gap between individuals, households, businesses and geographic areas at different socioeconomic levels with regard both to their opportunities to access communication technologies (ICTs) and to make use of the internet for a wide variety of activities". Thus not only does this early definition focus on access but also on the activities made possible by that access. The move from an access-based perspective towards eParticipation comes about as authors' focus attention not on whether a citizen has access to ICTs and the internet but rather what they do with that access. This refocusing raises questions around digital inclusion where attention is on skills and usage (Warschauer, 2003a; Bavel et al., 2004). However, even though this 'second' divide centred on use was identified over a decade ago (Attewell, 2001) with research on how tools are actually used has received less attention than the first (Peng, 2010).

For some authors the objective is to improve users' proficiency (Blignaut, 2009). This proficiency in term it is argued may give them competitive advantages over non-users (Robles et al., 2011). Contextual and historical factors are relevant here in explaining differences in usage patterns. Ferro et al. (2011) argues that the multi-dimensional view almost assumes that access is present and focuses on individuals and their use of IT: it does not assume that groups use technologies inherently differently, quoting (Hines et al., 2001, p.15) who argue "*individuals and communities employ technologies for very specific goals, linked often to their histories and social barriers*".

There is increasing acceptance that the digital divide not only relates to (un)availability of ICT's but also social, political, cultural and institutional contexts which shape how ICT's are used (Madon et al., 2007). Even with access cultural differences affect how users access and interact with information (Recabarren et al., 2008). Differences in use may be attributed to socio-demographic factors (Vehovar et al., 2006). Garcia-Jimenez and Gomez-Barroso (2009) argue access is a sine qua non but still only a means to an end: adoption is also important and is based on the opportunities and experiences developed historically and offered in the present. Warschauer (2003a) argues that the division is not digital but rather social, coming from economic, cultural and linguistic contexts.

This means that for those targeted by the eParticipation strategy the divide was not just related to access but there also existed a cognitive divide. Indeed Fonseca (2010, p.25) conceptualises the digital divide as linked to a cognitive divide "*it is related to understand, learn, express, produce, show, collaborate, create, and innovate using technology*". Therefore even with access internet users may not have the virtual co-presence that exists among other users (Graham, 2011). IT literacy is seen by Warschauer (2003b) not as a cognitive skill but also entwined in a set of wider social practices.

While digital inclusion is encapsulated in the digital divide literature (Meneses & Momino, 2010) the former concept goes further with Rose and Sandford (2007) arguing that eInclusion is dependent on the digital divide literature. Digital inclusion is often equated with social inclusion within the digital divide literature (Seale et al., 2010). Not only does eInclusion promote ICTs and reduce usage gaps but is also concerned with ICTs being used to achieve wider inclusion objectives such as improving economic performance and employment opportunities as well as seeking to overcome exclusion to improve quality of life, cohesion and social participation (Znotina et al., 2008). Rodousakis and Santos (2008) quoting the Riga Declaration 2006 identified six priority areas relating to eInclusion:

- Needs of older workers and elderly people.
- Reducing the geographical digital divide.
- Improving e-accessability and usability.
- Improving digital literacy skills.
- The promotion of cultural diversity in regard to e-Inclusion.
- Improving e-Government.

The eParticipation concept is wide-ranging: based on their literature review of 99 articles identified as very relevant (Sandford & Rose, 2007) identified a number of themes: eDemocracy, eGovernance, eAccessability, eActivism, eCam-paigning, eCommunity, eConsultation, eDecision Making, eDeliberation, eInclusion, ePetition, ePolitics, ePolling, eRulemaking, and eVoting. This is not surprising as eParticipation is an evolution, due to the internet, of many existing activities (Saebo et al., 2008) and has been defined by Gatautis (2010, p.483) as "*employing ICT within politics in regard of participatory, self-organized democracy and grassroots communication and discussion purposes*". Macintosh and Whyte (2008, p.17) define eParticipation as "*the use of ICTs to support information provision, top-down engagement which is concerned with support for government-led initiatives, and ground-up empowerment which is mainly concerned with support to enable citizens, civil society organizations and other democratically constituted groups to engage with their elected representatives and officials*".

There are a number of degrees of eParticipation: citizen-engagement such as consultation, deliberation, information provision etc. (Gatautis, 2010) with Saebo et al. (2008) arguing that there is an implication that technology has the ability to transform or change citizen involvement in both the process deliberation and decision making.

One aspect of eParticipation focuses on the interaction of civil society and the formal politics sphere (Sandford & Rose, 2007) empowering citizens political capabilities (Gatautis, 2010). This can be achieved by, for example, The objective of eParticipation is to empower people to engage in bottom-up decision making that enables politicians make informed decisions as well as citizens contributing their ideas, requests and suggestions to the political discourse which has the potential to modify democratic participation if such acts are accepted and supported (Gatautis, 2010). This results in citizens developing political responsibility (Gatautis, 2010). This means that through ICT mediation eParticipation extends and transforms democratic processes, (Sandford & Rose, 2007).

The participation part may take place within or outside the formal political process (Saebo et al., 2008). In addition to the formal politics sphere eParticipation may also take place between civil society and the administrative sphere (Sandford & Rose, 2007). It may also seek to empower citizens' and organisations' cultural and socio-technical capabilities thus enabling them to become involved in the information society (Gatautis, 2010) as well as increasing their ability to participate in digital governance (Saebo et al., 2008).

eParticipation initiatives have been developed at various governmental levels as well as through citizen organization and experimentation (Boyd, 2008), civil society (Macintosh & Whyte, 2008; Sandford & Rose, 2007) and the private sector, but as Guyader (2009) argues as a result of the 'global crisis' the private sector will focus their resources on customers and immediate goals. Guyader (2009) argues that public authorities concentrate on 'enabling conditions' around access infrastructure rather than on what motivates citizens to participate in the knowledge society. There is a danger that eInclusion initiatives will be 'patchy' and not achieve visible critical mass without 'sturdy coordination by public authorities' and a 'sternness' to enforce commitments (Guyader, 2009). The toughest issue around eInclusion is coordination (among private, public sectors and civil society) to harmonise public initiatives over different layers of public governance (Guyader, 2009). In the section that follows a case study is presented whereby multiple state agencies worked together to develop a coordinated eParticipation strategy over the course of a year.

Methodology

Our goal as coordinators of the strategy development process was to provide that various stakeholders with the skills to observe, reflect, plan and develop the strategy rather than provide them with a specific set of processes and series of questions that might restrict or reflect our perceived expertise in this emerging exercise. Action research is either research initiated to solve an immediate problem or a reflective process of progressive problem solving led by individuals working with others in teams or as part of a community of practice to improve the way they address issues and solve problems (Denscombe, 2010; Greenwood & Levin, 2007; Lewin, 1958). As our goal in developing the strategy was very much action and participative it was logical that a participatory action research methodology be used. Our action research is of a reflective process of the various stages outlined in the case study with a community of stakeholders. Denscombe (2010, p. 6) writes that an action research strategy's purpose is to solve a particular problem and to produce guidelines for best practice, these were very much the goals of the research.

CASE STUDY

Limerick Community Connect (LCC) whose mission was to support, promote and deliver collaborative and innovative approaches to the use of ICT in communities at risk of digital exclusion set up a separate committee to develop an eParticipation strategy group. The development of a Limerick Community Connect e-participation strategy arose after many disjointed initiatives and digital community projects over a period of ten years. With a declining availability of funding and a requirement for improved monitoring of projects a number of groups came together and proposed the need for a strategy as result of the poor performance of the disadvantaged communities relative to other regions in the city despite the large amount of funding and support groups who had been working in the area for over a decade.

Evidence of the poor results came from research relating to Limerick that was carried out by O'Dwyer (2008) who compared 7 disadvantaged to 1 non-disadvantaged community. He found over twice as many respondents in non-disadvantaged communities were using internet cafes, broadband

and on-line shopping. In the disadvantaged areas surveyed 47% had never used a computer, with internet connections 50% below the national average.

For those without a home computer just over 10% used internet cafes and school/college respectively, with only 15% using community centres. Even though access in the form of computers in community locations were provided these were not being utilised fully for three reasons:

1. People did not know of the location or felt that the resources were not easy to access
2. Respondents did not see computers as relevant to their lives and had no interest in using community resources.
3. There was a fear of failure- particularly when this would occur in a public, open centre.

Therefore, for these particular disadvantaged communities in Limerick the 'first' digital divide is relevant with access to computers and the internet as a problem.

One particular socio-demographic factor relevant to ICT usage in Limericks disadvantaged areas was education. In the city those leaving school aged 15 or younger was 22.2% compared to a national average of 17.9%: figures for early school leavers in disadvantaged communities ranged from 33.7% to a high of 55.4%, (Limerick Health Promotion, 2008) based on data from (Census, 2006). This meant that there were relatively low levels of general literacy as well as limited opportunities to engage with formal ICT programmes.

This cognitive divide can be seen in recent research who found that 35% of those in disadvantaged communities said that computers/the internet were irrelevant to them. Of those without a home computer 47.4% said that there was nothing that would encourage them to start using a computer/the internet, (O'Dwyer, 2008).

As can be seen from Table 1 these communities have typically faced very high inter-generational

unemployment even when Ireland was doing well economically. Thus, proficiency of ICT in order to gain employment was relatively less important given the degree of early school leaving and high unemployment in an economic boom. However, given their higher reliance on state assistance and services there was potential to provide opportunities to increase electronic access and participation in the area of e-Government.

Many of these priority areas were also or relevance to limerick as O'Dwyer, (2008) found that of those not using a computer:

*   80% of over 55's
*   61% of unemployed
*   77% of those engaged in home duties
*   82% of those retired.

A problem with eParticipation in the limerick case was that recent research Humphreys and Dineen (2007) found lower levels of social capital and low levels of institutional trust in disadvantaged neighbourhoods. In addition (Limerick Health Promotion, 2008) identified the issue of 'learned helplessness' whereby members of the disadvantaged communities had become over reliant on state support services and agencies.

This was the background to the LCC requirement to develop a working strategy that might address the fundamental social, political, educational and access challenges that were core to the improvement of eparticipation in the disadvantaged communites.

Strategy Development Stages

This section details the steps taken in chronological order to develop an eParticipation strategy. As well as outlining the actions taken at each stage and the issues that arose the section also tries to outline lessons learned and provide advice for similar initiatives.

Table 1. Unemployment rates in target areas.

Area	2002	2006
Moyross	21.3%	24.6%
Southill	24.8%	29.2%
St. Munchin's	15.0%	14.0%
St. Mary's	30.4%	27.4%
Our Lady of Lourdes	21.6%	21.5%
Ireland	8.8%	8.5%

Source: (Census, 2002; Census, 2006)

1. Strategy Group Creation Meeting 1

The strategy group could only meet 4 times over a year, the time allocated to the strategy development exercise. Some administrative support was provided in the form of an administrator, made available for 1 day per week. This administrator had the advantage of working in the relevant communities for the rest of the week and this gave her constant access to both community representatives and all the main service providers. Because she had work with all strategy group members (except the facilitators) over an extended period of time she had built up a level of trust and understood the key actors roles and perspectives. The composition of the group is outlined in Table 2. The group composition involved participants from a number of sectors: (1) Educational Establishments (UL, LIT, VEC, FAS), (2) National, Regional (Shannon Development) and City (Limerick Regeneration and PAUL) Development Groups (3) Disadvantaged Community Representatives.

It was decided at the first formal meeting that one of the authors, seen as independent, would chair the meetings and oversee the strategy development process. The chair/facilitator was seen as

Table 2. Group Composition

Organisation Name	Organisation Task/Perspective
University of Limerick (UL)	Facilitators (2)
FAS	Government Training Provider
Community Action Centre	Youth Centre Manger (Also Chair of LCC- Parent Group)
Shannon Development	Regional Development (including Broadband roll-out)
South Hill House	Community Worker (Also Secretary Parent Group)
Limerick Institute of Technology (LIT)	Third Level- Access Officer Postgraduate Development Officer
St Munchins Family Resource Centre	Community Worker
SIE	Second Level Liason
Limerick Regeneration	Renovating/rebuilding disadvantaged communities in Limerick. Chief Executive Officer Project Manager: Education & Training
City of Limerick Vocational Education Committee (VEC)	Sub-degree level education. Learning Technology Development Officer
People Action Against Unemployment Limited (PAUL)	Grant Provider Co-ordinator of Social Programmes
Dublin City University	Community Development Officer
Limerick Community Connect	ICT Development Worker (Also part-time Strategy Group Administrator)
Department of Communications & Natural Resource	Digital Inclusion Officer

having no vested interest and not seen as closely aligned to any particular perspectives. It should be noted that over the first few weeks (prior to the second formal meeting) and a number of additional members were co-opted on to the group during this time. These members came from the civil service department charged with eParticipation, as well as an expert on the topic from a (non-Limerick) based university.

It was found that where organisations had a number of people on the group attendance at meetings could alternate and so some degree of continuity was lost. Senior members of organisations, placed on the committee, though carrying power were more difficult to schedule for meetings and so, due to other commitments, did not have the opportunity to contribute as much as would have been optimal for the project.

At this meeting there were some initial discussions around the nature of what a digital inclusion strategy should include. While most of the group members (excluding the facilitators) knew each other both from interacting as part of their employment and as members of the parent group the suggestions made at this meeting reflected the perspectives of the members. For example those with an organisational remit to increase broadband penetration saw the problem as a 'first order' digital divide problem to which access was a solution similar to authors such as Adriani and Becchetti (2003) and Compaine (2001). This view however suited their organisational agenda (such as the objective of Shannon Development to increase the availability of broadband as they were involved in the roll out of a metropolitan area network MAN in the city). Some of those in middle management roles saw the need for information systems to support their own reporting responsibilities. Interestingly those group members who interacted daily with those in the disadvantaged communities began from an eParticipation perspective. They questioned the need for infrastructure solutions being discussed before what they saw as the key question was answered:

what would access to digital technology allow disadvantaged citizens to do and in what ways would any initiatives increase quality of life in a way that was sustainable. In this view they echoed authors such as (Warschauer, 2003b). While managers in support agencies raised questions around the exclusion of the disadvantaged communities community workers went further. They questioned from what people in these communities would be excluded? The latter's focus was on identifying new projects, or existing projects with a potential digital aspect, in which community members could usefully participate.

2. Identification of Stakeholder Views (Individual Group Meetings)

Given the limit on the number of formal meetings of the full group the role of the Chair and administrator was critical in taking the terms of references and wishes of the main group and translating these in to a series of activities and outcomes to be reported back to the next full meeting. Though not appreciated fully at the time by the facilitators it was possible to identify at this first meeting that different people espoused reflected the fact that their organisations were at different stages of understanding the development of concepts around the digital divide, digital inclusion and eParticipation as discussed in literature above. At this time it was seen as a diversity of opinions and views on the same phenomena it was decided that the next step would be individual meetings to better understand the diverse views expressed by group members.

Because the authors/facilitators were seen as impartial but were relatively new to the area these meetings were arranged to increase their knowledge or relevant organisations. The meetings were found to be very valuable as they enabled participants to outline their views on how the strategy could be developed from their own perspective: they outlined their resources and capabilities as well as ways in which their own organisation was already involved and the other organisations with whom they interacted in service delivery to the disadvantaged communities. During the course of these meetings it was possible to identify differences in emphasis among members of the strategy group. These meetings also enabled the authors' identify key areas of interest among members and reinforce the independence of the authors. The meetings also suggested the steps members felt other participants should take and improvements that would help to advance the strategy.

An opportunity was taken during this time to co-opt a number of additional members on to the strategy group. These were an academic specialising in digital inclusion and working as a development officer between a university and its local community (to provide a theoretical perspective) as well as a head of a digital inclusion section in a (national) government department (to provide a national and European perspective).

A lesson learned when arranging these meetings was to not only seek to meet the strategy group member but also suggest the inclusion of any relevant/interested parties from the organisation. This sometimes provided access to the views of workers with more day-to-day experience working with the citizens. It also provided a wider network of contacts to clarify points and access information and feedback during later stages. This was useful as in some instances these additional meeting participants had very practical suggestions and feedback on previous projects. In hindsight an opportunity was missed: as well as seeking to understand stakeholders current needs the meetings it would have also been valuable to raise issues of eParticipation and 'second order' effects (Attewell, 2001) with those who saw the strategy in terms of the 'first order' access problem.

3. 'Theme' Identification

Having individually met the strategy group's members the two facilitators structured the views expressed under three headings. The objective here

was to identify a small number of broad themes that would take into account the differing work of all participants. The themes needed to be sufficiently encompassing so as ensure all relevant aspects were taken into account but still remain focused on digital inclusion and increased digital participation. The latter was vital due to the multifaceted nature of eParticipation (Warschauer, 2003b; Saebo et al., 2008; Madon et al., 2007) discussions often had a tendency to drift to wider societal and economic issues outside the group's remit. Analysis of interviews revealed three key areas which could be considered analytically separate but nonetheless were interlinked under which researchers assembled the relevant views of all participants.

Theme 1: Community Participation: Hearing and Heeding the Community Voice.

This theme was developed by those working closest with the relevant communities and who were focused on seeking ways to engage in eParticipation to improve peoples' quality of life. Because eParticipation was low in the relevant communities (O'Dwyer, 2008) it was decided that any initiatives needed to show how participation could be beneficial to the 'lived experience' of the targeted groups. By seeking to link eParticipation to everyday activities and existing projects in the targeted areas it was hoped to increase sustainability. Focusing on the experiences of the communities also had value for the strategy group's parent organisation. By using its network to facilitate the development of a community voice Limerick Community Connect could help identify new and innovative forms of eParticipation. This was seen as having the potential to provide a number of useful outcomes. Firstly, it provided the LCC group with a useful additional coordinative role. It could draw upon its community members' contacts to develop new ideas for eParticipation and draw on other members organisational resources to trial these ideas. Secondly, where the ideas proved successful they could be incorporated into members' mainstream activities. The allowed this theme to provide an effective 'R&D' facility as well as 'proof of concept' for ideas. This was particularly valuable to public sector organisations who did not wish, in economically straitened circumstances, to be seen to waste public money on unsuccessful projects. Thirdly, linking it closely with the communities increased the chances of acceptance, sustainability and success.

Theme 2: Improving Community Group Processes.

A key issue among community groups was a need to implement more efficient processes to manage their work. They saw a need for 'evidence-based reporting' from government bodies as well as private philanthropic funders on communities' activities as becoming a requirement for seeking and sustaining funding streams. These systems could not only aid the community groups in terms of information collection and processing but they also saw a use in tracking citizens use of their service so as to suggest how to target future initiatives.

Theme 3: Coordination among Service Providers.

Given the different missions of the various LCC members it was important to identify when and how coordination would take place. This was seen as the most difficult theme. During individual meetings a number of members expressed concern that there was duplication of service provision with a need to clarify the role of each organisation. In the previous number of years, when Irelands economy had been growing strongly, there had been increased funding provided for disadvantaged communities: this allowed organisations to increase their range of services including internet access, digital inclusion and electronic government, but not necessarily in a coordinated way. Because at the time the strategy was being

developed Ireland was in a recession, with service providers facing year-on-year budget cuts (requiring them to concentrate on core service provision) this proved to be a good time to raise the question of who would take responsibility to implement portions of the strategy and what aspects would require coordinated action.

Due to the fact that the researchers were new to the area and to ensure that the 'three pillars' of the eParticipation strategy were inclusive and encompassing a second meeting was called.

4. Theme Development Meeting

This meeting was run as a workshop. At the beginning the three themes were outlined by the chair, providing, for each theme, examples and issues to show how the various perspectives were represented within each theme and the linkages between the themes. Three rapporteurs were approached prior to the meeting and asked to take charge of an theme in which they were identified as having a particular interest. The strategy group was then divided into three and asked to augment or provide additional detail to the themes as outlined at the start of the meeting. Groups were rotated so all members commented on all themes. Rapporteurs took detailed notes of all contributions. It was decided to specifically exclude the researchers and administrator from this role to ensure the theme development process was led by group members. The feedback on the workshop was that members felt the format enabled more participation (due to the discussions taking place in smaller groups) and felt that there was a high degree of participation. Each rapporteur converted their notes into an electronic document that was e-mailed to the facilitators.

Though not necessary in this instance where members represented different organisations, in a situation where an organisation had a number of members on such a strategy development group it could be useful to 'break up natural coalitions' (Garvin & Roberto, 2001) by allocating members from the same organisation to different theme groups. This would avoid dominance in any particular group and provide the maximum awareness of other viewpoints.

Though successful, in retrospect a number of changes would have aided the process. Firstly, it would have been useful when seeking agreement of members to act as rapporteurs if they were given a briefing session on the theme. It was found that at the previous stage detailed discussions had taken place between the facilitators and giving the rapporteurs some sense of this background information would have aided their job in the workshop. Secondly, each rapporteur reported their theme in coherent but different formats: some prior guidelines would have ensured more consistency across the documents.

This stage provided much more detail on each theme. It was also possible to identify which theme(s) were more core/peripheral to particular members. The inclusive nature of the workshop ensured that no relevant issues had been overlooked and that any new issues fitted under existing themes. If any significantly different new themes had emerged it would have been possible to structure the workshop so that rapporteurs could report this and to develop a new theme as part of a plenary session of the full group before the workshop ended. The way the meeting was structured acted not only to provide more detail on issues but also indicated particular local initiatives in particular communities or by constituent organisations. The workshop structure also acted to ensure participation and commitment across all group members.

A key issue arose around this time was the power and influence each member of the strategy development group had within their organisation. It was found that the more core eParticipation was to an organisation's mission the higher the level of the representative they sent. For some organisations (such as limerick city county council) eParticipation, while important, was not their core activity. This led them to nominate a person,

often technical, and at a lower organisational level than other members. In these circumstances it was important that the person could act as an evangelist in their host organisation to ensure any actions suggested in the final strategy would be implemented by their organisation.

A related problem, partly related to the recession requiring efficiencies in service provision, was that there were changes in how some of the members' organisations were structured. FAS the state employment and training body (previously a national body with regional offices) was to be broken up and reorganised under the auspices of the VECs (vocational education committees). The number of VECs was also rationalised at this time so that Limerick city and Limerick County were merged. In addition the Limerick Regeneration agency, previously an autonomous body with an independent budget, was to be placed under the control of the city/county council. This meant that the composition of the group changed over the course of the year. These changes meant that the strategy, as it developed, could highlight proposed initiatives but without necessarily knowing which body would ultimately be charged with implementing particular initiatives. Because the missions of some service providers were in the process of being changed it required that the strategy be left 'open' for members to update it in light of wider events. It would also require the strategy formulation process to be very open and transparent so that changes that other members made could be seen by the group. This turbulent environment was particularly suited to being supported by a wiki technology. The success of this support was predicated on members firstly becoming aware of relevant changes in a timely manner and secondly modifying the developing strategy accordingly.

5. Wiki Development

The facilitators analysed and reflected on the electronic reports received from the rapporteurs, developing them into a sequence of actions for each theme. Given the technical capabilities of the group, and to ensure transparency of the work being undertaken by the facilitators in aiding the strategy development,it was decided to develop a wiki to support the strategy development process. This was initially structured to create a homepage from which members could access a webpage for each theme. Each theme page contained firstly a section that outlined the rapporteur's workshop notes. Below this was a section where those notes were restructured by the facilitators. This was used to increase transparency around the restructuring process and sought to show how the actions developed flowed from the workshop contributions. All members were given full rights to read and edit as well as leave comments on any thematic webpage. The ability to add pages was reserved for the facilitators. It also allowed them to add relevant material to what it was envisaged would become an expanding document. It was decided that members would not delete the work of others.

Where facilitators lacked sufficient expertise on an issue or required more detail or data they posed explicit questions highlighted in the relevant section of a theme's web page. These could then be answered or discussed in more detail by any of the main group with relevant experience. It was envisaged that the outcome of this stage would be a record of detailed actions and suggestions nuanced by member's experiences including some instances of disagreement. These would then serve to provide the agenda for the next meeting of the full group where limited time could be used for a full discussion and resolution of issues rather than developing the material itself (the job to be accomplished by the wiki).

In retrospect the utilisation of the on-line wiki component could have been improved if there had been more convergence on the objectives of the strategy. Where there was divergence of opinion members wanted this to be resolved in an (off-line) meeting format. Wiki usage would have been increased if it were made clear that a purpose of adding to the wiki was to highlight

differences in emphasis. In practice once an approach had been advocated other members were reluctant to add contrary or alternative views. This could have been advanced as a positive rather than negative action. It would have been beneficial if differences in emphasis around the nature eParticipation versus access had been addressed at an earlier stage. At this stage, when particular action items were being drafted these were being written by some members at different 'developmental' stages. What had initially been seen as diverse perspectives now had the potential to become divergent thinking. There needed to be a convergence of views on what specific actions needed to be included in the strategy.

6. Feedback Meeting

The format of this meeting had to be revised based on how the wiki was used by members. Firstly, only some members used the wiki. This was a surprise to the facilitators given the technical nature of the group; charged with creating a digital strategy. Secondly, those members who did interact through the site chose to use the comment feature rather than directly edit pages. This resulted in short general comments on how the theme could be developed, without the detail it was hoped would be provided to develop such views. Alternatively the comment focused on suggesting alternative terminology, an issue that was present but not fully appreciated in the earlier stages. While both were useful they were limited in scope. Interestingly, comments, placed at the bottom of the web page carried the author's login name, identifying them which may have been an inhibiting factor for some. Had they edited the thematic web page their comments would have been more anonymous as these only identified the last person to edit, but not the changes that had been made.

An improvement to the process would have been to provide details of expected norms of interaction at the previous meeting- this had instead been conveyed afterward in an e-mail from the administrator. In addition, the facilitators should have monitored activity on the wiki and informally contacted members to provide additions to themes in which they were particularly interested.

Because of the lack of progress developing themes on the wiki the next group meeting required more time to be spent discussion the themes and the general direction of the strategy. These comments were noted by the facilitators who again had to reflect on how to modify the wiki to reflect the wishes of the group expressed in the meeting. Some of this involved creating additional pages to reflect expected sections of the final strategy report. While this advanced the project the groups reliance on the facilitators was becoming more central and administrative with members contributions only occurring at meetings.

7. Focused Wiki Editing

Having updated the wiki to reflect the (third) meeting the facilitators sought to increase the group's own development of the eParticipation strategy. Based on members' contributions during group and individual meetings each member was e-mailed individually. They were asked to address a specific theme or sub-theme and edit that section of the wiki. It was felt that this individualised approach would place more emphasis and responsibility on each member, particularly when the e-mail identified how their contribution would help develop the overall strategy. This helped identify their role in context of the strategy and asked them to reflect on how aspects of the strategy could affect their organisation. To encourage participation deadlines were set, participation by members monitored, and reminder e-mails sent. The need for tight deadlines had to be tempered by the fact that this project was not, in many cases the core activity of some members who had to prioritise other work.

One group were identified as not engaging with the wiki development, even at the comment

level: the local communities' representatives. This group had the deepest level of involvement with the target areas. As such they were ideally placed to identify the communities' needs and how these could be enhanced through eParticipation. The facilitators were fortunate that the administrator had worked closely with these representatives over a long number of years and had built up a high level of trust with them. It was agreed that the administrator would meet community representatives individually and in small groups. She would write up their views (under the various themes- especially theme 1) and she would then add these to the relevant sections of the wiki.

By focusing the wiki it was possible to allow a particular view to be developed in a more detailed manner. Because of the way the task was segmented it was possible to accommodate members at different 'stages'. Plans for access could be developed by those with that organisational remit while those interested in participation (local community group workers and representatives) could focus on the projects possible assuming a sufficient infrastructure.

8. Contextualising for Stakeholders

Reflection and re-structuring was again used after the members' focused editing stage. This involved an 'opening up' of the details provided. Members' motivations were increased by seeking details on how their own organisation could become involved in certain theme sections. Their contributions were naturally organisation-centric and space needed to be created in the document to allow other future contributions to augment themes: particularly for areas of close collaboration or where resource sharing might be possible. Because of their overview on all aspects of the three themes and knowledge of the member's perspectives facilitators played a useful role in identifying possible areas for coordination or collaboration. This ensured that the contributions were contextualised and ready for the next stage.

Setting individualised tasks and tight deadlines was found to advance the project quickly, even though this section was completed over the summer when certain people took their holidays. This delayed the process somewhat. It would have been useful to have known holiday arrangements in advance when segmenting and sequencing work and setting deadlines.

9. General Wiki Editing

Once focused contributions were added to the wiki (stage 7) and the pages were opened up (stage 8) the wiki was now available for all participants to make contributions to other sections. One structural change was made at this stage. The facilitators reviewed similar strategy documents to identify a suitable structure for the final report. While the three themes did not change other pages were restructured and added, which allowed the main page of the wiki to become a table of contents for the eventual strategy.

Facilitators allocated review and editing work to all group members with deadlines. This ensured that additional perspectives on content were captured. In addition to assigning this work facilitators indicated to participants' specific areas to see if coordination of actions across agencies was desirable and comment on this. At this stage members were looking to see how the overall strategy would affect their organisations. Therefore, more nuanced and deeper reflection was required of the group. A key objective of this part of the strategy stage was identifying initiatives and projects on which organisations had a defined role or could see how their own objectives could be advanced by parts of the strategy.

The role of the facilitators was to outline possible ways in which participants' organisations could support eParticipation, as enunciated in the document, even by suggesting new areas of work and responsibility. It is also important at this stage to identify 'contact points' between organisations and define these relationships in terms sufficiently specific to avoid subsequent disagreement and non-cooperation while avoiding an eventual strategy that is too prescriptive and detailed. Where time is available arranging a series of bi-lateral meetings between affected members would enhance this stage. When developing a time-line for this activity consideration should also be given to the level of power each member possessed as in this case study several members had an eParticipation role within a wider organisation that had to be convinced to allocate resources to initiatives developed. To an extent the eventual strategy could be used as a form of legitimation for individual organisational changes.

10. Conversion from Wiki to Draft Strategy Document

By the time this stage was reached all members were aware of the content of the strategy. The various pages were converted from a hyperlinked series of web-pages to a linear document. The role of the facilitators was to ensure that the various inputs were brought together to form a coherent narrative. Another consideration when producing an eParticipation strategy, where there were multiple actors and perspectives was the possibility to use the material developed to write customised versions of the strategy for various audiences (potential funders, similar organisations, government etc.). A particular external audience was that of existing and potential funders of projects. This would not involve changing the strategy but rather presenting elements of the strategy in a different order to emphasise issues of importance, for example the development of methods to collect evidence on the success of projects.

Several contributors embedded hyperlinks to external web-sites in their contributions. These were produced as references on the final document but as the strategy was also made available as a PDF it was possible to have a slightly different document that retained the links and made it easier for reader to access external material. Though not used in this case it would also be possible to create a strategy web-site, providing more detail (e.g. audio-visual material of success stories, case studies etc.) that would show how other organisations had developed projects. If such a support web-site were present it could also act to showcase successes and also act as an archive artefact which could be drawn upon in future strategy iterations.

11. Ensuring final alignment Meeting

Once the final document was produced it was brought back to the fourth and final group meeting. Because LCC had delegated authority to develop the strategy to this group it was important that a formal meeting discussed and ratified the document before the group was effectively disbanded and the strategy was presented to the parent organisation. It is important to notes that because all the strategy group members were drawn from the wider parent group it was important that they should be committed to its implementation and act to support its development in LCC. This underlines the importance of group composition of the strategy formulation group from the start. Ideally strategy group members would have nurtured support of the strategy in advance of the publication of the strategy within their organisations.

DISCUSSION

This chapter seeks to provide suggestions regarding developing an eParticipation strategy for disadvantaged communities in a city where the development process required the input from several stakeholder groups.

A key issue at the start of such a process is to identify and clarify stakeholders' perspective i.e. do they wish to achieve eParticipation (and the associated second-order effects) or limit the strategy to enabling eInclusion and access to ICT and the internet. It was important to surface these perspectives and identify if they were mutually

compatible (some stakeholders could focus on access while others could concentrate on eParticipation initiatives) or whether a common viewpoint was required. Where the agencies involved held differing briefs it is important to identify and scope suitable themes and ensure that all participants can see how their organisation has to potential to contribute to a theme or themes.

The open and reconfigurable nature of wiki technology allowed participants to freely add to thematic web pages but there were problems with lack of usage initially. Clear expectations, tight but manageable deadlines and an initial round of assigned editing was needed to increase usage.

A balance need to be struck between allowing participants modify and extend thematic wiki pages, allowing sometimes divergent ideas and the need for the group to physically meet, to reach an agreed, convergent, position.

There are a number of lessons both for community management practice and information lessons. Clearly the contextual factors will make each study somewhat unique

Lessons for management practice in relation to community digital strategy were;

- The importance of unbiased or affiliated leadership of the process.
- Ensuring the broadest involvement of as many of the relevant stakeholders.
- Establishing a clear and mutual agreement on terms of reference.
- The development of a shared meaning in relation to scope and understanding of the key concepts of inclusion, participation and digital divide.
- Embracing variety of stakeholders agendas and perspectives where possible.
- An open and transparent consultation process.
- The targeting of realistic goals and actions that are immediately implementable.

A number of lessons in relation to Information Management practice were also identified:

- The creation of a dynamic content management system that mirrored the community development process.
- Democratising of the creation of the strategy content with equal access and open collaboration.
- The use of a content management system that will develop and facilitate future ongoing work.
- The need to support and encourage use of accessible collaboration tools.

LIMITATIONS

Limitations of the study have been highlighted throughout the process descriptions however a number of general limitations of the study need to be outlined. As the authors were participants in developing and managing the development of the community strategy, bias with regard to interpretation of results cannot be ruled out. Additionally the generalizability of the process and methods used need to considered as the stages emerged from the both the initial framing of the problem and was reframed based on the input from that particular set of stakeholders and was conditioned by the happenings that were taking place with their various organisations.

SUGGESTED FURTHER RESEARCH

The paper does not elaborate on the details of the final strategy that was developed, further work and research can address the success of the strategy as it was rolled out and managed within the community setting. It was anticipated that the wiki would play a pivotal role in capturing and supporting the implementation of the strategy. Early indications were that this was only partly happening and

would require further analysis. Finally the evolving nature of the technology and our understanding of e-participation would mean that tracking the particular project implementations as an ongoing dynamic event that will need periodic evaluation in order to capture and enhance our understanding of these critical digital technologies that are constantly redefining how our communities are shaped. A comparison with similar initiative in other cities and in other countries to

REFERENCES

Adriani, F., & Becchetti, L. (2003). *Does the digital divide matter? The role of ICT across country level and growth estimates*. CEIS Tor Vergata.

Attewell, P. (2001). The First and Second Digital Divides. *Sociology of Education*, 74(3), 252–259. doi:10.2307/2673277

Ayanso, A., Cho, F. I., & Lertwachara, K. (2010). The digital divide: Global and regional ICT leaders and followers. *Information Technology for Development*, 16(4), 304–319. doi:10.1080/02681102.2010.504698

Barzilai-Nahon, K. (2006). Gaps and Bits: Conceptualizing Measurements for Digital Divides. *The Information Society*, 22(5), 269–279. doi:10.1080/01972240600903953

Bavel, R. V., Punie, Y., et al. (2004). ICTs and Social Capital in the Knowledge Society.

Belanger, F., & Carter, L. (2009). The impact of the digital divide on e-Government use. *Communications of the ACM*, 52(4), 132–135. doi:10.1145/1498765.1498801

Blignaut, P. (2009). A Bilateral Perspective on the Digital Divide in South Africa. *Perspectives on Global Development and Technology*, 8(4), 581–601. doi:10.1163/156915009X12583611836091

Borgida, E., Sullivan, J. L., Oxendine, A., Jackson, M. S., Riedel, E., & Gangl, A. (2002). Civic culture meets the digital divide: The role of community electronic networks. *The Journal of Social Issues*, *58*(1), 125–141. doi:10.1111/1540-4560.00252

Boyd, O. P. (2008). Differences in eDemocracy parties' eParticipation systems. *Information Policy*, *13*, 167–188.

Census of Population. (2002). Dublin, Central Statistics Office.

Census of Population (2006). Dublin, Central Statistics Office.

Coley, R., & Cradler, J. et al. (1997). *Computers and Classrooms: The Status of Technology in U.S. Schools*. Princeton, NJ: Educational Testing Service.

Compaine, B. (2001). *Re-examining the digital divide: Internet and telecom consortium*. Cambridge, MA: MIT Press.

Dewan, S., & Riggins, F. J. (2005). The Digital Divide: Current and Future Research Directions. *Journal of the Association for Information Systems*, *6*(12), 298–337.

Ferlander, S., & Timms, D. (2006). Bridging the Dual Digital Divide: A Local Net and an IT-Cafe in Sweden. *Information Communication and Society*, *9*(2), 137–159. doi:10.1080/13691180600630732

Ferro, E., Helbig, N. C., & Gil-Garcia, J. R. (2011). The role of IT literacy in defining digital divide policy needs. *Government Information Quarterly*, *28*(1), 3–10. doi:10.1016/j.giq.2010.05.007

Fonseca, C. (2010). The Digital Divide and the Cognitive Divide: Reflections on the Challenge of Human Development in the Digital Age. *Annenberg School for Communication & Journalism*, *6*, 25–30.

Garcia-Jimenez, M., & Gomez-Barroso, J. (2009). Universal Service in a Broader Perspective: The European Digital Divide. *Informatica Economica*, *13*(2), 155–165.

Garvin, D. A., & Roberto, M. A. (2001). What you don't know about making decisions. *Harvard Business Review*, 108–116. PMID:11550627

Gatautis, R. (2010). Creating public value through eParticipation: Wave project. *Economics and Management*, *15*, 483–490.

Graham, M. (2011). Time machine and virtual portals: The spatialities of the digital divide. *Progress in Development Studies*, *11*(3), 211–227. doi:10.1177/146499341001100303

Guyader, H. L. (2009). eInclusion public policies in Europe. Brussels, European Comission: Information Society and Media.

Hines, A. H., & Nelson, A. et al. (2001). *Hidden Circuits. Technicolor. A. H. Hines, A. Nelson and T. L. N. Tu*. New York: New York University Press.

Humphreys, E., & Dineen, D. (2007). *Evaluation of Social Capital in Limerick City*. Limerick: University of Limerick.

Limerick Health Promotion. (2008). *Health Impact Assessment of Early School Leaving, Absenteeism and Truancy*. Limerick: Health Service Executive.

Macintosh, A., & Whyte, A. (2008). Towards an evaluation framework for eParticipation. *Transforming Government: People. Process and Policy*, *2*(1), 16–30.

Madon, S., Reinhard, N., et al. (2007). Digital Inclusion Projects in Developing Countries: Processes of Institutionalisation. Proceedings of the 9th International Conference on Social Implications of Computers in Developing Countries. Sao Paula, Brazil.

Meneses, J., & Momino, J. M. (2010). Putting Digital Literacy in Practice: How Schools Contribute to Digital Inclusion in the Network Society. *The Information Society*, 26(3), 197–208. doi:10.1080/01972241003712231

O'Dwyer, S. (2008). *Identifying ICT Needs in Disadvantaged Communities within Limerick City*. Limerick City Community ICT Steering Group.

Peng, G. (2010). Critical Mass, Diffusion Channels, and the Digital Divide. *Journal of Computer Information Systems*, 63–71.

Pretto, N. D. L., & Bailey, O. G. (2010). Digital culture in Brazil: Building 'peeracy'? *International Journal of Media and Cultural Politics*, 6(3), 265–281. doi:10.1386/mcp.6.3.265_1

Recabarren, M., Nussbaum, M., & Leiva, C. (2008). Cultural divide and the internet. *Computers in Human Behavior*, 24(6), 2917–2926. doi:10.1016/j.chb.2008.04.013

Robles, J. M., & Torres-Albero, C. et al. (2011). Spanish E-government and the Third Digital Divide: A Sociological View. *Journal of US-China Public Administration*, 8(4), 401–412.

Rodousakis, N. and A. M. d. Santos (2008). "The development of inclusive e-Government in Austria and Portugal: a comparison of two success stories." Innovation: the European Journal of Social Science Research **21**(4): 283-316.

Rose, J., & Sandford, C. (2007). Mapping eParticipation Research: Four Central Challenges. *Communications of the Association for Information Systems*, 20, 909–943.

Sacchi, A., Giannini, E., Bochic, R., Reinhard, N., & Lopes, A. B. (2009). Digital Inclusion with the McInternet: Would You Like Fries With That? *Communications of the ACM*, 52(3), 113–116. doi:10.1145/1467247.1467275

Saebo, O., Rose, J., & Skiftenes Flak, L. (2008). The shape of eParticipation: Characterizing an emerging research area. *Government Information Quarterly*, 25(3), 400–428. doi:10.1016/j.giq.2007.04.007

Salvador, A. C., Rojas, S., & Susinos, T. (2010). Weaving Networks: An Educational Project for Digital Inclusion. *The Information Society*, 26(2), 137–143. doi:10.1080/01972240903562795

Sandford, C., & Rose, J. (2007). Characterizing eParticipation. *International Journal of Information Management*, 27(6), 406–421. doi:10.1016/j.ijinfomgt.2007.08.002

Seale, J., Draffan, E. A., & Wald, M. (2010). Digital agility and digital decision-making: Conceptualising digital inclusion in the context of disabled learners in higher education. *Studies in Higher Education*, 35(4), 445–461. doi:10.1080/03075070903131628

Servon, L. (2002). *Bridging the digital divide: Technology, community and public policy*. London: Blackwell. doi:10.1002/9780470773529

Srinuan, C., & Bohlin, E. (2011). What makes people go on line? An empirical analysis of the digital divide in Thailand. Proceedings of the Annual International Conference on Micro and Macro Economics.

Stephenson, S. (2009). Digital Divide: A Discursive Move Away from the Real Inequities. *The Information Society*, 25(1), 1–22. doi:10.1080/01972240802587539

Understanding the digital divide. (2001OECD. Paris: Directorate for Science, Technology and Industry.

Vehovar, V., Sicherl, P., Hüsing, T., & Dolnicar, V. (2006). Methodological Challenges of Digital Divide Measurements. *The Information Society*, 22(5), 279–290. doi:10.1080/01972240600904076

Warschauer, M. (2003). Dissecting the 'Digital Divide': A Case Study in Egypt. *The Information Society, 19*(4), 297–304. doi:10.1080/01972240309490

Warschauer, M. (2003). *Technology and social inclusion: Rethinking the digital divide.* Cambridge, MA: MIT Press.

Wenglinsky, H. (1998). *Does it Computer? The Relationship between Educational Technology and Student Achievement in Mathematics.* Princeton, NJ: Policy Information Centre of the Educational Testing Service.

Wimmer, M. A. (2007). *The Role of Research in Successful E-Government Implementation E-Government Guide Germany. A. Zechner* (pp. 79–91). Stuttgart: Fraunhofer.

Chapter 14
Wheelchair Controlled by Hands Gestures Recognition:
A Natural User Interface

Arminda Guerra Lopes
Polytechnic Institute of Castelo Branco, Portugal

ABSTRACT

This chapter presents the development of a new human-machine interface - a wheelchair controlled by the recognition of human hands' static gestures. The application will allow the occupant of an intelligent wheelchair to communicate with certain objects in order to facilitate their daily life. The suggested methodology draws on the use of computational processes and low-cost hardware. The development of the application involved dealing with computer vision issues in a comprehensive way. It was based on the steps of video image capture, image segmentation, feature extraction, pattern recognition and classification. In terms of its relevance and impact, the application described in the chapter promotes a more natural and intuitive mode of interaction for disabled individuals, which is expected to improve their quality of life.

INTRODUCTION

The growth of road accidents and the increased number of individuals who suffer severe consequences and associated mobility problems are trends in contemporary societies. This situation inevitably affects the physical, psychological and social well-being of individuals. Historically, technological developments moved towards the facilitation of life. Daily, we use resources particularly developed to assist and simplify the dynamics of everyday life, such as pens, cars, computers, telephones, an endless catalog of tools, which are already an integral part of our routine.

Individuals with mobility disabilities have consistently claimed for the development of assistive technologies that could provide them with a better quality of life. An alternative means of mobility is the wheelchair. However, the use of a wheelchair does not allow complete mobility in its fullest sense. In particular for example, carrying out autonomous and independent actions (such as picking up a small object) without the help of others is a matter of serious concern.

DOI: 10.4018/978-1-4666-8833-9.ch014

The main objective of the work reported in this chapter was the development of a system for static gesture recognition using one hand only, located in front of a webcam, in a simple and uniform background scenario, without the support of any kind of assistive item, equipment, or product. The system was implemented in the C++ programming language with the aid of OpenCV library. The development of this proposal was greatly influenced by Radabaugh (2012), who argued that for people without disabilities, technology makes things easier. For people with disabilities, technology makes things possible.

To help making things possible for individuals that face mobility challenges, a gestural interface was developed based on a review of the literature, case studies, conceptual theories, and the requirements elicited in interviews conducted with participants.

THE STARTING POINT: NATURAL USER INTERFACES

Natural User Interfaces (NUI) can be considered as any technology that allows a user to interact more intuitively and directly with machines and their information. This new technological generation uses new methods of data entry, such as multi-touch, voice, pen, finger, tracking motion or fiducial markers. This implies a new philosophy of interaction with devices (Blake, 2010). We can therefore conceive NUI to interact with the environment through devices that may be embedded in houses appliances, or even in our clothes.

Natural user interfaces aim to open opportunities for fundamental natural interactions with the user, rejecting mechanical devices to access information. The first developments of NUI date back to 1991, when Mark Weiser presented his vision around two fundamental concepts that still guide the scientific research in the area of Human-machine interface. The first concept is ubiquitous computing mainly covering the hardware (Weiser, 1991). The aim was to make the human-computer interaction so natural that it could integrate the informatics with individuals' natural actions and behaviors. The second concept was related to the "calm technology" where Weiser pondered about a technology to design the interaction based on calm and comfort, giving primacy to the relationship between the user and the content (Weiser & Brown, 1995).

Natural interfaces are the logical step to achieve this form of interaction, where the user interacts with the computer, using speech, gestures, voice, or even eye movement. For Monson-Haefel (2010) the term NUI is defined as an interface that models the aspects of direct interactions between people and their natural environment. The same term is defined by Blake (2010) as a user interface, designed to use natural human behaviors, to interact directly with the content. However, the easiest way to understand the NUI is to compare it with other more traditional types of interfaces, such as graphical user interfaces (GUI) and interfaces for command line (CLI).

With that in mind, we align with definition offered by Blake (2010): "a Natural interface is an interface designed to reuse existing skills that the user needs to interact directly with the content" (Blake, 2010). According to Blake (2010) both CLI and GUI use artificial elements on their interfaces; CLI uses text for input and output of information and GUI uses, for example, the mouse for input and windows, menus, icons as output information. However, if CLI and GUI definitions are at the level of the input devices, NUI belongs to the domain of how the interaction is performed. It refers to a style of interface that is so easy to control that it seems invisible to the user.

In Blake (2010) proposes an interface designed in order that humans can use natural behaviors such as touch, gestures or speech, for interaction with the content focusing on the interactions themselves, instead of focusing on the interface. Therefore, in a natural interface, any technology can be used, since the interaction is based on the reuse of existing computational skills innate or acquired through practice, experience and interaction with the surrounding environment (Buxton, 2010).

The application of these capabilities inherent to human beings can be adapted to different tasks as a major advantage of natural interfaces. The learning curve is quite steep through the observation of another person having the ability once or twice (Blake, 2010). These capabilities still hold characteristics and fluency feelings of naturalness as people interact with the real world. These features are based on different interaction technologies and we can typify them in gestural interfaces, touch, multi-touch, tangible, based on speech recognition, based on eye tracking and multimodal.

Multimodal Interfaces

Multimodal input systems have the ability to process a combination of modalities such as speech, touch, handwriting, gestures, gaze, head movements and body - coordinated with the output systems. They recognize the natural forms of language and human behavior and consequently they support the human-machine interaction in a transparent, flexible, efficient and expressive way (Oviatt, 2003).

Sarter focuses on multimodal interfaces output, and he emphasises the use of visual, audible and tactile feedback for creating systems whose income is synergy, redundancy and increased capacity of information transfer (Sarter, 2006).

Each of the non-traditional forms of input features presents series of constraints namely the full handwriting recognition with the free hand or the gestures, and facial/body expressions. The incorporation of these forms of communication in input interfaces is an enormous technological challenge. The input format can be as simple as two pointing devices or it may include voice and image recognition. The integration of these multiple skills will achieve complementarity of

expression to the user and at the same time, the system provides the ability to choose what forms of input and output are the most appropriate for each situation.

Tactile Interfaces

Tactile interfaces interact with the user through touch, which can be constructed from different types of receivers allowing several approaches to synthesize feeling (light touch, heavy touch, pressure, pain, vibration, heat and cold). Telemedicine and robotics are an example of areas that have benefited with the development of this technology. The project "The Haptic Radar" (Cassinelli, Zerroug & Ishikawa, 2009) is an interesting application whose objective is to increase spatial awareness, and the feeling of the environment around the user. This is subsequently translated into vibrations and other sensory stimuli. As a result, a blind user is able to avoid colliding with objects that are few feet from them. The potential of this project is tremendous because it may serve to avoid collisions in dangerous environments for individuals with visual disabilities and? Or to enhance drivers' awareness.

Tangible Interfaces

These interfaces can be defined as those that include interactions carried out with physical artifacts as stimuli to interfere in context and representations of digital information. The ability of tangible user interfaces (TUI) to recognize objects and interactions applied in the context of a computational system opens up new possibilities to make interactions with computers closest to real-world processes. In the field of emergency management, for example, real-time information of the situation in a place of occurrence may represent better care, reducing damages. This feature is very important in environments with critical processes, where rapid understanding of the current situation can provide an improvement in decision-making (Radicchi, Nunes, & Botega, 2010). A different application of this technology is proposed with Siftables (Merrill, Kalanithi, & Maes, 2007). These are blocks that can think and can become any number of interactive applications, such as mathematical games or music sequencers.

Voice Recognition Interfaces

The ability to communicate by voice with our devices is promising. Driving a car, cooking a meal, repairing an engine or performing a surgery are examples of activities that could benefit from interactions via voice recognition. Currently there are already several applications in this area, particularly the speech-to-text or voice dialling on mobile phones.

Moreover, to facilitate the interaction of disabled individuals with computers, Chathuranga, Samarawickrama, Chandima, Chathuranga, & Abeykoon (2010) present a comprehensive solution to the problem where, as an alternative to the mouse, VC techniques and speech recognition technologies are used: through voice commands users can perform actions relating to the handling of the mouse. The hardware consists of a digital video camera and a microphone.

The voice recognition is expanding into various areas of application, for example, a universal translator in real time.

Eye Tracking Interfaces

Crawling Eye (Eye Tracking) is a system that tracks eye movement and records the entire journey. In using the system, it is possible to analyze reading patterns and visual queries of the users. The domains of advertising and marketing are very interested in the evolution of this technology, as it is based on the aggregation of information about where the eye of the consumer persists. In the domain of rehabilitation and medicine an eye-tracking system for rehabilitation of eye move-

ment impairments has also been developed (Lina, Huana, Chana, Yehb, & Chiua, 2004).

Other authors show how face detection combined with real-time eye tracking can be used in gaming environments (Corcoran, Nanu, Petrescu & Bigioi, 2012). The information gathered can be used to manage and to improve the design of interfaces for games being adaptable to certain user behaviours: change of mood for example.

Gestural Interfaces

Gesture recognition based interfaces are currently available, mostly developed by the games industry. The success of Nintendo Wii and Microsoft Kinect are already part of everyday life for many families. Influenced by this level of availability, the number of research on Gestural Interfaces is high, which is also due to the consolidation of techniques of images recognition, objects and movements in the area of Computer Vision (Buxton et al., 1994). In this type of interface, the interaction with a given system occurs through the recognition of gestures performed with the head, arms, hands and other limbs of the human body. An interesting example dates back to 1986 with the System Very Nervous System (VNS) developed by Rokeby (2010), which provides a sophisticated level of gestural interaction through a video camera. The computer detects the location of all the gestures of all members of the human body, interprets them, and maps these with sounds and other musical parameters.

However, the scope of the work presented in this chapter is limited to gestural interfaces through the recognition of hand gestures. Therefore, we will present in more detail this type of interfaces beginning with the definition of hand gestures. From this point on, when we refer to gestures, we mean specifically gestures performed by hands.

Hand Gestures

Over time, research done on gesture recognition has pursued the creation of a system that can identify specific human gestures in order to use them in the transmission of information or control devices. People often communicate through gestures. They are used for everything. There is evidence that gestures benefit spoken language, being part of a language process (McNeill & Levy, 1982).

We define gesture as body movement, especially movement of the head arms and in particular hands to express ideas or feelings (Porto Editora, 2012). However, there are numerous definitions and discussions on the definition of gesture.

Biologically and sociologically, the definition of gesture is somehow vague, opening the opportunity for researchers to classify gestures openly: "the notion of gesture is to embrace all kinds of situations in which an individual employs movements whose communicative intent is paramount" (Nespoulous, Perron, & Roch, 1986).

Gestures associated with speech are referenced as gesticulation. Those who operate independently of communication are referred to as autonomous. These can be organized in a language of communication, but may also represent movement commands.

According to Mulder, it is possible to characterize the human gesture in three functional roles: semiotic, ergotic and epistemic (Mulder, 1996). The semiotic function of gesture intends to communicate meaningful information. Its structure is conventional and follows a shared cultural experience. The gesture "goodbye" or the sign language itself illustrates this function. The ergotic function of gesture is associated with the notion of work, corresponding to the ability of humans to manipulate the real world to create artefacts or to change the state of the environment by "direct manipulation". The epistemic function of gesture allows humans to learn about the environment through tactile experiences. An illustrative example of the epistemic function occurs when we place our hands on an object and we find out which material it is made of.

Another method of classification categorizes gestures into four dichotomies: symbol-act, transparency-opacity, semiotics-multi-semiotics autonomy and centripetal-centrifugal (Nespoulous, Perron, & Roch, 1986). The two latter are not relevant for the purposes of this study as they are not related to the control of an object or to interpersonal communication.

The dichotomy symbol-act indicates that some gestures are pure actions, while others serve as symbols. A gesture of action occurs when a person, for example, counts their money, while a symbolic gesture occurs when a person places their thumb to hitchhike. This idea points to the possibility of using gestures that are representative of real movements in HMI devices.

The dichotomy of transparency-opacity refers to how easily individuals may interpret gestures. Transparency is associated with universality, which states that some standard cross-cultural gestures have agreed upon meanings. In reality, the gestures have standard meanings, but do not have the same meaning in all societies (Birdwhistell, 1970). Fortunately, this means that the signals used to control HMI devices can be chosen freely.

Another possibility for the classification of pattern gestures uses three categories: mimetic, deictic and arbitrary (Nespoulous, Perron, & Roch, 1986). In mimetic gestures, movements form a representation of an object or resource. For example, placing a hand on the chin and moving it down can be used to represent a beard. These gestures are amply used in representations of sign language.

The deictic are used to point to objects; they are transparent in their context and represent real intentions. Pointing with the hand to a chair for permission to sit is a practical example of such gestures. Like its predecessors, they are very useful in sign language.

Arbitrary gestures are those whose interpretation has to be studied due to its opacity. Although not common from the cultural point of view, they can be used without any additional verbal information. Therefore, these may be created for specific use of an HMI device.

Contrasting the presented taxonomy, the interaction with current computers is made freely, and the dominant paradigm is direct manipulation. However, we can speculate about this direct manipulation, because the gestures offered seem restricted with how they operate in our daily lives. This deficiency becomes obvious when considering the proficiency of human beings in the use of gestures in their day-to-day.

Dynamic and Static Gestures

Studies of human-computer interaction systems through gestures focus generally on the input and output interfaces. The gestures require the use of hands to instruct a machine, and its meaning depends on the system that integrates and evaluates it. In these systems, the gestures are created by a hand in pose or by a physical movement in two or three dimensions, translated into computer commands or movement commands. The symbolic gestures of stop, start, grab-and-drop are quite common in our society and can be used in both cases.

Pavlovic et al., (1997) offers a definition of manual gesture that combines the evolution of posture and position in time, with the intention to communicate or manipulate. Gestures are differenced into two types: dynamic and static.

Dynamic gestures necessarily imply temporal evolution (Birk, Moeslund, & Madsen, 1997) and require movement to convey the intended message. The gesture of saying "goodbye" is an example of a dynamic gesture with an open hand that only has meaning if it is made with movement.

On the other hand, with static gestures there is no need to move and to transmit the message. The same open hand static, if performed without movement, conveys information from "stop". In terms of computer vision, a static configuration is a gesture of the hand pose, which can be represented by a single image, and a dynamic

gesture is a gesture with movement, represented by a sequence of images.

Thus, based on the use of human gestures, there are some requirements and tasks to design an ideal system for gesture recognition architecture:

- Choosing gestures that fit the environment in a useful way;
- Creating a system that can recognize human gestures that are not perfect;
- Creating a system that can simultaneously use both static and dynamic gestures as components of the transmission of information;
- Designing the gesture as fast as possible, even if the gesture is incomplete;
- Employing a recognition method that uses a small amount of processing time and memory;
- Producing an expandable system that can recognize other types of gestures;
- Creating an environment that enables the use of gestures to control remote devices.

Gestural Based Systems

The importance given to applications based on gestures lies in its potential for use in human-computer interaction. Gestures can naturally increase the interaction between the user and the computer by replacing devices like mouse, keyboard, joystick or buttons on the machine. However, the main thrust for the development of gesture interfaces arises from the growth of applications in virtual environments (Krueger, 1991), for example, to simulate surgeries.

In most of these applications, the gestures are seen as controls for virtual objects that can be generated by computer, simulating 2D or 3D objects or abstractions of real objects, such as robotic arms. However, not all gestures based applications are designed in order to manipulate objects, they can also be employed to transmit messages; moreover, the use in communication through sign language or teleconferencing provides us this kind of opportunities (Pavlovic et al., 1997).

From the literature, we notice that there are numerous examples of techniques that use Computer Vision to develop systems of gesture recognition applied in different areas. We note that most studies on this topic focuses on some specific areas of interest.

There are several applications of gestural interfaces such as the development of techniques of forensic identification, young children interaction with computers, patients monitoring emotional states or television remote control (Acharya, 2007). The following studies are underlined.

Fourney et al. (2010) present Maestro, a gesture recognition system for direct interaction with electronic presentations that allows users to use gestures to control the navigation of presentations (Fourney et al., 2010). The hand segmentation process consists in thresholding the image through color, but users need a pair of gloves, one red and one blue. The motion recognition uses matching templates and features of the trajectory of the hands, such as the location of start and end of the gesture path length, moment of inertia, among others.

According to Roccetti et al. (2011), systems based on gesture recognition can support interaction with computer games without the help of any controller. The main novelty in this approach resides in the use of contextual information that can be inferred from the game setting and creating algorithms able to recognize the interactions of a player (Roccetti et al., 2011). The algorithm for recognizing the hand, receives the video stream captured and analyzed, frame by frame, to detect and identify a set of key points of the hands and forearms of a player. The tracking algorithm of hands determines the exact position of both hands. Finally, the recognition algorithm verifies actions, in terms of time and trajectory, the action taken by the user.

Rautaray (2010) presents a work that implements gesture recognition techniques to develop a software interface to control VLC Player through gestures. The application developed is composed of a core module, which uses the Principal Component Analysis algorithm to find the feature vectors of gestures. The algorithm of K-Nearest Neighbor (KNN) does the gesture recognition. A theoretical analysis of the approach informs the process of recognizing a static background. The training images are made by the cut of the static background gesture; and the Lucas Kanade algorithm does motion detection.

Static Gesture Recognition

Static gesture is represented by an image. The recognition is based on feature extraction discriminants of the image. We can, for instance, extract features from the directions of the fingers or the contours of the hand.

The position of the palm of the hand and of the fingers has been widely used for gesture recognition (MacLean et al., 2001; Kim & Fellner, 2001). We can also treat other information concerning hands such as angles (Sato et al., 2001), roughness (Jang et al., 2005) or sampling points on the boundary region of the hand (Hamada et al., 2002; Hamada et al., 2000).

Another category of resources amply used implies the notion of moment. It is a weighted average of the pixels intensities of an image, usually chosen to have some interpretation. We can find statistical moments (Lee et al., 2000), Zernike moments (Sribooruang et al., 2004) and Hu moments (Hu, 1962), which are most frequently used. Fourier analysis can also be applied for representing the limits of the hand (Licsár & Szirányi, 2004).

The feature extraction is a complex computational problem because it requires perfect background characteristics and high computational resources. Disorganized background images with changes in lighting conditions become very difficult to handle. Allied to this, the algorithms used require loading the whole image into memory, which complicates the management of the computer resources.

After extracting the features, then we can classify the gestures. The more simplistic way of static hand recognition is to count the number of fingers (Kim & Fellner, 2001). Nevertheless, recognition can be seen as a matching process, applying cluster algorithms (Licsár & Szirányi, 2004; Zhou et al., 2004). In this case, recognition consists of finding the best match between images that represent static gestures. We may also do the same correspondence with Chamfer distance algorithm (Athitsos & Sclaroff, 2001). In addition, the Neural Networks are widely used in the hand postures detection and classification using two or three layers of neurons (Marcel et al., 2000). More recently, techniques of face detection have been applied to this problem. The Viola and Jones (2003) system that leverages the features Haar is consensual among researchers (Jones & Viola, 2003).

SMART WHEELCHAIRS: STATE OF THE ART

Since the 80s, researchers have devoted effort towards assisting the locomotion of people dependent on motorized wheelchairs, by developing techniques based on mobile robotics. Initially, the proposals addressed the chair as self-driving vehicles, designed to operate in industrial parks. Tags were placed in the environment, and the location of the vehicle was found by recognizing the tags that automatically generate optimal trajectory for a certain location established (Madarasz, Heiny, Cromp & Mazur, 1986). In addition, magnetic lines were placed on the floor of the environment, being all the possible trajectories pre-established (Wakaumi, Nakamura & Matsumura, 1992).

Research was focused on vehicles able to follow paths and turn away from obstacles that were fitted with sensors such as video cameras and ultrasound and leaned out around the issues of control, navigation and obstacle avoidance without giving much importance to the user. The vehicle acted like a mobile robot and the user as cargo to be transported from one point to another in an environment adapted to a robot. (Mazo et al. 1995), (Katevas et al, 1997), and (Wang et al., 1997).

In the 90s, that paradigm has changed with the introduction of the idea of assisted control for obstacle avoidance (Bell, Borenstein, Levine, Koren & Jaros, 1994). Later, and for the first time, an autonomous vehicle for the differently-abled users was presented, known as VAHM, introducing innovations at the control level. This vehicle had three navigation modes: manual, assisted and autonomous, allowing the user to choose the desired level of control (Bourhis and Pino, 1996).

This new approach has opened new issues for research. It included several areas and it became necessary to reconcile professionals of the exact sciences and natural sciences. From there, the work focused mainly on control techniques and assisted adaptive, easy to interact with the user, then the term intelligent wheelchair arose (Tahboub and Asada, 1999; Luo, Chen & Lin, 1999; Nakanishi, Kuno, Shimada & Shirai, 1999). Today, these chairs represent a key development in the maximization of the wheelchairs' functionality, comfort, and users' independence and user self-esteem. Biomechanics technologies, ergonomics, interfaces and control have been incorporated, which allow user navigation and obstacle avoidance, making mobility safer and more comfortable.

Wheelchair Types

The literature features various proposals for smart wheelchairs and their contribution to navigation and obstacle avoidance. However, the great majority of studies relates to the movement of the chair exclusively, with no concerns about complete mobility. In fact, this relationship is not fully effective for the kind of obstacles and difficulties person with no mobility needs to overcome.

The work of Jia et al.(2007) presents a control system for hands-free wheelchair that relies on an intelligent interface based on visual recognition of user's head the "RoboChair". The recognized gestures are used to generate the control commands for controlling digital signal movements. Face detection uses Adaboost algorithms; CamShift is used for object tracking. The combined systems achieve accurate face detection, tracking and gesture recognition in real time. This is a useful system for users who have restricted limb movements caused by diseases such as Parkinson's disease and quadriplegia.

Shan, Tan & Wei (2007) used two approaches, in object recognition, to develop a control interface for a wheelchair with robotic hand: the Particle Filtering and Meanshift approaches.

Kobayashi et al., (2009) proposed an intelligent robotic wheelchair that observes the user and the surrounding environment. It understands the user's intentions from their behaviors and the environmental information, even when the user is out of the wheelchair. The chair recognizes the commands indicated by hand gestures. The system is based on face recognition, however it can be changed to recognize the movements of the mouth, eyes or other body parts being adapted to the user necessities.

Other authors (Tsui et al., 2011) developed a complete system that, through a robotic arm, allows the user to autonomously collect a desired object from a shelf. The object's position is calculated by stereoscopic vision. A camera is placed on the shoulder of the user, and the robot's arm moves to the most suitable position adjusting its orientation, if necessary, so that its claw is perpendicular to the intended object. The robot arm compares the camera image with the images database and chooses the best combination. Then, the robot's arm moves to align the selected feature points, it moves forwards and shuts its claw for grasping the object. The interface is very intuitive and has two operation modes: via a touch screen or a joystick.

In addition, Kumar and Dinesh (2012) presented a proposal where the core idea was to control the wheelchair using gesture recognition for people with physical disabilities. The authors focused on the kinds of gestures to study and how they affect the recognition through the computer. They found that there are specific gestures for each role, which capture and store for the formulation of a specific pattern used in the process of obtaining results. A video camera to capture images of hand gestures is used which are compared with the pre-defined data and stored and then, a signal to the microcontroller that controls the specific motor to move the wheelchair is sent.

A methodology to apply techniques of gesture recognition, voice recognition and eye tracking in the control of the wheelchairs movement is presented by Chhabria and Dharaskar (2012). In terms of the gestural interface, a scheme that reduces the gestures database size was presented. This was used to store different postures of humans. To interact through the eyes, they proposed a new algorithm for eye movement recognition from left or right. The algorithm also used the eye blinking to control the starting and stopping of the wheelchair.

Table 1 presents a general view about the main projects considering wheelchairs that use computational vision techniques.

Interface Design: Process Description

In this section we present the basic concepts related to digital image processing. This information is required for a better understanding of the approach we subsequently propose. We begin with some basic concepts inherent in a work of this scope, and then the most currently used methods of digital image processing, feature extraction, object recognition and classification. This will be followed by interface description.

Table 1. Main Wheelchair Projects

Project's Name	Description
Autonomous Wheelchair (Madarasz, Heiny, Cromp, & Mazur, 1986)	Autonomous navigation using a map in cluttered environments.
Smart Wheelchair (Nisbet, Craig, Odor, & Aitken, 1995)	Used to aid in mobility training. Follows lines and moves backward when it collides with objects.
CPWNS (Yoder, Baumgartner, & Skaar, 1996)	Play routes that are taught to the system by manually steering the wheelchair between the start point and the end point.
The Intelligent Wheelchair (Gribble, Browning, Hewett, Remolina, & Kuipers, 1998)	Autonomous navigation by artificial recognition marks on the floor.
Tetra Nauta (Balcells & Gonzalez, 1998)	Autonomous navigation by artificial recognition marks on the floor.
Wheelesley (Yanco, 1998)	Assisted navigation.
Rolland (Roefer & Lankenau, 2000)	Monitors and learns the characteristics of the environment while browsing for planning trajectories. Through previous training, also learns the obstacle avoidance.
LOUSON III (Tse & Luo, 2000)	Control to follow a target.
Intelligent Wheelchair System (Murakami, Kuno, Shimada, & Shirai, 2001)	The user controls the wheelchair through facial expressions recognition. The response of the chair adapts to the environment in which it operates.

COLOR SPACES

Color is a visual perception recognized by humans. It derives from the light spectrum that interacts in the eye and it transmits information through the optic nerve to the nervous system. This phenomenon is not completely understood, but we know that colors are determined by the nature of the light reflected from objects.

We can define color space as a mathematical model used to describe each color from representative formulas of color components. The representation of any color may be obtained from the combination of these components.

There are several color models, with different characteristics and properties, adapted to diverse situations as the construction of equipment for HCI. Two of the most commonly use models are RGB and HSV.

The RGB model is based on the observation that by mixing red (R), green (G) and blue (B) in various proportions, it is possible to obtain a wide range of colors. Therefore, we can build a color image using the red component, green and light blue detected for each pixel. The color of each of these is then determined by the weight of each primary color. In an image according to the RGB model, the value of each pixel can be thought of as a vector with three components with values of red, green and blue. Thus, the color space can be exposed so that R, G and B are considered as the orthogonal axes in three dimensional color spaces that can be represented in terms of a color cube.

In a digital image, the pixels of the image will have three values one for the red, green and blue components. Therefore, a color image can be represented by the composition of three-color channels, corresponding to the three primary colors (r, g, b). The red channel will have the values of all the red pixels, the green channel values of all green pixels and the blue channel blue values of all pixels. Generally, 8 bits represent each of the three-color components.

The HSV model is widely used because the color information contained in the hue (H) and saturation (S) can be dissociated from the brightness (V). The hue specifies the dominant color, the pure color can be any color of the color spectrum. The saturation measures the amount contained in the pure white color by varying the color clarity. Thus, hue and saturation specify the color information. The brightness is used to represent hue's light and saturation i.e., an object in sunlight or in shade will have different brightness values.

Image in Grayscale

A grayscale image has no information about the color, only has information about the intensity of light. These images are the result of a calculation of the intensity of light at each pixel for each color. Each pixel value is a single sample of a color space that ranges from black as the lowest intensity and white as higher intensity.

To convert an image in RGB color space to grayscale, it is necessary to calculate the average of the three channels (r, g, b) and store this information in a single color channel.

Histograms

A histogram of an image is a graph of the relative frequency of occurrence of each of the color values allowed for each pixel (Breckon & Solomon, 2011). Usually represented by a bar chart, each of these values provides, for each color level the number or percentage of pixels corresponding to the image. For a single gray scale image, the histogram may be constructed by counting the numbers of times each gray scale value (0-255) occur within the image. The horizontal axis represents the gray level values. Each vertical bar represents the number of times that the corresponding gray level in the image occurred. The identification of objects in an image is not simply a matter of finding the peaks and valleys of the histogram, but this can provide qualitative and other quantitative information, such as the gray level minimum, maximum, average, or predominant bright or dark pixels.

Filters

A digital filter is a generic term to refer to a mathematical operation applied to an image. it is used as tool to improve image quality or to bring out certain objects or image features.

There are different approaches to the application level of filters to PDI, but we can divide them into two broad categories: low-pass filters and high-pass filters. In the first category filters with values close to zero are applied to high frequencies; they are also used to reduce the noise by smoothing the image. In the second category filters with values close to zero for low frequencies are applied. This filter makes the transitions between different regions of the image to become sharper but, instead, they emphase the noise that may exist in the image.

Binary Image

A binary image is a digital image in which there are only two possible values for each pixel. The colors used for the representation of these values are black and white, normally. These images have enormous benefits in terms of simplicity and speed of treatment. They are widely used in digital image processing, where a color represents the object and the other is the background.

SYSTEM DESCRIPTION

This section presents the system description. The proposed solution, the hardware, software and the gestural database design. The diverse steps encountered within the interface development are explained in detail. The digital image processing took us the principal labor since it was the main challenge to be achieved, which is the reason for the detailed description presented.

Proposed Solution

The rationale for the proposal that follows is based on our concern for individuals who need to have access to an object placed on a surface with a large area, which inhibits autonomous actions.

The permanent evolution of acquisition and image processing technologies allows the creation of a computational system that allows a machine to recognize human gestures. The construction of this system requires the use of various complex-programming algorithms. We list general procedures that entail: (1) image capture, (2) human hand segmentation, (3) feature extraction, (4) classification of gestures.

Different kinds of algorithms for gestural recognition have been studied; however, the challenge lies in the fact of making this interaction device independent, in a way that allows easier human hand identification, such as gloves or motion capture sensors. Therefore, the gestural algorithms development, based on low cost webcams, is a great stimulus in Human-Machine Interaction.

Given the obtained results during the course of this investigation, we proposed a system to help the occupant of a wheelchair to interact with the world, especially, to have access to certain objects in order to facilitate their daily life (Figure 1a & b).

In terms of hardware, the prototype consisted of an intelligent wheelchair, a laptop with a built-in webcam and a robotic arm. The software contained in static gesture recognition, performed in real time, through a hand located in front of webcam.

Against this background, to give effect to this concept of mobility, every executed gesture was transposed to a robotic arm action. This transposition is set from six gestures that we present in Figure 2. Each gesture fulfills a specific function in the context of the individual mobility facilitation, namely: (a) pause; (b) stretch mechanical arm with speed 1 (c) stretch mechanical arm with speed 2 (d) open claw, (e) close claw; (f) move arm to the starting position.

With this method, it is possible to build a human-machine interaction system, facilitating the life of the individual with disabilities, with an acceptable level of environmental restrictions. Forcing the person to use a glove, or any other device that aids the identification of the human hand, also inhibits the individual action's freedom and autonomy.

The scope of this work is limited to the recognition of gestures; we aim to identify the static gesture shown by the occupant of the chair, between a set of pre-defined gestures system.

The Hardware Design

In terms of hardware, the prototype consists of an intelligent wheelchair, a laptop with a built-in webcam and a mechanical arm.

The hardware used to develop this project was undercurrent hardware with no special requirements to integrate the software. We used a processor Intel Core 2 Quad 9400 @2.6GHz, a motherboard ASUSTek P5Q-PRO, the memory was DDR2 4 GB and the hard drive was Western Digital 1TB 7200rpm.

The main concern is the digital camera. The digital camera should provide a stable signal without large variations in brightness. This is of enormous importance because it may represent the exclusion of several problems. In this project the camera used to capture video did not provide a stable signal to the brightness level, and therefore the software, sometimes, displayed unconformities in the colors recognition and targeting. A digital camera from Logitech with the following characteristics was used: Logitech Webcam C100, video capture 640x480 pixels, video resolution: 30 squares per second, interface: USB 2.0. The objective was to use cheap and easy to find hardware available to everybody.

Figure 1. a: Proposed Solution; b: Proposed Solution

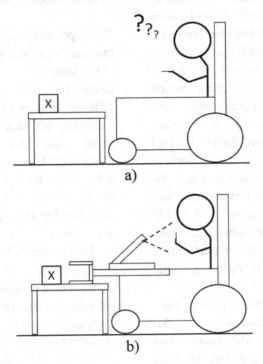

The Software Design

The software consisted of a static gesture recognition system, operationalized in real time through a hand located in front of webcam.

In Computer Vision software the dedicated libraries, Matlab application and OpenCV were the most important. The Matlab software is generically designed for different uses: numerical calculation, calculation of matrices and signal processing. Its

Figure 2. Hand Recognition Gestures

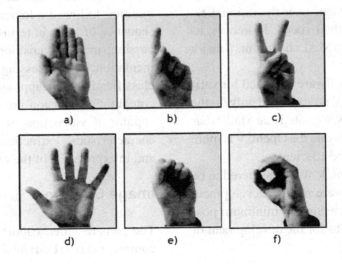

scripting language uses commands very similar to how we write algebraic expressions and it does not require to the programmer the concern to include libraries, to declare variables or to manage memory. However, Matlab is built in on the Java language that is built on the C language, which makes it slow in the code implementation, and difficult to use for image processing in real time.

OpenCV is a cross-platform library free and open source, consisting of a set of functions in the areas of Image Processing and Computer Vision. OpenCV was considered fast and efficient in all its versions (Linux, Windows, OS X and Android). The OpenCV library introduces basic data structures, which is ideal for performing matrix operations. It uses highly optimized code for image processing.

To arrive at a software choice we compared and reflected about its attributes and outcomes. Although Matlab displays good results in parameters related to usability, and having a good learning curve based on its development environment, as well as an efficient memory management and an excellent help section, the code execution is slow and its price is also a disadvantage.

Conversely, the OpenCV library provides the best results with regard to the attributes related to the efficiency of the final product. OpenCV requires an extra effort from the programmer regarding the memory management and debugging, but it has huge advantages over the rationalization of resources and their speed. Moreover, its huge speed compared to MatLab presents a major benefit.

Matlab is generic software designed for various uses, while OpenCV is developed only for the image processing. Thus, we noted that Matlab has a better learning curve while the OpenCV is more difficult to use but more efficient.

In conclusion, OpenCV was considered to be the most suitable software for the development of an effective system using the minimum possible resources as well as for the development of programming skills.

The Gestural Database

The representative images of the gestures were randomly selected. We wanted several productions of the same gesture with average variations intra-gesture but with significantly variations between different classes of gestures (inter-gesture high variance). It was not necessary that the gestures of the same class were perfectly equal in each element of the feature vector, but there should be at least one element in the array that was different in order to simulate the naturalness of gestures performed by different individuals that could use our system.

The gestural database was created through the following procedures: video images capture with various different positions and handpicked six poses as standard gestures to be recognized; the application running and exporting each frame; exporting of images randomly selected; exporting of the respective feature vectors for each frame; storage of the feature vector in a database. Each gesture in the database was represented by 100 images. For the purposes of testing, five different individuals each contributed another 100 images for each gesture.

The System

The method used for the symbolic gesture recognition followed a logical and complementary sequence of tasks in terms of digital image processing: image acquisition; preprocessing; segmentation; post processing; feature extraction and classification. The approach followed tracks the computational vision problems based on steps: capture of video images, image segmentation, characteristics' extraction, pattern recognition and interpretation of the results.

Image Capture

The camera video capture is connected to the computer via the USB interface and positioned by

Figure 3. Captured marker with a well-positioned hand

a bracket in front of the human hand to perform gestures. The distance between the human hand chambers should be such that the human hand occupies nearly the whole gestures marker represented in the captured image. (Figure 3)

Each frame captured by the camera is treated as a static image, and it should be captured from the original video. It has a resolution of 640x480 pixels reproduced in RGB color space and 8 bits represent each color channel.

The next phase was the pre-processing where the information required for the segmentation task was selected. The area with the human hand and the information we intended to work was defined. The remaining part of the image was discarded because it does not offer relevant data. With this, we significantly reduced the number of pixels that will be treated. Then, a filter is applied for smoothing the captured image. This is a simple operation of image processing often used in order to eliminate some noise that may be present in the image. The filter used is low-pass Gaussian with mask of 5x5.

Segmentation

The segmentation is the main part of the process and involves a sequence of logical tasks. The goal is the separation of the human hand and the background image. All frames collected by the video camera go through this process. The stages are: normalized RGB conversion, red channel extraction, background subtraction, histogram processing and image threshold. The first step of the process is to classify each pixel as belonging or not to a particular object. The RGB color space has problems when changes in illumination occur, because colors vary substantially. This seriously affects the desired classification. To overcome this obstacle, different color spaces can be used to separate the information from the pixel brightness.

The color spaces that exhibit the desired characteristics are: normalized RGB, HSV, HSL and YCbCr. Each of these color spaces has three components. One of the main important is the brightness parameter, normalized for RGB spectrum. In this parameter the color values remain the same even when changes in brightness occur. Colors in RGB can be transformed to RGB normalized using the following formulas:

$$r = \frac{R}{R+G+B}$$
$$g = \frac{G}{R+G+B}$$
$$b = \frac{B}{R+G+B}$$

Any one of three values $(r + g + b = 1)$ may be discarded since it is redundant. The normalized RGB is recognized by some authors as advantageous for the segmentation of color (Aryuanto & Limpraptono, 2009) because it eliminates the effect of variations in color intensity in pixels. After clarifying the choice regarding the color space, the segmentation process is presented. The procedure begins with the conversion of frames captured by video for the standard RGB color space camera.

Then, the background image of the red channel is normalized. The background subtraction permits to obtain an image in gray scale with changes in color intensity between the background and the hand. The next step is the histogram conception. The image segmentation based on histograms is a one of the simplest technique used to select the gray levels that occurs in the separation of pixels into regions. We considered that in a simple image there are only two entities: the background and the object. The background is generally a gray level and occupies most of the image. The gray level is a large peak in the histogram. The object image is another gray level, which is another peak with spacing relative to the first.

Through the histogram, we calculate the optimal value of the threshold method using the Valley. This method proposes that the deepest valley between the two peaks should be set as the threshold. So, we got an acceptable separation between the background and the object.

The Post-Processing

At this stage, the information gathered by applying morphological filters to the binaries image is refined. The aim is to eliminate small holes and edges inside the segmented image. The filters used were filter dilation and erosion filter. The two filters operate in inner and outer edges of objects. The amount and the way objects dilate or shrink obey to the election of the mask. The dilation permits the objects to dilate or increase in size, while erosion allows them to shrink. In this case, morphological filters were applied. The sequence of application of the filters was: first dilation and then the dilated image erosion. With the expansion, the aim is firstly expand the object through its inner and outer edges, to fill any gaps and to expand the edges uniformly. After applying morphological erosion filter in the dilated image, it seeks to return to the original object; only the outer edges will be affected, because the holes already fully populated in the expansion phase will be maintained. Figure 4 shows the results after the application of the morphological filters.

The previous steps provided an image where we can find the edge pixels that separate the hand from the background, but no information about the edges as entities in them had still be found, thus, the next step was to gather the whole pixels on the edge contours surrounding the stain of the segmented hand. Contour is a curve (sequence of points) that defines the edge of an object in an image and is represented by a vector of points. This phase detect all contours surrounding the stain of the segmented hand and it has as main objective to locate all pixels belonging to the contour of the hand. Through the extracted contour we can calculate several structures such as convex hull, contour edges, fingers and surrounding rectangles.

Feature Extraction

The feature extraction allows obtaining a set of vectors of features, also called descriptors that can distinguish accurately each hand gesture based on the use of geometric features with Hu invariant moments. The presented features were the most discriminatory from the six gestures chosen: con-

Figure 4. Image after the application of morphological filters

tour size; contour circularity; contour eccentricity; convex hull size; bounding box proportion; bounding box area; rotated bounding box area; main inertia axe; Hu Moments.

Some problems during the gesture recognition may occur if there is a large rotational movement, because the shape and proportions of features that represent the gesture may change. These features are easy to extract, are independent and are sufficient to distinguish the amount of gestures chosen by us, however, these are not suitable for all types of gestures.

Pattern Recognition and Classification

In terms of pattern recognition and classification, the Support Vector Machines (SVM) was the chosen technique. This technique has been used for different pattern recognition tasks frequently with results superior to those achieved by similar techniques in many applications. Its main characteristics are (Smola 1999): Good generalizability; Robustness in larger dimensions; Well-defined theory in Mathematics and Statistics.

The SVM are linear classifiers that maximize the geometric distance between the vector subspaces of classes. This technique is based on the construction of a hyper-plane as a decision surface, to maximize the margin of separation among classes.

However, it is not always possible to directly establish a linear separation between classes (Figure 5). The input data are mapped by a mathematical function (kernel) to a new domain of feature vectors. This conversion increases the size of the space, which allows the definition of a linear hyper-plane that minimizes misclassification. To solve the problem, we selected the following parameters:

- **Problem:** Support for vector classification with N classes allowing the imperfect separation of classes;
- **Type of Kernel:** Linear. The linear discrimination was made in the original feature space. It was the fastest option;
- **Criteria for Termination of the Process:** We defined 1000 as the maximum possible iterations and an accuracy of 0.000001.

DISCUSSION

The objective of the interface described in this chapter was the development of a system for static gesture recognition using one hand only. The hand should be located in front of a webcam, in a uniform background scenario, without the support of any kind of assistive item, equipment, or product.

After the explanation and description of the proposed solution, there are some reflections that merit emphasis.

Considering the color space chosen for the segmentation we conclude that the normalized RGB, HSV or YCbCr could be used because the changes of color spaces do not help in the detection of skin due to the variety of colors that it can have. Thus, an extra computational effort in the conversion of RGB space for any other is unnecessary. For the purposes of our work, the importance of segmentation emerges from the choice of the optimal threshold value. Where

Figure 5. Separation between Classes using SVM Algorithm

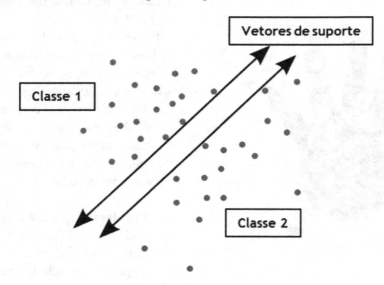

images display color variations we should use an approach with multilevel adaptive threshold in the diverse sections of the image.

A major advantage of the approach presented is the removal of the influence of brightness during the segmentation process, so that it becomes less dependent on the lighting conditions, which has always been a critical obstacle to image recognition. Figure 6 illustrates the stages of segmentation, where each column represents a necessary step for segmentation and lines represent the actions taken in low light, great and high, respectively.

For the different types of lighting, we can see changes throughout the segmentation process, except in the final step - detection features. In the column of images representing gestures in standard RGB color space, we can attest that skin color is always more noticeable than other colors in the image. In addition, the method applied to find the optimal threshold proves itself to be quite useful as it eliminates most reflections, as can be seen in the column segmentation's images.

The small imperfections found are eliminated in the stage of detection of features since our algorithm only takes into account the largest outer contour found in the image. The only restriction

is related to the size of objects in skin color that we find in the image, as if they are larger than the hand, they will be the target of extracting contours. Figure 7 presents some examples to illustrate the described situations.

Regarding the application of the smoothing filter, this could have been applied only with a mask of vertical smoothing. The horizontal softening benefits the elimination of noise from the television signals, losing image resolution in vertical columns shape. The vertical smoothing permits the grainy image elimination. The image quality suffers in the form of horizontal lines. By applying the two types of smoothing we lose picture detail. The application of two filters did not value the image definition because, in this case, the missing details were irrelevant. The edges of human hand were significant.

The approach presented in this chapter proposes the use of geometric characteristics together with Hu invariant moments. The use of moments comes from its uniformity even in gestures with different rotations and scales. Then, it was necessary to normalize the features to make the data consistent. Normalization aims at ensuring that all values are in a proportional spatial distribu-

Figure 6. Segmentation steps with various types of lighting

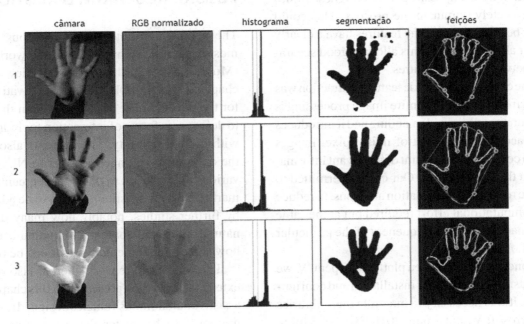

Figure 7. Irregular Background Segmentation

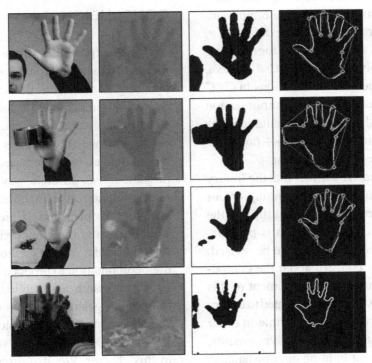

tion, making it impossible for the highest values to completely dominate the process. This could occur because some of the features have a clearly higher absolute value. This allows a good separation between linear gestures.

The choice of geometric features extraction was performed because the entire image processing is computationally very demanding and it introduces an unacceptable amount of noise (pixel images with a considerable amount of irrelevant information in the background). Our choice permitted to reduce redundant information and, thus, to reduce the computational effort required but at the same time maintaining the uniqueness of the particular object of interest.

Concerning the chosen platform, OpenCV, we emphasize their complex installation and configuration. It was necessary to integrate their libraries in Microsoft Visual Studio 2010 Express Edition C ++ platform. This configuration was demanding because the documentation that came with the OpenCV package required certain improvements, but overall its performance was fairly reliable.

OpenCV supports several programming languages, by using wrappers. These exist for C #, Java and Python. Aware that the programming itself would probably be easier in C # or Java, we decided to use the original functions in C / C ++ due to the computational effort minimization on non-essential tasks. The documentation was provided in the languages C and C ++ programming although it needs improvement.

Finally, we emphasize the fact that the library is constantly evolving. At the beginning of our work, the existing version was 2.3 at the end the version it was 2.4.2. This evolution is positive, however it exposes errors that should be revised.

We underline our concern about the computational cost throughout the development of this work. The algorithms were implemented to ensure an acceptable performance in real time in order to perform segmentation in indoor environments, conditional on different lighting circumstances.

FUTURE RESEARCH DIRECTIONS

The natural user interfaces are among the ten most innovative technologies in the world today (Moore, 2008). In the literature review for this chapter it was possible to find an innovative basis for the development of an application that helps to define new forms of interaction for individuals with limited mobility. The chapters also makes the case for a continued interest in NUI and its various applications to different segments of the market. Several questions remain to be addressed by further studies, notably how many different natural interfaces may exist simultaneously, or how can accidental communications be treated.

In terms of future work, there is also scope to extend the approach presented in this chapter into assistive autonomous vehicles designed to execute multitasks such as material transport, fire fighting, explosives disarmament and other activities that can place humans at risk.

CONCLUSION

This chapter presents the key concepts and stages that led to the development of a system for recognizing static gestures to control wheelchairs. Several different views for each of the constituent steps of the work described were presented in detail. Various color spaces for the representation of images, multiple types of filters to remove possible noise, different ways of disaggregating regions of interest from the background and various types of object classification were described. This illustrated the complexity surrounding the selection of the various methods to be applied and their combination to produce the expected result.

The research and bibliographic analysis on the topic - gesture recognition algorithms, the segmentation and classification of images and the VC library OpenCV – was extensively discussed in this chapter. We also discussed a number of techniques that could make the proposed work operational, in real time, thus allowing the detection of hand gestures in a conventional work environment, based on threshold algorithms and contours detection. A database was designed with images of one hand without any restrictions during image acquisition and five different individuals tested them. A system for static gestures recognition from the acquisition and phase-to-phase identification was developed.

However there limitations to the work reported in this chapter: the construction of the highlighted prototype would not be possible to build based on the available resources. Therefore the scope of the work was restricted to a gesture recognition system. The goal was the identification of the static gesture shown by the occupant of the wheelchair.

The objectives of this work were based on the study, implementation and improvement of existing techniques applied to the recognition of static hand gestures, more specifically: recognition based on hand geometry systems. The system works efficiently and accurately with dissimilar gestures, but may show some weakness in the use of identical gestures such as sign language.

The segmentation method used reveals some inaccuracy with the variation of the conditions of the background scenery and lighting. We suggest the study of other methods that have a better response to color variation as well as to the presence of objects in the gestures scenario capture. We anticipate that the algorithms that will respond better to these conditions may be based on neural networks.

Overall, the system's implementation using the geometric characteristics of the hand for gesture recognition was achieved. The limitations found in existing systems such as the restrictions imposed on the hand capture phase, in the system's performance and in the selection/ accuracy of the extracted features were overcome. Thus, considering the ambient conditions and limitations, the proposed system can be characterized as a natural user interface, suitable for use in human-computer applications.

ACKNOWLEGMENT

A special thank you goes to Ricardo Proença who contributed to this paper: for his valuable work and for sharing his knowledge.

REFERENCES

Acharya, T., & Ray, A. K. (2007). *Image processing: Principles and Applications*. John Wiley & Sons.

Athitsos, V., & Sclaroff, S. (2001). An appearance-based framework for 3d hand shape classification and camera viewpoint estimation. Proceedings of the Fifth IEEE International Conference on Automatic Face and Gesture Recognition.

Bell, D., Borenstein, J., Levine, S., Koren, Y., & Jaros, J. (1994). An assistive navigation system for wheelchairs based upon mobile robot obstacle avoidance. Proceedings of the *IEEE International Conference on Robotics and Automation*, San Diego. doi:10.1109/ROBOT.1994.351167

Bersch, R. (2009). Design de um serviço de tecnologia assistiva em escolas públicas. Retrieved from http://www.lume.ufrgs.br/handle/10183/18299

Birdwhistell, R. (1970). *Kinesics and Context; essays on body motion communication*. Philadelphia: University of Pennsylvania Press.

Birk, H., Moeslund, T. B., & Madsen, C. B. (1997). Real-Time Recognition of Hand Alphabet Gestures Using Principal Component Analysis. Proceedings of the 10th Scandinavian Conference on Image Analysis.

Blake, J. (2010). *Natural User Interfaces in. NET*. Manning Publications.

Blake, J. (2010). *Multi-touch Development with WPF and Silverlight*. Manning Publications.

Bourhis, G., & Pino, P. (1996). Mobile robotics and mobility assistance for people with motor impairments: Rational justification for the VAHM project. *IEEE Transactions on Rehabilitation Engineering*, 4(1), 7–12. doi:10.1109/86.486052 PMID:8798067

Buxton, B. (2010). CES 2010: NUI with Bill Buxton [Interview].

Buxton, W., Billinghurst, M., Guiard, Y., Sellen, A., & Zhai, S. (1994). *Human Input to Computer Systems: Theories, Techniques and Technology*. Retrieved from http://www.billbuxton.com/input-Manuscript.html

Cassinelli, A., Zerroug, A., & Ishikawa, M. (2009), Virtual Haptic Radar. Obtido de Ishikawa Oku Laboratory: http://www.k2.t.u-tokyo.ac.jp/perception/VirtualHapticRadar/

Chathuranga, S., Samarawickrama, K., Chandima, H., Chathuranga, K., & Abeykoon, A. (2010). Hands free interface for Human Computer Interaction. 2010 5th International Conference on Information and Automation for Sustainability (ICIAFs) 359-364. IEEE.

Chhabria, S., & Dharaskar, R. (2012). Multimodal Interface for Disabled Persons. *International Journal of Computer Science and Communication*, V, 223–228.

Corcoran, P., Nanu, F., Petrescu, S., & Bigioi, P. (2012). Real-Time Eye Gaze Tracking for Gaming Design and Consumer Electronics Systems. *IEEE Transactions on Consumer Electronics*, 58(2), 347–355. doi:10.1109/TCE.2012.6227433

Fourney, A., Terry, M., & Mann, R. (2010). Gesturing in the wild: understanding the effects and implications of gesture-based interaction for dynamic presentations. *Proceedings of BCS HCI*

Hamada, Y., Shimada, N., & Shirai, Y. (2000). Hand shape estimation using image transition network. Proceedings of the HUMO '00 Proceedings of the Workshop on Human Motion. doi:10.1109/HUMO.2000.897387

Hamada, Y., Shimada, N., & Shirai, Y. (2002). Hand Shape Estimation Using Sequence of Multi-Ocular Images Based on Transition Network. Proceedings of the International Conference on Vision Interface.

Hu, M. K., (1962). Visual Pattern Recognition by Moment Invariants. *IRE Trans. Info. Theory*, IT(8), 179-187.

Jang, H. Jun-Hyeong, Jin-Woo, D. J., & Bien, Z. Z. (2005). Two-staged hand-posture recognition method for softremocon system. Proceedings of Systems, Man and Cybernetics, 2005 IEEE International Conference on, Volume (1).

Jia, P., Hu, H., Lu T., & Yuan, K., (2007). Head Gesture Recognition for Hands-free Control of an Intelligent Wheelchair. Industrial Robot: An International Journal, Volume (34), 60-68.

Jones, M. J., & Viola, P. (2003). Face recognition using boosted local features. Proceedings of the International Conference on Computer Vision.

Katevas, N., Sgouros, N., Tzafestas, S., Papakonstantinou, G., Beattie, P., Bishop, J., Tsanakas, P., & Koutsouris, D. (1997). The autonomous mobile robot SENARIO: a sensor aided intelligent navigation system for powered wheelchairs," *Robotics & Automation Magazine,* 60-70.

Kim, H., & Fellner, D. W. (2001). Interaction with Hand Gesture for a Back-Projection Wall. *CGI '04 Proceedings of the Computer Graphics International*, Washington.

Kobayashi, Y., Kinpara, Y., Shibusawa, T., & Kuno, Y. (2009). Robotic wheelchair based on observations of people using integrated sensors. Proceedings of the 2009 IEEE/RSJ international conference on intelligent robots and systems, 2013-2018. doi:10.1109/IROS.2009.5353933

Krueger, W. M. (1991). *Artificial Reality II*. Addison-Wesley.

Kumar, K. M., & Dinesh, M., (2012). Hand gesture recognition for wheelchair controlled by digital image processing. *International Journal of Communications and Engineering.*

Lee, L. K., Kim, S., Choi, Y. K., & Lee, M. H. (2000). Recognition of hand gesture to human-computer interaction. Proceedings of the 26th Annual Conference of the IEEE Industrial Electronics Society (Vol. 3).

Licsár, A., & Szirányi, T. (2004). Dynamic training of hand gesture recognition system. Proceedings of the 17th International Conference on Pattern Recognition (ICPR'04) (Vol. 4). doi:10.1109/ICPR.2004.1333935

Lina, C.-S., Huana, C.-C., Chana, C.-N., Yehb, M.-S., & Chiua, C.-C. (2004). Design of a computer game using an eye-tracking device for eye's activity rehabilitation. *Optics and Lasers in Engineering*, 42(1), 91–108. doi:10.1016/S0143-8166(03)00075-7

Luo, R., Chen, T. M., & Lin, M. H. (1999). Automatic guided intelligent wheelchair system using hierarchical grey-fuzzy motion decision-making algorithms. Proceedings of the 1999 IEEE/RSJ International Conference on Intelligent Robots and Systems. doi:10.1109/IROS.1999.812794

MacLean, J., Pantofaru, C., Wood, L., Herpers, R., Derpanis, K., Topalovic, D., & Tsotsos, J. (2001). Fast Hand Gesture Recognition for Real-Time Teleconferencing Applications. Proceedings of the IEEE ICCV Workshop on Recognition, Analysis, and Tracking of Faces and Gestures in Real-Time Systems, Vancouver. doi:10.1109/RATFG.2001.938922

Madarasz, R. L., Heiny, L. C., Cromp, R. F., & Mazur, N. M. (1986). The design of an autonomous vehicle for the disabled. *IEEE Journal on Robotics and Automation*, RA-2(3), 117–126. doi:10.1109/JRA.1986.1087052

Marcel, S., Bernier, O., Viallet, J. E., & Collobert, D. (2000). Hand gesture recognition using inpu/output hidden markov models. Proceedings of the Fourth IEEE International Conference on Automatic Face and Gesture Recognition. doi:10.1109/AFGR.2000.840674

Mazo, M., Rodriguez, F. J., Lazaro, L., Urena, J., Santiso, E., Revenga, P., & Garcia, J. J. (1995). Wheelchair for physically disabled people with voice, ultrasonic and infrared sensor control. *Autonomous Robots*, 2(3), 203. doi:10.1007/BF00710857

McNeill, D., & Levy, E. (1982). *Conceptual Representations in Language Activity and Gesture.* John Wiley and Sons Ltd.

Merrill, D., Kalanithi, J., & Maes, P. (2007). Siftables: Towards Sensor Network User Interfaces. *Proceedings of the First International Conference on Tangible and Embedded Interaction (TEI'07).* Louisiana: ACM. doi:10.1145/1226969.1226984

Mitra S., & Acharya, T., (2007). Gesture recognition: A survey. In *IEEE Transactions on Systems, Man, and Cybernetics*, Part C: Applications and Reviews.

Monson-Haefel, R. (2010). Proposed Definition of Natural User Interface (NUI). Retrieved from http://theclevermonkey.blogspot.pt

Mulder, A. (1996). *Hand gestures for hci.* Vancouver: Simon Fraser University.

Nakanishi, S., Kuno, Y., Shimada, N., & Shirai, Y. (1999). Robotic wheelchair based on observations of both user and environment. Proceedings of the 1999 IEEE/RSJ International Conference on Intelligent Robots and Systems. doi:10.1109/IROS.1999.812796

Nespoulous, J.-L., Perron, P., & Roch, A. (1986). *The Biological Foundations of Gestures: Motor and Semiotic Aspects.* Hillsdale: Lawrence Erlbaum Associates.

Oviatt, S. (2003). Multimodal interfaces. In J. Jacko & A. Sears (Eds.), *The Human-Computer Interaction Handbook (p. 286.304)*. New Jersey: Lawrence Erlbaum and Associates.

Pavlovic, V. I., Sharma, R., & Huang, T. S. (1997). Visual Interpretation of Hand Gestures for Human Computer Interaction: A Review. *IEEE Transactions on Pattern Analysis and Machine Intelligence*, *19*(7), 677–695. doi:10.1109/34.598226

Radabaugh, M. P. (2012). NIDRR's Long Range Plan - Technology for Access and Function Research. Retrieved from http://www.ncddr.org/new/announcements/lrp/fy1999-2003/lrp_techaf.html

Radicchi, A., Nunes, A., & Botega, L. (2010). Proposta de Desenvolvimento de Interface Tangível para Aplicações de Gerenciamento de Emergência. Proceedings of the XI Symposium on Virtual and Augmented Reality. Natal.

Rautaray S., & Agrawal, A. (2010). A Vision based Hand Gesture Interface for Controlling VLC Media Player," International Journal of Computer Applications.

Roccetti, M., Marfia, G., & Semeraro, A. (2011). A Fast and Robust Gesture Recognition System for Exhibit Gaming Scenario *Proceedings of the 4th International ICST Conference on Simulation Tools and Techniques*, Barcelona.

Rokeby, D. (2010). Very Nervous System 1986-1990. Retrieved from http://www.davidrokeby.com/vns.html

Sarter, N. B. (2006). Multimodal information presentation: Design guidance and research challenges. *International Journal of Industrial Ergonomics*, *36*(5), 439–445. doi:10.1016/j.ergon.2006.01.007

Sato, Y., Saito, M., & Koik, H. (2001). Real-Time Input of 3D Pose and Gestures of a User's Hand and Its Applications for HCI. Proceedings of the 2001 IEEE Virtual Reality Conference, Yokohama.

Shan, C., Tan, T., & Wei, Y. (2007). Real-time hand tracking using a mean shift embedded particle filter. Journal Pattern Recognition, New York.

Smola, A. (1999). Geometry and invariance in kernel based methods. In Advances in Kernel Methods: Support Vector Learning, (pp. 89-116). MIT Press.

Sribooruang, Y., Kumhom, P., & Chamnongthai, K. (2004). *Hand posture classification using wavelet moment invariant," in Virtual Environments*. Human-Computer Interfaces and Measurement Systems.

Tahboub, K., & Asada, H. H. (1999). A semi-autonomous control architecture applied to robotic wheelchairs. *Proceedings of the 1999 IEEE/RSJ International Conference on Intelligent Robots and Systems*. doi:10.1109/IROS.1999.812795

Tsui, K. M., Kimb, D.J., Behal, A., Kontak D., & Yancoa, H. A. (2011). I Want That: Human-in-the-Loop Control of a Wheelchair-Mounted Robotic Arm. *Applied Bionics and Biomechanics*, 127-147.

Wakaumi, H., Nakamura, K., & Matsumura, T. (1992). Development of an automated wheelchair guided by a magnetic ferrite marker lane. *Journal of Rehabilitation Research and Development*, *29*(1), 27–34. doi:10.1682/JRRD.1992.01.0027 PMID:1740776

Weiser, M. (1991). The Computer for the 21st Century. *Scientific American*, *265*(3), 94–104. doi:10.1038/scientificamerican0991-94

Weiser, M., & Brown, J. S. (1995). Designing Calm Technology. Retrieved from http://www.ubiq.com/weiser/calmtech/calmtech.htm

Zhou, H., Lin, D. J., & Huang, T. S. (2004). Static hand gesture recognition based on local orientation histogram feature distribution model. Proceedings of the Conference on Computer Vision and Pattern Recognition Workshop (CVPRW'04) (Vol. 10).

Chapter 15
The Roles of Business Process Modeling and Business Process Reengineering in E–Government

Kijpokin Kasemsap
Suan Sunandha Rajabhat University, Thailand

ABSTRACT

This chapter reveals the roles of business process modeling (BPM) and business process reengineering (BPR) in eGovernment, thus describing the concepts of eGovernment and BPM; BPM methodologies; business process modeling notation (BPMN); the importance of BPR in government-to-citizen (G2C) e-commerce; the relationship between BPM and eGovernment-based citizen satisfaction; the application of BPR in eGovernment; and the implementation of eGovernment through BPM. eGovernment is a modern trend that is driven by the advances in BPM and BPR as well as the aspirations of citizens who place increasing demands on governments' service. By modeling business processes in eGovernment, public sector organizations can achieve improvements in transparency and reduction in costs and resource requirements, resulting in improved business performance and compliance. The chapter argues that applying BPM and BPR in eGovernment has the potential to enhance public sector performance and achieve organizational goals in public sector organizations.

INTRODUCTION

Business processes constitute a significant portion of organizational costs. Managing business processes offers significant opportunities for improving market share, managerial decision making, and performance (Seethamraju, 2012). eGovernment phenomenon has become more important with the increasing number of implementations worldwide (Ozkan & Kanat, 2011).

eGovernment is a variety of electronic communications between governments, business, and citizens (Tohidi, 2011). eGovernment is defined as the provision of public information and services through the use of information and communications technology (ICT) (Andersen & Henriksen, 2006; Helbig, Ramón Gil-García, & Ferro, 2009).

The increase in citizens' use of eGovernment becomes a long-term trend because a growing number of people have recognized and experi-

DOI: 10.4018/978-1-4666-8833-9.ch015

enced greater efficiency, effectiveness, and convenience in using various government functions via eGovernment and digital connections with conventional channels (Nam, 2014). eGovernment has the potential to improve the provision of public services and foster citizens' participation in public policy process. Many governments have increasingly adopted ICT to provide services and information, thus limiting direct contacts with service recipients (Asongwe, 2012; Chun, Shulman, Sandoval, & Hovy, 2010).

Business process is considered as a critical corporate asset (Seethamraju, 2012). BPM is one of the effective techniques that can be used for understanding business process and for improving business performance (Abu Rub & Issa, 2012). BPM enables a common understanding and analysis of business process (Gandhewar & Wadegaonkar, 2012). BPR is a business approach aiming at improving the efficiency and effectiveness of business processes within and across organizations (Toor & Dhir, 2011).

The strength of this chapter is on the thorough literature consolidation of utilizing BPM and BPR in eGovernment. The extant literatures of BPM and BPR provide a contribution to practitioners and researchers by describing a comprehensive view of the functional applications of BPM and BPR to appeal to different segments of BPM and BPR in order to maximize the public sector impact of BPM and BPR in eGovernment.

BACKGROUND

Since the late 1990s, a number of countries have launched the eGovernment projects, with a particular emphasis on using information technology (IT) to provide electronic information and services to citizens and businesses, thus combining the purposes of increasing efficiency and becoming more customer-responsive (Chen & Gant, 2001). From the beginning of the 1990s, public administration has been confronted by a process of new

demands. The public society has been transformed by the influence of new technologies. With the development of the World Wide Web (WWW) and its establishment as the most important platform through which data and services are accessible for humans and programs, a new business challenge is raised concerning not only the management of workflows within an organization, but also the management of business processes that span the boundaries of organizations (van der Aalst, 1999).

eGovernment systems are built based on the website technology (Sensuse & Ramadhan, 2012). eGovernment practically transforms the nature of relationships from command and control hierarchy to interactive collaboration among governments, citizens, businesses, public sector employees, and other governments (Sarantis, Charalabidis, & Askounis, 2011). eGovernment has the potential to promote the free flow of public information and provision of public services to citizens, promote government transparency and accountability, and facilitate citizens' involvement in the public policy process (Bertot, Jaeger, & Grimes, 2010; Bwalya, 2009; Relly & Sabharwal, 2009). eGovernment has the ability to improve the efficiency of public service provision through electronic transactions and interactions with citizens, businesses, and other branches of government (Bertot et al., 2010).

eGovernment has the capability of building citizens' trust in government by providing citizens with the freedom and ability to participate in the political, social, and economic life of their countries (Parent, Vandebeek, & Gemino, 2005). eGovernment services reduce operating costs and provide direct communications between citizens, companies, and governmental organizations (Aydinli, Brinkkemper, & Ravesteyn, 2009). Two-way communications between government and citizens can effectively build citizens' trust in their governments (Tolbert & Mossberger, 2006; Yang & Rho, 2007). For example, voting online has the potential to increase voters' turnout and confidence in the results of elections (Parent et al., 2005).

The basic purpose of eGovernment is to make the government and its policies more effective by providing citizens with efficient access to public information (Heeks, 2003). Engaging citizens in government is one of the key visions of eGovernment advancement (Caillier, 2009; Jones, Hackney, & Irani, 2007; Thomas & Streib, 2003). eGovernment offers the potential to bring citizens closer to their governments (Hsu, Chen, & Wang, 2009). eGovernment can provide citizens with easy access to information and services regarding social and political rights, thus allowing them to safeguard their basic human rights (Charif & Ramadan, 2003; Yang & Rho, 2007).

Because of the lack of consensus on the definition of eGovernment, there are challenges and obstacles for the development of a general framework for the implementation of eGovernment in many countries (Almarabeh & AbuAli, 2010). eGovernment enhances transparency, accountability, and responsiveness among different branches of governments, government agencies, citizens, and businesses (Ahn & Bretschneider, 2011; Bertot, Jaeger, & Grimes, 2012). eGovernment encourages democracy and reduces the distance between citizens and government (Macintosh, Robson, Smith, & Whyte, 2003). Addressing the challenges of eGovernment requires collaboration and action for trusted identities in cyberspace among government, citizens, private sector organizations, civil society, academia, and public media (Asongwe, 2012).

The increase in eGovernment efficiency has strengthened the quality of government services to citizens and business sector (Millard, 2006; Relyea, 2002). Many businesses have initiated and managed measures to strengthen the organization of business processes (Becker, Algermissen, & Niehaves, 2006). Business process is a set of linked procedures and activities which collectively realize business objective and policy goal, normally within the context of an organizational structure defining functional roles and relationships (Sensuse & Ramadhan, 2012). BPM is essential within

a BPR life cycle (Lin, Yang, & Pai, 2002). BPR is a popular term since the 1990s (Davenport, 1993; Hammer & Champy, 1993). BPR is defined as an essential design of business processes in order to gain powerful improvements in the contemporary measures of business performance such as cost, quality, service, and speed (Hammer & Champy, 1993).

BUSINESS PROCESS MODELING AND BUSINESS PROCESS REENGINEERING IN E-GOVERNMENT

This section describes the concepts of eGovernment and BPM; BPM methodologies; BPMN; the importance of BPR in G2C e-commerce; the relationship between BPM and eGovernment-based citizen satisfaction; the application of BPR in eGovernment; and the implementation of eGovernment through BPM.

Concept of E-Government

The application of IT to government services has given rise to eGovernment (Ozkan & Kanat, 2011). The Internet revolution and advances in ICT have dramatically changed how citizens and businesses interact with their government (Tavana, Zandi, & Katehakis, 2013). eGovernment first began in the mid-1990s. Since then it has been embraced by almost all Member States of the United Nations, although there has been significant variation among nations in its development (United Nations, 2012).

The common definition of eGovernment is the delivery of information and services to citizens, businesses, and public agencies (Carter & Belanger, 2005; Sipior & Ward, 2005; West, 2004). eGovernment has the ability to transform relations with citizens, businesses, and other areas of government (Mnjama & Wamukoya, 2007). For the delivery of information and services, public administration has experienced a change from the bureaucratic, inward-looking approach to a citizen-centric, outward-looking approach that prioritizes the needs of users (Ho, 2002; Thompson, Rust, & Rhoda, 2005).

eGovernment is a dynamic concept that has an enormous impact on the effective delivery of government services to citizens, business partners, and other government entities (Davies, 2002). eGovernment is about having centralized operations to reduce communication and information cost (Jaeger & Thompson, 2003) and to maximize effectiveness (Landsbergen & Wolken, 2001), speed, productivity, and service delivery (Holmes, 2001; Wimmer, 2002). eGovernment is the provision of routine government information and transactions using Internet technologies through public kiosks (Marche & McNiven, 2003).

eGovernment services include information for research, government forms and services, public policy information, employment and business opportunities, voting information, tax filing, license registration, payment of fines, and submission of comments to government officials (Larsen & Rainie, 2002). eGovernment is a fundamental element in the modernization of any government, serving as a process toward enhancing transparency, accountability, and good governance (Aggelidid & Chatzoglou, 2008). eGovernment can be used to promote the transparency of government operations and enhance citizens' trust in government (Tolbert & Mossberger, 2006; Ubaldi, 2011). Tavana et al. (2013) stated that eGovernment initiatives are deployed to enhance citizen services and cost savings in government administration and to improve transparency and accountability in government functions.

One of the most prominent factors contributing toward the success of eGovernment has been the adoption and diffusion of services offered online (Moon, 2002), aiming at facilitating the enhancement of public service delivery systems (Lean, Zailani, Ramayah, & Fernando, 2009). eGovernment is the delivery of government information and services to citizens, businesses, government employees, and other agencies online through the Internet (West, 2004). The most significant development in service delivery is that technology has changed the traditional government service by enabling a reduction in face-to-face interaction. Citizens can directly access the government service that they require without negotiating a government hierarchy (Akesson & Edvardsson, 2008).

Many countries are aware of benefits that eGovernment can improve service delivery to citizens (Mutula & Mostert, 2010). Weerakkody et al. (2012) stated that the countries with economies in transition need better alignment of their national ICT strategies with various eGovernment projects. There are many benefits of transforming traditional public services into eGovernment services (i.e., the cost-effective delivery of services, the integration of services, the reduction in administrative costs, a single integrated view of citizens across government services, and faster adaptation to citizens' needs) (Akman, Yazici, Mishraa, & Arifoglu, 2005; Venkatesh, Chan, & Thong, 2012). The advantages of eGovernment in timeliness, responsiveness, and cost containment are substantial (Evans & Yen, 2006).

eGovernment initiatives of varying scope and complexity have been implemented at the municipal, state, and federal government levels around the world (Torres, Pina, & Acerete, 2005). Siau and Long (2006) chose a slightly different approach by using the theory of growth and development to understand the differences of eGovernment development among countries and reported that the three factors (i.e., income levels, development status, and region) can explain these differences on a global scale.

As the implementation of eGovernment projects becomes important in both public and private sector organizations, the need to successfully tackle project management emerges (Sarantis et al., 2011). eGovernment projects are widely implemented around the world as a core of national strategy, but with different degree of success (Sultan, AlArfaj, & AlKutbi, 2012). The great potential that ICT possesses to support government processes has been recognized worldwide (Yildiz, 2007). Valdés et al. (2011) stated that the implementation of eGovernment programs in a country is accompanied by the redesign of processes that support the new models of service delivery, by structural reforms in the public agencies responsible for promoting and managing new technologies, and by major efforts to modernize the legal framework to support and regulate the utilization of ICT in public sector organizations.

eGovernment is introduced to public administration in the aspect of private sector adoption of e-business and e-commerce (Gauld & Goldfinch, 2006). E-business changes the business world, thus revolutionizing the procedure of effective communication between internal and external customers within an organization (Kasemsap, 2015a). The use of e-commerce positively impacts the organization in various ways ranging from operational benefits to strategic benefits (Kasemsap, 2015b). Governments can utilize e-commerce to improve business processes (McAdam & Donaghy, 1999). Through the use of e-commerce technologies, organizations are challenged to redesign their processes in order to achieve the benefits of increased efficiencies, cost reductions, and better customer service (Warkentin, Gefen, Pavlou, & Rose, 2002).

eGovernment is a complex socio-technical system, highly dependent upon overall institutional maturity, regulatory policy frameworks, and socio-cultural considerations (Dale & Goldfinch, 2006). Irani et al. (2012) stated that eGovernment is an effective mechanism for increasing government productivity and a key enabler of citizen-centric services. Luna-Reyes et al. (2012) identified that eGovernment includes the four main dimensions: e-services (providing public services), e-management (improving managerial effectiveness), e-democracy (promoting democratic values and mechanisms), and e-policy (developing public policies).

The benefits of e-services are grouped into two categories (i.e., tangible benefits and intangible benefits). Tangible benefits involve saving time and saving money, whereas intangible benefits include the quality of information, service, and system. Information quality is correlated with the information provided by an e-service website involving accuracy, currency, and ease of understanding (Alanezi, Kamil, & Basri, 2010; Gilbert, Balestrini, & Littleboy, 2004; Rai, Lang, & Welker, 2002), timeliness, consistency, relevance, and completeness (DeLone & McLean, 2003).

Regarding e-services, safety, trust, and security are considered as the important factors that explain users' acceptance of e-services (Featherman & Pavlou, 2003; Pavlou, 2003). However, not all the public services are easily transferable to the e-service environment (O'Donnell & Humphreys, 2003). In e-services, the possibility of losing users' information privacy is the most crucial risk that can be incurred since government agencies are required by law to share users' information with other government agencies and with public officers (Yang, Jun, & Peterson, 2004). E-participation is recognized in the context of e-democracy, which is considered as an online medium for public involvement (Gronlund, 2003; Jaeger & Thompson, 2004). eGovernment capabilities can vary from the provision of simple information via website to the ability to conduct financial transactions and participate in e-democracy, concerning e-voting and policy development over the Internet (Holden, Norris, & Fletcher, 2003).

The development of eGovernment involves many important factors (i.e., the quality of information, technological infrastructure, organizational characteristics, legal and regulatory environment, and economic and social contexts) (Luna-Reyes et al., 2012). eGovernment factors contribute to an increase in the efficiency of government (Dearstyne, 2001). The relationships between constituents and eGovernment stages should be incorporated into the process of decision making when government considers the movement from one stage of eGovernment to other stages of eGovernment (Belanger & Hiller, 2006).

eGovernment is recognized as a procedure to deliver government services to citizens, businesses, and other government entities (Watson & Mundy, 2001). eGovernment has the potential to transform not only the way in which most public services are delivered, but also the fundamental relationship between government and citizens (Watson & Mundy, 2001). While citizens experience good e-services from the private sector organizations with the higher levels of citizen satisfaction, they expect the high standards from government agencies (Edmiston, 2003). eGovernment imitates the private sector organizations by offering more efficient, transparent, and accessible public services to citizens and businesses (Irani, Elliman, & Jackson, 2007; Weerakkody, Jones, & Olsen, 2007).

eGovernment provides citizens with the added values of better quality and reduced turnaround times (Gouscos, Kalikakis, Legal, & Papadopoulou, 2007; Heeks, 2006; Kumar, Murkerji, Butt, & Persaud, 2007). eGovernment is the use of IT by public sector organizations (Heeks, 2006). The use of IT in the government sector offers great opportunities for enhancing service quality and efficiency and trimming down governmental expenses (Lin, Fofanah, & Liang, 2011). From the providers' perspective, government costs can be cut by reducing the frequency of face-to face service interactions with using eGovernment (Akesson & Edvardsson, 2008).

Effective eGovernment facilitates more efficient delivery of information and services to citizens, promotes productivity among public servants, encourages citizens' participation in government, and empowers all citizens (Kim, Kim, & Lee, 2009). eGovernment can be used as a tool to promote economic development, since it will enable businesses to more effectively transact with government (Badri & Alshare, 2008). Governments use the Internet in order to provide public services to their citizens (Watson & Mundy, 2001).

Governments should form better relationships with businesses and citizens by providing more effective government services (Al-Kibisi, De Boer, Mourshed, & Rea, 2001; Layne & Lee, 2001).

During the eGovernment era, the role of technology in the transformation of public sector organizations has significantly increased, while the relationship between ICT and organizational change in public sector organizations has become the subject of intensive research over the last decade (Nograšek & Vintar, 2014). The scope of eGovernment has been of interest to practitioners and researchers studying information system (Grant, 2005; Heeks & Bailur, 2006; Zhang, Guo, Chen, & Chau, 2009). There is an increasing recognition that various stakeholder groups for eGovernment have the significant roles to play in ensuring the long-term success of eGovernment enterprise (Rowley, 2011).

After some decades of eGovernment research and practice, an important body of knowledge is apparent in the literature suggesting that eGovernment becomes an established management field (Yildiz, 2007). eGovernment is one of the major concerns in management (Bornstein, 2000). The academic disciplines of business management studies have initiated the eGovernment issue (Davenport, 1993; Earl, 1994). eGovernment research area is symbolized by a multidisciplinary approach to government (Irani & Dwivedi, 2008), and has a relatively short history (Dwivedi, 2009). Another area of research that has received a lot of attention is the citizens' use of eGovernment and citizens' trust in government (Morgeson, VanAmburg, & Mithas, 2011).

Citizens' adoption of eGovernment services has been less than satisfactory in most countries (Carter & Weerakkody, 2008). Understanding citizens' trust in government is important and has a relationship to the development of eGovernment (Horsburgh, Goldfinch, & Gauld, 2011). While eGovernment seems to be a substantial growth in the development of eGovernment initiatives (Bednarz, 2002; Friel, 2002), it is not clear that citizens will embrace the use of eGovernment services. Some key concerns can limit eGovernment growth, including citizen privacy (Thibodeau, 2000). The operational benefits of using eGovernment include the availability of service, a reduction in response time, and a reduction in error rate (Al-Kibisi et al., 2001).

Citizens mistrust eGovernment initiatives, believing that eGovernment initiatives result in the invasion of citizen privacy by government (James, 2000). To be successful eGovernment implementation, ideal strategies and practices need to be identified for establishing and prioritizing business processes (Irani et al., 2012). eGovernment program needs to describe an obvious understanding of the proposed benefits to citizens about what challenges need to be effectively taken and the level of institutional change that needs to attain for it to be successful in a proposed eGovernment context (Hazlett & Hill, 2003).

Enhancing the effectiveness and efficiency of eGovernment services at affordable costs continues to be an interesting discussion (Hu, Shi, Pan, & Wang, 2012). The local and national government agencies face the challenging era of eGovernment (Belanger & Hiller, 2006). The implementation of eGovernment ensures that there is an improvement in processes within government agencies, efficiency is achieved, and public services are better managed and delivered (Irani et al., 2007). eGovernment exhibits the effective manner in which governments make use of the exchange of information and services related to citizens, individual businesses, and other government agencies (Welch, Hinnant, & Moon, 2004).

Concept of Business Process Modeling

Business processes have been the subjects of formal study from multiple perspectives over a long period from the start of the industrial age to the current IT-enabled services (ITES) age (Seethamraju, 2012). ICT has the potential to create radical changes in the classic bureaucratic structures of public sector organizations (Kim, Pan, & Pan, 2007; Pollitt, 2010; Weerakkody & Dhillon, 2008). In order to achieve corporate business objectives, a strong coherence between business and IT has become an important factor of competition on market places in industries (Kersten & Verhoef, 2003). The IT industry is one of the most dynamic industries in the world as it has an increased productivity (Abu Rub & Issa, 2012).

Bhaskar et al. (1994) stated that simulation has an important role in modeling and analyzing the activities in introducing BPR since it enables quantitative estimations to be made on the influence of the redesigned process on system performances. Many different methods and techniques can be used for modeling business processes in order to give an understanding of possible scenarios for improvement (Ould, 1995). Citizens and businesses are demanding faster delivery of public services and much better information (Ongaro, 2004). BPM can provide a method for discussing, communicating, and analyzing existing processes, an avenue for designing new processes, a baseline for continuing improvement, and a software program to control business processes (Huckvale & Ould, 1995).

BPM is a tool for knowledge management that allows the transformation of informal knowledge into formal knowledge and facilitates its externalization and sharing (Kalpic & Bernus, 2006). Saven (2003) stated that BPM becomes popular as it facilitates an analysis of business processes in a business enterprise. BPM can be used to learn about a process, make decisions about a process, and develop business process software (Saven, 2003).

Hammer and Champy (1993) stated that several companies and organizations report their successful experiences by applying revolutionary perspectives to obtain dramatic, radical, and fundamental changes. However, people rethink the myths of BPR after recognizing that 70 percent of BPR efforts fail (Davenport & Stoddard, 1994). Spencer (1999) stated that reengineering rejects the paradigm of separating tasks by using technology to join tasks into connected processes.

BPM is used for the application of functionality of business process, the sequence of activities and their relationships, and the resource usage characteristics. Vernadat (1996) suggested that BPM is used to achieve business benefits (i.e., the reduction in process complexity, the improved transparency of system's behavior related to better management of business processes, the clear understanding of entity in question, the capitalization of acquired business knowledge, and process improvement for enlarging the characteristics of business processes).

BPM is important for process engineering as a business approach that allows the transformation of informal knowledge into formal knowledge, and facilitates externalization, knowledge sharing, and subsequent knowledge internalization in organization (Kalpic & Bernus, 2006). BPM has the potential to establish the criteria for improving the availability and quality of captured knowledge due to its formal nature, increase reusability, and reduce the costs of knowledge transfer (Kalpic & Bernus, 2006).

Management fields such as process modeling and workflow management demonstrate a clear understanding of theory toward achieving a high standard of development (Becker et al., 2006). Gandhewar and Wadegaonkar (2012) indicated that BPM plays two important roles: to capture existing processes by structurally representing their activities and related elements; and to represent new processes in order to evaluate their performance. BPM in software engineering is the activity of representing processes of a business enterprise, so that the current process is analyzed and improved in the future (Toor & Dhir, 2011). The techniques for characterizing and analyzing business processes are related to BPM (Luo & Tung, 1999). Verginadis and Mentzas (2008) stated that business processes are dynamic and unpredictable.

Curtis et al. (1992) suggested that BPM can be used to achieve a number of objectives and goals in modern business. BPM can facilitate a business group to share their understanding of the process by using a common process representation. BPM can serve as the foundation for process improvement and management by supporting the analysis of process behavior and performance. BPM can automate process guidance and support (Curtis et al., 1992). BPM supports the understanding of current business processes, process improvement, process management, process development, and process execution (Curtis et al., 1992).

The important idea of eGovernment vision has emerged, and governments have taken promising steps to deploy eGovernment services (Chen, 2002; Scherlis & Eisenberg, 2003). The review of eGovernment is often limited to the provision of online services and public administrations' Internet portals. A business approach characterized by a focus on business processes can contribute to the management of changes in public sector organizations (McIvor, McHugh, & Cadden, 2002; Ongaro, 2004). Organizations are dispersed among different areas, countries, and continents. There is a decentralized ownership of tasks, information, and resources inside an organization regarding business processes. Different groups inside an organization autonomously act in order to manage the resources consumed, from whom and with which cost and time limits (Verginadis & Mentzas, 2008).

Beynon-Davies and Williams (2003) stated that there is not enough emphasis on the engineering of both business processes and systems in the UK. Facilitated by eGovernment, public agencies are looking for transformational change by making a fundamental improvement. While policy makers and practitioners in the public sector have branded their current improvements as BPR, the academic and research communities have avoided from making any comparisons. Compared with two cases of public sector transformation in the UK and Netherlands, eGovernment-induced change requires a plan for a basic improvement which, in contrast to BPR, is obtained by accumulative steps, and has a high level of participation (Weerakkody, Janssen, & Dwivedi, 2011).

eGovernment is presented as a promising reduction strategy in many countries. Organizational characteristics are the major factors of perceived burden reduction and implementation effectiveness. Arendsen et al. (2014) stated that the perceived organizational benefits positively relate to the overall confirmation of the former system adoption decision. Irani et al. (2003) stated that decision makers require the skill to evaluate the element of technology, and to assess its impact on the future of the organization and people. The analysis of business process from various industries and research areas helps in the identification of the special characteristics of processes that span across organizations (Verginadis & Mentzas, 2008). Organizations are involved in business processes, and each of them tries to maximize its business profit during an interorganizational workflow.

Business Process Modeling Methodologies

Kueng et al. (1996) categorized BPM approaches into four major categories: activity-oriented approaches, which tend to define a business process as a specific ordering of activities referred to tasks; object-oriented approaches, which are associated with object orientation, such as encapsulation, inheritance, and specialization; role-oriented approaches, which focus on roles as sets of activities, carrying out particular responsibilities; and speech act-oriented approaches, which are based on speech act theory or an action perspective. Luo and Tung (1999) proposed a framework for selecting BPM methods based on the business objectives of process modeling (i.e., communication, analysis, and control), perspectives of business modeling methods (i.e., object, activity, and role perspectives), and the characteristics of business

modeling methods (i.e., formality, scalability, enactability, and ease of use).

Applying information system within business architecture has the potential to increase business performance and gain competitive advantage in the digital age (Kasemsap, 2015c). BPM and BPR are the major topics in the discussion of enterprise modernization (Davenport, 1993). Several business methods, techniques, and tools have been developed and implemented to support process-oriented reorganization (Scheer, 2000). BPM methods can posses the capability in facilitating process evaluation and alternative selection (Gandhewar & Wadegaonkar, 2012). Different BPM methodologies have different business capabilities, and consider business processes from different perspectives (Luo & Tung, 1999). BPM methodologies can maintain the analysis capability of facilitating process evaluation and alternative selection (Lin et al., 2002).

BPM methodologies provide business users with the ability to model their business processes and to implement business models. BPM methodologies can supply transparency into business processes, as well as the centralization of corporate business process models and execution metrics (Toor & Dhir, 2011). Modeling functionality allows for pre-execution ''what-if'' modeling and simulation. Post-execution optimization is available based on the analysis of actual as-performed metrics.

The increasing popularity of BPM results in a rapidly growing number of modeling techniques and tools (Hommes & van Reijswound 2000). Examples of BPM methodologies are BPMN; Cognition enhanced Natural language Information Analysis Method (CogNIAM); Extended Business Modeling Language (xBML); Event-driven Process Chain (EPC); Icam DEFinition for Function Modeling (IDEF0); and Unified Modeling Language (UML) (Toor & Dhir, 2011). IDEF0, IDEF3, Petri Nets, System Dynamics, Knowledge-based Techniques, Activity Based Costing and

Discrete-Event Simulation are the examples of BPM techniques widely used (Eatock, Giaglis, Paul, & Serrano, 2000).

Architecture of Integrated Information Systems (ARIS) is an approach to enterprise modeling (Lankhorst, 2005). ARIS offers methods for analyzing processes and taking a holistic view of process design, management, workflow, and application processing. The ARIS approach provides a generic methodological framework and a BPM tool. ARIS uses a modeling language known as EPC, which is a significant aspect of the ARIS model. EPC is the center of the House of ARIS, and connects all other business views, as well as describes the movement of the business process.

ARIS includes the four major perspectives of techniques such as organizational view, data view, control view, and functional view. ARIS is a unique and internationally famous method for optimizing business process and implementing application systems. ARIS methods recognize business processes by means of UML, leading to an information model as the foundation for a methodical and intelligent method of developing application systems (Scheer, 2000).

BIZAGI is a software suite with two complementary products (i.e., a process modeler and a BPM suite). BIZAGI process modeler is a freeware application used to diagram, document, and simulate processes using the BPMN standard notation. BIZAGI BPM suite is a business process management and workflow solution that enables organizations to automate business processes and workflows. BONITA is an open-source business process management and workflow suite. BONITA BPM involves three major components: BONITA studio, BONITA BPM engine, and BONITA portal. BONITA BPM can be applied for several projects requiring complex workflows like supply chain management, eGovernment, human resources, and contract management in modern business.

Business Process Modeling Notation

The high competitiveness between business organizations demands a constant innovation and evolution in their productive processes, requiring information system to be produced and modified with the same swiftness (Chiarello, Emer, & Neto, 2014). BPMN is a graphical notation, maintained by the Object Management Group (OMG) and created for the representation of business processes based on workflows (OMG, 2013).

BPMN has been broadly accepted as the new standard for BPM toward widespread adoption in practice across various industries (Erickson & Penker, 2000). The four basic categories of elements in BPMN are the workflow objects (i.e., events, tasks, and decisions), connection objects (i.e., sequence messages and associations), swim lanes (i.e., pools and lanes), and artifacts (i.e., data objects, annotations, and groups) (OMG, 2013). Workflow objects are the main graphical elements expressing the behavior of a business process. Connection objects define the way flow objects are connected together. Swim lanes depict and highlight the various entities participating in the process. Artifacts are used to provide additional information to assist in better comprehension of model.

BPMN is a graphical representation for specifying business processes in BPM. BPMN is a standard for BPM that provides a graphical notation for specifying business processes in a Business Process Diagram (BPD), based on a flowcharting technique similar to activity diagrams from UML. The BPMN specification also provides a mapping between the graphics of the notation and the underlying constructs of execution languages, particularly Business Process Execution Language (BPEL).

The objective of BPMN is to support business process management, for both technical users and business users, able to represent complex process semantics. BPMN focuses on business processes without covering organizational aspects such as business rules, information data model, organizational resources, and strategy. The employment of BPM through BPMN can assist in the elicitation of requirements because it is possible to map the workflow and a process of information concerning activities and to identify existing information system and requirements for the construction of new systems (Hernandez, Rodriguez, & Martin, 2010).

A standard BPMN provides businesses with the capability of understanding their internal business procedures in a graphical notation, and gives organizations the ability to communicate these business procedures in a standard manner. The graphical BPMN facilitates a clear understanding of business performance collaborations and business transactions between and among organizations (Toor & Dhir, 2011).

Importance of Business Process Reengineering in Government-to-Citizen E-Commerce

Regarding e-commerce, eGovernment represents the introduction of a great movement of technological innovation as well as government reinvention. eGovernment shows an immense stimulus to move forward in the 21st century with higher quality, cost-effective government services, and a better relationship between citizens and government (Fang, 2002). Many government agencies in developed countries have taken modern steps toward the website and ICT use, thus adding coherence to all local activities on the Internet, enlarging local access and skills, expanding correlative services for local debates, and increasing citizens' participation in the promotion of territory (Graham & Aurigi, 1997).

G2C is the communication link between a government and private individuals or residents. Such G2C communication refers to that which reach through ICT, but can also involve direct mail and media campaigns. G2C can enter at the federal, state, and local levels. G2C category includes the interactions between government and citizens that can electronically achieve (Kumar, Umashankar, Rani, & Ramana, 2010). G2C applications allow citizens in order to pay taxes, receive payments and documents, communicate with government at any time from any location, improve accounting, record keeping, and reduce processing time. On the administrative side, the information can be stored in databases in various locations with the security of transactions. The practical implementations of G2C are in the fields of tourism and recreation, education, government services, and safety information. Many government agencies and departments are scheduling for more innovative e-services such as e-voting in public sector organizations.

G2C deals with the relationship between government and citizens (Ndou, 2004). eGovernment allows government agencies to talk, listen, and interact with citizens, thus supporting accountability, democracy, and improvements to public services. A broad collection of interactions can be developed ranging from the delivery of services and the provision of welfare and health benefits to regulatory and compliance oriented licensing (Riley, 2001). G2C allows customers to access government information and services from everywhere by using various electronic channels (i.e., cellular phone and wireless devices). G2C reinforces government participation in local community life in terms of sending an e-mail and contributing to an online discussion forum in public sector organizations (Ndou, 2004).

Developing eGovernment services that can effectively deal with changes is a challenge for public administrations (Apostolou, Mentzas, Stojanovic, Thoenssen, & Lobo, 2011). eGovernment experiences have presented poor results when compared with those achieved in private sector organizations. The errors are produced with a high rate of failures

(Heeks, 2003). Many difficulties occur from the requirement of transforming methods in which the activities of public sector organizations are usually executed to take advantage of new business technologies. This perspective forces the use of transformation tools, such as BPR, to carry out the dynamic business changes.

eGovernment activities are correlated with government planning, organizing, leading, and controlling (Kumar et al., 2010). Top management of public sector organizations is responsible for preparing a master schedule plan which sets both short-run conditions and long-run directions in organizations. It is the responsibility of government to get people to participate in its design and implementation (Kumar et al., 2010). Many public sector organizations are managing BPR projects in response to increased market competition (Luo & Tung, 1999). The failure of various eGovernment applications and activities can be effectively controlled with citizen partnership toward the success and prosperity of society through utilizing BPR.

Relationship between Business Process Modeling and E-Government-Based Citizen Satisfaction

Oliver (1999) defined satisfaction as the perception of a pleasurable fulfillment of a service. Citizen satisfaction is a composite performance indicator from various eGovernment aspects determined by citizens' needs (i.e., perceived services, expectation, and the level of G2C relationship) (Al Shafi & Weerakkody, 2007). Citizen satisfaction is the person's feeling toward a variety of factors affecting a given situation (Wixom & Todd, 2005). Citizen satisfaction is the individual's emotional state following a certain experience (Oliver, 1993). Satisfaction with eGovernment is considered as the ability of citizens to get the information they desire and have a service experience that solves their problems (Reddick & Roy, 2013).

Tsohou et al. (2013) stated that evaluating eGovernment services is essential for governments due to the capacity of e-services in order to transform public administrations and assist the interactions of governments with citizens, businesses, and other government agencies. There is a relationship between eGovernment and citizen satisfaction (Cohen, 2006). User satisfaction in information system research is taken to be a surrogate measure of success (Gatian, 1994), but user satisfaction has generated more controversy than agreement (Woodroof & Burg, 2003). A lack of attention to the theoretical aspects of user satisfaction construct has led to disagreements among researchers regarding its definition, measurement method, and research findings. eGovernment evaluation promotes eGovernment system because the essence of citizen satisfaction is measured to achieve citizen expectations and reduce government costs (Huang & Bwoma, 2003).

Shankar et al. (2003) measured citizen satisfaction in terms of transactional satisfaction and overall satisfaction. Transactional satisfaction refers to citizen satisfaction derived from individual transactions. The quality of citizen satisfaction varies from one transaction to other transactions (Shankar et al., 2003). The appropriate application of ICT by public sector organizations has the ability to increase citizen satisfaction with government (Irani et al., 2012). Current information, convenient services, and the new channels of communication reduce the information gap and increase citizen satisfaction in public sector organizations (Welch et al., 2004).

A major domain of eGovernment research is the examination of information delivery to citizens (Irani et al., 2012). eGovernment services involve communications and transactions between government and citizens. Horan and Abhichandani (2006) stated that the increase in eGovernment services has led to the requirement to improve citizen satisfaction regarding eGovernment services. Liu et al. (2010) explained that citizen satisfaction with

Internet service provision is a complex equation with various elements determining how well the online experience meets the needs of Internet users. Before endorsing eGovernment initiatives, citizens should trust government organizations that they have the intelligence and technical resources essential to implement eGovernment systems (Liu et al., 2010).

eGovernment service providers should increase the likelihood of improving citizen satisfaction in government (Irani et al., 2012). Jones et al. (2007) indicated that the variety of the constituency of local boroughs has a great influence from a social perspective, thus dictating their conclusive attitudes toward technology in government. As citizens progressively interact with eGovernment services, there are the wide-ranging prospects for effective service provision from eGovernment initiatives (Irani et al., 2012).

There are various assessments that apply citizen-centered eGovernment services to system evaluation (Welch et al., 2004). Wang et al. (2005) presented a model for assessing the performance of eGovernment system with a citizen-centered approach by concentrating on the process and outcome of eGovernment interaction. Carter and Belanger (2004) emphasized the adoption of eGovernment initiatives based on eGovernment approach.

Reddick (2005) analyzed the demand side of eGovernment related to the citizen-centered service of interacting with eGovernment systems. The measures of e-service performance should be able to indicate an eGovernment strategy (Irani et al., 2007). It is preferable to measure the direct effect of eGovernment initiatives to the citizens, the benefits to government, and the overall value of eGovernment improvement to the country (Irani et al., 2012). To advance the service provision, there is a profitable transition of citizens considering eGovernment as a successful collection of transactions toward accomplishing their citizens' needs (West, 2004).

Application of Business Process Reengineering in E-Government

The introduction of ICT within business processes lowers communication time and costs (Hammer & Mangurian, 1987; Malone, Yates, & Benjamin, 1987). BPR encompasses the envisioning of new work strategies, the actual process design activity, and the implementation of the change in its complex technological, human, and organizational dimensions (Davenport, 1993). BPR entails the redesign of business processes utilizing IT to bring about a quantum leap in performance (Thong, Yap, & Seah, 2000). Implementing eGovernment initiative effectively challenges endeavors in developing countries due to various factors such as insufficient resources and technology, as well as restrictive social conditions (van der Vyver & Rajapakse, 2012).

To increase public value, there is a need for eGovernment system to be knowledge based and user-centric (Ramani & Kumaraswamy, 2013). The use of technology modernizes business structures, processes, regulatory frameworks, human resources, and the culture of public administration (Centeno, van Bavel, & Burgelman, 2005). eGovernment becomes important however it cannot be successfully implemented without changes in business processes that are performed by government institutions (Stemberger & Jaklic, 2007).

The government redefines its business role from authoritative redistributor to service provider through using BPR (Hughes et al., 2006). An organization can redesign its business process, redesign business network, and redefine the process scope in organization. Venkatraman (1994) stated about the degree of business transformation in terms of evolutionary levels (i.e., localized exploitation and internal integration) and revolutionary levels (i.e., business process redesign, business network redesign, and business scope redefinition).

Layne and Lee (2001) identified the four major stages of business evolution in eGovernment (i.e., catalogue, transaction, vertical integration, and horizontal integration). The immediate impact to citizens can be judged in terms of ease of access, ease of use, and better efficiency. Providing a large group of forms from individual authorities in one location gives citizens the ease of access resulting in time savings. Concerning political considerations, a complete business process redesign will never be possible as the existing authorities must remain in place.

In order to achieve more powerful range of business benefits, the government needs to move up to the first revolutionary level and engage in the process of BPR (Hughes, Scott, & Golden, 2006). An understanding of bureaucratic process that forms citizen services is necessary so that it is possible to identify business processes and the elements of business processes that can be redesigned, redefined, automated, and left unchanged. However, this interval portal presents the transformation stages of business process that need to be managed in order to deliver any level of eGovernment.

The development of BPR platform represents the fulfillment of business network redesign as the BPR platform completely impacts on the nature of the exchange among various participants through new IT capabilities (Hughes et al., 2006). Individual authorities should participate in a centralized mechanism of utilizing business process toward achieving eGovernment.

BPR platform encourages business movement toward electronic information sharing capable of promoting effective interconnectivity, process linkage, and knowledge management (Hughes et al., 2006). Business redefinition is presented by the strategic shift in government policy toward citizen-centered eGovernment services enabled by a BPR system. While public sector organizations have adopted IT to improve their operational efficiency, the changing environment requires more radical changes to improve the quality of public service (Thong et al., 2000). The development of local authority websites represents the situation of localized exploitation that is the implementa-

tion of IT within a business at a practical level requiring little process change.

Regarding service delivery process, BPR-related citizen participation introduces a new business process of citizen identification to which the local authority is a passive participant (Hughes et al., 2006). Participation facilitates electronic access to services, although this aspect requires almost no process change is still conducted in a conventional manner with the citizen receiving electronic or physical notification of service completion. Government by its nature is a collection of business processes (i.e., agencies and departments in organization).

Implementation of E-Government through Business Process Modeling

eGovernment implementation is an explanation of e-readiness form of country to participate in the global information society (Mutula & Mostert, 2010). eGovernment readiness is an important measure of a community's overall readiness to utilize opportunities provided by ICT (Al-Omari & Al-Omari, 2006; Kovacic, 2005). An effective eGovernment readiness assessment framework is a necessary condition for advancing eGovernment (Ayanso, Chatterjee, & Cho, 2011). Gender egalitarianism, institutional collectivism, performance orientation, and uncertainty avoidance values are the key determinants of eGovernment readiness (Khalil, 2011).

An understanding of the e-readiness of a country or community is necessary for providing baseline information that can be used for planning and making comparisons across organizations and countries (Mutula & Mostert, 2010). The assessment of e-readiness can be utilized as an information gathering mechanism to assist governments while planning strategies for conduction ICT integration and making improvements on specific e-readiness components (Mutula & Van Brakel, 2006). Huang and Shyu (2008) explained how eGovernment infrastructure provides its citizens and organizations with easy access to government information and eGovernment services.

The implementation of eGovernment initiatives has been reported in many researches, thus stimulating business process change, increasing internal efficiency, expanding the levels of information sharing, developing innovation and competitiveness, and promoting social inclusion, greater transparency, and greater proximity to citizens (Guijarro, 2007; Kaylor, 2005; Scholl, 2001). National and local governments can provide new and better business responses to essential standing issues such as poverty reduction, wealth creation, as well as education, equity, and social justice (Mutula & Van Brakel, 2006).

The implementation of eGovernment earns government costs. The greater eGovernment is available for financial strength and the easier eGovernment is suitable for a city council to introduce eGovernment services and public contents via the Internet (Serrano-Cinca, Rueda-Tomas, & Portillo-Tarragona, 2009). Reddick (2005) stated that citizens' Internet experience and citizens' income level positively affect the adoption of eGovernment regarding both online transactions and information searches.

FUTURE RESEARCH DIRECTIONS

Although eGovernment has increased transparency and improved communication and access to information by citizens, digital diffusion of information is often achieved at high cost to government agencies and taxpayers. In moving toward a broad business process-oriented and IT-supported modernization of an administration, the development of a reference process model as a store of domain knowledge has the potential to extremely reduce the complexity of using eGovernment projects and to simplify their implementation by means of a business process orientation around reference processes.

Growing demands on using BPM and BPR methodologies arising from the special features of the eGovernment domain are not being entirely met by existing applications. eGovernment success will mostly depend on the improvement gained as a result of BPM and BPR implementation. Reaching higher eGovernment levels is related to business process redesign toward taking advantage of IT capabilities. One portal working on front office to get requests is not enough. Government should prepare the quick and high quality services in public sector organizations. However, this issue means a new level of business integration that government agencies must face in operation, thus requiring the use of BPM and BPR.

Many current eGovernment applications appear at basic levels, regardless of the future benefits that may appear at superior levels. The delay of eGovernment utilization is the result of the difficulty in implementing BPM and BPR in public sector organizations. In order to accomplish eGovernment benefits, leaders in the public sector organizations should generate effective BPM and BPR methodologies and software tools to achieve competitive advantage through business process integration.

Utilizing BPM and BPR methodologies in eGovernment can enhance the government applicability in the implementation of eGovernment and provide a valuable insight into the successful completion of citizen-centered eGovernment services in governments and departments. The important areas for future research are to investigate the unique nature of business processes in both public and private sector organizations so that business process integration can be further developed through using BPM and BPR methodologies.

CONCLUSION

This chapter revealed the roles of BPM and BPR in eGovernment, thus describing the concepts of eGovernment and BPM; BPM methodologies; BPMN; the importance of BPR in G2C e-commerce; the relationship between BPM and eGovernment-based citizen satisfaction; the application of BPR in eGovernment; and the implementation of eGovernment through BPM. This chapter also provided valuable insights into how citizen-centered eGovernment services can be attained, and highlighted the importance of managing business processes in the implementation of BPM and BPR concerning eGovernment.

eGovernment is a modern trend that is driven by the advances in BPM and BPR as well as the aspirations of citizens who place increasing demands on governments' service. Leaders in the public sector organizations should involve both employees and citizens in business processes during the introduction of BPM and BPR in eGovernment services. eGovernment services must be redesigned to ensure that the benefits of ICT systems are fully realized. The business process connects local and central systems through the use of a centralized database that maintains the authenticated data of the individual citizens in using eGovernment services.

While serving as a successful example of a movement to eGovernment services, it is related to a citizen-centered eGovernment platform. The business process provision of the technical business infrastructure and the redesign of local business processes in using BPM and BPR have been identified as the major elements determining the success of business process. Localized business exploitation is achieved by directing government authorities to implement individual websites. The development of citizen-focused portal sites promotes a business process shift from departmental orientation to citizen-centered eGovernment satisfaction.

The portals and elements of BPM and BPR platform are the examples of internal business process integration in eGovernment services. Throughout BPM and BPR stages, providing effective BPM and BPR systems focusing on the citizen-centered eGovernment satisfaction encourages citizens' usage of BPM. The ability to indicate BPM and BPR systems is facilitated by the learning that appears while developing the initial eGovernment initiatives in the evolutionary stages. In addition, the establishment of a special government entity has greatly contributed to the success of business process integration.

BPM and BPR play the important roles to identify and manage the major business process success factors involved in delivering eGovernment utilized by citizens. The most suitable business model and technical infrastructure are implemented to leverage expertise in using eGovernment services. The use of existing expertise proves greatly successful in terms of developing successful business process infrastructures in a limited time frame. eGovernment interactions between independent agencies are successfully coordinated to ensure the delivery of eGovernment service-related quality. The maintenance of the citizens' satisfaction by providing high quality of eGovernment services through website portals.

eGovernment initiatives that fit within the evolutionary classification can be achieved in a timely manner. More revolutionary initiatives are achievable but that the development of these business process initiatives requires efficient BPM and BPR methodologies. eGovernment services must be redesigned to ensure that the benefits of ICT systems are completely realized. The utilization of BPM and BPR related to eGovernment requires more time to aid citizens who are in need of support from employees; and the time that is saved as a result of the introduction of BPM and BPR in eGovernment must be effectively utilized by BPM and BPR methodologies. Applying BPM and BPR in eGovernment has the potential to increase public sector performance and reach competitive advantage in public sector organizations.

REFERENCES

Abu Rub, F. A., & Issa, A. A. (2012). A business process modeling-based approach to investigate complex processes: Software development case study. *Business Process Management Journal, 18*(1), 122–137. doi:10.1108/14637151211215046

Ahn, M. J., & Bretschneider, S. (2011). Politics of e-government: E-government and the political control of bureaucracy. *Public Administration Review, 71*(3), 414–424. doi:10.1111/j.1540-6210.2011.02225.x

Akesson, M., & Edvardsson, B. (2008). Effects of e-government on service design as perceived by employees. *Managing Service Quality, 18*(5), 457–478. doi:10.1108/09604520810898839

Akman, I., Yazici, A., Mishraa, A., & Arifoglu, A. (2005). E-government: A global view and an empirical evaluation of some attributes of citizens. *Government Information Quarterly, 22*(2), 239–257. doi:10.1016/j.giq.2004.12.001

Al-Kibisi, G., De Boer, K., Mourshed, M., & Rea, N. (2001). Putting citizens on-line, not inline. *The McKinsey Quarterly*, (2): 64.

Al-Omari, A., & Al-Omari, H. (2006). E-government readiness assessment model. *Journal of Computer Science, 2*(11), 841–845. doi:10.3844/jcssp.2006.841.845

Al Shafi, S., & Weerakkody, V. (2007). Implementing and managing e-government in the state of Qatar: A citizens' perspective. *Electronic government. International Journal (Toronto, Ont.), 4*(4), 436–450.

Alanezi, M., Kamil, A., & Basri, S. (2010). A proposed instrument dimensions for measuring e-government service quality. *International Journal of u- and e-Service Science and Technology, 3*(4), 1–17.

Almarabeh, T., & AbuAli, A. (2010). A general framework for e-government: Definition maturity challenges, opportunities, and success. *European Journal of Scientific Research, 39*(1), 29–42.

Andersen, K. V., & Henriksen, H. Z. (2005). The first leg of e-government research: Domains and application areas 1998-2003. Copenhagen, Netherlands: Center for Research on IT in Policy Settings (CIPS), Copenhagen Business School.

Apostolou, D., Mentzas, G., Stojanovic, L., Thoenssen, B., & Lobo, T. P. (2011). A collaborative decision framework for managing changes in e-Government services. *Government Information Quarterly, 28*(1), 101–116. doi:10.1016/j.giq.2010.03.007

Arendsen, R., Peters, O., ter Hedde, M., & van Dijk, J. (2014). Does e-government reduce the administrative burden of businesses? An assessment of business-to-government systems usage in the Netherlands. *Government Information Quarterly, 31*(1), 160–169. doi:10.1016/j.giq.2013.09.002

Asongwe, P. N. (2012). E-government and the Cameroon cybersecurity legislation 2010: Opportunities and challenges. *The African Journal of Information and Communication, 2*(12), 157–163.

Ayanso, A., Chatterjee, D., & Cho, D. I. (2011). E-government readiness index: A methodology and analysis. *Government Information Quarterly, 28*(4), 522–532. doi:10.1016/j.giq.2011.02.004

Aydinli, O. F., Brinkkemper, S., & Ravesteyn, P. (2009). Business process improvement in organizational design of e-Government services. *Electronic. Journal of E-Government, 7*(2), 123–134.

Badri, M. A., & Alshare, K. (2008). A path analytic model and measurement of the business value of e-government: An international perspective. *International Journal of Information Management, 28*(6), 524–535. doi:10.1016/j.ijinfomgt.2006.10.004

Becker, J., Algermissen, L., & Niehaves, B. (2006). A procedure model for process oriented e-government projects. *Business Process Management Journal*, *12*(1), 61–75. doi:10.1108/14637150610643760

Bednarz, A. (2002). Getting plugged in to e-government. *New World (New Orleans, La.)*, *19*(27), 36–39.

Belanger, F., & Hiller, J. S. (2006). A framework for e-government: Privacy implications. *Business Process Management Journal*, *12*(1), 48–60. doi:10.1108/14637150610643751

Bertot, J. C., Jaeger, P. T., & Grimes, J. M. (2010). Using ICTs to create a culture of transparency: E-government and social media as openness and anti-corruption tools for societies. *Government Information Quarterly*, *27*(3), 264–271. doi:10.1016/j.giq.2010.03.001

Bertot, J. C., Jaeger, P. T., & Grimes, J. M. (2012). Promoting transparency and accountability through ICTs, social media, and collaborative e-government. *Transforming Government: People. Process and Policy*, *6*(1), 78–91.

Beynon-Davies, P., & Williams, M. D. (2003). Evaluating electronic local government in the UK. *Journal of Information Technology*, *18*(2), 137–149. doi:10.1080/0268396032000101180

Bhaskar, R., Lee, H. S., Levas, A., Petrakian, R., Tsai, F., & Tulskie, B. (1994). *Analysing and reengineering business processes using simulation*. Paper presented at the 1994 Winter Simulation Conference, Lake Buena Vista, FL. doi:10.1109/WSC.1994.717510

Bornstein, I. W. (2000). Keeping our sights on the horizon: GFOA's survey on emerging issues. *Government Finance Review*, *16*(6), 40–43.

Bwalya, J. K. (2009). Factors affecting adoption of e-government in Zambia. *The Electronic Journal of Information Systems in Developing Countries*, *28*(4), 1–13.

Caillier, J. G. (2009). Centralized customer service: What local government characteristics influence its acceptance and usage of information? *Public Administration and Management*, *14*(2), 292–322.

Carter, L., & Belanger, F. (2004). The influence of perceived characteristics of innovating on e-government adoption. *The Electronic. Journal of E-Government*, *2*(1), 11–20.

Carter, L., & Belanger, F. (2005). The utilization of e-government services: Citizen trust, innovation and acceptance factors. *Information Systems Journal*, *15*(1), 5–25. doi:10.1111/j.1365-2575.2005.00183.x

Carter, L., & Weerakkody, V. (2008). E-government adoption: A cultural comparison. *Information Systems Frontiers*, *10*(4), 473–482. doi:10.1007/s10796-008-9103-6

Centeno, C., van Bavel, R., & Burgelman, J. C. (2005). A prospective view of e-government in the European Union. *The Electronic Journal of E-Government*, *3*(2), 59–66.

Charif, H., & Ramadan, M. (2003). E-government attempts in ESCWA member countries. In M. A. Wimmer (Ed.), *Knowledge management in electronic government* (pp. 310–318). New York, NY: Springer–Verlag. doi:10.1007/3-540-44836-5_33

Chen, H. (2002). Digital government: Technologies and practices. *Decision Support Systems*, *34*(3), 223–227. doi:10.1016/S0167-9236(02)00118-5

Chen, Y. C., & Gant, J. (2001). Transforming local e-government services: The use of application service providers. *Government Information Quarterly, 18*(4), 343–355. doi:10.1016/S0740-624X(01)00090-9

Chiarello, M. A., Emer, M. C. F. P., & Neto, A. G. S. S. (2014). An approach of software requirements elicitation based on the model and notation business process (BPMN). *Lecture Notes on Software Engineering, 2*(1), 65–70. doi:10.7763/LNSE.2014.V2.96

Chun, S. A., Shulman, S., Sandoval, R., & Hovy, E. (2010). Government 2.0: Making connections between citizens, data and government. *Information Polity: The International Journal of Governance and Democracy in the Information Age, 15*(1/2), 1–9.

Cohen, J. E. (2006). Citizen satisfaction with contacting government on the Internet. *Information Policy, 11*(1), 51–65.

Curtis, B., Kellner, M. I., & Over, J. (1992). Process modeling. *Communications of the ACM, 35*(9), 75–90. doi:10.1145/130994.130998

Dale, T., & Goldfinch, S. (2006). *Dangerous enthusiasms: E-government, computer failure, and information system development*. Dunedin, New Zealand: Otago University Press.

Davenport, T. H. (1993). *Process innovation: Reengineering work through information technology*. Boston, MA: Harvard Business School Press.

Davenport, T. H., & Stoddard, D. B. (1994). Reengineering: Business change of mythic proportions. *Management Information Systems Quarterly, 18*(2), 121–127. doi:10.2307/249760

Davies, T. R. (2002). Throw e-gov a lifeline. *Governing, 15*(9), 72.

Dearstyne, B. W. (2001). E-business, e-government & information proficiency. *Information Management Journal, 34*(4), 16.

DeLone, W., & McLean, E. (2003). The DeLone and McLean model of information systems success: A ten-year update. *Journal of Management Information Systems, 19*(4), 9–30.

Dwivedi, Y. K. (2009). Viewpoint: An analysis of e-government research published in Transforming Government: People, Process and Policy (TGPPP). *Transforming Government: People. Process and Policy, 3*(1), 7–15.

Earl, M. J. (1994). The new and the old of business process redesign. *The Journal of Strategic Information Systems, 3*(1), 5–22. doi:10.1016/0963-8687(94)90003-5

Eatock, J., Giaglis, G. M., Paul, R. J., & Serrano, A. (2000). The implications of information technology infrastructure capabilities for business process change success. In P. Henderson (Ed.), *Systems engineering for business process change* (pp. 127–137). London, UK: Springer–Verlag. doi:10.1007/978-1-4471-0457-5_11

Edmiston, K. D. (2003). State and local e-government: Prospects and challenges. *American Review of Public Administration, 33*(1), 20–45. doi:10.1177/0275074002250255

Erickson, H., & Penker, M. (2000). *Business modeling with UML: Business patterns at work*. New York, NY: John Wiley & Sons.

Evans, D., & Yen, D. C. (2006). E-government: Evolving relationship of citizens and government, domestic, and international development. *Government Information Quarterly, 23*(2), 207–235. doi:10.1016/j.giq.2005.11.004

Fang, Z. (2002). E-government in digital era: Concept, practice and development. *International Journal of the Computer, 10*(2), 1–22.

Featherman, M., & Pavlou, P. (2003). Predicting e-services adoption: A perceived risk facets perspective. *International Journal of Human-Computer Studies, 59*(4), 451–474. doi:10.1016/S1071-5819(03)00111-3

Friel, B. (2002). GovBenefits.gov. *Government Executive, 34*(15), 38.

Gandhewar, V. V., & Wadegaonkar, A. P. (2012). Guidelines for business process modeling and its application to training process. *International Journal of Modeling and Optimization, 2*(6), 705–707. doi:10.7763/IJMO.2012.V2.215

Gatian, A. W. (1994). Is user satisfaction a valid measure of system effectiveness? *Information & Management, 26*(3), 119–131. doi:10.1016/0378-7206(94)90036-1

Gauld, R., & Goldfinch, S. (2006). *Dangerous enthusiasms: E-government, computer failure and information systems development*. Dunedin, New Zealand: Otago University Press.

Gilbert, D., Balestrini, P., & Littleboy, D. (2004). Barriers and benefits in the adoption of e-government. *International Journal of Public Sector Management, 17*(4/5), 286–301. doi:10.1108/09513550410539794

Gouscos, D., Kalikakis, M., Legal, M., & Papadopoulou, S. (2007). A general model of performance and quality for one-stop e-government service offerings. *Government Information Quarterly, 24*(4), 860–885. doi:10.1016/j.giq.2006.07.016

Graham, S., & Aurigi, A. (1997). Virtual cities, social polarization, and the crisis in urban public space. *Journal of Urban Technology, 4*(1), 19–52. doi:10.1080/10630739708724546

Grant, G. (2005). Realizing the promise of electronic government. *Journal of Global Information Management, 13*(1), 1–4. doi:10.4018/jgim.2005010101

Gronlund, A. (2003). e-Democracy: In search of tools and methods for effective participation. *Journal of Multi-Criteria Decision Analysis, 12*(2/3), 93–100. doi:10.1002/mcda.349

Guijarro, L. (2007). Interoperability frameworks and enterprise architectures in e-government initiatives in Europe and the United States. *Government Information Quarterly, 24*(1), 89–101. doi:10.1016/j.giq.2006.05.003

Hammer, M., & Champy, J. (1993). *Reengineering the corporation: A manifesto for business revolution*. New York, NY: Harper Business.

Hammer, M., & Mangurian, G. E. (1987). The changing value of communications technology. *MIT Sloan Management Review, 28*(2), 65–71.

Hazlett, S., & Hill, F. (2003). E-government: The realities of using IT to transform the public sector. *Managing Service Quality, 13*(6), 445–452. doi:10.1108/09604520310506504

Heeks, R. (2003). *Reinventing government in the information age: International practice, IT-enabled public sector reform*. London, UK: Routledge.

Heeks, R. (2006). *Implementing and managing eGovernment: An international text*. London, UK: Sage.

Heeks, R., & Bailur, S. (2006). Analyzing e-Government research: Perspectives, philosophies, theories, methods, and practice. *Government Information Quarterly, 24*(2), 243–265. doi:10.1016/j.giq.2006.06.005

Helbig, N., Ramón Gil-García, J., & Ferro, E. (2009). Understanding the complexity of electronic government: Implications from the digital divide literature. *Government Information Quarterly, 26*(1), 89–97. doi:10.1016/j.giq.2008.05.004

Hernandez, U. I., Rodriguez, F. J. A., & Martin, M. V. (2010). *Use processes modeling requirements based on elements of BPMN and UML use case diagrams*. Paper presented at the Second International Conference on Software Technology and Engineering (ICSTE 2010), San Juan, Puerto Rico, United States. doi:10.1109/ICSTE.2010.5608758

Ho, A. T. (2002). Reinventing local governments and the e-government initiative. *Public Administration Review, 62*(4), 434–444. doi:10.1111/0033-3352.00197

Holden, S. H., Norris, D. F., & Fletcher, P. D. (2003). Electronic government at the local level: Progress to date and future issues. *Public Performance and Management Review, 26*(4), 325–344. doi:10.1177/15309576030260004002

Holmes, D. (2001). *E-business strategies for government*. London, UK: Nicholas Brealey Publishing.

Hommes, B., & van Reijswoud, V. (2000). *Assessing the quality of business process modeling techniques*. Paper presented at the 33rd Hawaii International Conference on System Sciences, Maui, Hawaii. doi:10.1109/HICSS.2000.926591

Horan, T. A., & Abhichandani, T. (2006). Evaluating user satisfaction in an e-government initiative: Results of structural equation modeling and focus group discussions. *Journal of Information Technology Management, 17*(4), 33–44.

Horsburgh, S., Goldfinch, S., & Gauld, R. (2011). Is public trust in government associated with trust in e-government? *Social Science Computer Review, 29*(2), 232–241. doi:10.1177/0894439310368130

Hu, G., Shi, J., Pan, W., & Wang, J. (2012). A hierarchical model of e-government service capability: An empirical analysis. *Government Information Quarterly, 29*(4), 564–572. doi:10.1016/j.giq.2012.04.007

Huang, J., & Shyu, S. H. (2008). E-government Web site enhancement opportunities: A learning perspective. *The Electronic Library, 26*(4), 545–560. doi:10.1108/02640470810893783

Huang, Z., & Bwoma, O. P. (2003). An overview of critical issues of e-government. *International Association for Computer Information Systems, 4*(1), 164–170.

Huckvale, T., & Ould, M. (1995). Process modeling – Who, what and how: Role activity diagramming. In V. Grover & W. J. Kettinger (Eds.), *Business process change: Reengineering concepts, methods and technologies* (pp. 330–349). London, UK: Idea Group Publishing.

Hughes, M., Scott, M., & Golden, W. (2006). The role of business process redesign in creating e-government in Ireland. *Business Process Management Journal, 12*(1), 76–87. doi:10.1108/14637150610643779

Irani, Z., & Dwivedi, Y. K. (2008). Editorial. *Transforming Government: People. Process and Policy, 2*(4), 221–224.

Irani, Z., Elliman, T., & Jackson, P. (2007). Electronic transformation of government in the UK: A research agenda. *European Journal of Information Systems, 16*(4), 327–335. doi:10.1057/palgrave.ejis.3000698

Irani, Z., Themistocleous, M., & Love, P. E. D. (2003). The impact of enterprise application integration on information system lifecycles. *Information & Management, 41*(2), 177–187. doi:10.1016/S0378-7206(03)00046-6

Irani, Z., Weerakkody, V., Kamal, M., Hindi, N. M., Osman, I. H., & Anouze, A. L. et al. (2012). An analysis of methodologies utilized in e-government research: A user satisfaction perspective. *Journal of Enterprise Information Management, 25*(3), 298–313. doi:10.1108/17410391211224417

Jaeger, P. T. (2003). The endless wire: E-government as global phenomenon. *Government Information Quarterly, 20*(4), 323–331. doi:10.1016/j.giq.2003.08.003

Jaeger, P. T., & Thompson, K. M. (2004). Social information behavior and the democratic process: Information poverty, normative behavior, and electronic government in the United States. *Library & Information Science Research, 26*(1), 94–107. doi:10.1016/j.lisr.2003.11.006

James, G. (2000). Empowering bureaucrats. *MC Technology Marketing Intelligence*, *20*(12), 62–68.

Jones, S., Hackney, R., & Irani, Z. (2007). Towards e-Government transformation: Conceptualizing "citizen engagement": A research note. *Transforming Government: People. Process and Policy*, *1*(2), 145–152.

Jones, S., Irani, Z., & Sharif, A. (2007). *E-government evaluation: Reflections on three organizational case studies*. Paper presented at the 40th Hawaii International Conference on System Sciences, Waikoloa, Big Island, HI. doi:10.1109/HICSS.2007.189

Kalpic, B., & Bernus, P. (2006). Business process modeling through the knowledge management perspective. *Journal of Knowledge Management*, *10*(3), 40–56. doi:10.1108/13673270610670849

Kasemsap, K. (2015a). The role of e-business adoption in the business world. In N. Ray, D. Das, S. Chaudhuri, & A. Ghosh (Eds.), *Strategic infrastructure development for economic growth and social change* (pp. 51–63). Hershey, PA: IGI Global. doi:10.4018/978-1-4666-7470-7.ch005

Kasemsap, K. (2015b). The role of electronic commerce in the global business environments. In F. Cipolla-Ficarra (Ed.), *Handbook of research on interactive information quality in expanding social network communications* (pp. 304–324). Hershey, PA: IGI Global. doi:10.4018/978-1-4666-7377-9.ch019

Kasemsap, K. (2015c). The role of information system within enterprise architecture and their impact on business performance. In M. Wadhwa & A. Harper (Eds.), *Technology, innovation, and enterprise transformation* (pp. 262–284). Hershey, PA: IGI Global. doi:10.4018/978-1-4666-6473-9.ch012

Kaylor, C. (2005). The next wave of e-government: The challenges of data architecture. *Bulletin of the American Society for Information Science and Technology*, *31*(2), 18–22. doi:10.1002/bult.1720310207

Kersten, B., & Verhoef, C. (2003). IT portfolio management: A banker's perspective on IT. *Cutter IT Journal*, *16*(4), 34–40.

Khalil, O. E. M. (2011). e-Government readiness: Does national culture matter? *Government Information Quarterly*, *28*(3), 388–399. doi:10.1016/j.giq.2010.06.011

Kim, H. J., Pan, G., & Pan, S. L. (2007). Managing IT-enabled transformation in the public sector: A case study on e-government in South Korea. *Government Information Quarterly*, *24*(2), 338–352. doi:10.1016/j.giq.2006.09.007

Kim, S., Kim, H. J., & Lee, H. (2009). An institutional analysis of an e-government system for anti-corruption: The case of OPEN. *Government Information Quarterly*, *26*(1), 42–50. doi:10.1016/j.giq.2008.09.002

Kovacic, Z. J. (2005). The impact of national culture on worldwide e-government readiness. *Informing Science: International Journal of an Emerging Discipline*, *8*, 143–158.

Kueng, P., Kawalek, P., & Bichler, P. (1996). *How to compose an object-oriented business process model?* Paper presented at the IFIP WG8.1/WG8.2 Working Conference, Atlanta, GA. doi:10.1007/978-0-387-35080-6_7

Kumar, S. P., Umashankar, C., Rani, J. K., & Ramana, V. V. V. (2010). e-Governance applications for citizens: Issues and framework. *International Journal on Computer Science and Engineering*, *2*(7), 2362–2365.

Kumar, V., Murkerji, B., Butt, I., & Persaud, A. (2007). Factors for successful e-government adoption: A conceptual framework. *The Electronic Journal of E-Government*, *5*(1), 63–76.

Landsbergen, D. J. Jr, & Wolken, G. J. Jr. (2001). Realizing the promise: Government information systems and the fourth generation of information technology. *Public Administration Review*, *61*(2), 206–220. doi:10.1111/0033-3352.00023

Lankhorst, M. (2005). *Enterprise architecture at work: Modelling, communication, and analysis.* Berlin, Germany: Springer–Verlag.

Larsen, E., & Rainie, L. (2002). *The rise of the e-citizen: How people use government agencies' web sites.* Washington, DC: Pew Internet and American Life Project.

Layne, K., & Lee, J. (2001). Developing fully functional e-government: A four stage model. *Government Information Quarterly*, *18*(2), 122–136. doi:10.1016/S0740-624X(01)00066-1

Lean, O. K., Zailani, S., Ramayah, T., & Fernando, Y. (2009). Factors influencing intention to use e-government services among citizens in Malaysia. *International Journal of Information Management*, *29*(6), 458–475. doi:10.1016/j.ijinfomgt.2009.03.012

Lin, F., Fofanah, S. S., & Liang, D. (2011). Assessing citizen adoption of e-Government initiatives in Gambia: A validation of the technology acceptance model in information systems success. *Government Information Quarterly*, *28*(2), 271–279. doi:10.1016/j.giq.2010.09.004

Lin, F. R., Yang, M. C., & Pai, Y. H. (2002). A generic structure for business process modeling. *Business Process Management Journal*, *8*(1), 19–41. doi:10.1108/14637150210418610

Liu, Y., Zhou, C., & Chen, Y. (2010). *Customer satisfaction measurement model of e-government service.* Paper presented at the 2010 IEEE International Conference on Service Operations and Logistics and Informatics (SOLI), Qingdao, China. doi:10.1109/SOLI.2010.5551542

Luna-Reyes, L. F., Gil-Garcia, J. R., & Romero, G. (2012). Towards a multidimensional model for evaluating electronic government: Proposing a more comprehensive and integrative perspective. *Government Information Quarterly*, *29*(3), 324–334. doi:10.1016/j.giq.2012.03.001

Luo, W., & Tung, Y. (1999). A framework for selecting business process modeling methods. *Industrial Management & Data Systems*, *99*(7), 312–319. doi:10.1108/02635579910262535

Macintosh, A., Robson, E., Smith, E., & Whyte, A. (2003). Electronic democracy and young people. *Social Science Computer Review*, *21*(1), 43–54. doi:10.1177/0894439302238970

Malone, T. W., Yates, J., & Benjamin, R. I. (1987). Electronic markets and electronic hierarchies. *Communications of the ACM*, *30*(6), 484–497. doi:10.1145/214762.214766

Marche, S., & McNiven, J. D. (2003). E-government and e-governance: The future isn't what it used to be. *Canadian Journal of Administrative Sciences*, *20*(1), 74–86. doi:10.1111/j.1936-4490.2003.tb00306.x

McAdam, R., & Donaghy, J. (1999). Business process re-engineering in the public sector: A study of staff perceptions and critical success factors. *Business Process Management Journal*, *5*(1), 33–49. doi:10.1108/14637159910249135

McIvor, R., McHugh, M., & Cadden, C. (2002). Internet technologies: Supporting transparency in the public sector. *International Journal of Public Sector Management*, *15*(3), 170–187. doi:10.1108/09513550210423352

Millard, J. (2006). User attitudes to e-government citizen services in Europe. *International Journal of Electronic Government Research*, *2*(2), 49–58. doi:10.4018/jegr.2006040103

Mnjama, N., & Wamukoya, J. (2007). E-government and records management: An assessment tool for e-records readiness in government. *The Electronic Library*, 25(3), 274–284. doi:10.1108/02640470710754797

Moon, M. J. (2002). The evolution of e-government among municipalities: Rhetoric or reality. *Public Administration Review*, 62(4), 424–433. doi:10.1111/0033-3352.00196

Morgeson, F. V., VanAmburg, D., & Mithas, S. (2011). Misplaced trust? Exploring the structure of the e-government–citizen trust relationship. *Journal of Public Administration: Research and Theory*, 21(2), 257–283. doi:10.1093/jopart/muq006

Mutula, S. M., & Mostert, J. (2010). Challenges and opportunities of e-government in South Africa. *The Electronic Library*, 28(1), 38–53. doi:10.1108/02640471011023360

Mutula, S. M., & Van Brakel, P. (2006). Assessment of e-readiness of small and medium-sized enterprises (SMEs) in the ICT sector in Botswana with respect to information access. *The Electronic Library*, 24(3), 402–417. doi:10.1108/02640470610671240

Nam, T. (2014). Determining the type of e-government use. *Government Information Quarterly*, 31(2), 211–220. doi:10.1016/j.giq.2013.09.006

Ndou, V. (2004). E-government for developing countries: Opportunities and challenges. *The Electronic Journal on Information Systems in Developing Countries*, 18(1), 1–24.

Nograšek, J., & Vintar, M. (2014). E-government and organisational transformation of government: Black box revisited? *Government Information Quarterly*, 31(1), 108–118. doi:10.1016/j.giq.2013.07.006

O'Donnell, O., & Humphreys, P. C. (2003). *E-government and the decentralization of service delivery*. Dublin, Ireland: Institute of Public Administration.

Oliver, R. L. (1993). Cognitive, affective, and attribute bases of the satisfaction response. *The Journal of Consumer Research*, 20(3), 418–430. doi:10.1086/209358

Oliver, R. L. (1999). Whence consumer loyalty. *Journal of Marketing*, 63(4), 33–44. doi:10.2307/1252099

Business process model and notation (BPMN). (2013, March). OMG. Retrieved from http://www.omg.org/spec/BPMN/2.0/

Ongaro, E. (2004). Process management in the public sector: The experience of one-stop shops in Italy. *International Journal of Public Sector Management*, 17(1), 81–107. doi:10.1108/09513550410515592

Ould, M. A. (1995). *Business processes: Modelling and analysis for re-engineering and improvement*. New York, NY: John Wiley & Sons.

Ozkan, S., & Kanat, I. E. (2011). e-Government adoption model based on theory of planned behavior: Empirical validation. *Government Information Quarterly*, 28(4), 503–513. doi:10.1016/j.giq.2010.10.007

Parent, M., Vandebeek, C. A., & Gemino, A. C. (2005). Building citizen trust through e-government. *Government Information Quarterly*, 22(4), 720–736. doi:10.1016/j.giq.2005.10.001

Pavlou, P. (2003). Consumer acceptance of electronic commerce: Integrating trust and risk with the technology acceptance model. *International Journal of Electronic Commerce*, 7(3), 69–103.

Pollitt, C. (2010). Technological change: A central yet neglected feature of public administration. *NISPAcee Journal of Public Administration and Policy*, *3*(2), 31–53. doi:10.2478/v10110-010-0003-z

Rai, A., Lang, S., & Welker, R. (2002). Assessing the validity of IS success models: An empirical test and theoretical analysis. *Information Systems Research*, *13*(1), 50–69. doi:10.1287/isre.13.1.50.96

Ramani, S., & Kumaraswamy, Y. S. (2013). The role of business process model in customer centric eGovernment system. *International Journal of Computers and Applications*, *72*(12), 13–23. doi:10.5120/12545-9003

Reddick, C. G. (2005). Citizen interaction with e-government: From the streets to servers? *Government Information Quarterly*, *22*(1), 38–57. doi:10.1016/j.giq.2004.10.003

Reddick, C. G., & Roy, J. (2013). Business perceptions and satisfaction with e-government: Findings from a Canadian survey. *Government Information Quarterly*, *30*(1), 1–9. doi:10.1016/j.giq.2012.06.009

Relly, J. E., & Sabharwal, M. (2009). Perceptions of transparency of government policymaking: A cross-national study. *Government Information Quarterly*, *26*(1), 148–157. doi:10.1016/j.giq.2008.04.002

Relyea, H. C. (2002). E-gov: Introduction and overview. *Government Information Quarterly*, *19*(1), 9–35. doi:10.1016/S0740-624X(01)00096-X

Riley, B. T. (2001). *Electronic governance and electronic democracy: Living and working in the connected world. Brisbane, Australia*. Australia: Commonwealth Centre for Electronic Governance.

Rowley, J. (2011). e-Government stakeholders: Who are they and what do they want? *International Journal of Information Management*, *31*(1), 53–62. doi:10.1016/j.ijinfomgt.2010.05.005

Sarantis, D., Charalabidis, Y., & Askounis, D. (2011). A goal-driven management framework for electronic government transformation projects implementation. *Government Information Quarterly*, *28*(1), 117–128. doi:10.1016/j.giq.2009.10.006

Saven, S. (2003). Business process modeling: Review and framework. *International Journal of Production Economics*, *90*(2), 129–149. doi:10.1016/S0925-5273(03)00102-6

Scheer, A. W. (2000). *ARIS – Business process modeling*. Berlin, Germany: Springer–Verlag. doi:10.1007/978-3-642-57108-4

Scherlis, W. L., & Eisenberg, J. (2003). IT research, innovation, and e-government. *Communications of the ACM*, *46*(1), 67–68. doi:10.1145/602421.602455

Scholl, H. (2001). *Applying stakeholder theory to e-government: Benefits and limits*. Albany, NY: Center for Technology in Government, University at Albany.

Seethamraju, R. (2012). Business process management: A missing link in business education. *Business Process Management Journal*, *18*(3), 532–547. doi:10.1108/14637151211232696

Sensuse, D. I., & Ramadhan, A. (2012). The relationships of soft systems methodology (SSM), business process modeling and e-Government. *International Journal of Advanced Computer Science and Applications*, *3*(1), 179–183.

Serrano-Cinca, C., Rueda-Tomas, M., & Portillo-Tarragona, P. (2009). Determinants of e-government extension. *Online Information Review*, *33*(3), 476–498. doi:10.1108/14684520910969916

Shankar, V., Smith, A. K., & Rangaswamy, A. (2003). Customer satisfaction and loyalty in online and offline environments. *Journal of Research in Marketing*, *20*(2), 153–175. doi:10.1016/S0167-8116(03)00016-8

Siau, K., & Long, Y. (2006). Using social development lenses to understand e-government development. *Journal of Global Information Management*, *14*(1), 47–62. doi:10.4018/jgim.2006010103

Sipior, J. C., & Ward, B. T. (2005). Bridging the digital divide for e-government inclusion: A United States case study. *The Electronic. Journal of E-Government*, *3*(3), 137–146.

Spencer, E. P. (1999). The reengineering concept: A graphic model. *Journal of Business Education*, *74*(5), 311–315. doi:10.1080/08832329909601704

Stemberger, M. I., & Jaklic, J. (2007). Towards e-government by business process change: A methodology for public sector. *International Journal of Information Management*, *27*(4), 221–232. doi:10.1016/j.ijinfomgt.2007.02.006

Sultan, A., AlArfaj, K. A., & AlKutbi, G. A. (2012). Analytic hierarchy process for the success of e-government. *Business Strategy Series*, *13*(6), 295–306. doi:10.1108/17515631211286146

Tavana, M., Zandi, F., & Katehakis, M. N. (2013). A hybrid fuzzy group ANP–TOPSIS framework for assessment of e-government readiness from a CiRM perspective. *Information & Management*, *50*(7), 383–397. doi:10.1016/j.im.2013.05.008

Thibodeau, P. (2000). E-government spending to soar through 2005. *Computerworld*, *34*(17), 12–13.

Thomas, J. C., & Streib, G. (2003). The new face of government: Citizen-initiated contacts in the era of e-Government. *Journal of Public Administration: Research and Theory*, *13*(1), 83–102. doi:10.1093/jpart/mug010

Thompson, D. V., Rust, R. T., & Rhoda, J. (2005). The business value of e-government for small firms. *International Journal of Service Industry Management*, *16*(4), 385–407. doi:10.1108/09564230510614022

Thong, J. Y. L., Yap, C. S., & Seah, K. L. (2000). Business process reengineering: The case of the Housing Development Board in Singapore. *Journal of Management Information Systems*, *17*(1), 245–270.

Tohidi, H. (2011). E-government and its different dimensions: Iran. *Procedia-Computer Science Journal*, *3*, 1101–1105. doi:10.1016/j.procs.2010.12.179

Tolbert, C. J., & Mossberger, K. (2006). The effects of e-government on trust and confidence in government. *Public Administration Review*, *66*(3), 354–369. doi:10.1111/j.1540-6210.2006.00594.x

Torres, L., Pina, V., & Acerete, B. (2005). E-government developments on delivering public services among EU cities. *Government Information Quarterly*, *22*(2), 217–238. doi:10.1016/j.giq.2005.02.004

Tour, T. P. S., & Dhir, T. (2011). Benefits of integrated business planning, forecasting, and process management. *Business Strategy Series*, *12*(6), 275–288. doi:10.1108/17515631111185914

Tsohou, A., Lee, H., Irani, Z., Weerakkody, V., Osman, I. H., Anouze, A. L., & Medeni, T. (2013). Proposing a reference process model for the citizen-centric evaluation of e-government services. *Transforming Government: People, Process and Policy*, *7*(2), 240–255.

Ubaldi, B. (2011). The impact of the economic and financial crisis on e-government in OECD member countries. *European Journal of ePractise, 11*, 5–18.

United Nations. (2012). *United Nations e-government survey 2012: E-government for the people.* New York, NY: United Nations.

Valdés, G., Solar, M., Astudillo, H., Iribarren, M., Concha, G., & Visconti, M. (2011). Conception, development and implementation of an e-Government maturity model in public agencies. *Government Information Quarterly*, *28*(2), 176–187. doi:10.1016/j.giq.2010.04.007

van der Aalst, W. M. P. (1999). Process-oriented architectures for electronic commerce and interorganizational workflow. *Information Systems, 24*(8), 639–671. doi:10.1016/S0306-4379(00)00003-X

van der Vyver, A., & Rajapakse, J. (2012). E-government adoption and business process reengineering in developing countries: Sri Lankan and South African case studies. *International Journal of Innovation. Management and Technology, 3*(6), 778–783.

Venkatesh, V., Chan, F., & Thong, J. (2012). Designing e-government services: Key service attributes and citizens' preference structures. *Journal of Operations Management, 30*(1/2), 116–133. doi:10.1016/j.jom.2011.10.001

Venkatraman, V. (1994). IT-enabled business transformation: From automation to business scope redefinition. *Sloan Management Review, 35*(2), 73–87.

Verginadis, Y., & Mentzas, G. (2008). Agents and workflow engines for inter-organizational workflows in e-government cases. *Business Process Management Journal, 14*(2), 188–203. doi:10.1108/14637150810864925

Vernadat, F. (1996). *Enterprise modelling and integration: Principles and applications.* London, UK: Chapman & Hall.

Wang, L., Bretschneider, S., & Gant, J. (2005). *Evaluating web-based e-government services with a citizen-centric approach.* Paper presented at the 38th Annual Hawaii International Conference on Systems Sciences, Big Island, HI. doi:10.1109/HICSS.2005.252

Warkentin, M., Gefen, D., Pavlou, P., & Rose, G. (2002). Encouraging citizen adoption of e-government by building trust. *Electronic Markets, 12*(3), 157–162. doi:10.1080/101967802320245929

Watson, R. T., & Mundy, B. (2001). A strategic perspective of electronic democracy. *Communications of the ACM, 44*(1), 27–30. doi:10.1145/357489.357499

Weerakkody, V., & Dhillon, G. (2008). Moving from e-government to t-government: A study of process reengineering challenges in a UK local authority perspective. *International Journal of Electronic Government Research, 4*(4), 1–16. doi:10.4018/jegr.2008100101

Weerakkody, V., El-Haddadeh, R., Sabol, T., Ghoneim, A., & Dzupka, P. (2012). E-government implementation strategies in developed and transition economies: A comparative study. *International Journal of Information Management, 32*(1), 66–74. doi:10.1016/j.ijinfomgt.2011.10.005

Weerakkody, V., Janssen, M., & Dwivedi, Y. K. (2011). Transformational change and business process reengineering (BPR): Lessons from the British and Dutch public sector. *Government Information Quarterly, 28*(3), 320–328. doi:10.1016/j.giq.2010.07.010

Weerakkody, V., Jones, S., & Olsen, E. (2007). E-government: A comparison of strategies in local authorities in the UK and Norway. *International Journal of Electronic Business, 5*(2), 141–159. doi:10.1504/IJEB.2007.012970

Welch, E. W., Hinnant, C. C., & Moon, M. J. (2004). Linking citizen satisfaction with e-government and trust in government. *Journal of Public Administration: Research and Theory, 15*(3), 371–391. doi:10.1093/jopart/mui021

West, D. M. (2004). E-government and the transformation of service delivery and citizen attitudes. *Public Administration Review, 64*(1), 15–27. doi:10.1111/j.1540-6210.2004.00343.x

Wimmer, M. (2002). A European perspective towards online one-stop government: The eGOV project. *Electronic Commerce Research and Applications, 1*(1), 92–103. doi:10.1016/S1567-4223(02)00008-X

Wixom, B. H., & Todd, P. (2005). A theoretical integration of user satisfaction and technology acceptance. *Information Systems Research, 16*(1), 85–102. doi:10.1287/isre.1050.0042

Woodroof, J., & Burg, W. (2003). Satisfaction/dissatisfaction: Are users predisposed? *Information & Management, 40*(4), 317–324. doi:10.1016/S0378-7206(02)00013-7

Yang, K., & Rho, S. Y. (2007). E-government for better performance: Promises, realities, and challenges. *International Journal of Public Administration, 30*(11), 1197–1217. doi:10.1080/01900690701225556

Yang, Z., Jun, M., & Peterson, R. (2004). Measuring costumer perceived online service quality: Scale development and managerial implications. *International Journal of Operations & Production Management, 24*(11/12), 1149–1174. doi:10.1108/01443570410563278

Yildiz, M. (2007). E-government research: Reviewing the literature, limitations, and ways forward. *Government Information Quarterly, 24*(3), 646–665. doi:10.1016/j.giq.2007.01.002

Zhang, N., Guo, X., Chen, G., & Chau, P. (2009). Impact of perceived fit on e-Government user evaluation: A study with a Chinese cultural context. *Journal of Global Information Management, 17*(1), 49–69. doi:10.4018/jgim.2009010103

ADDITIONAL READINGS

Belanger, F., & Carter, L. (2012). Digitizing government interactions with constituents: An historical review of e-government research in information systems. *Journal of the Association for Information Systems, 13*(5), 363–394.

Blasini, J., & Leist, S. (2013). Success factors in process performance management. *Business Process Management Journal, 19*(3), 477–495. doi:10.1108/14637151311319914

Bouchbout, K., Akoka, J., & Alimazighi, Z. (2012). An MDA-based framework for collaborative business process modeling. *Business Process Management Journal, 18*(6), 919–948. doi:10.1108/14637151211283357

Dwivedi, Y. K., Weerakkody, V., & Janssen, M. (2012). Moving towards maturity: Challenges to successful e-government implementation and diffusion. *ACM SIGMIS Database, 42*(4), 11–22. doi:10.1145/2096140.2096142

Fady, R., & Abd El Aziz, R. (2012). Process architecture and process modeling in the Egyptian industry: The case of Incom. *International Journal of Enterprise Network Management, 5*(1), 33–42.

Grimmelikhuijsen, S. (2012). Linking transparency, knowledge and citizen trust in government: An experiment. *International Review of Administrative Sciences, 78*(1), 50–73. doi:10.1177/0020852311429667

Gruhn, V., & Laue, R. (2013). A heuristic method for detecting problems in business process models. *Business Process Management Journal, 16*(5), 806–821.

Hanson, K., Kararach, G., & Shaw, T. M. (2012). *Rethinking development challenges for public policy: Insights from contemporary Africa.* Hampshire, UK: Palgrave Macmillan. doi:10.1057/9780230393271

Hernaus, T., Bach, M. P., & Vuksic, V. B. (2012). Influence of strategic approach to BPM on financial and non-financial performance. *Baltic Journal of Management, 7*(4), 376–396. doi:10.1108/17465261211272148

Iden, J. (2012). Investigating process management in firms with quality systems: A multi-case study. *Business Process Management Journal, 18*(1), 104–121. doi:10.1108/14637151211215037

Isik, O., Mertens, W., & Van den Bergh, J. (2013). Practices of knowledge intensive process management: Quantitative insights. *Business Process Management Journal, 19*(3), 515–534. doi:10.1108/14637151311319932

Kang, B., Kim, D., & Kang, S. H. (2012). Periodic performance prediction for real-time business process monitoring. *Industrial Management & Data Systems, 112*(1), 4–23. doi:10.1108/02635571211193617

Liang, S. W., & Lu, H. P. (2013). Adoption of e-government services: An empirical study of the online tax filing system in Taiwan. *Online Information Review, 37*(3), 424–442. doi:10.1108/OIR-01-2012-0004

Lin, H. F. (2013). The effects of knowledge management capabilities and partnership attributes on the stage-based e-business diffusion. *Internet Research, 23*(4), 439–464. doi:10.1108/IntR-11-2012-0233

Magal, S. R., & Word, J. (2012). *Integrated business processes with ERP systems*. Hoboken, NJ: John Wiley & Sons.

Mergel, I. (2012). The social media innovation challenge in the public sector. Information Polity. *The International Journal of Government & Democracy in the Information Age, 17*(3/4), 281–292.

Nisbet, E. C., Stoycheff, E., & Pearce, K. E. (2012). Internet use and democratic demands: A multinational, multilevel model of Internet use and citizen attitudes about democracy. *Journal of Communication, 62*(2), 249–265. doi:10.1111/j.1460-2466.2012.01627.x

Norris, D. F., & Reddick, C. G. (2013). Local e-government in the United States: Transformation or incremental change? *Public Administration Review, 73*(1), 165–175. doi:10.1111/j.1540-6210.2012.02647.x

Ofner, M. H., Otto, B., & Osterle, H. (2012). Integrating a data quality perspective into business process management. *Business Process Management Journal, 18*(6), 1036–1067. doi:10.1108/14637151211283401

Olufemi, F. J. (2012). Electronic governance: Myth or opportunity for Nigerian public administration? *International Journal of Academic Research in Business and Social Sciences, 2*(9), 1–19.

Solaimani, S., & Bouwman, H. (2012). A framework for the alignment of business model and business processes: A generic model for trans-sector innovation. *Business Process Management Journal, 18*(4), 655–679. doi:10.1108/14637151211253783

Stavenko, Y., Kazantsev, N., & Gromoff, A. (2013). Business process model reasoning: From workflow to case management. *Procedia Technology, 9*, 806–811. doi:10.1016/j.protcy.2013.12.089

Sultan, A., AlArfaj, K. A., & AlKutbi, G. A. (2012). Analytic hierarchy process for the success of e-government. *Business Strategy Series, 13*(6), 295–306. doi:10.1108/17515631211286146

Thiault, D. (2012). *Managing performance through business processes*. Seattle, WA: CreateSpace.

Tzikopoulos, A., Manouselis, N., Kastrantas, K., & Costopoulou, C. (2012). An online information system to support blended training of rural SMEs on e-government. *Program: Electronic Library and Information Systems*, *46*(1), 123–143. doi:10.1108/00330331211204593

Voutinioti, A. (2013). Determinants of user adoption of e-government services in Greece and the role of citizen service centres. *Procedia Technology*, *8*, 238–244. doi:10.1016/j.protcy.2013.11.033

Zhao, F. (2013). An empirical study of cultural dimensions and e-government development: Implications of the findings and strategies. *Behaviour & Information Technology*, *32*(3), 294–306. doi:10.1080/0144929X.2011.644580

KEY TERMS AND DEFINITIONS

Business Process Management: A management technique that scrutinizes the processes that a company goes through to perform certain tasks.

Business Process Modeling: The documentation of a business system using a combination of text and graphical notation.

Business Process Reengineering: The thorough rethinking of all business processes, job definitions, management systems, organizational structure, work flow, and underlying assumptions and beliefs.

Citizen: A person who is entitled to enjoy all the legal rights and privileges granted by a state to people comprising its constituency.

eGovernment: The use of information and communications technology (ICT) to improve the activities of public sector organizations.

Government: The act or process of governing, especially the control and administration of public policy in a political unit.

Information Technology: A broad term that includes the development, installing and use of anything to do with computing and telecommunications.

Public Sector: The part of the economy that is controlled or funded by the government.

Chapter 16
Customer Experience Management System at a University's Student Support Services:
An Organizational Ambidexterity Perspective

Amevi Kouassi
The University of Sheffield, UK

Jorge Tiago Martins
The University of Sheffield, UK

Andreea Molnar
Portsmouth University, UK

ABSTRACT

The study reported in this chapter evaluates how the Customer Experience Management System (CEMS) used by a University's Student Support Services (StuSS) responds to the objectives of capturing, storing, extracting, interpreting, distributing, using and reporting customer experience information for creating organisational value. Theoretically, the study draws on the concept of organizational ambidexterity. Concerning the research design, the study was undertaken using qualitative methods of data collection and interpretivist methods of data analysis. It has been inductively discovered that the availability of customer experience information obtained through the CEMS allows StuSS to respond effectively to different student needs. Organizationally, there is clarity concerning the ownership and management of customer relationships. Individual student data is collected, coordinated and distributed across lines of business. Because of this, StuSS is able to consistently identify customers across touch points and channels. Further suggestions are advanced to improve StuSS's analytical investigation capability to derive descriptive and predictive customer information, through applying data mining models to the information that is currently collected.

DOI: 10.4018/978-1-4666-8833-9.ch016

INTRODUCTION

In the context of Higher Education (HE), the quality of students' experience can be considered a key component in the total quality management process (Douglas, McClelland, & Davis, 2008; Kanji, Malek, & Tambi, 1999; Tsinidou, Gerogiannis, & Fitsilis, 2010; Zineldin, Akdag, & Vasicheva, 2011), and consequently a fertile ground for the study of customer experience management systems (CEMS).

The emergent adoption and use of information systems to improve the student-institution relationship is expected to facilitate a more student-centric focus, improve customer data and process management, increase student loyalty, and contribute to students' overall satisfaction with their institution's programs and services (Seeman, & O'Hara, 2006; Hilbert, Schönbrunn, & Schmode, 2007; Daradoumis, Rodriguez-Ardura, Faulin, Juan, Xhafa, & Martinez-Lopez, 2010).

It is not open to debate that Higher Education Institutions (HEIs) strive to offer the best possible learning experience to their students. There is also a growing stream of literature embracing the student-customer model (Browne, Kaldenberg, Browne, & Brown, 1998; Munteanu, Ceobanu, Bobalca, & Anton, 2010; Wright, 2008), and indeed arguing that a customer focus in HE "provides a framework for ensuring student satisfaction by embedding quality into the learning process through quality instruction, quality assessment, and greater attention to students' needs" (Mark, 2013, p. 8). Consequently, HEIs are continuously seeking ways to improve the quality of the total learning experience by investigating approaches to quality systems (Rowley, 1996). Being aligned with this objective, the study reported in this chapter aims to evaluate the CEMS used by the Student Support Services (StuSS) at a UK-based HEI, serving a population of over 25.000 students.

The mission of StuSS is to help students with enquiries that pertain to their records (student status documentation, certifying letters, atten-

dance monitoring, exam services, summary of results and transcripts of qualification), and to point students to the most relevant academic and well-being information sources and services. Their CEMS is based on a customer experience survey that is sent to students personally visiting or contacting StuSS online. The survey collects customer experience information through basic indicators such as: (1) initial categorisation of feedback information (compliment, comment, suggestion, complaint, other); (2) specification of service requested; (3) degree of service satisfaction; (4) open elicitation of what StuSS has done well; (5) open elicitation of what StuSS can improve; and (6) open elicitation of what would the user tell a friend about StuSS. Data collected from the survey is stored at an enquiry recording system – a web-based application that provides StuSS with information about not only how many users the service that served but also who they were and which enquiries they have made.

The wider objective of the chapter is to understand how this system responds to the objectives of capturing, storing, extracting, interpreting, distributing, using and reporting customer experience information for creating organisational value, understood here as the ability to simultaneously satisfy existing customers while using competitive pressure to innovate (Schreuders, & Legesse, 2012). This duality is at the core of organisational ambidexterity, or in other words "the ability to simultaneously pursue both incremental and discontinuous innovation and change" (Tushman, & O'Reilly, 1996). In that sense, it becomes necessary to understand the ways in which CEMS is currently used as a pathway to building organisational ambidexterity at StuSS.

The remainder of the chapter develops as follows. The "Background" section provides a literature review on the concepts of "customer experience management", "organizational ambidexterity", and "information systems evaluation". An understanding of these intersecting frameworks is necessary before delving into the empirical stage of the study and will prepare the reader for the interpretive evaluation performed on the CEMS, with the view to understand how it supports the refinement of current practice and the search for innovation in practice. The "Methodology" section offers an overview of the study's alignment in terms of research philosophy, research methodology and research design. The following section "Customer Centricity" reports the findings in the form of a Grounded Theory narrative. The chapter closes with a section on "Solutions and Recommendations" where we recommend an extension of StuSS's data mining capabilities, and a "Conclusion" section where the conceptual links between customer experience management and organizational ambidexterity are reprised.

BACKGROUND

Customer Experience Management

The concept of 'customer experience' has progressively expanded as an area of concern to scholars, practitioners, and service managers. Being initially considered as an issue pertaining essentially to entertainment organisations, it has now captured the interest of various sectors, with a growing body of research emphasising the centrality of experience beyond the simple action of offering consumers a product or service (Mascarenhas, Kesavan, &Bernacchi, 2006; Gentile, Spiller, & Noci, 2007; Verhoef, Lemon, Parasuraman, Roggeveen, Tsiros, & Schlesinger, 2009; Johnston, & Kong, 2011), and embracing the dimensions of emotional and functional benefits to the consumer (Ryder, 2007). The wide encompassing scope of the concept is apprehended by the definition advanced by Laming and Mason (2014), who understand customer experience as "the physical and emotional experiences occurring through the interactions with the product and/or service offering of a brand from point of first direct, conscious contact, through the total journey to

the post-consumption stage" Laming and Mason (2014). This will be the operational definition of customer experience throughout the study reported in this chapter.

In keeping with this definition, the internal and subjective points of view (Nagasawa, 2008), as well the direct or indirect responses that customers extract from any contact with an organisation are manifestations of customer experience. This accentuates the pervasive character of experience, particularly if we consider that individuals interact with organisations through a variety of channels: personal face-to-face communications, telephone, e-mails and web presence all promote contact with customers, all concur to meet individual customer needs, and all contribute to the shaping of some sort of experience. Thus, the growth of customer contact points is an opportunity for organisations to practice positive customer responsiveness and use these points to communicate their understanding and ability to meet individual customers' needs (Matthews, & Lawley, 2006).

Comprehending what customers expect, what factors influence customer expectations and how service providers satisfy customers' different needs are increasingly becoming critical success factors (Hsieh and Yuan, 2010). The evaluation of services' reliability is also increasingly dependent on the information available on experience (Galetzka, Verhoeven, & Pruyn, 2006). Furthermore, since customer experience can easily revert into words-of-mouth recommendations or criticism, advertising, news reports and reviews, the interest in the concept has increased considerably in recent years (Rageh Melewar, & Woodside, 2013).

Poor customer experience reduces the potential customer base of an organisation and in turn the organisation's performance itself (Svari, Slantten, Svensson,& Edvardsson, 2011). Indeed, a negative customer experience not only forces the existing customers to migrate to competitors but may also result in increased difficulties to attract new customers (Tseng, Qinhai & Su, 1999).

When collected and used strategically, customer experience information enhances organisational performance in the design of integrated areas of activity such as marketing, human resources management, operations, and information systems management (Teixeira, Patricio, Nunes, Nobrega, Raymond, & Constantine, 2012). Being ascribed greater prestige and recognition is another related benefit if organisations succeed in building a strong and well-balanced relationship with their customers (Aurier, & Siadou-Martine, 2007).

However, the challenge remains as to how organisations can systematically manage their customers' experiences in order to make them not only better for the customer but also better for the organisation's staff, and more efficient (Johnston, & Kong, 2011).

A natural departure point is to consider how relationships with customers evolve and contribute towards shaping experience. As the relationship becomes deeper, relational parties start gaining experience (Dagger, & O'Brien, 2009). In this process, empowering and involving the internal staff is an important step towards a real customer experience management because customer experience management will not succeed if it is not clearly understood and properly practiced by managers and employees who directly interact with the customers (Smith, 2006). In addition, organisations' personnel are instrumental in the creation and provision of quality services and products (Smith and Lewis, 1989), and quality is seen as a major contributor to the effectiveness of service provision in a context of increased competition.

It is also important to assert that the ultimate purpose of customer experience management is brand success and differentiation from competitors. Experience has indeed been labelled as the next competitive battleground (Teixeira, Patricio, Nunes, Nobrega, Raymond, & Constantine, 2012). This strategic orientation implies a concern with the consistent production of positive experiences as a driver of business profitability and growth (Frow, & Payne, 2007). However, it cannot be a simple exercise in relationship marketing. It requires the recognition of customer experience management as an intellectual integrator of service, quality, relationship and brand (Palmer, 2010). Most significantly, it requires applying customer experience knowledge to improve and innovate. In turn, pursuing the innovation endeavour implies balancing the competing demands of refining current organisational practices and searching for new practices and courses of action. This tension is more clearly understood within the framework of organisational learning theory (March, 1991), where it is proposed that organisations' search strategies related to innovation may be determined by performance feedback (Levinthal, & March, 1991), of which we propose knowledge on customer experience is a good example. Organisations compare performance aspirations with actual performance and it is in this confrontation with performance gaps that strategic choices occur between taking risks and searching for new strategies or searching for the refinement of current practices (Baum, Rowley, Shipilov, & Chuang, 2005).

Organisational Ambidexterity

Organizational theory argues that in order to ensure viability, organizations must achieve a proper balance between exploitation and exploration, where exploitation refers to "refinement, efficiency, selection and implementation" and exploration refers to "search, variation, experimentation and innovation (March, 1991, p.71). However, the persisting idea that organizational success is based on a choice between exploiting current capabilities and pursuing new sources of competitive advantage through exploration is challenged by the concept of ambidextrous organisations, which accounts for organizations' dynamic capability to simultaneously improve existing products and services (exploitation) and entering new product/ service domains (exploration) (Tushman, & O'Reilly, 1996). Ambidextrous organizations excel at "exploit[ing] existing competencies and exploring new opportunities" (Raisch, Birkinshaw, Probst, & Tushman, 2009). Indeed, research on ambidextrous organizations has provided evidence that the simultaneous pursuit of exploration and exploitation is beneficial to organizational performance (Tushman, & O'Reilly, 1996; Gibson, & Birkinshaw, 2004; He, & Wong, 2004; O'Reilly, & Tushman, 2004; van Loy, Martens, & Debackere, 2005; Smith, & Tushman, 2005; Cao, Gedajlovic, & Zhang, 2009; Carmeli, & Halevi, 2009; Jansen, Tempelaar, van den Bosch, & Volberda, 2009; Nemanich, & Vera, 2009; Rothaermel, & Alexandre, 2009; O'Reilly, Harrel, & Tushman, 2010).

An important anchor of organizational ambidexterity is the set of dynamic capabilities that organizations must use in order to perform activities that are not only based on existing knowledge and processes but also on the absorption of new knowledge. These dynamic capabilities can be described as the organization's "ability to integrate, build, and reconfigure internal and external competencies to address rapidly changing environments" (Teece, Pisano, & Schuen, 1997). More recently, they have been related to the ability to sense changes in the competitive environment in terms of customers, technology and competition, but also to the active recognition of opportunities and threats (O'Reilly, & Tushman, 2011). In terms of key managerial traits this requires managers who are capable of hosting contradictions: exploiting old certainties to navigate current business demands, and the renewal of skills, knowledge and expertise with a view to exploring new possibilities and better coping with future changes (Mom, van den Bosch, & Volberda, 2007; Mom, van den Bosch, & Volberda, 2009).

Information Systems Evaluation

The previous sections were concerned with: (1) establishing an understanding of customer experience management as a strategic process that is focused on "a customer's entire experience with a product or a company" (Schmitt, 2003), and (2) relating customer experience management to organizational exploratory and exploitative practices. These practices are greatly helped by CEMS - a "set of tools which allow the management of the user experience and the associated business aspects of the provisioned service" (Perkis et al., 2014). This set of tools typically deals with: (1) the acquisition of customer experience information through basic indicators; (2) the transformation of basic indicators into customer experience metrics; (3) and the production of actions that improve customer satisfaction (Cuadra, Cutanda, Aurelius, Brunnstrom, Lopez de Vergara, Varela, Laulajainen, Morais, Cavalli, Mellouk, Augustin, & Perez-Mateos, 2013).

In order to understand how StuSS makes use of CEMS we endeavour to conduct an evaluation of the system. Evaluating information systems has become a controversial field for numerous scholars and practitioners. Organisations themselves are under pressure to engage in information systems evaluation practices to "benchmark and define costs, benefits, risks and implications of investing in IT/IS systems and infrastructures" (Irani, Sharif, & Love, 2005).

A dominant view on evaluation follows a cost-benefit approach (Willcocks, 1992) and defines the ultimate goal of evaluation as the assessment and improvement of information systems (Remenyi and Sherwood-Smith, 1999). According to this perspective, evaluation can be formal or informal and rooted on financial criteria and technical requirements (Serafeimidis, & Smithson, 2003), as evaluation results are typically used by organisations to plan and perform improvement actions (Lagsten, & Goldkuhl, 2008). However, goal-free evaluation is also possible if the evaluators engage in assessing the information system's effects in fulfilling demonstrated needs of the socio-technical environment in which the system is expected to imprint change (Chen, Osman, & Peng, 2013). Furthermore, according to standard linear models of information systems evaluation that focus on a temporal perspective, evaluation can either be formative or summative, depending on whether it develops during the process of design and development of the information system, or at the end of this process (Beynon-Davies, Owens, & Williams, 2004).

However, in recognising that information systems evaluation is deeply related with social and organisational processes, this chapter will not follow functionalistic evaluation methods and will instead align with an interpretive evaluation approach (Symons, & Walsham, 1988; Avgerou, 1995; Farbey, Land, & Targett, 1999). Information systems are predominately social systems. Consequently the social aspects need to be taken in consideration during an evaluation exercise, as different organisational actors make sense of their situation and interactions with information systems (Jones, & Hughes, 2001). It is therefore expected that, by emphasising the situatedness of social action and knowledge, an interpretive approach to information systems evaluation will promote increased stakeholder commitment and greater opportunities for organisational learning (Hirschheim, & Smithson, 1999; Walsham, 1999).

METHODOLOGY

Research Philosophy

As a field of research, Information Systems has been dominated by the positivist research paradigm, and its emphasis on the design and formalization of subjectivity-free systems (Klein, & Lyytinen, 1984). However, and as argued in the previous section, this chapter advocates an interpretive orientation that values important subjective and inter-subjective dimensions such as power, politics, and related socially constructed variables (Markus, 1983) that are amenable to

inductive understanding and typically apprehended by qualitative research designs. Indeed the inductive approach pursued here implies that the researchers look at data first in order to formulate theoretical hypotheses, whereas a deductive approach would imply submitting a set of a priori determined hypotheses to verification through test (Fernandez, 2004).

In epistemological terms, the strength of Information Systems qualitative research lies in its ambitious undertaking of uncovering "subtleties of process and impact related to the use of information technology" (Trauth, 2001, p.5) in a variety of settings: organisational transformation resulting from business reengineering; socio-cultures of computer-supported collaborative work; assessment of communication systems, etc. Accordingly, Information Systems investigations that are conducted from a qualitative perspective are a manifestation of the discipline's maturity and realisation that information systems are fundamentally social rather than technical systems (Hirschheim, 1992; Luna-Reyes, Zhang, Gil-Garcia, & Cresswell, 2005).

In reviewing the Information Systems literature, it is possible to find studies embodying solutions that focus on the systemic analysis of functional organisational systems whilst methodologically transcending the typical limits on interpretability conveyed by quantitatively analysed data. These studies (e.g. Toraskar, 1991; Orlikowski, 1993; Urquhart, 1997; Lehmann, & Gallupe, 2005; Allan, 2007; Coleman, & O'Connor, 2007; Rodon, & Pastor, 2007; Martins, & Nunes, 2011) elevate the study of systems dynamics to the status of main targets of research. We join the authors of such studies in the same interest for a deeper understanding IS phenomena, which "emerge[s] when the technolog[ical] and the behavioural interact, much like different chemical elements reacting to one another when they form a compound" (Lee, 2001).

Research Methodology

This empirical component of this study followed the Grounded Theory methodology (Glaser and Strauss, 1967). This choice reflects growing calls for a shift in Information Systems research and for a refocusing on "contextual and processual elements as well as the action of key players associated with organizational change elements that are often omitted in IS studies" (Orlikowski, 1993). Similarly, Watson (2001), Weber (2003) and Seidel and Recker (2009) claim for more theory development-focused Information Systems research, whilst Myers (1997) and Urquhart (2001) highlight Grounded Theory's usefulness in developing context-based, process-oriented descriptions and explanations of Information Systems phenomena.

More recently, Fendt and Sachs (2007) posited that the Grounded Theory method is "engaged with the world and helps, especially with the constant comparison and theoretical sampling techniques, to come skin close to the lived experience and incidents of the management world and make sense of them" (p. 448). This is particularly relevant for Information Systems research, in which "it is often that organizational cases are the dominant unit of analysis" (Lehmann, & Fernandez, 2007, p. 7).

Grounded Theory incorporates iterative interaction with the social-technical environment under study, through direct contact with either human informants or other resources (Martins, Nunes, Alajamy, & Zhou, 2013). This interaction results in a closely linked process of data collection and analysis, and is operated through coding, memoing and constant comparison at each stage of the analysis. The theory construction in the methodology is based on the construction of analytical codes and concepts from data (not from logically deducted hypotheses). These procedures are well explained and defined and offer the Information Systems researcher a sense of assurance by means of a concrete set of methods that promise validity

(e.g. theoretical sampling; theoretical saturation) and lead to the emergence of theory.

Research Design

The data collection developed through semi-structured interviews with different participants, selected according to the principles of theoretical sampling (Strauss, & Corbin, 1998). The informants included the Service manager, the Student communications coordinator, the Customer service improvement assistant, and the Information assistant that compose StuSS's team and that deal with the CEMS on a daily basis. Each interview lasted for approximately one hour. Since we were interested in the socio-technical dynamics of the system, the interview guide (*vide* Appendix 1) was arranged to invite informants to speak about their experiences of use, institutional support, organisational culture, drivers, and barriers.

The interviews were in-depth, semi-structured conversations between researchers and informant, focusing on the informant's "perception of self, life and experience, expressed in his or her words" (Minichiello, Aroni, Timewell, & Alexander, 1995, p.61). This was in line with the fundamental assumption of qualitative interviewing that informants are experts of their lives and beliefs, as well as of the meanings they ascribe to experiential life "as it is lived, felt, undergone, made sense of, and accomplished (…)" (Schwandt, 2001, p. 84). Indeed it was felt that the qualitative interviews engaged the researchers and the informants in a meaningful conversation that granted access to personal experiences and to the realms of socially constructed reality. These realms are composed of "scenic details, participants' motivations and intentions, and the web of social relations in which events happened" (Schultze, & Avital, 2011, p.3). Relying on quantitative methods to understand them would imply reducing the richness of human behaviour to the description of statistical patterns of frequencies, distributions and constructs' interdependent relationships (Brekhus,

Galliher, & Gubrium, 2005). Conversely, qualitative interviews experienced as conversations gave informants the opportunity to tell their story in their own words and in their own way.

The process of data analysis was concomitant with data collection and followed the tripartite coding process – i.e. open, axial, and selective coding – proposed by Strauss and Corbin (1998).

CUSTOMER CENTRICITY

The outcome of a Grounded Theory analysis is the generation of theory. Accordingly this section introduces the key categories that were extracted from coding to produce a rich contextual account) that explains how CEMS is currently used by StuSS as a pathway to building organisational ambidexterity at StuSS.

As represented visually in Figure 1, CEMS is perceived to facilitate three interrelated processes represented here as near core categories: the extraction of deeper customer insight; the promotion of enhanced customer interaction; and the improvement of future interaction outcomes. These processes, which will be explained in greater detail in the subsequent sections, converge into the dominant category of 'customer centricity', which refers to StuSS's attempt to orient their operating model around customers. In practical terms it refers to carefully defined customer segmentation that informs product development, demand generation, and the production and scheduling of services to students. Accordingly, customer centricity represents StuSS's use of CEMS to: (1) better distinguish and more effectively allocate resources to customers through the cycle of customer identification, customer attraction and customer development; (2) better understand each customer's behaviour, characteristics and needs through a built-up of systematic details and knowledge.

Deep Customer Insight

The near core category 'deep customer insight' represents a deep understanding of customer needs and the drivers of customer behaviour. It comprises managing quality customer data, profiling and segmentation, and prediction of customer behaviour.

The management of quality customer data is what allows an integrated view of the customer. It enables the extraction of knowledge about individual customers based on comprehensive, current and complete information. Amongst participants there was agreement that the enquiry recording system at StuSS allows staff to know exactly what students' needs are as well to find the best way to fulfil them:

Students come to us for all kinds of reason; so many times they are quite confused. We have to make a welcoming environment for them. That is the most important thing really, and from there we can spend some time working out what exactly they are after and how far we can fulfil that. That is when the information system comes in really.

Profiling and segmentation refer to an understanding of the defining features that differentiate customers. A fine grained profiling and segmentation allows a differentiation of customers according to needs that naturally worth of the service to the customer. CEMS gives StuSS the possibility not only to know who their customers are but also to understand what their pattern of interaction with the service is. This ability to acquire information on students' experience of StuSS's services is perceived to be critical in the delivery of more personalized services:

Our students feel that they can approach us and come to talk to us whether this happens at the front desk, over the phone, or through our website. And obviously we are a front desk environment, so you know, customer service is so important. We need

Figure 1.

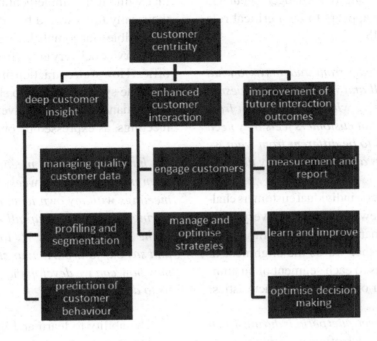

to present ourselves in a good way to students. Now information systems are very important to that what we do here and in how much we know about each student. We have our system where we can record all the enquiries.

Finally, prediction of customer behaviour is all about anticipating customers' needs and behaviour. It implies proactively answering the question 'Which product is most likely to be needed and wanted by a specific type of customer?'. The answers to this question will enable the intelligent change of service provision towards individual customers' needs and preferences in order to maximize efficiencies and to minimize risks. Participants seem to agree that every interaction with customers is recorded in the system for future reference and for better customer management. The system provides real-time information on the patterns of students visiting StuSS, pre-and-post service use behaviour and potential factors that may lead students to come back to StuSS:

Using the system tells us that around Easter time lots of students want to travel, so international students will need documents to take to embassies. Obviously exam times information will be high on demand at the end of each semester, but enquiries to happen earlier now.

Enhanced Customer Interaction

The near core category 'enhanced customer interaction' refers to the dialogical relationships with customers, from which segmentation and customization of strategy ensues. It comprises engaging customers, and managing and optimizing relationship strategies.

The engagement of customers' stems from the acquisition of descriptive knowledge on each individual customer, and from the acquisition of customers' impressions on the quality of the service provided. Amongst participants there are a shared understanding around the importance of customers feeling that they dialogue they establish StuSS is mutually beneficial. Customers feeling listened to and realizing that changes occur via customer influence appears to be a critical role performed by CEMS:

It is getting that feedback from students as to what they find works well and what they find doesn't, that helps determining what students want from us and you know, what customers feels they need sometimes happens to be different from what we as service providers actually think they need.

When knowledge on individual customers challenges prevailing views on service delivery, what follows next is the management and optimization of strategies or in other words the alignment of tactics and resources to each segment of customers based upon their own unique characteristics:

We know when to expect quiet periods during which we can focus on the back office work but we now we also know when things are likely to get very busy and we try to get as many staff as possible to support demand. So the system gives us a big picture on trends and shapes our performance during the year, so we can adapt our practice according to that information.

Improvement of Future Interaction Outcomes

The near core category 'improvement of future interaction outcomes' refers to the learning that is necessary to occur for the StuSS to improve services and guide the allocation of resources. It comprises robust mechanisms of measurement and reporting, the ability to learn and improve, and the optimization of decision making.

Measurement and report refers to StuSS's ability to link customer experience to the assessment of both individual and organizational performance. It emerged from the interviews with participants that the information system has been created with the intention to fully support current and future service delivery plans. All interviewees recognized

that without the implementation of this system, their daily tasks would be difficult and virtually impossible to accomplish. The system is pervasive in all service delivery areas, from front desk to back office. However, extraction of critical information from the system in order to shape organizational performance seems to revolve mainly around staff meetings, as expressed by one participant:

We have very regular meetings, you know, big team meetings once a week, we have individual meetings with my own team quite regularly and during those we pick up all our ideas and look at the staffs' strengths. We look at staff strength and say ok, your particular strength is this area, now how can we develop that further and enable us to do more?

The ability to learn and improve stems from paying attention to what is important to customers. Participants expressed a common concern with StuSS's ability to retain, organize and update customer information so that it could be used meaningfully in order to improve customer experience across the university. As explained by one informant:

We do hold reviews as well, we meet on a monthly basis and look at customers' responses and we discuss how we responded to individual questions and how else we can respond. That does bring on patterns and trends at particular points in the academic year, when certain key issues are expected to arise.

Finally, the optimization of decision making refers to grounding decision making on the weighing of insights from empirical examination of customer experience data. This experiential data should guide the allocation of resources and/ or promote change in services/ processes. When reflecting on the affordances of CEMS, participants consider them to impact decision-making. They all maintained that the feedback received through

CEMS assisted them in ultimate decision making, particularly if there was convergence around specific areas in need of attention. As noted by one participant:

We look through the system to read customers' experiences and act on them. If we get lot of similar comments, we can look back into our service and change; we can talk about things and discuss how to improve our service.

SOLUTIONS AND RECOMMENDATIONS

The theoretical and empirical work presented in this chapter suggests that practitioners are under increasing pressure to evaluate Information Systems in order to target and better determine value and benefits. Indeed Information Systems evaluation has become a major concern for various organizations (Jones, & Hughes, 2001), and the evaluation presented in this chapter is a good instantiation of this trend.

StuSS has perceived the advantage of adding information on customer experience to the information managed by its core enquiry recording system. The findings suggest that through collecting customers' opinions on service provision and service satisfaction StuSS is aggregating revelant customer knowledge: they know who the customers are (customer profiling and segmentation) and they determine the typical behavioural patterns customers follow. StuSS appears to be a customer enthusiast, as individual student data is collected, coordinated and distributed across lines of business. Because of this, StuSS is able to consistently identify customers across touch points and channels (students physically visiting the office or inquiring online) over time. The availability of customer knowledge allows StuSS to respond effectively to different student needs. Organizationally there is clarity concerning the ownership and management of customer relationships. All informants considered that collecting and processing student s' opinions is an extremely important step to evaluate customer experience. Another recurrent pattern in the data collected was a shared understanding that the workforce is empowered and aligned with the business objectives and values of StuSS, and have a strong bond between them.

However, student profiling seems to contain mostly basic descriptive information (based on requests metrics). Indeed student communications are increasingly customized to enhance relevance by addressing known needs. The resulting business benefit is beginning to be measured and acknowledged, however this happens in face-to-face meetings where customer experience information is analysed. A more advanced analytical investigation capability can be put in place to derive descriptive and predictive customer insight in a more efficient way (e.g. using statistical process, control methodologies). It is crucial for StuSS to re-engineer their CEMS into producing automated reviews of service delivery instead of having to meet on such a regular basis.

It is possible advance specific recommendations on how the system can benefit from applying data mining models to the information that is collected and stored. Indeed, data mining tools in customer relationship management (CRM) is an emerging trend within the global economy and its application can help StuSS to analyse and understand customer behaviour, which is a foundation of competitive customer experience strategy (Ngai, Xiu & Chu, 2008).

Appropriate data mining tools would allow StuSS to extract and identify useful information and knowledge from the enquiry system, enabling decision-making based on customer experience. Because the consistent use of organizational data can guide decision making, the following data mining models are suggested as an operational framework to assist StuSS in approaching the information collected on customer experience as a business driven process:

- **Classification:** It is the most commonly used model to segment and predict future customer behaviour. The common tools used are networks, decision trees and if-then-else rules (Kim, Jung, Suh, & Hwang, 2006);
- **Forecasting:** This model estimates the future value based on a record's patterns. For example, demand forecast is amongst the most common. The tools used are neutral networks and survival analysis (Etzion, Fisher, & Wasserkrug, 2005);
- **Sequence Discovery:** This model seeks to identify associations or pattern over time. Common tools used are statistics and set theory (Chen, Chiu, & Chang, 2005);
- **Visualization:** It is a data presentation method in which users can view complex patterns. This model is used in conjunction with other data mining models to provide a clear understanding of discovery patterns or relationships (Turban, Aronson, Liang, & Sharda, 2007).

CONCLUSION

By focusing on the current experience of customers, CEMS complement the traditional business value of Customer Relationship Management systems that tend to focus on the recorded history (Verhoef, Lemon, Parasyraman, Roggeveen, Tsiros, & Schesinger, 2009). This adds both externally and internally-oriented value since it helps organizations enhance their marketing capabilities (Chang, Park & Chaiy, 2010), and improve their business architecture capabilities (Coltman, Devinney, & Midgley, 2011). It also helps maximizing long-term success since it combines operating simultaneously with mechanisms of efficiency, regularity and predictability (Far-joun, 2010), and with mechanisms of innovation and flexibility that facilitate reconfiguration in response to external challenges (Gibson, & Bir-

kinshaw, 2004). In the specific context of StuSS this duality is visible in activities that deal with the response to current demands, and in activities that communicate an intention to adjust or change strategies and services. The former (e.g. managing customer data, profiling and segmenting customers, engaging customers and measurement and reporting), seem to represent exploitative business and a critical focus on the efficiency of operations. The latter (e.g. prediction of customer behaviour, management and optimization of strategy, optimization of decision making) appear to convey concern with exploratory business and a critical focus on adaptability, flexibility and experimentation. The coexistence of both pathways reveals StuSS's commitment to both efficiency and innovation activities. Rather than perceiving exploitation and exploration as two polar ends in a continuum, StuSS seems to use its CEMS to explore new customer knowledge that will in time be exploited, as it becomes assimilated into the main operations.

REFERENCES

Allan, G. (2007). The use of the grounded theory methodology in investigating practitioners' integration of COTS components in information systems. *Proceedings of the ICIS*. Paper 149, Montreal.

Aurier, P., & Siadou-Martine, B. (2007). Perceived justice and consumption experience evaluations: A qualitative and experimental investigation. *International Journal of Service Industry Management, 18*(5), 450–471. doi:10.1108/09564230710826241

Avgerou, C. (1995). Evaluating information systems by consultation and negotiation. *International Journal of Information Management, 15*(6), 427–436. doi:10.1016/0268-4012(95)00046-A

Baum, J. A. C., Rowley, T. J., Shipilov, A. V., & Chuang, Y.-T. (2005). Dancing with strangers: Aspiration performance and the search for underwriting syndicate partners. *Administrative Science Quarterly*, *50*(4), 536–575.

Beynon-Davies, P., Owens, I., & Williams, M. D. (2004). Information systems evaluation and information systems development process. *Journal of Enterprise Information Management*, *17*(4), 276–282. doi:10.1108/17410390410548689

Brekhus, W. H., Galliher, J. F., & Gubrium, J. F. (2005). The need for thin description. *Qualitative Inquiry*, *16*(6), 1–19.

Browne, B. A., Kaldenberg, D. O., Browne, W. E. G., & Brown, D. J. (1998). Student as customer: Factors affecting student satisfaction and assessments of institutional quality. *Journal of Marketing for Higher Education*, *8*(3), 1–14. doi:10.1300/J050v08n03_01

Cao, Q., Gedajlovic, R., & Zhang, H. (2009). Unpacking organizational ambidexterity: Dimensions, contingencies, and synergistic effects. *Organization Science*, *20*(4), 781–796. doi:10.1287/orsc.1090.0426

Carmeli, A., & Halevi, M. Y. (2009). How top management team behavioral integration and behavioral complexity enable organizational ambidexterity. *The Leadership Quarterly*, *20*(2), 207–218. doi:10.1016/j.leaqua.2009.01.011

Chang, W., Park, J. E., & Chaiy, S. (2010). How does CRM technology transform into organizational performance? A mediating role of marketing capability. *Journal of Business Research*, *63*(8), 849–855. doi:10.1016/j.jbusres.2009.07.003

Chen, M. C., Chiu, A. L., & Chang, H. H. (2005). Mining changes in customer behavior in retail marketing. *Expert Systems with Applications: An International Journal*, *28*(4), 773–781. doi:10.1016/j.eswa.2004.12.033

Chen, S., Osman, N. M., & Peng, G. C. (2013). Information systems evaluation: methodologies and practical case studies. In P. Isaias & M. B. Nunes (Eds.), *InformationSsystems Research and Exploring Social Artifacts: Aapproaches and Methodologies* (pp. 333–354). Hershey, PA: IGI; doi:10.4018/978-1-4666-2491-7.ch017

Coleman, G., & O'Connor, R. (2007). Using grounded theory to understand software process improvement: A study of Irish software product companies. *Information and Software Technology*, *49*(6), 531–694. doi:10.1016/j.infsof.2007.02.011

Coltman, T., Devinney, T. M., & Midgley, D. F. (2011). Customer relationship management and firm performance. *Journal of Information Technology*, *26*(3), 205–219. doi:10.1057/jit.2010.39

Cuadra, A., Cutanda, M., Aurelius, A., & Brunnstrom, K., Lopez de Vergara, J.E., Varela, M., Laulajainen, J.-P., Morais, A., Cavalli, A., Mellouk, A., Augustin, B., & Perez-Mateos, I. (2013). Ecosystem for customer experience assurance. *Proceedings of International Conference on Smart Communications in Network Technologies*, 1-5, Paris:IEEE.

Dagger, T. S., & O'Brien, T. K. (2009). Does experience matter? Differences in relationship benefits, satisfaction, trust, commitment and loyalty for novice and experienced service users. *European Journal of Marketing*, *44*(9/10), 1528–1552. doi:10.1108/03090561011062952

Daradoumis, T., Rodriguez-Ardura, I., Faulin, J., Juan, A. A., Xhafa, F., & Martinez-Lopez, F. (2010). Customer Relationship Management applied to higher education: Developing an e-monitoring system to improve relationships in electronic learning environments. *International Journal of Services Technology and Management*, *14*(1), 103–125. doi:10.1504/IJSTM.2010.032887

Douglas, J., McClelland, R., & Davies, J. (2008). The development of a conceptual model of student satisfaction with their experience in higher education. *Quality Assurance in Education*, *16*(1), 19–35. doi:10.1108/09684880810848396

Etzion, O., Fisher, A., & Wasserkrug, S. (2005). E-CLV: A modeling approach for customer lifetime evaluation in e-commerce domain, with an application and case study for online auction. *Information Systems Frontiers*, *7*(4-5), 421–434. doi:10.1007/s10796-005-4812-6

Farbey, B., Land, F., & Targett, D. (1999). The moving staircase. Problems of appraisal and evaluation in a turbulent environment. *Information Technology & People*, *12*(3), 238–252. doi:10.1108/09593849910278196

Farjoun, M. (2010). Beyond dualism: Stability and change as duality. *Academy of Management Review*, *35*(2), 202–225. doi:10.5465/AMR.2010.48463331

Fendt, J., & Sachs, W. (2007). Grounded theory method in management research: Users' perspectives. *Organizational Research Methods*, *11*(3), 430–455. doi:10.1177/1094428106297812

Fernandez, W. D. (2004). The Glaserian approach and emerging business practices in information systems management: achieving relevance through conceptualization. *Proceedings of the 3rd European Conference on Research Methods in Business and Management* (pp. 177-186).

Frow, P., & Payne, A. (2007). Towards the 'perfect' customer experience. *Journal of Brand Management*, *15*(2), 89–101. doi:10.1057/palgrave.bm.2550120

Galetzka, M., Verhoeven, J., & Pruyn, A. T. H. (2006). Service validity and service reliability of search, experience and credence services. *International Journal of Service Industry Management*, *17*(3), 271–283. doi:10.1108/09564230610667113

Gentile, C., Spiller, N., & Noci, G. (2007). How to sustain the customer experience: An overview of experience components that co-create value with the customer. *European Management Journal*, *25*(5), 395–410. doi:10.1016/j.emj.2007.08.005

Gibson, C. B., & Birkinshaw, J. (2004). The antecedents, consequences, and mediating role of organizational ambidexterity. *Academy of Management Journal*, *47*(2), 209–226. doi:10.2307/20159573

Glaser, B., & Strauss, A. (1967). *The Discovery of Grounded Theory: Strategies for Qualitative Research*. New York: Aldine.

He, Z. L., & Wong, P. K. (2004). Exploration vs. exploitation: An empirical test of the ambidexterity hypothesis. *Organization Science*, *15*(4), 481–194. doi:10.1287/orsc.1040.0078

Hilbert, A., Schönbrunn, K., & Schmode, S. (2007). Student Relationship Management in Germany – Foundations and Opportunities. *Management Review*, *18*(2), 204–219.

Hirschheim, R. (1992). Information Systems Epistemology: An Historical Perspective. In R. D. Galliers (Ed.), *Information Systems Research – Issues, Methods, and Practical Guidelines* (pp. 61–88). Henley-on-Thames, England: Alfred Waller Ltd.

Hirschheim, R., & Smithson, S. (1999). Evaluation of information systems: a critical assessment. In L. P. Willcocks & S. Lester (Eds.), *Beyond the IT productivity paradox* (pp. 381–410). Chichester: John Wiley & Sons.

Hsieh, Y. H., & Yuan, S. T. (2010). Modelling service experience design process with customer expectation management: A systems dynamics perspective. *Kybernetes*, *39*(7), 1128–1144. doi:10.1108/03684921011062746

Irani, Z., Sharif, A. M., & Love, P. E. D. (2005). Linking knowledge transformation to Information Systems Evaluation. *European Journal of Information Systems, 14*(3), 213–228. doi:10.1057/palgrave.ejis.3000538

Jansen, J. J. P., Tempelaar, M., van den Bosch, F. A. J., & Volberda, H. (2009). Structural differentiation and ambidexterity: The mediating role of integration mechanisms. *Organization Science, 20*(40), 797–811. doi:10.1287/orsc.1080.0415

Johnston, R., & Kong, X. (2011). The customer experience: A road-map for improvement. *Managing Service Quality, 21*(1), 5–24. doi:10.1108/09604521111100225

Jones, S., & Hughes, J. (2001). Understanding IS evaluation as a complex social process: A case study of UK local authority. *European Journal of Information Systems, 10*(4), 189–203. doi:10.1057/palgrave.ejis.3000405

Kanji, G. K., Malek, A., & Tambi, B. A. (1999). Total quality management in UK higher education institutions. *Total Quality Management, 10*(1), 129–153. doi:10.1080/0954412998126

Kim, S. Y., Jung, T. S., Suh, E. H., & Hwang, H. S. (2006). Customer segmentation and strategy development based on customer lifetime value: A case study. *Expert Systems with Applications, 31*(1), 101–107. doi:10.1016/j.eswa.2005.09.004

Klein, H. K., & Lyytinen, K. (1984). The Poverty of Scientism in Information Systems in Research methods in Information Systems. *Proceedings of the IFIP WG Colloquium* (pp. 131-162).

Lagsten, J., & Goldkuhl, G. (2008). Interpretative IS Evaluation: Results and Uses. *The Electronic Journal of Information Systems Evaluation, 11*(2), 97–108.

Laming, C., & Mason, K. (2014). Customer experience – an analysis of the concept and its performance in airline brands. *Research in Transportation Business and Management, 10*, 15–25. doi:10.1016/j.rtbm.2014.05.004

Lee, A. S. (2001). Challenges to qualitative researchers in information systems. In E. M. Trauth (Ed.), *Qualitative research in information systems: issues and trends* (pp. 240–270). London: Idea Group Publishing. doi:10.4018/978-1-930708-06-8.ch010

Lehmann, H., & Fernandez, W. (2007). Adapting the grounded theory method for information systems research. In D. Pauleen (Ed.), *Proceedings of QualIT Conference*, 1-8.

Lehmann, H. P., & Gallupe, R. B. (2005). Information Systems for Multinational Enterprises – Some Factors at Work in their Design and Implementation. *Journal of International Management, 11*(4), 28–49.

Levinthal, D., & March, J. G. (1981). A model of adaptive organizational search. *Journal of Economic Behavior & Organization, 2*(4), 307–333. doi:10.1016/0167-2681(81)90012-3

Luna-Reyes, L. F., Zhang, J., Gil-Garcia, J. R., & Cresswell, A. M. (2005). Information systems development as emergent socio-technical change: A practice approach. *European Journal of Information Systems, 14*(1), 93–115. doi:10.1057/palgrave.ejis.3000524

March, J. G. (1991). Exploration and exploitation in organizational learning. *Organization Science, 2*(1), 71–87. doi:10.1287/orsc.2.1.71

Mark, E. (2013). Student satisfaction and the customer focus in higher education. *Journal of Higher Education Policy and Management, 35*(1), 2–10. doi:10.1080/1360080X.2012.727703

Markus, M. L. (1983). Power, Politics and MIS Implementation. *Communications of the ACM*, *26*(6), 430–444. doi:10.1145/358141.358148

Martins, J. T., & Nunes, M. B. (2011). On Trust and Assurance: Towards a Risk Mitigation Normative Framework for eLearning Adoption. [British Columbia: ACI.]. *Proceedings of ICEL*, *2011*, 209–218.

Martins, J. T., Nunes, M. B., Alajamy, M., & Zhou, L. (2013). Grounded theory in practice: a discussion of cases in information systems research. In P. Isaias & M. B. Nunes (Eds.), *Information Systems Research and Exploring Social Artifacts: Approaches and Methodologies* (pp. 142–160)., doi:10.4018/978-1-4666-2491-7.ch008

Mascarenhas, O. A., Kesavan, R., & Bernacchi, M. (2006). Lasting customer loyalty: A total customer experience approach. *Journal of Consumer Marketing*, *23*(7), 397–405. doi:10.1108/07363760610712939

Matthews, S. S., & Lawley, M. (2006). Improving customer service: Issues in customer contact management. *European Journal of Marketing*, *40*(1), 218–232. doi:10.1108/03090560610637392

Minichiello, V., Aroni, R., Timewell, E., & Alexander, L. (1995). *In-depth interviewing: principles, techniques, analysis*. Melbourne: Longman.

Mom, T. J. M., van den Bosch, F. A. J., & Volberda, H. W. (2007). Investigating managers' exploration and exploitation activities: The influence of top-down, bottom-up, and horizontal knowledge inflows. *Journal of Management Studies*, *44*(6), 910–931. doi:10.1111/j.1467-6486.2007.00697.x

Mom, T. J. M., van den Bosch, F. A. J., & Volberda, H. W. (2009). Understanding variation in managers' ambidexterity: Investigating direct and indirect effects of formal structural and personal coordination mechanisms. *Organization Science*, *20*(4), 812–828. doi:10.1287/orsc.1090.0427

Munteanu, C., Ceobanu, C., Bobalca, C., & Anton, O. (2010). An analysis of customer satisfaction in a higher education context. *International Journal of Public Sector Management*, *23*(2), 124–140. doi:10.1108/09513551011022483

Myers, M. C. (1997). Qualitative research in information systems. *Management Information Systems Quarterly*, *21*(2), 241–242. doi:10.2307/249422

Nagasawa, S. (2008). Customer experience management: Influencing on human Kansei to management of technology. *The TQM Journal*, *20*(4), 312–323. doi:10.1108/17542730810881302

Nemanich, L., & Vera, D. (2009). Transformational leadership and ambidexterity in the context of an acquisition. *The Leadership Quarterly*, *20*(1), 19–33. doi:10.1016/j.leaqua.2008.11.002

Ngai, E. W., Xiu, L., & Chu, D. C. K. (2008). Application of data mining techniques in customer relationship management: A literature review and classification. *Expert System with Applications: An International Journal*, *36*(2), 2592–2602. doi:10.1016/j.eswa.2008.02.021

O'Reilly, C. A. III, Harreld, J. B., & Tushman, M. L. (2010). Organizational ambidexterity: IBM and emerging business opportunities. *California Management Review*, *51*(4), 75–99. doi:10.2307/41166506

O'Reilly, C. A., & Tushman, M. L. (2004). The ambidextrous organization. *Harvard Business Review*, *82*, 74–82. PMID:15077368

O'Reilly, C. A. III, & Tushman, M. L. (2011). Organizational ambidexterity in action. *California Management Review*, *53*(4), 5–22. doi:10.1525/cmr.2011.53.4.5

Orlikowski, W. J. (1993). CASE Tools as Organisational Change: Investigating Incremental and Radical Changes in Systems Development. *Management Information Systems Quarterly*, *17*(3), 309–340. doi:10.2307/249774

Palmer, A. (2010). Customer experience management: A critical review of an emerging idea. *Journal of Services Marketing, 24*(3), 196–208. doi:10.1108/08876041011040604

Perkis, A., Reichl, P., & Beker, S. (2014). Business Perspectives on Quality of Experience. Moller, S., & Raake, A. (Eds), Quality of experience: advanced concepts, applications and methods (pp. 97-108). Berlin: Springer. doi:10.1007/978-3-319-02681-7_7

Rageh, A., Melewar, T. C., & Woodside, A. (2013). Using netnography research method to reveal the underlying dimensions of the customer/tourist experience. *Qualitative Market Research. International Journal (Toronto, Ont.), 16*(2), 126–149.

Raisch, S., Birkinshaw, J., Probst, G., & Tushman, M. L. (2009). Organizational ambidexterity: Balancing exploitation and exploration for sustained performance. *Organization Science, 20*(4), 685–695. doi:10.1287/orsc.1090.0428

Remenyi, D., & Sherwood-Smith, M. (1999). Maximise information systems value by continuous participative evaluation. *Logistics Information Management, 12*(1/2), 14–31. doi:10.1108/09576059910256222

Rodon, J., & Pastor, A. (2007). Applying Grounded Theory to Study the Implementation of an Inter-Organizational Information System. *The Electronic Journal of Business Research Methods, 5*(2), 71–82.

Rothaermel, F. T., & Alexandre, M. T. (2009). Ambidexterity in technology sourcing: The moderating role of absorptive capacity. *Organization Science, 20*(4), 759–780. doi:10.1287/orsc.1080.0404

Ryder, I. (2007). Customer experience. *Journal of Brand Management, 15*(2), 85–88. doi:10.1057/palgrave.bm.2550127

Schmitt, B. (2003). *Customer experience management: a revolutionary approach to connecting with your customers*. New York: Wiley.

Schreuders, J., & Legesse, A. (2012). Organizational ambidexterity: How small technology firms balance innovation and support. *Technology Innovation Management Review, 2*(2), 17–21.

Schultze, U., & Avital, M. (2011). Designing Interviews to Generate Rich Data for Information Systems Research. *Information and Organization, 21*(1), 1–16. doi:10.1016/j.infoandorg.2010.11.001

Schwandt, T. A. (2001). *Dictionary of qualitative inquiry*. Thousand Oaks, CA: Sage.

Seeman, E. D., & O'Hara, M. (2006). Customer relationship management in higher education: Using information systems to improve the student-school relationship. *Campus-Wide Information Systems, 23*(1), 24–34. doi:10.1108/10650740610639714

Seidel, S., & Recker, J. (2009). Using Grounded Theory for Studying Business Process Management Phenomena. In S. Newell, E. Whitley, N. Pouloudi, J. Wareham, & L. Mathiassen (Eds.), *Proceedings of the 17th European Conference on Information Systems* (pp. 490-501).

Serafeimidis, V., & Smithson, S. (2003). Information systems evaluation as an organizational institution- experience from a case study. *Information Systems Journal, 13*(30), 251–274. doi:10.1046/j.1365-2575.2003.00142.x

Smith, A. (2006). CRM and customer service: strategic asset or corporate overhead. Handbook of Business Strategy, 7(1), 87-93.

Smith, A. M., & Lewis, B. R. (1989). Customer Care in Financial Service Organisations. *International Journal of Bank Marketing, 7*(5), 13–22. doi:10.1108/02652328910131917

Smith, W. K., & Tushman, M. L. (2005). Managing strategic contradictions: A top management model for managing innovation streams. *Organization Science*, *16*(5), 522–536. doi:10.1287/orsc.1050.0134

Strauss, A., & Corbin, J. (1998). *Basics of qualitative research: techniques and procedures for developing grounded theory*. London: Sage.

Svari, S., Slantten, T., Svensson, G., & Edvardsson, B. (2011). A SOS construct of negative emotion in customers' service experience (CSE) and service recovery by firms (SRF). *Journal of Services Marketing*, *24*(5), 323–335. doi:10.1108/08876041111149685

Symons, V., & Walsham, G. (1988). The evaluation of information systems: A critique. *Journal of Applied Systems Analysis*, *15*, 119–132.

Teece, D. J., Pisano, G., & Schuen, A. (1997). Dynamic capabilities and strategic management. *Strategic Management Journal*, *18*(7), 509–533. doi:10.1002/(SICI)1097-0266(199708)18:7<509::AID-SMJ882>3.0.CO;2-Z

Teixeira, J., Patricio, L., Nunes, N. J., Nobrega, L., Raymond, P. F., & Constantine, L. (2012). Customer experience modelling: From customer experience to service design. *Journal of Service Management*, *23*(3), 362–376. doi:10.1108/09564231211248453

Toraskar, K. V. (1991). How managerial uses evaluate their decision-support: A Grounded Theory Approach. *Journal of Computer Information Systems*, *7*, 195–225.

Trauth, E. (2001). The Choice of Qualitative Methods in IS Research. In E. Trauth (Ed.), *Qualitative research in IS: issues and trends* (pp. 1–19). London: Idea Group Publishing. doi:10.4018/978-1-930708-06-8.ch001

Tseng, M. M., Qinhai, M., & Su, C.-J. (1999). Mapping customers' service experience for operation improvement. *Business Process Management*, *5*(1), 50–64. doi:10.1108/14637159910249126

Tsinidou, M., Gerogiannis, V., & Fitsilis, P. (2010). Evaluation of the factors that determine quality in higher education: An empirical study. *Quality Assurance in Education*, *18*(3), 227–244. doi:10.1108/09684881011058669

Turban, E., Aronson, J. E., Liang, T. P., & Sharda, R. (2007). *Decision support and business intelligence systems*. New Jersey: Pearson Education.

Tushman, M. L., & O'Reilly, C. A. III. (1996). Ambidextrous organizations: Managing evolutionary and revolutionary change. *California Management Review*, *38*(4), 8–30. doi:10.2307/41165852

Urquhart, C. (1997). Exploring analyst-client communication: using grounded theory techniques to investigate informal requirements gathering. In Lee, A. S., Libenau, J., & DeGross, J. L. (Eds), Proceedings of the International Conference on Information Systems and Qualitative Research (pp. 149-181). doi:10.1007/978-0-387-35309-8_10

Urquhart, C. (2001). An encounter with grounded theory: Or reinforcing old prejudices? A brief reply to Bryant. *Journal of Information Technology Theory and Application*, *4*(3), 43–54.

van Loy, B., Martens, T., & Debackere, K. (2005). Organizing for continuous innovation: On the sustainability of ambidextrous organizations. *Creativity and Innovation Management*, *14*(3), 208–221. doi:10.1111/j.1467-8691.2005.00341.x

Verhoef, P. C., Lemon, K. N., Parasuraman, A., Roggeveen, A., Tsiros, M., & Schlesinger, L. A. (2009). Customer experience creation: Determinants, dynamics and management strategies. *Journal of Retailing*, *85*(1), 31–41. doi:10.1016/j.jretai.2008.11.001

1. Walsham, G. (1999). Interpretive evaluation design for information systems. In Beyond the IT Productivity Paradox. In L. P. Willcocks & S. Lester (Eds.), *Beyond the IT productivity paradox* (pp. 363–380). Chichester: John Wiley & Sons.

1. Watson, R. (2001). Research in information systems: What we haven't learned. *Management Information Systems Quarterly*, *25*, v–xv.

1. Weber, R. (2003). Editor's comments: Theoretically speaking. *Management Information Systems Quarterly*, *27*, iii–xii.

1. Willcocks, L. (1992). Evaluating information technology investments: Research findings and reappraisal. *Journal of Information Systems*, *2*(2), 243–268. doi:10.1111/j.1365-2575.1992.tb00081.x

1. Wright, R. E. (2008). Targeting, segmenting, and positioning the market for college students to increase customer satisfaction and overall performance. *College Student Journal*, *42*(3), 891–894.

1. Zineldin, M., Akdag, H. C., & Vasicheva, V. (2011). Assessing quality in higher education: New criteria for evaluating students' satisfaction. *Quality in Higher Education*, *17*(2), 231–243. doi:10.1080/13538322.2011.582796

KEY TERMS AND DEFINITIONS

Customer Centricity: A strategic approach to managing organizations' relationships with customers that revolves around customers and their needs. Being customer centric implies the ability to extract valuable insights on customer needs with the objective of delivering products or services that fulfil those needs in a way that is meaningful to customers.

Customer Experience: The totality of critical moments when customers interact with an organization and its offerings. It cannot be apprehended by a snapshot in time. It is composed of perceptions – both conscious and subconscious – that are the result of continuing interactions with an organization during the customer life cycle. It therefore reflects the perspective of an end-to-end journey, as well as the history of interactions with an organization's services, products, channels or employees.

Customer Experience Management: A strategy that requires organizations to know what is important to customers at each stage of the customer journey. It assumes a hedonic component, since it corresponds to the notion of quality based on experience. The skillful management of customer experience – which can include awareness-raising, attraction, cultivation and advocacy efforts – enhances customer satisfaction and delivers gains throughout organizations. Its ultimate goal is to optimize interactions from the customer's point of view, and, as a result, develop enhanced customer loyalty.

Customer Experience Management System: An information system that allows organizations to track, oversee and organize every interaction between a customer and the organization throughout the customer lifecycle. This typically implies measuring and analyzing customers' emotions and acting on customers' feedback through the design and re-design of the total customer experience.

Grounded Theory: A systematic, inductive qualitative research methodology particularly suited for theory generation and development. In interpretive Information Systems research it typically involves iterative interaction with the socio-technical environment under study. The methodology advocates a closely linked process of data collection and analysis. The latter operates through coding, memoing and constant comparison.

Organizational Ambidexterity: Refers to an organizations' simultaneous ability to exploit existing knowledge for efficiency, and to explore new knowledge for innovation.

APPENDIX 1: INTERVIEW GUIDE

1. Why is a customer care policy so important for StuSS, and how do you think information systems help operationalize StuSS's vision on service quality?
2. What do you think are the specific needs of your customers?
3. How do you think a customer experience management system respond to the objectives of StuSS's customer care policy?
4. When and why was the system developed? Can you trace the history of development, including requirement analysis, constitution of project team, and involvement of staff in decision-making, implementation?
5. Was there an internal analysis of which processes and workflows were being targeted for change, as a consequence of implementing the customer experience management system?
6. Do you feel you had the chance to provide input into the development cycle and the implementation process? Do you feel this affects to some extent your views on the system?
7. Does the customer experience management system help you address what customers expect from StuSS's products and services? How is this translated in terms of strategic planning, decision-making and on an operational level?
8. In technical terms, how is the follow-up survey integrated into StuSS's enquiry recording system?
9. How does the collection of data from customers enable StuSS to make sure products and services are appropriate to the needs of your customers?
10. How do you act on the information collected? Where is it stored? How and when is it reviewed and interpreted? Do you have access to it? If not, how do you think having access to it would be beneficial for your work practice?
11. How do you learn as an organization from the information collected, and how do you use that information to change internal work practices?
12. Do you think StuSS is ready to use the information collected to streamline business processes? Can you give specific examples?
13. In terms of perceived improved operational efficiency, can you tell us how the data collected by the system is used to:
    a. Improve decision-making?
    b. Streamline business processes?
14. How do you evaluate the value of customer experience? Based on criteria such as performance, delivery time, budget and quality?
15. What would you change in terms of readiness to extract value from the system?
16. What changes in your work practice did the implementation of the customer experience management system introduce?
17. How do you see the value and benefit of such changes? What would you change if you could?
18. How do you feel the customer experience management system impacts the levels of communication, collaboration and trust between staff at StuSS?

Chapter 17
Degree of Openness in Public Policies:
A Conceptual Proposal

Antonio Bob Santos
ISCTE-IUL, University Institute of Lisbon, Portugal

ABSTRACT

Research conducted around the topic of open innovation has been mainly empirical in nature and primarily focused on firms. For a better understanding of open innovation, it is important to conduct further research beyond the "firm environment", particularly in areas related to public policy. This chapter addresses the topic of open innovation, relating it to public policy, analyzing the framework conditions that can stimulate the development of open innovation in organizations. More specifically, the chapter uses the Portuguese public policies as a case study. A methodology is proposed and discussed for analyzing the degree of openness in public policy, concerning policy orientation to support the development of open innovation.

INTRODUCTION[1]

The topic of open innovation has been one of the most researched in the literature of innovation management, having increasing attention in disciplines such as economics, psychology or sociology (Huizingh, 2011). Research conducted around open innovation has been mainly empirical in nature and primarily focused on firms (Chesbrough and Bogers, 2014; Chesbrough and Schwartz, 2007; Helfat and Quinn, 2006). For a better understanding of open innovation, it is important to have further research out of the firm environment,

particularly in areas such as innovation systems or public policies, given their importance to the creation of conditions to stimulate open innovation activities (Chesbrough and Bogers, 2014). In this sense, this Chapter brings up the topic of open innovation to the area of public policy, analyzing the framework conditions for the development of open innovation, using the Portuguese public policies as a case study. In this Chapter it is proposed a methodology to analyse the degree of openness of public policies, concerning their orientation to support the adoption of open innovation by companies and other organizations.

DOI: 10.4018/978-1-4666-8833-9.ch017

METHODOLOGY

This Chapter is developed as follows: a) backgroung and literature review about the relevance of public policies in supporting innovation and open innovation; b) identification of the most relevant public policies to stimulate open innovation, based in the conceptual framework proposed by de Jong *et al.* (2010); c) analysis of the most relevant public programs to promote open innovation, based in the Portuguese case (12 programs were found); d) within these 12 programs, 35 typologies of project were identified in total, being analyzed the respective Rules and Legislation, identifying their eligible expenditures (expenditures that beneficiaries - companies or other entities - can benefit when they submit their projects for public funding); e) proposal of a classification of the "degree of openness" and the "level of openness" of each public program, concerning their orientation towards open innovation; f) conclusion and future research directions.

BACKGROUND: PUBLIC POLICIES AND OPEN INNOVATION- A CONCEPTUAL OVERVIEW

The term "open innovation" emerged in 2003 from the observation and analysis of innovation practices present in multinational companies (based in the United States of America - USA), where it was found that these practices functioned as an open system, with multiple interconnections with external actors. This work was initially developed by Professor Henry Chesbrough (2003a), which distinguished this open innovation model from the vertically integrated model – the dominant model in the twentieth century - in which companies had all the control of the innovation process - traditional innovation model (West *et al.*, 2014).

The conclusions of Chesbrough indicated that large multinationals did not abandoned the traditional innovation model (vertically integrated) definitively, but that it was complemented with a set of external demand for technology and its incorporation in the company's production process, as well as through the monitoring of the technology flows generated internally that were targeted to markets, through licensing processes, for example (Chesbrough, 2006, pp. 2-3). This form of organization of innovation has been designated by the term open innovation (original term):

Open innovation means that valuable ideas can come from inside or outside the company and can go to market from inside or outside the company as well. This approach places external ideas and external paths to market on the same level of importance as that reserved for internal ideas and paths to market during the Closed Innovation Era. (Chesbrough, 2003a, p. 43).

Chesbrough and Bogers (2014) introduced new insights to this definition, namely through the notions of pecuniary and non-pecuniary mechanisms associated with knowledge flows:

… we define open innovation as a distributed innovation process based on purposively managed knowledge flows across organizational boundaries, using pecuniary and non-pecuniary mechanisms in line with the organization's business model. (Chesbrough and Bogers, 2014, p. 17).

In this definition is highlighted the importance of knowledge flows management, including in R&D activities. These flows can be managed in an intentional way by organizations, through inflows of external knowledge and outflows of not used internal knowledge (Chesbrough and Bogers, 2014, pp.12-13). In the last decade, research on open innovation has been conducted essentially in an empirical base, focused more on countries that are in the technological frontier and on companies with global strategies, and at the firm level (Chesbrough and Bogers, 2014; Helfat and Quinn 2006). Nevertheless, the analysis of open innovation at other levels, such as at innovation systems or at public policy, it`s necessary to have a deeper understanding of the concept and of its relevance as a field of research (West *et al.*, 2014). Concerning public policy, the understanding of the impact of public policies in promoting open innovation has been an underresearched topic in open innovation literature.

Economic literature appoints market failures (neoclassic approach) and systemic failures (evolutionary approach) as justifications for Government (public policies) intervention in the market (Dosi *et al.*, 1988; Freeman, 1987; Lundvall, 1988; Nelson and Rosenberg 1993). Systemic failures are also called systemic problems, given that the evolutionary approach does not consider possible the equilibrium of the system, i.e., there are no optimal or ideal systems (Chaminade and Equist, 2010). In this approach (evolutionary), innovation results from interactive processes and from the existence of multiple channels/links between the stages of invention and wealth creation, as well as from feedback channels between these phases, where various actors and intermediaries play an important role. Are also regarded as fundamental in the innovation process: institutions (rules, norms, culture, etc.); the cumulative nature of knowledge; tacit knowledge; the iterative process of learning; and the dissemination of knowledge (Lundvall *et al.*, 2012). According to the evolutionary approach, these failures can be mitigated by the action of public policies, promoting the cooperation in various policy areas, as well as stimulating the interactions between the various actors involved in the innovation process. The evolutionary approach has analyzed in depth the issues addressed by the literature on open innovation, including collaborative networks (formal and informal), corporate entrepreneurship, intellectual property management, absorptive capacity, knowledge flows, the interactions between of companies and R&D institutions (Laursen and Salter, 2005). Thus, we can consider the open innovation approach in a systemic and evolutionary perspective, stressing

the importance of public policy in promoting it, being the reasons for the public intervention similar to the reasons that justify the intervention of the public policies in promoting innovation systems and innovation in general. The literature of open innovation refers that the support of public policies should focus, not only on promoting innovation activities in companies, but also on improving the environment and the functioning of innovation systems. It is also stressed the need for a better coordination of the various policy areas, in order to achieve a greater stimulus to open innovation activities (de Jong *et al.*, 2008, 2010).

In fact, public policies play an important role for the development of the innovation process (Foray, 2009; Mazzucato, 2011), including open innovation activities, in areas like financial and tax policy or in the regulatory framework where the company operates – external environment of the firm (Chesbrough and Bogers, 2014; de Jong *et al.*, 2010). Public policies can promote innovation diffusion, recombination and its transformation, contributing to the balance between three types of policy instruments in the context of global open innovation (Herstad *et al.*, 2010; Wessner and Wolff, 2012): to promote R&D activities, stimulating the capacity of knowledge absorption and accumulation and its dissemination to business; to encourage innovation networks, promoting dissemination channels and recombination of knowledge; to stimulate internal networks (at the firm level) and international connections, since the absorptive capacity of firms are subject to resource constraints (e.g., budget restrictions). Also OECD (2009) considers that public policy needs to adopt a more open and flexible approach to innovation, where collaboration and competition coexist in the innovation process, implying greater coherence and interdisciplinarity of public policies to promote innovation.

According to Santos (2015), one of the few research articles that examine the role of public policies in the creation of conditions to the development of open innovation was carried out by de

Jong *et al.* (2010). In this research, public policies oriented to stimulate open innovation should take into account two dimensions: the internal dimension of the organizations and their external dimension, which may or may not be favorable to the adoption of open innovation. These two dimensions are influenced by public policies, and seven relevant policy areas have been identified to stimulate open innovation in a given economy. Based on this conceptual model, de Jong *et al.* (2008, 2010) conducted a comparative analysis of public policies to support open innovation in the Netherlands, Belgium and Estonia. The main findings of that research will be discussed in the following sections, with an application of the methodology (an extended version) to the Portuguese case.

PUBLIC POLICIES TO SUPPORT OPEN INNOVATION - AN EXTENDED FRAMEWORK

The research of Jong *et al* (2008, 2010) indicates that public policies can create a proper environment towards the development of open innovation, taking into account the internal dimension of organizations as well their surrounding conditions (external dimension), which can be favorable or unfavorable to the adoption of open innovation. From an analysis of the literature, these authors found that organizations (companies, in that case) organize their open innovation practices (internal dimension) according to five areas (Table 1): networks (informal in nature, aimed at acquiring and maintaining relationships with external entities); formal collaborations (with external entities, such as customers, suppliers, universities, etc., that can stimulate innovation); corporate entrepreneurship (strategies to develop ideas generated internally by its employees, as well as internalize ideias and knowledge generated by external entities); intellectual property strategy (IP); and R&D management (development of absorptive capacity and

knowledge retention through internal R&D or the use of R&D generated outside the organization).

These five areas can be influenced and determined, in particular, by the legal and institutional framework where the organization operates, being very determined by the action of public policies (Torkkeli *et al.*, 2009). The same conclusions are pointed by de Jong *et al* (2008, 2010), which identifies three characteristics of the external environment that could affect the adoption of open innovation (Table 1): 1) a strong public knowledge base (higher education and research institutions; incentives for the industry-university collaboration); 2) mobility and qualification of the labour market (encouraging the connection between innovation stakeholders; policies for adult`s education and training); 3) access to finance (public policy intervention due to the existing of market failures, particularly asymmetric information - between companies and financial institutions - and market uncertainty – lack of credit or foreign funds access, etc.).

The work of de Jong *et al.* (2008, 2010) also mentions that both internal dimension and the external environment in which the organization operates can be influenced by seven areas of public policy (Table 1): 1) R&D policy, oriented to stimulate R&D in companies; 2) networking policy, promoting the connections between innovation actors and backing clusters; 3) entrepreneurship policy, stimulating the creation of spin-offs and the development of an entrepreneurship culture; 4) science policy, renewing the knowledge stock available and disseminating R&D and knowledge to business and society; 5) education and training policy, promoting a high qualified education and training system; 6) labour market policy, promoting the mobility of human resources and the attraction of skilled workers from other countries; 7) competition policy, decreasing the barriers of access to markets, monopolistic/oligopolistic positions and the lack of transparency in the markets. Within each of the seven policy areas, there were identified the main public policy action lines that

Table 1. Conceptual model of the areas of public policy and action lines that can stimulate open innovation

Policy Area	Action Line of Public Policy	Organization of Open Innovation Activities (Internal Conditions)					External Conditions		
		Networks	Collaboration	Corporate Entrepreneurship	IP Management	R&D Management	Base of Public Knowledge	Mobility/ Qualification of Human Resorces	Financial Instruments
R&D policy	10. Financial and fiscal incentives	x	x		x	x	x		
	11. IP system				x	x	x		
	12. Standards and Certification					x			
	13. User innovation					x			
Collaboration policy	14. Networking skills	x	x	x	x				
	15. Incentives to collaboration	x	x	x	x				
	16. Technological markets	x	x		x				
	17. Technological intermediaries	x	x						
	18. Backup *clusters*								
Entrepreneurship policy	10. Support to corporate entrepreneurship				x	x	x		x
	11. Access to finantial instruments				x				
	12. Support to start-ups/spin-offs								
Science policy	13. Incentives and funding						x		
	14. Balanced incentives						x		
	15. Focus on excelence						x		
	16. Difusion and cooperatiob						x		
Education and Training policy	17. Entrepreneurship education			x				x	
	18. Lifelong learning education							x	
Labour market policy	19. Human resources mobility							x	
	20. Attraction of qualified human resources from abroad							x	
Competition policy	21. Competition stimulus				x				x
eGovernment policy	22. Co-creation/user innovation	x	x		x	x	x		
	23. Open standards /Open Source					x			
	24. eProcurement					x			
	25. Open data								

Source: adapted from de Jong *et al*. (2008, 2010).

Note: The "eGovernment Policy" is a new proposal for this Chapter, to complement the previous analyzes of de Jong *et al*. (2008, 2010).

may have impact in the adoption of open innovation by organizations. In total, they proposed 21 action lines (Table 1), that allows the analysis of how public policies can influence the adoption of open innovation.

Based on literature review, it is proposed in this Chapter the extension of the framework used by de Jong *et al*. (2010), proposing a new policy area that can have a major impact on the adop-

tion of open innovation by organizations - the eGovernment policy – i.e., the simplification and modernization strategies of Public Administration, supported by information and communication technologies (ICT). The eGovernment policy can influence positively or negatively the adoption of open innovation by organizations, particularly in small and medium enterprises (Assar *et al*., 2011), as follows:

- By providing to society the knowledge generated by the entities of Public Administration (open knowledge /open access) or general interest data (open data), under which companies can create economic value (OECD, 2011; Ubaldi, 2013);
- Developing technological solutions based on non-proprietary technology (open source), open formats (open standards), as well as technologically neutral infrastructures (open connectivity), important to stimulate the development of new products and services, especially by SMEs and start-ups (Di Natale *et al.*, 2003; Mutkoski, 2011);
- Adopting a more flexible intellectual property policy, (creative commons, IP licensing, etc.): as big buyer of technologies, Public entities may encourage the commercialization of technologies developed in sectors where it is the largest client (Dolfsma and Seo, 2013);
- Developing services and solutions for Public Administration with the involvement of citizens, through collaborative developments processes - such as co-creation (Prahalad and Ramaswamy, 2000) or user innovation (Bogers *et al.*, 2010) - implying that the traditional management practices in Public Administration (top-down) walk towards a network and collaborative model (O' Reilly, 2013);
- Stimulating electronic procurement (eProcurement), essential to boost innovation from the demand side, i.e, in companies and other private organizations (European Commission, 2006; Edquist and Zabala-Iturriagagoitia, 2012).

Thus, it is proposed "eGovernment" as a new policy area that can influence the adoption of open innovation by organizations, in addition to the framework of de Jong *et al.* (2008, 2010). The inclusion of a new policy area also implies the inclusion of action lines that can stimulate the adoption of open innovation. Based in the analisys above, it is considered the following eGovernment action lines (four in total): "co-creation/ user innovation", "open standards /open source", "eProcurement" and "open data". In Table 1, and after the inclusion of the eGovernment area, eight areas of public policy that influence the adoption of open innovation by organizations can be identified, in a total of 25 action lines.

This conceptual model (without eGovernment policy area) was used and applied to the reality of three European countries (Netherlands, Belgium and Estonia) being analysed how public policies responded to the 21 action lines proposed (de Jong *et al.*, 2008, 2010). Based on that, and extending the model with the inclusion of eGovernment policy area, the proposal in this Chapter is to apply this methodology to the Portuguese case, analysing public policies in an open innovation perspective. The main results are presented in the next Section.

ANALISYS OF PUBLIC POLICIES IN PORTUGAL, IN AN OPEN INNOVATION PERSPECTIVE

Following the conceptual framework proposed in the previous Section, it were identified the main public programs in each of the eight public policy areas (according to Table 1). The time period of the analysis was between 2007-2013, that was the implementation period of the main financial instrument to support public policies on competitiveness and innovation - the QREN - National Strategic Reference Framework (QREN, 2011). Thus, in the current analysis, it is considered the programs under QREN that responde to each of the eight policy areas (discussed in the previous section), as well as other programs financed by the State budget that are relevant to promote innovation, as the case of the tax benefits to private R&D. In

Figure 1. Major Programs to Support Innovation and areas of Public Policy – the Portuguese case (2007-2013)
Source: own elaboration

Policy areas							
R&D Policy	Entrepreneurship Policy	Science Policy	Networks / Clusters Policy	Education and Training Policy	Labour Market Policy	eGovernment Policy	Competition Policy
R&D Incentice System (SI I&DT) ➢ Individual projects ➢ Copromotion projects ➢ R&D vouchers ➢ Coletive R&D projects ➢ R&D centres in companies ➢ R&D promotion	**Qualification and Internacionalization Incentive System (SI Q&I)** ➢ Innovation vouchers ➢ Joint projects ➢ Cooperation projects ➢ Individual projects	**Science Program** ➢ Qualified HR attraction ➢ S&T International Partnerships ➢ HR advanced training (PhD scholarships)	**Colective Eficiency Strategy** ➢ Poles ➢ Clusters	**New Opportunities Program** ➢ Youth Axe ➢ Adults Axe	**INOV Program** ➢ INOV Contact ➢ INOV Youth ➢ INOV Mundus ➢ INOV Social ➢ INOV Arts ➢ INOV Vasco da Gama	**SIMPLEX Program** ➢ Simplex 2006-2011	**Competition Law**
R&D Fiscal Incentives ➢ SIFIDE	**Innovation Incentives System (SI Inovation)** ➢ Productive innovation projects ➢ Special projects ➢ Strategic projects ➢ Qualified entrepreneurship	**Scientific and Technological Entities Support System (SAESCTN)** ➢ Mobility of human resources ➢ Technological centres ➢ C&T Parks					
Venture Capital ➢ Portugal Ventures ➢ InovCapital ➢ Finicia							

total, there are 12 programs that fall within the eight areas of public policy (Figure 1):

These 12 programs include 35 typologies of projects/initiatives, having been analysed concerning their Rules and Legislation, identifying their eligible expenditures, according to the 25 action lines identified in Table 1. The detailed analysis is shown in Annex B. Based in the descriptive analysis of Annex B, a further analysis was performed, crossing the eight policy areas and the 25 action lines (considered in Table 1) with the 12 public programs (Figure 1), originating a new table, where it is possible to analyse the eligible expenditures that are oriented towards open innovation (Table 1.1, Annex A). In the next section, and based in the analysis of the Table 1.1 (Annex A) and in Annex B, it is proposed a classification of each typology of program, according to their degree of openness.

DEGREE AND LEVEL OF OPENNESS OF PUBLIC POLICIES - A PROPOSAL

The evaluation of public policies have been a common practice in some countries and in international organizations, such as the OECD and the World Bank (Furubo *et al.*, 2002), despite the difficulties of this process and the administrative and cultural barriers at level of public administrations (Thoenig, 1999, p 684.). However, it is recognized that the existence of an evaluation process and its institutionalization as a regular procedure may have a positive effect on public administration improvements and innovations (Bemelmans-Videc, 1994; Hall and Taylor, 1996; Koelble, 1996). Given the non-existence in Portugal of public policy evaluations concerning their support to open innovation activities, and given that a comprehensive evaluation process requires an impact assessment of these policies (Derlien and Rist, 2002) - for which we do not have data - was chosen, in this chapter, to make an evaluation exercise based on the analysis of the eligible expenditures supported by public programs, analyzing their orientation to support open innovation activities.

From the analysis of the public programs and their typologies of projetc (descriptive analysis in Annex B, summarized in Annex A, Table 1.1), we proceed to their classification according to the number of action lines covered by their eligible expenditures (that we call "degree of openness", measuring the depth of that support). Subsequently, based on that classification, we grouped the programs and their typologies according to similar degrees of openness (that we call "level of openness"), in order to have a better perception of the scope of public policies to support open innovation activities.

Degree of Openness (Depth)

Based in the results of Table 1.1 (Annex A), is now proposed a classification of each programe and typology of project, in order to have a better perception of their support to promote open innovation activities[2], following similar metholodogy applyed in other studies (e.g., Jacob and Varone, 2004), with the following considerations:

- The 25 action lines are extended to 30 action lines, in order to fit to the specificities of the Portuguese public policies (see Table 1.1, Annex A);
- Each of the 30 action lines of public policy was coded in binary variables ("0" and "1") indicating their coverage or not by the elegible expenditures of the typologies of project[3]. Since binary variables are used to verify (or not) a particular phenomenon (Greene, 1997), it was considered that they are the most appropriate type of variables

to use in this case. Each action line takes the value of:
  - ○ "1", if they are covered by the elegible expenditures of each of the typologies of project;
  - ○ "0", if they are not covered.
- In the case of the programs (that aggregate the typologies of project), the procedure is similar: each of the 30 action lines also assume the value of "1" if they are covered by at least one of their typology of project, and the value of "0" if they are not;
- In each typology of project, the total sum of the 30 action lines is "30" (maximum value) if all are covered by the elegible expenditures of each typology, assuming the minimum value of "0" if there are no action lines covered;
- The openness of each typology of project is given by the arithmetic mean (X)[4]: the ratio between the sum of action lines covered by their eligible costs (minimum value of "0" and maximum of "30") and the maximum value possible of action lines that may be eligible by each typology of project (maximum value of "30"), that is, the degree of openness of the typologies of project assumes a value between "0" and "1";
- The degree of openness of the programs (that aggregate the typologies of project) is also given by an arithmetic mean: the ratio between the sum of the action lines covered by their typologies of project (minimum "0" and maximum "30"), and the highest possible number of action lines covered by their tipology of project (maximum value of "30"), so that the resulting variable assumes a minimum value of "0" and a maximum of "1".

Given these assumptions, it is possible to analyze all the binary variables (Table 1.2, Annex A), as well as the degree of openness of each typology and program (Table 1.3, Annex A). In Figure 2 are

Figure 2. 1 and 2.2 - Degree of Openness of Typologies of Projects and Programs
Source: own ellaboration

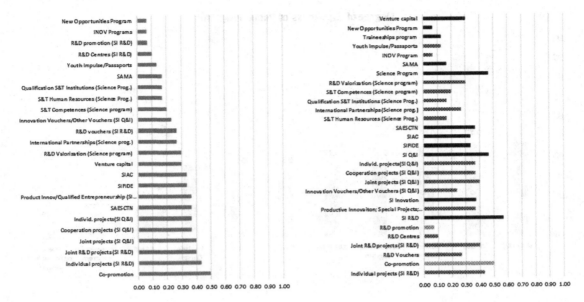

summarized the found values for each typology and program, ranging between 0.07 (in the New Opportunities program, INOV programs and in the typology of project "Promotion of R&D") and 0.5 (typology "Co-Promotion"), meaning that the eligible expenditures of the typologies cover between 7 percent and 50 percent of the action lines that cover open innovation activities.

In Figure 2.1 it`s possible to see the typologies with the highest degree of openness: "Co-promotion Projects", "Individual Projects" and "Collective R&D Projects" (under the SI I&D program, with values between 0.4 and 0.5), followed by the "Joint Projects", "Projects in Cooperation" and "Individual Projects" (under SI Q&I program, with values between 0.37 and 0.4). Projects under SAESCTN program, SI Innovation, SIFIDE and SIAC appear in the following positions, with values between 0.33 and 0.37. On the opposite side, projects that have a lower degree of openness are those that fall within the New Opportunities program (0.07), the INOV program (0.07), as well as the typologies of project "R&D

promotion" (0.07) and "R&D Centres" (0.10) - these two under the SI I&DT program.

It is also possible to analyze the typologies of projects grouped by the respective programs, having a better perception of their degree of openness. Thus, in Figure 2.2, it can be seen that the typologies with higher "openness" (i.e., more oriented to support open innovation activities) are: in SI I&D program, the typologies "Co-promotion Projects" and "Individual Projects"; in SI Q&I program, the "Joint Projects"; in Science program, the typologies "Valorization of R&D" and "International Partnerships in Science and Technology"; and in SI Innovation program, the four typologies of project have the same degree of openness.

The aggregate analysis by program allows to see which offers a greater coverage of the 30 action lines, through the eligible expenditures of their typologies of program, that is, a higher degree of openness. In Figure 3 it is possible to perceive that the SI I&DT program is the one that has a higher degree of openness (with a value of 0.57 – i.e., the eligible expenditures of

Figure 3. Degree of Openness of Public Policy Programs
Source: own elaboration

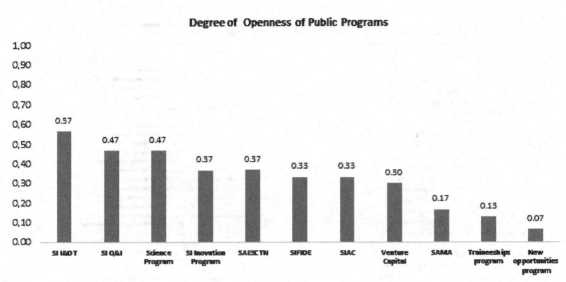

the typologies of project of SI I&DT program, on the whole, cover 57 percent of the 30 action lines of public policy), followed by SI Q&I and the Science program (both with a value of 0.47), the SI Innovation and SAESCTN (0.37).

It has also to be noted that the programs that have a lower degree of openness are the SAMA program (0.17), the Traineeships program/internships (0.13) and the New Opportunities program (0.07). This classification allows us to see that the programs that have a greater degree of openness are those that directly support R&D activities and enterprises innovation (followed by programs that support R&D and S&T institutions), while the programs directed to the environment context (external to the company) have a smaller degree of openness.

Level of Openness

The typologies of project and the programs analysed can be grouped by levels of openness (i.e., in groups with similar degree of openness), in order to have a better perception of those who support more broadly open innovation activities. Given

that this is a qualitative analysis, it is proposed the transformation of the degree of openness values (values ranging between "0" and "1", as shown in Figure 2) into categorical variables, which is the most appropriate in this type of analysis (Mertler and Vannatta, 2002). These variables correspond to different levels of openness: "weak", "moderate", "high" and "strong" (Table 2). This methodology is inspired by the ones used by some international innovation rankings, such as the IUS - Innovation Union Scoreboard (European Commission, 2014), although in this case are grouped countries and not public policies (in the IUS, the EU27 countries are grouped in four separate categories, according to their performance innovation, with values vary between "0" and "1"). The four levels of openness here proposed are justified due to the existence of several programs and typologies of projects in analysis (12 programs, including 35 typologies), allowing a more detailed classification and visually identify the most comprehensive in terms of support to open innovation activities (Table 2).

The classification according to the level of openness allows to find that most part of the programs and typologies of projects have a moderate

Table 2. Classification of the Level of Openness

Degree of Openness (between 0-1)	Level of Openness	Description
< 0.25	1- Weak level of openness	The degree of openness of the typologies of project and programs assumes a value less than 0.25 (i.e., their eligible expenses cover less than 25 percent of the open innovation action lines).
0.25-0.49	2- Moderate level of openness	The degree of openness of the typologies of project and programs assumes a value between 0.25-0.49 (i.e., their eligible expenses cover between 25 percent and 49 percent of the open innovation action lines).
0.5-0.74	3- High level of openness	The degree of openness of the typologies of project and programs assumes a value between 0.5-0.74 (i.e., their eligible expenses cover between 50 percent and 74 percent of the open innovation action lines).
> 0.74	4- Strong level of openness	The degree of openness of the typologies of project and programs assumes a value higher than 0.74 (i.e., their eligible expenses cover between 75 percent and 100 percent of the open innovation action lines).

Source: own elaboration

(0.25-0.49) or weak (< 0.25) level of openness, and that there are no programs (or typologies) with a strong level of openness (> 0.74). Only one program has a high level of openness – the R&D incentive system (SI R&D, with a value higher than 0.49) – the same with the typology "Co-promotion Projects" (included in SI R&D program). The Science program and the incentive system to Qualification and Internationalization (SI Q&I) are the ones that are highest rated in the moderate level group (a value of 0.47 for both programs), i.e, very close to have a high level of openness (Figure 4).

This classification reveals that the majority of public programs have a weak or moderate level of innovation openness, reflecting the absence of programs that cover the majority of open innovation activities (with the exception of R&D programs), i.e., most part of the programs have incentives to support only some open innovation activities. That means that companies (and other organizations) must submit their projects to different public programs (in this case, 35 typologies under 12 programs), in order to have financial support for the different innovation areas, which can put in disadvantage small and medium sized companies, generally with fewer resources to deal with the procedures necessary for the preparation

and submission of funding proposals, in relation to larger companies.

Such as in the degree of openness, the analysis of the level of openness shows that the programs (and typologies) that support R&D activities (including R&D co-promotion) are thee ones that have a higher level of openness. In the moderate level of openness we find a mix of programs and typologies of project targeted for companies and for the scientific and technological system institutions, while in the weak level of openness are located essentially the programs oriented to the external conditions of organizations (including the ones related with human resources).

CONCLUSION AND FUTURE RESEARCH DIRECTIONS

This Chapter allows the analysis of open innovation in a context outside the firm environment - which has been the main focus of the research in open innovation by the academic literature in the last decade - placing the analysis in the context of public policy. This is a first contribute to realize how public policy can encourage the adoption of open innovation by organizations, taking into account their impact on their activities (internal

Figure 4. Level of Openness – a Classification of the Public Programs and Typologies of Projects
Source: own elaboration

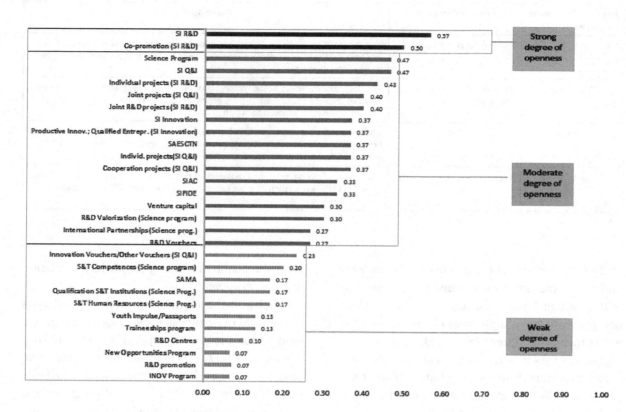

context) and in the environment in which they operate (external context).

To that end, and based on the case of Portugal, it were analysed the eligible expenditures of the public programs and their typology of projects in an open innovation perspective, complemented by a classification of their degree and level of openness, which allowed us to see which ones are more or less oriented to support open innovation activities. This classification aims to provide a methodology to analyze the degree of openness of public policies, which can be used by policy makers to design new measures to stimulate open innovation or to redesign or redirect existing programs and initiatives in that direction.

The main findings of this analysis shows that public programs and typologies of projects, in the Portuguese case, allow financially support to open innovation activities (in general), having as eligible the expenditures presented by organizations (companies or other entities) related to these activities. However, if considered individually, most part of the programs and typologies have a moderate or weak level of openness. With regard to the public programs more oriented to support open innovation (i.e., covering more incentives), it appears that there is a wider range of incentives (financial and fiscal incentives) directed to private R&D, particularly supporting R&D personnel hiring and IP registration costs, as well as joint projects with firms and scientific and technological institutions. One area where a greater focus on open innovation is needed is at the level of incentives for cooperation and networking, in particular by strengthening the establishment and consolidation of clusters. The areas with the lowest number of policy-oriented initiatives to stimulate open innovation are those that act at the level of context (external conditions), namely the labour market policy, education and training policy and eGovernment policy. Also worth noting that there are two areas without any specific public support: user innovation (in R&D policy) and intrapreneurship (in Entrepreneurship policy).

As a limitation of this study, it has to be pointed out that the analysis performed only shows the orientation of public policies for open innovation, based on the eligible expenditures of its programs and typologies of projects, i.e., allows us to see whether or not the projects presented by organizations (firms or other entities) can be covered by public funding in their open innovation activities. However, it`s not clear how this coverage possibility match with the projects submitted in fact. Thus, as a future research direction, it`s necessary to say that it would be enriching another analysis that includes the eligible expenditures that had been financed by each typology of project or programs. Also a deeper analysis of the issues and problems related to the lack of support to some open innovation activities by public policies could be done using, for example, the Business Process Modeling/Business Process Reengineering methodologies, allowing the aligning of public policies objectives/mission with the wants and needs of companies and other organizations.

REFERENCES

Assar, S., Boughzala, I., & Isckia, T. (2011). eGovernment trends in the web 2.0 era and the open innovation perspective: an exploratory field study. Electronic Government, Lecture Notes in Computer Science, (Vol. 6846, pp. 210-222). Springer Berlin Heidelberg.

Bemelmans-Videc, M.-L., Eriksen, B., & Golenberg, N. (1994). Facilitating organizational learning: human resource management and program evaluation. In F. Leeuw, R. Rist, & R. Sonnichsen (Eds.), *Can Government Learn? Comparative Perspective on Evaluation and Organizational Learning*. New Brunswick: Transaction Publishers.

Bergman, M., Charles, D., & Hertog, P. (2001). In pursuit of innovative clusters. In *OECD, Innovative clusters: drivers of national innovation systems*. Paris: OECD.

Bogers, M., Afuah, A., & Bastian, B. (2010). Users as innovators: A review, critique, and future research directions. *Journal of Management, 36*(4), 857–875. doi:10.1177/0149206309353944

Breschi, S., & Malerba, F. (2005). *Clusters, Networks and Innovation*. Oxford University Press.

Chaminade, C., & Edquist, C. (2010). Rationales for public policy intervention in the innovation process: systems of innovation approach. In R. Smits, S. Kuhlmann & P. Shapira (Eds.) (2010), The Theory and Practice of Innovation Policy.

Chesbrough, H. (2003a). *Open Innovation: The New Imperative for Creating and Profiting from Technology*. Boston, MA: Harvard Business School Press.

Chesbrough, H. (2003b). *The era of open innovation*. MIT Sloan Management Review.

Chesbrough, H. (2004). Managing open innovation. *Industrial Research Institute, 47*(1), 23–26.

Chesbrough, H. (2006). Open innovation: a new paradigm for understanding industrial innovation. In H. Chesbrough, W. Vanhaverbeke, & J. West (Eds.), Open Innovation: Researching a New Paradigm. Oxford University Press.

Chesbrough, H., & Bogers, M. (2014). Explicating Open Innovation: Clarifying an Emerging Paradigm for Understanding Innovation. In H. Chesbrough, W. Vanhaverbeke & J. West (Eds.), New Frontiers in Open Innovation. Oxford: Oxford University Press.

Chesbrough, H., & Schwartz, K. (2007). Innovating business models with codevelopment partnerships. *Industrial Research Institute*, *50*(1), 55–59.

Chesbrough, H., & Vanhaverbeke, W. (2011). *Open innovation and public policy in Europe*. Science Business Publishing Ltd.

Chesbrough, H., Vanhaverbeke, W., & West, J. (Eds.). (2008). *Open Innovation: Researching a New Paradigm*. Oxford University Press.

Cohen, W. M., & Levinthal, D. A. (1990). Absorptive Capacity: A New Perspective on Learning and Innovation. *Administrative Science Quarterly*, *35*(1), 128–152. doi:10.2307/2393553

Cooke, P. (2005). Regional knowledge capabilities and open innovation: Regional innovation systems and clusters in the asymmetric knowledge economy. *Research Policy*, *34*(8), 1128–1149. doi:10.1016/j.respol.2004.12.005

Dahlander, L., & Gann, D. (2010). How open is innovation? *Research Policy*, *39*(6), 699–709. doi:10.1016/j.respol.2010.01.013

De Jong, J. P. J., Kalvet, T., & Vanhaverbeke, W. (2008). *Policies for Open Innovation: Theory, Framework and Cases*. Helsinki: VISION Era-Net.

De Jong, J. P. J., Kalvet, T., & Vanhaverbeke, W. (2010). Exploring a theoretical framework to structure the public policy implications of open innovation. *Technology Analysis and Strategic Management*, *22*(8), 877–896. doi:10.1080/09537325.2010.522771

Derlien, H.-U., & Rist, R. (2000). Policy Evaluation in International Comparison. In J.-E. Furubo, R. Rist, & R. Sandahal (Eds.), *International Atlas of Evaluation*. London, New Brunswick: Transaction Publishers.

Di Natale, M., Cucinotta, T. & Kolachalam, S. (2003). A modular Open-source Architecture for ICT Services in the Public Administration. *Electronic Government,* (167-172). Springer Berlin Heidelberg.

Dolfsma, W., & Seo, D. (2013). Government policy and technological innovation - a suggested typology. *Technovation*, *33*(6-7), 173–179. doi:10.1016/j.technovation.2013.03.011

Dosi, G., & Freeman, C. (Eds.). (1988). *Technical Change and Economic Theory*. London: Pinter.

Dreyfuss, R. (2011). Policy Forum: Privatising Science, Evaluating the Public Impact of Open Innovation. *The Australian Economic Review*, *44*(1), 66–72. doi:10.1111/j.1467-8462.2010.00621.x

Edquist, C. (2001, June 12-15). *The Systems of Innovation Approach and Innovation Policy: An account of the state of the art.* Lead paper presented at the DRUID Conference, Aalborg.

Edquist, C., & Zabala-Iturriagagoitia, J. M. (2012). Public Procurement for Innovation as mission-oriented innovation policy. *Research Policy*, *41*(10), 1757–1769. doi:10.1016/j.respol.2012.04.022

Edquist, E. & Chaminade, C. (2006, July*)*. Industrial policy from a systems of innovation perspective. *EIB papers, 11*(1&2).

Foray, D. (Ed.). (2009). *The New Economics of Technology Policy*. Edward Elgar. doi:10.4337/9781848449169

Fredberg, T., Elmquist, M. & Ollila, S. (2008). Managing open innovation: present findings and future directions. *Vinnova report, VR 2008:02*.

Freeman, C. (1987). *Technology and Economic Performance: Lessons from Japan.* London: Pinter.

Furubo, J.-E., Rist, R., & Sandahl, R. (Eds.). (2002). *International Atlas of Evaluation.* London, New Brunswick: Transaction Publishers.

Greene, W. H. (1997). *Econometric Analysis* (3rd ed.). Upper Saddle River, New Jersey: Prentice-Hall.

Hagedoorn, J., & Ridder, A.-K. (2012). Open innovation, contracts, and intellectual property rights: an exploratory empirical study.

Hall, P. A., & Taylor, R. C. (1996). Political Science and the Three New Institutionalisms. *Political Studies, 44*(5), 936–957. doi:10.1111/j.1467-9248.1996.tb00343.x

Helfat, C., & Quinn, J. (2006). Off the shelf book review – Open Innovation: The new imperative for creating and profiting from technology. *The Academy of Management Perspectives, 20*(2), 86–88. doi:10.5465/AMP.2006.20591014

Herstad, S., Bloch, C., Ebersberger, B., & De Velde, E. (2010). National innovation policy and global open innovation: Exploring balances, tradeoffs and complementarities. *Science & Public Policy, 37*(2), 113–124. doi:10.3152/030234210X489590

Hoyer, B. (2011). *Unlocking the digital future through open innovation – an intellectual capital approach. Directorate-General for the Information Society and Media.* European Commission.

Huizingh, E. K. R. E. (2011). Open innovation: State of the art and future perspectives. *Technovation, 31*(1), 2–9. doi:10.1016/j.technovation.2010.10.002

Innovation Union Scoreboard 2014. (2014 European Commission.

Jacob, S., & Varone, F. (2004). Institutionnalisation de L'évaluation et Nouvelle Gestion Publique: Un État des Lieux Comparatif. *Revue Internationale de Politique Comparée, 11*(2).

Koelble, T. A., Cook, K. S., Levi, M., Granovetter, M., Swedberg, R., & March, J. G. et al. (1996). The New Institutionalism in Political Science and Sociology. *Comparative Politics, 27*(2), 231–243. doi:10.2307/422167

Laursen, K., & Salter, A. J. (2005). Open Innovation: The Role of Openness in Explaining Innovation Performance Among U.K. Manufacturing Firms. *Strategic Management Journal, 27*(2), 131–150. doi:10.1002/smj.507

Laursen, K., & Salter, A. J. (2014). The paradox of openness: Appropriability, external search and collaboration. *Research Policy, 43*(5), 867–878. doi:10.1016/j.respol.2013.10.004

Lundvall, B.-A. (1988). Innovation as an interactive process: from user-producer interaction to the national system of innovation. In G. Dosi, C. Freeman, R. Nelson, G. Silverberg, & L. Soete (Eds.), Technical Change and Economic Theory (349-369). London: Pinter.

Lundvall, B.-Å., Johnson, B., Andersen, E. S., & Dalum, B. (2002). National systems of production, innovation and competence building. *Research Policy, 31*(2), 213–231. doi:10.1016/S0048-7333(01)00137-8

Malecki, E. (2011). Connecting local entrepreneurial ecosystems to global innovation networks: Open innovation, double networks and knowledge integration. *International Journal of Entrepreneurship and Innovation Management, 14*(1), 36–59. doi:10.1504/IJEIM.2011.040821

Mazzucato, M. (2011). *The Entrepreneurial State.* London, UK: Demos.

Mertler, C., & Vannatta, R. (2002). *Advanced and Multivariate Statistical Methods.* Pyrczak Publishing.

Mutkoski, S. (2011). *Defining Open Standards: A comparison of policy and practice.* 7th International Conference on Standardization and Innovation in Information Technology (SIIT), 1-12. IEEE. doi:10.1109/SIIT.2011.6083616

Nelson, R., & Rosenberg, N. (1993). Technical innovation and national systems. In R. R. Nelson (Ed.), *National Innovation Systems: A comparative analysis.* New York: Oxford University Press.

Observatório do QREN. (2011). *QREN - Quadro de Referência Estratégico Nacional.* Observatório do QREN. Retrieved from www.qren.pt

OECD. (2008). *Open Innovation in Global Networks.* Paris: OECD.

OECD. (2009). *The OECD Innovation Strategy: draft interim report.* Paris: OECD.

OECD. (2011). *Measuring the Economics of Big Data. DSTI/ICCP/IIS (2011) 4, OECD. O`Reilly, T. (2013). Government as a Platform, Open Government: Collaboration, Transparency and Participation in Practice.* O`Reilly Media, Inc.

Prahalad, C. K., & Ramaswamy, V. (2000). Co-Opting Customer Experience. *Harvard Business Review.*

Pre-commercial Procurement - Public sector needs as a driver of Innovation. (2006, September). European Commission.

Santos, A. B. (2015). Open Innovation research: trends and influences – a Bibliometric Analysis. *Journal of Innovation Management, 3*(2), 131-165.

Spithoven, A., Clarysse, B., & Knockaert, M. (2010). Building absorptive capacity to organize inbound open innovation in traditional industries. *Technovation, 30*(2), 130–141. doi:10.1016/j.technovation.2009.08.004

Teece, D. (2006). Reflections on "Profiting from Innovation". *Research Policy, 35*(8), 1131–1146. doi:10.1016/j.respol.2006.09.009

Thoenig, J.-C. (1999). L'évaluation, sources de connaissances applicables aux réformes de la gestion publique. *Revue française d'administration publique, n° 92.*

Ubaldi, B. (2013). Open Government Data: Towards Empirical Analysis of Open Government Data Initiatives. *OECD Working Papers on Public Governance.*

UMIC. (2011). *Relatório de Atividades 2011.* Ministério da Educação e Ciência.

Vanhaverbeke, W., West, J., & Chesbrough, H. (2014). Surfing the new wave of open innovation research. In H. Chesbrough, W. Vanhaverbeke, & J. West (Eds.), New Frontiers in Open Innovation. Oxford: Oxford University Press. doi:10.1093/acprof:oso/9780199682461.003.0015

Wessner, C., & Wolff, A. (2012). *Rising to the Challenge, U.S. Innovation Policy for the Global Economy.* Washington, D.C.: The National Academies Press.

West, J., Ammon, S., Vanhaverbeke, W., & Chesbrough, H. (2014). Open innovation: The next decade. *Research Policy, 43*(5), 805–811. doi:10.1016/j.respol.2014.03.001

ENDNOTES

[1] The author thanks to the two anonymous referees for their helpful comments and suggestions to this chapter. The author also thanks the insights from the participants of the 1st World Open Innovation Conference (4-5 December 2014, Napa Valley, São Francisco), specially the comments from Professor Wim Vanhaverbeke (Hasselt University and ESADE). The author is also grateful to Professor Sandro Mendonça, from ISCTE-IUL (Lisbon) by the useful insights to this Chapter.

2   The exception is the program "Legal Regime of Competition", that was not classified, due its regulatory nature of the economic activity, i.e, it`s not an incentive program.

3   The decision to assign the same value of "1" to the action lines that are eligible, instead of using weighted values, is justified by the fact that the importance of each action line to stimulate open innovation depends on the characteristics of firms and of the environment in which they operate (Chesbrough *et al.*, 2006; Chesbrough and Vanhaverbeke, 2011; de Jong *et al.*, 2010). An action line can be more important for a company (or sector / cluster) than for other company, for example.

4   The arithmetic mean is the ratio of the sum of all observed values and the total number of observations.

APPENDIX A

Table 3. Analysis of the eligible expenditures of the typology of projects, according to the 30 action lines of public policy for open innovation (Part I)

Policy Area	Program / Action Lines of Public Policy Supporting Open Innovation (1 - 30)	R&D Incentive System						Innovation Incentive System	Qualification and Internationalization Incentive System				SIFIDE	Collective Eficiency / SIAC
		Individual Projects	Copromotion Projects	R&D Vouchers	Colective R&D Projects	R&D Centres in Companies	R&D Promotion Projects	Productive Innovation; Special Projects; Strategic Projects; Qualified Entrepreneurship	Innovation Vouchers/ Entrepreneurship Vouchers/ Energy Vouchers/ Internationalization Vouchers	Joint Projects	Cooperation Projects	Individual Projects	SIFIDE	Poles and Clusters
R&D Policy	**Financial/Fiscal Incentives**													
	1. R&D hiring incentives	x	x			x		x		x	x	x	x	
	2. R&D activities/ Consultant services	x	x	x	x				x	x	x	x	x	
	Intelectual Property Support													
	3. Patents/Trademarks registration	x	x		x			x		x	x	x	x	
	Standards and Certification													
	4. R&D and innovation management certification process	x	x			x		x		x	x	x		
	5. User innovation													
Colaboration/ Network Policy	**Network Skills**													
	6. R&D activities/ Consultant services	x	x	x	x				x	x	x	x	x	x
	7. International promotion	x	x		x			x		x	x	x		x
	Colaboration and Partnerships Support													
	8. Consortium/ Partnerships between companies and universities/R&D institutions		x		x			x					x	x
	Technological Markets													
	9. Patents acquisition	x	x	x	x			x					x	x
	10. Licensing of patents (acquisition to other entities)	x	x	x	x			x						
	Technological Intermediation													
	11. R&D activities/ Consultant services	x	x	x	x				x	x	x	x	x	x
	Support to Clusters													
	12. Networks and clusters		x		x									x
	13. Intrapreneurship incentives													

continued on following page

Table 3. Continued

Policy Area	Program (Action Lines of Public Policy Supporting Open Innovation (1 - 30))	R&D Incentive System						Innovation Incentive System	Qualification and Internationalization Incentive System				SIFIDE	Collective Eficiency / SIAC
		Individual Projects	Copromotion Projects	R&D Vouchers	Colective R&D Projects	R&D Centres in Companies	R&D Promotion Projects	Productive Innovation; Special Projects; Strategic Projects; Qualified Entrepreneurship	Innovation Vouchers/ Entrepreneurship Vouchers/ Energy Vouchers/ Internationalization Vouchers	Joint Projects	Cooperation Projects	Individual Projects	SIFIDE	Poles and Clusters
Entrepreneurship Policy	14. Access to financial instruments			x					x					x
	Support to Start-Ups/Spin-Offs/High-Growth Companies													
	15. R&D activities/ Consultant services	x	x	x	x				x	x	x	x	x	x
Science Policy	16. Incentives and financial support			x					x					
	17. Adequate incentives													
	18. Focus on Excellence													
	Diffusion and Cooperation Incentives													
	19. R&D hiring incentives	x	x			x		x		x	x	x	x	
	20. Demonstration/ Dissemination of R&D results	x	x		x		x	x		x			x	x
	21. International promotion	x	x		x			x		x	x	x		
Education and Training Policy	22. Entrepreneuship education													
	23. Human Resources (HR) qualification and Lifelong learning							x	x	x	x	x		x
Labour Market Policy	24. HR mobility													
	25. Qualified HR attraction													
Competition Policy	26. Competition stimulus													
eGovernment Policy	27. Cocreation													
	28. Open Standards													
	29. eProcurement													
	30. Open data													

Table 4. Analysis of the eligible expenditures of the typology of projects, according to the 30 action lines of public policy for open innovation (Part II)

Policy Area	Action Lines of Public Policy Supporting Open Innovation (1 - 30)	S & T Support System — HR Mobility; S&T Parks (R&D Projects, R&D Results Exploitation, 7° Framework Program R&D)	Science Program 2007-2013 — HR Training; Scientific and Technological Culture (Doctoral and R&D Grants; PhD Hiring for R&D Institutions; Experimental Teaching of Sciences	Internationalization of the Scientific and Technological System-S&T International Partnerships; ESA / ESO Projects; Eureka / Eurostars	Qualification of Entities from S&T System; Liaison of R&D Institutions with Companies; Public and Private R&D Thematic Networks (after 2012)	Scientific and Technical Expertise (Attraction of Highly Qualified Staff at Scientific and Technical Level)	R&D Economic Exploitation (UTEN Network; University-Enterprise Programs	SAMA – Administrative Modernization Support System — Qualification and Administrative Simplification of the Public Services to Citizens and Businesses	Professional traineeship Programs — "INOV" Programs (INOVContact; INOVMundus; INOVArt; INOVExport; INOVJovem; INOVSocial; INOV Energy)	"Impulso Jovem" Initiative "Passports" Initiative	New Opportunities Program — Youth Axis Adult Axis	Venture Capital Programs — INOFIN FINOV; SAPFRI Portugal Ventures FSCR FCGM FGTC Business Angels
	Financial/Fiscal Incentives											
R&D Policy	1. R&D hiring incentives	x										
R&D Policy	2. R&D activities/ Consultant services	x										
	Intelectual Property Support											
R&D Policy	3. Patents/ Trademarks registration	x					x					
	Standards and Certification											
R&D Policy	4. R&D and innovation management certification process											
R&D Policy	5. User innovation											
	Network Skills											
Collaboration Policy	6. R&D activities/ Consultant services											x
Collaboration Policy	7. International promotion											x
	Collaboration and Partnerships Support											
Collaboration Policy	8. Consortium/ Partnerships between companies and universities/ R&D institutions	x		x	x		x					x
	Technological Markets											
Collaboration Policy	9. Patents acquisition					x						x
Collaboration Policy	10. Licensing of patents (acquisition to other entities)											x

continued on following page

Table 4. Continued

Policy Area	Action Lines of Public Policy Supporting Open Innovation (1 - 30)	S & T Support System	Science Program 2007-2013					SAMA – Administrative Modernization Support System	Professional traineeship Programs		New Opportunities Program	Venture Capital Programs
		HR Mobility; S&T Parks (R&D Projects, R&D Results Exploitation, 7° Framework Program R&D	HR Training; Scientific and Technological Culture (Doctoral and R&D Grants; PhD Hiring for R&D Institutions; Experimental Teaching of Sciences	Internationalization of the Scientific and Technological System-S&T International Partnerships; ESA / ESO Projects; Eureka / Eurostars	Qualification of Entities from S&T System; Liaison of R&D Institutions with Companies; Public and Private R&D Thematic Networks (after 2012)	Scientific and Technical Expertise (Attraction of Highly Qualified Staff at Scientific and Technical Level)	R&D Economic Exploitation (UTEN Network; University-Enterprise Programs	Qualification and Administrative Simplification of the Public Services to Citizens and Businesses	"INOV" Programs (INOVContact; INOVMundus; INOVArt; INOVExport; INOVJovem; INOVSocial; INOV Energy)	"Impulso Jovem" Initiative "Passports" Initiative	Youth Axis Adult Axis	INOFIN FINOV; SAPFRI Portugal Ventures FSCR FCGM FGTC Business Angels
Technological Intermediation												
Collaboration Policy	11. R&D activities/ Consultant services						x					x
Support to Clusters												
	12. Networks and Clusters											x
Entrepreneurship Policy	13. Intrapreneurship incentives											
	14. Access to financial instruments											x
Support to Start-Ups/Spin-Offs/High-Growth Companies												
	15. R&D activities/ Consultant services											x
Science Policy	16. Incentives and financial support	x		x	x							
	17. Adequate incentives	x		x	x	x						
	18. Focus on Excellence	x		x	x	x	x					
Diffusion and Cooperation Incentives												
	19. R&D hiring incentives	x	x	x	x	x	x					
	20. R&D demonstration/ Dissemination of R&D results	x	x			x	x					
	21. International promotion	x		x		x	x					

continued on following page

Table 4. Continued

Policy Area	Program / Action Lines of Public Policy Supporting Open Innovation (1 - 30)	S & T Support System — HR Mobility; S&T Parks (R&D Projects, R&D Results Exploitation, 7° Framework Program R&D)	Science Program 2007-2013 — HR Training; Scientific and Technological Culture (Doctoral and R&D Grants; PhD Hiring for R&D Institutions; Experimental Teaching of Sciences)	Internationalization of the Scientific and Technological System-S&T International Partnerships; ESA / ESO Projects; Eureka / Eurostars	Qualification of Entities from S&T System; Liaison of R&D Institutions with Companies; Public and Private R&D Thematic Networks (after 2012)	Scientific and Technical Expertise (Attraction of Highly Qualified Staff at Scientific and Technical Level)	R&D Economic Exploitation (UTEN Network; University-Enterprise Programs)	SAMA – Administrative Modernization Support System — Qualification and Administrative Simplification of the Public Services to Citizens and Businesses	Professional traineeship Programs — "INOV" Programs (INOVContact; INOVMundus; INOVArt; INOVExport; INOV Jovem; INOVSocial; INOV Energy)	"Impulso Jovem" Initiative "Passports" Initiative	New Opportunities Program — Youth Adult Axis	Venture Capital Programs — INOFIN FINOV; SAPFRI Portugal Ventures FSCR FCGM FGTC Business Angels
Education and Training Policy	22. Entrepreneurship education	x	x								x	
	23. Human Resources (HR) qualification and Lifelong learning		x					x	x	x	x	
Labour Market Policy	24. HR mobility	x		x		x			x	x	
	25. Qualified HR attraction			x		x						
Competition Policy	25. Competition stimulus											
eGovernment Policy	27. Cocriation							x				
	28. Open Standards							x				
	29. eProcurement							x				
	30. Open Data							x				

Source: own elaboration

Table 5. Analysis of the eligible expenditures of the typology of projects, according to the 30 action lines of public policy for open innovation - proposed classification (Part I)

Policy Area	Program / Action Lines of Public Policy Supporting Open Innovation (1 - 30)	R&D Incentive System (SI R&D)							Innovation Incentive System	Qualification and Internationalization Incentive System (SI Q&I)					SIFIDE	Collective Eficiency Strategy / SIAC
		Individual Projects	Co-Promotion Projects	R&D Vouchers	Colective R&D Projects	R&D Centres in Companies	R&D Promotion Projects	SI R&D (Total)	Productive Innovation; Special Projects; Strategic Projects; Qualified Entrepreneurship	Innovation Vouchers/Entrepreneurship Vouchers/Energy Vouchers/Internationalization Vouchers	Joint Projects	Cooperation Projects	Individual Projects	SI Q&I (Total)	Tax Incentives	Poles and Clusters
R&D Policy	**Financial/Fiscal Incentives**															
	1. R&D hiring incentives	1	1	0	0	1	0	1	1	0	1	1	1	1	1	0
	2.R&D activities/ Consultant services	1	1	1	1	0	0	1	0	1	1	1	1	1	1	0
	Intelectual Property Incentives															
	3.Patents/Trademarks registration	1	1	0	1	0	0	1	1	0	1	1	1	1	1	0
	Standards and Certification															
	4.R&D and innovation management certification process	1	1	0	0	1	0	1	1	0	1	1	1	1	0	0
	5.User innovation	0	0	0	0	0	0	0	0	0	0	0	0	0	0	*0*
Colaboration/ Network Policy	**Network Skills**															
	6.R&D activities/ Consultant services	1	1	1	1	0	0	1	0	1	1	1	1	1	1	1
	7.International promotion	1	1	0	1	0	0	1	1	0	1	1	1	1	0	1
	Colaboration and Partnerships Stimulus															
	8.Consortium/Partnerships between companies and universities/R&D institutions	0	1	0	1	0	0	1	1	0	0	0	0	0	1	1
	Technological Markets															
	9.Patents acquisition	1	1	1	1	0	0	1	1	0	0	0	0	0	1	1
	10.Licensing of patents (acquisition to other entities)	1	1	1	1	0	0	1	1	0	0	0	0	0	0	0
	Technological Intermediation															
	11.R&D activities/ Consultant services	1	1	1	1	0	0	1	0	1	1	1	1	1	1	1
	Support to Clusters															
	12.Networks and clusters	0	1	0	1	0	0	1	0	0	0	0	0	0	0	1

continued on following page

Table 5. Continued

Policy Area	Program / Action Lines of Public Policy Supporting Open Innovation (1 - 30)	R&D Incentive System (SI R&D)							Innovation Incentive System	Qualificatiom and Internationalization Incentive System (SI Q&I)					SIFIDE	Collective Eficiency Strategy / SIAC
		Individual Projects	Co-Promotion Projects	R&D Vouchers	Colective R&D Projects	R&D Centres in Companies	R&D Promotion Projects	SI R&D (Total)	Productive Innovation; Special Projects; Strategic Projects; Qualified Entrepreneurship	Innovation Vouchers/ Entrepreneurship Vouchers/ Energy Vouchers/ Internationalization Vouchers	Joint Projects	Cooperation Projects	Individual Projects	SI Q&I (Total)	Tax Incentives	Poles and Clusters
Entrepreneurship Policy	13. Intrapreneurship incentives	0	0	0	0	0	0	0	0	0	0	0	0	0	0	0
	14. Access to financial instruments	0	0	1	0	0	0	1	0	1	0	0	0	1	0	1
	Support to Start-Ups/Spin-Offs/High-Growth Companies															
	15. R&D activities/ Consultant services	1	1	1	1	0	0	1	0	1	1	1	1	1	1	1
	16. Incentives and financial support	0	0	1	0	0	0	1	0	1	0	0	0	1	0	0
Science Policy	17. Adequate incentives	0	0	0	0	0	0	0	0	0	0	0	0	0	0	0
	18. Focus on Excellence	0	0	0	0	0	0	0	0	0	0	0	0	0	0	0
	Difusion and Cooperation															
	19. R&D hiring incentives	1	1	0	0	1	0	1	1	0	1	1	1	1	1	0
	20. R&D demonstration/ Dissemination of R&D results	1	1	0	1	0	1	1	1	0	1	0	0	1	1	1
	21. International promotion	1	1	0	1	0	1	1	1	0	1	1	1	1	0	0
	22. Entrepreneuship education	0	0	0	0	0	0	0	0	0	0	0	0	0	0	0
Education and training Policy	23. Human Resources (HR) qualification and Lifelong learning	0	0	0	0	0	0	0	1	1	1	1	1	1	0	1
	24. HR mobility	0	0	0	0	0	0	0	0	0	0	0	0	0	0	0
Labour Market Policy	25. Qualified HR attraction	0	0	0	0	0	0	0	0	0	0	0	0	0	0	0
Competition Policy	26. Competition stimulus	0	0	0	0	0	0	0	0	0	0	0	0	0	0	0
	27. Cocreation	0	0	0	0	0	0	0	0	0	0	0	0	0	0	0
eGovernment Policy	28. Open Standards	0	0	0	0	0	0	0	0	0	0	0	0	0	0	0
	29. eProcurement	0	0	0	0	0	0	0	0	0	0	0	0	0	0	0
	30. Open data	0	0	0	0	0	0	0	0	0	0	0	0	0		0

Source: own elaboration

Table 6. Analysis of the eligible expenditures of the typology of projects, according to the 30 action lines of public policy for open innovation - proposed classification (Part II)

Policy Area	Action Lines of Public Policy Supporting Open Innovation (1 - 30)	S&T Support System SAESCTN	Science Program 2007-2013							SAMA – Administrat. Modernization Support System	Professional Traineeship Programs		New Opportunities Program	Venture Capital Programs	Competition Law
		HR Mobility; S&T Parks (R&D Projects, R&D Results Exploitation, 7° Framework Program R&D	HR Training; Scientific and Technological Culture (Doctoral and R&D Grants; PhD Hiring for R&D Institutions; Experimental Teaching of Sciences	Internationalization of the Scientific and Technological System-S&T International Partnerships; ESA / ESO Projects; Eureka / Eurostars	Qualification of Entities from S&T System; Liaison of R&D Institutions with Companies; Public and Private R&D Thematic Networks (After 2012)	Scientific and Technical Expertise (Attraction of Highly Qualified Staff at Scientific and Technical Level)	R&D Economic Exploitation (UTEN Network; University-Enterprise Programs	Science Program (Total)	Qualification and Administrative Simplification of the Public Services to Citizens and Businesses	"INOV" Programs (INOVContact; INOVMundus; INOVArt; INOVExport; INOVJovem; INOVSocial; INOV Energy)	"Impulso Jovem" Initiative "Passports" Initiative	Youth Axis Adult Axis	INOFIN FINOV; SAPFRI Portugal Ventures FSCR FCGM FGTC Business Angels	Anti-Competition Practices; Studies, Inspections and Audits; Public Aid
R&D policy	**Financial/Fiscal Incentives**													
	1. R&D hiring incentives	1	0	0	0	0	0	0	0	0	0	0	0	0
	2.R&D activities/ Consultant services	1	0	0	0	0	0	0	0	0	0	0	0	0
	Intellectual Property Incentives													
	3.Patents/ Trademarks registration	1	0	0	0	0	1	1	0	0	0	0	0	0
	Standards and Certification													
	4.R&D and innovation management certification process	0	0	0	0	0	0	0	0	0	0	0	0	0
	5.User innovation	0	0	0	0	0	0	0	0	0	0	0	0	0
	Network Skills													
	6.R&D activities/ Consultant services	0	0	0	0	0	0	0	0	0	0	0	1	0

continued on following page

Table 6. Continued

Policy Area	Action Lines of Public Policy Supporting Open Innovation (1 - 30)	S&T Support System SAESCTN — HR Mobility; S&T Parks (R&D Projects, R&D Results Exploitation, 7° Framework Program R&D)	Science Program 2007-2013 — HR Training; Scientific and Technological Culture (Doctoral and R&D Grants; PhD Hiring for R&D Institutions; Experimental Teaching of Sciences)	Internationalization of the Scientific and Technological System-S&T International Partnerships; ESA / ESO Projects; Eureka / Eurostars	Qualification of Entities from S&T System; Liaison of R&D Institutions with Companies; Public and Private R&D Thematic Networks (After 2012)	Scientific and Technical Expertise (Attraction of Highly Qualified Staff at Scientific and Technical Level)	R&D Economic Exploitation (UTEN Network; University-Enterprise Programs)	Science Program (Total)	SAMA – Administrat. Modernization Support System — Qualification and Administrative Simplification of the Public Services to Citizens and Businesses	Professional Traineeship Programs — "INOV" Programs (INOVContact; INOVMundus; INOVArt; INOVExport; INOVJovem; INOVSocial; INOV Energy)	"Impulso Jovem" Initiative "Passports" Initiative	New Opportunities Program — Youth Axis Adult Axis	Venture Capital Programs — INOFIN FINOV; SAPFRI Portugal Ventures FSCR FCGM FGTC Business Angels	Competition Law — Anti-Competition Practices; Studies, Inspections and Audits; Public Aid
Colaboration/Network Policy	7. International promotion	0	0	0	0	0	0	0	0	0	0	0	1	0
	Colaboration and Partnerships Stimulus													
	8. Consortium/ Partnerships between companies and universities/ R&D institutions	1	0	1	1	0	1	1	0	0	0	0	1	0
	Technological Markets													
	9. Patents acquisition	0	0	0	0	0	1	1	0	0	0	0	1	0
	10. Licensing of patents (acquisition to other entities)	0	0	0	0	0	0	0	0	0	0	0	1	0
	Technological Intermediation													
	11. R&D activities/ Consultant services	0	0	0	0	0	1	1	0	0	0	0	1	0
	Support to Clusters													
	12. Networks and clusters	0	0	0	0	0	0	0	0	0	0	0	1	0
Entrepreneurship Policy	13. Intrapreneurship support	0	0	0	0	0	0	0	0	0	0	0	0	0
	14. Access to financial instruments	0	0	0	0	0	0	0	0	0	0	0	1	0
	Support to Start-Ups/Spin-Offs/High-Growth Companies													
	15. R&D activities/ Consultant services	0	0	0	0	0	0	0	0	0	0	0	1	0

continued on following page

Table 6. Continued

Policy Area	Action Lines of Public Policy Supporting Open Innovation (1 - 30)	S&T Support System SAESCTN — HR Mobility; S&T Parks (R&D Projects, R&D Results Exploitation, 7ª Framework Program R&D	Science Program 2007-2013 — HR Training; Scientific and Technological Culture (Doctoral and R&D Grants; PhD Hiring for R&D Institutions; Experimental Teaching of Sciences	Internationalization of the Scientific and Technological System–S&T International Partnerships; ESA / ESO Projects; Eureka / Eurostars	Qualification of Entities from S&T System; Liaison of R&D Institutions with Companies; Public and Private R&D Thematic Networks (After 2012)	Scientific and Technical Expertise (Attraction of Highly Qualified Staff at Scientific and Technical Level)	R&D Economic Exploitation (UTEN Network; University-Enterprise Programs	Science Program (Total)	SAMA – Administrat. Modernization Support System — Qualification and Administrative Simplification of the Public Services to Citizens and Businesses	Professional Traineeship Programs — "INOV" Programs (INOVContact; INOVMundus; INOVArt; INOVExport; INOVJovem; INOVSocial; INOV Energy)	"Impulso Jovem" Initiative "Passports" Initiative	New Opportunities Program — Youth Axis Adult Axis	Venture Capital Programs — INOFIN FINOV; SAPFRI Portugal Ventures FSCR FCGM FGTC Business Angels	Competition Law — Anti-Competitition Practices; Studies, Inspections and Audits; Public Aid
Science Policy	16. Incentives and financial support	1	0	1	1	0	0	1	0	0	0	0	0	0
	17. Adequate incentives	1	0	1	1	1	0	1	0	0	0	0	0	0
	18. Focus on Excellence	1	0	1	1	1	1	1	0	0	0	0	0	0
	Difusion and Cooperation													
	19. R&D staff hiring	1	1	1	1	1	1	1	0	0	0	0	0	0
	20. R&D demonstration/ Dissemination of R&D results	1	1	0	0	1	1	1	0	0	0	0	0	0
	21. International promotion	1	0	1	0	1	1	1	0	0	0	0	0	0
Education and Training Policy	22. Entrepreneurship education	1	1	0	0	0	0	1	0	0	0	1	0	0
	23. HR qualification and Lifelong learning	0	1	0	0	0	0	1	1	1	1	1	0	0
Labour Market Policy	24. HR Mobility	0	1	1	0	0	1	1	0	1	1	0	0	0
	25. Qualified HR attraction	0	0	1	0	1	0	1	0	0	0	0	0	0

continued on following page

Table 6. Continued

Policy Area	Action Lines of Public Policy Supporting Open Innovation (1 - 30)	S&T Support System SAESCTN	Science Program 2007-2013					Science Program (Total)	SAMA – Administrat. Modernization Support System	Professional Traineeship Programs		New Opportunities Program	Venture Capital Programs	Competition Law
		HR Mobility; S&T Parks (R&D Projects, R&D Results Exploitation, 7° Framework Program R&D	HR Training; Scientific and Technological Culture (Doctoral and R&D Grants; PhD Hiring for R&D Institutions; Experimental Teaching of Sciences	Internationalization of the Scientific and Technological System–S&T International Partnerships; ESA / ESO Projects; Eureka / Eurostars	Qualification of Entities from S&T System; Liaison of R&D Institutions with Companies; Public and Private R&D Thematic Networks (After 2012)	Scientific and Technical Expertise (Attraction of Highly Qualified Staff at Scientific and Technical Level)	R&D Economic Exploitation (UTEN Network; University-Enterprise Programs		Qualification and Administrative Simplification of the Public Services to Citizens and Businesses	"INOV" Programs (INOVContact; INOVMundus; INOVArt; INOVExport; INOVJovem; INOVSocial; INOV Energy)	"Impulso Jovem" Initiative "Passports" Initiative	Youth Axis Adult Axis	INOFIN FINOV; SAPFRI Portugal Ventures FSCR FCGM FGTC Business Angels	Anti-Competitition Practices; Studies, Inspections and Audits; Public Aid
Competition Policy — 26. Competition stimulus		0	0	0	0	0	0	0	0	0	0	0	0	1
eGovernment Policy — 27. Cocreation		0	0	0	0	0	0	0	1	0	0	0	0	0
28. Open Standards		0	0	0	0	0	0	0	1	0	0	0	0	0
29. eProcurement		0	0	0	0	0	0	0	1	0	0	0	0	0
30. Open data		0	0	0	0	0	0	0	1	0	0	0	0	0

Source: own elaboration

Table 7. Degree of openness of the typologies of projects (based on the eligible expenditures of Table 1 and Table 2) (Part I)

	Programs and typologies of project													
	R&D Incentives System (SI R&D) - Typologies of Project							Innovation Incentives System (SI Innovation) - Typologies of Project		Qualification and Internationalization Incentives System (SI Q&I) - Typologies of Project				
	Individual Projects	Copromotion Projects	R&D Vouchers	Colective R&D Projects	R&D Centres in Companies	R&D Promotion Projects	SI R&D (Total)	Productive Innovation; Special Projects; Strategic Projects; Qualified Entrepreneurship	SI Innovation (Total)	Innovation Vouchers/ Entrepreneurship Vouchers/ Energy Vouchers/ Internationalization Vouchers	Joint Projects	Cooperation Projects	Individual Projects	SI Q&I (Total)
Action lines covered by the elegible expenditures (1)	13	15	8	12	3	2	17	11	11	7	12	11	11	14
Total number of possible action lines covered (2)	30	30	30	30	30	30	30	30	30	30	30	30	30	30
Degree of Openness (1/2)	0.43	0.50	0.27	0.40	0.10	0.07	0.57	0.37	0.37	0.23	0.40	0.37	0.37	0.47

Source: own elaboration

Table 8. Degree of openness of the typologies of projects (based on the eligible expenditures of Table 1 and Table 2) (Part II)

	Programs and Typologies of Project														
				Science Program – Tipology of Projects							Professional Traineeship Programs – Tipology of Projects				
	SIFIDE	EEC/ SIAC (Poles/Clusters)	SAESCTN (HR Mobility; Tecn. Centres; S&T Parks)	S&T HR	International Partnerships	Qualification of Entities from Scientific and Technological System	Scientific and Technical Expertise	R&D Exploitation	Science Program (total)	SAMA – Administrative Modernization Support System	INOV Programs (Youth; Contact; Mundus; V.Gama; Social; Arts; Energy)	Impulso Jovem Initiative Passports	Professional Traineeship Programs (Total)	New Opportunities Program (Youth and Adults Axis)	Venture Capital programs
Action lines covered by the elegible expenditures (1)	10	10	11	5	8	5	6	9	14	5	2	4	4	2	9
Total number of possible action lines covered (2)	30	30	30	30	30	30	30	30	30	30	30	30	30	30	30
Degree of Openness (1/2)	0.33	0.33	0.37	0.17	0.27	0.17	0.20	0.30	0.47	0.17	0.07	0.13	0.13	0.07	0.30

Source: own elaboration

APPENDIX B

Descriptive Analysis of the Programs and Typologies of Project, According to the Orientation of their Eligible Expenditures towards Open Innovation

SI I&DT Program: Incentive System to Research and Technological Development

The SI I&DT aims to intensify the efforts of business R&D, stimulating the insertion of companies in international networks of knowledge and innovation, and to promote the coordination between companies and scientific and technological entities (SCTN). Based on the analysis of the eligible expenditures (from the Rules of SI I&DT program), the action lines that have a higher coverage by the eligible expenditures are those that fall in the policy areas "R&D Policy" and "Networks/Collaboration Policy". In terms of "R&D Policy", both the typology of projects "Individual Projects" and "Co-promotion" (Table 1 in Annex A) have eligible expenditures for hiring R&D personnel and consultancy in R&D (financial incentives), patenting (intellectual property) and the costs with management R&D and innovation certification process (standards and certification). The typology "R&D Vouchers" is oriented toward the acquisition of consultancy and R&D services, delivered by entities of the SCTN. This is an important tool for the access of SMEs to technology transfer and knowledge, essential in the open innovation process (Laursen and Salter, 2005, 2014). Stand-still, there are no incentives in SI I&DT program to stimulate innovation coming from the users (user innovation).

With regard to the action lines which fall into the "Network and Collaboration Policy", the development of network skills and the stimulus to the cooperation between enterprises and research institutions is enhanced in the projects "Co-promotion" and " Collective R&D", while the cost of acquisition and/or licensing of patents (promotion of technological markets) and the acquisition of R&D activities (technology intermediation) are eligible in all projects, except in "R&D Centres" (Table 1, in Annex A). The expenditures with R&D demonstration is also contemplated by SI I&DT program in all the typologies of project, except in the "R&D Vouchers" typology. There is also a specific project for the dissemination of R&D results - "Demonstration Projects" - although it only had two calls (June, 2008 and December, 2009). These kind of projects are important for the demonstration and technology dissemination of innovative products and services, encouraging the diffusion of innovation and knowledge, key issue in open innovation (Chesbrough, 2006).

System of Incentives for Innovation: SI Innovation Program

The SI Innovation program aims to promote innovation in companies, the development of products and added value services (that are oriented towards international markets), the technological development and to promote qualified entrepreneurship. Companies are the only beneficiaries of this program, with the eligible expenditures common to all the typologies of projects of SI Innovation: "Productive Innovation", "Special Regime Projects", "Strategic Interest Projects" and "Qualified Entrepreneurship" (Table 1, in Annex A).

The SI Innovation includes, in its eligible expenditures, the main action lines of intervention for open innovation with respect to business R&D, namely financial incentives (to hire R&D staff), intellectual property costs (patenting) and expenses with standards and certification in R&D management. The SI

Innovation is also designed to include as eligible expenditure the international promotion of innovation and their outcomes, as well as partnerships between companies and research entities (action line "stimulus to collaboration/partnerships") and the acquisition of patents and patent licensing (action line "promotion of technological markets"), that are important for the adoption of open innovation by firms (Chesbrough, 2003b, 2006). Also the eligibility of expenditures on demonstration and dissemination of the results of R&D and contracting R&D personnel contribute to the dissemination policies and cooperation within the "Science Policy" (Table 1, in Annex A). Since April 2008, SI Innovation program also has as eligible expenditures with training activities associated with the developed of the projects approved, including the expenditures with trainees, trainers or the preparation, implementation, monitoring and evaluation of projects. This question is important in an open innovation perspective, due to the importance of the existance of qualified human resources in companies to increase the absorptive capacity of external knowledge (Laursen and Salter, 2005; Spithoven *et al.*, 2010).

Incentive System of Qualification and Internationalisation: SI Q&I Program

The SI Q&I program aims to support projects streamlined by companies (individually ones or in cooperation) or projects dynamized by public institutions, business associations and research entities, although they have to have as target innovative small and medium enterprises (SMEs). Are also targeted to be supported joint projects developed by companies and research entities, as well as the acquisition of specialized services by SMEs delivered by research entities (in the case of "Innovation Voucher" typology, as well as in the typologies created in November 2012 - the "Entrepreneurship Voucher", "Energy Voucher" and "Internationalization Voucher").

Based on the analysis of the eligible expenditures included in the SI Innovation program (Table 1, in Annex A), it is possible to note that the typologies "Joint Projects", "Projects in Cooperation" and "Individual Projects" are the ones that include eligible expenditures conductive to open innovation. In fact, these three typologies include expenditures with R&D personnel (action lines "financial incentives", "network skills", "dissemination and cooperation"), R&D activities and consultancy services (action lines "financial incentives", "technological intermediation"), patenting (acrtion line "intellectual property") or R&D certification and management (action line "standards and certification"). The "Joint Projects" typology also includes as elegible, expenditures with demonstration and dissemination of R&D results, important for the process of open innovation. The "Innovation Voucher" typology (as well as the "Entrepreneurship Voucher", "Energy Voucher" and "Internationalization Voucher") allow SMEs to hire R&D services from research institutions, stimulating th technological intermediation activities, strengthening networking skills, thus, benefiting the emergence of new technology-based firms oriented to global markets, important in the open innovation process (Malecki, 2011).

Under the SI Q&I program, was launched a call (in 2011) in the typology "Individual Projects", which only covers the cost of registration of patents, utility models and trademarks, having a higher financial incentive the projects that aim the future commercialization and licensing of patents (or brands) - which is one of the important aspects in open innovation with regard to the adoption of more flexible forms of industrial property protection (Chesbrough, 2004; Helfat and Quinn, 2006). As in the SI Innovation program, also the SI Q&I has (since April 2008) as eligible expenditures, investments in training associated with the development of projects, including the expenses with trainees, trainers or the preparation, implementation, monitoring and evaluation of the projects approved.

Fiscal Incentives System for Business R&D: SIFIDE Program

SIFIDE is a system of tax incentives for business R&D, particularly SMEs. It is a system that allows a tax credit of 32.5% of the total expenditure on R&D of the company, which can add 50% of this spending over the average of the previous two years, up to 1.5 million euros. In the limit, the total deduction can reach 82.5% of the investment in R&D.

As it is shown in Table 1 (Annex A), SIFIDE allows companies to include a wide range of costs related to R&D activities – that are key activities in the process of open innovation (de Jong *et al.*, 2008) - in particular: expenses with R&D personnel (tax incentives); R&D consulting activities and intellectual property registration (action lines that fall within the "R&D Policy"); expenses related to the acquisition of expert services (technological intermediation) or the acquisition of intellectual property services, through technological markets (action lines of "Collaboration Policy"); and costs with demonstration and dissemination of the results of R&D, essential in the open innovation process (action lines that fall in "Science Policy").

Collective Efficiency Strategy: SIAC Program (Poles of Competitiveness and Clusters)

SIAC is an instrument created to complement and enhance the existing programs analysed above, and to stimulate the creation or consolidation of industrial clusters or poles of competitiveness, as well as other networks associated with collective efficiency strategies. SIAC supports initiatives that boost the competitiveness of enterprises, business associations, technology centers and research entities. Projects can be developed by one or more entities, in this case organized in co-promotion.

The relevance of clusters and networks is concerned with the impact it has on the creation of innovation dynamics (Breschi and Malerba, 2005), also contributing to the development of practices of open innovation (Cooke, 2005). If we analyze the eligible expenditure and projects supported by SIAC, it is possible to find that they are targeted to promote cooperation and collaboration among firms and between firms and research entities, and to support initiatives that encourage the creation of new businesses. In fact, are included eligible expenses with consultancy services (studies, research and diagnostics directly related to the design, implementation and evaluation of the project), technical and scientific assistance (including R&D activities), that stimulate competence network, as well as expenditure with the creation and promotion of networks that support businesses and entrepreneurs, clusters and poles of competitiveness, promoting cooperation between enterprises and research entities (action line of the "Collaboration Policy"). Since November 2012, SIAC includes the support to entrepreneurship initiatives, in particular developed by young people, under the "Impulso Jovem" program. In 2012, it was lauched (under SIAC) a contest to encourage the participation of national entities in EU Programs for R&D (in particular in the 7th Framework Programe of R&D) stimulating cooperation between research entities and companies.

Support System to the Entities of the Scientific and Technological System: SAESCTN program

SAESCTN is an instrument oriented to strengthening the scientific and technological system, making it more competitive internationally, and to promote their coordination and collaboration with companies.

According to the Rules of SAESCTN, the projects should be promoted by scientific and research entities, individually or collectively, and may involve companies and other public or private entities. Two types of projects are supported: projects aiming scientific research and technological development and projects that promote scientific and technological culture, crosscutting.

If we analyze the eligible expenses in an open innovation perspective, we find that most of them fall under the "R&D Policy" (Table 3, Annex A). Eligible expenditures are directly related to R&D activities, including expenditure on human resources (e.g., costs with research fellows), missions abroad related to the projects, costs with registration of intellectual property abroad - patents, copyrights, utility models and designs, brands or models (including fees, surveys to the state of the art and consultancy fees). The relationship between intellectual property and open innovation has attracted the attention of several authors, and there is a growing consensus that the protection of intellectual property is critical to stimulate open innovation, being essential the development of business models that enable the creation of value with IP (Chesbrough, 2004; Teece, 2006; Fredberg *et al.*, 2008; Chesbrough and Vanhaverbeke, 2011; Hoyer, 2011; Hagedoorn and Ridder, 2012).

SAESCTN also considered as eligible expenditures with demonstration, promotion and dissemination of the project results, responding to the policy area "Science Policy" (Table 3, Annex A). There are also supported projects that aim to promote scientific and technological culture ("Education for Entrepreneurship" Policy) or national and international projects involving companies ("Collaboration Policy"). SAESCTN has been an instrument that financed many of the initiatives launched under the "Science Programs" (see next program analysis).

"Science Programs"

Science policy has been materialized, in Portugal, in the "Commitment for Science" initiative (launched on March 29, 2006), that aimed to close the gap between Portugal and EU27 average in terms of scientific and technological development. Although it was originally scheduled to run until 2009, the "Commitment to Science" initiative has been successively renewed and strengthened, particularly in the events " Ciência 2007", "Ciência 2008", Ciência 2009", "Ciência 2010" and "Ciência 2012".

If we analyze the types of projects supported, we realize that most of them respond to the action lines that fall within the "Science Policy", also having impact on the action lines of the "Education and Training Policy" and of the "Collaboration Policy". In fact, projects that fall within the typology "reeinforcement of scientific and technical skills" are oriented to create high quality infrastructures that promote access to knowledge, as well as to the creation of new knowledge using distributed technologies. In this typology of projects, there is also an initiative to attract highly qualified human resorces (at technical and scientific level), which fall under the "Labour Market Policy" (Table 3, Annex A).

In the typology "Advanced Human Resource Training and Promotion of the Scientific and Technological Culture", most of the projects launched relate to the support of PhD scholarships and postdoctoral, as well as for the integration of researchers and for hiring PhDs for research institutions, contributing to the creation of a skilled human resource base and to encourage greater mobility in the scientific and technological system. This question is important in open innovation: the advanced training of human resources is essential to increase the cumulative and absorptive capacity in R&D and in innovation activities (Cohen and Levinthal, 1990). It should also be noted the importance for the process of innovation, of the promotion and dissemination of the scientific and technological culture, also promoting a culture of entrepreneurship in the education system (Edquist, 2001). In this field, the initiative "Ciência Viva/ Life Science" was created to introduce experimental science teaching in the 1st cicle of basic education.

The typology of projects that fall under the "Qualification of R&D Institutions" action line aim to become more competitive internationally and tp raise the level of excellence of national R&D institutions (public or private). In this action line, it is necessary to highlight initiatives such as the "Reform of State Laboratories" or the "Improvement of the functioning of Associated Laboratories", which are assessed internationally on a regular basis. These assessments are essential for the State, in order to grant the status of "Associated Laboratory" to entities with excellency at scientific and technical level, and also to determin the levels of public funding grants to R&D institutions (the literature on open innovation - as Chesbrough (2003a), Herstad *et al* (2010) and Dreyfuss (2011) - refers to the importance of appropriate funding mechanisms for R&D and Science, based on the excellence of the institutions internationally evaluated). The "Ciência 2012" initiative provides the stimulus for the creation of "Research Centers of Excellence" in public and private sector, based on these evaluation criteria. In this context, highlighting the creation of "Thematic Networks for Research and Innovation", promoting cooperation between enterprises and organizations of the scientific system (in response to the action line "Stimulating Collaboration and Coordination with Scientific and Technological System Entities), as exemplified by the networks created under the CMU-Portugal partnership or the MIT-Portugal partnership (UMIC, 2011).

As in the previous typology, also projects under the "Internationalisation, Excelence and Evaluation" typology focuses on public funding based on criteria of excellence and international assessment, as are examples of the projects submitted to the 7th Framework Program for R&D (from the European Commission) or the Eureka/Eurostars projects, which are evaluated internationally in a competitive base. These projects involve companies and entities from the scientific and technological system, both nationally and internationally, encouraging collaboration among researchers, mobility and knowledge flows (responding to the action lines under the "Science Policy", "Collaboration Policy", "Education and Training Policy" and "Labour Market Policy").

Projects developed under the "Commitment to Science" initiative and the annual editions of "Science Programs" have been incorporating the suport to the economic exploitation of the results of R&D. For example, the creation of the UTEN Network (University Technology Enterprise Network), which was created under the Austin/Texas-Portugal partnership, aimed to promote in the market the results of the activities of that partnership, being extended to other international partnerships that exist in Portugal (MIT-Portugal, CMU-Portugal, Fraunhofer and Harvard Medical School), as well as to the Offices of Technology Transfer that exist in higher education institutions. It is also necessary to highlight the initiative "PhD in business environment", stimulating cooperation between enterprises and research entities, promoting mobility of researchers and workers between these two areas, as well as the initiative to "promote intellectual property registration" (which was reinforced in 2011, with stimulus provided to international intellectual property licensing, that is important for the process of open innovation).

INOV Programs / Internships Program ("Passaportes" Program)

In order to enable enterprises (SMEs) with qualified human resources and to facilitate the integration of young people into the labour market, was launched the INOV Jovem program (in 2005), which included financial support for placements/internships of young professionals in SMEs. In later years, similar initiatives have been launched in several areas, including the arts (INOV Art), cooperation (INOV Mundus), in the area of exports (Export INOV), in the social area (Social INOV), in the energy sector (Energy INOV) and internationalization (INOV Contact).

If we analyze these initiatives in accordance with the approach of open innovation, we find that all INOV initiatives respond to the action line "Training and Lifelong Learning" (Education and Training Policy). We can say that the action line "Mobility of Human Resources" (Labour Market policy) is covered by the initiatives INOV, not only because they are targeted to support internships in companies and in international organizations - as in INOV Contact, INOV Art, INOV Mundus or even in INOV Export - but also because they include youth throughout the country that can be hired for an internship in companies that are located anywhere in the country, encouraging labour mobility – in INOV Jovem initiative, Social INOV and Energy INOV. Chesbrough (2003a, 2004; 2006) finds that labour mobility is one of the factors that contributes to the spread of knowledge and, thus, to a greater openness of the innovation process.

In 2012, the "Impulso Jovem" program had also incentives for the hiring of young people by firms, also expected to include training activities (like in the INOV programs). Inside the "Impulso Jovem" program, the measure "Employment Passport" aims to promote the development of human resources in the tradable goods and services sectors, while "Employment Passport to Social Economy", the "Agriculture Passport" and the "Employment Associations and Federations Youth and Sports Passport" intended to promote the development of competencies in the respective areas of coverage. Under the "Impulso Jovem" program, the "Passport to Entrepreneurship" measure was released in 2012, which consists in a funding for entrepreneurs develop their business project, with the support of a National Network of Mentors, in order to get business advice, as well as by the access to technical assistance for the development of the business project. In an open innovation perspective, these measures contribute (like the INOV programs) for the action lines under "Education and Training Policy" and "Labour Market Policy" policy, as well as to the "Entrepreneurship Policy", as in the case of "Employment Passport" initiative.

Adult and Youth Qualification: New Opportunities Program (Novas Oportunidades)

To combat skills shortages of the Portuguese population, was released (in September 2005) the New Opportunities program, covering all age levels and forms of learning (formal, non-formal and informal). The initiative had two priorities for intervention - "Youth" and "Adults".

The "Young" priority was intended to combat school failure and dropping out of the education system, diversifying the offers in the education and training system, through the growth of vocational courses, as well as increasing the offers of post-secondary (non-degree) courses. To that, were established as priorities to achieve half of young people of secondary education courses in vocational training, as well as make the 12th year the minimum level of education for all young people. The priority "Adults" intended to qualify active adult population, with a dual certification approach - academic and vocational – with instruments such as the creation of the "New Opportunities Centres", the legal regime of education courses and adult education or the "Referential of Key Competencies for Education and Training for Adults at Secondary Level". The designation "New Opportunities" was used between 2005-2011, and thereafter ceased to be used, keeping, however, most part of the tools developed in the priorities "Youth" and "Adults" (although with lower budgets assossiated).

In an open innovation approach, we can say that the New Opportunities program falls within the framework of the "Education and Training Policy", thereby stimulating lifelong learning and skills of entrepreneurship among young people (Table 3, Annex A).

Administrative Modernisation Support System: SAMA Program

The Administrative Modernisation Support System aims to create conditions for a more efficient and effective Public Administration (PA), through the development of approaches to reduce the "red tape" in its relationship with citizens and business. According to the Rules of SAMA program, the goals are: qualification of Government services, by streamlining, reengineering and dematerialisation of processes; development of the Public Administration Network, using the intensive use of ICT; and the promotion of integrated modernization initiatives, ensuring coordination between the three main areas of intervention - people, organization and technology. The implementation of the projects supported by SAMA is aligned with an open innovation approach (Table 3, Annex A), in particular with regard to the following principles:

- The development project should be supported by interoperability platforms, using open standards and systems (open stardards), enabling interconnection between different departments of the PA and the provision of electronic services across multiple channels. In this context, it is necessary to highlight the development of the Platform for Interoperability, which supports initiatives such as the Citizen Card, or the Law 36/2011, concerning the adoption of open standards in the computer systems of the PA;
- Adoption of electronic public procurement as a way to make more effective the process of public procurement, generating savings, including through the negotiation processes and the reduction of transaction costs. Portugal has been a pioneer in this field in European terms, given the experience accumulated since 2003, with the work done by UMIC, and pursued under the Simplex initiative;
- The availability of information with general interest - "open data" - so that they can be used, re-used and distributed, either commercially or non-commercial, by any person, entity or company. In Portugal was recently developed a public open data platform, through the "Dados.gov" initiative, where one can find some applications developed by citizens based on the reuse of public data (co-creation / user innovation).

Like in SI Innovation, SI Q&I and SIAC programs, SAMA considers eligible investments in training actions associated with the development of projects, including the expenditures with trainees, trainers or the preparation, implementation, monitoring and evaluation of projects.

Venture Capital Instruments

The period 2005-2013 was marked by a restructuring of public instruments of venture capital, aiming to increase efficiency of supported projectsa and the development of the various stages of the life cycle of the company (from "pre-seed" stage to the stage of internationalization). In legislative terms, we can highlight the Decree -Law 319/2002, of 28 December (as amended by Decree-Law 151/2004 of 29 June, and 52/ 2006 of 15 March), which recognizes the importance of venture capital as an instrument of consolidation and development of business, as well as the Decree -Law 375/2007 of 8 November, more comprehensive, simplifying and restructuring the activity of risk capital, as well as recognizing for the first time, the activity of "business angels". It also has to be noted the importance of the creation of Portugal Ventures company (in 2012), which resulted from the merger of three public companies of venture capital.

These tools, combined with others, such as those aimed at risk sharing, are important for stimulating the activities of open innovation, facilitating companies' access to external capital and alternative financing sources (Chesbrough, 2003a, 2003b). In this context, highlight the launch and consolidation of the following instruments: INOFIN (Framework Program of Financial Innovation to Market SMEs), launched in 2006; FINOVA (Support Fund for Financing Innovation), launched in 2008, which had as its goals the participation in risk capital funds; SAFPRI (Support System Financing and Risk Sharing Innovation), launched in 2008, which aimed at the dissemination of financial instruments, with a complementary mechanism of financing and risk sharing innovation; and Portugal Ventures company, launched in 2012, that reorganized public venture capital instruments, having concentrated the activity of public venture capital for SMEs in a single public operator.

Towards sustaining the financing capacity of public instruments and encourage the sharing of risk in relation to the operators of the venture capital market, it is necessary to highlight the instruments "Counter-guarantee Mutual Fund", "Guarantee Fund for Securitization" and "Venture Capital Syndication Fund". Another important area in stimulating open innovation is the existence of an environment favorable to business angel activity, by the Decree -Law 375/2007 of 8 November, that set the legal and fiscal framework for the activity of individual investors venture capital (business angels).

Legal Framework for Competition

Competition policy is fundamental for open innovation, stressing the importance of well-functioning markets, including the stimulus to competition, limitaitons of cartels and preventing the abuse of dominant market positions (de Jong *et al.*, 2008, 2010). In this sense, it is highlighted, in the period 2005-2013, the adoption of Law no. ° 19/2012 of 8 May, on the Legal Regime of Competition, repealing the previous Laws on the subject. This new scheme clarifies the anti-competition practices, including agreements, concerted practices and decisions by associations of undertakings, abuse of dominant position, the abuse of economic dependence, as well as the sanctioning process on restrictive practices. Moreover, this law also defines the procedures for merger control and sanctions proceedings, relating to concentrations between undertakings, the powers of inspection and audit, the limitations of public aid, as well as violations and associated penalties.

The New Legal Framework for Competition also defines the powers, tasks and powers of the Competition Authority and its relationship to industry regulators. In a perspective of open innovation, the new Legal Framework for Competition falls under the area of "Competition Policy", and cross all economic activity (i.e., is not an instrument for funding or incentives for companies).

Chapter 18
Aligning Knowledge Management with Research Knowledge Governance

Isabel Pinho
University of Aveiro, Portugal

Cláudia Pinho
University of Aveiro, Portugal

ABSTRACT

Research Knowledge production is the result from knowledge processes that happen at diverse networks spaces. Those spaces are supported by a cascade of systems (Data Management Systems, Information Management Systems, Knowledge Management Systems, Evaluation Systems and Monitoring Systems) that must be aligned to avoid formation of silos and barriers to the flows of information and knowledge. The energy that powers consists of the people and their connections; so there is crucial to understand and govern formal and informal networks. By take a holistic approach, we propose to join benefits of an efficient knowledge management with the implementation of knowledge governance mechanisms in order to improve Research Knowledge production and its impacts.

1. INTRODUCTION

Research knowledge production and knowledge use in the context of research-oriented Higher Education Institutions can be improved. Research and knowledge production deals with great complexity. It is therefore necessary to align knowledge management and research knowledge governance to enlarge and enhance capabilities by connecting multiple research networks and knowledge networks.

Although universities are knowledge intensive environments, there seems to be a lack of alignment between organizational knowledge management and the governance of scientific knowledge at institutional, national and supranational levels.

Knowledge creation is the result of collaborations across institutional and organizational boundaries. The facilitation of access to distributed knowledge and the establishment of networks spaces are tasks that appeal to new forms of management and governance. By taking a holistic ap-

DOI: 10.4018/978-1-4666-8833-9.ch018

Figure 1. Conceptual Model

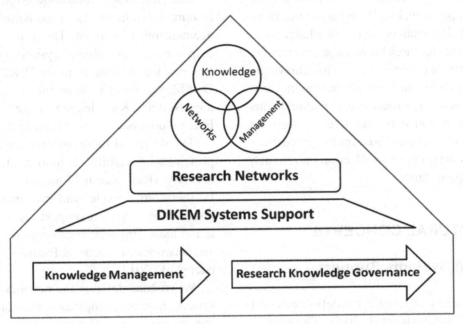

proach, we can understand such networking spaces of knowledge co-creation and identify potential benefits of aligning knowledge management and research knowledge governance.

At all levels of governance, it is crucial that institutions, agencies and organizations seek out for solutions to value knowledge, through adequate data, information and knowledge management.

Our starting point is the fact that the production of knowledge is a social process that must be managed. Adopting this knowledge–based perspective, we build a conceptual model that structures this chapter and that can serve as a content navigation guide (Figure 1).

By taking this approach we have chosen three key concepts that are interconnected, namely: knowledge, networks and management.

Knowledge is the main resource (input) and the most value product (output) of research processes. Networks are the context, virtual spaces and shared mental spaces that give energy to those research processes. Management should focus on

this resource and also in the environment on which those processes develop.

Research networks are special spaces where tacit knowledge - existing within individuals' heads - can be shared and increased via interpersonal interaction and social relationships. Thus, beyond information technology to support digital capture, storage, retrieval and distribution of an organization's documented, it is necessary to cultivate knowledge management practices that look at hard and soft factors pertaining to knowledge processes (Pinho *et al.*, 2012). This kind of knowledge management can be perceived as a service that can improve scientific knowledge production and also can add value to this new knowledge.

In order to deal with the complexity of knowledge production at micro, meso and macro levels, we can integrate the knowledge management definition advanced by Carla O'Dell & Jackson Grayson (1998, p.6) - "the conscious strategy of getting the right knowledge to the right people at the right time and helping people share and put information into action in ways that strive to improve organizational performance" – with a knowledge governance approach. Finally, we argue that there should be an alignment between knowledge management and the research knowledge governance, in order to match common efforts to achieve the scientific objectives and desired societal impacts.

In terms of its organization the chapter begins with structural concepts and later focuses on research networks. From those multifaceted theoretical bases we propose a reflection on research knowledge governance.

2. STRUCTURAL CONCEPTS

2.1 DIKEM Systems Support

There is a variety of knowledge definitions and taxonomies (Kakabadse et al., 2003). The various definitions of what knowledge is depend on the perspective from which knowledge is observed (Alavi & Leidner, 2001; Chen & Chen, 2006). The concept of knowledge is more clearly understood when compared with the concepts of data and information. There is a relationhip between these three concepts, but they are not synonymous. Zack (1999) defines data as observation or facts, information as data in a meaningful context and knowledge as meaningfully organized accumulation of information.

In an earlier conceptualisation, Polanyi (1967) divided the human knowledge in two dimensions: explicit (written, codified and easy to transfer) and tacit knowledge (internalised, personal and highly difficult to communicate). This division helps to simplify our approach to knowledge, but it remains essential to establish that explicit knowledge and tacit knowledge are complementary and its conversion creates chances for the creation of knowledge (Nonaka, 1991). While some researchers view the two knowledge dimensions as distinct, Alavi and Leiner (2001, p. 112) suggest that they are "not dichotomous states of knowledge, but mutually dependent and reinforcing qualities of knowledge".

Data, information and knowledge are the main resources that Information and Knowledge Management must focus on. This process is greatly helped by an ensemble of systems (see Table 1) – which we propose to name DIKEM systems: Data Management Systems, Information Management Systems, Knowledge Management Systems, Evaluation Systems and Monitoring Systems.

The design of these systems must follow the principles of usability (Pinho et al., 2008) and security (Rubenstein-Montano et al., 2001). Furthermore, if made available open access they also can be seen as a support service to benefit individuals, projects, organizations, institutions and networks (Schroeder & Pauleen, 2007; Schroeder et al., 2012).

When considered at the network level, these systems require appropriate governance to reduce transaction costs and help: a) accessing and using data and information; b) making informed decisions; c) implementing programs and; d) solving conflicts among stakeholders.

2.2 Governance and Knowledge Governance

Similarly to "knowledge", there are several definitions for the concept of "governance". The most fundamental narratives from which the dominant definitions draw are governance in corporate management and governance in political sciences (Windsor, 2009).

Rhodes (1996, p. 652) defines governance as "self-organizing inter-organizational networks" characterized by:

1. Interdependence between organizations. Governance is broader than government, covering non-state actors. Changing the boundaries of the state meant the boundaries between public, private and voluntary sectors are diffuse and opaque;

Table 1. DIKEM Systems Support

Type of Systems	Issues
Data Management Systems	Real time data, available in open access
Information Management Systems	Explicit knowledge
Knowledge Management Systems	Explicit Knowledge + Tacit knowledge + Knowledge processes
Evaluation Systems	Alignment evaluation and monitoring
Monitoring Systems	

2. Continuing interactions between network members, caused by the need to exchange resources and negotiate shared purposes;
3. Game-like interactions, rooted in trust and regulated by the rules of the game negotiated and agreed by network participants;
4. A significant degree of autonomy from the state. Networks are not accountable to the state; they are self-organising.

Also according to Rhodes (1996, 2007), the concept of governance is currently used in contemporary social sciences with at least six different uses: the minimal state, corporate governance, new public management, good governance, social-cybernetic systems and self-organized networks. It originates from the need to craft an umbrella term that covered diverse meanings not enclosed by the traditional concept of "government"; and it is linked to emergent managerialist narratives (Ball, 2009; Santiago & Carvalho, 2012).

Pahl-Wostl (2009) developed a conceptual framework for analysing adaptive capacity and multi-level learning processes in resource governance regimes, looking for differences in governance modes of bureaucratic hierarchies, markets and networks regarding the degree of formality of institutions and the importance of state and non-state actors (Figure 2).

Markets and hierarchies are complemented with networks; those networks are composed of a rich multiplicity of actors coupled to one another. All those entities can be regarded as "governing structures for authoritatively allocating resources and exercising control and co-ordination" (Rhodes, 1996, p. 652).

Another important concept is that of "knowledge governance". Knowledge governance is closely related to knowledge management; both seek to capitalize knowledge or creating value from knowledge, but at different scopes. Knowledge management is concerned with knowledge processes at organizational level, Knowledge governance refers to choosing structures and mechanisms that can influence the processes of knowledge looking the interrelation between micro, meso and macro levels, with a strategic focus (Acworth, 2008; Alavi & Leidner, 2001; Davenport & Prusak, 1998; Foss, 2009; Foss, 2007; Foss & Mahoney, 2010; Grandori, 2001; Grandori & Furnari, 2008; Karvalics, 2012; Miller, 2007; Pinho et al., 2012; Schroeder & Pauleen, 2007).

2.3 Networks and Governance Networks

Collaboration is related to the connectivity phenomenon, which surrounds networks and the aggregate behavior of people. A network "consists of a set actors or nodes along with a set of ties of a specified type that link them" (Borgatti & Halgin, 2011, p. 1169). Networks are a theoretical and practical research event in the field of research in all fields of knowledge. This exponentially grows convergence appeals to the contributions of various disciplines and to the need of an integration of all those knowledge (Börner et al., 2007; Dorogovtsev & Mendes, 2002).

Figure 2. Governance modes (hierarchies, markets and networks)
Source: Pahl-Wostl (2009)

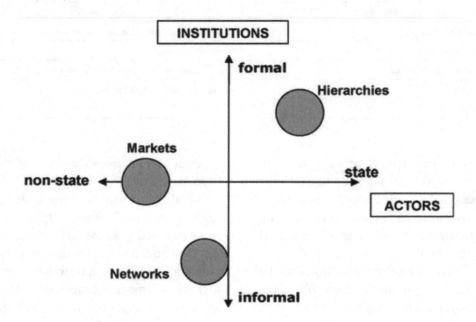

3. RESEARCH NETWORKS

3.1 Research Networks Levels of Analysis

Governance networks can be described as a "pluricentric governance system" in contrast to a unicentric system of state rule and the multicentric system of market competition (Kersbergen & Waarden, 2004). Governance networks have been defined by Sorensen and Torfing (2005, p. 3) as:

- "A relatively stable horizontal articulation of interdependent, but operationally autonomous actors,
- Who interact through negotiations that involve bargaining, deliberation and intense power struggles,
- Which take place within a relatively institutionalized framework of contingently articulated rules, norms, knowledge and social imaginations,
- That is self-regulating within limits set by external agencies, and
- Which contribute to the production of public purpose in the broad sense of visions, ideas, plans and regulations."

The diversity of different network spaces offers a broad spectrum of understanding, interpretations and operationalization of research networks at micro, meso and macro levels (Dopfer et al., 2004; He et al., 2011). A synthesis of these levels is presented in Table 2.

The categorization presented here ranges from the individual level, such as ego-networks, to the global level, such as knowledge network. Micro meta-level includes "researcher networks" and "project research and group research". We considered "Organizational" and "Institutional" levels belong to the Meso meta-level. Finally, at Macro meta-level it is possible to find "National Research Systems", "International and Global Research Systems" and "disciplines or scientific fields".

Table 2. Levels of Analysis

Dimension	Categories	Issues	Articles Examples
Micro (Individual)	Researcher networks	Ego-network	Bozeman & Corley, 2004; Everett & Borgatti, 2005; Lowrie & McKnight, 2004
	Project research or group research	Project networks group networks	Anzai et al., 2012; Blevins et al., 2010
Meso (Institutional)	Organizational	Research Centre Network	Boardman & Corley, 2008; Teixeira et al., 2011
	Institutional	Department and University networks	Jong, 2008; Quintella et al., 2009
Macro (System)	National Research System	Country or Nation	Glänzel et al., 2006; Gülgöz et al., 2002; Leta et al., 2006; Packer & Meneghini, 2006
	International and Global Research Systems	EU Latin America Africa	Grimes & Collins, 2003; Ladle et al., 2012; López López et al., 2010; Pohoryles, 2002; Toivanen & Ponomariov, 2011; Zingerli, 2010
	Disciplines or scientific fields	Knowledge Network	Leydesdorff & Persson, 2010; Manning, 2007; Newman, 2007; Sun & Manson, 2011

This sequence is hierarchical but only from a dimension point of view, i.e. no level is more important than other. Each level must be used according to each research question. Sometimes it is possible to use more than one level, i.e. one might examine the impact of science policy and related programs (macro) that promote formal networks, on an institutional level (meso).

Although this proposed framework (Table 2) classifies research networks into three dimensions (micro networks, meso networks and macro networks) there are other available classifications that are useful for the analysis of networks: formal vs. informal networks (Allen et al., 2007); short-term vs. long term duration networks (Lemarchand, 2012); highly bounded vs. more fluid networks (Lowrie & McKnight, 2004); simple vs. complex networks (Newman, 2003); internal and external networks (Helble & Chong, 2004); international vs. domestic (Glänzel et al., 2006; Glanzel & Schubert, 2005; Leta et al., 2006).

3.2 Research Networks Governance

Similarly to the process of drawing a map, choosing an appropriate scale to work with is an important task that allows to structure work, clarify findings and integrate new knowledge in a logical manner. This cartographic metaphor may help to understand and locate the various research networks within a territory of collaboration that can be observed with different lenses. These networks' territories are not mutually exclusive, rather, they are intrinsically embedded. This adds a great deal of complexity to the process of taking a governance approach, since it is necessary to understand research networks at each level and across levels (Foss, 2007). Rather than separating research networks by levels, we must consider them holistically, integrate results on all levels, grasping patterns in order to find the underlying mechanisms. This is not in contradiction with the levels presented earlier in this chapter, as an integrated understanding requires some framework or structure.

The practice of research network governance is dependent on a number of enablers and/or precursors, namely:

- Collaborative research and collaborative writing is becoming increasingly frequent (Katz & Martin, 1997; Lemarchand, 2012);
- The number of co-authored scientific publication and citation impact has increased in all subject fields during the last decades (Adams, 2012; Adler et al., 2009; Persson et al., 2004);
- The boundary challenges of managing researchers (Goffee & Jones, 2007; Jayasingam et al., 2010);
- The role played by common purpose, effective links that enable interaction at different levels, shared leadership, independence of members to act on various networks (Brannback, 2003);
- The need for a clear direction and objectives (Agranoff & McGuire, 2001).

Modeling research network governance is a tool to support thinking about to how to improve knowledge production, within a network research environment (Pidd, 2010). In this chapter we aim to propose a Research Networks Governance Model (RNGM), which results from a review and synthesis of the existent body of theory.

Research networks do not unfold in an institutional and policy research vacuum. Accordingly, beyond endogenous elements of a network it is also necessary to understand its exogenous elements and its support mechanisms. Drawing on conceptual discussion taking place across a variety of disciplines – networks science, sociology of knowledge and knowledge management - we propose a RNGM. This model highlights eight main elements: four endogenous elements (research networks structure, research networks mechanisms/processes, research networks inputs and research networks outputs); three exogenous elements (research networks contexts, research networks impacts, science policy cycle); and the existence of supporting DIKEM Systems (see Figure 3).

The robust governance of research networks requires a combination of quantitative approaches (numerical, large scale data to provide context at macro and meso levels (Leydesdorff & Persson, 2010) and qualitative approaches (interview and observation-based, providing small-scale and rich information at micro level (Zingerli, 2010)). The integration of the two approaches can serve different objectives of management, governance and science policy (Lowndes & Skelcher, 1998; Wixted & Holbrook, 2012).

The RNGM makes it possible to derive propositions and develop a research design to collect and analyze qualitative network data (Cornelissen et al., 2011; Newell & Swan, 2000; Zingerli, 2010) and quantitative network data (Acedo et al., 2006; Barabasi et al., 2002; Gaughan & Ponomariov, 2008; Laudel, 2002). We define research network governance as a set of instruments and mechanisms that coordinate participant elements to deliver outcomes and impacts, by understanding and respecting different forms of knowledge production and policy contexts. This position argues that the governance of research networks aims to support intellectual freedom where a balance between control and creativity is allowed. As Johnson et al. (2010) argue network science provides insights that not only document the evolution of research networks, but also may be prescriptive of mechanisms to enhance their success, efficiency and effectiveness.

4. TOWARDS RESEARCH KNOWLEDGE GOVERNANCE

Knowledge production can be seen as a result of collaboration (i.e. working together to achieve a common goal) and, more specifically, research collaboration as "the working together of researchers to achieve the common goal of producing new

Figure 3. Research Networks Governance Model

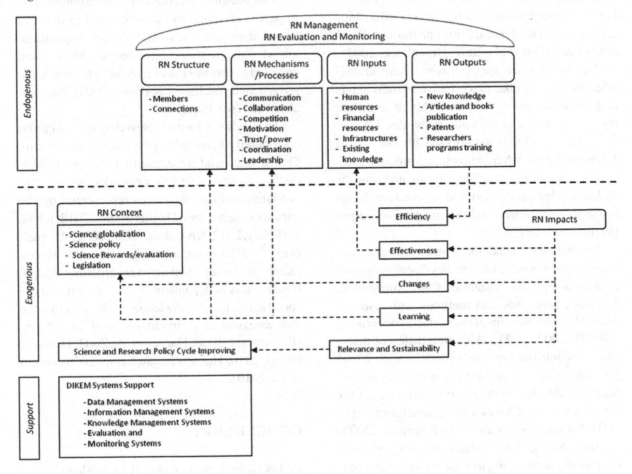

scientific knowledge" (Katz & Martin, 1997, p. 7). Considering research collaboration as a process that transforms existing knowledge and social capital into new knowledge, it is possible to think of how to manage this process in order to improve knowledge production.

All organizations have a common denominator: they are based on knowledge (Alvesson, 1993). However, some organizations have knowledge as their core output, supply knowledge to the public, or aggregate workers who are mainly experts developing and providing knowledge (Starbuck, 1992). More and more organizations acknowledge that their main activities are related to the management of knowledge, and that knowledge is a

strategic resource that must be governed to achieve and sustain competitive advantage (Argote et al., 2003; Nahapiet & Ghoshal, 1998).

Our focus is on Universities and academic research networks that stand as examples of organizations where knowledge governance is key. Universities are very special settings, because they are at the heart of knowledge creation and simultaneously they operate within knowledge networks. Accordingly, universities showcase a significant level of knowledge management activities associated with the creation and maintenance of knowledge repositories, improving knowledge access, enhancing knowledge environment and valuing knowledge (Rowley, 2000). This is particularly important for the transfer of knowledge occurring through university-business relationships (Agrawal & Henderson, 2002) or through R&D networks (Allen et al., 2007; Brannback, 2003).

Universities are social spaces where knowledge exchanges take place between individuals and organisations of various fields of expertise through formal and informal networks. Universities are knowledge networks (Chirikov, 2013; Johnson, 2005), where knowledge processes develop (acquisition, creation, sharing and transfer of knowledge processes) and where knowledge is the main resource and the most value output (Pinho et al., 2012).

Furthermore, academics and researcher are knowledge workers, i.e. "professionals engaged in the conception or creation of new knowledge, products, processes and methods and systems, and in the management of the projects concerned" (OECD, 2002, p. 93). Although different disciplinary contributions are called into play and integration challenges are frequent, it is widely accepted that research networks are critical for the production of knowledge (Almendral et al., 2007; Bozeman & Corley, 2004; Brannback, 2003; Castells, 2000). There is also supporting evidence correlating networking to improved research outputs and impact (Garner et al., 2012; Good, 2012; Kearney & Lincoln, 2013).

Regrettably, the traditional management of researchers, research projects and research institutions has neglected the phenomenon of knowledge co-production and research networks (Carayannis & Campbell, 2009; Carneiro, 2000; Neely et al., 2001).

If increasing the levels of research outputs and impact is an objective, it is essential to improve knowledge processes (knowledge acquisition, knowledge creation, knowledge sharing and knowledge transfer), and to establish knowledge governance mechanisms (Foss, 2007; Pinho et al., 2012) (see Figure 4).

The design of formal research networks can be considered a knowledge governance mechanism. On the one hand we argue that it is possible to design formal research networks taking into consideration the objectives represented by the various stakeholders (Gagliardi et al., 2012; Klenk & Hickey, 2012; Kretschmer et al., 2001; Wormell et al., 2002). On the other hand we acknowledge that there is no optimal network structural design, because this is dependent on the context and the specific modes of knowledge production that are characteristic of different areas of knowledge (Bonaccorsi, 2008; Harvey et al., 2002; Heitor & Bravo, 2010; Hessels & van Lente, 2008; Jansen et al., 2010).

CONCLUSION

In this chapter, we introduced a knowledge management and research knowledge governance alignment framework. The challenge of modeling multiple knowledge production spaces requires the contribution of several disciplines. Starting from three key concepts - knowledge, networks, management- we reflected on the role of research networks as social spaces, formal and informal

Figure 4. Research Knowledge Governance framework

structures where complex research activities are developed.

The performance of research knowledge production (quality and quantity) depends not only on integrated data system support, information, knowledge, assessment and monitoring but also on individual performance, teams, projects, and research institutions. Thus, knowledge management must take into account both hard and soft factors in order to manage these areas of collaboration and competition.

The proposed concept of research knowledge governance indicates a move from hierarchical spaces of knowledge production to self-organizing networks with multi-level governance scales. Connecting knowledge and people requires the integration of macro, meso and micro social spaces. This means creating environments that facilitate knowledge sharing. Also, we need to understand individuals, groups and the larger systems within which they operate.

Through the interactions of knowledge governance mechanisms and knowledge management processes it is possible to create value and improve research performance. This is a great challenge that opens a new and promising avenue of research and practice, which is of interest for academia, science, industry and government.

In a time of increasing specialization and apparent knowledge silos, it becomes crucial to have a comprehensive picture where the integration of various components and their relationships is clear. In sum, a people-centric knowledge management approach is our proposed way to capitalise information systems and knowledge processes.

REFERENCES

Acedo, F. J., Barroso, C., Casanueva, C., & Galan, J. L. (2006). Co-authorship in management and organizational studies: An empirical and network analysis. *Journal of Management Studies*, *43*(5), 957–983. doi:10.1111/j.1467-6486.2006.00625.x

Acworth, E. B. (2008). University-industry engagement: The formation of the Knowledge Integration Community (KIC) model at the Cambridge-MIT Institute. *Research Policy*, *37*(8), 1241–1254. doi:10.1016/j.respol.2008.04.022

Adams, J. (2012). Collaborations: The rise of research networks. *Nature*, *490*(7420), 335–336. doi:10.1038/490335a PMID:23075965

Adler, R., Ewing, J., & Taylor, P. (2009). Citation statistics. *Statistical Science*, *24*(1), 1–14. doi:10.1214/09-STS285

Agranoff, R., & McGuire, M. (2001). Big Questions in Public Network Management Research. *Journal of Public Administration: Research and Theory*, *11*(3), 295–326. doi:10.1093/oxfordjournals.jpart.a003504

Agrawal, A., & Henderson, R. (2002). Putting Patents in Context: Exploring Knowledge Transfer from MIT. *Management Science*, *48*(1), 44–60. doi:10.1287/mnsc.48.1.44.14279

Alavi, M., & Leidner, D. E. (2001). Review: Knowledge management and knowledge management systems: conceptual foundations and research issues. *Management Information Systems Quarterly*, *25*(1), 107–136. doi:10.2307/3250961

Allen, J., James, A. D., & Gamlen, P. (2007). Formal versus informal knowledge networks in R&D: A case study using social network analysis. *R & D Management*, *37*(3), 179–196. doi:10.1111/j.1467-9310.2007.00468.x

Almendral, J. A., Oliveira, J. G., López, L., Mendes, J. F. F., & Sanjuán, M. A. F. (2007). The network of scientific collaborations within the European framework programme. *Physica A: Statistical Mechanics and its Applications*, *384*(2), 675-683.

Alvesson, M. (1993). Organizations as Rhetoric-knowledge-intensive firms and the Struggle with Ambiguity. *Journal of Management Studies*, *30*(6), 997–1015. doi:10.1111/j.1467-6486.1993.tb00476.x

Anzai, T., Kusama, R., Kodama, H., & Sengoku, S. (2012). Holistic observation and monitoring of the impact of interdisciplinary academic research projects: An empirical assessment in Japan. *Technovation*, *32*(6), 345–357. doi:10.1016/j.technovation.2011.12.003

Argote, L., McEvily, B., & Reagans, R. (2003). Managing Knowledge in Organizations: An Integrative Framework and Review of Emerging Themes. *Management Science*, *49*(4), 571–582. doi:10.1287/mnsc.49.4.571.14424

Ball, S. J. (2009). Privatising education, privatising education policy, privatising educational research: Network governance and the 'competition state'. *Journal of Education Policy*, *24*(1), 83–99. doi:10.1080/02680930802419474

Barabasi, A. L., Jeong, H., Neda, Z., Ravasz, E., Schubert, A., & Vicsek, T. (2002). Evolution of the social network of scientific collaborations. *Physica a-Statistical Mechanics and Its Applications, 311*(3-4), 590-614.

Blevins, D., Farmer, M. S., Edlund, C., Sullivan, G., & Kirchner, J. E. (2010). Collaborative research between clinicians and researchers: A multiple case study of implementation. *Implementation Science; IS*, *5*(1), 76–76. doi:10.1186/1748-5908-5-76 PMID:20946658

Boardman, P. C., & Corley, E. A. (2008). University research centers and the composition of research collaborations. *Research Policy*, *37*(5), 900–913. doi:10.1016/j.respol.2008.01.012

Bonaccorsi, A. (2008). Search regimes and the industrial dynamics of science. *Minerva*, *46*(3), 285–315. doi:10.1007/s11024-008-9101-3

Borgatti, S. P., & Halgin, D. S. (2011). On Network Theory. *Organization Science*, *22*(5), 1168–1181. doi:10.1287/orsc.1100.0641

Börner, K., Sanyal, S., & Vespignani, A. (2007). Network science. *Annual Review of Information Science & Technology*, *41*(1), 537–607. doi:10.1002/aris.2007.1440410119

Bozeman, B., & Corley, E. (2004). Scientists' collaboration strategies: Implications for scientific and technical human capital. *Research Policy*, *33*(4), 599–616. doi:10.1016/j.respol.2004.01.008

Brannback, M. (2003). R&D collaboration: Role of Ba in knowledge-creating networks. *Knowledge Management Research & Practice*, *1*(1), 28–38. doi:10.1057/palgrave.kmrp.8500006

Carayannis, E. G., & Campbell, D. F. J. (2009). 'Mode 3' and 'Quadruple Helix': Toward a 21st century fractal innovation ecosystem. *International Journal of Technology Management*, *46*(3-4), 201–234. doi:10.1504/IJTM.2009.023374

Carneiro, A. (2000). How does knowledge management influence innovation and competitiveness? *Journal of Knowledge Management*, *4*(2), 87–98. doi:10.1108/13673270010372242

Castells, M. (2000). *The Rise of The Network Society: The Information Age: Economy, Society and Culture*. San Francisco: John Wiley & Sons.

Chen, M. Y., & Chen, A. P. (2006). Knowledge management performance evaluation: A decade review from 1995 to 2004. *Journal of Information Science*, *32*(1), 17–38. doi:10.1177/0165551506059220

Chirikov, I. (2013). Research universities as knowledge networks: The role of institutional research. *Studies in Higher Education*, *38*(3), 456–469. doi:10.1080/03075079.2013.773778

Cornelissen, F., van Swet, J., Beijaard, D., & Bergen, T. (2011). Aspects of school-university research networks that play a role in developing, sharing and using knowledge based on teacher research. *Teaching and Teacher Education*, *27*(1), 147–156. doi:10.1016/j.tate.2010.07.011

Davenport, T. H., & Prusak, L. (Eds.). (1998). *Working Knowledge: How Organisations Manage What They Know*. Boston, MA: Harvard Business School Press.

Dopfer, K., Foster, J., & Potts, J. (2004). Micro-meso-macro. *Journal of Evolutionary Economics*, *14*(3), 263–279. doi:10.1007/s00191-004-0193-0

Dorogovtsev, S. N., & Mendes, J. F. F. (2002). *Evolution of networks: from biological nets to the Internet and WWW*. Oxford: Oxford University Press.

Everett, M., & Borgatti, S. P. (2005). Ego network betweenness. *Social Networks*, *27*(1), 31–38. doi:10.1016/j.socnet.2004.11.007

Foss, N. (2009). Alternative research strategies in the knowledge movement: From macro bias to micro-foundations and multi-level explanation. *Eur Manage Rev*, *6*(1), 16–28. doi:10.1057/emr.2009.2

Foss, N. J. (2007). The Emerging Knowledge Governance Approach: Challenges and Characteristics. *Organization*, *14*(1), 29–52. doi:10.1177/1350508407071859

Foss, N. J., & Mahoney, J. T. (2010). Exploring Knowledge Governance. *International Journal of Strategic Change Management*, *2*(2-3), 93–101. doi:10.1504/IJSCM.2010.034409

Gagliardi, A. R., Brouwers, M. C., & Bhattacharyya, O. K. (2012). The guideline implementability research and application network (GIRAnet): an international collaborative to support knowledge exchange: study protocol. *Implementation Science; IS*, *7*(1), 26–26. doi:10.1186/1748-5908-7-26 PMID:22471937

Garner, J. G., Porter, A. L., Newman, N. C., & Crowl, T. A. (2012). Assessing research network and disciplinary engagement changes induced by an NSF program. *Research Evaluation*, *21*(2), 89–104. doi:10.1093/reseval/rvs004

Gaughan, M., & Ponomariov, B. (2008). Faculty publication productivity, collaboration, and grants velocity: Using curricula vitae to compare center-affiliated and unaffiliated scientists. *Research Evaluation*, *17*(2), 103–110. doi:10.3152/095820208X287180

Glänzel, W., Leta, J., & Thijs, B. (2006). Science in Brazil. Part 1: A macro-level comparative study. *Scientometrics*, *67*(1), 67–86. doi:10.1007/s11192-006-0055-7

Glanzel, W., & Schubert, A. (2005). Domesticity and internationality in co-authorship, references and citations. *Scientometrics*, *65*(3), 323–342. doi:10.1007/s11192-005-0277-0

Goffee, R., & Jones, G. (2007). Leading clever people. *Harvard Business Review*, *85*(3), 72. PMID:17348171

Good, B. (2012). Assessing the effects of a collaborative research funding scheme: An approach combining meta-evaluation and evaluation synthesis. *Research Evaluation*, *21*(5), 381–391. doi:10.1093/reseval/rvs026

Grandori, A., & Furnari, S. (2008). A chemistry of organization: Combinatory analysis and design. *Organization Studies*, *29*(3), 459–485. doi:10.1177/0170840607088023

Grimes, S., & Collins, P. (2003). Building a knowledge economy in Ireland through European research networks. *European Planning Studies*, *11*(4), 395–414. doi:10.1080/09654310303641

Gülgöz, S., Yedekçioğlu, O. A., & Yurtsever, E. (2002). Turkey's output in social science publications: 1970-1999. *Scientometrics*, *55*(1), 103–121. doi:10.1023/A:1016055121274

Harvey, J., Pettigrew, A., & Ferlie, E. (2002). The Determinants of Research Group Performance: Towards Mode 2? *Journal of Management Studies*, *39*(6), 747–774. doi:10.1111/1467-6486.00310

He, B., Ding, Y., & Ni, C. Q. (2011). Mining Enriched Contextual Information of Scientific Collaboration: A Meso Perspective. *Journal of the American Society for Information Science and Technology*, *62*(5), 831–845. doi:10.1002/asi.21510

Heitor, M., & Bravo, M. (2010). Portugal at the crossroads of change, facing the shock of the new: People, knowledge and ideas fostering the social fabric to facilitate the concentration of knowledge integrated communities. *Technological Forecasting and Social Change*, *77*(2), 218–247. doi:10.1016/j.techfore.2009.10.006

Helble, Y., & Chong, L. C. (2004). The importance of internal and external R&D network linkages for R&D organisations: Evidence from Singapore. *R & D Management*, *34*(5), 605–612. doi:10.1111/j.1467-9310.2004.00366.x

Hessels, L. K., & van Lente, H. (2008). Re-thinking new knowledge production: A literature review and a research agenda. *Research Policy*, *37*(4), 740–760. doi:10.1016/j.respol.2008.01.008

Jansen, D., von Görtz, R., & Heidler, R. (2010). Knowledge production and the structure of collaboration networks in two scientific fields. *Scientometrics*, *83*(1), 219–241. doi:10.1007/s11192-009-0022-1

Jayasingam, S., Ansari, M. A., & Jantan, M. (2010). Influencing knowledge workers: The power of top management. *Industrial Management & Data Systems*, *110*(1), 134–151. doi:10.1108/02635571011008443

Johnson, J. C., Christian, R. R., Brunt, J. W., Hickman, C. R., & Waide, R. B. (2010). Evolution of Collaboration within the US Long Term Ecological Research Network. *Bioscience*, *60*(11), 931–940. doi:10.1525/bio.2010.60.11.9

Johnson, J. D. (2005). Knowledge networks: Dilemmas and paradoxes. *International Journal of Information Management*(0).

Jong, S. (2008). Academic organizations and new industrial fields: Berkeley and Stanford after the rise of biotechnology. *Research Policy*, *37*(8), 1267–1282. doi:10.1016/j.respol.2008.05.001

Kakabadse, N. K., Kakabadse, A., & Kouzmin, A. (2003). Reviewing the knowledge management literature: Towards a taxonomy. *Journal of Knowledge Management*, *7*(4), 75–91. doi:10.1108/13673270310492967

Karvalics, L. (2012). Transcending Knowledge Management, Shaping Knowledge Governance. In P. H. T. Hou (Ed.), *New Research on Knowledge Management Models and Methods*.

Katz, J. S., & Martin, B. R. (1997). What is research collaboration? *Research Policy*, *26*(1), 1–18. doi:10.1016/S0048-7333(96)00917-1

Kearney, M.-L., & Lincoln, D. (2013). Research universities: Networking the knowledge economy. *Studies in Higher Education*, *38*(3), 313–315. doi:10.1080/03075079.2013.778682

Kersbergen, K. V., & Waarden, F. V. (2004). 'Governance' as a bridge between disciplines: Cross-disciplinary inspiration regarding shifts in governance and problems of governability, accountability and legitimacy. *European Journal of Political Research*, *43*(2), 143–171. doi:10.1111/j.1475-6765.2004.00149.x

Klenk, N. L., & Hickey, G. M. (2012). Improving the social robustness of research networks for sustainable natural resource management: Results of a Delphi study in Canada. [SPP]. *Science & Public Policy*, *39*(3), 357–372. doi:10.1093/scipol/scs024

Kretschmer, H., Liming, L., & Kundra, R. (2001). Foundation of a global interdisciplinary research network (COLLNET) with Berlin as the virtual centre. *Scientometrics*, *52*(3), 531–537. doi:10.1023/A:1014268505676

Ladle, R. J., Todd, P. A., & Malhado, A. C. M. (2012). Assessing insularity in global science. *Scientometrics*, 1–6.

Laudel, G. (2002). What do we measure by co-authorships? *Research Evaluation, 11*(1), 3–15. doi:10.3152/147154402781776961

Lemarchand, G. A. (2012). The long-term dynamics of co-authorship scientific networks: Iberoamerican countries (1973-2010). *Research Policy, 41*(2), 291–305. doi:10.1016/j.respol.2011.10.009

Leta, J., Glänzel, W., & Thijs, B. (2006). Science in Brazil. Part 2: Sectoral and institutional research profiles. *Scientometrics, 67*(1), 87–105. doi:10.1007/s11192-006-0051-y

Leydesdorff, L., & Persson, O. (2010). Mapping the geography of science: Distribution patterns and networks of relations among cities and institutes. *Journal of the American Society for Information Science and Technology, 61*(8), 1622–1634.

López López, W., García-Cepero, M. C., Aguilar Bustamante, M. C., Silva, L. M., & Aguado López, E. (2010). Panorama general de la producción académica en la psicología iberoamericana, 2005-2007. *Papeles del Psicólogo, 31*(3), 296–309.

Lowndes, V., & Skelcher, C. (1998). The dynamics of multi-organizational partnerships: An analysis of changing modes of governance. *Public Administration, 76*(2), 313–333. doi:10.1111/1467-9299.00103

Lowrie, A., & McKnight, P. J. (2004). Academic research networks: A key to enhancing scholarly standing. *European Management Journal, 22*(4), 345–360. doi:10.1016/j.emj.2004.06.011

Manning, S. (2007). Linking educational research activities across Europe: A review of the WIFO Gateway to Research on Education in Europe. *European Educational Research Journal, 6*(4), 446–450. doi:10.2304/eerj.2007.6.4.446

Miller, C. A. (2007). Democratization, International Knowledge Institutions, and Global Governance. *Governance: An International Journal of Policy, Administration and Institutions, 20*(2), 325–357. doi:10.1111/j.1468-0491.2007.00359.x

Nahapiet, J., & Ghoshal, S. (1998). Social Capital, Intellectual Capital, and the organizational advantage. *Academy of Management Review, 23*(2), 242–266.

Neely, A., Chris, A., & Crowe, P. (2001). The performance prism in practice. *Measuring Business Excellence, 5*(2), 6–13. doi:10.1108/13683040110385142

Newell, S., & Swan, J. (2000). Trust and inter-organizational networking. *Human Relations, 53*(10), 1287–1328.

Newman, H. B. (2007). Networking for High Energy and Nuclear Physics. *Computer Physics Communications, 177*(1/2), 224–230. doi:10.1016/j.cpc.2007.02.002

Newman, M. E. J. (2003). The structure and function of complex networks. *SIAM Review, 45*(2), 167–256. doi:10.1137/S003614450342480

Nonaka, I. (1991). The knowledge-creating company. *Harvard Business Review, 69*(6), 96–104.

O' Dell, C. S., & Grayson, C. J. (1998). *If only we knew what we know: the transfer of internal knowledge and best practice.* New York: Free Press.

OECD. (2002). *The Measurement of Scientific and Technical Activities: Proposed Standard Practice for Surveys of Research and Development.* Paris: OECD.

Packer, A. L., & Meneghini, R. (2006). Articles with authors affiliated to Brazilian institutions published from 1994 to 2003 with 100 or more citations: I - The weight of international collaboration and the role of the networks. *Anais da Academia Brasileira de Ciencias, 4*(78), 841–853. PMID:17143417

Pahl-Wostl, C. (2009). A conceptual framework for analysing adaptive capacity and multi-level learning processes in resource governance regimes. *Global Environmental Change, 19*(3), 354–365. doi:10.1016/j.gloenvcha.2009.06.001

Persson, O., Glänzel, W., & Danell, R. (2004). Inflationary bibliometric values: The role of scientific collaboration and the need for relative indicators in evaluative studies. *Scientometrics, 60*(3), 421–432. doi:10.1023/B:SCIE.0000034384.35498.7d

Pidd, M. (2010). Why modelling and model use matter. *The Journal of the Operational Research Society, 61*(1), 14–24. doi:10.1057/jors.2009.141

Pinho, I., Rego, A., & Cunha, M. P. (2012). Improving knowledge management processes: A hybrid positive approach. *Journal of Knowledge Management, 16*(2), 215–242. doi:10.1108/13673271211218834

Pinho, I., Rego, A., & Kastenholz, E. (2008). Factores satisfacientes e insatisfacientes dos utilizadores de websites: Um estudo de caso. *Tékhne-Polytechnical Studies Review, 6*(10), 51–71.

Pohoryles, R. J. (2002). The Making of the European Research Area—a View from Research Networks. *Innovation: The European Journal of Social Sciences, 15*(4), 325–340.

Polanyi, M. (1967). *The Tacit Dimension*. London: Routledge.

Quintella, R. H., Freitas, E. J. S. M., Ventura, A. C., Santos, M. A., & Antonio, L. Q. (2009). Network dynamics in scientific knowledge acquisition: An analysis in three public universities in the state of Bahia. *Revista de Administração Pública, 43*(6), 1279–1314. doi:10.1590/S0034-76122009000600004

Rhodes, R. A. W. (1996). The new governance: Governing without government. *Political Studies, 44*(4), 652–667. doi:10.1111/j.1467-9248.1996.tb01747.x

Rhodes, R. A. W. (2007). Understanding governance: Ten years on. *Organization Studies, 28*(8), 1243–1264. doi:10.1177/0170840607076586

Rowley, J. (2000). Is higher education ready for knowledge management? *International Journal of Educational Management, 14*(7), 325–333. doi:10.1108/09513540010378978

Rubenstein-Montano, B., Buchwalter, J., & Liebowitz, J. (2001). Knowledge management: A U.S. Social Security Administration case study. *Government Information Quarterly, 18*(3), 223–253. doi:10.1016/S0740-624X(01)00078-8

Santiago, R., & Carvalho, T. (2012). Managerialism rhetorics in Portuguese higher education. *Minerva, 50*(4), 511–532. doi:10.1007/s11024-012-9211-9

Schroeder, A., & Pauleen, D. (2007). KM governance: Investigating the case of a knowledge intensive research organisation. *Journal of Enterprise Information Management, 20*(4), 414–431. doi:10.1108/17410390710772696

Schroeder, A., Pauleen, D., & Huf, S. (2012). KM Governance: The mechanisms for guiding and controlling KM programs. *Journal of Knowledge Management, 16*(1), 1–1. doi:10.1108/13673271211198918

Sørensen, E., & Torfing, J. (2005). The Democratic Anchorage of Governance Networks. *Scandinavian Political Studies, 28*(3), 195–218. doi:10.1111/j.1467-9477.2005.00129.x

Starbuck, W. H. (1992). Learning by knowledge-intensive firms. *Journal of Management Studies, 29*(6), 713–740. doi:10.1111/j.1467-6486.1992.tb00686.x

Sun, S., & Manson, S. M. (2011). Social Network Analysis of the Academic GIScience Community. *The Professional Geographer, 63*(1), 18–33. doi:10.1080/00330124.2010.533560

Teixeira, M. O., Machado, C. J. S., Filipecki, A. T. P., Cortes, B. A., & Klein, H. E. (2011). Descrição e análise do uso de um instrumento de coordenação em um instituto público de pesquisa em biomedicina. *Ciencia & Saude Coletiva, 16*(3), 1835–1847. doi:10.1590/S1413-81232011000300019 PMID:21519673

Toivanen, H., & Ponomariov, B. (2011). African regional innovation systems: Bibliometric analysis of research collaboration patterns 2005-2009. *Scientometrics, 88*(2), 471–493. doi:10.1007/s11192-011-0390-1

Windsor, D. (2009). Tightening corporate governance. *Journal of International Management, 15*(3), 306–316. doi:10.1016/j.intman.2009.02.003

Wixted, B., & Holbrook, J. A. (2012). Environmental complexity and stakeholder theory in formal research network evaluations. *Prometheus, 30*(3), 291–314. doi:10.1080/08109028.2012.727276

Wormell, I., Bothma, T. J. D., & Ralebipi, R. M. D. (2002). DISSAnet: Development of an information science research network in the Republic of South Africa 1998-2000. *Education for Information, 20*(1), 45–56.

Zack, M. H. (1999). Developing a Knowledge Strategy. *California Management Review, 41*(3), 125–145. doi:10.2307/41166000

Zingerli, C. (2010). A sociology of international research partnerships for sustainable development. *European Journal of Development Research, 22*(2), 217–233. doi:10.1057/ejdr.2010.1

504

Compilation of References

Abu Rub, F. A., & Issa, A. A. (2012). A business process modeling-based approach to investigate complex processes: Software development case study. *Business Process Management Journal, 18*(1), 122–137. doi:10.1108/14637151211215046

Acedo, F. J., Barroso, C., Casanueva, C., & Galan, J. L. (2006). Co-authorship in management and organizational studies: An empirical and network analysis. *Journal of Management Studies, 43*(5), 957–983. doi:10.1111/j.1467-6486.2006.00625.x

Acemoglu, D., Mostagir, M., & Ozdaglar, A. (2014, January). Managing Innovation in a Crowd. *National Bureau of Economic Research* [Working Paper 19852].

Acharya, T., & Ray, A. K. (2007). *Image processing: Principles and Applications.* John Wiley & Sons.

Acharyya, S., Koyejo, O., & Ghosh, J. (2012). Learning to rank with bregman divergences and monotone retargeting. *arXiv preprint arXiv:1210.4851.*

Acworth, E. B. (2008). University-industry engagement: The formation of the Knowledge Integration Community (KIC) model at the Cambridge-MIT Institute. *Research Policy, 37*(8), 1241–1254. doi:10.1016/j.respol.2008.04.022

Adams, J. (2012). Collaborations: The rise of research networks. *Nature, 490*(7420), 335–336. doi:10.1038/490335a PMID:23075965

Adler, B. T., & De Alfaro, L. (2007). *A content-driven reputation system for the Wikipedia.* Paper presented at the Proceedings of the 16th international conference on World Wide Web. doi:10.1145/1242572.1242608

Adler, B. T., Chatterjee, K., De Alfaro, L., Faella, M., Pye, I., & Raman, V. (2008). *Assigning trust to Wikipedia content.* Paper presented at the Proceedings of the 4th International Symposium on Wikis.

Adler, R., Ewing, J., & Taylor, P. (2009). Citation statistics. *Statistical Science, 24*(1), 1–14. doi:10.1214/09-STS285

Adriani, F., & Becchetti, L. (2003). *Does the digital divide matter? The role of ICT across country level and growth estimates.* CEIS Tor Vergata.

Agranoff, R., & McGuire, M. (2001). Big Questions in Public Network Management Research. *Journal of Public Administration: Research and Theory, 11*(3), 295–326. doi:10.1093/oxfordjournals.jpart.a003504

Agrawal, A., & Henderson, R. (2002). Putting Patents in Context: Exploring Knowledge Transfer from MIT. *Management Science, 48*(1), 44–60. doi:10.1287/mnsc.48.1.44.14279

Ahn, M. J., & Bretschneider, S. (2011). Politics of e-government: E-government and the political control of bureaucracy. *Public Administration Review, 71*(3), 414–424. doi:10.1111/j.1540-6210.2011.02225.x

Ajzen, I., & Fishbein, M. (1980). *Understanding Attitudes and Predicting Social Behavior* (2nd ed.). New Jersey: Prentice Hall.

Akesson, M., & Edvardsson, B. (2008). Effects of e-government on service design as perceived by employees. *Managing Service Quality, 18*(5), 457–478. doi:10.1108/09604520810898839

Akman, I., Yazici, A., Mishraa, A., & Arifoglu, A. (2005). E-government: A global view and an empirical evaluation of some attributes of citizens. *Government Information Quarterly, 22*(2), 239–257. doi:10.1016/j.giq.2004.12.001

Al Shafi, S., & Weerakkody, V. (2007). Implementing and managing e-government in the state of Qatar: A citizens' perspective. *Electronic government. International Journal (Toronto, Ont.)*, *4*(4), 436–450.

Alanezi, M., Kamil, A., & Basri, S. (2010). A proposed instrument dimensions for measuring e-government service quality. *International Journal of u- and e-Service Science and Technology*, *3*(4), 1–17.

Alavi, M., & Leidner, D. E. (2001). Review: Knowledge management and knowledge management systems: Conceptual foundations and research issues. *Management Information Systems Quarterly*, *25*(1), 107–136. doi:10.2307/3250961

Albors, J., Ramos, J. C., & Hervas, J. L. (2008). New learning network paradigms: Communities of objectives, crowdsourcing, wikis and open source. *International Journal of Information Management*, *28*(3), 194–202. doi:10.1016/j.ijinfomgt.2007.09.006

Alcobia, P. (2001). Atitudes e Satisfação no Trabalho. In J. M. C. Ferreira, J. Neves, & A. Caetano (Eds.), *Manual de Psicossociologia das Organizações* (pp. 531–565). Lisbon: McGraw-Hill.

Alghaith, T., Brown, D., & Worthington, D. (2013). *Stakeholder saliency dynamics in strategic ICT projects in the Saudi public healthcare system: appreciative systems perspective. (Doctor of Philosphy)*. United Kingdom: Lancaster University Management School.

Al-Hatmi, B. (2013). *Public IT Investment: The Success of IT Projects*. Singapore: Partridge Publishing.

Al-Kibisi, G., De Boer, K., Mourshed, M., & Rea, N. (2001). Putting citizens on-line, not inline. *The McKinsey Quarterly*, (2): 64.

Allan, G. (2007). The use of the grounded theory methodology in investigating practitioners' integration of COTS components in information systems. *Proceedings of the ICIS*. Paper 149, Montreal.

Allen, J., James, A. D., & Gamlen, P. (2007). Formal versus informal knowledge networks in R&D: A case study using social network analysis. *R & D Management*, *37*(3), 179–196. doi:10.1111/j.1467-9310.2007.00468.x

Allport, G. (1954). Attitudes in the History of Social Psychology. In G. Lindsey & A. Aronson (Eds.), *Handbook of Social Psychology*. Reading: Addison-Wesley.

Almalki, M., Fitzgerald, G., & Clark, M. (2011). Health care system in Saudi Arabia: An overview. *Eastern Mediterranean Health Journal*, *17*(10). PMID:22256414

Almarabeh, T., & AbuAli, A. (2010). A general framework for e-government: Definition maturity challenges, opportunities, and success. *European Journal of Scientific Research*, *39*(1), 29–42.

Almendral, J. A., Oliveira, J. G., López, L., Mendes, J. F. F., & Sanjuán, M. A. F. (2007). The network of scientific collaborations within the European framework programme. *Physica A: Statistical Mechanics and its Applications, 384*(2), 675-683.

Al-Omari, A., & Al-Omari, H. (2006). E-government readiness assessment model. *Journal of Computer Science, 2*(11), 841–845. doi:10.3844/jcssp.2006.841.845

Alpaydin, E. (2004). *Introduction to machine learning*. MIT press.

Alvesson, M. (1993). Organizations as Rhetoric-knowledge-intensive firms and the Struggle with Ambiguity. *Journal of Management Studies*, *30*(6), 997–1015. doi:10.1111/j.1467-6486.1993.tb00476.x

Amaral, L., & Varajão, J. (2007). Planeamento de sistemas de informação, FCA - Editora de Informática, Lda, Lisboa, 4ª ed, p. 247.

Amaral, L. (1994). PRAXIS: Um referencial para o planeamento de sistemas de informação.

American Institutes for Research (AIR). *Most teachers "highly qualified" under NCLB standards, but teacher qualifications lag in many high poverty and high minority schools.* (2013). Retrieved from http://www.air.org/reports-products/index.cfm?fa=viewContent&content_id=417

Amrollahi, A., Ghapanchi, A., & Talaei-Khoei, A. (2014a). *A systematic review of the current theory base in the crowdsourcing literature.* Paper presented at the ANZAM 2014 Conference, Sydney, Australia.

Amrollahi, A., Ghapanchi, A., & Talaei-Khoei, A. (2014b). *Using Crowdsourcing Tools for Implementing Open Strategy: A Case Study in Education*. Paper presented at the Twentieth Americas Conference on Information System (AMCIS 2014).

Amrollahi, A., Khansari, M., & Manian, A. (2014a). How Open Source Software Succeeds? A Review of Research on Success of Open Source Software. *International Journal of Information and Communication Technology Research*, 6(2), 67–77.

Amrollahi, A., Khansari, M., & Manian, A. (2014b). Success of Open Source in Developing Countries: The Case of Iran.[IJOSSP]. *International Journal of Open Source Software and Processes*, 5(1), 50–65. doi:10.4018/ijossp.2014010103

Andersen, K. V., & Henriksen, H. Z. (2005). The first leg of e-government research: Domains and application areas 1998-2003. Copenhagen, Netherlands: Center for Research on IT in Policy Settings (CIPS), Copenhagen Business School.

Anderson, M. (2011). Crowdsourcing Higher Education: A Design Proposal for Distributed Learning. *MERLOT Journal of Online Learning and Teaching*, 7(4), 576–590.

Anderson, V. (2008). Communities of practice and part-time lecturers: opportunities and challenges in Higher Education. In C. Kimble, P. Hildreth, & I. Bourdon (Eds.), *Communities of practice. Creating learning environments for educators* (pp. 83–103). North Carolina: Information Age Publishing.

Andrews, M., Bruns, G., Dogru, K. M., & Lee, H. (2013). Understanding Quota Dynamics in Wireless Networks. *Proceedings of the third conference on the Analysis of Mobile Phone Datasets. NetMob. Cambridge, USA.* doi:10.1145/2663494

Andriof, J., & Waddock, S. (2002). Unfolding stakeholder engagement. In J. Andriof, S. Waddock, B. Husted, & S. S. Rahman (Eds.), *Unfolding stakeholder thinking: theory, responsibility, and engagement*. Sheffield, UK: Greenleaf Publishing Limited. doi:10.9774/GLEAF.978-1-909493-28-5_3

Antin, J. (2011). *My kind of people?: perceptions about wikipedia contributors and their motivations*. Paper presented at the Proceedings of the SIGCHI Conference on Human Factors in Computing Systems. doi:10.1145/1978942.1979451

Antràs, P., Garicano, L., & Rossi-Hansberg, E. (2006). Offshoring in a knowledge economy. *The Quarterly Journal of Economics*, 121, 31–77.

Anzai, T., Kusama, R., Kodama, H., & Sengoku, S. (2012). Holistic observation and monitoring of the impact of interdisciplinary academic research projects: An empirical assessment in Japan. *Technovation*, 32(6), 345–357. doi:10.1016/j.technovation.2011.12.003

Apostolou, D., Mentzas, G., Stojanovic, L., Thoenssen, B., & Lobo, T. P. (2011). A collaborative decision framework for managing changes in e-Government services. *Government Information Quarterly*, 28(1), 101–116. doi:10.1016/j.giq.2010.03.007

Arazy, O., & Nov, O. (2010). *Determinants of wikipedia quality: the roles of global and local contribution inequality*. Paper presented at the Proceedings of the 2010 ACM conference on Computer supported cooperative work. doi:10.1145/1718918.1718963

Arbuckle, J. L. (2006). IBM SPSS Amos Student.

Arendsen, R., Peters, O., ter Hedde, M., & van Dijk, J. (2014). Does e-government reduce the administrative burden of businesses? An assessment of business-to-government systems usage in the Netherlands. *Government Information Quarterly*, 31(1), 160–169. doi:10.1016/j.giq.2013.09.002

Argote, L., McEvily, B., & Reagans, R. (2003). Managing Knowledge in Organizations: An Integrative Framework and Review of Emerging Themes. *Management Science*, 49(4), 571–582. doi:10.1287/mnsc.49.4.571.14424

Argyris, C. (2002). Double-Loop Learning, Teaching and Research. *Academy of Management Learning & Education*, 1(2), 206–218. doi:10.5465/AMLE.2002.8509400

Argyris, C., Putnam, R., & Smith, D. (1985). *Action Science: Concepts, Methods, and Skills for Research and Intervention*. San Francisco, CA: Jossey-Bass.

Argyris, C., & Schon, D. (1974). *Theory in practice: increasing professional effectiveness*. San Francisco, CA: Jossey-Bass.

Argyris, C., & Schon, D. A. (1989). Participatory Action Research and Action Science Compared: A Commentary. *The American Behavioral Scientist*, *32*(5), 612–623. doi:10.1177/0002764289032005008

Armenakis, A. A., Harris, S. G., & Mossholder, K. W. (1993). Creating readiness for organizational change. *Human Relations*, *46*(6), 681–703. doi:10.1177/001872679304600601

Artto, K., Kujala, J., Dietrich, P., & Martinsuo, M. (2008). What is project strategy? *International Journal of Project Management*, *26*(1), 4–12. doi:10.1016/j.ijproman.2007.07.006

Asadi, N., & Lin, J. (2013). *Training efficient tree-based models for document ranking. Advances in Information Retrieval. 146 – 157*. Springer.

Aslam, J. A., Kanoulas, E., Pavlu, V., Savev, S., & Yilmaz, E. (2009). Document selection methodologies for efficient and effective learning-to-rank.*Proceedings of the 32nd international ACM SIGIR conference on Research and development in information retrieval* (pp. 468–475). doi:10.1145/1571941.1572022

Asongwe, P. N. (2012). E-government and the Cameroon cybersecurity legislation 2010: Opportunities and challenges. *The African Journal of Information and Communication*, *2*(12), 157–163.

Asrilhant, B., Dyson, R. G., & Meadows, M. (2004). Strategic projects on the sector of oil exploration and production.*Revista de Administração de Empresas*,*44*(1), 82–95. doi:10.1590/S0034-75902004000100006

Assar, S., Boughzala, I., & Isckia, T. (2011). eGovernment trends in the web 2.0 era and the open innovation perspective: an exploratory field study. Electronic Government, Lecture Notes in Computer Science, (Vol. 6846, pp. 210-222). Springer Berlin Heidelberg.

Athitsos, V., & Sclaroff, S. (2001). An appearance-based framework for 3d hand shape classification and camera viewpoint estimation. Proceedings of the Fifth IEEE International Conference on Automatic Face and Gesture Recognition.

Atsalakis, G. S., & Valavanis, K. P. (2009a). Surveying stock market forecasting techniques – Part II: Soft computing methods. *Expert Systems with Applications*, *36*(3), 5932–5941. doi:10.1016/j.eswa.2008.07.006

Atsalakis, G. S., & Valavanis, K. P. (2009b). Forecasting stock market short-term trends using a neuro-fuzzy based methodology. *Expert Systems with Applications*, *36*(7), 10696–10707. doi:10.1016/j.eswa.2009.02.043

Attewell, P. (2001). The First and Second Digital Divides. *Sociology of Education*, *74*(3), 252–259. doi:10.2307/2673277

Aurier, P., & Siadou-Martine, B. (2007). Perceived justice and consumption experience evaluations: A qualitative and experimental investigation. *International Journal of Service Industry Management*, *18*(5), 450–471. doi:10.1108/09564230710826241

Avgerou, C. (1995). Evaluating information systems by consultation and negotiation. *International Journal of Information Management*, *15*(6), 427–436. doi:10.1016/0268-4012(95)00046-A

Avison, D., Jones, J., Powell, P., & Wilson, D. (2004a). Using and validating the strategic alignment model. *The Journal of Strategic Information Systems*, *13*(3), 223–246. doi:10.1016/j.jsis.2004.08.002

Avison, D., & Malaurent, J. (2007). Impact of cultural differences: A case study of ERP introduction in China. *International Journal of Information Management*,*27*(5), 368–374. doi:10.1016/j.ijinfomgt.2007.06.004

Avlonitis, G. J., & Panagopoulos, N. G. (2005). Antecedents and consequences of CRM technology acceptance in the sales force. *Industrial Marketing Management*, *34*(4), 355–368. doi:10.1016/j.indmarman.2004.09.021

Ayanso, A., Chatterjee, D., & Cho, D. I. (2011). E-government readiness index: A methodology and analysis. *Government Information Quarterly*, *28*(4), 522–532. doi:10.1016/j.giq.2011.02.004

Ayanso, A., Cho, F. I., & Lertwachara, K. (2010). The digital divide: Global and regional ICT leaders and followers. *Information Technology for Development*, *16*(4), 304–319. doi:10.1080/02681102.2010.504698

Aydinli, O. F., Brinkkemper, S., & Ravesteyn, P. (2009). Business process improvement in organizational design of e-Government services. *Electronic. Journal of E-Government, 7*(2), 123–134.

Badri, M. A., & Alshare, K. (2008). A path analytic model and measurement of the business value of e-government: An international perspective. *International Journal of Information Management, 28*(6), 524–535. doi:10.1016/j.ijinfomgt.2006.10.004

Baghat, S., & Bolton, B. (2008). Corporate governance and firm performance. *Journal of Corporate Finance, 14*(3), 257–273. doi:10.1016/j.jcorpfin.2008.03.006

Bagrow, J. P., Wang, D., & Barabási, A.-L. (2011). Collective Response of Human Populations to Large-Scale Emergencies. *PLoS ONE, 6*(3), e17680. doi:10.1371/journal.pone.0017680 PMID:21479206

Ballantine, J. A., & Cunningham, N. (Eds.). (1999). *Strategic information systems planning: applying private sector frameworks in UK public healthcare.*

Ball, S. J. (2009). Privatising education, privatising education policy, privatising educational research: Network governance and the 'competition state'. *Journal of Education Policy, 24*(1), 83–99. doi:10.1080/02680930802419474

Barabasi, A. L., Jeong, H., Neda, Z., Ravasz, E., Schubert, A., & Vicsek, T. (2002). Evolution of the social network of scientific collaborations. *Physica a-Statistical Mechanics and Its Applications, 311*(3-4), 590-614.

Barki, H., Rivard, S., & Talbot, J. (1993). Toward an assessment of software development risk. *Journal of Management Information Systems, 10*(2), 203–225.

Barzilai-Nahon, K. (2006). Gaps and Bits: Conceptualizing Measurements for Digital Divides. *The Information Society, 22*(5), 269–279. doi:10.1080/01972240600903953

Bates, T. (2000). *Managing technological change. Strategies for college and university leaders.* San Francisco: Jossey-Bass.

Bates, T. (2005). *Technology, e-learning and Distance Education.* London: Routledge. doi:10.4324/9780203463772

Batty, M., Desyllas, J., & Duxbury, E. (2003). The discrete dynamics of small-scale spatial events: Agent-based models of mobility in carnivals and street parades. *International Journal of Geographical Information Science, 17*(7), 673–697. doi:10.1080/1365881031000135474

Baum, J. A. C., Rowley, T. J., Shipilov, A. V., & Chuang, Y.-T. (2005). Dancing with strangers: Aspiration performance and the search for underwriting syndicate partners. *Administrative Science Quarterly, 50*(4), 536–575.

Bavel, R. V., Punie, Y., et al. (2004). ICTs and Social Capital in the Knowledge Society.

Bawane, J., & Spector, J. M. (2009). Prioritization of online instructor roles: Implications for competency-based teacher education programs. *Distance Education, 30*(3), 383–397. doi:10.1080/01587910903236536

Beaulieu, S., & Pasquero, J. (2002). Reintroducing stakeholder dynamics in stakeholder thinking: A negotiated-order perspective. *Journal of Corporate Citizenship, 6*(6), 53–69. doi:10.9774/GLEAF.4700.2002.su.00007

Becker, J., Algermissen, L., & Niehaves, B. (2006). A procedure model for process oriented e-government projects. *Business Process Management Journal, 12*(1), 61–75. doi:10.1108/14637150610643760

Becker, R. A., Caceres, R., Hanson, K., Loh, J. M., Urbanek, S., Varshavsky, A., & Volinsky, C. (2011). Route Classification Using Cellular Handoff Patterns. *Proceedings of the 13th International Conference on Ubiquitous Computing* (pp. 123–132). New York, NY, USA: ACM. doi:10.1145/2030112.2030130

Bednarz, A. (2002). Getting plugged in to e-government. *New World (New Orleans, La.), 19*(27), 36–39.

Beer, M., & Nohria, N. (2000). Cracking the code of change. *Harvard Business Review, 78*(3), 133–141. PMID:11183975

Beggs, A. W. (2001). Queues and hierarquies. *The Review of Economic Studies, 68*(2), 297–322. doi:10.1111/1467-937X.00170

Behrend, T. S., Sharek, D. J., Meade, A. W., & Wiebe, E. N. (2011). The viability of crowdsourcing for survey research. *Behavior Research Methods, 43*(3), 800–813. doi:10.3758/s13428-011-0081-0 PMID:21437749

Belanger, F., & Carter, L. (2009). The impact of the digital divide on e-Government use. *Communications of the ACM*, *52*(4), 132–135. doi:10.1145/1498765.1498801

Belanger, F., & Hiller, J. S. (2006). A framework for e-government: Privacy implications. *Business Process Management Journal*, *12*(1), 48–60. doi:10.1108/14637150610643751

Bell, D., Borenstein, J., Levine, S., Koren, Y., & Jaros, J. (1994). An assistive navigation system for wheelchairs based upon mobile robot obstacle avoidance. Proceedings of the *IEEE International Conference on Robotics and Automation*, San Diego. doi:10.1109/ROBOT.1994.351167

Bemelmans-Videc, M.-L., Eriksen, B., & Golenberg, N. (1994). Facilitating organizational learning: human resource management and program evaluation. In F. Leeuw, R. Rist, & R. Sonnichsen (Eds.), *Can Government Learn? Comparative Perspective on Evaluation and Organizational Learning*. New Brunswick: Transaction Publishers.

Benbasat, I., Goldstein, D. K., & Mead, M. (1987). The case research strategy in studies of information systems. *Management Information Systems Quarterly*, *11*(3), 369–386. doi:10.2307/248684

Bendersky, M., Metzler, D., & Croft, W. B. (2010). Learning concept importance using a weighted dependence model.*Proceedings of the third ACM international conference on Web search and data mining* (pp. 31–40). doi:10.1145/1718487.1718492

Bengtsson, L., Lu, X., Thorson, A., Garfield, R., & von Schreeb, J. (2011). Improved Response to Disasters and Outbreaks by Tracking Population Movements with Mobile Phone Network Data: A Post-Earthquake Geospatial Study in Haiti. *PLoS Medicine*, *8*(8), e1001083. doi:10.1371/journal.pmed.1001083 PMID:21918643

Bennett, R. E., & Gitomer, D. H. (2009). Transforming K-12 assessment: Integrating accountability testing, formative assessment and professional support. In C. Wyatt-Smith & J. J. Cumming (Eds.), Educational assessment in the 21st century, 43-61. New York, NY: Springer.

Ben-Zvi, T. (2012). Measuring the perceived effectiveness of decision support systems and their impact on performance. *Decision Support Systems*, *54*(1), 248–256. doi:10.1016/j.dss.2012.05.033

Bergman, M., Charles, D., & Hertog, P. (2001). In pursuit of innovative clusters. In *OECD, Innovative clusters: drivers of national innovation systems*. Paris: OECD.

Bergstrom, M., & Stehn, L. (2005). Matching industrialised timber frame housing needs and enterprise resource planning: A change process. *International Journal of Production Economics*, *97*(2), 172–184. doi:10.1016/j.ijpe.2004.06.052

Berle, A., & Means, G. (1932). *The Modern Corporation and Private Property*. Chicago: Commerce Clearing House.

Bersch, R. (2009). Design de um serviço de tecnologia assistiva em escolas públicas. Retrieved from http://www.lume.ufrgs.br/handle/10183/18299

Bertot, J. C., Jaeger, P. T., & Grimes, J. M. (2010). Using ICTs to create a culture of transparency: E-government and social media as openness and anti-corruption tools for societies. *Government Information Quarterly*, *27*(3), 264–271. doi:10.1016/j.giq.2010.03.001

Bertot, J. C., Jaeger, P. T., & Grimes, J. M. (2012). Promoting transparency and accountability through ICTs, social media, and collaborative e-government. *Transforming Government: People. Process and Policy*, *6*(1), 78–91.

Beynon-Davies, P., Owens, I., & Williams, M. D. (2004). Information systems evaluation and information systems development process. *Journal of Enterprise Information Management*, *17*(4), 276–282. doi:10.1108/17410390410548689

Beynon-Davies, P., & Williams, M. D. (2003). Evaluating electronic local government in the UK. *Journal of Information Technology*, *18*(2), 137–149. doi:10.1080/0268396032000101180

Bhandari, P., Nunes, M., & Annansingh, F. (2005). Analysing the penetration of knowledge management practices in organisations through a survey of case studies. *Proceedings of the 4th European Conference on Research Methodology for Business and Management Studies (ECRM 2005)*. Université Paris Dauphine, Paris, France.

Bhaskar, R., Lee, H. S., Levas, A., Petrakian, R., Tsai, F., & Tulskie, B. (1994). *Analysing and reengineering business processes using simulation.* Paper presented at the 1994 Winter Simulation Conference, Lake Buena Vista, FL. doi:10.1109/WSC.1994.717510

Bhattacherjee, A. (2001). Understanding information systems continuance: An expectation-confirmation model. *Management Information Systems Quarterly, 25*(3), 351–370. doi:10.2307/3250921

Biancalana, C., Gasparetti, F., Micarelli, A., & Sansonetti, G. (2011). Social Tagging for Personalized Location-Based Services. *Social Recommender Systems (SRS), a Workshop of the ACM Conference on Computer Supported Cooperative Work.* Retrieved from http://citeseerx.ist.psu.edu/viewdoc/download?doi=10.1.1.475.8892&rep=rep1&type=pdf

Biggs, J. (1999). What the student does: Teaching for enhanced learning. *Higher Education Research & Development, 18*(1), 57–75. doi:10.1080/0729436990180105

Birdwhistell, R. (1970). *Kinesics and Context; essays on body motion communication.* Philadelphia: University of Pennsylvania Press.

Birk, H., Moeslund, T. B., & Madsen, C. B. (1997). Real-Time Recognition of Hand Alphabet Gestures Using Principal Component Analysis. Proceedings of the 10th Scandinavian Conference on Image Analysis.

Bitterman, J. E. (2008). Concepts in adult education doctoral study. In *Communities of Practice.* In C. Kimble, P. Hildreth, & I. Bourdon (Eds.), *Communities of practice. Creating learning environments for educators* (pp. 311–333). North Carolina: Information Age Publishing.

Blackmore, C. (2005). Learning to appreciate learning systems for environmental decision making: A 'work-in-progress' perspective. *Systems Research and Behavioral Science, 22*(4), 329–341. doi:10.1002/sres.697

Blake, J. (2010). *Multi-touch Development with WPF and Silverlight.* Manning Publications.

Blake, J. (2010). *Natural User Interfaces in. NET.* Manning Publications.

Blank, S. C. (1992). Chaos in futures markets? a nonlinear dynamical analysis. *Journal of Futures Markets, 11*(6), 711–728. doi:10.1002/fut.3990110606

Blevins, D., Farmer, M. S., Edlund, C., Sullivan, G., & Kirchner, J. E. (2010). Collaborative research between clinicians and researchers: A multiple case study of implementation. *Implementation Science; IS, 5*(1), 76–76. doi:10.1186/1748-5908-5-76 PMID:20946658

Blignaut, P. (2009). A Bilateral Perspective on the Digital Divide in South Africa. *Perspectives on Global Development and Technology, 8*(4), 581–601. doi:10.1163/156915009X12583611836091

Bloom, N., Garicano, L., Sadun, R., & Van Reenen, J. (2013). The distinct effects of Information Technology and Communication Technology on firm organization [Unpublished paper]. Retrieved from http://www.stanford.edu/~nbloom

Blumenstock, J. E. (2008). *Size matters: word count as a measure of quality on wikipedia.* Paper presented at the Proceedings of the 17th international conference on World Wide Web. doi:10.1145/1367497.1367673

Blunden, M. (1984). Geoffrey Vickers—an intellectual journey. Open Systems Group (Ed.), The Vickers papers, 3-42.

Boardman, P. C., & Corley, E. A. (2008). University research centers and the composition of research collaborations. *Research Policy, 37*(5), 900–913. doi:10.1016/j.respol.2008.01.012

Bogers, M., Afuah, A., & Bastian, B. (2010). Users as innovators: A review, critique, and future research directions. *Journal of Management, 36*(4), 857–875. doi:10.1177/0149206309353944

Bonaccorsi, A. (2008). Search regimes and the industrial dynamics of science. *Minerva, 46*(3), 285–315. doi:10.1007/s11024-008-9101-3

Borgatti, S. P., & Halgin, D. S. (2011). On Network Theory. *Organization Science, 22*(5), 1168–1181. doi:10.1287/orsc.1100.0641

Borgida, E., Sullivan, J. L., Oxendine, A., Jackson, M. S., Riedel, E., & Gangl, A. (2002). Civic culture meets the digital divide: The role of community electronic networks. *The Journal of Social Issues, 58*(1), 125–141. doi:10.1111/1540-4560.00252

Born in another time: Ensuring educational technology meets the needs of students today – and tomorrow. (2012, December). *National Association of States Boards of Education*. Arlington, VA: Author.

Börner, K., Sanyal, S., & Vespignani, A. (2007). Network science. *Annual Review of Information Science & Technology*, *41*(1), 537–607. doi:10.1002/aris.2007.1440410119

Bornstein, I. W. (2000). Keeping our sights on the horizon: GFOA's survey on emerging issues. *Government Finance Review*, *16*(6), 40–43.

Boss, G, P. Malladi, S. Quan, L. Legregni, and H. Hall (2007). Cloud computing [Technical Report]. *IBM high performance on demand solutions.*

Bourhis, G., & Pino, P. (1996). Mobile robotics and mobility assistance for people with motor impairments: Rational justification for the VAHM project. *IEEE Transactions on Rehabilitation Engineering*, *4*(1), 7–12. doi:10.1109/86.486052 PMID:8798067

Bourne, H., & Jenkins, M. (2013). Organizational Values: A Dynamic Perspective. *Organization Studies*, *34*(4), 495–514. doi:10.1177/0170840612467155

Bowman, B., G. Davis & J. Wetherbe (1993). Three stage of MIS planning. *Information and Management*, 6, 1, 1983.

Box, G., & Jenkins, G. (1970). *Time Series Analysis: Forecasting and Control*. Holden-Day.

Boyd, E. M., & Fales, A. W. (1983). Reflective learning: Key to learning from experience. *Journal of Humanistic Psychology*, *23*(2), 99–117. doi:10.1177/0022167883232011

Boyd, N. M., & Nowell, B. (2014). Psychological Sense of Community: A New Construct for the Field of Management. *Journal of Management Inquiry*, *23*(2), 107–122. doi:10.1177/1056492613491433

Boyd, O. P. (2008). Differences in eDemocracy parties' eParticipation systems. *Information Policy*, *13*, 167–188.

Bozeman, B., & Corley, E. (2004). Scientists' collaboration strategies: Implications for scientific and technical human capital. *Research Policy*, *33*(4), 599–616. doi:10.1016/j.respol.2004.01.008

Brabham, D. C. (2008a). Crowdsourcing as a model for problem solving an introduction and cases. *Convergence (London)*, *14*(1), 75–90. doi:10.1177/1354856507084420

Brabham, D. C. (2008b). Moving the crowd at iStockphoto: The composition of the crowd and motivations for participation in a crowdsourcing application. *First Monday*, *13*(6). doi:10.5210/fm.v13i6.2159

Brabham, D. C. (2009). Crowdsourcing the public participation process for planning projects. *Planning Theory*, *8*(3), 242–262. doi:10.1177/1473095209104824

Brändle, A. (2005). Too Many Cooks Don't Spoil the Broth.

Brannback, M. (2003). R&D collaboration: Role of Ba in knowledge-creating networks. *Knowledge Management Research & Practice*, *1*(1), 28–38. doi:10.1057/palgrave.kmrp.8500006

Braun, V., & Clarke, V. (2006). Using thematic analysis in psychology. *Qualitative Research in Psychology*, *3*(2), 77–101. doi:10.1191/1478088706qp063oa

Breiman, L. (2001). Random forests. *Machine Learning*, *45*(1), 5–32. doi:10.1023/A:1010933404324

Brekhus, W. H., Galliher, J. F., & Gubrium, J. F. (2005). The need for thin description. *Qualitative Inquiry*, *16*(6), 1–19.

Breschi, S., & Malerba, F. (2005). *Clusters, Networks and Innovation*. Oxford University Press.

Brock, W. A., Hsieh, D., & LeBaron, B. (1991). *Nonlinear Dynamics, Chaos, and Instability: Statistical Theory and Economic Evidence*. Cambridge, MA: MIT Press.

Brookfield, S. D. (1995). *Becoming a critically reflective teacher*. San Francisco, CA: Jossey-Bass.

Brown-Brumfield, D., & DeLeon, A. (2010). Adherence to a medication safety protocol: Current practice for labeling medications and solutions on the sterile field. *Association of Operating Room Nurses*. AORN Journal, 91(5), 610-610-7. doi:10.1016/j.aorn.2010.03.002

Browne, B. A., Kaldenberg, D. O., Browne, W. E. G., & Brown, D. J. (1998). Student as customer: Factors affecting student satisfaction and assessments of institutional quality. *Journal of Marketing for Higher Education*, *8*(3), 1–14. doi:10.1300/J050v08n03_01

Brummer, J. J. (1991). *Corporate responsibility and legitimacy: An interdisciplinary analysis.* Greenwood Press New York.

Bryant, S. L., Forte, A., & Bruckman, A. (2005). *Becoming Wikipedian: transformation of participation in a collaborative online encyclopedia.* Paper presented at the Proceedings of the 2005 international ACM SIGGROUP conference on Supporting group work. doi:10.1145/1099203.1099205

Bryman, A. (2001). *Social research methods.* Bath, England: Oxford University Press.

Bryman, A., & Bell, E. (2003). *Business research methods.* Oxford, England: Oxford University Press.

Bryman, A., & Cramer, D. (2005). *Quantitative data analysis with SPSS 12 and 13: a guide for social scientists.* East Sussex: Routledge.

Brynjolfsson, Erik and Andrew McAfee (2014). *The Second Machine Age.* W. W. Norton & Company. Kindle edition.

Brynjolfsson, E., & McAffe, A. (2011). *Race against the Machine.* Digital Frontier Press.

Buchanan, D., & Bryman, A. (Eds.). (2011). *The organizational research context: properties and implications in Sage handbook of organizational research methods.* Thousand Oaks, CA: SAGE Publications.

Buonanno, G., Faverio, P., Pigni, F., Ravarini, A., Sciuto, D., & Tagliavini, M. (2005). Factors affecting ERP system adoption: A comparative analysis between SMEs and large companies. *Journal of Enterprise Information Management, 18*(4), 384–426. doi:10.1108/17410390510609572

Burges C. (2010). From ranknet to lambdarank to lambdamart: An overview.

Burges, C., Renshaw, T. S. E., Lazier, A., Deeds, M., Hamilton, N., & Hullender, G. (2005). Learning to rank using gradient descent. *Proceedings of the 22nd international conference on Machine learning* (pp. 89–96).

Burke, C., Stagl, K., Klein, C., Goodwin, G., Salas, E., & Halpin, S. (2006). What types of leadership behaviors are functional in teams? A meta-analysis. *The Leadership Quarterly, 17*(3), 288–307. doi:10.1016/j.leaqua.2006.02.007

Burke, W., & Litwin, G. (1992). A causal model of organizational performance and change. *Journal of Management, 18*(3), 523–545. doi:10.1177/014920639201800306

Busa-Fekete, R., Kégl, B., Éltető, T., & Szarvas, G. (2013). Tune and mix: Learning to rank using ensembles of calibrated multi-class classifiers. *Machine Learning, 93*(2-3), 261–292. doi:10.1007/s10994-013-5360-9

Business process model and notation (BPMN). (2013, March). OMG. Retrieved from http://www.omg.org/spec/BPMN/2.0/

Buxton, B. (2010). CES 2010: NUI with Bill Buxton [Interview].

Buxton, W., Billinghurst, M., Guiard, Y., Sellen, A., & Zhai, S. (1994). *Human Input to Computer Systems: Theories, Techniques and Technology.* Retrieved from http://www.billbuxton.com/inputManuscript.html

Bwalya, J. K. (2009). Factors affecting adoption of e-government in Zambia. *The Electronic Journal of Information Systems in Developing Countries, 28*(4), 1–13.

Cadle, J., & Yeate, D. (2001). *Project management for information systems.* Harlow, Essex, England: Financial Times/Prentice Hall.

Caetano, A. (2001). Mudança e Intervenção Organizacional. In J. M. C. Ferreira, J. Neves, & A. Caetano (Eds.), *Manual de Psicossociologia das Organizações* (pp. 531–565). Lisbon: McGraw-Hill.

Caillier, J. G. (2009). Centralized customer service: What local government characteristics influence its acceptance and usage of information? *Public Administration and Management, 14*(2), 292–322.

Calabrese, F., Colonna, M., Lovisolo, P., Parata, D., & Ratti, C. (2011). Real-Time Urban Monitoring Using Cell Phones: A Case Study in Rome. *IEEE Transactions on Intelligent Transportation Systems, 12*(1), 141–151. doi:10.1109/TITS.2010.2074196

Calabrese, F., Pereira, F. C., Di Lorenzo, G., Liu, L., & Ratti, C. (2010). The Geography of Taste: Analyzing Cell-phone Mobility and Social Events. *Proceedings of the 8th International Conference on Pervasive Computing* (pp. 22–37). Berlin, Heidelberg: Springer-Verlag. doi:10.1007/978-3-642-12654-3_2

Calauzènes, C., Usunier, N., & Gallinari, P. (2013). Calibration and regret bounds for order-preserving surrogate losses in learning to rank. *Machine Learning*, *93*(2-3), 227–260. doi:10.1007/s10994-013-5382-3

Cameron, K., Dutton, J., & Quinn, R. (2003). An Introduction to Positive Organizational Scholarship. In K. Cameron, J. Dutton, & R. Quinn (Eds.), *Positive Organizational Scholarship* (pp. 3–13). San Francisco, CA: Berrett-Koehler.

Cameron, K., & Quinn, R. (1998). *Diagnosing and changing organizational culture: based on the competing values framework*. Reading: Addison-Wesley.

Campbell, D. T., & Stanley, J. C. (1963). Experimental and quasi-experimental designs for research on teaching. In N. L. Gage (Ed.), *Handbook of research on teaching* (pp. 171–246). Chicago, IL: Rand McNally.

Candeias, A. A. (2008). Criatividade: Perspectiva integrativa sobre o conceito e a sua avaliação. In M. F. M. S. Bahia (Ed.), *Criatividade: conceito, necessidades e intervenção*. Braga: Psiquilibrios.

Can, E. F., Croft, W. B., & Manmatha, R. (2014). Incorporating query-specific feedback into learning-to-rank models. *Proceedings of the 37th international ACM SIGIR conference on Research and development in information retrieval* (pp. 1035 – 1038).

Cao, M., Zhang, Q., & Seydel, J. (2005). B2C e-commerce web site quality: An empirical examination. *Industrial Management & Data Systems*, *105*(5), 645–661. doi:10.1108/02635570510600000

Cao, Q., Gedajlovic, R., & Zhang, H. (2009). Unpacking organizational ambidexterity: Dimensions, contingencies, and synergistic effects. *Organization Science*, *20*(4), 781–796. doi:10.1287/orsc.1090.0426

Cao, Y., Xu, J., Liu, T., Li, H., Huang, Y., & Hon, H. (2006). Adapting ranking svm to document retrieval. *Proceedings of the 29th annual international ACM SIGIR conference on Research and development in information retrieval* (pp. 186–193).

Cao, Z., Qin, T., Liu, T., Tsai, M., & Li, H. (2007). Learning to rank: from pairwise approach to listwise approach. *Proceedings of the 24th international conference on Machine learning* (pp. 129–136). doi:10.1145/1273496.1273513

Capocci, A., Servedio, V. D., Colaiori, F., Buriol, L. S., Donato, D., Leonardi, S., & Caldarelli, G. (2006). Preferential attachment in the growth of social networks: The internet encyclopedia Wikipedia. *Physical Review E: Statistical, Nonlinear, and Soft Matter Physics*, *74*(3), 036116. doi:10.1103/PhysRevE.74.036116 PMID:17025717

Carayannis, E. G., & Campbell, D. F. J. (2009). 'Mode 3' and 'Quadruple Helix': Toward a 21st century fractal innovation ecosystem. *International Journal of Technology Management*, *46*(3-4), 201–234. doi:10.1504/IJTM.2009.023374

Carillo, K., & Okoli, C. (2011). Generating quality open content: A functional group perspective based on the time, interaction, and performance theory. *Information & Management*, *48*(6), 208–219. doi:10.1016/j.im.2011.04.004

Carmeli, A., & Halevi, M. Y. (2009). How top management team behavioral integration and behavioral complexity enable organizational ambidexterity. *The Leadership Quarterly*, *20*(2), 207–218. doi:10.1016/j.leaqua.2009.01.011

Carneiro, A. (2000). How does knowledge management influence innovation and competitiveness? *Journal of Knowledge Management*, *4*(2), 87–98. doi:10.1108/13673270010372242

Carrizosa, M. T. (2006). *Firm growth, persistence and multiplicity of equilibria: An analysis of Spanish manufacturing and service industries* [Unpublished PhD Dissertation]. University Rovira I Virgili, Spain.

Carroll, N. (2013). E-learning – the McDonaldization of education. *European Journal of Higher Education*, *3*(4), 342–356. doi:10.1080/21568235.2013.833405

Carter, L., & Belanger, F. (2004). The influence of perceived characteristics of innovating on e-government adoption. *The Electronic. Journal of E-Government*, *2*(1), 11–20.

Carter, L., & Belanger, F. (2005). The utilization of e-government services: Citizen trust, innovation and acceptance factors. *Information Systems Journal*, *15*(1), 5–25. doi:10.1111/j.1365-2575.2005.00183.x

Carter, L., & Weerakkody, V. (2008). E-government adoption: A cultural comparison. *Information Systems Frontiers*, *10*(4), 473–482. doi:10.1007/s10796-008-9103-6

Cassinelli, A., Zerroug, A., & Ishikawa, M. (2009), Virtual Haptic Radar. Obtido de Ishikawa Oku Laboratory: http://www.k2.t.u-tokyo.ac.jp/perception/VirtualHapticRadar/

Castells, M. (2000). *The Rise of The Network Society: The Information Age: Economy, Society and Culture*. San Francisco: John Wiley & Sons.

Castells, M. (2005). *The Network Society: A Cross-cultural Perspective*. Northampton, MA: Edward Elgar Publishing.

Castiglione, F. (2001). Forecasting Price Increments Using an Artificial Neural Network. *Advances in Complex Systems*, *3*(01), 45–56. doi:10.1142/S0219525901000097

Cavalcanti, J. C. (2014). *Effects of IT on Enterprise Architecture, Governance and Growth*. Pensylvannia, USA: IGI-Global.

Cave, C. (2013). Creativity Web - Resources for Creativity and Innovation.

Census of Population (2006). Dublin, Central Statistics Office.

Census of Population. (2002). Dublin, Central Statistics Office.

Centeno, C., van Bavel, R., & Burgelman, J. C. (2005). A prospective view of e-government in the European Union. *The Electronic Journal of E-Government*, *3*(2), 59–66.

Chaminade, C., & Edquist, C. (2010). Rationales for public policy intervention in the innovation process: systems of innovation approach. In R. Smits, S. Kuhlmann & P. Shapira (Eds.) (2010), The Theory and Practice of Innovation Policy.

Chang, W., Park, J. E., & Chaiy, S. (2010). How does CRM technology transform into organizational performance? A mediating role of marketing capability. *Journal of Business Research*, *63*(8), 849–855. doi:10.1016/j.jbusres.2009.07.003

Chan, Y. E., & Reich, B. H. (2007). IT alignment: What have we learned? *Journal of Information Technology*, *22*(4), 297–315. doi:10.1057/palgrave.jit.2000109

Chapelle, O., & Chang, Y. (2011). Yahoo! learning to rank challenge overview. *Journal of Machine Learning Research-Proceedings Track*, *14*, 1–24.

Chapelle, O., Chang, Y., & Liu, T. (2011). Future directions in learning to rank. *Proceedings of Yahoo!* (pp. 91–100). Learning to Rank Challenge.

Chapelle, O., Metlzer, D., Zhang, Y., & Grinspan, P. (2009). Expected reciprocal rank for graded relevance. *Proceedings of the 18th ACM conference on Information and knowledge management* (pp. 621–630).

Chapman, C., & Ward, S. (1997). *Project risk: management processes, techniques and insights*. New York, NY: Wiley.

Charette, R. (1989). *Software engineering risk analysis and management*. New York, NY: McGraw-Hill.

Charif, H., & Ramadan, M. (2003). E-government attempts in ESCWA member countries. In M. A. Wimmer (Ed.), *Knowledge management in electronic government* (pp. 310–318). New York, NY: Springer–Verlag. doi:10.1007/3-540-44836-5_33

Chathuranga, S., Samarawickrama, K., Chandima, H., Chathuranga, K., & Abeykoon, A. (2010). Hands free interface for Human Computer Interaction. 2010 5th International Conference on Information and Automation for Sustainability (ICIAFs) 359-364. IEEE.

Chatterjee, S., Chakraborty, S., Sarker, S., Sarker, S., & Lau, F. Y. (2009). Examining the success factors for mobile work in healthcare: A deductive study. *Decision Support Systems*, *46*(3), 620–633. doi:10.1016/j.dss.2008.11.003

Chawla, A., & Kelloway, E. K. (2004). Predicting openness and commitment to change. *Leadership and Organization Development Journal*, *25*(5/6), 485–498. doi:10.1108/01437730410556734

Cheah, C. Y. J., & Garvin, M. J. (2004). An open framework for corporate strategy in construction. *Engineering, Construction, and Architectural Management*, *11*(3), 176–188. doi:10.1108/09699980410535787

Checkland, P. (2005). Webs of significance: The work of Geoffrey Vickers. *Systems Research and Behavioral Science*, *22*(4), 285–290. doi:10.1002/sres.692

Checkland, P., & Casar, A. (1986). Vickers' concept of an appreciative system: A systemic account. *Journal of Applied Systems Analysis*, (13): 3–17.

Chelaru, S., Orellana-Rodriguez, C., & Altingovde, I. S. (2013). How useful is social feedback for learning to rank YouTube videos?[WWW]. *World Wide Web (Bussum)*, 1–29.

Chen, J., Ren, Y., & Riedl, J. (2010). *The effects of diversity on group productivity and member withdrawal in online volunteer groups*. Paper presented at the Proceedings of the SIGCHI Conference on Human Factors in Computing Systems. doi:10.1145/1753326.1753447

Chen, D. Q., Mocker, M., Preston, D. S., & Teubner, A. (2010). Information systems strategy: Reconceptualization, measurement, and implications. *Quarterly*, 34(2), 233–259.

Chen, H. (2002). Digital government: Technologies and practices. *Decision Support Systems*, 34(3), 223–227. doi:10.1016/S0167-9236(02)00118-5

Chen, H., Chiang, R. H. L., & Storey, V. C. (2012, December). Business Intelligence and Analytics: From Big Data to Big Impact. *Management Information Systems Quarterly*, 36(4), 1165–1188.

Chen, H., Nunes, M., Zhou, L., & Peng, G. (2011). The role of electronic records management in information systems development: Gathering, recording and managing evidence of crucial communication and negotiations with customers. *Aslib Proceedings*, 63(2/3), 168–187. doi:10.1108/00012531111135646

Chen, M. C., Chiu, A. L., & Chang, H. H. (2005). Mining changes in customer behavior in retail marketing. *Expert Systems with Applications: An International Journal*, 28(4), 773–781. doi:10.1016/j.eswa.2004.12.033

Chen, M. Y., & Chen, A. P. (2006). Knowledge management performance evaluation: A decade review from 1995 to 2004. *Journal of Information Science*, 32(1), 17–38. doi:10.1177/0165551506059220

Chen, S., Osman, N. M., & Peng, G. C. (2013). Information systems evaluation: methodologies and practical case studies. In P. Isaias & M. B. Nunes (Eds.), *InformationSsystems Research and Exploring Social Artifacts: Aapproaches and Methodologies* (pp. 333–354). Hershey, PA: IGI; doi:10.4018/978-1-4666-2491-7.ch017

Chen, Y. C., & Gant, J. (2001). Transforming local e-government services: The use of application service providers. *Government Information Quarterly*, 18(4), 343–355. doi:10.1016/S0740-624X(01)00090-9

Chesbrough, H. (2006). Open innovation: a new paradigm for understanding industrial innovation. In H. Chesbrough, W. Vanhaverbeke, & J. West (Eds.), Open Innovation: Researching a New Paradigm. Oxford University Press.

Chesbrough, H., & Bogers, M. (2014). Explicating Open Innovation: Clarifying an Emerging Paradigm for Understanding Innovation. In H. Chesbrough, W. Vanhaverbeke & J. West (Eds.), New Frontiers in Open Innovation. Oxford: Oxford University Press.

Chesbrough, H. (2003a). *Open Innovation: The New Imperative for Creating and Profiting from Technology*. Boston, MA: Harvard Business School Press.

Chesbrough, H. (2003b). *The era of open innovation*. MIT Sloan Management Review.

Chesbrough, H. (2004). Managing open innovation. *Industrial Research Institute*, 47(1), 23–26.

Chesbrough, H., & Schwartz, K. (2007). Innovating business models with codevelopment partnerships. *Industrial Research Institute*, 50(1), 55–59.

Chesbrough, H., & Vanhaverbeke, W. (2011). *Open innovation and public policy in Europe*. Science Business Publishing Ltd.

Chesbrough, H., Vanhaverbeke, W., & West, J. (Eds.). (2008). *Open Innovation: Researching a New Paradigm*. Oxford University Press.

Chesney, T. (2007). An empirical examination of Wikipedia's credibility. *First Monday*, 11(11). doi:10.5210/fm.v11i11.1413

Chhabria, S., & Dharaskar, R. (2012). Multimodal Interface for Disabled Persons. *International Journal of Computer Science and Communication*, V, 223–228.

Chiarello, M. A., Emer, M. C. F. P., & Neto, A. G. S. S. (2014). An approach of software requirements elicitation based on the model and notation business process (BPMN). *Lecture Notes on Software Engineering*, 2(1), 65–70. doi:10.7763/LNSE.2014.V2.96

Chien, S.-W., & Tsaur, S.-M. (2007). Investigating the success of ERP systems: Case studies in three Taiwanese high-tech industries. *Computers in Industry*, *58*(8), 783–793. doi:10.1016/j.compind.2007.02.001

China economic yearbook. (2004). Beijing, China: China Economic Yearbook Editing Committee.

Chin, W. W. (1998). Commentary: Issues and Opinion on Structural Equation Modeling. *Management Information Systems Quarterly*, *22*(1), vii–xvi. doi:10.2307/249674

Chirikov, I. (2013). Research universities as knowledge networks: The role of institutional research. *Studies in Higher Education*, *38*(3), 456–469. doi:10.1080/03075079.2013.773778

Cho, V., & Wayman, J. C. (2009, April). *Knowledge management and educational data use*. Paper presented at the 2009 Annual Meeting of the American Educational Research Association, San Diego, CA.

Cho, V., & Wayman, J. C. (2012). Districts' efforts for data use and computer data systems: The role of sensemaking in system use and implementation. Proceedings of the *2012 Annual Meeting of the American Educational Research Association, Vancouver, British Columbia, Canada*. Retrieved from http://www.vincentcho.com/uploads/9/6/5/2/9652180/cho__wayman_aera_2012_final.pdf

Cho, V., & Wayman, J. C. (2013). District leadership for computer data systems: Technical, social, and organizational challenges in implementation. Proceedings of the *UCEA Convention*, Indianapolis, IN. Retrieved from http://www.vincentcho.com/uploads/9/6/5/2/9652180/ucea_2013_co_data_systems_final.pdf

Choi, B., Alexander, K., Kraut, R. E., & Levine, J. M. (2010). *Socialization tactics in wikipedia and their effects*. Paper presented at the Proceedings of the 2010 ACM conference on Computer supported cooperative work. doi:10.1145/1718918.1718940

Chou, D. C., Tripuramallu, H. B., & Chou, A. Y. (2005). BI and ERP integration. *Information Management & Computer Security*, *13*(5), 340–349. doi:10.1108/09685220510627241

Chou, S. W., & Chang, Y. C. (2008). The implementation factors that influence the ERP (enterprise resource planning) benefits. *Decision Support Systems*, *46*(1), 149–157. doi:10.1016/j.dss.2008.06.003

Chrissis, M., Konrad, M., & Shrum, S. (2011). CMMI for development: guidelines for process integration and product improvement, 3rd Ed. SEI Series in Software Engineering. Boston: Pearson Education.

Chun, S. A., Shulman, S., Sandoval, R., & Hovy, E. (2010). Government 2.0: Making connections between citizens, data and government. *Information Polity: The International Journal of Governance and Democracy in the Information Age*, *15*(1/2), 1–9.

Cicmil, S., Williams, T., Thomas, J., & Hodgson, D. (2006). Rethinking project management: Researching the actuality of projects. *International Journal of Project Management*, *24*(8), 675–686. doi:10.1016/j.ijproman.2006.08.006

Clarke, D., & Hollingsworth, H. (2002). Elaborating a model of teacher professional growth. *Teaching and Teacher Education*, *18*(8), 947–967. doi:10.1016/S0742-051X(02)00053-7

Clegg, C., Axtell, C., Damadoran, L., Farbey, B., Hull, R., Lloyd-Jones, R., & Tomlinson, C. (1997). Information technology: A study of performance and the role of human and organizational factors. *Ergonomics Journal*, *40*(9), 851–871. doi:10.1080/001401397187694

CMMI for Development, Version 1.3 [Technical Report]. (2010). *CMMI Product Team*.

Coburn, C. E., Honig, M. I., & Stein, M. K. (2009). What's the evidence on districts' use of evidence? In J. Bransford, D. J. Stipek, N. J. Vye, L. Gomez, & D. Lam (Eds.), The role of research in educational improvement, 67-88. Cambridge, MA: Harvard Education Press.

Coch, L., & French, J. R. P. (1948). Overcoming resistance to change. *Human Relations*, *2*(4), 512–532. doi:10.1177/001872674800100408

Cochrane, T., Black, B., Lee, M., Narayan, V., & Verswijvelen, M. (2013). Rethinking e-learning supporting strategies. *The International Journal for Academic Development*, *18*(3), 276–293. doi:10.1080/1360144X.2012.733884

Coghlan, D. (2006). Insider action research doctorates: Generating actionable knowledge. *Higher Education, 54*(2), 293–306. doi:10.1007/s10734-005-5450-0

Coghlan, D., & Brannick, T. (2010). *Doing action research in your own organization* (3rd ed.). Thousand Oaks, CA: Sage Publications.

Cohen, J. E. (2006). Citizen satisfaction with contacting government on the Internet. *Information Policy, 11*(1), 51–65.

Cohen, W. M., & Levinthal, D. A. (1990). Absorptive Capacity: A New Perspective on Learning and Innovation. *Administrative Science Quarterly, 35*(1), 128–152. doi:10.2307/2393553

Cohen, W. W., Schapire, R. E., & Singer, Y. (1999). Learning to order things. *Journal of Artificial Intelligence Research, 10*, 243–270.

Coleman, G., & O'Connor, R. (2007). Using grounded theory to understand software process improvement: A study of Irish software product companies. *Information and Software Technology, 49*(6), 531–694. doi:10.1016/j.infsof.2007.02.011

Coley, R., & Cradler, J. et al. (1997). *Computers and Classrooms: The Status of Technology in U.S. Schools.* Princeton, NJ: Educational Testing Service.

Collis, B. A., & Wende, M.C. van der (Eds.) (2002). *Models of Technology and future use of ICT in Higher Education.* Enschede: University of Twente

Collis, J., & Hussey, R. (2003). *Business research: A practical guide for undergraduates and postgraduate students.* Hampshire, England: Palgrave McMillan.

Coltman, T., Devinney, T. M., & Midgley, D. F. (2011). Customer relationship management and firm performance. *Journal of Information Technology, 26*(3), 205–219. doi:10.1057/jit.2010.39

Combs, G. (2004). Why teachers hate tech training... and what to do about it. *MultiMedia & Internet@Schools, 11*(1), 8-8.

Compaine, B. (2001). *Re-examining the digital divide: Internet and telecom consortium.* Cambridge, MA: MIT Press.

Conti, T. (1997). *Organizational Self-assessment.* London: Chapman & Hall.

Cooke, F. L. (2000). Manpower restructuring in the state-owned railway industry of China: The role of the state in human resource strategy. *International Journal of Human Resource Management, 11*(5), 904–924. doi:10.1080/095851900422348

Cooke, P. (2005). Regional knowledge capabilities and open innovation: Regional innovation systems and clusters in the asymmetric knowledge economy. *Research Policy, 34*(8), 1128–1149. doi:10.1016/j.respol.2004.12.005

Cooper, R. B. (2000). Information technology development creativity: A case study of attempted radical change. *Management Information Systems Quarterly, 24*(2), 245–275. doi:10.2307/3250938

Cooperrider, D., & Whitney, D. (2005). *Appreciative Inquiry: a Positive Revolution in Change.* San Francisco: Berrett-Koehler Publishers.

Corbin, J. M., & Strauss, A. L. (2008). *Basics of qualitative research: Techniques and procedures for developing grounded theory.* Los Angeles, Calif.: Sage Publications, Inc.

Corcoran, P., Nanu, F., Petrescu, S., & Bigioi, P. (2012). Real-Time Eye Gaze Tracking for Gaming Design and Consumer Electronics Systems. *IEEE Transactions on Consumer Electronics, 58*(2), 347–355. doi:10.1109/TCE.2012.6227433

Cornelissen, F., van Swet, J., Beijaard, D., & Bergen, T. (2011). Aspects of school-university research networks that play a role in developing, sharing and using knowledge based on teacher research. *Teaching and Teacher Education, 27*(1), 147–156. doi:10.1016/j.tate.2010.07.011

Cossock D., & Zhang T. (2006). Subset ranking using regression. *Learning theory*, 605–619.

Council of Health Services. (2009). Healthcare Strategies in the Kingdom of Saudi Arabia. (B/39175). Saudi Arabia.

Coutinho, C. P. (2011). *Metodologia da Investigação em ciências sociais e humanas – Theory and Practice.* Coimbra: Almedina.

Crammer, K., & Singer, Y. (2001). Pranking with ranking. *Advances in Neural Information Processing Systems, 14,* 641–647.

Craswell, N., Fetterly, D., Najork, M., Robertson, S., & Yilmaz, E. (2009). *Microsoft research at trec 2009. web and relevance feedback tracks. Technical report.* DTIC Document.

Creswell, J. (2003). *Research design: Qualitative, quantitative, and mixed methods approaches.* London: Sage.

Crowston, K., Annabi, H., & Howison, J. (2003). Defining open source software project success.

Crowston, K., Annabi, H., Howison, J., & Masango, C. (2005). *Effective work practices for FLOSS development: A model and propositions.* Paper presented at the System Sciences, 2005. HICSS'05. Proceedings of the 38th Annual Hawaii International Conference on. doi:10.1109/HICSS.2005.222

Crowston, K., Howison, J., & Annabi, H. (2006). Information systems success in free and open source software development: Theory and measures. *Software Process Improvement and Practice, 11*(2), 123–148. doi:10.1002/spip.259

Cuadra, A., Cutanda, M., Aurelius, A., & Brunnstrom, K., Lopez de Vergara, J.E., Varela, M., Laulajainen, J.-P., Morais, A., Cavalli, A., Mellouk, A., Augustin, B., & Perez-Mateos, I. (2013). Ecosystem for customer experience assurance. *Proceedings of International Conference on Smart Communications in Network Technologies,* 1-5, Paris:IEEE.

Cummings, T., & Worley, C. (2009). Organizational Development & Change, 9th Edition. Mason: South-Western Cengage Learning.

Curtis, B., Kellner, M. I., & Over, J. (1992). Process modeling. *Communications of the ACM, 35*(9), 75–90. doi:10.1145/130994.130998

Dagger, T. S., & O'Brien, T. K. (2009). Does experience matter? Differences in relationship benefits, satisfaction, trust, commitment and loyalty for novice and experienced service users. *European Journal of Marketing, 44*(9/10), 1528–1552. doi:10.1108/03090561011062952

Dahlander, L., & Gann, D. (2010). How open is innovation? *Research Policy, 39*(6), 699–709. doi:10.1016/j.respol.2010.01.013

Dale, T., & Goldfinch, S. (2006). *Dangerous enthusiasms: E-government, computer failure, and information system development.* Dunedin, New Zealand: Otago University Press.

Daly, J., Kellehear, A., & Gliksman, M. (1997). *The public health researcher: a methodological approach.* Melbourne: Oxford University Press.

Dang, V., Bendersky, M., & Croft, W. B. (2013). Two-stage learning to rank for information retrieval. In Advances in Information Retrieval, 423–434. doi:10.1007/978-3-642-36973-5_36

Daradoumis, T., Rodriguez-Ardura, I., Faulin, J., Juan, A. A., Xhafa, F., & Martinez-Lopez, F. (2010). Customer Relationship Management applied to higher education: Developing an e-monitoring system to improve relationships in electronic learning environments. *International Journal of Services Technology and Management, 14*(1), 103–125. doi:10.1504/IJSTM.2010.032887

Davenport, T. (2014). *big data @ work: Dispelling the Myths, Uncovering the Opportunities.* Harvard Business Press. doi:10.15358/9783800648153

Davenport, T. H. (1993). *Process innovation: Reengineering work through information technology.* Boston, MA: Harvard Business School Press.

Davenport, T. H. (1998). Putting the enterprise into the enterprise system. *Harvard Business Review, 76*(4), 121–131. PMID:10181586

Davenport, T. H., & Harris, J. G. (2007). *Competing on Analytics: The New Science of Winning.* Harvard Business Press.

Davenport, T. H., & Prusak, L. (Eds.). (1998). *Working Knowledge: How Organisations Manage What They Know.* Boston, MA: Harvard Business School Press.

Davenport, T. H., & Stoddard, D. B. (1994). Reengineering: Business change of mythic proportions. *Management Information Systems Quarterly, 18*(2), 121–127. doi:10.2307/249760

Davenport, T., Harris, J. G., & Morison, R. (2010). *Analytics at Work: Smart Decisions Better Results*. Harvard Business Press.

Davies, T. R. (2002). Throw e-gov a lifeline. *Governing*, *15*(9), 72.

Davis, M. R. (2013, October1). Managing the digital district: Intelligent data analysis helps predict needs. [Bethesda, MD: Editorial Projects in Education.]. *Education Week*, *33*(06), 20–21.

Dawson, S. (2009). 'Seeing' the learning community: An exploration of the development of a resource for monitoring online student networking. *British Journal of Educational Technology*, *41*(5), 736–752. doi:10.1111/j.1467-8535.2009.00970.x

Dawson, S., Macfadyen, L., Lockyer, L., & Mazzochi-Jones, D. (2011). Using Social Network Metrics to Assess the Effectiveness of Broad-Based Admission Practices. *Australasian Journal of Educational Technology*, *27*(1), 16–27.

De Brún, C. (2007). Knowledge management and the national health service in England. In R. Bali & A. Dwivedi (Eds.), *Healthcare knowledge management: Issues, advances, and successes* (pp. 179–188). New York: Springer New York. doi:10.1007/978-0-387-49009-0_13

De Jong, J. P. J., Kalvet, T., & Vanhaverbeke, W. (2008). *Policies for Open Innovation: Theory, Framework and Cases*. Helsinki: VISION Era-Net.

De Jong, J. P. J., Kalvet, T., & Vanhaverbeke, W. (2010). Exploring a theoretical framework to structure the public policy implications of open innovation. *Technology Analysis and Strategic Management*, *22*(8), 877–896. doi:10.1080/09537325.2010.522771

De Laat, P. B. (2010). How can contributors to open-source communities be trusted? On the assumption, inference, and substitution of trust. *Ethics and Information Technology*, *12*(4), 327–341. doi:10.1007/s10676-010-9230-x

De Montjoye, Y.-A., Hidalgo, C. A., Verleysen, M., & Blondel, V. D. (2013). Unique in the Crowd: The privacy bounds of human mobility. *Scientific Reports*, *3*. doi:10.1038/srep01376 PMID:23524645

De Mulder, Y., Danezis, G., Batina, L., & Preneel, B. (2008). Identification via Location-profiling in GSM Networks.*Proceedings of the 7th ACM Workshop on Privacy in the Electronic Society* (pp. 23–32). New York, NY, USA: ACM. doi:10.1145/1456403.1456409

Dearstyne, B. W. (2001). E-business, e-government & information proficiency. *Information Management Journal*, *34*(4), 16.

Decoster, G. P., Labys, W. C., & Mitchell, D. W. (1992). Evidence of chaos in commodity futures prices. *Journal of Futures Markets*, *12*(3), 291–305. doi:10.1002/fut.3990120305

Dejean, S., & Jullien, N. (2012). Enrolled since the beginning. an assessment of the Wikipedia contributors' behavior regarding their first contribution: Marsouin working paper.

DeLone, W. H. (1988). Determinants of success for computer usage in small business. *Management Information Systems Quarterly*, *12*(1), 51–61. doi:10.2307/248803

Delone, W. H. (2003). The DeLone and McLean model of information systems success: A ten-year update. *Journal of Management Information Systems*, *19*(4), 9–30.

DeLone, W. H., & McLean, E. R. (1992). Information systems success: The quest for the dependent variable. *Information Systems Research*, *3*(1), 60–95. doi:10.1287/isre.3.1.60

Delone, W. H., & Mclean, E. R. (2004). Measuring e-commerce success: Applying the DeLone & McLean information systems success model.*International Journal of Electronic Commerce*, *9*(1), 31–47.

Demsetz, H. (1983). The structure of ownership and the theory of the firm. *Journal of Law and Economics, No*, *26*(June).

Derlien, H.-U., & Rist, R. (2000). Policy Evaluation in International Comparison. In J.-E. Furubo, R. Rist, & R. Sandahal (Eds.), *International Atlas of Evaluation*. London, New Brunswick: Transaction Publishers.

Desai, C., Wright, G., & Fletcher, K. (1998). Barriers to successful implementation of database marketing: A cross-industry study. *International Journal of Information Management*, *18*(4), 265–276. doi:10.1016/S0268-4012(98)00015-2

DeWalt, D. A. (2010). Ensuring safe and effective use of medication and health care: Perfecting the dismount. *Journal of the American Medical Association*, *304*(23), 2641–2642. doi:10.1001/jama.2010.1844 PMID:21119075

Dewan, S., & Riggins, F. J. (2005). The Digital Divide: Current and Future Research Directions. *Journal of the Association for Information Systems*, *6*(12), 298–337.

Dewey, J. (1933). *How we think: a restatement of the relation of reflective thinking to the educative process*. Boston, MA: Heath.

Dewey, J. (1938). *Experience and Education*. New York: Touchstone.

Dezdar, S., & Ainin, S. (2011). Measures of success in projects implementing enterprise resource planning. *International Journal of Business Performance Management*, *12*(4), 334–353. doi:10.1504/IJBPM.2011.042012

Di Lorenzo, G., & Calabrese, F. (2011). Identifying human spatio-temporal activity patterns from mobile-phone traces. *Proceedings of the 2011 14th International IEEE Conference on Intelligent Transportation Systems (ITSC)* (pp. 1069–1074). doi:10.1109/ITSC.2011.6082974

Dias, P. (2008). *E-Conteúdos para E-Formadores. TecMinho/ Gabinete de Formação Contínua*. Braga: Universidade do Minho.

Ding, D. X., Hu, P. J.-H., Verma, R., & Wardell, D. G. (2009). The impact of service system design and flow experience on customer satisfaction in online financial services. *Journal of Service Research*.

Ding, D. Z., Goodall, K., & Warner, M. (2000). The end of the 'iron rice-bowl': Whither Chinese human resource management? *International Journal of Human Resource Management*, *11*(2), 217–236. doi:10.1080/095851900339837

Dobusch, L., & Kapeller, J. (2013). *Open Strategy between Crowd and Community: Lessons from Wikimedia and Creative Commons*. Paper presented at the Academy of Management Proceedings. doi:10.5465/AMBPP.2013.15831abstract

Dolfsma, W., & Seo, D. (2013). Government policy and technological innovation - a suggested typology. *Technovation*, *33*(6-7), 173–179. doi:10.1016/j.technovation.2013.03.011

Donaldson, T., & Preston, L. E. (1995). The stakeholder theory of the corporation: Concepts, evidence, and implications. *Academy of Management Review*, 65–91.

Donmez, P., & Carbonell, J. G. (2008). Optimizing estimated loss reduction for active sampling in rank learning. *Proceedings of the 25th international conference on Machine learning* (pp. 248–255). doi:10.1145/1390156.1390188

Dopfer, K., Foster, J., & Potts, J. (2004). Micro-meso-macro. *Journal of Evolutionary Economics*, *14*(3), 263–279. doi:10.1007/s00191-004-0193-0

Dorogovtsev, S. N., & Mendes, J. F. F. (2002). *Evolution of networks: from biological nets to the Internet and WWW*. Oxford: Oxford University Press.

Dosi, G., & Freeman, C. (Eds.). (1988). *Technical Change and Economic Theory*. London: Pinter.

Douglas, J., McClelland, R., & Davies, J. (2008). The development of a conceptual model of student satisfaction with their experience in higher education. *Quality Assurance in Education*, *16*(1), 19–35. doi:10.1108/09684880810848396

Downes, S. (2009). Learning Networks and Connective Knowledge. Retrieved from http://www.downes.ca/post/36031

Downs, A. (2012). Resistance to change as a positive influencer: An introduction. *Journal of Organizational Change Management*, *25*(6), 784. doi:10.1108/jocm.2012.02325faa.001

Dreyfuss, R. (2011). Policy Forum: Privatising Science, Evaluating the Public Impact of Open Innovation. *The Australian Economic Review*, *44*(1), 66–72. doi:10.1111/j.1467-8462.2010.00621.x

Drori, O. (1997). From theory to practice or how not to fail in developing information systems. *Software Engineering Notes*, *22*(1), 85–87. doi:10.1145/251759.251875

Dubey, S., & Hefley, W. E. (2011). *Greening ITIL: Expanding the ITIL lifecycle for Green IT*. Paper presented at the Technology Management in the Energy Smart World (PICMET), 2011 Proceedings of PICMET'11.

Duchi, J. C., Mackey, L., & Jordan, M. I. (2013). The asymptotics of ranking algorithms. *Annals of Statistics*, *41*(5), 2292–2323. doi:10.1214/13-AOS1142

Duh, K., & Fujino, A. (2012). Flexible sample selection strategies for transfer learning in ranking. *Information Processing & Management*, 48(3), 502–512. doi:10.1016/j.ipm.2011.05.002

Dwivedi, Y. K. (2009). Viewpoint: An analysis of e-government research published in Transforming Government: People, Process and Policy (TGPPP). *Transforming Government: People. Process and Policy*, 3(1), 7–15.

Earl, M. (1989). *Management strategies for information technologies*. London: Prentice Hall.

Earl, M. J. (1994). The new and the old of business process redesign. *The Journal of Strategic Information Systems*, 3(1), 5–22. doi:10.1016/0963-8687(94)90003-5

Easterby-Smith, M., Thorpe, R., & Lowe, A. (2002). *Management research*. London: Sage.

Easterby-Smith, M., Thorpe, R., & Lowe, A. (2002). *Management research: An introduction*. London, Thousand Oaks: Sage Publications Ltd.

Eatock, J., Giaglis, G. M., Paul, R. J., & Serrano, A. (2000). The implications of information technology infrastructure capabilities for business process change success. In P. Henderson (Ed.), *Systems engineering for business process change* (pp. 127–137). London, UK: Springer–Verlag. doi:10.1007/978-1-4471-0457-5_11

Ed Tech Ticker. (2011, March 18). Data-driven instruction survey released. *Tech & Learning: Ideas and Tools for Ed Tech Leaders*. Retrieved from http://www.techlearning.com/default.aspx?tabid=67&entryid=5837

Eden, C., & Ackermann, F. (1998). *Making strategy: The journey of strategic management*. Sage Publications Ltd.

Edjalali, R. (2011). *Information 20/20: Focus, Connect and Lead with Information*. Gartner.

Edmiston, K. D. (2003). State and local e-government: Prospects and challenges. *American Review of Public Administration*, 33(1), 20–45. doi:10.1177/0275074002250255

Edquist, C. (2001, June 12-15). *The Systems of Innovation Approach and Innovation Policy: An account of the state of the art*. Lead paper presented at the DRUID Conference, Aalborg.

Edquist, C., & Zabala-Iturriagagoitia, J. M. (2012). Public Procurement for Innovation as mission-oriented innovation policy. *Research Policy*, 41(10), 1757–1769. doi:10.1016/j.respol.2012.04.022

EFQM-A. (2013). *EFQM Excellence Model*. Brussels: European Foundation for Quality Management.

Egan, T. M. (2002). Organization development: An examination of definitions and dependent variables. *Organization Development Journal*, 20(2), 59–71.

Eikebrokk, T. R., & Olsen, D. H. (2007). An empirical investigation of competency factors affecting e-business success in European SMEs. *Information & Management*, 44(4), 364–383. doi:10.1016/j.im.2007.02.004

Eisenberg, E., & Riley, P. (2001). Organizational Culture. In F. Jablin & L. Putnam (Eds.), *The New Handbook of Organizational Communication* (pp. 291–323). Thousand Oaks, CA: SAGE Publications.

Eisenhardt, K. M. (1989). Building theories from case study research. *Academy of Management Review*, 532–550.

Elman, J. L. (1990). Finding structure in time. *Cognitive Science*, 14(2), 179–211. doi:10.1207/s15516709cog1402_1

Engwall, M. (2003). No project is an island: Linking projects to history and context. *Research Policy*, 32(5), 789–808. doi:10.1016/S0048-7333(02)00088-4

Erickson, H., & Penker, M. (2000). *Business modeling with UML: Business patterns at work*. New York, NY: John Wiley & Sons.

Erwin, D. G., & Garman, A. N. (2010). Resistance to organizational change: Linking research and practice. *Leadership and Organization Development Journal*, 31(1), 39–56. doi:10.1108/01437731011010371

Etzion, O., Fisher, A., & Wasserkrug, S. (2005). E-CLV: A modeling approach for customer lifetime evaluation in e-commerce domain, with an application and case study for online auction. *Information Systems Frontiers*, 7(4-5), 421–434. doi:10.1007/s10796-005-4812-6

Evans, D., & Yen, D. C. (2006). E-government: Evolving relationship of citizens and government, domestic, and international development. *Government Information Quarterly*, 23(2), 207–235. doi:10.1016/j.giq.2005.11.004

Everett, M., & Borgatti, S. P. (2005). Ego network betweenness. *Social Networks*, 27(1), 31–38. doi:10.1016/j.socnet.2004.11.007

Fama, E. F. (1965). The behaviour of stock market prices. *The Journal of Business*, 38(1), 34–106. doi:10.1086/294743

Fama, E. F. (1970). Efficient capital markets: A review of theory and empirical work. *The Journal of Finance*, 25(2), 383–417. doi:10.2307/2325486

Fang, Z. (2002). E-government in digital era: Concept, practice and development. *International Journal of the Computer*, 10(2), 1–22.

Farbey, B., Land, F., & Targett, D. (1999). The moving staircase. Problems of appraisal and evaluation in a turbulent environment. *Information Technology & People*, 12(3), 238–252. doi:10.1108/09593849910278196

Faria, A., Heppen, J., Li, Y., Stachel, S., Jones, W., & Sawyer, K. … Palacios, M. (2012, Summer). *Charting success: Data use and student achievement in urban schools*. Council of the Great City Schools and the American Institutes for Research. Retrieved from http://www.cgcs.org/cms/lib/DC00001581/Centricity/Domain/87/Charting_Success.pdf

Farjoun, M. (2010). Beyond dualism: Stability and change as duality. *Academy of Management Review*, 35(2), 202–225. doi:10.5465/AMR.2010.48463331

Farrell, T. S. C. (2004). *Reflective practice in action: 80 reflection breaks for busy teachers*. Thousand Oaks, CA: Corwin Press.

Faul, F., Erdfelder, E., Buchner, A., & Lang, A.-G. (2009). Statistical power analyses using G*Power 3.1: Tests for correlation and regression analyses. *Behavior Research Methods*, 41(4), 1149–1160. Statistical power analyses using G*Power 3.1: Tests for correlation and regression analyses doi:10.3758/BRM.41.4.1149 PMID:19897823

Featherman, M., & Pavlou, P. (2003). Predicting e-services adoption: A perceived risk facets perspective. *International Journal of Human-Computer Studies*, 59(4), 451–474. doi:10.1016/S1071-5819(03)00111-3

Fendt, J., & Sachs, W. (2007). Grounded theory method in management research: Users' perspectives. *Organizational Research Methods*, 11(3), 430–455. doi:10.1177/1094428106297812

Fereday, J., & Muir-Cochrane, E. (2006). Demonstrating rigor using thematic analysis: A hybrid approach of inductive and deductive coding and theme development. *International Journal of Qualitative Methods*, 5(1), 1–11.

Ferlander, S., & Timms, D. (2006). Bridging the Dual Digital Divide: A Local Net and an IT-Cafe in Sweden. *Information Communication and Society*, 9(2), 137–159. doi:10.1080/13691180600630732

Fernandez, W. D. (2004). The Glaserian approach and emerging business practices in information systems management: achieving relevance through conceptualization. *Proceedings of the 3rd European Conference on Research Methods in Business and Management* (pp. 177-186).

Ferro, E., Helbig, N. C., & Gil-Garcia, J. R. (2011). The role of IT literacy in defining digital divide policy needs. *Government Information Quarterly*, 28(1), 3–10. doi:10.1016/j.giq.2010.05.007

Field, A. (2005). *Discovering statistics using SPSS: and sex, drugs and rock'n'roll* (2nd ed.). London: SAGE.

Fishbein, M., & Ajzen, I. (1975). *Belief, Attitude, Intention and Behavior: An Introduction to Theory and Research*. Reading: Addison-Wesley.

Fisher, K. (2003). Demystifying critical reflection: Defining criteria for assessment. *Higher Education Research & Development*, 22(3), 313–325. doi:10.1080/0729436032000145167

Flanagan, N. (2007). Teacher in a strange land: yet more reflections on reflecting. Retrieved from http://teacherleaders.typepad.com/teacher_in_a_strange_land/2007/01/yet_more_reflec.html

Fletcher, K., & Wright, G. (1995). Organisational, strategic and technical barriers to successful implementation of database marketing. *International Journal of Information Management*, 15(2), 115–126. doi:10.1016/0268-4012(95)00005-R

Flyvbjerg, B. (2006). Five misunderstandings about case-study research. *Qualitative Inquiry*, 12(2), 219–245. doi:10.1177/1077800405284363

Fogarty, R. (1994). *The mindful school: how to teach for metacognitive reflection.* Palatine, IL: IRI/Skylight Publishing.

Fonseca, C. (2010). The Digital Divide and the Cognitive Divide: Reflections on the Challenge of Human Development in the Digital Age. *Annenberg School for Communication & Journalism, 6,* 25–30.

Foray, D. (Ed.). (2009). *The New Economics of Technology Policy.* Edward Elgar. doi:10.4337/9781848449169

Forte, A., & Bruckman, A. (2008). *Why do people write for Wikipedia? Incentives to contribute to open–content publishing.* Paper presented at the Proceedings of 41st Annual Hawaii International Conference on System Sciences (HICSS).

Foss, N. (2009). Alternative research strategies in the knowledge movement: From macro bias to micro-foundations and multi-level explanation. *Eur Manage Rev, 6*(1), 16–28. doi:10.1057/emr.2009.2

Foss, N. J. (2007). The Emerging Knowledge Governance Approach: Challenges and Characteristics. *Organization, 14*(1), 29–52. doi:10.1177/1350508407071859

Foss, N. J., & Mahoney, J. T. (2010). Exploring Knowledge Governance. *International Journal of Strategic Change Management, 2*(2-3), 93–101. doi:10.1504/IJSCM.2010.034409

Fourney, A., Terry, M., & Mann, R. (2010). Gesturing in the wild: understanding the effects and implications of gesture-based interaction for dynamic presentations. *Proceedings of BCS HCI*

Frank, M. Z., & Stengos, T. (1988). Some evidence concerning macroeconomic chaos. *Journal of Monetary Economics, 22*(3), 423–438. doi:10.1016/0304-3932(88)90006-2

Freeman, C. (1987). *Technology and Economic Performance: Lessons from Japan.* London: Pinter.

Freeman, R. E. (1984). Strategic management: A stakeholder approach. *Analysis, 38*(01).

Freeman, R. E., Harrison, J. S., & Wicks, A. C. (2007). *Managing for stakeholders: Survival, reputation, and success.* Yale University Press.

Freund, Y., Iyer, R., Schapire, R. E., & Singer, Y. (2003). An efficient boosting algorithm for combining preferences. *Journal of Machine Learning Research, 4,* 933–969.

Freund, Y., & Schapire, R. E. (1995). A desicion-theoretic generalization of on-line learning and an application to boosting. In *Computational learning theory* (pp. 23–37). Springer. doi:10.1007/3-540-59119-2_166

Frias-Martinez, E., Williamson, G., & Frias-Martinez, V. (2011). An Agent-Based Model of Epidemic Spread Using Human Mobility and Social Network Information. *Proceedings of the 2011 IEEE Third International Conference on Privacy, Security, Risk and Trust (PASSAT) and 2011 IEEE Third Inernational Conference on Social Computing (SocialCom)* (pp. 57–64). doi:10.1109/PASSAT/SocialCom.2011.142

Friedman, A. L., & Miles, S. (2002). Developing stakeholder theory. *Journal of Management Studies, 39*(1), 1–21. doi:10.1111/1467-6486.00280

Friedman, J. H. (2001). Greedy function approximation: A gradient boosting machine.(english summary). *Annals of Statistics, 29*(5), 1189–1232. doi:10.1214/aos/1013203451

Friel, B. (2002). GovBenefits.gov. *Government Executive, 34*(15), 38.

Frooman, J. (1999). Stakeholder influence strategies. *Academy of Management Review,* 191–205.

Frow, P., & Payne, A. (2007). Towards the 'perfect' customer experience. *Journal of Brand Management, 15*(2), 89–101. doi:10.1057/palgrave.bm.2550120

Furubo, J.-E., Rist, R., & Sandahl, R. (Eds.). (2002). *International Atlas of Evaluation.* London, New Brunswick: Transaction Publishers.

Gagliardi, A. R., Brouwers, M. C., & Bhattacharyya, O. K. (2012). The guideline implementability research and application network (GIRAnet): an international collaborative to support knowledge exchange: study protocol. *Implementation Science; IS, 7*(1), 26–26. doi:10.1186/1748-5908-7-26 PMID:22471937

Galetzka, M., Verhoeven, J., & Pruyn, A. T. H. (2006). Service validity and service reliability of search, experience and credence services. *International Journal of Service Industry Management*, *17*(3), 271–283. doi:10.1108/09564230610667113

Galliers, R. D. (1993). IT strategies: Beyond competitive advantage. *The Journal of Strategic Information Systems*, *2*(4), 283–291. doi:10.1016/0963-8687(93)90007-W

Galliers, R., & Leidner, D. (Eds.). (2003). *Strategic Information Management: Challenges and Strategies in Managing Information Systems*. Oxford, Great Britain: Butterworth-Heinemann.

Gandhewar, V. V., & Wadegaonkar, A. P. (2012). Guidelines for business process modeling and its application to training process. *International Journal of Modeling and Optimization*, *2*(6), 705–707. doi:10.7763/IJMO.2012. V2.215

Gao, W., & Yang, P. (2014). Democracy is good for ranking: Towards multi-view rank learning and adaptation in web search.*Proceedings of the 7th ACM international conference on Web search and data mining* (pp. 63—72). doi:10.1145/2556195.2556267

Garcia-Jimenez, M., & Gomez-Barroso, J. (2009). Universal Service in a Broader Perspective: The European Digital Divide. *Informatica Economica*, *13*(2), 155–165.

Garet, M., Porter, A., Desimone, L., Birman, B., & Yoon, K. (2001). What makes professional development effective? Results from a national sample of teachers. *American Educational Research Journal*, *38*(4), 915–945. doi:10.3102/00028312038004915

Gargeya, V. B., & Brady, C. (2005). Success and failure factors of adopting SAP in ERP system implementation. *Business Process Management Journal*, *11*(5), 501–516. doi:10.1108/14637150510619858

Garicano, L., & Prat, A. (2013). Organizational economics with cognitive costs. Proceedings of *Advances in Economics and Econometrics:Tenth World Congress* (Volume 1, 342), Cambridge University Press.

Garicano, Luis and Esteban Rossi-Hansberg (2006). The Knowledge Economy at the Turn of the Twentieth Century: The Emergence of Hierarchies. *Journal of the European Economic Association*. April-May. 4(2-3): 393-403.

Garicano, L. (2000). Hierarchies and the Organization of Knowledge in Production. *Journal of Political Economy*, *108*(5), 874–904. doi:10.1086/317671

Garicano, L., & Rossi-Hansberg, E. (2012). Organizing growth. *Journal of Economic Theory*, *147*(2), 623–656. doi:10.1016/j.jet.2009.11.007

Garnaut, R., Song, L., Tenev, S., & Yao, Y. (2005). China's ownership transformation: process, outcomes and prospects. Washington, D.C: International Finance Corporation (World Bank Group).

Garner, J. G., Porter, A. L., Newman, N. C., & Crowl, T. A. (2012). Assessing research network and disciplinary engagement changes induced by an NSF program. *Research Evaluation*, *21*(2), 89–104. doi:10.1093/reseval/rvs004

Garrison, D. R. (2011). *E-Learning in the 21st Century: A Framework for Research and Practice*. London: Routledge.

Garvin, D. A., & Roberto, M. A. (2001). What you don't know about making decisions. *Harvard Business Review*, 108–116. PMID:11550627

Gatautis, R. (2010). Creating public value through eParticipation: Wave project. *Economics and Management*, *15*, 483–490.

Gatian, A. W. (1994). Is user satisfaction a valid measure of system effectiveness? *Information & Management*, *26*(3), 119–131. doi:10.1016/0378-7206(94)90036-1

Gattiker, T. F., & Goodhue, D. L. (2005). What happens after ERP implementation: Understanding the impact of interdependence and differentiation on plant-level outcomes. *Management Information Systems Quarterly*, *29*(3), 559–585.

Gaughan, M., & Ponomariov, B. (2008). Faculty publication productivity, collaboration, and grants velocity: Using curricula vitae to compare center-affiliated and unaffiliated scientists. *Research Evaluation*, *17*(2), 103–110. doi:10.3152/095820208X287180

Gauld, R., & Goldfinch, S. (2006). *Dangerous enthusiasms: E-government, computer failure and information systems development*. Dunedin, New Zealand: Otago University Press.

Generett, G. G., & Hicks, M. A. (2004). Beyond reflective competency: Teaching for audacious hope-in-action. *Journal of Transformative Education, 2*(3), 187–203. doi:10.1177/1541344604265169

Geng, X., Liu, T., Qin, T., & Li, H. (2007). Feature selection for ranking. *Proceedings of the 30th annual international ACM SIGIR conference on Research and development in information retrieval* (pp. 407–414).

Geng, X., Qin, T., Liu, T., Cheng, X., & Li, H. (2011). Selecting optimal training data for learning to rank. *Information Processing & Management, 47*(5), 730–741. doi:10.1016/j.ipm.2011.01.002

Gentile, C., Spiller, N., & Noci, G. (2007). How to sustain the customer experience: An overview of experience components that co-create value with the customer. *European Management Journal, 25*(5), 395–410. doi:10.1016/j.emj.2007.08.005

George, A. L., & Bennett, A. (2005). *Case studies and theory development in the social sciences.* The MIT Press.

Geurts, P., & Louppe, G. (2011). Learning to rank with extremely randomized trees. *JMLR: Workshop and Conference Proceedings* (Vol. 14).

Gibson, C. B., & Birkinshaw, J. (2004). The antecedents, consequences, and mediating role of organizational ambidexterity. *Academy of Management Journal, 47*(2), 209–226. doi:10.2307/20159573

Gilbert, D., Balestrini, P., & Littleboy, D. (2004). Barriers and benefits in the adoption of e-government. *International Journal of Public Sector Management, 17*(4/5), 286–301. doi:10.1108/09513550410539794

Gilbert, P. K., & Dabbagh, N. (2005). How to structure online discussions for meaningful discourse: A case study. *British Journal of Educational Technology, 36*(1), 5–18. doi:10.1111/j.1467-8535.2005.00434.x

Giles, J. (2005). Internet encyclopedias go head to head. *Nature.com*.

Giles, J., Park, A., & Zhang, J. (2005). What is China's true unemployment rate? *China Economic Review, 16*(2), 149–170. doi:10.1016/j.chieco.2004.11.002

Gil-Garcia, J. R. (2012). *Enacting Electronic Government Success.* Springer. doi:10.1007/978-1-4614-2015-6

Gil-Garcia, J. R., Chengalur-Smith, I., & Duchessi, P. (2007). Collaborative e-Government: Impediments and benefits of information-sharing projects in the public sector. *European Journal of Information Systems, 16*(2), 121–133. doi:10.1057/palgrave.ejis.3000673

Gil-García, J. R., & Pardo, T. A. (2005). E-government success factors: Mapping practical tools to theoretical foundations. *Government Information Quarterly, 22*(2), 187–216. doi:10.1016/j.giq.2005.02.001

Gill, J., & Johnson, P. (1991). *Research methods for managers.* London: Paul Chapman.

Glänzel, W., Leta, J., & Thijs, B. (2006). Science in Brazil. Part 1: A macro-level comparative study. *Scientometrics, 67*(1), 67–86. doi:10.1007/s11192-006-0055-7

Glanzel, W., & Schubert, A. (2005). Domesticity and internationality in co-authorship, references and citations. *Scientometrics, 65*(3), 323–342. doi:10.1007/s11192-005-0277-0

Glaser, B., & Strauss, A. (1967). *The Discovery of Grounded Theory: Strategies for Qualitative Research.* New York: Aldine.

Glasswell, K. (2012). Building teacher capacity and raising reading achievement. *Australian Council Educational Research Conference 2012, Session R, 112-115.* Queensland, Australia: Australian Council Educational Research.

Glesne, C., & Peshkin, A. (1992). *Becoming qualitative researchers.* New York, NY: Longman.

Glott, R., Schmidt, P., & Ghosh, R. (2010). Wikipedia survey–overview of results. *United Nations University: Collaborative Creativity Group.*

Glynn, L. G., MacFarlane, A., Kelly, M., Cantillon, P., & Murphy, A. W. (2006). Helping each other to learn - a process evaluation of peer assisted learning. *BMC Medical Education, 6*(18), 1–9. PMID:16524464

Goffee, R., & Jones, G. (2007). Leading clever people. *Harvard Business Review, 85*(3), 72. PMID:17348171

Goldberg, D. E. (1989). *Genetic Algorithm in Search, Optimization, and Machine Learning.* Addison Wesley.

González, M. C., Hidalgo, C. A., & Barabási, A.-L. (2008). Understanding individual human mobility patterns. *Nature*, *453*(7196), 779–782. doi:10.1038/nature06958 PMID:18528393

Goodall, K., & Warner, M. (1997). Human resources in Sino-foreign joint ventures: Selected case studies in Shanghai, compared with Beijing. *International Journal of Human Resource Management*, *8*(5), 569–594. doi:10.1080/095851997341397

Good, B. (2012). Assessing the effects of a collaborative research funding scheme: An approach combining meta-evaluation and evaluation synthesis. *Research Evaluation*, *21*(5), 381–391. doi:10.1093/reseval/rvs026

Goodman, D. P., & Hambleton, R. K. (2004). Student test score reports and interpretive guides: Review of current practices and suggestions for future research. *Applied Measurement in Education*, *17*(2), 145–220. doi:10.1207/s15324818ame1702_3

Gorgeon, A., & Swanson, E. B. (2009). *Organizing the Vision for Web 2.0: A Study of the Evolution of the Concept in Wikipedia.* Paper presented at the Proceedings of the 5th international Symposium on Wikis and Open Collaboration. doi:10.1145/1641309.1641337

Gottschalk, P. (1999a). Strategic information systems planning: The IT strategy implementation matrix. *European Journal of Information Systems*, *8*(2), 107–118. doi:10.1057/palgrave.ejis.3000324

Gounaris, S. P., Panigyrakis, G. G., & Chatzipanagiotou, K. C. (2007). Measuring the effectiveness of marketing information systems: An empirically validated instrument. *Marketing Intelligence & Planning*, *25*(6), 612–631. doi:10.1108/02634500710819978

Gouscos, D., Kalikakis, M., Legal, M., & Papadopoulou, S. (2007). A general model of performance and quality for one-stop e-government service offerings. *Government Information Quarterly*, *24*(4), 860–885. doi:10.1016/j.giq.2006.07.016

Graham, J. L., & Lam, N. M. (2004). The Chinese negotiation. In Harvard business review on doing business in China, 31-56. Boston: Harvard Business School Publishing.

Graham, M. (2011). Time machine and virtual portals: The spatialities of the digital divide. *Progress in Development Studies*, *11*(3), 211–227. doi:10.1177/146499341001100303

Graham, S., & Aurigi, A. (1997). Virtual cities, social polarization, and the crisis in urban public space. *Journal of Urban Technology*, *4*(1), 19–52. doi:10.1080/10630739708724546

Grandori, A., & Furnari, S. (2008). A chemistry of organization: Combinatory analysis and design. *Organization Studies*, *29*(3), 459–485. doi:10.1177/0170840607088023

Grant, G. (2005). Realizing the promise of electronic government. *Journal of Global Information Management*, *13*(1), 1–4. doi:10.4018/jgim.2005010101

Greene, W. H. (1997). *Econometric Analysis* (3rd ed.). Upper Saddle River, New Jersey: Prentice-Hall.

Greiner, L. E. (1972). Evolution and Revolution as Organizations Grow. *Harvard Business Review*, *50*(4), 37–46. PMID:10179654

Grimes, S., & Collins, P. (2003). Building a knowledge economy in Ireland through European research networks. *European Planning Studies*, *11*(4), 395–414. doi:10.1080/09654310303641

Gronlund, A. (2003). e-Democracy: In search of tools and methods for effective participation. *Journal of Multi-Criteria Decision Analysis*, *12*(2/3), 93–100. doi:10.1002/mcda.349

Grossman, S. J., & Hart, O. D. (1986). The Costs and Benefits of Ownership: A Theory of Vertical and Lateral Integration. *Journal of Political Economy*, *94*(4), 691–719. doi:10.1086/261404

Growth Policy Analysis. (2013). *China's healthcare system-overview and quality improvements.* Sweden: Swedish Agency for Growth Policy Analysis.

Guijarro, L. (2007). Interoperability frameworks and enterprise architectures in e-government initiatives in Europe and the United States. *Government Information Quarterly*, *24*(1), 89–101. doi:10.1016/j.giq.2006.05.003

Gülgöz, S., Yedekçioglu, O. A., & Yurtsever, E. (2002). Turkey's output in social science publications: 1970-1999. *Scientometrics, 55*(1), 103–121. doi:10.1023/A:1016055121274

Gummesson, E. (2000). *Qualitative Methods in Management Research* (2nd ed.). Thousand Oaks, CA: Sage Publications.

Gupta, P. (2011). Learning to rank: Using bayesian networks. *PhD Thesis*.

Guyader, H. L. (2009). eInclusion public policies in Europe. Brussels, European Comission: Information Society and Media.

Habermas, J. (1979). *Communication and the evolution of society* (T. McCarthy, Trans.). Boston: Beacon.

Hackman, J. (1987). The design of work teams. In J. W. Lorsch (Ed.), *Handbook of organizational behavior* (pp. 315–342). Englewood Cliffs, NJ: Prentice-Hall.

Hagedoorn, J., & Ridder, A.-K. (2012). Open innovation, contracts, and intellectual property rights: an exploratory empirical study.

Halawi, L. A., McCarthy, R. V., & Aronson, J. E. (2007). An empirical investigation of knowledge management systems' success. *Journal of Computer Information Systems, 48*(2).

Halfaker, A., Kittur, A., & Riedl, J. (2011). *Don't bite the newbies: how reverts affect the quantity and quality of Wikipedia work.* Paper presented at the Proceedings of the 7th international symposium on wikis and open collaboration. doi:10.1145/2038558.2038585

Halfaker, A., Kittur, A., Kraut, R., & Riedl, J. (2009). *A jury of your peers: quality, experience and ownership in Wikipedia.* Paper presented at the Proceedings of the 5th International Symposium on Wikis and Open Collaboration. doi:10.1145/1641309.1641332

Hall, P. A., & Taylor, R. C. (1996). Political Science and the Three New Institutionalisms. *Political Studies, 44*(5), 936–957. doi:10.1111/j.1467-9248.1996.tb00343.x

Halpin, J., & Cauthen, L. (2011, July31). The education dashboard. *Center for Digital Education's Converge Special Report, 2*(3), 2–36.

Hamada, Y., Shimada, N., & Shirai, Y. (2000). Hand shape estimation using image transition network. Proceedings of the HUMO '00 Proceedings of the Workshop on Human Motion. doi:10.1109/HUMO.2000.897387

Hamada, Y., Shimada, N., & Shirai, Y. (2002). Hand Shape Estimation Using Sequence of Multi-Ocular Images Based on Transition Network. Proceedings of the International Conference on Vision Interface.

Hambleton, R. K. (2002). How can we make NAEP and state test score reporting scales and reports more understandable? In R. W. Lissitz & W. D. Schafer (Eds.), Assessment in educational reform (pp. 192-205). Boston, MA: Allyn & Bacon.

Hambleton, R. K., & Slater, S. C. (1996). *Are NAEP executive summary reports understandable to policymakers and educators?* Paper presented at the annual meeting of the National Council on Measurement in Education, New York.

Hamel, G. (2012). *What Matters Now: How to Win in a World of Relentless Change, Ferocious Competition, and Unstoppable Innovation.* Jossey-Bass.

Hammer, M., & Champy, J. (1993). *Reengineering the corporation: A manifesto for business revolution.* New York, NY: Harper Business.

Hammer, M., & Mangurian, G. E. (1987). The changing value of communications technology. *MIT Sloan Management Review, 28*(2), 65–71.

Hampton, T. (2007). Groups urge warning label for medical devices containing toxic chemical.[JAMA]. *Journal of the American Medical Association, 298*(11), 1267. doi:10.1001/jama.298.11.1267 PMID:17878415

Han, Q., & Ferreira, P. (2013). Determinants of Subscriber Churn in Wireless Networks: The Role of Peer Influence.*26th European Conference on Operational Research, Telecommunication, Networks, and Social Networks Stream, Roma, Italy.* doi:10.1145/2639968.2640057

Harman, D. (1995). Overview of the second text retrieval conference (trec-2). *Information Processing & Management, 31*(3), 271–289. doi:10.1016/0306-4573(94)00047-7

Hart, O. D., & Moore, J. (1990). Property rights and the theory of the firm. *Journal of Political Economy, 48*(6), 1119–1158. doi:10.1086/261729

Hart, T. (2008). Interiority and education. Exploring the neurophenomenology of contemplation and its potential role in learning. *Journal of Transformative Education, 6*(4), 235–250. doi:10.1177/1541344608329393

Harvey, J., Pettigrew, A., & Ferlie, E. (2002). The Determinants of Research Group Performance: Towards Mode 2? *Journal of Management Studies, 39*(6), 747–774. doi:10.1111/1467-6486.00310

Hasan Dalip, D., André Gonçalves, M., Cristo, M., & Calado, P. (2009). *Automatic quality assessment of content created collaboratively by web communities: a case study of wikipedia.* Paper presented at the Proceedings of the 9th ACM/IEEE-CS joint conference on Digital libraries. doi:10.1145/1555400.1555449

Hasan, S., Zhan, X., & Ukkusuri, S. V. (2013). Understanding Urban Human Activity and Mobility Patterns Using Large-scale Location-based Data from Online Social Media. *Proceedings of the 2Nd ACM SIGKDD International Workshop on Urban Computing* (pp. 6:1–6:8). New York, NY, USA: ACM. doi:10.1145/2505821.2505823

Hastie, T., Tibshirani, R., & Friedman, J. (2009). *The elements of statistical learning.* Berlin: Springer. doi:10.1007/978-0-387-84858-7

Hattie, J. (2010). Visibly learning from reports: The validity of score reports. *Online Educational Research Journal.* Also: Paper presented at the annual meeting of the National Council for Measurement in Education (NCME), San Diego, CA. Retrieved from http://www.oerj.org/View?action=viewPaper&paper=6 Hattie, J., & Timperley, H. (2007, March). The power of feedback. *Review of Educational Research, 77*(1), 81-112. doi: 10.3102/003465430298487

Häyrinen, K., Saranto, K., & Nykänen, P. (2008). Definition, structure, content, use and impacts of electronic health records: A review of the research literature. *International Journal of Medical Informatics, 77*(5), 291–304. doi:10.1016/j.ijmedinf.2007.09.001 PMID:17951106

Hazlett, S., & Hill, F. (2003). E-government: The realities of using IT to transform the public sector. *Managing Service Quality, 13*(6), 445–452. doi:10.1108/09604520310506504

He, B., Ding, Y., & Ni, C. Q. (2011). Mining Enriched Contextual Information of Scientific Collaboration: A Meso Perspective. *Journal of the American Society for Information Science and Technology, 62*(5), 831–845. doi:10.1002/asi.21510

He, C., Wang, C., Zhong, Y., & Li, R. (2008). A survey on learning to rank. *Proceedings of International Conference on Machine Learning and Cybernetics* (pp. 1734—1739).

Heeks, R. (2003). *Reinventing government in the information age: International practice, IT-enabled public sector reform.* London, UK: Routledge.

Heeks, R. (2006). *Implementing and managing eGovernment: An international text.* London, UK: Sage.

Heeks, R., & Bailur, S. (2006). Analyzing e-Government research: Perspectives, philosophies, theories, methods, and practice. *Government Information Quarterly, 24*(2), 243–265. doi:10.1016/j.giq.2006.06.005

Heeks, R., & Bhatnagar, S. (Eds.). (1999). *Understanding success and failure in information age reform.*

HEFCE. *HEFCE strategy for e-learning.* (2005). London: HEFCE.

Heilman, K.M., Nadeau, S.E., & Beversdorf, D.Q. (2003). Creative innovation: possible brain mechanisms. *Neurocase, 9*(5), 369-379.

Heitor, M., & Bravo, M. (2010). Portugal at the crossroads of change, facing the shock of the new: People, knowledge and ideas fostering the social fabric to facilitate the concentration of knowledge integrated communities. *Technological Forecasting and Social Change, 77*(2), 218–247. doi:10.1016/j.techfore.2009.10.006

Helbig, N., Ramón Gil-García, J., & Ferro, E. (2009). Understanding the complexity of electronic government: Implications from the digital divide literature. *Government Information Quarterly, 26*(1), 89–97. doi:10.1016/j.giq.2008.05.004

Helble, Y., & Chong, L. C. (2004). The importance of internal and external R&D network linkages for R&D organisations: Evidence from Singapore. *R & D Management*, *34*(5), 605–612. doi:10.1111/j.1467-9310.2004.00366.x

Helfat, C., & Quinn, J. (2006). Off the shelf book review – Open Innovation: The new imperative for creating and profiting from technology. *The Academy of Management Perspectives*, *20*(2), 86–88. doi:10.5465/AMP.2006.20591014

Henderson, J. C., & Venkatraman, N. (1993). Strategic alignment: Leveraging information technology for transforming organizations. *IBM Systems Journal*, *32*(1), 4–16. doi:10.1147/sj.382.0472

Henri, F., & Pudelko, B. (2003). Understanding and analysing activity and learning in virtual communities. *Journal of Computer Assisted Learning*, *19*(4), 472–487. doi:10.1046/j.0266-4909.2003.00051.x

Herbrich, R., Graepel, T., & Obermayer, K. (1999). Large margin rank boundaries for ordinal regression. *Advances in Neural Information Processing Systems*, 115–132.

Hernandez, U. I., Rodriguez, F. J. A., & Martin, M. V. (2010). *Use processes modeling requirements based on elements of BPMN and UML use case diagrams*. Paper presented at the Second International Conference on Software Technology and Engineering (ICSTE 2010), San Juan, Puerto Rico, United States. doi:10.1109/ICSTE.2010.5608758

Heron, J., & Reason, P. (1997). A participatory inquiry paradigm. *Qualitative Inquiry*, *3*(3), 274–294. doi:10.1177/107780049700300302

Herr, K., & Anderson, G. (2005). *The Action Research Dissertation – a guide for students and faculty*. Thousand Oaks, CA: SAGE Publications, Inc.

Herstad, S., Bloch, C., Ebersberger, B., & De Velde, E. (2010). National innovation policy and global open innovation: Exploring balances, tradeoffs and complementarities. *Science & Public Policy*, *37*(2), 113–124. doi:10.3152/030234210X489590

Heskett, J. L., Jones, T. O., Loveman, G. W., Sasser, W. E. Jr, & Schlesinger, L. A. (2000). *Putting the service-profit chain to work. (Product No. 4460, HBR On Point)*. Cambridge, MA: Harvard Business School Publishing Corporation.

Hessels, L. K., & van Lente, H. (2008). Re-thinking new knowledge production: A literature review and a research agenda. *Research Policy*, *37*(4), 740–760. doi:10.1016/j.respol.2008.01.008

He, Z. L., & Wong, P. K. (2004). Exploration vs. exploitation: An empirical test of the ambidexterity hypothesis. *Organization Science*, *15*(4), 481–194. doi:10.1287/orsc.1040.0078

Hilbert, A., Schönbrunn, K., & Schmode, S. (2007). Student Relationship Management in Germany – Foundations and Opportunities. *Management Review*, *18*(2), 204–219.

Hines, A. H., & Nelson, A. et al. (2001). *Hidden Circuits. Technicolor. A. H. Hines, A. Nelson and T. L. N. Tu*. New York: New York University Press.

Hirschheim, R. (1992). Information systems epistemology: An historical perspective. In R. Galliers (Ed.), *Information Systems Research: Issues, Methods and Practical Guidelines* (pp. 28–60). London: Blackweel Scientific Publications.

Hirschheim, R. (1992). Information Systems Epistemology: An Historical Perspective. In R. D. Galliers (Ed.), *Information Systems Research – Issues, Methods, and Practical Guidelines* (pp. 61–88). Henley-on-Thames, England: Alfred Waller Ltd.

Hirschheim, R., & Smithson, S. (1999). Evaluation of information systems: a critical assessment. In L. P. Willcocks & S. Lester (Eds.), *Beyond the IT productivity paradox* (pp. 381–410). Chichester: John Wiley & Sons.

Hitt, M., Ireland, R., & Hoskinsson, R. (2009). Strategic Management: Competitiveness and Globalization (Concepts and Cases) (8th ed.). Mason: South-Western Cengage Learning.

Ho, A. T. (2002). Reinventing local governments and the e-government initiative. *Public Administration Review*, *62*(4), 434–444. doi:10.1111/0033-3352.00197

Hofmann, K., Whiteson, S., & de Rijke, M. (2013). Balancing exploration and exploitation in listwise and pairwise online learning to rank for information retrieval. *Information Retrieval, 16*(1), 63–90. doi:10.1007/s10791-012-9197-9

Hofstede, G. (2001). *Culture's consequences: comparing values, behaviours, institutions, and organizations across nations* (2nd ed.). London: Sage.

Holden, S. H., Norris, D. F., & Fletcher, P. D. (2003). Electronic government at the local level: Progress to date and future issues. *Public Performance and Management Review, 26*(4), 325–344. doi:10.1177/1530957603026004002

Hollnagel, E. (2000). Barrier analysis and accident prevention. Retrieved from http://human-factors.arc.nasa.gov/april01-workshop/EH_barrier_analysis.pdf

Holmes, D. (2001). *E-business strategies for government.* London, UK: Nicholas Brealey Publishing.

Holsapple, C. W., & Lee-Post, A. (2006). Defining, Assessing, and Promoting E-Learning Success: An Information Systems Perspective*. *Decision Sciences Journal of Innovative Education, 4*(1), 67–85. doi:10.1111/j.1540-4609.2006.00102.x

Hommes, B., & van Reijswoud, V. (2000). *Assessing the quality of business process modeling techniques.* Paper presented at the 33rd Hawaii International Conference on System Sciences, Maui, Hawaii. doi:10.1109/HICSS.2000.926591

Horan, T. A., & Abhichandani, T. (2006). Evaluating user satisfaction in an e-government initiative: Results of structural equation modeling and focus group discussions. *Journal of Information Technology Management, 17*(4), 33–44.

Horkay, N., Bennett, R. E., Allen, N., Kaplan, B., & Yan, F. (2006, November). Does it matter if I take my writing test on computer? An empirical study of mode effects in NAEP. *The Journal of Technology, Learning, and Assessment, 5*(2), 1–50. Retrieved from http://ejournals.bc.edu/ojs/index.php/jtla/article/view/1641/

Horsburgh, S., Goldfinch, S., & Gauld, R. (2011). Is public trust in government associated with trust in e-government? *Social Science Computer Review, 29*(2), 232–241. doi:10.1177/0894439310368130

Horsti, A., Tuunainen, V. K., & Tolonen, J. (2005). *Evaluation of electronic business model success: Survey among leading finnish companies.* Paper presented at the System Sciences, 2005. HICSS'05. Proceedings of the 38th Annual Hawaii International Conference on. doi:10.1109/HICSS.2005.253

Horton, K. S., & Dewar, R. G. (2001). Evaluating creative practice in information systems strategy formation: the application of Alexandrian patterns. Proceedings of the 34th Hawaii International Conference on System Sciences. doi:10.1109/HICSS.2001.927123

Howe, J. (2006a). Crowdsourcing: A definition. *URL. Retrieved from* [REMOVED HYPERLINK FIELD]http://www.crowdsourcing.com/cs/2006/06/crowdsourcing_a.html

Howe, J. (2006b). The rise of crowdsourcing. *Wired magazine, 14*(6), 1-4.

Howe, J. (2008). *Crowdsourcing: How the power of the crowd is driving the future of business.* Random House.

Hoyer, B. (2011). *Unlocking the digital future through open innovation – an intellectual capital approach. Directorate-General for the Information Society and Media.* European Commission.

Hsieh, D. (1991). Chaos and nonlinear dynamics: Applications to financial markets. *The Journal of Finance, 46*(5), 1839–1878. doi:10.1111/j.1540-6261.1991.tb04646.x

Hsieh, T.-J., Hsiaso, H.-F., & Yeh, W.-C. (2011). Forecasting stock markets using wavelet transforms and recurrent neural networks: An integrated system based on artificial bee colony algorithm. *Applied Soft Computing, 11*(2), 2510–2525. doi:10.1016/j.asoc.2010.09.007

Hsieh, Y. H., & Yuan, S. T. (2010). Modelling service experience design process with customer expectation management: A systems dynamics perspective. *Kybernetes, 39*(7), 1128–1144. doi:10.1108/03684921011062746

Hu, M. K., (1962). Visual Pattern Recognition by Moment Invariants. *IRE Trans. Info. Theory,* IT(8), 179-187.

Hua, G., Zhang, M., Liu, Y., Ma, S., & Ru, L. (2010). Hierarchical feature selection for ranking. *Proceedings of the 19th international conference on World Wide Web* (pp. 1113–1114). doi:10.1145/1772690.1772830

Huang, J., & Shyu, S. H. (2008). E-government Web site enhancement opportunities: A learning perspective. *The Electronic Library*, 26(4), 545–560. doi:10.1108/02640470810893783

Huang, S.-C., & Wu, T.-K. (2010). Integrating recurrent SOM with wavelet-based kernel partial least square regressions for financial forecasting. *Expert Systems with Applications*, 37(8), 5698–5705. doi:10.1016/j.eswa.2010.02.040

Huang, S., Chang, I., Li, S., & Lin, M. (2004). Assessing risk in ERP projects: Identify and prioritize the factors. *Industrial Management & Data Systems*, 104(8), 681–688. doi:10.1108/02635570410561672

Huang, Z., & Bwoma, O. P. (2003). An overview of critical issues of e-government. *International Association for Computer Information Systems*, 4(1), 164–170.

Huckvale, T., & Ould, M. (1995). Process modeling – Who, what and how: Role activity diagramming. In V. Grover & W. J. Kettinger (Eds.), *Business process change: Reengineering concepts, methods and technologies* (pp. 330–349). London, UK: Idea Group Publishing.

Hu, G., Shi, J., Pan, W., & Wang, J. (2012). A hierarchical model of e-government service capability: An empirical analysis. *Government Information Quarterly*, 29(4), 564–572. doi:10.1016/j.giq.2012.04.007

Hughes, B., & Cotterell, M. (2002). *Software project management*. London: McGraw-Hill.

Hughes, M., Scott, M., & Golden, W. (2006). The role of business process redesign in creating e-government in Ireland. *Business Process Management Journal*, 12(1), 76–87. doi:10.1108/14637150610643779

Huizingh, E. K. R. E. (2011). Open innovation: State of the art and future perspectives. *Technovation*, 31(1), 2–9. doi:10.1016/j.technovation.2010.10.002

Humphreys, E., & Dineen, D. (2007). *Evaluation of Social Capital in Limerick City*. Limerick: University of Limerick.

Hurson, T. (2007). *Think Better: An innovator's guide to productive thinking*. New York: McGraw-Hill.

Hussein, R., Karim, N. S. A., & Selamat, M. H. (2007). The impact of technological factors on information systems success in the electronic-government context. *Business Process Management Journal*, 13(5), 613–627. doi:10.1108/14637150710823110

Husu, J., Toom, A., & Patrikainen, S. (2008). Guided reflection as a means to demonstrate and develop student teachers' reflective competencies. *Reflective Practice*, 9(1), 37–51. doi:10.1080/14623940701816642

Huvila, I. (2010). Where does the information come from. *Information Research*, 15(3), 28–28.

Hyde, A. (2009). Thought piece: reflective endeavours and evidence-based practice: directions in health sciences theory and practice. *Reflective Practice*, 10(1), 117–120. doi:10.1080/14623940802652938

Ibrahim, M., & Carman, M. (2014a). Undersampling Techniques to Re-balance Training Data for Large Scale Learning-to-Rank. *Proceedings of the 10th Asia Information Retrieval Society Conference, Malaysia* (pp. 444-457). doi:10.1007/978-3-319-12844-3_38

Ibrahim, M., & Carman, M. (2014b). Improving Scalability and Performance of Random Forest Based Learning-to-Rank Algorithms by Aggressive Subsampling. *Proceedings of the 12th Australasian Data Mining Conference, Brisbane, Australia*.

Ikemoto, G. S., & Marsh, J. A. (2008). Chapter 5: Cutting through the "data-driven" mantra: different conceptions of data-driven decision making. Evidence and Decision Making: Yearbook of the National Society for the Study of Education, 106(1), 105-131. Santa Monica, CA: RAND Corporation and National Society for the Study of Education.

Ingram, D., Louis, K. S., & Schroeder, R. G. (2004). Accountability policies and teacher decision making: Barriers to the use of data to improve practice. *Teachers College Record*, 106(6), 1258–1287. doi:10.1111/j.1467-9620.2004.00379.x

Innovation Union Scoreboard 2014. (2014European Commission.

International Data Corporation. (2012). *Digital Universe Study*.

Irani, Z., & Dwivedi, Y. K. (2008). Editorial. *Transforming Government: People. Process and Policy*, *2*(4), 221–224.

Irani, Z., Elliman, T., & Jackson, P. (2007). Electronic transformation of government in the UK: A research agenda. *European Journal of Information Systems*, *16*(4), 327–335. doi:10.1057/palgrave.ejis.3000698

Irani, Z., Sharif, A. M., & Love, P. E. D. (2005). Linking knowledge transformation to Information Systems Evaluation. *European Journal of Information Systems*, *14*(3), 213–228. doi:10.1057/palgrave.ejis.3000538

Irani, Z., Themistocleous, M., & Love, P. E. D. (2003). The impact of enterprise application integration on information system lifecycles. *Information & Management*, *41*(2), 177–187. doi:10.1016/S0378-7206(03)00046-6

Irani, Z., Weerakkody, V., Kamal, M., Hindi, N. M., Osman, I. H., & Anouze, A. L. et al. (2012). An analysis of methodologies utilized in e-government research: A user satisfaction perspective. *Journal of Enterprise Information Management*, *25*(3), 298–313. doi:10.1108/17410391211224417

Isaacman, S., Becker, R., Cáceres, R., Kobourov, S., Martonosi, M., Rowland, J., & Varshavsky, A. (2011). Identifying Important Places in People's Lives from Cellular Network Data. Proceedings of the 9th International Conference on Pervasive Computing (pp. 133–151). Berlin, Heidelberg: Springer-Verlag. Retrieved from http://dl.acm.org/citation.cfm?id=2021975.2021988

Isaacman, S., Becker, R., Cáceres, R., Kobourov, S., Rowland, J., & Varshavsky, A. (2010). A Tale of Two Cities. *In Proceedings of the Eleventh Workshop on Mobile Computing Systems & Applications* (pp. 19–24). New York, NY, USA: ACM. doi:10.1145/1734583.1734589

Issitt, M. (2003). Reflecting on reflective practice for professional education and development in health promotion. *Health Education Journal*, *62*(2), 173–188. doi:10.1177/001789690306200210

Iveroth, E., Fryk, P., & Rapp, B. (2013). Information technology strategy and alignment issues in health care organizations. *Health Care Management Review*, *38*(3), 188–200. doi:10.1097/HMR.0b013e31826119d7 PMID:22722318

Jackson, P. (1994). *Desk research*. London: Kogan Page.

Jacob, S., & Varone, F. (2004). Institutionnalisation de L'évaluation et Nouvelle Gestion Publique: Un État des Lieux Comparatif. *Revue Internationale de Politique Comparée*, *11*(2).

Jaeger, P. T. (2003). The endless wire: E-government as global phenomenon. *Government Information Quarterly*, *20*(4), 323–331. doi:10.1016/j.giq.2003.08.003

Jaeger, P. T., & Thompson, K. M. (2004). Social information behavior and the democratic process: Information poverty, normative behavior, and electronic government in the United States. *Library & Information Science Research*, *26*(1), 94–107. doi:10.1016/j.lisr.2003.11.006

Jalote, P. (2002). *Software project management in practice*. Boston, MA: Addison-Wesley Professional.

James, G. (2000). Empowering bureaucrats. *MC Technology Marketing Intelligence*, *20*(12), 62–68.

Jang, H. Jun-Hyeong, Jin-Woo, D. J., & Bien, Z. Z. (2005). Two-staged hand-posture recognition method for softremocon system. Proceedings of Systems, Man and Cybernetics, 2005 IEEE International Conference on, Volume (1).

Jang, J. S. R. (1993). ANFIS: Adaptive-network-based fuzzy inference system. *IEEE Transactions on Systems, Man, and Cybernetics*, *23*(3), 665–685. doi:10.1109/21.256541

Jansen, D., von Görtz, R., & Heidler, R. (2010). Knowledge production and the structure of collaboration networks in two scientific fields. *Scientometrics*, *83*(1), 219–241. doi:10.1007/s11192-009-0022-1

Jansen, J. J. P., Tempelaar, M., van den Bosch, F. A. J., & Volberda, H. (2009). Structural differentiation and ambidexterity: The mediating role of integration mechanisms. *Organization Science*, *20*(40), 797–811. doi:10.1287/orsc.1080.0415

Janvrin, D., Bierstaker, J., & Lowe, D. J. (2008). An examination of audit information technology use and perceived importance. *Accounting Horizons*, *22*(1), 1–21. doi:10.2308/acch.2008.22.1.1

Järvelin, K., & Kekäläinen, J. (2000). IR evaluation methods for retrieving highly relevant documents. *Proceedings of the 23rd annual international ACM SIGIR conference on Research and development in information retrieval* (pp. 41–48).

Järvelin, K., & Kekäläinen, J. (2002). Cumulated gain-based evaluation of ir techniques.[TOIS]. *ACM Transactions on Information Systems, 20*(4), 422–446. doi:10.1145/582415.582418

Jarvis, P. (1992). Reflective practice and nursing. *Nurse Education Today, 12*(3), 174–181. doi:10.1016/0260-6917(92)90059-W PMID:1625667

Javanmardi, S., Ganjisaffar, Y., Lopes, C., & Baldi, P. (2009). *User contribution and trust in Wikipedia.* Paper presented at the Collaborative Computing: Networking, Applications and Worksharing, CollaborateCom 2009, 5th International Conference. doi:10.4108/ICST.COLLABORATECOM2009.8376

Jayasingam, S., Ansari, M. A., & Jantan, M. (2010). Influencing knowledge workers: The power of top management. *Industrial Management & Data Systems, 110*(1), 134–151. doi:10.1108/02635571011008443

Jennex, M. E., Smolnik, S., & Croasdell, D. (2007). *Towards defining knowledge management success.* Paper presented at the System Sciences, 2007. HICSS 2007. 40th Annual Hawaii International Conference on. doi:10.1109/HICSS.2007.571

Jennex, M. E., & Olfman, L. (2006). A model of knowledge management success.[IJKM]. *International Journal of Knowledge Management, 2*(3), 51–68. doi:10.4018/jkm.2006070104

Jennex, M., & Olfman, L. (2005). Assessing knowledge management success.[IJKM]. *International Journal of Knowledge Management, 1*(2), 33–49. doi:10.4018/jkm.2005040104

Jia, P., Hu, H., Lu T., & Yuan, K., (2007). Head Gesture Recognition for Hands-free Control of an Intelligent Wheelchair. Industrial Robot: An International Journal, Volume (34), 60-68.

Joachims, T. (2002). Optimizing search engines using clickthrough data. *Proceedings of the 8th ACM SIGKDD international conference on Knowledge discovery and data mining* (pp. 133–142).

Johnson, J. D. (2005). Knowledge networks: Dilemmas and paradoxes. *International Journal of Information Management*(0).

Johnson, J. C., Christian, R. R., Brunt, J. W., Hickman, C. R., & Waide, R. B. (2010). Evolution of Collaboration within the US Long Term Ecological Research Network. *Bioscience, 60*(11), 931–940. doi:10.1525/bio.2010.60.11.9

Johnston, R., & Kong, X. (2011). The customer experience: A road-map for improvement. *Managing Service Quality, 21*(1), 5–24. doi:10.1108/09604521111100225

Jones, M. J., & Viola, P. (2003). Face recognition using boosted local features. Proceedings of the International Conference on Computer Vision.

Jones, S., Irani, Z., & Sharif, A. (2007). *E-government evaluation: Reflections on three organizational case studies.* Paper presented at the 40th Hawaii International Conference on System Sciences, Waikoloa, Big Island, HI. doi:10.1109/HICSS.2007.189

Jones, K. S., Walker, S., & Robertson, S. E. (2000). A probabilistic model of information retrieval: development and comparative experiments: Part 1. *Information Processing & Management, 36*(6), 779–808. doi:10.1016/S0306-4573(00)00015-7

Jones, L., Watson, B., Gardner, J., & Gallois, C. (2004). Organizational Communication: Challenges for the new century. *Journal of Communication, 54*(4), 722–750. doi:10.1111/j.1460-2466.2004.tb02652.x

Jones, S., Hackney, R., & Irani, Z. (2007). Towards e-Government transformation: Conceptualizing "citizen engagement": A research note. *Transforming Government: People. Process and Policy, 1*(2), 145–152.

Jones, S., & Hughes, J. (2001). Understanding IS evaluation as a complex social process: A case study of UK local authority. *European Journal of Information Systems, 10*(4), 189–203. doi:10.1057/palgrave.ejis.3000405

Jong, S. (2008). Academic organizations and new industrial fields: Berkeley and Stanford after the rise of biotechnology. *Research Policy*, *37*(8), 1267–1282. doi:10.1016/j.respol.2008.05.001

Jordan, M. I. (1986). Attractor dynamics and parallelism in a connectionist sequential machine, *Proceedings of the Eighth Annual IEEE Conference of the Cognitive Science Society*, New York, 53, 1-520.

Jorgensen, H., Owen, L., & Neus, A. (2008). *IBM Global Making change work study report*. USA: IBM Global Services.

Jullien, N. (2012). What We Know About Wikipedia: A Review of the Literature Analyzing the Project (s).

JUSE. (2013). *The Application Guide for The Deming Prize 2013, For Companies and Organizations Overseas*. Japan: The Deming Prize Committee, Union of Japanese Scientists and Engineers.

Kaiser, M. G., & Ahlemann, F. (2010). Measuring Project Management Information Systems Success: Towards a Conceptual Model and Survey Instrument.

Kakabadse, N. K., Kakabadse, A., & Kouzmin, A. (2003). Reviewing the knowledge management literature: Towards a taxonomy. *Journal of Knowledge Management*, *7*(4), 75–91. doi:10.1108/13673270310492967

Kalpic, B., & Bernus, P. (2006). Business process modeling through the knowledge management perspective. *Journal of Knowledge Management*, *10*(3), 40–56. doi:10.1108/13673270610670849

Kanji, G. K., Malek, A., & Tambi, B. A. (1999). Total quality management in UK higher education institutions. *Total Quality Management*, *10*(1), 129–153. doi:10.1080/0954412998126

Kao, L.-J., Chiu, C.-C., Lu, C.-J., & Chang, C.-H. (2013). A hybrid approach by integrating wavelet-based feature extraction with MARS and SVR for stock index forecasting. *Decision Support Systems*, *54*(3), 1228–1244. doi:10.1016/j.dss.2012.11.012

Kappelman, L. A., McKeeman, R., & Zhang, L. (2006). Early warning signs of IT project failure: The dominant dozen. *Information Systems Management*, *23*(4), 31–36. doi:10.1201/1078.10580530/46352.23.4.20060901/95110.4

Karray, F. O., & De Silva, C. (2004). *Soft Computing and Intelligent Systems Design: Theory, Tools and Applications*. Pearson Education.

Karvalics, L. (2012). Transcending Knowledge Management, Shaping Knowledge Governance. In P. H. T. Hou (Ed.), *New Research on Knowledge Management Models and Methods*.

Kasemsap, K. (2015a). The role of e-business adoption in the business world. In N. Ray, D. Das, S. Chaudhuri, & A. Ghosh (Eds.), *Strategic infrastructure development for economic growth and social change* (pp. 51–63). Hershey, PA: IGI Global. doi:10.4018/978-1-4666-7470-7.ch005

Kasemsap, K. (2015b). The role of electronic commerce in the global business environments. In F. Cipolla-Ficarra (Ed.), *Handbook of research on interactive information quality in expanding social network communications* (pp. 304–324). Hershey, PA: IGI Global. doi:10.4018/978-1-4666-7377-9.ch019

Kasemsap, K. (2015c). The role of information system within enterprise architecture and their impact on business performance. In M. Wadhwa & A. Harper (Eds.), *Technology, innovation, and enterprise transformation* (pp. 262–284). Hershey, PA: IGI Global. doi:10.4018/978-1-4666-6473-9.ch012

Kashanchi, R., & Toland, J. (2008). Investigating the social dimension of alignment: Focusing on communication and knowledge sharing. Proceedings of *ACIS 2008 (Vol. 2)*.

Katevas, N., Sgouros, N., Tzafestas, S., Papakonstantinou, G., Beattie, P., Bishop, J., Tsanakas, P., & Koutsouris, D. (1997). The autonomous mobile robot SENARIO: a sensor aided intelligent navigation system for powered wheelchairs," *Robotics & Automation Magazine,* 60-70.

Katz, J. S., & Martin, B. R. (1997). What is research collaboration? *Research Policy*, *26*(1), 1–18. doi:10.1016/S0048-7333(96)00917-1

Kaylor, C. (2005). The next wave of e-government: The challenges of data architecture. *Bulletin of the American Society for Information Science and Technology*, *31*(2), 18–22. doi:10.1002/bult.1720310207

Kearney, M.-L., & Lincoln, D. (2013). Research universities: Networking the knowledge economy. *Studies in Higher Education, 38*(3), 313–315. doi:10.1080/03075079.2013.778682

Kearns, G. S., & Sabherwal, R. (2007). Strategic alignment between business and information technology: A knowledge-based view of behaviors, outcome, and consequences. *Journal of Management Information Systems, 23*(3), 129–162. doi:10.2753/MIS0742-1222230306

Keil, M., Cule, P., Lyytinen, K., & Schmidt, R. (1998). A framework for identifying software project risks. *Communications of the ACM, 20*(11), 76–83. doi:10.1145/287831.287843

Kelly, J. (2013, December 14). *Big data: Hadoop, Business Analytics and Beyond: A Big Data manifesto from the Wikibon Community*. Retrieved from http://wikibon.org/wiki/v/Big_Data:_Hadoop,_Business_Analytics_and_Beyond

Kemmis, S. (1982). Action research. In T. Husen, Postlethwaite (Eds.), International Encyclopedia of Education: Research & Studies. Oxford: Pergamon Press.

Kersbergen, K. V., & Waarden, F. V. (2004). 'Governance' as a bridge between disciplines: Cross-disciplinary inspiration regarding shifts in governance and problems of governability, accountability and legitimacy. *European Journal of Political Research, 43*(2), 143–171. doi:10.1111/j.1475-6765.2004.00149.x

Kersten, B., & Verhoef, C. (2003). IT portfolio management: A banker's perspective on IT. *Cutter IT Journal, 16*(4), 34–40.

Khalil, O. E. M. (2011). e-Government readiness: Does national culture matter? *Government Information Quarterly, 28*(3), 388–399. doi:10.1016/j.giq.2010.06.011

Kimble, C., Hildreth, P., & Bourdon, I. (2008). Communities of Practice. Creating Learning Environments for Educators (Vol. 1 & 2). North Carolina: Information Age Publishing.

Kim, H. J., Pan, G., & Pan, S. L. (2007). Managing IT-enabled transformation in the public sector: A case study on e-government in South Korea. *Government Information Quarterly, 24*(2), 338–352. doi:10.1016/j.giq.2006.09.007

Kim, H., & Fellner, D. W. (2001). Interaction with Hand Gesture for a Back-Projection Wall. *CGI '04 Proceedings of the Computer Graphics International*, Washington.

Kim, H.-J., & Shin, K.-S. (2007). A hybrid approach based on neural networks and genetic algorithms for detecting temporal patterns in stock markets. *Applied Soft Computing, 7*(2), 569–576. doi:10.1016/j.asoc.2006.03.004

Kim, S. S. (1998). Time-delay recurrent neural network for temporal correlations and prediction. *Neurocomputing, 20*(1-3), 253–263. doi:10.1016/S0925-2312(98)00018-6

Kim, S. Y., Jung, T. S., Suh, E. H., & Hwang, H. S. (2006). Customer segmentation and strategy development based on customer lifetime value: A case study. *Expert Systems with Applications, 31*(1), 101–107. doi:10.1016/j.eswa.2005.09.004

Kim, S., Kim, H. J., & Lee, H. (2009). An institutional analysis of an e-government system for anti-corruption: The case of OPEN. *Government Information Quarterly, 26*(1), 42–50. doi:10.1016/j.giq.2008.09.002

King, N. (2008). *Template analysis*. Retrieved from http://www2.hud.ac.uk/hhs/research/template_analysis

King, N., & Horrocks, C. (2010). *Interviews in qualitative research*. London: Sage.

Kittur, A., & Kraut, R. E. (2008). *Harnessing the wisdom of crowds in wikipedia: quality through coordination*. Paper presented at the Proceedings of the 2008 ACM conference on Computer supported cooperative work. doi:10.1145/1460563.1460572

Kleim, R. L., & Ludin, I. S. (2000). *Reducing project risks*. Hampshire: Gower Publishing Ltd.

Klein, H. K., & Lyytinen, K. (1984). The Poverty of Scientism in Information Systems in Research methods in Information Systems.*Proceedings of the IFIP WG Colloquium* (pp. 131-162).

Klenk, N. L., & Hickey, G. M. (2012). Improving the social robustness of research networks for sustainable natural resource management: Results of a Delphi study in Canada.[SPP]. *Science & Public Policy, 39*(3), 357–372. doi:10.1093/scipol/scs024

Kliem, R., & Ludin, I. (2000). *Reducing project risk*. Aldershot, England: Gower Publishing Limited.

Knapp, M. S., Swinnerton, J. A., Copland, M. A., & Monpas-Hubar, J. (2006). *Data-informed leadership in education*. Seattle, WA: Center for the Study of Teaching and Policy.

Knight, A., & Ruddock, L. (2008). *Advanced research methods in the built environment*. Blackwell Pub.

Kobayashi, Y., Kinpara, Y., Shibusawa, T., & Kuno, Y. (2009). Robotic wheelchair based on observations of people using integrated sensors. Proceedings of the 2009 IEEE/RSJ international conference on intelligent robots and systems, 2013-2018. doi:10.1109/IROS.2009.5353933

Kock, N.F., McQueen, R.J., & Scott., J.L. (1997). Can action research be made more rigorous in a positivist sense? The contribution of an iterative approach. *Journal of Systems & Information Technology*, 1(1), 1-24.

Koelble, T. A., Cook, K. S., Levi, M., Granovetter, M., Swedberg, R., & March, J. G. et al. (1996). The New Institutionalism in Political Science and Sociology. *Comparative Politics*, 27(2), 231–243. doi:10.2307/422167

Kolowski, S., Watola, D., Jensen, J., Kim, B., & Botero, I. (2009). Developing adaptive teams: a theory of dynamic team leadership. In E. Salas, G. Goodwin, & C. Burke (Eds.), *Team effectiveness in complex organizations: cross-disciplinary perspectives and approaches* (pp. 113–154). USA: Psychology Press, Taylor & Francis Group.

Kotter, J. P. (1996). *Leading Change*. Boston, Massachusetts: Harvard Business School Press.

Kotter, J. P., & Schlesinger, L. A. (1979). Choosing strategies for change. *Harvard Business Review*, (March-April): 106–114. PMID:10240501

Kovacic, Z. J. (2005). The impact of national culture on worldwide e-government readiness. *Informing Science: International Journal of an Emerging Discipline*, 8, 143–158.

Kramer, M., Gregorowicz, A., & Iyer, B. (2008). *Wiki trust metrics based on phrasal analysis*. Paper presented at the Proceedings of the 4th International Symposium on Wikis. doi:10.1145/1822258.1822291

Kretschmer, H., Liming, L., & Kundra, R. (2001). Foundation of a global interdisciplinary research network (COLNET) with Berlin as the virtual centre. *Scientometrics*, 52(3), 531–537. doi:10.1023/A:1014268505676

Krone, K., Kramer, M., & Sias, P. (2010). Theoretical developments in organizational communication research. In *The Handbook of communication science* (2nd ed.). Thousand Oaks, CA: SAGE Publications. doi:10.4135/9781412982818.n10

Krueger, W. M. (1991). *Artificial Reality II*. Addison-Wesley.

Kuehn, B. M. (2009). FDA focuses on drugs and liver damage: Labeling and other changes for acetaminophen.[JAMA]. *Journal of the American Medical Association*, 302(4), 369–371. doi:10.1001/jama.2009.1019 PMID:19622807

Kueng, P., Kawalek, P., & Bichler, P. (1996). *How to compose an object-oriented business process model?* Paper presented at the IFIP WG8.1/WG8.2 Working Conference, Atlanta, GA. doi:10.1007/978-0-387-35080-6_7

Kulkarni, U. R., Ravindran, S., & Freeze, R. (2007). A knowledge management success model: Theoretical development and empirical validation. *Journal of Management Information Systems*, 23(3), 309–347. doi:10.2753/MIS0742-1222230311

Kumar, K. M., & Dinesh, M., (2012). Hand gesture recognition for wheelchair controlled by digital image processing. *International Journal of Communications and Engineering*.

Kumar, S. P., Umashankar, C., Rani, J. K., & Ramana, V. V. V. (2010). e-Governance applications for citizens: Issues and framework. *International Journal on Computer Science and Engineering*, 2(7), 2362–2365.

Kumar, V., Murkerji, B., Butt, I., & Persaud, A. (2007). Factors for successful e-government adoption: A conceptual framework. *The Electronic Journal of E-Government*, 5(1), 63–76.

Kung, K. S., Greco, K., Sobolevsky, S., & Ratti, C. (2014). Exploring Universal Patterns in Human Home-Work Commuting from Mobile Phone Data. *PLoS ONE*, 9(6), e96180. doi:10.1371/journal.pone.0096180 PMID:24933264

Lachman, N., & Pawlina, W. (2006). Integrating professionalism in early medical education: The theory and application of reflective practice in the anatomy curriculum. *Clinical Anatomy (New York, N.Y.)*, *19*(5), 456–460. doi:10.1002/ca.20344 PMID:16683241

Ladle, R. J., Todd, P. A., & Malhado, A. C. M. (2012). Assessing insularity in global science. *Scientometrics*, 1–6.

Lagsten, J., & Goldkuhl, G. (2008). Interpretative IS Evaluation: Results and Uses. *The Electronic Journal of Information Systems Evaluation*, *11*(2), 97–108.

Lahmiri, S. (2014c). Wavelet low and high frequency components as features to predict stock prices with backpropagation neural networks. *Journal of King Saud University - Computer and Information Sciences*, *26*, 218-227.

Lahmiri, S. (2013). Forecasting S&P500 Directions using Wavelets and Support Vector Machines. *International Journal of Strategic Decision Sciences*, *4*, 78–88. doi:10.4018/jsds.2013010105

Lahmiri, S. (2014a). Entropy-based technical analysis indicators selection for CAC40 fluctuations prediction using support vector machines. *Fluctuation and Noise Letters*, *13*. doi:10.1142/S0219477514500138

Lahmiri, S. (2014b). Improving forecasting accuracy of the S&P500 intra-day price direction using both wavelet low and high frequency coefficients. *Fluctuation and Noise Letters*, *13*(01), 1450008. doi:10.1142/S0219477514500084

Lahmiri, S., & Boukadoum, M. (2015a). An Ensemble System Based on hybrid EGARCH-ANN with Different Distributional Assumptions to Predict S&P500 Intraday Volatility. *Fluctuation and Noise Letters*, *14*(01), 1550001. doi:10.1142/S0219477515500017

Lahmiri, S., & Boukadoum, M. (2015b). Intelligent ensemble forecasting system of stock market fluctuations based on symmetric and asymmetric wavelet functions. *Fluctuation and Noise Letters*, 1550033. doi:10.1142/S0219477515500339

Lahmiri, S., Boukadoum, M., & Chartier, S. (2014a). A supervised classification system of financial data based on wavelet packet and neural networks. *International Journal of Strategic Decision Sciences*, *4*(4), 72–84. doi:10.4018/ijsds.2013100105

Lahmiri, S., Boukadoum, M., & Chartier, S. (2014b). Exploring Information Categories and Artificial Neural Networks Numerical Algorithms in S&P500 Trend Prediction: A Comparative Study. *International Journal of Strategic Decision Sciences*, *5*(1), 76–94. doi:10.4018/IJSDS.2014010105

Lai, H., Pan, Y., Tang, Y., & Yu, R. (2013). FSMRank: Feature Selection Algorithm for Learning to Rank. *IEEE Transactions on Neural Networks and Learning Systems*, *24*(6), 940–952. doi:10.1109/TNNLS.2013.2247628 PMID:24808475

Lam, S. K., Karim, J., & Riedl, J. (2010). *The effects of group composition on decision quality in a social production community*. Paper presented at the Proceedings of the 16th ACM international conference on Supporting group work. doi:10.1145/1880071.1880083

Laming, C., & Mason, K. (2014). Customer experience – an analysis of the concept and its performance in airline brands. *Research in Transportation Business and Management*, *10*, 15–25. doi:10.1016/j.rtbm.2014.05.004

Landsbergen, D. J. Jr, & Wolken, G. J. Jr. (2001). Realizing the promise: Government information systems and the fourth generation of information technology. *Public Administration Review*, *61*(2), 206–220. doi:10.1111/0033-3352.00023

Lankhorst, M. (2005). *Enterprise architecture at work: Modelling, communication, and analysis*. Berlin, Germany: Springer–Verlag.

Lan, Y., Liu, T., Ma, Z., & Li, H. (2009). Generalization analysis of listwise learning-to-rank algorithms. *Proceedings of the 26th Annual International Conference on Machine Learning* (pp. 577–584).

Lan, Y., Liu, T., Qin, T., Ma, Z., & Li, H. (2008). Querylevel stability and generalization in learning to rank. *Proceedings of the 25th international conference on Machine learning* (pp. 512–519).

Larsen, E., & Rainie, L. (2002). *The rise of the e-citizen: How people use government agencies' web sites*. Washington, DC: Pew Internet and American Life Project.

Laudel, G. (2002). What do we measure by co-authorships? *Research Evaluation, 11*(1), 3–15. doi:10.3152/147154402781776961

Lau, F., Price, M., Boyd, J., Partridge, C., Bell, H., & Raworth, R. (2012). Impact of electronic medical record on physician practice in office settings: A systematic review. *BMC Medical Informatics and Decision Making, 12*(1), 10. doi:10.1186/1472-6947-12-10 PMID:22364529

Laurillard, D. (2013). *Rethinking university teaching: a conversational framework for the effective use of learning technologies*. London: Routledge.

Laursen, K., & Salter, A. J. (2005). Open Innovation: The Role of Openness in Explaining Innovation Performance Among U.K. Manufacturing Firms. *Strategic Management Journal, 27*(2), 131–150. doi:10.1002/smj.507

Laursen, K., & Salter, A. J. (2014). The paradox of openness: Appropriability, external search and collaboration. *Research Policy, 43*(5), 867–878. doi:10.1016/j.respol.2013.10.004

Lave, J., & Wenger, E. (1990). *Situated learning: legitimate peripheral participation*. Cambridge, MA: University of Cambridge Press.

Lawrence, M. (2003). Are you up to it? *The Computer Bulletin for Information Systems Professionals, 45*(2), 22.

Lawrence, P. R. (1969). *How to deal with resistance to change*. Harvard Business Review, January - February.

Layne, K., & Lee, J. (2001). Developing fully functional e-government: A four stage model. *Government Information Quarterly, 18*(2), 122–136. doi:10.1016/S0740-624X(01)00066-1

Le Deu, F., Parekh, R., Zhang, F., & Zhou, G. (2012). *Health care in China: Entering 'uncharted waters*. Shanghai, China: McKinsey & Company.

Lean, O. K., Zailani, S., Ramayah, T., & Fernando, Y. (2009). Factors influencing intention to use e-government services among citizens in Malaysia. *International Journal of Information Management, 29*(6), 458–475. doi:10.1016/j.ijinfomgt.2009.03.012

Lederer, A. L., & Sethi, V. (1991). Critical dimensions of strategic information systems planning. *Decision Sciences, 22*(1), 104–119. doi:10.1111/j.1540-5915.1991.tb01265.x

Lee, L. K., Kim, S., Choi, Y. K., & Lee, M. H. (2000). Recognition of hand gesture to human-computer interaction. Proceedings of the 26th Annual Conference of the IEEE Industrial Electronics Society (Vol. 3).

Lee, A. S. (2001). Challenges to qualitative researchers in information systems. In E. M. Trauth (Ed.), *Qualitative research in information systems: issues and trends* (pp. 240–270). London: Idea Group Publishing. doi:10.4018/978-1-930708-06-8.ch010

Lee, G. O. M., & Warner, M. (2002). Labour-market policies in Shanghai and Hong Kong: A study of "one country, two systems" in Greater China. *International Journal of Manpower, 23*(6), 505–526. doi:10.1108/01437720210446379

Lee, S. (2013). IT Governance Issues in Korean Government Integrated Data Center. *International Journal of Advancement in Computing Technology, 5*(11), 438–444. doi:10.4156/ijact.vol5.issue11.54

Lee, S. Y. T., Kim, H.-W., & Gupta, S. (2009). Measuring open source software success. *Omega, 37*(2), 426–438. doi:10.1016/j.omega.2007.05.005

Lee, S.-K., & Yu, J.-H. (2012). Success model of project management information system in construction. *Automation in Construction, 25*, 82–93. doi:10.1016/j.autcon.2012.04.015

Lehmann, H. P., & Gallupe, R. B. (2005). Information Systems for Multinational Enterprises – Some Factors at Work in their Design and Implementation. *Journal of International Management, 11*(4), 28–49.

Lehmann, H., & Fernandez, W. (2007). Adapting the grounded theory method for information systems research. In D. Pauleen (Ed.), *Proceedings of QualIT Conference*, 1-8.

Lemarchand, G. A. (2012). The long-term dynamics of co-authorship scientific networks: Iberoamerican countries (1973-2010). *Research Policy, 41*(2), 291–305. doi:10.1016/j.respol.2011.10.009

LeRoy, S. F. (1989). Efficient capital markets and martingales. *Journal of Economic Literature, 27*, 1538–1621.

Lester, S. (1999). An introduction to phenomenological research.

Leta, J., Glänzel, W., & Thijs, B. (2006). Science in Brazil. Part 2: Sectoral and institutional research profiles. *Scientometrics*, *67*(1), 87–105. doi:10.1007/s11192-006-0051-y

Leveraging the power of state longitudinal data systems: Building capacity to turn data into useful information. (2011). *Data Quality Campaign*. Retrieved from http://www.dataqualitycampaign.org/files/DQC-Research%20capacity%20May17.pdf

Levinthal, D., & March, J. G. (1981). A model of adaptive organizational search. *Journal of Economic Behavior & Organization*, *2*(4), 307–333. doi:10.1016/0167-2681(81)90012-3

Lewin, K. (1946). Action research and minority problems. *The Journal of Social Issues*, 2.

Lewin, K. (1951). *Field theory in Social Science*. New York: Harper & Row.

Lewin, K. (1951). *Field theory in social sciences*. New York: Harper Torchbooks.

Lewis, S., Pea, R., & Rosen, J. (2010). Beyond participation to co-creation of meaning: Mobile social media in generative learning communities. *Social Sciences Information. Information Sur les Sciences Sociales*, *49*(3), 351–369. doi:10.1177/0539018410370726

Leydesdorff, L., & Persson, O. (2010). Mapping the geography of science: Distribution patterns and networks of relations among cities and institutes. *Journal of the American Society for Information Science and Technology*, *61*(8), 1622–1634.

Licsár, A., & Szirányi, T. (2004). Dynamic training of hand gesture recognition system. Proceedings of the 17th International Conference on Pattern Recognition (ICPR'04) (Vol. 4). doi:10.1109/ICPR.2004.1333935

Lientz, B. P., & Larssen, L. (2006). *Risk management for IT projects: how to deal with 150 issues and risks*. Oxford: Butterworth-Heinemann Ltd.

Li, H. (2011). Learning to rank for information retrieval and natural language processing.[Morgan and Claypool Publishers.]. *Synthesis Lectures on Human Language Technologies*, *4*(1), 1–113. doi:10.2200/S00348ED-1V01Y201104HLT012

Li, H., & Xu, J. (2012). Beyond bag-of-words: machine learning for query-document matching in web search. *Proceedings of the 35th international ACM SIGIR conference on Research and development in information retrieval* (pp. 1177–1177). doi:10.1145/2348283.2348528

Lih, A. (2004). Wikipedia as participatory journalism: Reliable sources? metrics for evaluating collaborative media as a news resource. *Nature*.

Li, L., & Lin, H. (2007). Ordinal regression by extended binary classification. *Advances in Neural Information Processing Systems*, *19*, 865–872.

Limayem, M., & Cheung, C. M. (2008). Understanding information systems continuance: The case of Internet-based learning technologies. *Information & Management*, *45*(4), 227–232. doi:10.1016/j.im.2008.02.005

Lim, D., Lanckriet, G., & McFee, B. (2013). Robust structural metric learning. *Proceedings of The 30th International Conference on Machine Learning* (pp. 615—623).

Limerick Health Promotion. (2008). *Health Impact Assessment of Early School Leaving, Absenteeism and Truancy*. Limerick: Health Service Executive.

Lina, C.-S., Huana, C.-C., Chana, C.-N., Yehb, M.-S., & Chiua, C.-C. (2004). Design of a computer game using an eye-tracking device for eye's activity rehabilitation. *Optics and Lasers in Engineering*, *42*(1), 91–108. doi:10.1016/S0143-8166(03)00075-7

Lin, C., Tan, B., & Chang, S. (2008). An exploratory model of knowledge flow barriers within Healthcare Organisations. *Information & Management*, *45*(5), 331–339. doi:10.1016/j.im.2008.03.003

Lincoln, Y. S., Lynham, S. A., & Guba, E. G. (2011). Paradigmatic controversies, contradictions, and emerging confluences revisited. In N. K. Denzin & Y. S. Lincoln (Eds.), *The SAGE Handbook of Qualitative Research*. Thousand Oaks, CA: SAGE Publications, Inc.

Lin, F. R., Yang, M. C., & Pai, Y. H. (2002). A generic structure for business process modeling. *Business Process Management Journal*, *8*(1), 19–41. doi:10.1108/14637150210418610

Lin, F., Fofanah, S. S., & Liang, D. (2011). Assessing citizen adoption of e-Government initiatives in Gambia: A validation of the technology acceptance model in information systems success. *Government Information Quarterly*, *28*(2), 271–279. doi:10.1016/j.giq.2010.09.004

Lin, H.-F. (2007). Measuring online learning systems success: Applying the updated DeLone and McLean model. *Cyberpsychology & Behavior*, *10*(6), 817–820. doi:10.1089/cpb.2007.9948 PMID:18085970

Lin, K., Jan, T., & Lin, H. (2013). Data selection techniques for large-scale learning to rank.*Proceedings of Conference on Technologies and Applications of Artificial Intelligence. Taipei, Taiwan*, (pp. 25 – 30).

Li, P., Burges, C., & Wu, Q. (2007). Learning to rank using classification and gradient boosting. *Advances in Neural Information Processing Systems*, *19*, 897–904.

Lipka, N., & Stein, B. (2010). *Identifying featured articles in Wikipedia: writing style matters.* Paper presented at the Proceedings of the 19th international conference on World wide web. doi:10.1145/1772690.1772847

Lippit, R., Watson, J., & Westley, B. (1958). *The Dynamics of Planned Change*. New York: Harcourt, Brace and World.

Lipsey, R. G., Carlaw, K. I., & Bekar, C. T. (2006). *Economic Transformations: General Purpose Technologies and Long Term Economic Growth*. Oxford University Press.

Little, J. W. (1997). The persistence of privacy: Autonomy and initiative in teachers' professional relations. *Teachers College Record*, *91*, 509–536.

Liu, Y., Zhou, C., & Chen, Y. (2010). *Customer satisfaction measurement model of e-government service.* Paper presented at the 2010 IEEE International Conference on Service Operations and Logistics and Informatics (SOLI), Qingdao, China. doi:10.1109/SOLI.2010.5551542

Liu, T. (2011). *Learning to rank for information retrieval.* Berlin: Springer. doi:10.1007/978-3-642-14267-3

Lo, A. W., & MacKinley, A. C. (1999).*A non-random walk down Wall Street*. Princeton: Princeton University Press.

Loh, T. C., & Koh, S. C. L. (2004). Critical elements for a successful enterprise resource planning implementation in small-and medium-sized enterprises. *International Journal of Production Research*, *42*(17), 3433–3455. doi:10.1080/00207540410001671679

Long, B., Chapelle, O., Zhang, Y., Chang, Y., Zheng, Z., & Tseng, B. (2010). Active learning for ranking through expected loss optimization.*Proceedings of the 33rd international ACM SIGIR conference on Research and development in information retrieval* (pp. 267–274). doi:10.1145/1835449.1835495

López López, W., García-Cepero, M. C., Aguilar Bustamante, M. C., Silva, L. M., & Aguado López, E. (2010). Panorama general de la producción académica en la psicología iberoamericana, 2005-2007. *Papeles del Psicólogo*, *31*(3), 296–309.

Loughran, J. J. (2002). Effective reflective practice: In search of meaning in learning about teaching. *Journal of Teacher Education*, *53*(1), 33–43. doi:10.1177/0022487102053001004

Louridas, P. (2006). Using wikis in software development. *Software, IEEE*, *23*(2), 88–91. doi:10.1109/MS.2006.62

Lowndes, V., & Skelcher, C. (1998). The dynamics of multi-organizational partnerships: An analysis of changing modes of governance. *Public Administration*, *76*(2), 313–333. doi:10.1111/1467-9299.00103

Lowrie, A., & McKnight, P. J. (2004). Academic research networks: A key to enhancing scholarly standing. *European Management Journal*, *22*(4), 345–360. doi:10.1016/j.emj.2004.06.011

Lucas, H. (1999). *Information Technology and the Productivity Paradox: Assessing the Value of Investing in IT: Assessing the Value of Investing in IT*. New York: Oxford University Press.

Lukin, L. E., Bandalos, D. L., Eckhout, T. J., & Mickelson, K. (2004). Facilitating the development of assessment literacy. *Educational Measurement: Issues and Practice*, *23*(2), 26–32. doi:10.1111/j.1745-3992.2004.tb00156.x

Luna-Reyes, L. F., Gil-Garcia, J. R., & Romero, G. (2012). Towards a multidimensional model for evaluating electronic government: Proposing a more comprehensive and integrative perspective. *Government Information Quarterly, 29*(3), 324–334. doi:10.1016/j.giq.2012.03.001

Luna-Reyes, L. F., Zhang, J., Gil-Garcia, J. R., & Cresswell, A. M. (2005). Information systems development as emergent socio-technical change: A practice approach. *European Journal of Information Systems, 14*(1), 93–115. doi:10.1057/palgrave.ejis.3000524

Lundvall, B.-A. (1988). Innovation as an interactive process: from user-producer interaction to the national system of innovation. In G. Dosi, C. Freeman, R. Nelson, G. Silverberg, & L. Soete (Eds.), Technical Change and Economic Theory (349-369). London: Pinter.

Lundvall, B.-Å., Johnson, B., Andersen, E. S., & Dalum, B. (2002). National systems of production, innovation and competence building. *Research Policy, 31*(2), 213–231. doi:10.1016/S0048-7333(01)00137-8

Luo, R., Chen, T. M., & Lin, M. H. (1999). Automatic guided intelligent wheelchair system using hierarchical grey-fuzzy motion decision-making algorithms. Proceedings of the 1999 IEEE/RSJ International Conference on Intelligent Robots and Systems. doi:10.1109/IROS.1999.812794

Luo, W., & Tung, Y. (1999). A framework for selecting business process modeling methods. *Industrial Management & Data Systems, 99*(7), 312–319. doi:10.1108/02635579910262535

Lynch, T., & Gregor, S. (2004). User participation in decision support systems development: Influencing system outcomes. *European Journal of Information Systems, 13*(4), 286–301. doi:10.1057/palgrave.ejis.3000512

Lyons, N. (Ed.). (2010). *Handbook of reflection and reflective inquiry: mapping a way of knowing for professional reflective inquiry.* New York: Springer. doi:10.1007/978-0-387-85744-2

Ma, C. (2013). Research on two-way referral schema of information systems in Beijing.[in Chinese]. *Chinese Hospital Management, 33*(1), 73–74.

Macdonald, C., Santos, R. L. T., & Ounis, I. (2012). On the Usefulness of Query Features for Learning to Rank. *Proceedings of the 21st ACM international conference on Information and knowledge management* (pp. 2559–2562). doi:10.1145/2396761.2398691

Macdonald, C., Santos, R. L. T., & Ounis, I. (2013). The whens and hows of learning to rank for web search. *Information Retrieval, 16*(5), 584–628. doi:10.1007/s10791-012-9209-9

Macintosh, A., Robson, E., Smith, E., & Whyte, A. (2003). Electronic democracy and young people. *Social Science Computer Review, 21*(1), 43–54. doi:10.1177/0894439302238970

Macintosh, A., & Whyte, A. (2008). Towards an evaluation framework for eParticipation. *Transforming Government: People. Process and Policy, 2*(1), 16–30.

MacLean, J., Pantofaru, C., Wood, L., Herpers, R., Derpanis, K., Topalovic, D., & Tsotsos, J. (2001). Fast Hand Gesture Recognition for Real-Time Teleconferencing Applications. Proceedings of the IEEE ICCV Workshop on Recognition, Analysis, and Tracking of Faces and Gestures in Real-Time Systems, Vancouver. doi:10.1109/RATFG.2001.938922

Madarasz, R. L., Heiny, L. C., Cromp, R. F., & Mazur, N. M. (1986). The design of an autonomous vehicle for the disabled. *IEEE Journal on Robotics and Automation, RA-2*(3), 117–126. doi:10.1109/JRA.1986.1087052

Madon, S., Reinhard, N., et al. (2007). Digital Inclusion Projects in Developing Countries: Processes of Institutionalisation. Proceedings of the 9th International Conference on Social Implications of Computers in Developing Countries. Sao Paula, Brazil.

Magoulas, Thanos, Ainda Hadzic, Ted Saarikko & Kalevi Pessi (2012). Alignment in Enterprise Architecture: A Comparative Analysis of Four Architectural Approaches. *The Electronic Journal of Information Systems Evaluation, 15*(1), 88-101.

Maizes, V., Rakel, D., & Niemiec, C. (2009). Integrative medicine and patient-centred care. *Explore (New York, N.Y.), 5*(5), 277–289. doi:10.1016/j.explore.2009.06.008 PMID:19733814

Malecki, E. (2011). Connecting local entrepreneurial ecosystems to global innovation networks: Open innovation, double networks and knowledge integration. *International Journal of Entrepreneurship and Innovation Management, 14*(1), 36–59. doi:10.1504/IJEIM.2011.040821

Malkiel, B. G. (2003). The Efficient Market Hypothesis and Its Critics. *The Journal of Economic Perspectives, 17*(1), 59–82. doi:10.1257/089533003321164958

Malone, T. W., Yates, J., & Benjamin, R. I. (1987). Electronic markets and electronic hierarchies. *Communications of the ACM, 30*(6), 484–497. doi:10.1145/214762.214766

Manion, M. (1994). Survey research in the study of contemporary China: Learning from local samples. *The China Quarterly, 139*, 741–765. doi:10.1017/S0305741000043149

Manjoo, F. (2009). Is Wikipedia a victim of its own success? *Time Mag, 174*.

Manning, C. D., Raghavan, P., & Schütze, H. (2008). *Introduction to information retrieval* (Vol. 1). Cambridge: Cambridge University Press. doi:10.1017/CBO9780511809071

Manning, S. (2007). Linking educational research activities across Europe: A review of the WIFO Gateway to Research on Education in Europe. *European Educational Research Journal, 6*(4), 446–450. doi:10.2304/eerj.2007.6.4.446

Mann, K., Gordon, J., & MacLeod, A. (2009). Reflection and reflective practice in health professions education: A systematic review. *Advances in Health Sciences Education: Theory and Practice, 14*(4), 595–621. doi:10.1007/s10459-007-9090-2 PMID:18034364

Mantel, S., Meredith, J., Shafer, S., & Sutton, M. (2001). *Project management in practice*. New York, NY: Wiley.

Marcel, S., Bernier, O., Viallet, J. E., & Collobert, D. (2000). Hand gesture recognition using inpu/output hidden markov models. Proceedings of the Fourth IEEE International Conference on Automatic Face and Gesture Recognition. doi:10.1109/AFGR.2000.840674

Marche, S., & McNiven, J. D. (2003). E-government and e-governance: The future isn't what it used to be. *Canadian Journal of Administrative Sciences, 20*(1), 74–86. doi:10.1111/j.1936-4490.2003.tb00306.x

March, J. G. (1991). Exploration and exploitation in organizational learning. *Organization Science, 2*(1), 71–87. doi:10.1287/orsc.2.1.71

Mark, E. (2013). Student satisfaction and the customer focus in higher education. *Journal of Higher Education Policy and Management, 35*(1), 2–10. doi:10.1080/1360080X.2012.727703

Marks, M., Mathieu, J., & Zaccaro, S. (2001). A temporally based framework and taxonomy of team processes. *Academy of Management Review, 26*, 356–376.

Markus, M. L. (1983). Power, Politics and MIS Implementation. *Communications of the ACM, 26*(6), 430–444. doi:10.1145/358141.358148

Marnewick, C., & Labuschagne, L. (2005). A conceptual model for enterprise resource planning (ERP). *Information Management & Computer Security, 13*(2), 144–155. doi:10.1108/09685220510589325

Marsh, J. A., Pane, J. F., & Hamilton, L. S. (2006). *Making sense of data-driven decision making in education: Evidence from recent RAND research*. Santa Monica, CA: RAND Corporation.

Marston, S., Li, Z., Bandyopadhyay, S., Zhang, J., & Ghalsasi, A. (2011). Cloud computing- The business perspective. *Decision Support Systems, 51*(1), 176–189. doi:10.1016/j.dss.2010.12.006

Martins, J. T., & Nunes, M. B. (2011). On Trust and Assurance: Towards a Risk Mitigation Normative Framework for eLearning Adoption.[British Columbia: ACI.]. *Proceedings of ICEL, 2011*, 209–218.

Martins, J. T., Nunes, M. B., Alajamy, M., & Zhou, L. (2013). Grounded theory in practice: a discussion of cases in information systems research. In P. Isaias & M. B. Nunes (Eds.), *Information Systems Research and Exploring Social Artifacts: Approaches and Methodologies* (pp. 142–160)., doi:10.4018/978-1-4666-2491-7.ch008

Martinsons, M. G., & Hempel, P. S. (1998). Chinese business process re-engineering. *International Journal of Information Management, 18*(6), 393–407. doi:10.1016/S0268-4012(98)00031-0

Martinsons, M. G., & Westwood, R. I. (1997). Management information system in the Chinese business culture: An explanatory theory. *Information & Management, 32*(5), 215–228. doi:10.1016/S0378-7206(96)00009-2

Mascarenhas, O. A., Kesavan, R., & Bernacchi, M. (2006). Lasting customer loyalty: A total customer experience approach. *Journal of Consumer Marketing, 23*(7), 397–405. doi:10.1108/07363760610712939

Matthews, S. S., & Lawley, M. (2006). Improving customer service: Issues in customer contact management. *European Journal of Marketing, 40*(1), 218–232. doi:10.1108/03090560610637392

Maurer, R. (1996). Using resistance to build support for change. *Journal for Quality and Participation*, 56–63.

Mazo, M., Rodriguez, F. J., Lazaro, L., Urena, J., Santiso, E., Revenga, P., & Garcia, J. J. (1995). Wheelchair for physically disabled people with voice, ultrasonic and infrared sensor control. *Autonomous Robots, 2*(3), 203. doi:10.1007/BF00710857

Mazzucato, M. (2011). *The Entrepreneurial State*. London, UK: Demos.

McAdam, R., & Donaghy, J. (1999). Business process re-engineering in the public sector: A study of staff perceptions and critical success factors. *Business Process Management Journal, 5*(1), 33–49. doi:10.1108/14637159910249135

McCalla, R., Ezingeard, J.-N., & Money, K. (2004). The Evaluation of CRM Systems: A Behavior Based Conceptual Framework.

McCalla, R., Ezingeard, J.-N., & Money, K. (2003). A behavioural approach to CRM systems evaluation. *Electronic Journal of Information Systems Evaluation, 6*(2), 145–154.

McCluskey, P. C. (1993). *Feedforward and Recurrent Neural Networks and Genetic Programs for Stock Market and Time Series Forecasting* [Master's thesis]. Brown University, USA.

McConnell, D. (2005). Examining the dynamics of networked e-learning groups and communities. *Studies in Higher Education, 30*(1), 25–42. doi:10.1080/0307507052000307777

McCormac, A. (2010). *The e-Skills manifesto*. Brussels: European Schoolnet.

McCutcheon, G., & Jung, B. (1990). Alternative perspectives on action research. *Theory into Practice, 29*(3), 144–151. doi:10.1080/00405849009543447

McDonald, S., Andal, J., Brown, K., & Schneider, B. (2007). *Getting the evidence for evidence-based initiatives: How the Midwest states use data systems to improve education processes and outcomes (Issues & Answers Report, REL 2007–No. 016)*. Washington, DC: U.S. Department of Education, Institute of Education Sciences, National Center for Education Evaluation and Assistance, Regional Educational Laboratory Midwest.

Mcguinness, D. L., Zeng, H., Silva, P. P. D., Ding, L., Narayanan, D., & Bhaowal, M. (2006). *Investigation into trust for collaborative information repositories: A Wikipedia case study* Paper presented at the Workshop on Models of Trust for the Web.

McIvor, R., McHugh, M., & Cadden, C. (2002). Internet technologies: Supporting transparency in the public sector. *International Journal of Public Sector Management, 15*(3), 170–187. doi:10.1108/09513550210423352

McKay, J., & Marshall, P. (2007). Driven by two masters, serving both - The Interplay of Problem Solving and Research in Information Systems Action Research Projects. In N. Kock (Ed.), Information Systems Action Research: An Applied View of Emerging Concepts and Methods.

McKay, K., Kuntz, J., & Naswall, K. (2013). The Effect of Affective Commitment, Communication and Participation on Resistance to Change: The Role of Change Readiness. *New Zealand Journal of Psychology, 42*(2).

McKernan, J. (1988). The countenance of curriculum action research: Traditional, collaborative, and emancipatory-critical conceptions. *Journal of Curriculum and Supervision, 3*(3), 173–200.

McNeill, D., & Levy, E. (1982). *Conceptual Representations in Language Activity and Gesture*. John Wiley and Sons Ltd.

McPherson, M., & Nunes, J. M. (2008). Critical issues for e-learning delivery: What may seem obvious is not always put into practice. *Journal of Computer Assisted Learning, 24*(5), 433–445. doi:10.1111/j.1365-2729.2008.00281.x

Meaney, M., & Pung, C. (2008). McKinsey global results: Creating organizational transformations. *The McKinsey Quarterly*, (August), 1–7.

Meister, J. C. (1998). *Corporate Universities – lessons in building a world-class work force. Revised and updated edition*. New York: McGraw-Hill.

Meneses, J., & Momino, J. M. (2010). Putting Digital Literacy in Practice: How Schools Contribute to Digital Inclusion in the Network Society. *The Information Society*, *26*(3), 197–208. doi:10.1080/01972241003712231

Merrill, D., Kalanithi, J., & Maes, P. (2007). Siftables: Towards Sensor Network User Interfaces.*Proceedings of the First International Conference on Tangible and Embedded Interaction (TEI'07)*. Louisiana: ACM. doi:10.1145/1226969.1226984

Mertler, C., & Vannatta, R. (2002). *Advanced and Multivariate Statistical Methods*. Pyrczak Publishing.

Metzler, D., & Croft, W. B. (2007). Linear feature-based models for information retrieval. *Information Retrieval*, *10*(3), 257–274. doi:10.1007/s10791-006-9019-z

Metzler, D., Strohman, T., & Croft, W. B. (2006). *Indri at trec 2006: Lessons learned from three terabyte tracks. Technical report*. DTIC Document.

Meyer, J. P., & Allen, N. J. (1991). A three-component conceptualization of organizational commitment. *Human Resource Management Review*, *1*(1), 61–89. doi:10.1016/1053-4822(91)90011-Z

Meyer, J. P., Stanley, D. J., Herscovitch, L., & Topolnytsky, L. (2002). Affective, Continuance, and Normative Commitment to the Organization: A Meta-analysis of Antecedents, Correlates, and Consequences. *Journal of Vocational Behavior*, *61*(1), 20–52. doi:10.1006/jvbe.2001.1842

Mezirow, J. (1981). A critical theory of adult learning and education. *Adult Education*, *32*(1), 3–24. doi:10.1177/074171368103200101

Mezirow, J. (1990). How critical reflection triggers transformative learning. In J. Mezirow (Ed.), *Fostering critical reflection in adulthood: a guide to transformative and emancipatory learning* (pp. 1–20). San Francisco, CA: Jossy-Bass.

Mezirow, J. (1997). Transformative learning: Theory to practice. *New Directions for Adult and Continuing Education*, *1997*(74), 5–12. doi:10.1002/ace.7401

Michalko, M. (2006). *Thinkertoys: A handbook of creative-thinking techniques* (2nd ed.). Toronto: Ten Speed Press.

Millard, J. (2006). User attitudes to e-government citizen services in Europe. *International Journal of Electronic Government Research*, *2*(2), 49–58. doi:10.4018/jegr.2006040103

Miller, C. A. (2007). Democratization, International Knowledge Institutions, and Global Governance. *Governance: An International Journal of Policy, Administration and Institutions*, *20*(2), 325–357. doi:10.1111/j.1468-0491.2007.00359.x

Miller, V. D., Johnson, J. R., & Grau, J. (1994). Antecedents to willingness to participate in a planned organizational change. *Journal of Applied Communication Research*, *22*(1), 59–80. doi:10.1080/00909889409365387

Minichiello, V., Aroni, R., Timewell, E., & Alexander, L. (1995). *In-depth interviewing: principles, techniques, analysis*. Melbourne: Longman.

Minnici, A., & Hill, D. D. (May 9, 2007). Educational architects: Do state education agencies have the tools necessary to implement NCLB? Washington, D.C.: Center on Education Policy.

Mintzberg, H. (2009). Rebuilding companies as communities. *Harvard Business Review*, (July-August): 1–7.

Mishra, P., Koehler, M. J., & Zhao, Y. (2007). *Faculty development by design: integrating technology in higher education*. Charlotte, NC: Information Age Publishing.

Mitchell, R. K., Agle, B. R., & Wood, D. J. (1997). Toward a theory of stakeholder identification and salience: Defining the principle of who and what really counts. *Academy of Management Review*, 853–886.

Mitra S., & Acharya, T., (2007). Gesture recognition: A survey. In *IEEE Transactions on Systems, Man, and Cybernetics*, Part C: Applications and Reviews.

Mnjama, N., & Wamukoya, J. (2007). E-government and records management: An assessment tool for e-records readiness in government. *The Electronic Library*, *25*(3), 274–284. doi:10.1108/02640470710754797

Moghaddasi, H., Asadi, F., Hosseini, A., & Ebnehoseini, Z. (2012). E-health: A global approach with extensive semantic variation. *Journal of Medical Systems*, *36*(5), 3173–3176. doi:10.1007/s10916-011-9805-z PMID:22113437

Mohan, A. (2010). An empirical analysis on point-wise machine learning techniques using regression trees for web-search ranking [Thesis].

Mohan, A., Chen, Z., & Weinberger, K. Q. (2011). Web-search ranking with initialized gradient boosted regression trees. *Journal of Machine Learning Research-Proceedings Track*, *14*, 77–89.

Mom, T. J. M., van den Bosch, F. A. J., & Volberda, H. W. (2007). Investigating managers' exploration and exploitation activities: The influence of top-down, bottom-up, and horizontal knowledge inflows. *Journal of Management Studies*, *44*(6), 910–931. doi:10.1111/j.1467-6486.2007.00697.x

Mom, T. J. M., van den Bosch, F. A. J., & Volberda, H. W. (2009). Understanding variation in managers' ambidexterity: Investigating direct and indirect effects of formal structural and personal coordination mechanisms. *Organization Science*, *20*(4), 812–828. doi:10.1287/orsc.1090.0427

Monson-Haefel, R. (2010). Proposed Definition of Natural User Interface (NUI). Retrieved from http://theclever-monkey.blogspot.pt

Moon, M. J. (2002). The evolution of e-government among municipalities: Rhetoric or reality. *Public Administration Review*, *62*(4), 424–433. doi:10.1111/0033-3352.00196

Morais, M. F., & Bahia, S. (2008). *Criatividade*. Braga: Psiquilibrios.

Morgan, J. T., Mason, R. M., & Nahon, K. (2011). *Lifting the veil: The expression of values in online communities*. Paper presented at the Proceedings of the 2011 iConference. doi:10.1145/1940761.1940763

Morgeson, F. V., VanAmburg, D., & Mithas, S. (2011). Misplaced trust? Exploring the structure of the e-government–citizen trust relationship. *Journal of Public Administration: Research and Theory*, *21*(2), 257–283. doi:10.1093/jopart/muq006

Morton, N. A., & Hu, Q. (2008). Implications of the fit between organizational structure and ERP: A structural contingency theory perspective. *International Journal of Information Management*, *28*(5), 391–402. doi:10.1016/j.ijinfomgt.2008.01.008

Morville, P., & Rosenfeld, L. (2006). *Information architecture for the World Wide Web*. Sebastopol, CA: O'Reilly.

Motahari, S., Zang, H., & Reuther, P. (2012). The Impact of Temporal Factors on Mobility Patterns. *Proceedings of the 2012 45th Hawaii International Conference on System Science (HICSS)* (pp. 5659–5668). doi:10.1109/HICSS.2012.572

Mufti, M. H. (2000). *Healthcare Development Strategies in the Kingdom of Saudi Arabia*. New York: Kluwer Academic.

Mulder, A. (1996). *Hand gestures for hci*. Vancouver: Simon Fraser University.

Müller, S., Mathiassen, L., & Balshøj, H. (2010). Software Process Improvement as organizational change: A metaphorical analysis of the literature. *Journal of Systems and Software*, *83*(11), 2128–2146. doi:10.1016/j.jss.2010.06.017

Munteanu, C., Ceobanu, C., Bobalca, C., & Anton, O. (2010). An analysis of customer satisfaction in a higher education context. *International Journal of Public Sector Management*, *23*(2), 124–140. doi:10.1108/09513551011022483

Murrell, K. (1999). International and intellectual roots of appreciative inquiry. *Organization Development Journal*, *17*, 49–62.

Mutkoski, S. (2011). *Defining Open Standards: A comparison of policy and practice*. 7th International Conference on Standardization and Innovation in Information Technology (SIIT), 1-12. IEEE. doi:10.1109/SIIT.2011.6083616

Mutula, S. M., & Mostert, J. (2010). Challenges and opportunities of e-government in South Africa. *The Electronic Library*, *28*(1), 38–53. doi:10.1108/02640471011023360

Mutula, S. M., & Van Brakel, P. (2006). Assessment of e-readiness of small and medium-sized enterprises (SMEs) in the ICT sector in Botswana with respect to information access. *The Electronic Library, 24*(3), 402–417. doi:10.1108/02640470610671240

Mycoted (2013). Creativity, Innovation, Tools, Techniques, Books, Discussions, Puzzles, Brain Teasers, Training ...

Myers, M.D. (1997). Qualitative research in information systems. *MIS Quarterly, 21*(2), 241-242.

Myers, M. D., & Avison, D. (1997). Qualitative research in information systems. *Management Information Systems Quarterly, 21*(2), 241–242. doi:10.2307/249422

Nagasawa, S. (2008). Customer experience management: Influencing on human Kansei to management of technology. *The TQM Journal, 20*(4), 312–323. doi:10.1108/17542730810881302

Nahapiet, J., & Ghoshal, S. (1998). Social Capital, Intellectual Capital, and the organizational advantage. *Academy of Management Review, 23*(2), 242–266.

Nakanishi, S., Kuno, Y., Shimada, N., & Shirai, Y. (1999). Robotic wheelchair based on observations of both user and environment. Proceedings of the 1999 IEEE/RSJ International Conference on Intelligent Robots and Systems. doi:10.1109/IROS.1999.812796

Nallapati, R. (2004). Discriminative models for information retrieval. *Proceedings of the 27th annual international ACM SIGIR conference on Research and development in information retrieval* (pp. 64–71).

Namjae, C., & Kiho, P. (2003). Exploring a priori and posteriori IS Valuation Distortion: Comparing cases in SCM, ERP, and CRM. *International Journal of Digital Management.* Retrieved from http://digital.re.kr/ijdm/past.html

Nam, T. (2014). Determining the type of e-government use. *Government Information Quarterly, 31*(2), 211–220. doi:10.1016/j.giq.2013.09.006

National Institute of Standard and Technology. (2014). Retrieved from http://www.nist.gov/itl/csd/cloud-102511.cfm

Ndou, V. (2004). E-government for developing countries: Opportunities and challenges. *The Electronic Journal on Information Systems in Developing Countries, 18*(1), 1–24.

Neely, A., Chris, A., & Crowe, P. (2001). The performance prism in practice. *Measuring Business Excellence, 5*(2), 6–13. doi:10.1108/13683040110385142

Nelson, R. R. (2007). IT project management: Infamous failures, classic mistakes, and best practices. *MIS Quarterly Executive, 6*(2), 67–78.

Nelson, R., & Rosenberg, N. (1993). Technical innovation and national systems. In R. R. Nelson (Ed.), *National Innovation Systems: A comparative analysis.* New York: Oxford University Press.

Nemanich, L., & Vera, D. (2009). Transformational leadership and ambidexterity in the context of an acquisition. *The Leadership Quarterly, 20*(1), 19–33. doi:10.1016/j.leaqua.2008.11.002

Nemoto, K., Gloor, P., & Laubacher, R. (2011). *Social capital increases efficiency of collaboration among Wikipedia editors.* Paper presented at the Proceedings of the 22nd ACM conference on Hypertext and hypermedia. doi:10.1145/1995966.1995997

Nespoulous, J.-L., Perron, P., & Roch, A. (1986). *The Biological Foundations of Gestures: Motor and Semiotic Aspects.* Hillsdale: Lawrence Erlbaum Associates.

Newell, S., & Swan, J. (2000). Trust and inter-organizational networking. *Human Relations, 53*(10), 1287–1328.

Newman, H. B. (2007). Networking for High Energy and Nuclear Physics. *Computer Physics Communications, 177*(1/2), 224–230. doi:10.1016/j.cpc.2007.02.002

Newman, M. E. J. (2003). The structure and function of complex networks. *SIAM Review, 45*(2), 167–256. doi:10.1137/S003614450342480

Ng, A. Y., & Jordan, M. I. (2001). *On discriminative vs. generative classifiers: A comparison of logistic regression and naive bayes* (pp. 841–848). NIPS.

Ngai, E. W., Xiu, L., & Chu, D. C. K. (2008). Application of data mining techniques in customer relationship management: A literature review and classification. *Expert System with Applications: An International Journal, 36*(2), 2592–2602. doi:10.1016/j.eswa.2008.02.021

Nicolini, D., Powell, J., Conville, P., & Martinez-Solano, L. (2008). Managing knowledge in the healthcare sector: A review. *International Journal of Management Reviews*, *10*(3), 245–263. doi:10.1111/j.1468-2370.2007.00219.x

NIST. (2013). *Malcolm Baldrige National Quality Award 2013-2014 Criteria for Performance Excellence*. USA: National Institute of Standards and Technology.

Niu, S., Guo, J., Lan, Y., & Cheng, X. (2012). Top-k learning to rank: Labelling, ranking and evaluation.*Proceedings of the 35th international ACM SIGIR conference on Research and development in information retrieval* (pp. 751–760). doi:10.1145/2348283.2348384

Niu, S., Lan, Y., Guo, J., Cheng, X., & Geng, X. (2014). What makes data robust: A data analysis in learning to rank. *Proceedings of the 37th annual international ACM SIGIR conference on Research and development in information retrieval* (pp. 1191–1194). doi:10.1145/2600428.2609542

Nograšek, J., & Vintar, M. (2014). E-government and organisational transformation of government: Black box revisited? *Government Information Quarterly*, *31*(1), 108–118. doi:10.1016/j.giq.2013.07.006

Nonaka, I. (1991). The knowledge-creating company. *Harvard Business Review*, *69*(6), 96–104.

Northouse, P. (2007). *Leadership: Theory and Practice* (4th ed.). Thousand Oaks, CA: SAGE Publications, Inc.

Norusis, M. (2008). *SPSS 17.0 statistical procedures companion*. Prentice Hall Press.

Nota, G., & Aiello, R. (2014). Managing Uncertainty in Complex Projects. In M. Faggini & A. Parziale (Eds.), Complexity in Economics: Cutting Edge Research (pp. 81-97). Switzerland: Springer International Publishing. doi:10.1007/978-3-319-05185-7_5

Noulas, A., Scellato, S., Lambiotte, R., Pontil, M., & Mascolo, C. (2012). A Tale of Many Cities: Universal Patterns in Human Urban Mobility. *PLoS ONE*, *7*(5), e37027. doi:10.1371/journal.pone.0037027 PMID:22666339

Novaes, W., & Zingales, L. (1999). Capital structure choice under a takeover threat [University of Chicago working paper].

O' Dell, C. S., & Grayson, C. J. (1998). *If only we knew what we know: the transfer of internal knowledge and best practice*. New York: Free Press.

O'Donnell, O., & Humphreys, P. C. (2003). *E-government and the decentralization of service delivery*. Dublin, Ireland: Institute of Public Administration.

O'Reilly, C. A. III, Harreld, J. B., & Tushman, M. L. (2010). Organizational ambidexterity: IBM and emerging business opportunities. *California Management Review*, *51*(4), 75–99. doi:10.2307/41166506

O'Reilly, C. A. III, & Tushman, M. L. (2011). Organizational ambidexterity in action. *California Management Review*, *53*(4), 5–22. doi:10.1525/cmr.2011.53.4.5

O'Reilly, C. A., & Tushman, M. L. (2004). The ambidextrous organization. *Harvard Business Review*, *82*, 74–82. PMID:15077368

Observatório do QREN. (2011). *QREN - Quadro de Referência Estratégico Nacional*. Observatório do QREN. Retrieved from www.qren.pt

O'Dwyer, S. (2008). *Identifying ICT Needs in Disadvantaged Communities within Limerick City*. Limerick City Community ICT Steering Group.

OECD. (2002). *The Measurement of Scientific and Technical Activities: Proposed Standard Practice for Surveys of Research and Development*. Paris: OECD.

OECD. (2008). *Open Innovation in Global Networks*. Paris: OECD.

OECD. (2009). *The OECD Innovation Strategy: draft interim report*. Paris: OECD.

OECD. (2011). *Measuring the Economics of Big Data. DSTI/ICCP/IIS (2011) 4, OECD. O`Reilly, T. (2013). Government as a Platform, Open Government: Collaboration, Transparency and Participation in Practice*. O`Reilly Media, Inc.

Oliver, D., Whymark, G., & Romm, C. (2005). Researching ERP adoption: An internet-based grounded theory approach. *Online Information Review*, *29*(6), 585–603. doi:10.1108/14684520510638052

Oliver, R. L. (1993). Cognitive, affective, and attribute bases of the satisfaction response. *The Journal of Consumer Research*, *20*(3), 418–430. doi:10.1086/209358

Oliver, R. L. (1999). Whence consumer loyalty. *Journal of Marketing*, *63*(4), 33–44. doi:10.2307/1252099

Ongaro, E. (2004). Process management in the public sector: The experience of one-stop shops in Italy. *International Journal of Public Sector Management*, *17*(1), 81–107. doi:10.1108/09513550410515592

Oprean, C., Brumar, C. I., Cater, M., & Barbat, B. E. (2011). Sustainable development: E-teaching (now) for lifelong e-learning. *Procedia: Social and Behavioral Sciences*, *30*, 988–992. doi:10.1016/j.sbspro.2011.10.192

Oreg, S. (2006). Personality, context, and resistance to organizational change. *European Journal of Work and Organizational Psychology*, *15*(1), 73–101. doi:10.1080/13594320500451247

Organ, D. W. (1988). Organizational Citizenship Behavior: The good soldier syndrome. Lexington, MA.

Orlikowski, W. J. (1993). CASE Tools as Organisational Change: Investigating Incremental and Radical Changes in Systems Development. *Management Information Systems Quarterly*, *17*(3), 309–340. doi:10.2307/249774

Ortega, F., & Izquierdo-Cortazar, D. (2009). *Survival analysis in open development projects*. Paper presented at the Emerging Trends in Free/Libre/Open Source Software Research and Development, 2009. FLOSS'09. ICSE Workshop. doi:10.1109/FLOSS.2009.5071353

Osborn, A. F. (1993). *Applied imagination: principles and procedures of creative problem-solving* (3rd ed.). Creative Education Foundation.

Otieno, G. O., Hinako, T., Motohiro, A., Daisuke, K., & Keiko, N. (2008). Measuring effectiveness of electronic medical records systems: Towards building a composite index for benchmarking hospitals. *International Journal of Medical Informatics*, *77*(10), 657–669. doi:10.1016/j.ijmedinf.2008.01.002 PMID:18313352

Ottesen, E. (2007). Reflection in teacher education. *Reflective Practice*, *8*(1), 31–46. doi:10.1080/14623940601138899

Otto, P., & Simon, M. (2008). Dynamic perspectives on social characteristics and sustainability in online community networks. *System Dynamics Review*, *24*(3), 321–347. doi:10.1002/sdr.403

Ould, M. A. (1995). *Business processes: Modelling and analysis for re-engineering and improvement*. New York, NY: John Wiley & Sons.

Ouyang, T. (2010). *Research on the sharing of medical information resource on the basis of bidirectional referral medical care in community health service and tertiary hospital* [Unpublished master's dissertation]. Hefei Industrial University, Hefei.

Oviatt, S. (2003). Multimodal interfaces. In J. Jacko & A. Sears (Eds.), *The Human-Computer Interaction Handbook (p. 286.304)*. New Jersey: Lawrence Erlbaum and Associates.

Ozkan, S., & Kanat, I. E. (2011). e-Government adoption model based on theory of planned behavior: Empirical validation. *Government Information Quarterly*, *28*(4), 503–513. doi:10.1016/j.giq.2010.10.007

Ozkan, S., & Koseler, R. (2009). Multi-dimensional students' evaluation of e-learning systems in the higher education context: An empirical investigation. *Computers & Education*, *53*(4), 1285–1296. doi:10.1016/j.compedu.2009.06.011

Packer, A. L., & Meneghini, R. (2006). Articles with authors affiliated to Brazilian institutions published from 1994 to 2003 with 100 or more citations: I - The weight of international collaboration and the role of the networks. *Anais da Academia Brasileira de Ciencias*, *4*(78), 841–853. PMID:17143417

Page, L. (2001). Method for node ranking in a linked database: Google Patents.

Page, L., Brin, S., Motwani, R., & Winograd, T. (1999). *The pagerank citation ranking: Bringing order to the web*. Stanford InfoLab.

Pahl-Wostl, C. (2009). A conceptual framework for analysing adaptive capacity and multi-level learning processes in resource governance regimes. *Global Environmental Change*, *19*(3), 354–365. doi:10.1016/j.gloenvcha.2009.06.001

Palchykov, V., Mitrović, M., Jo, H.-H., Saramäki, J., & Pan, R. K. (2014). Inferring human mobility using communication patterns. *Scientific Reports*, *4*, 6174. doi:10.1038/srep06174 PMID:25146347

Palloff, R. M., & Pratt, K. (2004). *Collaborating online: learning together in community*. San Franscico, CA: Jossey-Bass.

Palmer, A. (2010). Customer experience management: A critical review of an emerging idea. *Journal of Services Marketing*, *24*(3), 196–208. doi:10.1108/08876041011040604

Palmer, P. (2007). *The courage to teach guide for reflection and renewal*. San Francisco, CA: Jossey-Bass.

Pan, F., Converse, T., Ahn, D., Salvetti, F., & Donato, G. (2009). Feature selection for ranking using boosted trees.*Proceedings of the 18th ACM conference on Information and knowledge management* (pp. 2025–2028). doi:10.1145/1645953.1646292

Pan, K., Nunes, J. M. B., & Peng, G. C. (2011). Risks affecting ERP viability: Insights from a very large Chinese manufacturing group. *Journal of Manufacturing Technology Management*, *22*(1), 107–130. doi:10.1108/17410381111099833

Papay, J.Harvard Graduate School of Education. (2007). *Aspen Institute datasheet: The teaching workforce*. Washington, DC: The Aspen Institute.

Parent, M., Vandebeek, C. A., & Gemino, A. C. (2005). Building citizen trust through e-government. *Government Information Quarterly*, *22*(4), 720–736. doi:10.1016/j.giq.2005.10.001

Park, S. Y. (2009). An analysis of the technology acceptance model in understanding university students' behavioral intention to use e-learning. *Journal of Educational Technology & Society*, *12*(3), 150–162.

Patton, M. Q. (2002). *Qualitative research & evaluation methods*. Thousand Oaks, CA. USA: Sage publication.

Pavlou, P. (2003). Consumer acceptance of electronic commerce: Integrating trust and risk with the technology acceptance model. *International Journal of Electronic Commerce*, *7*(3), 69–103.

Pavlov, D. Y., Gorodilov, A., & Brunk, C. A. (2010). Bagboo: a scalable hybrid bagging-the-boosting model. *Proceedings of the 19th ACM international conference on Information and knowledge management* (pp. 1897–1900).

Pavlovic, V. I., Sharma, R., & Huang, T. S. (1997). Visual Interpretation of Hand Gestures for Human Computer Interaction: A Review. *IEEE Transactions on Pattern Analysis and Machine Intelligence*, *19*(7), 677–695. doi:10.1109/34.598226

Pavlu, V. (2008). *Large scale ir evaluation*. ProQuest LLC.

Pedersen, J., Kocsis, D., Tripathi, A., Tarrell, A., Weerakoon, A., Tahmasbi, N., et al. (2013). *Conceptual foundations of crowdsourcing: A review of IS research*. Paper presented at the System Sciences (HICSS), 2013 46th Hawaii International Conference on. doi:10.1109/HICSS.2013.143

Peng, G. (2010). Critical Mass, Diffusion Channels, and the Digital Divide. *Journal of Computer Information Systems*, 63–71.

Peng, G. C., & Nunes, J. M. B. (2008, June 19-20). Issues and difficulties in doing participative research in China: lessons learned from a survey in information systems research. *Proceedings of the 7th European Conference on Research Methodology (ECRM) for Business and Management Studies*, London, UK (pp. 245-252).

Peng, G. C., & Nunes, J. M. B. (2009). Identification and assessment of risks associated with ERP post-implementation in China. *Journal of Enterprise Information Management*, *22*(5), 587–614. doi:10.1108/17410390910993554

Peng, G. C., & Nunes, J. M. B. (2009b). Surfacing ERP exploitation risks through a risk ontology. *Industrial Management & Data Systems*, *109*(7), 926–942. doi:10.1108/02635570910982283

Peng, G. C., & Nunes, J. M. B. (2010). Barriers to the successful exploitation of ERP systems in Chinese State-Owned Enterprises. *International Journal of Business and Systems Research*, *4*(5/6), 596–620. doi:10.1504/IJBSR.2010.035077

Peng, G. C., & Nunes, J. M. B. (2012). Establishing and verifying a risk ontology for ERP post-implementation. In M. Ahmad, R. M. Colomb, & M. S. Abdullah (Eds.), *Ontology-based Applications for Enterprise Systems and Knowledge Management*. Hershey, USA: IGI Global.

Penuel, W. R., Fishman, B. J., Yamaguchi, R., & Ghallagher, L. P. (2007). What makes professional development effective? Strategies that foster curriculum implementation. *American Educational Research Journal, 44*(4), 921–958. doi:10.3102/0002831207308221

Pepper, R., & Garrity, J. (2014). The Internet of Everything: How the Network Unleashes the Benefits of Big Data. In B. Bilbao-Osorio, S. Dutta, & B. Lanvin (Eds), *The Global Technology Report: Rewards and Risks of Big Data*. World Economic Forum.

Perez-Batres, L. A., Doh, J. P., Miller, V. V., & Pisani, M. J. (2012). Stakeholder pressures as determinants of CSR strategic choice: Why do firms choose symbolic versus substantive self-regulatory codes of conduct? *Journal of Business Ethics, 110*(2), 157–172. doi:10.1007/s10551-012-1419-y

Perkins, D. H. (1997). History, politics, and the sources of economic growth: China and the East Asian way of growth. In F. Itoh (Ed.), *China in the twenty-first century: politics, economy, and society* (pp. 25–47). Tokyo: United Nations University Press.

Perkis, A., Reichl, P., & Beker, S. (2014). Business Perspectives on Quality of Experience. Moller, S., & Raake, A. (Eds), Quality of experience: advanced concepts, applications and methods (pp. 97-108). Berlin: Springer. doi:10.1007/978-3-319-02681-7_7

Persson, O., Glänzel, W., & Danell, R. (2004). Inflationary bibliometric values: The role of scientific collaboration and the need for relative indicators in evaluative studies. *Scientometrics, 60*(3), 421–432. doi:10.1023/B:SCIE.0000034384.35498.7d

Petter, S., DeLone, W., & McLean, E. (2008). Measuring information systems success: Models, dimensions, measures, and interrelationships. *European Journal of Information Systems, 17*(3), 236–263. doi:10.1057/ejis.2008.15

Petter, S., & Fruhling, A. (2011). Evaluating the success of an emergency response medical information system. *International Journal of Medical Informatics, 80*(7), 480–489. doi:10.1016/j.ijmedinf.2011.03.010 PMID:21501969

Phophalia, A. (2011). A survey on learning to rank (letor) approaches in information retrieval}. Proceedings of *Nirma University International Conference on Engineering (NUiCONE)* (pp. 1—6).

Pidd, M. (2010). Why modelling and model use matter. *The Journal of the Operational Research Society, 61*(1), 14–24. doi:10.1057/jors.2009.141

Pinho, I., Rego, A., & Cunha, M. P. (2012). Improving knowledge management processes: A hybrid positive approach. *Journal of Knowledge Management, 16*(2), 215–242. doi:10.1108/13673271211218834

Pinho, I., Rego, A., & Kastenholz, E. (2008). Factores satisfacientes e insatisfacientes dos utilizadores de websites: Um estudo de caso. *Tékhne-Polytechnical Studies Review, 6*(10), 51–71.

Pitt, L. F., Watson, R. T., & Kavan, C. B. (1995). Service quality: A measure of information systems effectiveness. *Management Information Systems Quarterly, 19*(2), 173–187. doi:10.2307/249687

Poderi, G. (2009). Comparing featured article groups and revision patterns correlations in Wikipedia. *First Monday, 14*(5). doi:10.5210/fm.v14i5.2365

Pohoryles, R. J. (2002). The Making of the European Research Area—a View from Research Networks. *Innovation: The European Journal of Social Sciences, 15*(4), 325–340.

Polanyi, M. (1967). *The Tacit Dimension*. London: Routledge.

Polikoff, I., Coyne, R., & Hodgson, R. (2005). *Capability cases: a solution envisioning approach*. California: Wesley.

Pollitt, C. (2010). Technological change: A central yet neglected feature of public administration. *NISPAcee Journal of Public Administration and Policy, 3*(2), 31–53. doi:10.2478/v10110-010-0003-z

Ponte, J. M., & Croft, W. B. (1998). A language modeling approach to information retrieval. *Proceedings of the 21st annual international ACM SIGIR conference on Research and development in information retrieval* (pp. 275–281). doi:10.1145/290941.291008

Popovič, A., Hackney, R., Coelho, P. S., & Jaklič, J. (2012). Towards business intelligence systems success: Effects of maturity and culture on analytical decision making. *Decision Support Systems*, *54*(1), 729–739. doi:10.1016/j.dss.2012.08.017

Porras, J. I., & Robertson, P. J. (1992). Organization development: Theory, practice, and research. In M. Dunnette & L. Hough (Eds.), *Handbook of industrial and organizational psychology* (2nd ed., Vol. 3, pp. 719–822). Palo Alto: Consulting Psychologists Press.

Porter, A., Garet, M. S., Desimone, L. M., & Birman, F. (2003). Providing effective professional development: Lessons from the Eisenhower program. *Science Educator*, *12*(1), 23–40.

Post, J. E., Lawrence, A. T., & Weber, J. (1996). *Business and society: Corporate strategy, public policy, ethics*. McGraw-Hill New York.

Prahalad, C. K., & Ramaswamy, V. (2000). Co-Opting Customer Experience. *Harvard Business Review*.

Pre-commercial Procurement - Public sector needs as a driver of Innovation. (2006, September). European Commission.

Pretto, N. D. L., & Bailey, O. G. (2010). Digital culture in Brazil: Building 'peeracy'? *International Journal of Media and Cultural Politics*, *6*(3), 265–281. doi:10.1386/mcp.6.3.265_1

Pritchard, C. (2004). *The project management Communications*. London: Toolkit Artech House.

Pulselli, R. M., Romano, P., Ratti, C., & Tiezzi, E. (2008). Computing Urban Mobile Landscapes through Monitoring Population Density Based on Cell-Phone Chatting. *International Journal of Design & Nature and Ecodynamics*, *3*(2), 121–134. Retrieved from http://www.witpress.com/elibrary/dne-volumes/3/2/346 doi:10.2495/D&NE-V3-N2-121-134

Qin, T., Liu, T., Xu, J., & Li, H. (2010). Letor: A benchmark collection for research on learning to rank for information retrieval. *Information Retrieval*, *13*(4), 346–374. doi:10.1007/s10791-009-9123-y

Qin, Y., Wu, M., Pan, X., Xiang, Q., Huang, J., & Gu, Z. et al. (2011, February25). Reactions of Chinese adults to warning labels on cigarette packages: A survey in Jiangsu Province. *BMC Public Health*, *133*(11), doi:10.1186/1471-2458-11-133 PMID:21349205

Quah, T.-S. (2008). DJIA stock selection assisted by neural network. *Expert Systems with Applications*, *35*(1-2), 50–58. doi:10.1016/j.eswa.2007.06.039

Quintella, R. H., Freitas, E. J. S. M., Ventura, A. C., Santos, M. A., & Antonio, L. Q. (2009). Network dynamics in scientific knowledge acquisition: An analysis in three public universities in the state of Bahia. *Revista de Administração Pública*, *43*(6), 1279–1314. doi:10.1590/S0034-76122009000600004

Quoc, C., & Le, V. (2007). Learning to rank with non-smooth cost functions. *Proceedings of the Advances in Neural Information Processing Systems*, *19*, 193–200.

Radabaugh, M. P. (2012). NIDRR's Long Range Plan - Technology for Access and Function Research. Retrieved from http://www.ncddr.org/new/announcements/lrp/fy1999-2003/lrp_techaf.html

Radicchi, A., Nunes, A., & Botega, L. (2010). Proposta de Desenvolvimento de Interface Tangível para Aplicações de Gerenciamento de Emergência. Proceedings of the XI Symposium on Virtual and Augmented Reality. Natal.

Rageh, A., Melewar, T. C., & Woodside, A. (2013). Using netnography research method to reveal the underlying dimensions of the customer/tourist experience. *Qualitative Market Research. International Journal (Toronto, Ont.)*, *16*(2), 126–149.

Rai, A., Lang, S. S., & Welker, R. B. (2002). Assessing the validity of IS success models: An empirical test and theoretical analysis. *Information Systems Research*, *13*(1), 50–69. doi:10.1287/isre.13.1.50.96

Raisch, S., Birkinshaw, J., Probst, G., & Tushman, M. L. (2009). Organizational ambidexterity: Balancing exploitation and exploration for sustained performance. *Organization Science*, 20(4), 685–695. doi:10.1287/orsc.1090.0428

Ramani, S., & Kumaraswamy, Y. S. (2013). The role of business process model in customer centric eGovernment system. *International Journal of Computers and Applications*, 72(12), 13–23. doi:10.5120/12545-9003

Rankin, J. G. (2011). *Over-the-Counter Data Standards*. Retrieved from www.overthecounterdata.com/s/OTCD-Standards.pdf

Rankin, J. G. (2013). *Over-the-counter data's impact on educators' data analysis accuracy*. ProQuest Dissertations and Theses, 3575082. Retrieved from http://pqdtopen.proquest.com/doc/1459258514.html?FMT=ABS

Ransbotham, S., & Kane, G. C. (2011). Membership turnover and collaboration success in online communities: Explaining rises and falls from grace in Wikipedia. *MIS Quarterly-Management Information Systems*, 35(3), 613.

Ratti, C., Pulselli, R. M., Williams, S., & Frenchman, D. (2006). Mobile Landscapes: Using location data from cell phones for urban analysis. *Environment and Planning. B, Planning & Design*, 33(5), 727–748. doi:10.1068/b32047

Rautaray S., & Agrawal, A. (2010). A Vision based Hand Gesture Interface for Controlling VLC Media Player," International Journal of Computer Applications.

Ravishankar, M. N., Pan, S. L., & Leidner, D. E. (2010). (forthcoming). Examining the strategic alignment and implementation success of a KMS: A Subculture-Based Multilevel Analysis. *Information Systems Research*.

Raymond, L., & Bergeron, F. (2008). Project management information systems: An empirical study of their impact on project managers and project success. *International Journal of Project Management*, 26(2), 213–220. doi:10.1016/j.ijproman.2007.06.002

Raymond, L., Pare, G., & Bergeron, F. (1995). Matching information technology and organizational structure: An empirical study with implications for performance. *European Journal of Information Systems*, 4(1), 3–16. doi:10.1057/ejis.1995.2

Recabarren, M., Nussbaum, M., & Leiva, C. (2008). Cultural divide and the internet. *Computers in Human Behavior*, 24(6), 2917–2926. doi:10.1016/j.chb.2008.04.013

Reddick, C. G. (2005). Citizen interaction with e-government: From the streets to servers? *Government Information Quarterly*, 22(1), 38–57. doi:10.1016/j.giq.2004.10.003

Reddick, C. G., & Roy, J. (2013). Business perceptions and satisfaction with e-government: Findings from a Canadian survey. *Government Information Quarterly*, 30(1), 1–9. doi:10.1016/j.giq.2012.06.009

Reich, B. H., & Benbasat, I. (2000). Factors that influence the social dimension of alignment between business and information technology objectives. *Management Information Systems Quarterly*, 24(1), 81–113. doi:10.2307/3250980

Reimers, K. (2002). Implementing ERP systems in China. *Proceedings of the 35th Annual Hawaii International Conference on System Sciences*. Hawaii, USA. doi:10.1109/HICSS.2002.994311

Relly, J. E., & Sabharwal, M. (2009). Perceptions of transparency of government policymaking: A cross-national study. *Government Information Quarterly*, 26(1), 148–157. doi:10.1016/j.giq.2008.04.002

Relyea, H. C. (2002). E-gov: Introduction and overview. *Government Information Quarterly*, 19(1), 9–35. doi:10.1016/S0740-624X(01)00096-X

Remenyi, D., & Sherwood-Smith, M. (1999). Maximise information systems value by continuous participative evaluation. *Logistics Information Management*, 12(1/2), 14–31. doi:10.1108/09576059910256222

Remenyi, D., Williams, B., Money, A., & Swartz, E. (1998). *Doing research in business and Management: An introduction to process and method*. London: Sage. doi:10.4135/9781446280416

Renjifo, C., & Carmen, C. (2012). The discounted cumulative margin penalty: Rank-learning with a list-wise loss and pair-wise margins. *Proceedings of IEEE International Workshop on Machine Learning for Signal Processing (MLSP)* (pp. 1—6). doi:10.1109/MLSP.2012.6349807

Rennie Center for Education Research and Policy. (2006, February). *Data-driven teaching: Tools and trends.* Cambridge, MA: Rennie Center for Education Research and Policy.

Research, C. C. W. (2010). IT investments of the manufacturing sector reached RMB 52.9 billion in 2010. Retrieved from http://www.donews.com/it/201102/371478.shtm

Rhodes, R. A. W. (1996). The new governance: Governing without government. *Political Studies, 44*(4), 652–667. doi:10.1111/j.1467-9248.1996.tb01747.x

Rhodes, R. A. W. (2007). Understanding governance: Ten years on. *Organization Studies, 28*(8), 1243–1264. doi:10.1177/0170840607076586

Rice, P., & Ezzy, D. (1999). *Qualitative research methods: a health focus.* Melbourne: Oxford University Press.

Riley, B. T. (2001). *Electronic governance and electronic democracy: Living and working in the connected world. Brisbane, Australia.* Australia: Commonwealth Centre for Electronic Governance.

Robertson, S. E., Kanoulas, E., & Yilmaz, E. (2010). Extending average precision to graded relevance judgments.*Proceedings of the 33rd international ACM SIGIR conference on Research and development in information retrieval* (pp. 603–610). doi:10.1145/1835449.1835550

Robertson, S., Zaragoza, H., & Taylor, M. (2004). Simple bm25 extension to multiple weighted fields. In *Proceedings of the thirteenth ACM international conference on Information and knowledge management*, pages 42–49. doi:10.1145/1031171.1031181

Robles, J. M., & Torres-Albero, C. et al. (2011). Spanish E-government and the Third Digital Divide: A Sociological View. *Journal of US-China Public Administration, 8*(4), 401–412.

Robson, C. (2011). *Real world research: a resource for users of social research methods in applied settings* (3rd ed.). USA: John Wiley & Sons, Ltd.

Roccetti, M., Marfia, G., & Semeraro, A. (2011). A Fast and Robust Gesture Recognition System for Exhibit Gaming Scenario*Proceedings of the 4th International ICST Conference on Simulation Tools and Techniques*, Barcelona.

Rodon, J., & Pastor, A. (2007). Applying Grounded Theory to Study the Implementation of an Inter-Organizational Information System. *The Electronic Journal of Business Research Methods, 5*(2), 71–82.

Rodousakis, N. and A. M. d. Santos (2008). "The development of inclusive e-Government in Austria and Portugal: a comparison of two success stories." Innovation: the European Journal of Social Science Research **21**(4): 283-316.

Rodriguez, M. (2008, May 01). Learning how to incorporate technology in classrooms. *Inland Valley Daily Bulletin.* Retrieved from http://www.highbeam.com/doc/1P2-16433823.html

Roepke, R., Agarwal, R., & Ferratt, T. W. (2000). Aligning the IT human resource with business vision: The leadership initiative at 3M. *Management Information Systems Quarterly, 24*(2), 327–353. doi:10.2307/3250941

Rokeby, D. (2010). Very Nervous System 1986-1990. Retrieved from http://www.davidrokeby.com/vns.html

Rose, J., & Sandford, C. (2007). Mapping eParticipation Research: Four Central Challenges. *Communications of the Association for Information Systems, 20*, 909–943.

Rosenzweig, R. (2006). Can history be open source? Wikipedia and the future of the past. *The Journal of American History, 93*(1), 117–146. doi:10.2307/4486062

Rothaermel, F. T., & Alexandre, M. T. (2009). Ambidexterity in technology sourcing: The moderating role of absorptive capacity. *Organization Science, 20*(4), 759–780. doi:10.1287/orsc.1080.0404

Rowley, J. (2000). Is higher education ready for knowledge management? *International Journal of Educational Management, 14*(7), 325–333. doi:10.1108/09513540010378978

Rowley, J. (2011). e-Government stakeholders: Who are they and what do they want? *International Journal of Information Management, 31*(1), 53–62. doi:10.1016/j.ijinfomgt.2010.05.005

Rubenstein-Montano, B., Buchwalter, J., & Liebowitz, J. (2001). Knowledge management: A U.S. Social Security Administration case study. *Government Information Quarterly, 18*(3), 223–253. doi:10.1016/S0740-624X(01)00078-8

Rucks, A., & Ginter, P. (1982). Strategic MIS: Promises unfulfilled. *Journal of Systems Management, 8,* 16–19.

Rumelhart, D. E., Hinton, G. E., & Williams, R. J. (1996). Learning representations by back-propagating errors. *Nature, 323*(6088), 533–536. doi:10.1038/323533a0

Ruohonen, M., & Higgins, L. F. (1998). Application of creativity principles to IS planning. In Hugh J. Watson (Ed.), Proceedings of the Thirty-First Hawaii International Conference on System Sciences *(Vol. VI),* Los Alamitos, California. doi:10.1109/HICSS.1998.654798

Ryder, I. (2007). Customer experience. *Journal of Brand Management, 15*(2), 85–88. doi:10.1057/palgrave. bm.2550127

Saad, E., Prokhorov, D., & Wunsch, D. (1998). Comparative study of stock trend prediction using time delay, recurrent and probabilistic neural networks. *IEEE Transactions on Neural Networks, 9*(6), 1456–1470. doi:10.1109/72.728395 PMID:18255823

Sabbah, F. M. (2011). Designing more effective accountability report cards. *ProQuest Dissertations and Theses, AAT 3469488.* Retrieved from http://search.proquest.com/docview/893068662?accountid=28180

Sabherwal, R., & Chan, Y. E. (2001). Alignment between business and IS strategies: A study of prospectors, analyzers, and defenders. *Information Systems Research, 12*(1), 11–33. doi:10.1287/isre.12.1.11.9714

Sacchi, A., Giannini, E., Bochic, R., Reinhard, N., & Lopes, A. B. (2009). Digital Inclusion with the McInternet: Would You Like Fries With That? *Communications of the ACM, 52*(3), 113–116. doi:10.1145/1467247.1467275

Saebo, O., Rose, J., & Skiftenes Flak, L. (2008). The shape of eParticipation: Characterizing an emerging research area. *Government Information Quarterly, 25*(3), 400–428. doi:10.1016/j.giq.2007.04.007

Sagers, G. (2004). The influence of network governance factors on success in open source software development projects.

Salas, E., Goodwin, G., & Burke, C. (2009). Team Effectiveness in Complex Organizations: an Overview. In E. Salas, G. Goodwin, & C. Burke (Eds.), *Team effectiveness in complex organizations: cross-disciplinary perspectives and approaches* (pp. 3–16). USA: Psychology Press, Taylor & Francis Group.

Salas, E., Stagl, K., Burke, C., & Goodwin, G. (2007). Modeling complex systems: Motivation, cognition and social processes. In *Nebraska Symposium on Motivation* (pp. 185–243).

Salmon, G. (2000). *E-moderating: the key to teaching and learning online.* London: Kogan Page. doi:10.4324/9780203465424

Salton, G., & Buckley, C. (1988). Term-weighting approaches in automatic text retrieval. *Information Processing & Management, 24*(5), 513–523. doi:10.1016/0306-4573(88)90021-0

Salton, G., Wong, A., & Yang, C. (1975). A vector space model for automatic indexing. *Communications of the ACM, 18*(11), 613–620. doi:10.1145/361219.361220

Salvador, A. C., Rojas, S., & Susinos, T. (2010). Weaving Networks: An Educational Project for Digital Inclusion. *The Information Society, 26*(2), 137–143. doi:10.1080/01972240903562795

Sandford, C., & Rose, J. (2007). Characterizing eParticipation. *International Journal of Information Management, 27*(6), 406–421. doi:10.1016/j.ijinfomgt.2007.08.002

Santiago, R., & Carvalho, T. (2012). Managerialism rhetorics in Portuguese higher education. *Minerva, 50*(4), 511–532. doi:10.1007/s11024-012-9211-9

Santos, E., Morais, C., & Paiva, J. (2004). Formação de professores para a integração das TIC no ensino da matemática – a study of the Autonomous Region of Madeira. Proceedings of the 6th International Symposium on Computers in Education, Cáceres.

Santos, V., & Amaral, L. (2012a). Introdução de criatividade no processo de identificação de estratégias de qualidade de dados. Proceedings of the Creativity and Innovation in Information Systems and Engineering Workshop CRIISE2012, Madrid, Spain.

Santos, V., & Amaral, L. (2012b). Estratégias para a introdução de criatividade em diferentes abordagens de planeamento de sistemas de informação. Proceedings of the 11th Conference of the Portuguese Association of Information Systems, Guimarães, Portugal.

Santos, V., Amaral, L., & Mamede, H. (2011a). A methodology for creativity introduction in the information systems planning. Proceedings of the 8th International Conference on Information Systems and Technology Management - CONTECSI, São Paulo

Santos, V., Amaral, L., & Mamede, H. (2011b). Método para a introdução de criatividade no processo de planeamento de sistemas de informação. Proceedings of the 6th Iberian Conference on Information Systems and Technologies (CISTI) Chaves

Santos, V., Amaral, L., & Mamede, H. (2011c). Information systems planning - How to enhance creativity? Proceedings of the CENTERIS'2011 Conference on ENTERprise Information Systems, Vilamoura.

Santos, A. B. (2015). Open Innovation research: Trends and influences – a Bibliometric Analysis. *Journal of Innovation Management, 3*(2), 131–165.

Santos, O. C., Barrera, C., & Boticario, J. G. (2004). An overview of aLFanet: An adaptive iLMS based on standards. *Adaptive Hypermedia and Adaptive Web-based Systems. Lecture Notes in Computer Science, 3137,* 429–432. doi:10.1007/978-3-540-27780-4_67

Santos, V., & Mamede, H. (2007). Creative information systems. In M. Freire & M. Pereira (Eds.), *Encyclopedia of Internet Technologies and Applications* (pp. 126–131). USA: IGI Global. doi:10.4018/978-1-59140-993-9.ch019

Sarantis, D., Charalabidis, Y., & Askounis, D. (2011). A goal-driven management framework for electronic government transformation projects implementation. *Government Information Quarterly, 28*(1), 117–128. doi:10.1016/j.giq.2009.10.006

Sarter, N. B. (2006). Multimodal information presentation: Design guidance and research challenges. *International Journal of Industrial Ergonomics, 36*(5), 439–445. doi:10.1016/j.ergon.2006.01.007

Sato, Y., Saito, M., & Koik, H. (2001). Real-Time Input of 3D Pose and Gestures of a User's Hand and Its Applications for HCI. Proceedings of the 2001 IEEE Virtual Reality Conference, Yokohama.

Sauer, C., & Reich, B. H. (2009). Rethinking IT project management: Evidence of a new mindset and its implications. *International Journal of Project Management, 27*(2), 182–193. doi:10.1016/j.ijproman.2008.08.003

Saunders, M., Lewis, P., & Thornhill, A. (2009). *Research methods for business students.* New York: Prentice Hall.

Saven, S. (2003). Business process modeling: Review and framework. *International Journal of Production Economics, 90*(2), 129–149. doi:10.1016/S0925-5273(03)00102-6

Sawchuk, S. (2013, July14). When bad things happen to good NAEP data. *Education Week, 32*(37), 1–22. Retrieved from http://www.edweek.org/ew/articles/2013/07/24/37naep.h32.html?tkn=XWSFjintSc1tarwBowLttmHfKt77SXIkUIav&cmp=ENL-EU-NEWS1

SCAMPI Upgrade Team. (2011). *Standard CMMI Appraisal Method for Process Improvement A, Version 1.3 Model Definition Document. Handbook CMU/SEI-2011-HB-001.* USA: Carnegie Mellon University/Software Engineering Institute.

Schaffert, S. (2006). *IkeWiki: A semantic wiki for collaborative knowledge management.* Paper presented at the Enabling Technologies: Infrastructure for Collaborative Enterprises, 2006, International Workshop. doi:10.1109/WETICE.2006.46

Schamber, L., Eisenberg, M. B., & Nilan, M. S. (1990). A re-examination of relevance: Toward a dynamic, situational definition. *Information Processing & Management, 26*(6), 755–776. doi:10.1016/0306-4573(90)90050-C

Scheer, A. W. (2000). *ARIS – Business process modeling.* Berlin, Germany: Springer–Verlag. doi:10.1007/978-3-642-57108-4

Schein, E. (2009). *The Corporate Culture Survival Guide - New and* (Revised Edition). San Francisco, CA: Jossey Bass.

Scherlis, W. L., & Eisenberg, J. (2003). IT research, innovation, and e-government. *Communications of the ACM, 46*(1), 67–68. doi:10.1145/602421.602455

Schiaffino, S., Garcia, P., & Amandi, A. (2008). eTeacher: Providing personalized assistance to e-learning students. *Computers & Education*, *51*(4), 1744–1754. doi:10.1016/j.compedu.2008.05.008

Schildkamp, K., Lai, M. K., & Earl, L. (2013). Data-based decision making in education: Challenges and opportunities. Dordrecht, Netherlands: Springer Science+Business Media

Schmitt, B. (2003). *Customer experience management: a revolutionary approach to connecting with your customers*. New York: Wiley.

Schnherr, M. (2009). Towards a Common Terminology in the Discipline of Enterprise Architecture. In G. Feuerlicht, & W. Lamersdorf (Eds.), Service-Oriented Computing - ICSOC 2008 Workshops, *Lecture Notes in Computer Science* (Vol. 5472, pp. 400-413). Springer-Verlag, Berlin.

Scholl, H. (2001). *Applying stakeholder theory to e-government: Benefits and limits*. Albany, NY: Center for Technology in Government, University at Albany.

Schön, D. (1983). *The reflective practitioner: how professionals think in action*. New York: Basic Books.

Schreuders, J., & Legesse, A. (2012). Organizational ambidexterity: How small technology firms balance innovation and support. *Technology Innovation Management Review*, *2*(2), 17–21.

Schroeder, A., & Pauleen, D. (2007). KM governance: Investigating the case of a knowledge intensive research organisation. *Journal of Enterprise Information Management*, *20*(4), 414–431. doi:10.1108/17410390710772696

Schroeder, A., Pauleen, D., & Huf, S. (2012). KM Governance: The mechanisms for guiding and controlling KM programs. *Journal of Knowledge Management*, *16*(1), 1–1. doi:10.1108/13673271211198918

Schultze, U., & Avital, M. (2011). Designing Interviews to Generate Rich Data for Information Systems Research. *Information and Organization*, *21*(1), 1–16. doi:10.1016/j.infoandorg.2010.11.001

Schwalbe, K. (2010). *Information technology project management*. Course Technology Ptr.

Schwandt, T. A. (2001). *Dictionary of qualitative inquiry*. Thousand Oaks, CA: Sage.

Scott, J. E., & Vessey, I. (2000). Implementing enterprise resource planning systems: The role of learning from failure. *Information Systems Frontiers*, *2*(2), 213–232. doi:10.1023/A:1026504325010

Seale, J., Draffan, E. A., & Wald, M. (2010). Digital agility and digital decision-making: Conceptualising digital inclusion in the context of disabled learners in higher education. *Studies in Higher Education*, *35*(4), 445–461. doi:10.1080/03075070903131628

Seeman, E. D., & O'Hara, M. (2006). Customer relationship management in higher education: Using information systems to improve the student-school relationship. *Campus-Wide Information Systems*, *23*(1), 24–34. doi:10.1108/10650740610639714

Seethamraju, R. (2012). Business process management: A missing link in business education. *Business Process Management Journal*, *18*(3), 532–547. doi:10.1108/14637151211232696

Seibold, D., & Shea, C. (2001). Participation and Decision Making. In F. Jablin & L. Putnam (Eds.), *The New Handbook of Organizational Communication* (pp. 664–704). Thousand Oaks, CA: SAGE Publications.

Seidel, S., & Recker, J. (2009). Using Grounded Theory for Studying Business Process Management Phenomena. In S. Newell, E. Whitley, N. Pouloudi, J. Wareham, & L. Mathiassen (Eds.), *Proceedings of the 17th European Conference on Information Systems* (pp. 490-501).

Senge, P. (2006). The Leader's New Work - Building Learning Organizations. In J. V. Gallos (Ed.), *Organization development: a Jossey-Bass reader* (pp. 765–792). San Francisco, CA: Jossey Bass.

Sen, R. (2007). A strategic analysis of competition between open source and proprietary software. *Journal of Management Information Systems*, *24*(1), 233–257. doi:10.2753/MIS0742-1222240107

Sensuse, D. I., & Ramadhan, A. (2012). The relationships of soft systems methodology (SSM), business process modeling and e-Government. *International Journal of Advanced Computer Science and Applications*, *3*(1), 179–183.

Serafeimidis, V., & Smithson, S. (2003). Information systems evaluation as an organizational institution- experience from a case study. *Information Systems Journal*, *13*(30), 251–274. doi:10.1046/j.1365-2575.2003.00142.x

Serrano-Cinca, C., Rueda-Tomas, M., & Portillo-Tarragona, P. (2009). Determinants of e-government extension. *Online Information Review*, *33*(3), 476–498. doi:10.1108/14684520910969916

Servon, L. (2002). *Bridging the digital divide: Technology, community and public policy*. London: Blackwell. doi:10.1002/9780470773529

Shahmoradi, L., Ahmadi, M., & Haghani, H. (2007). Determining the most important evaluation indicators of healthcare information systems (HCIS) in Iran. *Health Information Management Journal*, *36*(1), 13. PMID:18195393

Shan, C., Tan, T., & Wei, Y. (2007). Real-time hand tracking using a mean shift embedded particle filter. Journal Pattern Recognition, New York.

Shang, S., & Seddon, P. B. (2002). Assessing and managing the benefits of enterprise systems: The business manager's perspective. *Information Systems Journal*, *12*(4), 271–299. doi:10.1046/j.1365-2575.2002.00132.x

Shani, A. R., & Pasmore, W. (1982, August). Towards a New Model of the Action Research Process. Academy of Management Proceedings.

Shankar, V., Smith, A. K., & Rangaswamy, A. (2003). Customer satisfaction and loyalty in online and offline environments. *Journal of Research in Marketing*, *20*(2), 153–175. doi:10.1016/S0167-8116(03)00016-8

Shashua, A., & Levin, A & Others. (2003). Ranking with large margin principle: Two approaches. *Advances in Neural Information Processing Systems*, *15*, 937–944.

Shehab, E. M., Sharp, M. W., Supramaniam, L., & Spedding, T. A. (2004). Enterprise resource planning: An integrative review. *Business Process Management Journal*, *10*(4), 359–386. doi:10.1108/14637150410548056

Shepard, L., Davidson, K., & Bowman, R. (2011). How middle school mathematics teachers use interim and benchmark assessment data. Los Angeles, CA: University of California, Los Angeles (UCLA), Center for Research on Evaluation, Standards, and Student Testing (CRESST), CRESST Report 807.

Sherer, S. A. (2004, Jan 5-8). Managing risk beyond the control of IS managers: the role of business management. *Proceedings of the 37th Hawaii International Conference on System Sciences*, 2004, Hawaii, USA. doi:10.1109/HICSS.2004.1265509

Shiller, R. J. (2003). From Efficient Markets Theory to Behavioral Finance. *The Journal of Economic Perspectives*, *17*(1), 83–104. doi:10.1257/089533003321164967

Shirk, S. L. (1994). *How China opened its door: the political success of the PRC's foreign trade and investment reform*. Washington, D.C.: Brookings Institution.

Siau, K., & Long, Y. (2006). Using social development lenses to understand e-government development. *Journal of Global Information Management*, *14*(1), 47–62. doi:10.4018/jgim.2006010103

Siemens, G. (2004). Connectivism: A Learning Theory for the Digital Age. Retrieved from http://www.elearnspace.org/Articles/connectivism.htm

Silverman, D. (2000). *Doing qualitative research: a practical handbook*. London: Sage.

Simmons, J., & Lovegrove, I. (2005). Bridging the conceptual divide: Lessons from stakeholder analysis. *Journal of Organizational Change Management*, *18*(5), 495–513. doi:10.1108/09534810510614977

Singhal, A., Salton, G., Mitra, M., & Buckley, C. (1996). Document length normalization. *Information Processing & Management*, *32*(5), 619–633. doi:10.1016/0306-4573(96)00008-8

Sipior, J. C., & Ward, B. T. (2005). Bridging the digital divide for e-government inclusion: A United States case study. *The Electronic. Journal of E-Government*, *3*(3), 137–146.

Smith, A. (2006). CRM and customer service: strategic asset or corporate overhead. Handbook of Business Strategy, 7(1), 87-93.

Smith, A. M., & Lewis, B. R. (1989). Customer Care in Financial Service Organisations. *International Journal of Bank Marketing*, 7(5), 13–22. doi:10.1108/02652328910131917

Smith, P. (2005). From flowers to palms: 40 years of policy for online learning. *ALT-J. Research in Learning Technology*, 13(2), 93–108. doi:10.1080/09687760500104054

Smith, W. K., & Tushman, M. L. (2005). Managing strategic contradictions: A top management model for managing innovation streams. *Organization Science*, 16(5), 522–536. doi:10.1287/orsc.1050.0134

Smola, A. (1999). Geometry and invariance in kernel based methods. In Advances in Kernel Methods: Support Vector Learning, (pp. 89-116). MIT Press.

Söderlind, E., & Kidby, S. (2005). Cross cultural cooperation – a field study about India and Sweden. Retrieved from http://www.diva-portal.org/sh/abstract.xsql?dbid=300

Söderlund, J., Vaagaasar, A. L., & Andersen, E. S. (2008). Relating, reflecting and routinizing: Developing project competence in cooperation with others. *International Journal of Project Management*, 26(5), 517–526. doi:10.1016/j.ijproman.2008.06.002

Song, C., Koren, T., Wang, P., & Barabási, A.-L. (2010a). Modelling the scaling properties of human mobility. *Nature Physics*, 6(10), 818–823. doi:10.1038/nphys1760

Song, C., Qu, Z., Blumm, N., & Barabási, A.-L. (2010b). Limits of Predictability in Human Mobility. *Science*, 327(5968), 1018–1021. doi:10.1126/science.1177170 PMID:20167789

Sørensen, E., & Torfing, J. (2005). The Democratic Anchorage of Governance Networks. *Scandinavian Political Studies*, 28(3), 195–218. doi:10.1111/j.1467-9477.2005.00129.x

Sousa, G. V. e. (1998). *Metodologia da investigação. Redacção e apresentação de trabalhos científicos*. Livraria Civilização.

Spencer, E. P. (1999). The reengineering concept: A graphic model. *Journal of Business Education*, 74(5), 311–315. doi:10.1080/08832329909601704

Spithoven, A., Clarysse, B., & Knockaert, M. (2010). Building absorptive capacity to organize inbound open innovation in traditional industries. *Technovation*, 30(2), 130–141. doi:10.1016/j.technovation.2009.08.004

Spoerri, A. (2007). *Visualizing the overlap between the 100 most visited pages on Wikipedia for September 2006 to January 2007.*

Sribooruang, Y., Kumhom, P., & Chamnongthai, K. (2004). *Hand posture classification using wavelet moment invariant," in Virtual Environments*. Human-Computer Interfaces and Measurement Systems.

Srinuan, C., & Bohlin, E. (2011). What makes people go on line? An empirical analysis of the digital divide in Thailand. Proceedings of the Annual International Conference on Micro and Macro Economics.

Stake, R. E. (1995). *The art of case study research*. Sage Publications, Inc.

Stake, R. E. (2005). Qualitative case studies. In N. Denzin & Y. Lincoln (Eds.), *The Sage handbook of qualitative research* (pp. 443–466). Thousand Oaks, CA: Sage Publications Ltd.

Stansbury, M. (2013, July). More training is key to better school data use: States have continued to make progress in building robust data systems—but stakeholders must know how to use student data effectively. *eSchool News*. Retrieved from http://www.eschoolnews.com/2012/11/16/more-training-is-key-to-better-school-data-use/?ast=104&astc=9990

Starbuck, W. H. (1992). Learning by knowledge-intensive firms. *Journal of Management Studies*, 29(6), 713–740. doi:10.1111/j.1467-6486.1992.tb00686.x

Statistical Reports on the Internet Development in China. (2011). Economic Yearbook Press Office China Internet Network Information Center. Retrieved from http://www.cnnic.net.cn/en/index/0O/02/index.htm

Stein, K., & Hess, C. (2007). *Does it matter who contributes: a study on featured articles in the german wikipedia*. Paper presented at the Proceedings of the eighteenth conference on Hypertext and hypermedia. doi:10.1145/1286240.1286290

Stemberger, M. I., & Jaklic, J. (2007). Towards e-government by business process change: A methodology for public sector. *International Journal of Information Management*, 27(4), 221–232. doi:10.1016/j.ijinfomgt.2007.02.006

Stephani, L., Mason, R., & Pegler, C. (2007). *The Educational Potential of e-Portfolios: Supporting Personal Development and Reflective Learning*. New York: Routledge.

Stephenson, S. (2009). Digital Divide: A Discursive Move Away from the Real Inequities. *The Information Society*, 25(1), 1–22. doi:10.1080/01972240802587539

Steward, M. (2001). Towards a global definition of patient centred care: The patient should be the judge of patient centred care. *British Medical Journal*, 322(7284), 444–445. doi:10.1136/bmj.322.7284.444

Stewart, K. J., Ammeter, A. P., & Maruping, L. M. (2006). Impacts of license choice and organizational sponsorship on user interest and development activity in open source software projects. *Information Systems Research*, 17(2), 126–144. doi:10.1287/isre.1060.0082

Stewart, K. J., & Gosain, S. (2006a). The impact of ideology on effectiveness in open source software development teams. *Management Information Systems Quarterly*, 291–314.

Stewart, K. J., & Gosain, S. (2006b). The moderating role of development stage in free/open source software project performance. *Software Process Improvement and Practice*, 11(2), 177–191. doi:10.1002/spip.258

Stiggins, R. (2002). Assessment for learning. *Education Week*, 21(26), 30, 32–33.

Straub, K. (1999). 1999 and beyond: IT's impact on the business of healthcare in the new millennium. *Health Management Technology*, 20(2), 40, 42–43. PMID:10346476

Strauss, A., & Corbin, J. (1998). *Basic of qualitative research: Techniques and procedures for developing grounded theory* (2nd ed.). London: Sage Publications.

Strauss, A., & Corbin, J. (1998). *Basics of qualitative research: techniques and procedures for developing grounded theory*. London: Sage.

Stringer, E. T. (1996). *Action research: A handbook for practitioners*. Thousand Oaks, CA: SAGE Publications, Inc.

Stufflebeam, D. (2000). *Guidelines for developing evaluation checklists: the checklists development checklist (CDC)*. Retrieved from http://www.wmich.edu/evalctr/archive_checklists/guidelines_cdc.pdf

Stvilia, B., Al-Faraj, A., & Yi, Y. J. (2009). Issues of cross-contextual information quality evaluation—The case of Arabic, English, and Korean Wikipedias. *Library & Information Science Research*, 31(4), 232–239. doi:10.1016/j.lisr.2009.07.005

Stvilia, B., & Gasser, L. (2008). An activity theoretic model for information quality change. *First Monday*, 13(4). doi:10.5210/fm.v13i4.2126

Subramaniam, C., Sen, R., & Nelson, M. L. (2009). Determinants of open source software project success: A longitudinal study. *Decision Support Systems*, 46(2), 576–585. doi:10.1016/j.dss.2008.10.005

Suchman, M. C. (1995). Managing legitimacy: Strategic and institutional approaches. *Academy of Management Review*, 571–610.

Sultan, A., AlArfaj, K. A., & AlKutbi, G. A. (2012). Analytic hierarchy process for the success of e-government. *Business Strategy Series*, 13(6), 295–306. doi:10.1108/17515631211286146

Sumner, M. (2000). Risk factors in enterprise-wide/ERP projects. *Journal of Information Technology*, 15(4), 317–327. doi:10.1080/02683960010009079

Sun, J. (2000). Organization development and change in Chinese state-owned enterprises: A human resource perspective. *Leadership and Organization Development Journal*, 21(8), 379–389. doi:10.1108/01437730010379267

Sun, Q., Zhang, A., & Li, J. (2005). A study of optimal state shares in mixed oligopoly: Implications for SOE reform and foreign competition. *China Economic Review*, 16(1), 1–27. doi:10.1016/j.chieco.2004.06.009

Sun, S., & Manson, S. M. (2011). Social Network Analysis of the Academic GIScience Community. *The Professional Geographer*, 63(1), 18–33. doi:10.1080/00330124.2010.533560

Surowiecki, J. (2005). *The Wisdom of Crowds.* New York: Anchor Books.

Susman, G. I., & Evered, R. D. (1978). An assessment of the scientific merits of action research. *Administrative Science Quarterly, 23*(4), 582–603. doi:10.2307/2392581

Svari, S., Slantten, T., Svensson, G., & Edvardsson, B. (2011). A SOS construct of negative emotion in customers' service experience (CSE) and service recovery by firms (SRF). *Journal of Services Marketing, 24*(5), 323–335. doi:10.1108/08876041111149685

Symons, V., & Walsham, G. (1988). The evaluation of information systems: A critique. *Journal of Applied Systems Analysis, 15*, 119–132.

Taha, T. A., & Ghosh, J. (1999). Symbolic interpretation of artificial neural networks. *IEEE Transactions on Knowledge and Data Engineering, 11*(3), 448–468. doi:10.1109/69.774103

Tahboub, K., & Asada, H. H. (1999). A semi-autonomous control architecture applied to robotic wheelchairs. *Proceedings of the 1999 IEEE/RSJ International Conference on Intelligent Robots and Systems.* doi:10.1109/IROS.1999.812795

Tan, H. (1997). Cascade ARTMAP: Integrating neural computation and symbolic knowledge processing. *IEEE Transactions on Neural Networks, 8*(2), 237–250. doi:10.1109/72.557661 PMID:18255628

Tan, M., Xia, T., Guo, L., & Wang, S. (2013). Direct optimization of ranking measures for learning to rank models.*Proceedings of the 19th ACM SIGKDD international conference on Knowledge discovery and data mining* (pp. 856—864). doi:10.1145/2487575.2487630

Tapscott, D., & Williams, A. (2008). *Wikinomics: How Mass Collaboration Changes Everything.* New York: Penguin Group.

Tapscott, D., & Williams, A. D. (2008). *Wikinomics: How mass collaboration changes everything.* Penguin.

Tarrida, A. C., & Femenia, D. C. (2008). Dirigir la creatividad: Una aproximación al funcionamiento intelectual de los directores de cine. In M.d.F. Morais & S. Bahia (Eds.) Criatividade: conceito, necessidades e intervenção. Psiquilibrios Braga.

Tatem, A. J., Huang, Z., Narib, C., Kumar, U., Kandula, D., & Pindolia, D. K. et al. (2014). Integrating rapid risk mapping and mobile phone call record data for strategic malaria elimination planning. *Malaria Journal, 13*(1), 52. doi:10.1186/1475-2875-13-52 PMID:24512144

Tavana, M., Zandi, F., & Katehakis, M. N. (2013). A hybrid fuzzy group ANP–TOPSIS framework for assessment of e-government readiness from a CiRM perspective. *Information & Management, 50*(7), 383–397. doi:10.1016/j.im.2013.05.008

Tavares, S. (2007). *O fenómeno da identificação organizacional: contributos para a sua explicação* [Unpublished Doctoral Dissertation]. ISCTE-IUL, Lisbon.

Taylor, J. (2003). *Managing information technology projects: Applying project management strategies to software, hardware and integration initiatives.* New York, NY: American Management Association.

Taylor, M., Guiver, J., Robertson, S., & Minka, T. (2008). Softrank: optimizing non-smooth rank metrics.*Proceedings of the international conference on Web search and web data mining* (pp. 77–86). doi:10.1145/1341531.1341544

Teece, D. (2006). Reflections on "Profiting from Innovation". *Research Policy, 35*(8), 1131–1146. doi:10.1016/j.respol.2006.09.009

Teece, D. J., Pisano, G., & Schuen, A. (1997). Dynamic capabilities and strategic management. *Strategic Management Journal, 18*(7), 509–533. doi:10.1002/(SICI)1097-0266(199708)18:7<509::AID-SMJ882>3.0.CO;2-Z

Teixeira, J., Patricio, L., Nunes, N. J., Nobrega, L., Raymond, P. F., & Constantine, L. (2012). Customer experience modelling: From customer experience to service design. *Journal of Service Management, 23*(3), 362–376. doi:10.1108/09564231211248453

Teixeira, M. O., Machado, C. J. S., Filipecki, A. T. P., Cortes, B. A., & Klein, H. E. (2011). Descrição e análise do uso de um instrumento de coordenação em um instituto público de pesquisa em biomedicina. *Ciencia & Saude Coletiva, 16*(3), 1835–1847. doi:10.1590/S1413-81232011000300019 PMID:21519673

Teo, T. S., Srivastava, S. C., & Jiang, L. (2008). Trust and electronic government success: An empirical study. *Journal of Management Information Systems*, *25*(3), 99–132. doi:10.2753/MIS0742-1222250303

Teubner, R. (2007). Strategic information systems planning: A case study from the financial services industry. *The Journal of Strategic Information Systems*, *16*(1), 105–125. doi:10.1016/j.jsis.2007.01.002

The Alaska Department of Natural Resources. (2003). RAPS feasibility study – technical assessment. Retrieved from http://www.dnr.state.ak.us/lup/Technical_Assessment_5.2.pdf

The eLearning Action Plan: Designing tomorrow's education. (2001). European Commission. Retrieved from http://www.uni-mannheim.de/edz/pdf/sek/2002/sek-2002-0236(01)-en.pdf

The next step: Using longitudinal data systems to improve student success. (2009). *Data Quality Campaign*. Retrieved from http://www.dataqualitycampaign.org/find-resources/the-next-step/

Thibodeau, P. (2000). E-government spending to soar through 2005. *Computerworld*, *34*(17), 12–13.

Thiry, M. (2002). Combining value and project management into an effective programme management model. *International Journal of Project Management*, *20*(3), 221–227. doi:10.1016/S0263-7863(01)00072-2

Thomas, J. C., & Streib, G. (2003). The new face of government: Citizen-initiated contacts in the era of e-Government. *Journal of Public Administration: Research and Theory*, *13*(1), 83–102. doi:10.1093/jpart/mug010

Thompson, D. V., Rust, R. T., & Rhoda, J. (2005). The business value of e-government for small firms. *International Journal of Service Industry Management*, *16*(4), 385–407. doi:10.1108/09564230510614022

Thong, J. Y. L., Yap, C. S., & Seah, K. L. (2000). Business process reengineering: The case of the Housing Development Board in Singapore. *Journal of Management Information Systems*, *17*(1), 245–270.

Tohidi, H. (2011). E-government and its different dimensions: Iran. *Procedia-Computer Science Journal*, *3*, 1101–1105. doi:10.1016/j.procs.2010.12.179

Toivanen, H., & Ponomariov, B. (2011). African regional innovation systems: Bibliometric analysis of research collaboration patterns 2005-2009. *Scientometrics*, *88*(2), 471–493. doi:10.1007/s11192-011-0390-1

Tolbert, C. J., & Mossberger, K. (2006). The effects of e-government on trust and confidence in government. *Public Administration Review*, *66*(3), 354–369. doi:10.1111/j.1540-6210.2006.00594.x

Tonellotto, N., Macdonald, C., & Ounis, I. (2013). Efficient and effective retrieval using selective pruning. *Proceedings of the sixth ACM international conference on Web search and data mining* (pp 6372. doi:10.1145/2433396.2433407

Toraskar, K. V. (1991). How managerial uses evaluate their decision-support: A Grounded Theory Approach. *Journal of Computer Information Systems*, *7*, 195–225.

Torres, L., Pina, V., & Acerete, B. (2005). E-government developments on delivering public services among EU cities. *Government Information Quarterly*, *22*(2), 217–238. doi:10.1016/j.giq.2005.02.004

Tour, T. P. S., & Dhir, T. (2011). Benefits of integrated business planning, forecasting, and process management. *Business Strategy Series*, *12*(6), 275–288. doi:10.1108/17515631111185914

Trauth, E. (2001). The Choice of Qualitative Methods in IS Research. In E. Trauth (Ed.), *Qualitative research in IS: issues and trends* (pp. 1–19). London: Idea Group Publishing. doi:10.4018/978-1-930708-06-8.ch001

Traveling through time: The forum guide to longitudinal data systems. Book Four of Four: Advanced LDS Usage (NFES 2011–802). (2011). *Education Statistics*. Washington, DC: National Center for Education Statistics, Institute of Education Sciences, U.S. Department of Education.

Traveling through time: The forum guide to longitudinal data systems. Book Two of Four: Planning and Developing an LDS (NFES 2011–804). (2010). *National Forum on Education Statistics*. Washington, DC: National Center for Education Statistics, Institute of Education Sciences, U.S. Department of Education.

Trestian, I., Ranjan, S., Kuzmanovic, A., & Nucci, A. (2009). Measuring Serendipity: Connecting People, Locations and Interests in a Mobile 3G Network. *Proceedings of the 9th ACM SIGCOMM Conference on Internet Measurement Conference* (pp. 267–279). New York, NY, USA: ACM. doi:10.1145/1644893.1644926

Truss, C., Gratton, L., Hope-Hailey, V., McGovern, P., & Stiles, P. (1997). Soft and hard models of human resource management: A reappraisal. *Journal of Management Studies*, *34*(1), 53–73. doi:10.1111/1467-6486.00042

Tsai, W.-H., Chou, W.-C., & Leu, J.-D. (2011). An effectiveness evaluation model for the web-based marketing of the airline industry. *Expert Systems with Applications*, *38*(12), 15499–15516.

Tsai, W., Lin, T. W., Chen, S., & Hung, S. (2007). Users' service quality satisfaction and performance improvement of ERP consultant selections. *International Journal of Business and Systems Research*, *1*(3), 280–301. doi:10.1504/IJBSR.2007.015830

Tseng, M. M., Qinhai, M., & Su, C.-J. (1999). Mapping customers' service experience for operation improvement. *Business Process Management*, *5*(1), 50–64. doi:10.1108/14637159910249126

Tsinidou, M., Gerogiannis, V., & Fitsilis, P. (2010). Evaluation of the factors that determine quality in higher education: An empirical study. *Quality Assurance in Education*, *18*(3), 227–244. doi:10.1108/09684881011058669

Tsohou, A., Lee, H., Irani, Z., Weerakkody, V., Osman, I. H., Anouze, A. L., & Medeni, T. (2013). Proposing a reference process model for the citizen-centric evaluation of e-government services. *Transforming Government: People, Process and Policy*, *7*(2), 240–255.

Tsui, F. (2004). Managing software projects. Sudbury, Massachusetts, America: Jones and Bartlett Publishers.

Tsui, K. M., Kimb, D.J., Behal, A., Kontak D., & Yancoa, H. A. (2011). I Want That: Human-in-the-Loop Control of a Wheelchair-Mounted Robotic Arm. *Applied Bionics and Biomechanics*, 127-147.

Turban, E., Aronson, J. E., Liang, T. P., & Sharda, R. (2007). *Decision support and business intelligence systems*. New Jersey: Pearson Education.

Tushman, M. L., & O'Reilly, C. A. III. (1996). Ambidextrous organizations: Managing evolutionary and revolutionary change. *California Management Review*, *38*(4), 8–30. doi:10.2307/41165852

Tushman, M. L., & Romanelli, E. (1985). Organizational evolution: A metamorphosis model of convergence and reorientation. In B. M. Staw & L. L. Cummings (Eds.), *Research in organizational behavior* (Vol. 7, pp. 171–222). Greenwich: JAI Press.

Tylecote, A., & Cai, J. (2004). China's SOE reform and technological change: A corporate governance perspective. *Asian Business & Management*, *3*(1), 57–84. doi:10.1057/palgrave.abm.9200070

Ubaldi, B. (2011). The impact of the economic and financial crisis on e-government in OECD member countries. *European Journal of ePractise*, *11*, 5–18.

Ubaldi, B. (2013). Open Government Data: Towards Empirical Analysis of Open Government Data Initiatives. *OECD Working Papers on Public Governance*.

Ulkuniemi, P. (2003). *Purchasing software components at the dawn of market*. University of Oulu.

Umble, E., Haft, R., & Umble, M. M. (2003). Enterprise Resource Planning: Implementation procedures and Critical Success Factors. *European Journal of Operational Research*, *146*(2), 246–257. doi:10.1016/S0377-2217(02)00547-7

UMIC. (2011). *Relatório de Atividades 2011*. Ministério da Educação e Ciência.

Understanding the digital divide. (2001OECD. Paris: Directorate for Science, Technology and Industry.

Underwood, J. S., Zapata-Rivera, D., & VanWinkle, W. (2008) Growing Pains: Teachers Using and Learning to Use IDMS®. *ETS Research Memorandum. RM-08-07.* Princeton, NJ: ETS.

Underwood, J. S., Zapata-Rivera, D., & VanWinkle, W. (2010). *An evidence-centered approach to using assessment data for policymakers (ETS Research Rep. No. RR-10-03)*. Princeton, NJ: ETS.

Ungerleider, C. (2008, September). *Evaluation of the Ontario Ministry of Education's student success / learning to 18 strategy: Final report.* Canadian Council on Learning (CCL). Retrieved from http://www.edu.gov.on.ca/eng/teachers/studentsuccess/ccl_sse_report.pdf

United Nations. (2012). *United Nations e-government survey 2012: E-government for the people.* New York, NY: United Nations.

United States Department of Education Office of Planning, Evaluation and Policy Development. (2009). Implementing data-informed decision making in schools: Teacher access, supports and use. United States Department of Education (ERIC Document Reproduction Service No. ED504191)

United States Department of Education Office of Planning, Evaluation and Policy Development. (2011). Teachers' ability to use data to inform instruction: Challenges and supports. United States Department of Education (ERIC Document Reproduction Service No. ED516494)

Urquhart, C. (1997). Exploring analyst-client communication: using grounded theory techniques to investigate informal requirements gathering. In Lee, A. S., Libenau, J., & DeGross, J. L. (Eds), Proceedings of the International Conference on Information Systems and Qualitative Research (pp. 149-181). doi:10.1007/978-0-387-35309-8_10

Urquhart, C. (2001). An encounter with grounded theory: Or reinforcing old prejudices? A brief reply to Bryant. *Journal of Information Technology Theory and Application, 4*(3), 43–54.

Valdés, G., Solar, M., Astudillo, H., Iribarren, M., Concha, G., & Visconti, M. (2011). Conception, development and implementation of an e-Government maturity model in public agencies. *Government Information Quarterly, 28*(2), 176–187. doi:10.1016/j.giq.2010.04.007

Van Beveren, J. (2003). Does health care for knowledge management? *Journal of Knowledge Management, 7*(1), 90–95. doi:10.1108/13673270310463644

Van de Ven, A. H., & Poole, M. S. (1995). Explaining Development and Change in Organizations. *Academy of Management Review, 20*(3), 510–540. doi:10.2307/258786

van der Aalst, W. M. P. (1999). Process-oriented architectures for electronic commerce and interorganizational workflow. *Information Systems, 24*(8), 639–671. doi:10.1016/S0306-4379(00)00003-X

Van der Heijden, H. (2004). User acceptance of hedonic information systems. *Management Information Systems Quarterly*, 695–704.

Van der Meij, H. (2008). Designing for user cognition and affect in a manual. Should there be special support for the latter? *Learning and Instruction, 18*(1), 18–29.

van der Vyver, A., & Rajapakse, J. (2012). E-government adoption and business process re-engineering in developing countries: Sri Lankan and South African case studies. *International Journal of Innovation. Management and Technology, 3*(6), 778–783.

van Loy, B., Martens, T., & Debackere, K. (2005). Organizing for continuous innovation: On the sustainability of ambidextrous organizations. *Creativity and Innovation Management, 14*(3), 208–221. doi:10.1111/j.1467-8691.2005.00341.x

Vanhaverbeke, W., West, J., & Chesbrough, H. (2014). Surfing the new wave of open innovation research. In H. Chesbrough, W. Vanhaverbeke, & J. West (Eds.), New Frontiers in Open Innovation. Oxford: Oxford University Press. doi:10.1093/acprof:oso/9780199682461.003.0015

VanWinkle, W., Vezzu, M., & Zapata-Rivera, D. (2011). *Question-based reports for policymakers* (ETS Research Memorandum No. RM-11-16). Princeton, NJ: ETS.

Vapnik, V. (1999). *The nature of statistical learning theory.* Berlin: Springer.

Vargas, R. (2005). *Os meios justificam os fins – a gestão baseada em valores: da ética individual à ética Empresarial.* Lisbon: Gradiva.

Vaughan, D. (1992). Theory elaboration: The heuristics of case analysis. In C. Ragin & B. H. (Eds.), What is a Case? Exploring the foundations of social inquiry (pp. 173-202): Cambridge University Press.

Vehovar, V., Sicherl, P., Hüsing, T., & Dolnicar, V. (2006). Methodological Challenges of Digital Divide Measurements. *The Information Society, 22*(5), 279–290. doi:10.1080/01972240600904076

Venkatesh, V., Chan, F., & Thong, J. (2012). Designing e-government services: Key service attributes and citizens' preference structures. *Journal of Operations Management, 30*(1/2), 116–133. doi:10.1016/j.jom.2011.10.001

Venkatraman, V. (1994). IT-enabled business transformation: From automation to business scope redefinition. *Sloan Management Review, 35*(2), 73–87.

Verginadis, Y., & Mentzas, G. (2008). Agents and workflow engines for inter-organizational workflows in e-government cases. *Business Process Management Journal, 14*(2), 188–203. doi:10.1108/14637150810864925

Verhoef, P. C., Lemon, K. N., Parasuraman, A., Roggeveen, A., Tsiros, M., & Schlesinger, L. A. (2009). Customer experience creation: Determinants, dynamics and management strategies. *Journal of Retailing, 85*(1), 31–41. doi:10.1016/j.jretai.2008.11.001

Vernadat, F. (1996). *Enterprise modelling and integration: Principles and applications*. London, UK: Chapman & Hall.

Vickers, G. (1968). Value systems and social process. London, Sydney etc.: Tavistock Publications.

Vickers, G. (1970). *Freedom in a rocking boat: changing values in an unstable society*. London: Allen Lane.

Vickers, G. (1973). *Making institutions work*. London: Associated Business Programmes Ltd.

Vickers, G. (1983). *Human systems are different*. London, New York: Harper & Row.

Vickers, S. G. (1965). *The art of judgement: a study of policy making*. Chapman & Hall.

Vitalari, N., & Shaughnessy, H. (2012). *The Elastic Enterprise: The New Manifesto for Business Revolution*. Telemachus Press, LLC.

Waddoups, G. L., Wentworth, N., & Earle, R. (2004). Principles of technology integration and curriculum development: A faculty design team approach. *Computers in the Schools, 21*(1/2), 15–23. doi:10.1300/J025v21n01_02

Wagner, C. (2004). Wiki: A technology for conversational knowledge management and group collaboration. *Communications of the Association for Information Systems, 13*(1), 58.

Wakaumi, H., Nakamura, K., & Matsumura, T. (1992). Development of an automated wheelchair guided by a magnetic ferrite marker lane. *Journal of Rehabilitation Research and Development, 29*(1), 27–34. doi:10.1682/JRRD.1992.01.0027 PMID:1740776

Waldersee, R., & Griffiths, A. (1996). *The changing face of organizational change*. Australia: Center for Corporate Change, Australian Graduate School of Management University of New South Wales.

Wanberg, C. R., & Banas, J. T. (2000). Predictors and outcomes of openness to changes in a reorganizing workplace. *The Journal of Applied Psychology, 85*(1), 132–132. doi:10.1037/0021-9010.85.1.132 PMID:10740964

Wang, L., Bretschneider, S., & Gant, J. (2005). *Evaluating web-based e-government services with a citizen-centric approach*. Paper presented at the 38th Annual Hawaii International Conference on Systems Sciences, Big Island, HI. doi:10.1109/HICSS.2005.252

Wang, Y., Wang, L., Li, Y., He, D., Liu, T., & Chen, W. (2013b). A theoretical analysis of ndcg type ranking measures. *arXiv preprint arXiv:1304.6480*.

Wang, B., Tang, J., Fan, W., Chen, S., Tan, C., & Yang, Z. (2013a). Query-dependent cross-domain ranking in heterogeneous network. *Knowledge and Information Systems, 34*(1), 109–145. doi:10.1007/s10115-011-0472-7

Wang, J.-Z., Wang, J.-J., Zhang, Z.-G., & Guo, S.-P. (2011). Forecasting stock indices with back propagation neural network. *Expert Systems with Applications, 38*, 14346–14355.

Wang, L., Bennett, P. N., & Collins-Thompson, K. (2012). Robust ranking models via risk-sensitive optimization. *Proceedings of the 35th international ACM SIGIR conference on Research and development in information retrieval* (pp. 761 – 770).

Wang, L., Lin, J., & Metzler, D. (2010). Learning to efficiently rank. *Proceedings of the 33rd international ACM SIGIR conference on Research and development in information retrieval* (pp. 138–145).

Wang, Y.-S., Wang, H.-Y., & Shee, D. Y. (2007). Measuring e-learning systems success in an organizational context: Scale development and validation. *Computers in Human Behavior*, *23*(4), 1792–1808. doi:10.1016/j.chb.2005.10.006

Ward, J., & Peppard, J. (2002). *Strategic planning for information systems* (Vol. 28). Wiley.

Warkentin, M., Gefen, D., Pavlou, P., & Rose, G. (2002). Encouraging citizen adoption of e-government by building trust. *Electronic Markets*, *12*(3), 157–162. doi:10.1080/101967802320245929

Warschauer, M. (2003). Dissecting the 'Digital Divide': A Case Study in Egypt. *The Information Society*, *19*(4), 297–304. doi:10.1080/01972240309490

Warschauer, M. (2003). *Technology and social inclusion: Rethinking the digital divide*. Cambridge, MA: MIT Press.

Watson, R. T., & Mundy, B. (2001). A strategic perspective of electronic democracy. *Communications of the ACM*, *44*(1), 27–30. doi:10.1145/357489.357499

Wauthier, F., Jordan, M., & Jojic, N. (2013). Efficient ranking from pairwise comparisons. *Proceedings of the 30th International Conference on Machine Learning* (pp. 109–117).

Wayman, J. C., & Cho, V. (2009). Preparing educators to effectively use student data systems. In T. J. Kowalski & T. J. Lasley II (Eds.), Handbook of data-based decision making in education (pp. 89-104). New York, NY: Routledge.

Wayman, J. C., Cho, V., & Shaw, S. M. (2009, December). *First-year results from an efficacy study of the Acuity data system*. Paper presented at the Twenty-fourth Annual Texas Assessment Conference, Austin, TX.

Wayman, J. C. (2005). Involving teachers in data-driven decision making: Using computer data systems to support teacher inquiry and reflection. *Journal of Education for Students Placed at Risk*, *10*(3), 295–308. doi:10.1207/s15327671espr1003_5

Wayman, J. C., Snodgrass Rangel, V. W., Jimerson, J. B., & Cho, V. (2010). *Improving data use in NISD: Becoming a data-informed district*. Austin, TX: The University of Texas at Austin.

Wazlawick, R. S. (2009). *Metodologia de pesquisa para ciência da computação Elsevier*. São Paulo.

Weerakkody, V., & Dhillon, G. (2008). Moving from e-government to t-government: A study of process reengineering challenges in a UK local authority perspective. *International Journal of Electronic Government Research*, *4*(4), 1–16. doi:10.4018/jegr.2008100101

Weerakkody, V., El-Haddadeh, R., Sabol, T., Ghoneim, A., & Dzupka, P. (2012). E-government implementation strategies in developed and transition economies: A comparative study. *International Journal of Information Management*, *32*(1), 66–74. doi:10.1016/j.ijinfomgt.2011.10.005

Weerakkody, V., Janssen, M., & Dwivedi, Y. K. (2011). Transformational change and business process reengineering (BPR): Lessons from the British and Dutch public sector. *Government Information Quarterly*, *28*(3), 320–328. doi:10.1016/j.giq.2010.07.010

Weerakkody, V., Jones, S., & Olsen, E. (2007). E-government: A comparison of strategies in local authorities in the UK and Norway. *International Journal of Electronic Business*, *5*(2), 141–159. doi:10.1504/IJEB.2007.012970

Weick, K. E., & Quinn, R. E. (1999). Organizational Change and Development. *Annual Review of Psychology*, *50*(1), 361–386. doi:10.1146/annurev.psych.50.1.361 PMID:15012461

Weill, P., & Broadbent, M. (1998). *Leveraging the New Infrastructure: How market leaders capitalize on IT*. Harvard Business School Press.

Weill, P., & Ross, J. W. (2004). *IT Governance: How Top Performers Manage IT Decision Rights for Superior Results. Center for Information Systems Research – CISR/MIT*. Harvard Business School Press.

Weinhardt, C., Blau, B., & Stößer, J. (2009). Cloud Computing – A Classification, Business Models, and Research Directions. *Business and Information Systems Engineering*. 5.

Weiser, M., & Brown, J. S. (1995). Designing Calm Technology. Retrieved from http://www.ubiq.com/weiser/calmtech/calmtech.htm

Weiser, M. (1991). The Computer for the 21st Century. *Scientific American, 265*(3), 94–104. doi:10.1038/scientificamerican0991-94

Weiss, J. W., & Anderson, D. Jr. (2004). CIOs and IT professionals as change agents, risk and stakeholder managers: A field study. *Engineering Management Journal, 16*(2), 13–18. doi:10.1080/10429247.2004.11415244

Welch, E. W., Hinnant, C. C., & Moon, M. J. (2004). Linking citizen satisfaction with e-government and trust in government. *Journal of Public Administration: Research and Theory, 15*(3), 371–391. doi:10.1093/jopart/mui021

Weller, M. (2007). The distance from isolation: Why communities are the logical conclusion in e-learning. *Computers & Education, 49*(2), 148–159. doi:10.1016/j.compedu.2005.04.015

Wenger, E. (1998). *Communities of practice: learning, meaning, and identity.* Cambridge: Cambridge University Press. doi:10.1017/CBO9780511803932

Wenglinsky, H. (1998). *Does it Computer? The Relationship between Educational Technology and Student Achievement in Mathematics.* Princeton, NJ: Policy Information Centre of the Educational Testing Service.

Wesolowski, A., Eagle, N., Tatem, A. J., Smith, D. L., Noor, A. M., Snow, R. W., & Buckee, C. O. (2012). Quantifying the Impact of Human Mobility on Malaria. *Science, 338*(6104), 267–270. doi:10.1126/science.1223467 PMID:23066082

Wessner, C., & Wolff, A. (2012). *Rising to the Challenge, U.S. Innovation Policy for the Global Economy.* Washington, D.C.: The National Academies Press.

West, D. M. (2004). E-government and the transformation of service delivery and citizen attitudes. *Public Administration Review, 64*(1), 15–27. doi:10.1111/j.1540-6210.2004.00343.x

West, J., Ammon, S., Vanhaverbeke, W., & Chesbrough, H. (2014). Open innovation: The next decade. *Research Policy, 43*(5), 805–811. doi:10.1016/j.respol.2014.03.001

Whittaker, B. (1999). What went wrong? Unsuccessful information technology projects. *Information Management & Computer Security, 7*(1), 23–29. doi:10.1108/09685229910255160

Whittington, R., Cailluet, L., & Yakis-Douglas, B. (2011). Opening strategy: Evolution of a precarious profession. *British Journal of Management, 22*(3), 531–544.

Wiley, D., & Hilton, J. (2009). Openness, dynamic specialization, and the disaggregated future of Higher Education. *International Review of Research in Open and Distance Learning, 10*(5).

Wilkinson, D. M., & Huberman, B. A. (2007a). Assessing the value of cooperation in Wikipedia. *arXiv preprint cs/0702140.*

Wilkinson, D. M., & Huberman, B. A. (2007b). *Cooperation and quality in wikipedia.* Paper presented at the Proceedings of the 2007 international symposium on Wikis. doi:10.1145/1296951.1296968

Willis, T. H., & Willis-Brown, A. H. (2002). Extending the value of ERP. *Industrial Management & Data Systems, 102*(1), 35–38. doi:10.1108/02635570210414640

Wimmer, M. (2002). A European perspective towards online one-stop government: The eGOV project. *Electronic Commerce Research and Applications, 1*(1), 92–103. doi:10.1016/S1567-4223(02)00008-X

Wimmer, M. A. (2007). *The Role of Research in Successful E-Government Implementation E-Government Guide Germany. A. Zechner* (pp. 79–91). Stuttgart: Fraunhofer.

Windsor, D. (2009). Tightening corporate governance. *Journal of International Management, 15*(3), 306–316. doi:10.1016/j.intman.2009.02.003

Winter, M., Smith, C., Morris, P., & Cicmil, S. (2006). Directions for future research in project management: The main findings of a UK government-funded research network. *International Journal of Project Management, 24*(8), 638–649. doi:10.1016/j.ijproman.2006.08.009

Winter, M., & Szczepanek, T. (2009). *Images of projects.* Gower Publishing, Ltd.

Wixom, B. H., & Todd, P. (2005). A theoretical integration of user satisfaction and technology acceptance. *Information Systems Research, 16*(1), 85–102. doi:10.1287/isre.1050.0042

Wixted, B., & Holbrook, J. A. (2012). Environmental complexity and stakeholder theory in formal research network evaluations. *Prometheus*, *30*(3), 291–314. doi:10.1080/08109028.2012.727276

Wohlstetter, P., Datnow, A., & Park, V. (2008). Creating a system for data-driven decision-making: Applying the principal-agent framework. *School Effectiveness and School Improvement*, *19*(3), 239–259. doi:10.1080/09243450802246376

Wöhner, T., & Peters, R. (2009). *Assessing the quality of Wikipedia articles with lifecycle based metrics.* Paper presented at the Proceedings of the 5th International Symposium on Wikis and Open Collaboration. doi:10.1145/1641309.1641333

Woodroof, J., & Burg, W. (2003). Satisfaction/dissatisfaction: Are users predisposed? *Information & Management*, *40*(4), 317–324. doi:10.1016/S0378-7206(02)00013-7

Woolf, B. P. (2008). *Building intelligent interactive tutors: student-centered strategies for revolutionizing e-Learning.* Burlington, CA: Morgan Kaufmann.

World Economic Forum- WEF. (2014). *The Global Technology Report: Rewards and Risks of Big Data.* Beñat Bilbao-Osorio, Soumitra Dutta, and Bruno Lanvin (editors).

Wormell, I., Bothma, T. J. D., & Ralebipi, R. M. D. (2002). DISSAnet: Development of an information science research network in the Republic of South Africa 1998-2000. *Education for Information*, *20*(1), 45–56.

Wright, G., & Donaldson, B. (2002). Sales information systems in the UK financial services industry: An analysis of sophistication of use and perceived barriers to adoption. *International Journal of Information Management*, *22*(6), 405–419. doi:10.1016/S0268-4012(02)00032-4

Wu, J., & Goh, K. Y. (2009). *Evaluating longitudinal success of open source software projects: A social network perspective.* Paper presented at the System Sciences, 2009. HICSS'09. 42nd Hawaii International Conference on.

Wu, J., Goh, K.-Y., & Tang, Q. (2007). Investigating success of open source software projects: A social network perspective.

Wu, J.-H., & Wang, Y.-M. (2006). Measuring ERP success: The ultimate users' view. *International Journal of Operations & Production Management*, *26*(8), 882–903. doi:10.1108/01443570610678657

Wu, Q., Burges, C. J. C., Svore, K. M., & Gao, J. (2010). Adapting boosting for information retrieval measures. *Information Retrieval*, *13*(3), 254–270. doi:10.1007/s10791-009-9112-1

Wutyi, H. (2012). *An exploratory Study of Factor Influencing IT Project Initiation Decision.* Auckland University of Information Technology.

Xavier, Z. F. H., Silveria, M. L., Almeida, M. J., Malab, S. H. C., Ziviani, A., & Marques-Neto, T. H. (2013). *Understanding Human Mobility Due to Large-Scale Events. Third conference on the Analysis of Mobile Phone Datasets.* NetMob. Cambridge, USA. Retrieved from http://perso.uclouvain.be/vincent.blondel/netmob/2013/NetMob2013-abstracts.pdf

Xia, F., Liu, T., & Li, H. (2009). Top-k consistency of learning to rank methods. *Advances in Neural Information Processing Systems*, *22*, 2098–2106.

Xia, F., Liu, T., Wang, J., Zhang, W., & Li, H. (2008). Listwise approach to learning to rank: theory and algorithm. *Proceedings of the 25th international conference on Machine learning* (pp. 1192–1199). doi:10.1145/1390156.1390306

Xia, F., Zhou, L., Yang, Y., & Zhang, W. (2007). Ordinal regression as multiclass classification. *International Journal of Intelligent Control and Systems*, *12*(3), 230–236.

Xiao, W., Chi, C., & Yang, M. (2007). *On-line collaborative software development via wiki.* Paper presented at the Proceedings of the 2007 international symposium on Wikis. doi:10.1145/1296951.1296970

Xiao, B., & Benbasat, I. (2007). E-commerce product recommendation agents: Use, characteristics, and impact. *Management Information Systems Quarterly*, *31*(1), 137–209.

Xie, M., Xie, G., & Zhang, Y. (2011). Construction of regional medical service mode of cooperation. [in Chinese]. *Modem Hospital Management*, *42*(3), 18–20.

Xue, Y., Liang, H., Boulton, W. R., & Snyder, C. A. (2005). ERP implementation failures in China: Case studies with implications for ERP vendors. *International Journal of Production Economics*, *97*(3), 279–295. doi:10.1016/j.ijpe.2004.07.008

Xu, J., & Li, H. (2007). Adarank: a boosting algorithm for information retrieval. *Proceedings of the 30th annual international ACM SIGIR conference on Research and development in information retrieval* (pp. 391–398). doi:10.1145/1277741.1277809

Xu, Q., Zhou, Y., Zhou, L., & Geng, Q. (2012). Study and implementation of cooperation for dual referral based on integrating healthcare enterprise cross-enterprise document sharing techniques.[in Chinese]. *Chinese Journal of Tissue Engineering Research*, *16*(22), 4112–4116.

Yang, K., & Rho, S. Y. (2007). E-government for better performance: Promises, realities, and challenges. *International Journal of Public Administration*, *30*(11), 1197–1217. doi:10.1080/01900690701225556

Yang, Z., Jun, M., & Peterson, R. (2004). Measuring costumer perceived online service quality: Scale development and managerial implications. *International Journal of Operations & Production Management*, *24*(11/12), 1149–1174. doi:10.1108/01443570410563278

Yao, J., & Tan, C. L. (2000). A case study on using neural networks to perform technical forecasting of Forex. *Neurocomputing*, *34*(1-4), 79–98. doi:10.1016/S0925-2312(00)00300-3

Yao, X. (1999). Evolving Artificial Neural Networks. *Proceedings of the IEEE*, *87*(9), 1423–1447. doi:10.1109/5.784219

Yates, D., & Paquette, S. (2011). Emergency knowledge management and social media technologies: A case study of the 2010 Haitian earthquake. *International Journal of Information Management*, *31*(1), 6–13. doi:10.1016/j.ijinfomgt.2010.10.001

Yen, G. (1994). Adaptive time-delay neural control in space structural platforms. Proceedings of *IEEE World Congress on Computational Intelligence* (Vol. 4, pp. 2622-2627). doi:10.1109/ICNN.1994.374635

Yi, C.-C., Liao, P.-W., Huang, C.-F., & Hwang, I.-H. (2009). Acceptance of mobile learning: a respecification and validation of information system success.

Yildiz, M. (2007). E-government research: Reviewing the literature, limitations, and ways forward. *Government Information Quarterly*, *24*(3), 646–665. doi:10.1016/j.giq.2007.01.002

Yin, R. (1994). *Case study research, design and methods.* Newbury Park, CA: Sage Publications.

Yin, R. K. (2003). *Case Study Research: Design and Methods* (Vol. 5). Thousand Oaks, CA: Sage Publications.

York-Barr, J. et al. (2006). *Reflective practice to improve schools: an action guide for educators.* Thousand Oaks, CA: Corwin Press.

Yost, D. S., Sentner, S. M., & Forlenza-Bailey, A. (2000). An examination of the construct of critical reflection: Implications for teacher education programming in the 21st century. *Journal of Teacher Education*, *51*(1), 39–49. doi:10.1177/002248710005100105

Yuan, B. (2012). Referral Anxiety. *China Health Human Resources*, *2012*(5), 29-31.

Yuan, J., Zheng, Y., & Xie, X. (2012). Discovering Regions of Different Functions in a City Using Human Mobility and POIs. *Proceedings of the 18th ACM SIGKDD International Conference on Knowledge Discovery and Data Mining* (pp. 186–194). New York, NY, USA: ACM. doi:10.1145/2339530.2339561

Yu, C. S. (2005). Causes influencing the effectiveness of the post-implementation ERP system. *Industrial Management & Data Systems*, *105*(1), 115–132. doi:10.1108/02635570510575225

Yue, Y., Finley, T., Radlinski, F., & Joachims, T. (2007). A support vector method for optimizing average precision. *Proceedings of the 30th annual international ACM SIGIR conference on Research and development in information retrieval* (pp. 271–278). doi:10.1145/1277741.1277790

Yu, H. (2005). SVM selective sampling for ranking with application to data retrieval. *Proceedings of the eleventh ACM SIGKDD international conference on Knowledge discovery in data mining* (pp 354–363). doi:10.1145/1081870.1081911

Yu, H., Oh, J., & Han, W. (2009). Efficient feature weighting methods for ranking. *Proceedings of the 18th ACM conference on Information and knowledge management* (pp. 1157–1166).

Yusuf, S., Nabeshima, K., & Perkins, D. H. (2006). Under new ownership: privatizing China's state-owned enterprises. California: Stanford University Press and Washington: The World Bank.

Yu, Z., Wu, F., Zhang, Y., Tang, S., Shao, J., & Zhuang, Y. (2014). Hashing with listwise learning to rank. *Proceedings of the 37th International ACM SIGIR Conference on Research and Development in Information Retrieval* (pp. 999-1002).

Zaccaro, S., Heinen, B., & Shuffler, M. (2009). Team Leadership and Team Effectiveness. In E. Salas, G. Goodwin, & C. Burke (Eds.), *Team effectiveness in complex organizations: cross-disciplinary perspectives and approaches* (pp. 83–111). USA: Psychology Press, Taylor & Francis Group.

Zaccaro, S., Rittman, A., & Marks, M. (2001). Team leadership. *The Leadership Quarterly, 12*(4), 451–483. doi:10.1016/S1048-9843(01)00093-5

Zachman, J. A. (1987). A framework for information systems architecture. *IBM Systems Journal, 26*(3), 276–292. doi:10.1147/sj.263.0276

Zack, M. H. (1999). Developing a Knowledge Strategy. *California Management Review, 41*(3), 125–145. doi:10.2307/41166000

Zadeh, L. A. (1965). Fuzzy sets. *Information and Control, 8*(3), 338–353. doi:10.1016/S0019-9958(65)90241-X

Zahra, S. A., & George, G. (2002). The net-enabled business innovation cycle and the evolution of dynamic capabilities. *Information Systems Research, 13*(2), 147–150. doi:10.1287/isre.13.2.147.90

Zaltman, G., & Duncan, R. (1977). *Strategies for planned change*. New York: Wiley.

Zang, H., & Bolot, J. (2011). Anonymization of Location Data Does Not Work: A Large-scale Measurement Study. *Proceedings of the 17th Annual International Conference on Mobile Computing and Networking* (pp. 145–156). New York, NY, USA: ACM. doi:10.1145/2030613.2030630

Zang, H., & Bolot, J. C. (2007). Mining Call and Mobility Data to Improve Paging Efficiency in Cellular Networks. *Proceedings of the 13th Annual ACM International Conference on Mobile Computing and Networking* (pp. 123–134). New York, NY, USA: ACM. doi:10.1145/1287853.1287868

Zapata-Rivera, D., & VanWinkle, W. (2010). A research-based approach to designing and evaluating score reports for teachers (*ETS Research Memorandum No. RM-10-01*). Princeton, NJ: ETS.

Zhang, J. (2007). Case study method in information system research. *Journal of Information, 5*, 88-89, 92.

Zhang, H. S. (2004). 国有及国有控股企业短期行为的制度经济学分析 (Economics analysis on the short-term behaviours of state-owned and state-holding enterprises) [In Chinese]. MSc. Political Economy, Shandong University. *China*.

Zhang, J., Dawes, S. S., & Sarkis, J. (2005). Exploring stakeholders' expectations of the benefits and barriers of e-government knowledge sharing. *Journal of Enterprise Information Management, 18*(5), 548–567. doi:10.1108/17410390510624007

Zhang, L., Pan, L., Guo, X., & Jiang, L. (2012). Study on measurement of workload for pharmaceutical service in clinician. [in Chinese]. *Journal of Clinical and Experimental Medicine, 11*(14), 99–1101. PMID:23086188

Zhang, M., Kuang, D., Hua, G., Liu, Y., & Ma, S. (2009). Is learning to rank effective for web search? *Proceedings of SIGIR 2008 workshop learning to rank for information retrieval (LR4IR)* (pp. 641-647).

Zhang, N., Guo, X., Chen, G., & Chau, P. (2009). Impact of perceived fit on e-Government user evaluation: A study with a Chinese cultural context. *Journal of Global Information Management, 17*(1), 49–69. doi:10.4018/jgim.2009010103

Zhao, R. (2011). *Research on sharing electronic medical record* [Unpublished masters dissertation]. Zhengzhou University, Henan, China.

Zheng, D., He, Y., Chu, Y., & Huang, L. (2006). Compared research of information systems research trend between mainland China and international. *Journal of Fudan University, 45*(5), 577–583.

Zheng, Z., Chen, K., Sun, G., & Zha, H. (2007). A regression framework for learning ranking functions using relative relevance judgments. *Proceedings of the 30th annual international ACM SIGIR conference on Research and development in information retrieval* (pp. 287–294). doi:10.1145/1277741.1277792

Zhong, H. (2009). The patient-centred care and hospital marketing strategies. *Management Observation (in Chinese), 2009*(10), 234-235.

Zhou, H., Lin, D. J., & Huang, T. S. (2004). Static hand gesture recognition based on local orientation histogram feature distribution model. Proceedings of the Conference on Computer Vision and Pattern Recognition Workshop (CVPRW'04) (Vol. 10).

Zhou, L., & Nunes, M. (2012). Identifying knowledge sharing barriers in the collaboration of traditional and western medicine professionals in Chinese hospitals: A case study. *Journal of Librarianship and Information Science, 44*(4), 238–248. doi:10.1177/0961000611434758

Zhou, L., Vasconcelos, A., & Nunes, M. (2008). Supporting decision making in risk management through an evidence-based information systems project risk checklist. *Information Management & Computer Security, 16*(2), 166–186. doi:10.1108/09685220810879636

Zhu, H., Kraut, R., & Kittur, A. (2012). *Effectiveness of shared leadership in online communities.* Paper presented at the Proceedings of the ACM 2012 conference on Computer Supported Cooperative Work. doi:10.1145/2145204.2145269

Zimmermann, H., Neuneier, R., & Grothmann, R. (2001). Multi-agent modeling of multiple FX-markets by neural networks. *IEEE Transactions on Neural Networks, 12*(4), 35–743. doi:10.1109/72.935087 PMID:18249909

Zingerli, C. (2010). A sociology of international research partnerships for sustainable development. *European Journal of Development Research, 22*(2), 217–233. doi:10.1057/ejdr.2010.1

Zusman, A. (1998). *Overview of creative methods.* Southfield, Michigan, USA: Ideation International Inc.

Zwick, R., Sklar, J., Wakefield, G., Hamilton, C., Norman, A., & Folsom, D. (2008). Instructional tools in educational measurement and statistics (ITEMS) for school personnel: Evaluation of three web-based training modules. *Educational Measurement: Issues and Practice, 27*(2), 14–27. doi:10.1111/j.1745-3992.2008.00119.x

About the Contributors

Jorge Tiago Martins is a Lecturer in Organisational Informatics at The University of Sheffield's Information School, UK. His overarching research and teaching area is the management and use of information technology (IT) in complex organisations. He is interested in the intersection between Information Management/ Knowledge Management systems and organisation, with particular emphasis on structures, cultures, work practices, behaviour, and change. These intersecting research interests form the basis of his dual affiliation to the Information Systems, and to the Knowledge and Information Management research groups.

Andreea Molnar is a Lecturer with the School of Creative Technologies, Portsmouth University, United Kingdom. Previously, she has been a postdoctoral researcher at Arizona State University, United States, Brunel University, United Kingdom and City University London, United Kingdom. She has a PhD in Technology Enhanced Learning from the National College of Ireland (under a scholarship funded by the Irish Research Council for Science, Engineering and Technology) and an MSc in Modelling and Simulations from Babes-Bolyai University, Cluj-Napoca, Romania. Prior to enrolling in the PhD programme she has worked as a Software Developer at Silnet Consulting, Italy and Fortech, Romania.

* * *

Taghred Alghaith is a visiting researcher in Lancaster University Management School. Alghaith is also the Strategy Follow-up head in the Council of Health Services in Saudi Arabia.

Luis Amaral was born in 1960 is Associate Professor at Department of Information Systems in the School of Engineering of University of Minho. Researches and teaches in the areas of Information Systems Planning, Information Systems Management and the Information Society, especially in the field of Public Administration. Chairman of the Board of the GCC - Computer Graphics Center since 2005. Pró-Rector of University of Minho between 2006 and 2009. President of the National College of Informatics (Order of Engineers) since 2010.

Alireza Amrollahi holds a master's degree in information technology management from the University of Tehran and currently is a PhD candidate at Griffith University, school of ICT. His research interests include open strategy, strategic planning for information systems, and open source and collaborative approaches for software and content development.

José Carlos S. Cavalcanti is an Associate Professor of Economics at the Department of Economics of the Federal University of Pernambuco – UFPE (Pernambuco/Brazil) and teaches Economics at the Center of Informatics of this University. He has a Civil Engineering undergraduate degree from the UFPE (Pernambuco/Brazil), a MSc. degree on Urban and Regional Planning from the Federal University of Rio de Janeiro – UFRJ (Rio de Janeiro/Brazil), and a Ph.D. degree on Economic History from the Manchester University (Manchester/England). His research focuses on technology (particularly information and communication technologies) and innovation economics. He has published many articles in the fields of economics and information systems in Brazil and elsewhere (including an IGI-Global publication). He has several years of experience in government positions and undertakes consultancy work.

Ramiro Gonçalves is an Associate Professor with Habilitation at the University of Trás-os-Montes e Alto Douro and Senior Research at INESC TEC, in Portugal where he lectures on information systems and digital platforms. His main research areas include the e-business and e-commerce, models and platforms, and accessibility web. He authored over 120 papers, in journals, books, and conferences and is part of the research teams of several projects including PLAYER and VITA.

Telmo Henriques holds a PhD in Information Science and Technology from ISCTE-Lisbon University Institute and a Master degree in Management from Universidade Autónoma de Lisboa. For over 23 years he has been a Manager at MillennuiumBCP Bank, mainly within Audit and IT areas. Currently he develops research activities at ISTAR-IUL. His interests are in the areas of Organizational Development & Change and Quality & Organizational Excellence, using Action Research within organizational context.

Muhammad Ibrahim is currently a final year PhD student in the Faculty of Information Technology, Monash University, Australia. He received his B.Sc. (Hons.) and M.S. degrees from the Dept. of Computer Science and Engineering, University of Dhaka, Bangladesh in the years 2008 and 2010 respectively. Prior to starting his PhD at Monash, he served as a lecturer in the Dept. of Computer Science and Engineering, Ahsanullah University of Science and Technology, Dhaka, Bangladesh (2010-2012). Muhammad Ibrahim has so far published six papers in international conferences, two journal papers, and a book chapter. His current research interests include information retrieval, machine learning and data mining.

Kijpokin Kasemsap received his BEng degree in Mechanical Engineering from King Mongkut's University of Technology Thonburi, his MBA degree from Ramkhamhaeng University, and his DBA degree in Human Resource Management from Suan Sunandha Rajabhat University. He is a Special Lecturer at Faculty of Management Sciences, Suan Sunandha Rajabhat University based in Bangkok, Thailand. He is a Member of International Association of Engineers (IAENG), International Association of Engineers and Scientists (IAEST), International Economics Development and Research Center (IEDRC), International Association of Computer Science and Information Technology (IACSIT), International Foundation for Research and Development (IFRD), and International Innovative Scientific and Research Organization (IISRO). He also serves on the International Advisory Committee (IAC) for International Association of Academicians and Researchers (INAAR). He has numerous original research articles in top international journals, conference proceedings, and book chapters on business management, human resource management, and knowledge management published internationally.

Mohammad Khansari received his B.Sc., M.Sc. and Ph.D. degrees in Computer Engineering all from Sharif University of Technology, Tehran, Iran. He has given more than fifty invited talks on FOSS and GNU/Linux localization topics in Iran and International conferences. He is the co-author of four books in Free/Open Source Software topics and has more than sixty papers in international conferences and journals. His main research interests are network science and complex networks, wireless multimedia/health sensor networks, multimedia over peer-to-peer networks, and Free/Open Source Software. Currently, he is the faculty member of Faculty of New Sciences and Technologies, University of Tehran.

Amevi Kouassi is an independent information systems professional.

Salim Lahmiri is professor at ESCA School of Management in Casablanca, Morocco. He holds a Ph.D degree in Cognitive Informatics from University of Quebec at Montreal and a master of engineering (M. Eng) degree within the department of electrical engineering at École de Technologie Supérieure, Montreal, Canada. His research interests are in pattern recognition, intelligent decision systems, and times series analysis and forecasting.

Arminda Guerra Lopes holds a PhD in Human Computer Interaction from Leeds Metropolitan University, U.K.; She is a Professor at Polytechnic Institute of Castelo Branco, Portugal and a researcher at Madeira Interactive Technologies Institute (M-ITI) Research Interests: Information Systems; Human Computer Interaction; Research Methodologies Other Research Interests: Social Informatics, Creativity and Innovation, Universal Design.

Henrique S. Mamede is an Auxiliary Professor at Departamento de Ciências e Tecnologia da Universidade Aberta, colaborador do INESC-TEC, consultor em sistemas de informação.

Fergal McGrath is a lecturer in Information Management at the Kemmy Business School in the University of Limerick. Dr McGrath is a graduate electronic engineer who worked in Australia and the United Kingdom and went on to establish an engineering design company, Seagull Electronics Ltd. Having completed an MBA in 1989 he has since pursued an academic career in the area of Information and Knowledge Management. He completed a doctorate in 2000 at the Henley Management College in the Brunel University. His research interests are in application of Institution Economics to Information and Knowledge Management. Dr. McGrath is the Director of the AIB Centre for Information and Knowledge Management, which researches organisational strategies in relation to the Information/Knowledge resource.

Gabriel-Miro Muntean (S'02-M'04) received the B.Eng. and M.Sc. degrees from the Computer Science Engineering Department, Politehnica University of Timisoara, Romania, in 1996 and 1997, respectively, and the Ph.D. degree from the School of Electronic Engineering, Dublin City University (DCU), Dublin, Ireland, in 2003 for his research on quality-oriented adaptive multimedia streaming over wired networks. He is currently a Senior Lecturer with the School of Electronic Engineering, DCU, co-Director of the DCU Performance Engineering Laboratory, and Consultant Professor with Beijing University of Posts and Telecommunications, China. He has published over 200 papers in prestigious international journals and conferences, has authored three books and 16 book chapters, and has edited six other books. His current research interests include quality-oriented and performance-related issues of adaptive multimedia delivery, performance of wired and wireless communications, energy-aware networking, and personalized e-learning. Dr. Muntean is an Associate Editor of the IEEE Transactions on Broadcasting, Associate Editor of the IEEE Communication Surveys and Tutorials, and a reviewer for other important international journals, conferences, and funding agencies. He is a member of the ACM, IEEE and the IEEE Broadcast Technology Society.

Manzur Murshed received the BScEngg (Hons) degree in computer science and engineering from Bangladesh University of Engineering and Technology (BUET), Dhaka, Bangladesh, in 1994 and the PhD degree in computer science from the Australian National University (ANU), Canberra, Australia, in 1999. He also completed his Postgraduate Certificate in Graduate Teaching from ANU in 1997. He is currently an Emeritus Professor Robert HT Smith Professor and Personal Chair at the Faculty of Science and Technology, Federation University Australia. Prior to this appointment, he served the School of Information Technology, Federation University Australia as the Head of School, from January 2014 to July 2014, the Gippsland School of Information Technology, Monash University as the Head of School 2007 to 2013. He was one of the founding directors of the Centre for Multimedia Computing, Communications, and Applications Research (MCCAR). His major research interests are in the fields of video technology, information theory, wireless communications, distributed computing, and security & privacy. He has so far published 180+ refereed research papers and received more than $1M nationally competitive research funding, including three Australian Research Council Discovery Projects grants in 2006, 2010, and 2013 on video coding and communications, and a large industry grant in 2011 on secured video conferencing. He has successfully supervised 19 and currently supervising 6 PhD students. He is an Editor of International Journal of Digital Multimedia Broadcasting and has had served as an Associate Editor of IEEE Transactions on Circuits and Systems for Video Technology in 2012 and as a Guest Editor of special issues of Journal of Multimedia in 2009-2012. He received the Vice-Chancellor's Knowledge Transfer Award (commendation) from the University of Melbourne in 2007, the inaugural Early Career Research Excellence award from the Faculty of Information Technology, Monash University in 2006, and a University Gold Medal from BUET in 1994. He is a Senior Member of IEEE.

Miguel Baptista Nunes, BSc, MSc, PhD, FHEA, FBCS, is a Senior Lecturer in Information Management at the Information School, University of Sheffield. Miguel is currently the Head of the Information Systems Research Group in the School and has been involved in research in information management and information systems for the last 20 years. He has published more than 150 refereed articles in both academic conferences and academic journals, published a book on action research for e-learning and served as programme chair for a number of International conferences.

Henrique O'Neill is Associated Professor of Information Systems and Operations Management at ISCTE – University Institute of Lisbon, Portugal. He received his M.Sc. degree from IST/UTL in Lisbon and the Ph.D. degree from the Cranfield University, United Kingdom. His research interests are broadly focused on the adoption of information systems and communication technologies to foster business performance, including business and IS/IT strategy, organizational analysis and processes design, and the quality of information systems in organizational contexts like healthcare, banking and finance, the public sector and manufacturing. He is co-author of 55 scientific papers and 3 books.

Alex Peng is a Lecturer in Information Systems in the Information School at the University of Sheffield, UK. He has been the PI of a number of projects funded by research councils and industrial partners, produced around 60 publications, and served as the chair of a number of international conferences.

Cláudia Pinho. Pinho's original research focused on Website Image Destination. Now, she is interested in a Qualitative Research focus on Content Analysis.

Isabel Pinho. PhD research focused on Knowledge Management at Research Centers. Now, Pinho is interested in Knowledge Networks and Research Networks.

Maria da Costa Potes is a full Professor at the higher School of Education, Polytechnic Institute of Santarem. She was an invited Associate Professor in UAB, Lisbon. Member of the Excellent Research Center CIDTFF Research Centre "Didatics and Technology in Education of Digital and Virtual Environments in Education (Technology literacy, Distance education and Learning. Personal Learning Environment. Collaborative member at the Information and Society Department (Foundation for Science and Technology) Potes has tenure in Education with specialty in elearning by the Universidade Aberta (UAB) Postdoctoral by the Universidade de Aveiro. PHD and Master Degree in Communication and Education Multimedia at the Universidade Aberta (Uab).

Jenny Grant Rankin has a Ph.D. in Education, specializing in School Improvement Leadership, and is a lifetime member of Mensa. She is a former award-winning teacher, site administrator, district administrator (overseeing data and assessment for a 35,000-student district), and Chief Education & Research Officer of Illuminate Education. Dr. Rankin presented on this chapter's topic at the U.S. Department of Education's Institute of Education Sciences (IES) National Center for Education Statistics (NCES) STATS-DC Conference; California Council on Teacher Education (CCTE) Conference; International Society for Technology in Education (ISTE) Conference; Society for Information Technology & Teacher Education (SITE) Conference; University of California, Los Angeles (UCLA) and National Center for Research on Evaluation, Standards, and Student Testing (CRESST) Conference; and other venues. Winning Teacher of the Year was a favorite honor, as was having the U.S. flag flown over the United States Capitol in recognition of Dr. Rankin's dedication to her students. Among other honors, Dr. Rankin served on research committees for the International Society for Technology in Education (ISTE), the Society for Information Technology & Teacher Education (SITE), and the California Council on Teacher Education (CCTE). She has also been an expert reviewer (reviewing for the journal *Educational Researcher*) for the American Educational Research Association (AERA) and a judge for edtech and Ivy League competitions. She regularly tweets at @OTCData and shares new research related to this chapter's topic at www.overthecounterdata.com, where information on her latest books can be found.

António Bob Santos is currently a Phd researcher in Economics at ISCTE-IUL (University Institute of Lisbon), with research focused on open innovation, clusters and innovation policy. He is also a coordinator of Smart City projects at CEiiA (Centre for Innovation and Creative Engineering). António is a former Advisor to the Portuguese Government in innovation policy. In the period 2011-2013 he had responsibilities in the definition and in the deputy-coordination of the Portuguese Digital Agenda, the Innovation and Entrepreneurship National Programme (+E+I) and the Clusters national program.

Before that (2005-2011) he had responsibilities in the deputy-coordination of the following programmes: the Technological Plan, the Digital Agenda 2015, the Lisbon Strategy and the EU2020 strategy in Portugal, the National Strategy for Sustainable Development (ENDS 2005-2015) and the European Year of Innovation and Creativity in Portugal (2009). In the period 2002-2005 Antonio worked at UMIC - Agency for Knowledge Society - where has designed initiatives like b-On (Online Knowledge Library), NEOTEC (Technology-based companies programme) or OTIC (Technology Transfer Offices). He was a visiting Assistant Professor at Polytechnic Institute of Santarém (2008-2012), with the coordination of the "eGovernment" chain in the Master of Multimedia Education and Communication. He is author of academic and non-academic articles about innovation, innovation policy, open innovation and clusters. Antonio is a member of the European Economic Association.

Vitor Santos, is an Assistant Professor at Instituto Superior de Estatística e Gestão de Informação da Universidade Nova de Lisboa and European University, teaching courses in Computer Science and Informatics Engineering Degrees. Before that, he was Professor at Trás os Montes e Alto Douro University (UTAD) and Minho University (UM). He integrates several national and international conferences scientific committees and has authored several academic publications. He was the Microsoft Portugal Academic Computer Science Program Manager for 8 years and he has 21 years of experience in IT projects. Vitor Santos holds a B.Sc in Informatics Engineering from Cocite, a Postgraduate course in Computer Science from Science Faculty of Lisbon University, a M.Sc. in information Systems Science from UM, a DEA from UM, a Computer Specialist title from polytechnic institutes of Guarda, Castelo Branco and Viseu and a PhD in Technology information Systems Science from Minho University (UM).

Mohammad Tahaei has studied master of computer engineering and he is currently working as a software engineer in a talented startup, his academic research includes use of machine learning algorithms in healthcare.

Ramona Trestian is a Lecturer with the Computer and Communications Engineering Department, School of Science and Technology, Middlesex University, London, UK. She was previously an IBM-IRCSET Exascale Postdoctoral Researcher with the Performance Engineering Laboratory (PEL) at Dublin City University (DCU), Ireland since December 2011. She was awarded the PhD from Dublin City University in March 2012 and the B.Eng. degree in Telecommunications from the Electronics, Telecommunications and the Technology of Information Department, Technical University of Cluj-Napoca, Romania in 2007. She has published in prestigious international conferences and journals and has two edited books. She is a reviewer for international journals and conferences and an IEEE member. Her research interests include mobile and wireless communications, multimedia streaming, handover and network selection strategies, and software-defined networks.

John Walsh is a Lecturer in Information Management at the Department of Management and Marketing, University of Limerick, Ireland where he teaches both undergraduate and post-graduate courses on Information & Knowledge Management. He received his PhD from Brunel University for his work on examining the effects of social practices on knowledge management repository re-use. His research interests focus on Sociomateriality, Knowledge Management, Digital Heritage and the Digital Divide.

Faisal Zaman is a Postdoctoral Research Fellow in Insight: Centre for Data Analytics, University College Dublin, Ireland. He received his PhD in Information Science from Kyushu Institute of Technology, Japan in 2011. He previously worked in Dublin City University and Kyushu Institute of Technology as Post Doctoral researcher. He also worked as a Statistical Programmer in Shafi Consultancy Ltd and lead analytical teams to analyse medical trial data. His main research interest is in developing data-specific statistical machine learning algorithms and he has hands-on experience in analyzing weather station, gene-expression, electro-magenitc discharge, credit-scoring, network trace and call details record data. He is program committee member of several data mining conferences. He has published 30 articles, conference proceedings, books, book chapters, conference papers, and technical reports. He has experience in supervising PhD and M.Sc. level students.

Lihong Zhou – BSc, MSc, PhD, is an Associate Professor at the School of Information Management in Wuhan University, China. He obtained his MSc and PhD in Information Studies from the Information School, the University of Sheffield. His research interests are in healthcare knowledge sharing, risk mitigation and management, and information systems project management.

Index

Information Resources Management Association

Become an IRMA Member

Members of the **Information Resources Management Association (IRMA)** understand the importance of community within their field of study. The Information Resources Management Association is an ideal venue through which professionals, students, and academicians can convene and share the latest industry innovations and scholarly research that is changing the field of information science and technology. Become a member today and enjoy the benefits of membership as well as the opportunity to collaborate and network with fellow experts in the field.

IRMA Membership Benefits:

- **One FREE Journal Subscription**

- **30% Off Additional Journal Subscriptions**

- **20% Off Book Purchases**

- Updates on the latest events and research on Information Resources Management through the IRMA-L listserv.

- Updates on new open access and downloadable content added to Research IRM.

- A copy of the Information Technology Management Newsletter twice a year.

- A certificate of membership.

IRMA Membership $195

Scan code to visit irma-international.org and begin by selecting your free journal subscription.

Membership is good for one full year.

Printed in the United States
By Bookmasters